WHY POLITICS MATTERS:
AN INTRODUCTION TO POLITICAL SCIENCE

WHY POLITICS MATTERS:
AN INTRODUCTION TO POLITICAL SCIENCE

Kevin L. Dooley
Dean of the Honors School
Associate Professor of Political Science
Monmouth University

Joseph N. Patten
Chair of the Department of Political Science and Sociology
Associate Professor of Political Science
Monmouth University

WADSWORTH
CENGAGE Learning

Australia • Brazil • Japan • Korea • Mexico • Singapore • Spain • United Kingdom • United States

WADSWORTH
CENGAGE Learning

Why Politics Matters: An Introduction to Political Science
Kevin L. Dooley, Joseph N. Patten

Senior Publisher: Suzanne Jeans

Executive Editor: Carolyn Merrill

Acquisitions Editor: Anita Devine

Development Editor: Rebecca Green

Assistant Editor: Laura Ross

Media Editor: Laura Hildebrand

Marketing Program Manager: Caitlin Green

Content Project Manager: Jessica Rasile

Art Director: Linda Helcher

Print Buyer: Fola Orekoya

Senior Rights Acquisition Specialist: Jennifer Meyer Dare

Production Service/Compositor: S4Carlisle Publishing Services

Text Designer: KeDesign

Cover Designer: Rokusek Design

Cover Image:
Patrick Baz/Staff/©Getty Images
Justin Guariglia/National
   Geographic/©Getty Images
Milos Bicanski/Contributor/©Getty Images
AP Photo/Andy Manis

For product information and technology assistance, contact us at
Cengage Learning Customer & Sales Support, 1-800-354-9706

For permission to use material from this text or product,
submit all requests online at **www.cengage.com/permissions**
Further permissions questions can be e-mailed to
permissionrequest@cengage.com.

Library of Congress Control Number: 2011937929

ISBN-13: 978-0-618-90715-1
ISBN-10: 0-618-90715-7

Wadsworth
20 Channel Center Street
Boston, MA 02210
USA

Cengage Learning is a leading provider of customized learning solutions with office locations around the globe, including Singapore, the United Kingdom, Australia, Mexico, Brazil and Japan. Locate your local office at **international.cengage.com/region**

Cengage Learning products are represented in Canada by Nelson Education, Ltd.

For your course and learning solutions, visit **www.cengage.com.**

Purchase any of our products at your local college store or at our preferred online store **www.cengagebrain.com.**

Instructors: Please visit login.cengage.com and log in to access instructor-specific resources.

Printed in Canada
1 2 3 4 5 6 7 15 14 13 12 11

To my wife Lauren and our children Jack and Megan.

—*K. L. D.*

To my parents, Veena, Nikhil, Jaya, and to the memory of U.S. Congressman Edward J. Patten.

—*J. N. P.*

BRIEF CONTENTS

CONTENTS

3 MODERN POLITICAL THEORY   58

PART II: AMERICAN GOVERNMENT

4 THE AMERICAN GOVERNMENT 90

CourseReader

5 THE AMERICAN CONGRESS 128

6 THE AMERICAN PRESIDENCY 164

CourseReader

7 THE AMERICAN JUDICIARY   198

CourseReader

PART III: COMPARATIVE GOVERNMENTS

10 AUTHORITARIAN STATES   296

PART IV: INTERNATIONAL RELATIONS

11 UNDERSTANDING INTERNATIONAL RELATIONS: TERMS AND THEORIES   324

CourseReader

12   WAR, DIPLOMACY, AND THE BEGINNING OF INTERNATIONAL RELATIONS   360

13 THE COLD WAR AND BEYOND: THE RISE OF THE UNITED STATES AND THE EMERGING GLOBAL ORDER   386

WHY POLITICS *SHOULD* MATTER TO YOU

With the start of each new semester comes the initial thrill of meeting new students enrolled in our introduction to political science course. At Monmouth University, where we teach, the introductory course has always been considered the "gateway" to the discipline; a general education requirement that attracts majors from across the academic spectrum. We meet students studying everything from accounting, marketing, and management to anthropology, biology, and music. Thus, the learning environment includes a wide variety of interesting and creative students majoring primarily in subjects other than political science. Although each section will also have a number of politically active, politically motivated undergrads, the classroom is mainly filled with non-majors. In many ways, it was this reality that made us begin to consider not only how *we* were teaching this course, but also how we could design an appropriate text for students from all academic disciplines.

Student Engagement Matters

Many of the books for this course are written for political science majors with a particular emphasis on comparative politics. But for today's students, a mix of majors and non-majors, and those completely new to political science, we wanted to offer a broader understanding of the discipline and an opportunity for you to discover which areas of political science are most interesting to you. Our solution was to design a curriculum that would keep both groups engaged in the learning process, major and non-major alike, by taking a "big picture" approach, evenly surveying the major areas within the field of political science, and emphasizing how the theoretical concepts of the discipline play out in the world around us.

The first thing you may have noticed about this book is this unique organization. We work outward from the student:

- **Part I:** Political Theory, you will learn about the foundations of ancient and modern political thought. This is an important place to start because it is here that the philosophical foundations for modern governments are formed. We believe it is crucial for you to have a general understanding of key political theorists in order for you to more effectively assess and critique the behavior of governments in our modern world.

- **Part II:** American Government, we build on the previous section by examining how the American Framers were influenced by ancient Greek and modern political philosophers when they drafted the American Constitution. Here you will become more familiar with how these political theorists influenced the structure of the American system of government, and survey modern issues associated with the American Congress, the American presidency, and the American judiciary. This section is given special emphasis because it was the "American experiment" toward popular government that ignited democratic fires across the globe, which continues to shape today's political landscape.

- **Part III:** Comparative Politics, you will learn about how other countries' systems are organized, where they differ and are alike, and how they tackle universal issues and those unique to their own particular societies. This section builds on the previous one in that we believe you will be in a much stronger position to compare other democratic and nondemocratic forms of government once you are able to use the principles behind your own system of government as a helpful reference point to understanding the foundational tenets of other forms of government.

- **Part IV:** International Relations, you will learn how this wide array of political systems and cultures interact with one another in our modern international system. Having a broad understanding of political systems and distinct regional cultures will shed light on why nations fight wars, what we can do to try to prevent them, and the challenges and opportunities we face as we attempt to solve global issues.

These sectional stepping-stones from Political Theory, to American Government, to Comparative Politics, to International Relations build upon each other, producing a scholar who is able to balance the knowledge of the domestic with that of the global. You will then be given the opportunity to reflect upon all of the issues previously covered in the text and possess the skills to see the world through the intellectual prism of the entire field of political science upon completion. We've found that this is an accessible and intuitive organization for students.

This foundational framework, paired with (1) a focus on application and critical thinking; (2) excerpts from the classic and contemporary thinkers who shaped this discipline; (3) the latest global events; and (4) vibrant illustrations bring political science to life! It is because we take so much pleasure in teaching political science to students from all academic majors that made writing this book a labor of love. It's fun to convey these important themes to our students, and we believe reading this book will be a stimulating, eye-opening, and enjoyable experience for you as well, as we set out to prove in the pages that follow.

Participation Matters

At the heart of this book, we strive to answer the questions we sometimes hear in the introduction to political science classroom: *Why do I have to take this course? I'm not a political science major and I don't plan to work in government, so why should this matter to me?* The answers surround each and every one of us, whether we know it or not. An understanding of politics is necessary for participation in a globalized world, a concept we stress in the book's opening chapter "Why Politics Matters" and throughout with a special feature entitled "Why Politics Matters to You!" You will come away aware of the challenges of the twenty-first century and with a new perspective on where political beliefs come from. You will be able to identify the opportunities available to you through which you can make an impact, and you will possess a strong confidence in your overview of the field at the book's completion. You are enthusiastically invited to join in this dialog. We've written the book in a conversational style, with thought-provoking questions at every turn.

Why Theory Matters—Applying Theory to Today!

Throughout, we'll look into the relationship between the theoretical underpinnings (theory) and the formation and interplay of political entities (practice). This theme is emphasized throughout the narrative and within special "Theory and Practice" features in every chapter, with the use of integrated readings through CourseReader. We highlight this important concept to encourage critical thought when assessing and interpreting our political world, as well as to help you apply these concepts to your life. You will come away with not just a series of case studies, but with the tools you'll need to analyze and affect your political surroundings well into the future.

FEATURES
that Teach

▼ **Why Politics Matters** brings the subject to life and encourages student interaction through engaging, conversational prose, a bold, full-color design with photographs, maps, figures, and other illustrations, and critical thinking questions in every boxed feature and throughout the narrative.

TABLE 1.1. Youth Voting: The Percentages of 18–24-Year-Old Citizens Who Voted in Recent Presidential Elections[2]

	Caucasian (%)	African American (%)	Native American (%)	Asian American (%)	Latinos (%)
1992	52	41	37	32	33
1996	38	34	25	35	24
2000	38	36	30	28	26
2004	50	47	37	36	33
2008	50	56	—	39	39

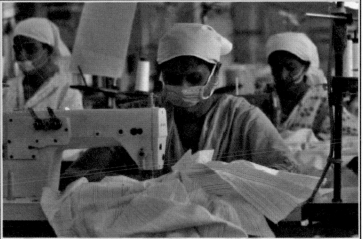

AP PHOTO/PAVEL RAHMAN

"both visually & intellectually interesting"
Keeley Mahanes,
Student at Northern Arizona University

Questions to Consider Before Reading this Chapter

1. What is power? What is the difference between hard power and soft power?

2. What are the three main assumptions of classical realism?

3. How can the three levels of analysis be useful to understanding issues of international conflict?

◀ **Questions to Consider before Reading this Chapter** open every chapter, serving as learning objectives to guide students' reading.

THEORY
and **Practice**

▼ **Theory and Practice** features demonstrate how political thought directly influences modern-day situat[...] institutions, and policies, in turn teaching students how to apply overarching political ideas to the current ev[...] and political practice around them and analyze both.

THEORY AND PRACTICE

The Greeks, the Roman Empire, and the Incorporation of Law into the State

The power of Aristotle's works prompted the Roman statesman Marcus Tullius Cicero (106–43 BCE) to refer to them as "a river of gold" centuries later. Cicero was a Roman statesman and philosopher who was an important link in the Greco-Roman tradition in that it was in part through Cicero that Greek philosophy came to play a role in the governing structure of the Roman Empire. In the *Republic* and *Laws*, Cicero advocated for a mixed constitution in the Roman Republic, consisting of the (1) consuls as the regional power; (2) the senate as the aristocratic power; and (3) the popular assembly.[43] Cicero's call for an aristocratic republic also influenced many of the American Founding Fathers.

Whereas Plato argued that justice in the Republic should be maintained through the leadership of the philosopher-king, Cicero instead argued that law, not philosophers, should guide the behavior of government. Cicero argued that leaders of society should be above all else knowledgeable in the realm of natural and positive law. He called for a unity between law and politics so that the political leader "is a speaking law, and the law a silent magistrate."[44] It is in part because of Cicero's emphasis on incorporating law into the State that many of the American Framers advocated creating a nation based on natural law.

Can you think of any existing law that places the well-being of special interests groups over the public good? If so, how would you change this law and how would this change improve our society?

THEORY AND PRACTICE

"I think it is vital to show how these theories work in practice and something that is missing from my current textbook....
I really like how this textbook is organized and written. It highlights the different sub-fields of political science giving equal time and energy to each, while providing excellent resources and tools within the textbook for the instructor to use. The book reflects my own philosophy of teaching an Intro to Politics course."

Ryan Fitzharris,
Pima Community College

"It does a great job relating the ideas to current issues, which makes it seem **relevant and therefore engaging.**"

Kaitlyn Andrey,
*Student at
Bloomsburg University of
Pennsylvania*

WHY POLITICS MATTERS
to YOU!

▼ **Why Politics Matters to You!** features show students how they can get involved and how politics and govment are influential in their lives.

WHY POLITICS MATTERS TO YOU!

Prisoner's Dilemma:
Are you more competitive than cooperative?

Hobbes argued that civil society will inevitably degenerate into civil war and death because people in the precontract state will not cooperate with each other out of a fear that placing trust in an untrustworthy person could have disastrous impacts. It is based on this finding that Hobbes argued we are by nature more competitive than cooperative. In 1950, Merrill Flood and Melvin Dresher from the Rand Corporation developed the prisoner's dilemma game theory to illustrate that people sometimes will not cooperate with each other even when it is their best interest to do so. Prisoner's Dilemma has been widely applied in the field of international relations and is highlighted again in Chapter 11.

Are you by nature a competitive or cooperative person? Pretend you and a classmate joined forces in robbing a bank. The two of you are later apprehended and brought to the police station for questioning. Because the police officers only have circumstantial evidence against you, they need to solicit a confession in order to ensure a conviction. One police officer takes you into an interrogation room while another police officer takes your classmate into an adjoining room. You are then each informed that it is in your best interest to cooperate with the investigation by admitting that you and your classmate were involved in the robbery. You then learn that if both you and your classmate remain quiet you will each do one year in prison. If you and your classmate both confess, you will each do five years in prison. If one confesses and the other remains quiet, the one who confesses will go free while the one who remains quiet will get 10 years in prison.

		Student A	
		Talk	Quiet
Student B	Talk	5 years each	A = 10 years B = 0 years
	Quiet	A = 0 years B = 10 years	1 year each

What would you choose to do?

WHY POLITICS MATTERS TO YOU!

"It's clear that this approach works… by **showing students how politics relates to their lives and actually matters….**
I really liked the material. I think the students liked it as well because the exam I gave them over the material gave me the highest average for a quiz/exam for the semester."

John Shively,
Longview Community College

"An engaging text with easy readability, leaving you with not only answers but the **desire to learn more, know more, and do more."**

Jaqueline P. Hess,
*Student at
San Diego Mesa College*

COURSEREADER
Assignments

◀ **CourseReader Assignments** appear alongside the n[...]tive, indicating where a primary source reading is a[...]able to enhance the discussion. Each provides a sum[...] of the reading and concludes with thought-prov[...] questions to help students identify the link betwee[...] selection and the chapter material.

CourseReader ASSIGNMENT

Log in to www.cengagebrain.com and open CourseReader to access the reading:

"Quantifying Arab Democracy: Democracy in the Middle East"
by Saliba Sarsar

In this article, Saliba Sarsar attempts to place a numeric value on the levels of freedom of the states of the Middle East. Taking into consideration a number of standard democratic values like media freedom, the presence of fair/free elections, the protection of women's rights, etc., Sarsar tries to determine if the Middle East is becoming more or less democratic.

- *What is the least democratic state in the Middle East?*
- *Are the numerous factors provided fair indicators of a state's level of democracy? If not, what other factors do you think are relevant?*

Chapter 1.
Politics: Who Gets What, When, How by Harold Lasswell
"Islam and the Arab Revolutions: A Golden Opprtunity" from *The Economist*
"Political Science in the United States: Past and Present" by David Easton

Chapter 2.
Civil Disobedience by Henry David Thoreau
Politics, Book 6 by Aristotle

Chapter 3.
Leviathan by Thomas Hobbes
The Second Treatise of Civil Government, Chapter II: Of the State of Nature by John Locke
"Declaration of Sentiments." History of Woman Suffrage. Ed. Elizabeth Cady Stanton, Susan B. Anthony, and Matilda Joslyn Gage. Vol. 1. 1881. 70–71

Chapter 4.
An Economic Interpretation of the Constitution by Charles A. Beard
McCulloch v. Maryland by John Marshall
Federalist Paper No. 10
Excerpt of *Democracy in America* by Alexis de Tocqueville

Chapter 5.
Congress: The Electoral Connection by David Mayhew
Home Style by Richard Fenno
"Pelosi's Bill: How She Did It" by Richard E. Cohen

Chapter 6.
"The Electoral College and the Framers' Distrust of Democracy" by James P. Pfiffner and Jason Hartke
Presidential Power excerpt by Richard Neustadt
Presidential Character excerpt by James David Barber

Chapter 7.
Federalist Paper # 78
Lawrence v. Texas
Citizen United v. Federal Election Commission (2010).

Chapter 8.
"Democracy as a Universal Value" by Amartya Sen
"How did Europe democratize?" by Daniel Ziblatt
"Quantifying Arab Democracy: Democracy in the Middle East" by Saliba Sarsar

Chapter 9.
The Spirit of Democracy by Larry Diamond
Viktor Yushchenko's *Inaugural Address, January 25, 200*[...]

Chapter 10.
"Authoritarianism in Pakistan" by Zoltan Barany
"Hitler's Propaganda Machine" by Roger Nelson

Chapter 11.
Barack Obama's *speech upon acceptance of the Nobel Peace Prize, Osio, Norway, 2009*
Communist Manifesto by Marx and Engels (excerpt), 1848

Chapter 12.
"The Concert of Europe: A Fresh Look at an International System" in World Politics, Vol. 28. No. 2 (Jan., 1976) pp. 159–174 by Richard B. Elrod
"Making the World Safe for Democracy" Speech by Woodrow Wilson's

Chapter 13.
"The Clash of Civilizations" by Samuel P. Huntington

FEATURES
that Teach

Visual timelines ▶

organize important historical events, political works, and the lives of political thinkers in each chapter, putting history into context and making it easy to see how events and concepts affect one another and connect.

"The first thing I enjoyed was the **enthusiasm and passion** the authors have towards their subject matter.... [they] do a good job in **making a host of complex topics user friendly for college students.**"

Cyrus Hayat,
Indiana University-Purdue University Indianapolis

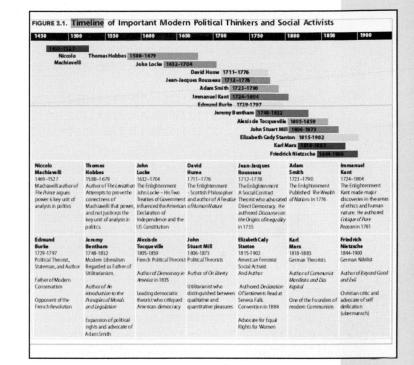

FIGURE 3.1. Timeline of Important Modern Political Thinkers and Social Activists

Realist: *a school of thought in international relations that emphasizes the furtherance of national interests and military security. Realists primarily believe nations exists within an anarchic international political system, and because of a tendency to distrust international organizations, believe nations must be prepared to militarily defend themselves at all times.*

▶ Critical thinking questions appear at the end of every boxed feature and in the margins within the narrative to spark discussion, application, and engage the reader.

◀ A Marginal glossary defines key terms as students read, and a list of **Key Terms** and **Key People** at the end of every chapter help students review the material.

SUPPLEMENTS
for Instructors & Students

CourseReader for *Why Politics Matters*
ISBN-10: 0618907157 | ISBN-13: 9780618907151 – *Why Politics Matters* with Printed Access Card for CourseReader
ISBN-10: 1133232124 | ISBN-13: 9781133232124 – Printed Access Card
ISBN-10: 1133232132 | ISBN-13: 9781133232131 – Instant Access Code
ISBN-10: 1133232116 | ISBN-13: 9781133232117 – SSO

In addition to the overviews of important political science theories and quoted excerpts included in the book, we have selected certain readings that highlight the focus of each chapter. Assigning readings can often be a difficult process. Within each chapter, you will come across reading assignments that are easily accessible within the Cengage Learning CourseReader. We have designed the CourseReader selections to tie in seamlessly with the section material. Keeping in mind that we must make the most of the time today's busy students can allocate to extra reading, we've handpicked two to four selections per chapter that will add the most to their study, reinforce the concepts from the text, and help them apply what they've learned to events around them. You may assign the questions that accompany the readings as graded or completion-based homework or use them to spark in-class discussion.

CourseReader is an easy-to-use and affordable option to create an online collection of readings for your course, and this is the first and only introductory book to political science offering a customizable e-reader. Instructors may assign the readings we've recommended for each chapter without any additional set-up, or you can choose to create and customize a reader specifically for your class from the thousands of text documents and media clips within CourseReader. You can also:

- add your own notes and highlight sections within a reading.
- edit the introductions to the readings.
- assign due dates using the pop-up calendar.
- easily organize your selections using the drag and drop feature.

You can view a demo of CourseReader at www.cengage.com/coursereader.

PowerLecture with ExamView® for *Why Politics Matters*
ISBN-10: 1111828180 | ISBN-13: 9781111828189

This DVD provides access to Interactive PowerPoint® Lectures, a Test Bank, and the Instructor's Manual. Interactive, book-specific PowerPoint lectures make it easy for you to assemble, edit, publish, and present custom lectures for your course. The slides provide outlines specific to every chapter of *Why Politics Matters*, 1st edition, and include tables, statistical charts, graphs, and photos from the book as well as outside sources. In addition, the slides are completely customizable for a powerful and personalized presentation. A test bank in Microsoft® Word and ExamView® computerized testing offers a large array of well-crafted multiple-choice and essay questions, along with their answers and page references. An Instructor's Manual includes learning objectives, chapter outlines, discussion questions, suggestions for class activities and projects, tips on integrating media into your class (including step-by-step instructions on how to create your own podcasts), suggested readings and Web resources. A section specifically designed for teaching assistants and adjuncts helps instructors get started teaching right away.

Companion Website for *Why Politics Matters*
ISBN-10: 1111941017 | ISBN-13: 9781111941017
cengagebrain.com/ISBN/0618907157

Students will find open access to learning objectives, tutorial quizzes, chapter glossaries, flashcards, and crossword puzzles, all correlated by chapter. Instructors also have access to the Instructor's Manual and PowerPoints.

"This online reader is an excellent idea. It allows the professor to individually design the class around what he/she considers most critical to the study."

Kevin Dockerty,
Kalamazoo Valley Community College

"I really enjoyed the CourseReader readings because of the connection to the chapter. They allowed for the real world application to be seen."

Christine Ludolph,
Student at Northern Arizona University

ACKNOWLEDGMENTS

We would like to express our sincere gratitude to the following instructors whose constructive feedback through reviews, focus groups, and class tests helped shape this first edition:

George Agbango	Bloomsburg University	**Victor Eno**	Florida A & M
Victor Aikhionbare	Palm Beach State College	**Jasmine Farrier**	University of Louisville
Daniel Allen	Anderson University	**Ryan Fitzharris**	Pima Community College
Brian Anderson	Mississippi University for Women	**Rick Foster**	Fort Lewis College
Chad Atkinson	Wright State University	**Amy Freedman**	Long Island University, C.W. Post
Kyeonghi Baek	Buffalo State College	**Steve Garrison**	Midwestern State University
Donald Baker	Long Island University, C.W. Post	**Donald Gawronski**	Mesa Community College
Abdallah Battah	Minnesota State University, Mankato	**David Goldberg**	College of DuPage
		Hans Hacker	Arkansas State University
Steven Bayne	Century College	**Michelle Hammes**	Saint Cloud State University
Kenneth Bernier	Central New Mexico Community College	**Sally Hansen**	Daytona State
		Cyrus Hayat	Indiana University, Purdue
Bradley Best	Buena Vista University	**Peter Heller**	Manhattan College
John Bing	Heidelberg College	**Timothy Jeske**	Yakima Valley Community College
Charles Boehmer	University of Texas El Paso	**Maorong Jiang**	Creighton University
Martin Bookbinder	Passaic County Community College	**Joon Kil**	Irvine Valley College
		Dongsoo Kim	West Liberty State College
Wendell Broadwell	Georgia Perimeter College	**Bob King**	Georgia Perimeter College
Matthew Burger	University of Maryland	**Edward Kissling**	Ocean County College
Peng-Khuan Chong	Plymouth State University	**Donnamarie Landsberg**	Johnson County Community College
Margery Coulson-Clark	Elizabeth City State University		
Stephen Crescenzi	Thomas Edison State College	**Christianna Leahy**	McDaniel College
Greg Culver	University of Southern Indiana	**Manwoo Lee**	Millersville University
John Davis	Howard University	**David Levenbach**	Arkansas State University
Wartyna Davis	William Paterson	**Richard Levy**	Salem State College
Tolga Demiryol	Quinnipiac College	**Timothy Lim**	California State University, Los Angeles
Chad DeWaard	University of Tennessee		
Jack DiSarno	University of North Carolina, Pembroke	**Lindsey Lupo**	Point Loma Nazarene University
		Shari MacLachlan	Palm Beach State College
Kevin Dockerty	Kalamazoo Valley Community College	**Sharon Manna**	North Lake College
		Samantha Mannion	Holyoke Community College
Tom Dolan	Columbus State University	**Andrae Marak**	California University of PA
Colleen Driscoll	Quinnipiac College	**Patrick McGovern**	Buffalo State College
Charles Ellison	Ivy Tech Community College	**Don Melton**	Arapahoe Community College
Walle Engedayehu	Prairie View A & M University	**John Mercurio**	San Diego City College

Melissa Michelson	Menlo College	Jason M. Seitz	Georgia Perimeter College
Stephen Morris	Middle Tennessee State University	John Shively	Longview Community College
Marcella Myers	Andrews University	Jonathan Schulman	Palm Beach State College
Bruce Nesmith	Coe College	Ginger Silvera	Cal State Dominguez Hills
Sunday Obazuaye	Cerritos College	Cigdem V. Sirin	University of Texas, El Paso
Daniel Ogbaharya	Western Illinois University	Shyam Sriram	Georgia Perimeter College
Evan Oxman	Lake Forest College	Robert T. Starks	Northeastern Illinois University
Don Ramlow	Kalamazoo Valley Community College	Adam P. Stone	Georgia Perimeter College
		Holley Tankersley	Coastal Caroline University
Sherri Replogle	Illinois State University	Kimberly Turner	College of DuPage
Erin E. Richards	Cascadia Community College	S.P. Udayakumar	South Asian Community Center for Education and Research
Michelle Rodriguez	San Diego Mesa College		
Mark Roeder	North Greenville University	Denise Vaughan	Bellevue College
Elgin Rogers	Ivy Tech State College, Bloomington	Greg Weeks	University of North Carolina, Charlotte
Leticia Sara	Red Rocks Community College	Stephen Wright	Northern Arizona University
Atsuko Sato	California State University, Los Angeles	Ming Xia	College of Staten Island, CUNY
		Bradford Young	Ocean County College
Robert A. Saunders	SUNY Farmingdale	Noah Zerbe	Humboldt State University
Shawn Scharf	Youngstown State University	Annalisa Zinn	Quinnipiac College

In addition, we'd like to thank our team at Wadsworth: Executive Acquiring Sponsoring Editor Carolyn Merrill, Acquisitions Editor Anita Devine, Development Editor Rebecca Green, Content Project Managers Sara Abbott and Jessica Rasile, and Senior Rights Specialist Jennifer Meyer Dare. We would also like to thank our Project Manager Perundevi Dhandapani with S4Carlisle Publishing Services and Photo Researcher Josh Garvin with the Bill Smith Group.

We would also like to thank Professors Rekha Datta, Nancy Mezey, Ken Mitchell, Kathryn Kloby, Enoch Nappen, Vincenzo Mele, Saliba Sarsar, and Ms. Kristen Gillette of the Monmouth University Department of Political Science and Sociology for their continued friendship and support.

ABOUT THE AUTHORS

Kevin L. Dooley is the dean of the Honors School and associate professor of political science at Monmouth University where he teaches courses in Political Theory, Ethics in International Relations, and Comparative European Politics. He received his Ph.D. from the Division of Global Affairs at Rutgers-Newark in 2005 and in 2011 was nominated for Monmouth University's Outstanding Teacher Award. He serves as the advisor to Monmouth University's Model United Nations Team.

Joseph N. Patten is chair of the Department of Political Science and Sociology and associate professor of political science at Monmouth University where he teaches courses in American Politics. He received his Ph.D. in political science from West Virginia University in 1996. In 2009, he received Monmouth University's Distinguished Teaching Award and was named Faculty Member of the Year at Buena Vista University in Iowa in 2002 and in 1999. He also serves as the coach of Monmouth University's Policy Debate Team and as the president of the New Jersey Political Science Association (2012).

Why Politics Matters:
An Introduction to Political Science

1

WHY POLITICS MATTERS

Egyptian anti-government demonstrators hold a huge national flag as others pray at Cairo's Tahrir Square on February 8, 2011 on the fifteenth day of demonstrations against the regime of President Hosni Mubarek. Three days later, Mubarek stepped down as president of Egypt after serving for 30 years. The Arab Spring (2011), which refers to pro-democratic popular uprisings throughout the Middle East and North Africa, began in Tunisia after a 26-year-old street produce merchant set himself on fire in protest of the police confiscating his belongings. The Arab Spring spread from Tunisia, to Egypt, and then on to Libya, Syria, and Yemen.

Questions to Consider Before Reading This Chapter

1. How have you been socialized by your family, friends, and peers? Have your political beliefs been challenged since you entered college?

2. What are political ideologies? What are the differences between left wing and right wing ideologies?

3. How can public opinion polls indicate your voting preferences or what you care most about?

4. What is the difference between "hard power" and "soft power" in the realm of international politics?

5. What do you think it takes to win a policy debate? How can the skills you learn in debate help you to influence policy issues?

6. What are the different areas that political scientists study? Why are theories so important to their research?

INTRODUCTION: WHAT IS POLITICAL SCIENCE?

There is an old adage that states one should never discuss religion or politics when attending dinner parties with casual acquaintances. Many of us have been taught that arguments focused on our cultural differences, recently enacted health care law, or partisan viewpoints frequently grow tense and might prevent friends from enjoying each others' company, or more importantly dessert. Those who adhere to the social etiquette of proper dinner conversation are probably smart to do so. A clashing of political views can bring about a stressful social environment and can cause awkward moments for unsuspecting dinner guests.

Lucky for you, however, you are in a political science class, which happens to be the most appropriate and exciting place to discuss such things. Here you are encouraged and even rewarded for respectfully engaging in a wide variety of political observations and cultural perspectives. Learning how to discuss politics in a civil manner requires practice and a thick skin. While we are certainly not required to agree with any particular outlook, we all have a responsibility to at least try to understand the viewpoints of others. We want to see that you, the next generation of citizens, are able to articulate and understand some of the challenges that face us in the coming century and to succeed in making this world a better and more secure place.

The challenges ahead are great. But so were the challenges that faced George Washington, Abraham Lincoln, Susan B. Anthony, Alice Paul, Mohandas Gandhi, Martin Luther King, Jr., and Nelson Mandela. All of these men and women demonstrated a commitment to change, but most of all, recognized that politics matters. In fact, it is probably one of the most defining features of the human experience. We are above all else as the great Greek philosopher Aristotle noted, "political animals." Unlike other members of the animal kingdom, humans possess the ability to reason and then through language carry that reason into action in the form of legally constructed

© PATRICK BAZ/AFP/GETTY IMAGES

3

communities. So, although you may never have thought of yourself or your friends as being *political*—you are. You have the ability to reason, the ability to articulate your ideas, and the ability to carry those thoughts into action.

So at times politics and debates about politics can become a passionate endeavor, one that can cause disagreements over what is considered right and wrong. Has there ever been a time when a fellow student said something you completely disagreed with? Or have you ever been offended by another's comments? If so, that is because each of us has been socialized by the many groups to which we belong. Political scientist Thomas M. Magstadt has defined **political socialization** as the process by which citizens develop the values, attitudes, beliefs, and opinions that enable them to support the political system.[1] In other words, the various groups that define our lives contribute to the way we view the world.

Students will likely process discussions that take place in this class differently from you because of the influences of their gender, race, religion, friends, sexual orientation, family, level of education, and socioeconomic status. These differences should be celebrated both in and beyond this class because learning from the experiences of others helps to inform our own beliefs. Perhaps Thomas Jefferson put it best when he said that he "never considered differences of opinion in politics, in religion, in philosophy, as cause for withdrawing from a friend."

Some political scientists examine how our differences influence whether and how we participate in the political process. Tables 1.1 to 1.3 highlight how race, gender, and education impact the voter turnout rates of college-age voters. These tables reveal that some college-age students belonging to certain social groups are more likely to vote than others. In Chapter 6 we examine how young voters played a large role in President Barack Obama's electoral victory over John McCain in 2008 and how young people are now more politically active than they have been in decades. On closer inspection Table 1.1 shows that young African Americans were more likely to vote than college-age students from other ethnic or racial groups. Approximately 56% of college-age African American voters participated in the 2008 presidential election, compared with 50% of Caucasians and 39% of young Asian and Hispanic voters.

Political socialization: *The process by which one's attitudes and values are shaped.*

Why do you believe some racial or ethnic groups vote in higher numbers than others? Why do you believe young people are more politically active than in previous decades?

TABLE 1.1. Youth Voting: The Percentages of 18–24-Year-Old Citizens Who Voted in Recent Presidential Elections[2]

	Caucasian (%)	African American (%)	Native American (%)	Asian American (%)	Latinos (%)
1992	52	41	37	32	33
1996	38	34	25	35	24
2000	38	36	30	28	26
2004	50	47	37	36	33
2008	50	56	—	39	39

TABLE 1.2. Youth Voting: The Percentage of 18–24-Year-Old Males and Females Who Voted in Recent Presidential Elections[3]

	Young Women (%)	Young Men (%)
1992	51	46
1996	38	33
2000	38	34
2004	50	44
2008	52	45

Why do you believe that college-age women are more likely to vote than college-age men?

TABLE 1.3. Youth Voting: The Percentage of 18–29-Year-Old College-Educated and Non-College-Educated Citizens Who Voted in Recent Elections[4]

	College Educated (%)	No College Education (%)	Difference in Voting Turnout (%)
1992	67.2	36.4	30.9
1996	52.0	26.0	26.0
2000	51.8	26.7	25.1
2004	61.1	33.7	27.4
2008	62.1	35.9	26.2

Why do you believe that educated college-age voters are more likely to vote than young people who do not attend college?

Table 1.2 also indicates that college-age women were more likely to vote than college-age men in the 2008 election, with 52 percent of 18–24-year-old women and 45 percent of college-age men casting a ballot. However, the most dramatic predictor of whether a young person is likely to vote is educational attainment. Table 1.3 highlights that young people with at least some experience in college (62 percent voter turnout) were much more likely to vote in the 2008 presidential election than young people without any college experience (36 percent voter turnout).

Although you may never have considered the influence that all or some of these groups have had on your life, certain political scientists have. For example, there are a number of political scientists who conduct and then analyze the results of public opinion polls. **Public opinion polls** allow individuals to see how certain *demographics* view certain political issues or problems. **Demographics,** which refer to some of the ways people are categorized (e.g., women, people of color, small business owners, union members, 18- to 24-year-olds with college degrees, Catholics, etc.), allow political scientists to determine if relationships exist between one's group and how one feels about a number of political issues. Public opinion polls may ask you your age, race/ethnicity, religion, and level of education and what you think about health

Public opinion polls:
Surveys that seek to determine how different groups of people perceive political issues.

Demographics:
Classifications of different groups of people that usually refer to one's race, class, ethnicity, gender, level of wealth, age, place of residence, employment status, level of education, and so on.

An American student at a high school near Santa Barbara, California, signs a petition for creating a nuclear-free world given to her by 18-year-old peace worker, Anmi Naruse from Nagasaki, Japan, on February 8, 2010. The city of Nagasaki was nearly destroyed by a U.S. atomic bomb that killed or injured approximately 150,000 people during the second World War on August 9, 1945.

care reform, gun control, homeland security, or President Obama. By answering these questions, political scientists can determine if there are relationships between one's demographic and one's opinions about the political world.

So in this very abstract way, you are already political. What this text attempts to do is to help you see that politics matters in a much deeper sense than the material covered on an exam or expressed in a research paper (although these also matter for obvious reasons).

POLITICAL SCIENCE AS THE STUDY OF POWER

In his 1936 book, the political scientist Harold Lasswell said that "politics is who gets what, when, and how." This very simple expression sums up the essence of this book and the entire field of political science at large. Political science is in many respects concerned with the study of *power*. In this book you will learn about how important ancient and modern political theorists viewed power and how political leaders exercise it in the current era. Political power can broadly be defined as the ability to get others to do what they would not do on their own. Socrates, Plato, Aristotle, and other ancient philosophers believed political power should only be applied as a means to the ends of social justice. These thinkers laid the theoretical foundation of Western civilization by maintaining that political power should be brandished by the wisest and most ethical members of society because leaders above all else have a responsibility to promote social harmony and the public good. They believed that only those educated on the virtues of justice should wield power because they will more likely place the public's interest over their own.

Niccolò Machiavelli's (1469–1527) book, *The Prince,* wandered away from this Greek view by asserting that "power" and not "justice" is the most important unit of analysis in politics. He claimed that in order to truly comprehend the nuances of politics, it is more important to have an understanding of how leaders can best acquire and maintain political control over the populace. Machiavelli's amoral approach to politics stressed that the primary purpose of government is to prevent civil unrest and to promote security at home and abroad.

The discussion of how governmental power should be structured is later joined by some of the leading **social contract theorists** such as Thomas Hobbes, John Locke, and Jean-Jacques Rousseau. These theorists focused mostly on the power relationship between government and the individual. In Chapter 3 we highlight how social contract theorists typically make observations on: (1) whether humans are more generally cooperative or competitive with one another; (2) the types of problems that are likely to occur in the absence of government; and (3) their preferred form of government for addressing these problems. Thomas Hobbes's (1588–1679) classic text *Leviathan* sets out to prove the correctness of Machiavelli's contention that power rather than justice is the most important variable in studying politics. It is here that Hobbes argued that the purpose of political power should not be used to primarily promote ethical governance, but should instead be used to promote the more limited goal of preventing social turmoil and war. Hobbes's social contract advocated for an *authoritarian system of government,* where individuals surrender all political power to the government so that government can more

Social contract theorists: *Thinkers beginning in the seventeenth century who sought to explain human nature by looking at the terms by which governments are set up in the first place.*

TABLE 1.4. Different Types of Political Systems, Economic Systems, and Political Ideologies[5]

Anarchism	A doctrine that advocates the abolition of organized authority. Anarchists believe all government is corrupt and evil.
Authoritarianism	A form of government in which a large amount of authority is invested in the state, at the expense of individual rights.
Autocracy	A government in which almost all power rests with the ruler. The Soviet Union under Stalin and Iraq under Saddam Hussein are examples of autocracies.
Capitalism	An economic system in which the means of production, such as land and factories, are privately owned and operated for profit.
Communism	The political system under which the economy, including capital, property, major industries, and public services, is controlled and directed by the state and in that sense is "communal."
Conservatism	A political philosophy that tends to support the status quo and advocates change only in moderation. Conservatism upholds the value of tradition and seeks to preserve all that is good about the past.
Direct democracy	Democracy in which the people as a whole make direct decisions, rather than have those decisions made for them by elected representatives.
Fascism	A nationalistic, authoritarian, anticommunist movement founded by Benito Mussolini in 1919. Fascism was a response to the economic hardship and social disorder that ensued after the end of World War I.
Feminism	The theory of the political, economic, and social equality of the sexes.
Feudalism	A medieval form of social economic and political organization. Feudalism had a pyramidal structure. At its head was the king; below the king was a hierarchal chain of nobles, down to the lords of individual manors—the manor being the basic social and economic unit.
Liberal	A person who believes it is the duty of government to ameliorate social conditions and create a more equitable society.
Libertarianism	The belief that government should not interfere in the lives of citizens, other than to provide police and military protection.
Marxism	The theory developed by Karl Marx and Friedrich Engels, which became the official doctrine of communism. According to Marxism, the key to how society operated was economics; all other aspects of society, such as politics and religion, were conditioned by the economic system.
Meritocracy	A society in which power is wielded by those who deserve it, based on their talents, industry, and success in competition, rather than through membership of a certain class or possession of wealth.
Monarchy	Form of rulership whereby a queen or king, empress or emperor holds absolute or limited power, usually inherited.
Nation-state	Usually used to describe the modern state, but strictly speaking applies only when the whole population of a state feels itself to belong to the same nation.
Oligarchy	A political system that is controlled by a small group of individuals, who govern in their own interests.
Pacifist	The doctrine that holds that war is never justified and that all disputes between nations should be settled peacefully.
Plutocracy	Government by the wealthy, or a group of wealthy people who control or influence a government.
Representative democracy	A system of government in which the people elect agents to represent them in a legislature.
Republic	The form of government in which ultimate power resides in the people, who elect representatives to participate in decision making on their behalf.
Social contract	The political theory that a state and its citizens have an unwritten agreement between them, a social contract into which they voluntarily enter.

TABLE 1.4. *(continued)*

Socialism	A political system in which the means of production, distribution, and exchange are mostly owned by the state, and used, at least in theory, on behalf of the people.
Terrorism	The pursuit of a political aim by means of violence and intimidation.
Theocracy	A state or government that is run by priests or clergy.
Totalitarianism	A system of government where the ruling authority extends its power over all aspects of society and regulates every aspect of life.
Utilitarianism	A political philosophy developed in England in the nineteenth century by thinkers such as Jeremy Bentham and John Stuart Mill, which says that the duty of government is to promote the greatest good for the greatest number.

efficiently prevent civil unrest and violence. In Table 1.4 we include definitions of different types of political systems and the economic systems and ideologies that influence them.

Other social contract theorists such as John Locke and Jean-Jacques Rousseau believed that power should be more widely dispersed among the people in *democratic systems of government* in order to achieve social harmony. John Locke (1632–1704) advocated for a *representative democracy* where government possesses limited powers and where the people select representatives to make decisions on their behalf. Locke's writings were particularly influential to the American Framers as they grappled with how best to form a new government in the late eighteenth century. Thomas Jefferson referenced Locke when he penned the U.S. Declaration of Independence in what has become one of the most widely cited sentences ever written: "We hold these truths to be self-evident that all men are created equal, that they are endowed by their Creator with certain unalienable Rights, that among these are life, liberty, and the pursuit of Happiness." It was this line of thinking that also paved the way for the expansion of political rights for ethnic minorities and women (see Theory and Practice box about female judges). Jean-Jacques Rousseau (1712–1778), on the other hand, criticized representative democracies claiming they facilitate the exploitation of the masses by political elites. He instead called for universal political participation in a direct democracy form of government, where the people as a whole make decisions for themselves.

Leading experts in American politics discuss political power in the context of the executive, legislative, and judicial branches of government. One major debate involves whether the American president has taken on "imperial" qualities and whether the executive branch has too much power over the other two branches of government. As we highlight in Chapter 6, famed presidential scholar Richard Neustadt, known by some as the American Machiavelli, argues that presidents must above all else have the political skills to "persuade" the Washington establishment and the American public to act on their agendas.

Do Female Justices View Legal Cases Differently than Male Justices?

Justice Elena Kagan was confirmed with little fanfare to the United States Supreme Court in August 2010. Out of the 112 Justices who have served on the Court throughout our history, only four of them have been women. Why is that? Do female Justices interpret legal facts differently from their male counterparts? There is some research in political science suggesting that female Justices might frame legal issues differently than male Justices when hearing oral arguments and drafting legal opinions.

Supreme Court Justice Ruth Bader Ginsberg, for example, was most vocal on a case questioning whether school officials in Arizona could legally strip-search a 13-year-old female student while searching for drugs. While some of the other male Justices downplayed the significance of the girl's embarrassment, Justice Ginsburg, as the lone female Justice on the Supreme Court at the time, empathized with the girl's humiliation. In a subsequent interview, Justice Ginsberg stated "they (meaning the other male judges) have never been a 13-year-old girl…it's a very sensitive age for a girl. I don't think my colleagues, some of them, quite understood."[6]

The first woman to serve on the Supreme Court was Sandra Day O'Connor, who was nominated to the bench by President Ronald Reagan in 1981. In 2010, Justice Kagan joined two other female Justices including Justice Ruth Bader Ginsberg, appointed by President Clinton in 1993, and Justice Sonia Sotomayor, nominated by President Obama in 2009. Having three female Justices serve together could impact the culture of the Court. One 2006 study of the U.S. business world, for instance, found that a critical mass of "three or more women can cause a fundamental change in the boardroom and enhance corporate governance."[7] Having three female Justices deliberating on cases might then expand the range of perspectives brought to legal discussions. However, another study in political science found no difference between the judicial decisions of male and female judges at the lower federal court level, except on the issue of sexual discrimination, where female judges were 10 percent more likely to rule in favor of the party bringing the suit.[8] In the

continued

United States, approximately 26.6 percent of all federal and state judges are women.[9] In comparison, women make up 26 percent of all judges in Canada, 46 percent of the judges in Finland, and 54 percent of the judges in France.[10]

> **Is the gender composition of the U.S. Supreme Court relevant to how it makes decisions?**
>
> **Should a person's gender, race, and/or ethnicity be taken into account when selecting judges? Why or why not?**

Political Power in International Affairs

The struggle for political power across the globe continues to shape our political landscape today. In 2011, popular movements against Middle Eastern despots spread from Tunisia to Egypt, and then on to Libya, Syria, and Yemen in what has been named the **Arab Spring**. Arab Spring refers to the democratic movements that have spread across the Middle East throughout 2011 as people across the region have taken to the streets in an attempt to wrestle power from authoritarian governments. This grassroots revolt against Middle Eastern autocrats was ignited after a 26-year-old Tunisian named Mohammed Bouazizi set himself on fire after a Tunisian police officer flipped his produce cart and confiscated his vegetable weighing scale because he was either unwilling or unable to pay a bribe.[11] His act of self-sacrifice against the Tunisian government sparked a citizen revolt that culminated in the toppling of the Tunisian president Ben Ali. Inspired by the Tunisian example, millions of Egyptians then took to the streets protesting police brutality, political corruption, the lack of free speech, and high inflation. They were also successful in toppling Egyptian president Hosni Mubarek. These protests and some continuing in the region are organized mostly by "young idealists, inspired by democracy, united by Facebook and excited by the notion of opening up to a wider world."[12]

In the realm of international politics Joseph Nye, Jr. makes distinctions between "hard power" and "soft power."[13] Nations exert hard power when they compel other nations to modify their behavior through military and/or economic force. However, nations can also influence the behavior of other nations by employing soft power, where leverage is gained through the sway of diplomatic and cultural persuasion.[14] The interplay between hard power and soft power is currently on display in U.S.

Arab Spring: *Refers to the pro-democratic political movements (2011) spreading throughout the Middle East and Northern Africa.*

CourseReader ASSIGNMENT

Log in to **www.cengagebrain.com** and open CourseReader to access the reading:

"Islam and the Arab Revolutions" and "Islam and the Arab Revolutions: A Golden Opportunity" from *The Economist,* April 2–8, 2011

These two articles from *The Economist* magazine highlight popular democratic movements in Tunisia, Egypt, Libya, Syria, and Yemen (a.k.a. the Arab Spring) that began in the spring of 2011. The articles also outline the potential role of Egypt's Islamic Brotherhood and other Islamic organizations in shaping the future direction of this grassroots movement in the region. Some view the Arab Spring through a positive lens and believe the uprisings will stabilize the region by spreading democracy, while others fear the uprisings might allow Islamic fundamentalists to take control in these countries.

- *Do you believe democracy is likely to take root in countries affected by the Arab Spring? Why or why not?*
- *What role if any should the international community play in shaping the future political direction in this region of the world?*

Counterterrorism:
A police or military strategy that employs offensive tactics to preempt or deter future terroristic attacks.

Counterinsurgency:
A military strategy that includes military, political, economic, and humanitarian efforts in an attempt to win over the hearts and minds of the domestic population.

foreign policy in Afghanistan. After the al-Qaeda-led terrorist attack on the United States on September 11, 2001, the U.S. government, led by President George W. Bush, exerted hard power in Afghanistan by using military force to remove the Taliban government. The United States then took the lead in drafting Afghanistan's new constitution and in establishing an interim government led by President Hamid Karzai in December 2004. Beginning in 2009, President Barack Obama increased the number of American troops in Afghanistan to 100,000. U.S. foreign policy in Afghanistan also transitioned from a **counterterrorism** policy to a **counterinsurgency** policy. The counterterrorism policy employed hard power in that it relied primarily on the American military to use force to eradicate al-Qaeda operatives from Afghanistan. More American troops were later dispatched to Afghanistan in order to implement a counterinsurgency policy, where the U.S. military employs both hard power and soft power in an attempt to win over the hearts and minds of the Afghan people.

Those advocating a counterinsurgency approach argue that in order to fight against terrorism effectively in Afghanistan, the United States needs to incorporate a soft power approach by assisting in the economic and political development of Afghanistan. The military has thus established relationships with Afghan tribal leaders, assisted in the building of roads, and helped to develop Afghanistan's economic and political system. Critics of the counterinsurgency policy oppose this form of nation-building on the grounds that it requires too many troops, is too costly, and is unlikely to win over the hearts and minds of the people. Many of these critics instead favor the counterterrorism approach because its more limited policy goal of fighting terrorists requires a less visible military presence. In May 2011, the United States dispatched helicopters filled with Navy Seals from Afghanistan to kill al-Qaeda's leader Osama bin Laden in a surprise raid of his secret compound in northwest Pakistan. However, the U.S. government still views the al-Qaeda network as a serious threat to its national security interests in Afghanistan and around the world.

In this handout image provided by the White House, President Barack Obama, Vice President Joe Biden, Secretary of State Hillary Clinton, and members of the national security team receive an update on the mission against Osama bin Laden in the Situation Room of the White House on May 1, 2011, in Washington, DC. Obama later announced that the United States had killed bin Laden in an operation led by U.S. Special Forces at a compound in Abbottabad, Pakistan.

THEORY AND PRACTICE

How You Can Engage Politics through Policy Debate

Resolved: *That the U.S. Government Should Modify Its Foreign Policy in Afghanistan from a Counterinsurgency Approach to a Counterterrorism Approach.*

One of the primary purposes of the field of political science is to help you become more informed and active members of our society. In the broadest sense this book hopes to inspire active citizenship and empower students with the skills necessary to engage our political system. Aristotle's *Politics* argued that political debate is the most highly valued political skill because it is through debate that we are able to carry reason into action. Debates also translate well into the classroom setting and can be formalized into the curriculum. The following represents a road map for structuring debates into the classroom setting.

continued ➡

The Affirmative Burden

The affirmative team has the burden of establishing three central points in order to win the debate round. While the affirmative team benefits from the element of surprise, in that it initiates the central arguments of the debate, it is disadvantaged by having to win three stock issue arguments.

The Plan

The affirmative team (typically two members) has the burden of offering an actionable plan. In this case it could read, *Resolved: The U.S. Government Should Modify Its Foreign Policy in Afghanistan from a Counterinsurgency Approach to a Counterterrorism Approach.* The affirmative plan is also advantaged with fiat powers, meaning debaters are to assume that the plan will be enacted into law, thus eliminating debate on the likelihood of congressional approval, and centering discourse on the merits of the proposal.

Observation One: Harms and Significance

In observation one, the affirmative team must establish "Harms and Significance." Here, the affirmative team must demonstrate that a substantial problem exists in our society. For example, in the case of the U.S. counterinsurgency approach in Afghanistan, the affirmative team can argue against counterinsurgency by emphasizing how and why the policy requires a large number of U.S. troops, the impact of the counterinsurgency policy on the U.S. budget, and more broadly provide evidence that the policy is not currently winning over the hearts and minds of the Afghan people. The affirmative team should persuasively argue that the evidence of their harmful acts represent significant problems in our society and requires swift legislative action.

Observation Two: Inherency

The affirmative team must also establish the inherency of their harms. The inherency argument establishes the need for policy action. The affirmative must convince judges that nothing in the status quo adequately addresses their harms. The affirmative team can lose the inherency argument, for instance, if the negative team uncovers pending legislation addressing their harms, suggesting no further action is required.

continued

Observation Three: Solvency

Lastly, in observation three, the affirmative team has the burden of establishing that their plan will significantly solve their harms. In this case the affirmative team must demonstrate that a counterterrorism policy will solve all or most of their harms analysis. In this example, the affirmative team should provide evidence that a counterterrorism policy requires fewer troops, costs less, and keeps Americans safe.

The Negative Team's Response

The primary characteristic of every great debate is a clashing of ideas, where oratory sparks and fireworks fill the room. It is the central responsibility of the negative team to ignite these fireworks by challenging the veracity of the affirmative team's evidence. It is therefore the negative team's responsibility to ensure that arguments do not suffer from the *two ships passing in the night* syndrome, as that would suggest the affirmative team's case is sailing through unchallenged.

On-Case Negative Arguments

The negative team can win the debate round by either attacking the affirmative case directly (i.e., on-case) or by making off-case arguments. Because the affirmative team is required to win the harms, inherency, and solvency argument, the negative team can win the debate by simply *taking out* one of the stock issues in the affirmative case. The negative team can therefore win the debate round if it can establish that the counterinsurgency policy is succeeding or if it can demonstrate that the affirmative's plan will not improve the status quo.

Off-Case Arguments: Disadvantages and Counterplans

It is sometimes difficult to attack the affirmative plan directly. There are glaring problems in society and some affirmative plans are logically sound. This places the negative team in a position where they are coerced into forwarding arguments that might defy common sense. In this event the negative team might strategically shift the debate toward off-case arguments. Off-case arguments represent a reversal of roles by allowing the negative team to go on the offensive. The negative team can place the affirmative team on the defensive by offering either a disadvantage or a counterplan.

continued

A disadvantage contends that an undesirable and unstated consequence will occur if the plan is passed. Disadvantages prevent the affirmative team from offering its plan in a vacuum in that they remind us that a solution to a particular problem might in fact cause more glaring problems in other areas. A counterplan offers the negative team another opportunity to win the debate without defending the status quo. Here, the negative team concedes the harms and inherency evidence of the affirmative plan and instead challenges the affirmative team with an alternative plan. The negative plan, however, must be mutually exclusive from the affirmative's plan, meaning the affirmative plan and the negative plan cannot coexist?

> Do you prefer the counterinsurgency approach over the counterterrorism approach in Afghanistan? Why or why not?
>
> In a policy debate, with whom does the burden of proof lie?
>
> Why is new evidence not allowed in a rebuttal?

POLITICAL SCIENCE AS AN ACADEMIC DISCIPLINE

Political science: *The academic discipline that seeks to understand the relationship between individuals and political institutions.*

Social sciences: *Any number of academic disciplines that seek to understand human behavior. Classically they have been understood to mean anthropology, archaeology, economics, criminology, political science, and psychology.*

Broadly speaking, **political science** (along with anthropology, criminal justice, economics, psychology, and sociology) is part of the academic tradition known as the **social sciences** because it examines and seeks to explain human behavior. In the same manner that psychologists through observation and research conduct experiments that seek to explain the human mind, political scientists seek to explain the relationship between human beings and their political institutions.

Since the beginning of philosophical inquiry, scholars have attempted to determine answers to questions about who should rule and which political institutions are best suited to bring peace and security to the people. In doing so, political scientists have developed a number of methods to help them conduct research. In the following section, we will briefly discuss some of these methods.

Approaches to Political Science

Historically, the field of political science has been divided into three major methodological traditions or schools of thought: traditionalism, behavioralism, and postbehavioralism. **Traditionalism** relies largely on **normative** evaluations. In other words, traditionalists seek answers to questions that try to determine if individuals within government institutions (like Congress) are acting how they "ought to be acting." For example, a traditionalist may examine the powers awarded to the U.S. Senate through a combination of history (how previous members voted) and philosophical inquiry (what the Constitution says about Congress, or the Founding Fathers) to determine if today's membership is representative of the true intention of the law. Traditionalists avoid numerical or **quantitative** determinations in their analyses because they seek value judgments in their outcomes, which are largely unquantifiable.

Adherents of **behavioralism,** on the other hand, look at the actual behavior of those in the political process and employ an *empirical* or data-driven approach. In the same manner that traditionalists attempt to determine how well one is living up to a constitutional or legal mandate, behavioralists try to determine why certain people behave the way they do. Behavioralists focus their research on quantitative analyses that attempt to use data to reinforce their arguments. In essence, behavioralists use mathematical or statistical models to explain different kinds of political and social behavior. They may seek to better understand the relationship between certain **variables** and attempt to find a **correlation** or relationship between them. For example, is there a correlation between one's gender and/or race and how one votes in the U.S. House of Representatives on issues related to an expansion of health care options? To answer this question, the behavioralist will examine the voting record of all of the members of Congress and then determine whether or not one's race and/or gender play a role in how one approaches the health care debate.

The last and most recent addition to the approaches political scientists use is known as **postbehavioralism.** The best way to understand the arguments of postbehavioralists is to see them as a hybrid of the previous two schools. Just as behavioralists critiqued traditionalists for being *too* "moral" or "value oriented" in their analyses, postbehavioralists have critiqued behavioralists for being *too* scientific and, in many ways, guilty of ignoring ethical responsibility to the field and to the citizenry at large. Postbehavioralists have tried to remind political scientists that in addition to conducting experiments or collecting data, they should try to answer some of the more important questions affecting the citizens, the states, and the world around them.

Although this has been a brief introduction to some of the ways political scientists approach the field, it is essential that you understand their differences before we move ahead. It is also essential that you understand the layout of this text and some of its unique features. Think of the following section as a road map to this text. It will begin with some of the text's chapter features and it will end with a brief description of each part.

Traditionalism: *The methodological tradition that seeks to understand if certain government or political institutions are behaving in accordance with how they "ought to behave."*

Normative: *A normative approach is any approach that seeks to determine how one "ought to live." You will see the normative approach more clearly in the discussion of Plato and Aristotle in Chapter 2.*

Quantitative analysis: *An analysis that uses data to interpret political phenomena. The data may come from survey research or established data sets to better understand the political world.*

Behavioralism: *The school of thought that looks at the "actual" behavior of certain persons or institutions. It is largely data driven and without a strong commitment to values.*

Variable: *Features or attributes of social science research. In particular, a variable might look at the relationship between race and voting, age and voting, or religious preference and voting.*

Correlation: *The relationship between two items or variables.*

Post-behavioralism: *The school of thought that seeks to combine elements of the traditional approach (especially the idea of values) with those of behavioralism.*

Why Politics Matters to YOU!

Throughout this book, you will see boxes entitled "Why Politics Matters to YOU!" These features are designed to help you make connections to others in the political world. Because we live in extraordinary times of financial, political, social, and technological interconnectedness, it is vital that you see a connection to your government and to the world beyond. Your generation, the Facebook generation, has the unique opportunity to gain access to events around the world instantaneously. However, this power can often breed a great deal of apathy and confusion toward domestic and global processes because it is quite overwhelming. The "Why Politics Matters to YOU!" boxes are our way of deconstructing some of the ways that modern life might overwhelm you and allow you to see that in these fantastic times, your understanding of and involvement in politics has never been more important.

To give you an example of how these boxes will read, we have included a brief story about cell phones and how you may not have realized the terror involved in their construction. This box (and all of the others for that matter) is designed to show you how interconnected you really are to the world at large and, more importantly, why politics matters. Now, we are not about to give you the common lecture about how technology has provided you with a global passport. But we are going to ask you to read the "Why Politics Matters to YOU!" feature and reexamine your relationship to the world through the very innocent example of cell phones. We ask you to open your mind and consider how the political world around you matters and how your role in it is truly important.

WHY POLITICS MATTERS TO YOU!

Your Cell Phone and the Democratic Republic of Congo

The Democratic Republic of Congo (DRC), which actually is neither democratic nor a republic, is a landlocked country in the heart of sub-Saharan Africa. Its history is one of colonialism, civil and regional war, exploitation, and genocide. According to the International Monetary Fund (IMF), an international agency committed to providing short-term relief to states that have experienced human catastrophes, the citizens of the DRC are some of the world's poorest. In the years following its independence from Belgium, the DRC (known as Zaire for a number of years) has experienced a never-ending cycle of civil unrest and political corruption culminating in a breakdown of its ability to prevent regional warlords from

continued

continued

destroying its political infrastructure. After the genocide that took place in neighboring Rwanda in 1994, a regional war broke out that is still raging and has left the country in shambles. To place this tragedy in an appropriate perspective, *New York Times* columnist Nicholas Kristof suggested that the death rate in the DRC as a result of this ongoing war is roughly 45,000 people per month.[15]

But at this point you are still probably wondering what this unimaginable tale of tragedy has to do with you. Well, in addition to mass casualties and a humanitarian crisis of epic proportions, the DRC also possesses the trinity of the modern electronic movement: tantalum, tin, and tungsten. These three minerals, in addition to gold, help fund the bank accounts of some of the country's worst warlords.

Tantalum, tin, and tungsten are the three most important elements in the production of cell phones. Tantalum, for instance, is a powdery mineral that has allowed the size of cell phones to shrink from the oversized ones of the 1980s to those that fit inside your shirt pocket today. It has allowed scientists to create "passive capacitators…[which] regulate voltage at high temperatures."[16] In short, it has provided cell phone developers

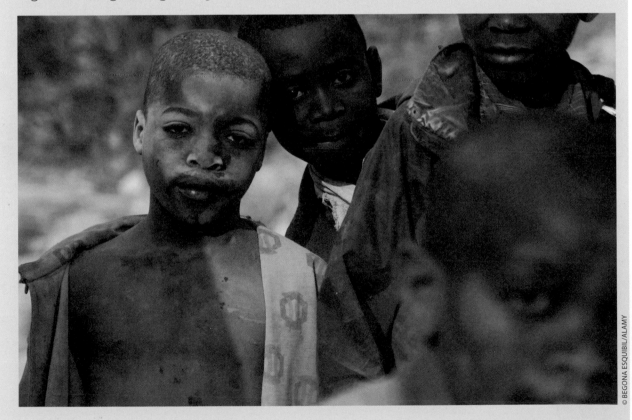

▲ Children workers of a mine in the Democratic Republic of Congo.

© BEGONA ESQUIBII/ALAMY

continued

the ability to control the high temperatures caused by cellular technology in a device that can fit in the palm of your hand without the risk of shock or fire. In scientific terms, tantalum has been a major breakthrough. In economic terms, however, it has seen the value of tantalum skyrocket, which in turn has made it quite valuable to those in Congo with access to the mines, many of whom employ less-than-savory labor practices.

Two investigative reporters, who have gained special access to the Congolese mines, provided the following eyewitness account of how the extraction of minerals takes place in the DRC:

> At the mines, we saw militiamen armed with AK-47 machine guns standing over miners and forcing them to work and pay bribes, including child miners as young as 11. We then crossed through army and rebel checkpoints, where smugglers paid off the commanders in U.S. dollars, and then witnessed how these same minerals were packed into barrels with Congolese flags on them and loaded onto planes and flown out of the country.
>
> We've seen how armed groups on all sides of the conflict are reaping hundreds of millions of dollars per year by controlling mines and trading routes, selling minerals to international traders and smelters, which in turn sell them to electronics and jewelry companies.[17]

The electronics companies then create the phones and manufacture precious jewels, market them to consumers, and ultimately bring them to the marketplace at a reasonable price.

So there you have it. The materials that allow your mobile devices to function with ease were probably mined by children in one of the most unstable countries on earth. Does this make you stop and think about other things you own and where they are made or mined? If so, you are on the road to seeing how this world of ours is really interconnected and some of the reasons why certain people have so much and others have so little.

Does the interconnectedness of the world make you question what items you choose to buy?

Why is there such a gap between the wealthy and poor in the world today?

Should large companies that deal with overseas markets and people change policies toward their workers?

© ISTOCKPHOTO.COM/SABLAMEK

Theory and Practice

Although the field of political science uses different approaches (which we will examine later in this chapter), an understanding of politics is still grounded in **theory.** Theories emerge when individuals seek answers to questions. For example, a popular question in the field of political science is, do governments with more females in positions of power create and then implement (bring into action) policies that are friendlier to women? While your inclination to this question might be to say that there is a correlation, this is still only a **hypothesis**, or an educated guess based on previously understood facts or logic. A theory emerges after one tests the hypothesis to see if a correlation exists. If it does, then one is said to make an argument in favor of the aforementioned theory.

Because theories are vital to good research, we have provided another type of learning box: the "Theory and Practice" feature. These learning boxes are designed to provide you with some of the theoretical underpinnings behind political issues and to provide you with a perspective that you might not have been aware of. They will shed light on what happens when theoretical concepts in political science are actually put into practice in our current political world.

Theory: *An idea that has been tested that aims to demonstrate a correlation between political phenomena.*

Hypothesis: *An educated guess about a particular experiment.*

Introducing You to the Field

Now that you have a basic understanding of some of the ways this book will incorporate theory into the practice of politics and the reasons why politics should matter to you, it is important to provide you with an overall layout of the book.

Introducing you to a field of study as broad as political science may seem quite demanding, so what we have done is to break it down into more manageable bites. If you think of political science as a large, or even better, an extra-large pizza, it may seem sloppy and overwhelming. But if we divide the subject into pieces, or what we call **subfields of political science**, and provide you with an entire semester to digest it, it becomes more manageable. In many ways, this is exactly the manner in which this book is constructed. We have taken the entire field and divided it four ways, with each part representing a major subfield within the overall discipline of political science. Thus, we have parts on political theory, American government, comparative politics, and international relations.

The parts follow a logical construction as well. Just as a foundation is the most important first step in the construction of a house, so too is political theory to the wider field of political science. Before we can embark on discussions concerning health care, foreign policy, or even the development of the Chinese and Indian economies, we need to first understand the classic philosophical arguments of ancient thinkers like Plato and Aristotle and the modern arguments of the social contract thinkers: Hobbes, Locke, and Rousseau. These ideas shaped the world of yesterday and will shape the world of tomorrow. Thus, it is vital that we begin with an understanding of the classics.

Subfields of political science: *The different content approaches within the overall discipline of political science. It can refer to political theory, American politics, comparative politics, and international relations.*

Since the political theory part ends with an examination of those social contract thinkers who contributed to the development of modern democratic thought, we have focused the second part on the world's longest lasting representative democracy, the United States. While this part deals with all aspects of the American political system, we pay particular attention to the major structural and behavioral components of the United States, including the fundamental principles of the American system of government as embodied in the U.S. Constitution, the political attitudes and activities of individual citizens and groups, and the structural arrangement as found in the legislative, executive, and judicial branches.

Comparative politics:
The subfield of political science that examines different types of institutions and issues within different countries. They are usually regionally based. For example, one may do comparative research on the area of the world known as the Middle East.

International Relations:
The field of political science that studies the way nations interact with one another and the influence of global trends on nation-states.

Part 3, which examines **comparative politics,** utilizes the information of the previous part and evaluates the policies, processes, and institutions of other states in relation to those of the United States. Definitions concerning types of government will include an analysis of the characteristics of authoritarian states and their democratic counterparts. In doing so, we will highlight certain states that are considered to be authoritarian or democratic. This will allow you the opportunity to see how other states choose and make policies, articulate and define issues pertaining to personal freedoms, and maintain and transfer power from one government to the next.

The last part, **international relations,** will build on the regional approach to comparative politics established in the preceding chapters. With special emphasis placed on concepts related to international relations theory, the development of the international system, international organizations, and globalization, this final part allows you to balance an understanding of domestic and global governance. This final part also allows you the opportunity to reflect on all of the issues covered in the text and to see the world through the intellectual prism of the entire field of political science.

SUMMARY

Overall, this book is designed to give you a greater understanding of both the theory and practice of politics. We intend to take away the intimidation of studying such thinkers as Plato and Aristotle, to make them more accessible and, we hope, more useful to future leaders. We'll also point out connections between your life and the world at large.

Today's world is highly interconnected and highly competitive. It is therefore important that you realize the roles you and your classmates play in it. Competition for jobs in the future will depend on some of the issues we address in this book. So enough said. Let's get started. Are you ready? Here we go...

© PATRICK BAZ/AFP/GETTY IMAGES

KEY TERMS

Anarchism p. 8

Arab Spring p. 11

Authoritarianism p. 8

Autocracy p. 8

Behavioralism p. 17

Capitalism p. 8

Communism p. 8

Comparative politics p. 22

Conservatism p. 8

Correlation p. 17

Counterinsurgency p. 12

Counterterrorism p. 12

Demographics p. 5

Direct democracy p. 8

Fascism p. 8

Feminism p. 8

Feudalism p. 8

Hypothesis p. 21

International Relations p. 22

Liberal p. 8

Libertarianism p. 8

Marxism p. 8

Meritocracy p. 8

Monarchy p. 8

Nation-state p. 8

Normative p. 17

Oligarchy p. 8

Pacifist p. 8

Plutocracy p. 8

Political science p. 16

Political socialization p. 4

Post-behavioralism p. 17

Public opinion polls p. 5

Quantitative analysis p. 17

Representative democracy p. 8

Republic p. 8

Social contract p. 8

Social contract theorists p. 7

Socialism p. 9

Social sciences p. 16

Subfields of political science p. 21

Terrorism p. 9

Theocracy p. 9

Theory p. 21

Totalitarianism p. 9

Traditionalism p. 17

Utilitarianism p. 9

Variable p. 17

2

ANCIENT POLITICAL THEORY

This statue of Plato can be seen in front of the Academy of Athens, which is located in Athens, Greece.

INTRODUCTION: HOW ANCIENT POLITICAL THOUGHT IMPACTS US TODAY

Ancient Greece is considered the cradle of Western civilization because it is here over 2,500 years ago that enormous strides were made in the areas of mathematics, science, architecture, politics, and philosophy that continue to shape our lives today. It is because of advancements made in ancient Greece that the American White House carries a loose resemblance to the Greek Parthenon, why modern doctors are required to pledge to do no harm when they take the Hippocratic Oath, why students all over the world study geometry, why billions across the globe tune into the Olympics, and why almost all of Western society now functions in some form of democratic government.

Ancient Greece was not a unified nation, but rather a collection of smaller city-states, encircled by farmland and typically only a few blocks long. Each of these city-states was referred to as a "polis," and inhabitants of each polis typically shared common cultural, political, economic, and religious customs. The word *politics* itself derives from the term *polis* and the name is still used today to describe modern city life (e.g., "metropolis" and "cosmopolitan"). It was the defined political structure of the polis that also helped to contextualize the works of three ancient Greek philosophers: Socrates, Plato, and Aristotle. It is fitting to emphasize these three philosophers because their observations laid the theoretical foundation from which all other Western political thought launches. A general understanding of the major theories associated with these early Greek thinkers can assist us in effectively critiquing and engaging our political world today.

Many of the questions raised by these early Greek thinkers are still hotly debated today. *What is the purpose of life? How can we find happiness? Which skills should our political leaders possess? What is the ideal form of government? Why is it important to be ethical?* These are the central questions raised by Socrates and appear throughout Plato's *The Republic* and Aristotle's *Politics*. These classic works are important because they not only offer a glimpse into ancient political

Questions to Consider Before Reading this Chapter

1. Why did Socrates accept his death sentence rather than flee his jail cell?

2. How did Plato make a connection between the Republic and the human soul?

3. Why did Plato believe democracies were inferior political systems?

4. What is the best path toward human happiness according to Plato?

5. Why does Aristotle believe that we are by nature political animals?

6. How did Plato and Aristotle differ with respect to their view of the ideal form of government?

7. In what ways did ancient Greek thinking influence and/or challenge early Christian thinking?

8. How did Plato and Aristotle influence the American system of government?

© JON HICKS/CORBIS

life, but also provoke us to think more broadly about the purpose of politics today. Socrates, Plato, and Aristotle started the theoretical discussion on politics and emphasized the need to select honest and competent leaders. For that reason it is helpful to have a general understanding of their viewpoints in order to more effectively evaluate our modern political system. This is of great consequence because discussions on ethical leadership have come to the forefront in American politics over the past 30 years. Chapter 5 on the American Congress highlights the corrosive nature of political corruption on American democracy in the discussion of the Abscam scandal, the Keating Five scandal, the Duke Cunningham scandal, and the Jack Abramoff scandal. Not coincidentally, public polling reveals that public mistrust of U.S. political leaders has grown over the past 30 years. Perhaps this trend can be reversed by reconnecting with some of the teachings advanced by Socrates, Plato, and Aristotle.

THE IONIANS

Ionians: *The earliest Greek philosophers who believed in using rationality rather than mythology to understand the universe.*

Ancient political thought and political science itself sprang from an ancient philosophical debate about whether *our universe behaves in a purposeful and systematic manner, or whether our universe instead is in a state of perpetual random change, devoid of any purpose or meaning.* The earliest Greek philosophers were the **Ionians**, who in the 6th century BCE rejected the cultural view reflected in Homer's mythological explanation that our universe was controlled by Zeus, Hera, Apollo, and other Greek gods and goddesses. The Ionians instead advocated employing greater rationality to the important questions of the day.

These early Greek philosophers concentrated on the material world, debating the form and substance of our universe. Thales of Miletus believed our universe was made of water, Anaximenes held that the universe was composed of air, while Heraclitus theorized that the universe was made of fire.[1] In the 5th century BCE, Democritus solved the conundrum with his discovery that all living things are instead composed of atoms. These early theorists asked deeper questions about our surroundings, such as what is the nature of our universe? Does the material world exist in a perpetual state of random change or is there an enduring life force guiding our universe?

Republican System of Government: *A system of government in which power is exercised indirectly through representatives that are voted into office by citizens of the state.*

Democracy: *A system of government in which the supreme power is vested in the people and exercised by them directly or indirectly through a system of representation usually involving periodically held free elections.*[51]

In this era, there were two rival and competing movements that organized around this question. The Greeks identified these philosophical camps as the *theory of becoming* and the *theory of being.*[2] The roots of all Western political thought are located in these two distinct philosophical schools.

Theory of Becoming

Those aligned with the *"theory of becoming"* argued that the universe was in a constant state of random and arbitrary change (or becoming) and could be understood in material terms. Democritus, for instance, conceived that all things in the universe

How Did the Greeks Influence the American Founding Fathers?

The teachings of Socrates, Plato, and Aristotle had a tremendous impact on the American Founding Fathers and the American system of government. American college entrance exams in the 18th century required students to be able to read and translate from the original Greek texts. Universities in this era offered very few elective courses and instead required students to study classical works. It was not unusual for Thomas Jefferson to study for 15 hours a day, and he was known to routinely carry with him several Greek grammar books. Furthermore, 30 of the 55 Delegates who attended the Constitutional Convention in Philadelphia in 1787 were college graduates. Most of the American Founding Fathers were therefore very well trained in the major theories associated with Plato's *The Republic* and Aristotle's *Politics*.

Carl J. Richard's text *Greeks & Romans Bearing Gifts: How the Ancients Inspired the Founding Fathers* highlights how early American political thought was shaped by the lessons learned from ancient Greece. The ill treatment of citizens in ancient Sparta inspired the Founding Father's belief in individual rights. In *Federalist Paper No. 6* Alexander Hamilton referred to ancient Sparta as "a little better than a well regulated camp," and John Adams referred to Spartan rules against private ownership as "stark mad."[3] The examples of Greek and Persian political structures led to the conviction that republican forms of government were superior to monarchies. They also learned of the potential for democracies to degenerate into mob rule from the example of ancient Athens. It is because of this that the term democracy is not included in the U.S. Constitution. James Madison's *Federalist Paper No.10* was chiefly concerned about whether our system of government could promote both majority rule and minority rights. Alexander Hamilton, John Adams, James Madison, and Thomas Jefferson learned from the classic texts that many Greek and Roman tyrants began their political careers as democratic reformers and feared that America might be vulnerable to a similar fate.

The American Founding Fathers were influenced by the Greeks when they created a representative democracy, whereby representatives are selected to make decisions on behalf of the people. Some American states allow for ballot initiatives whereby legislatures are bypassed and citizens make decisions on policy questions directly in the voting booth.

continued

Do you believe it is better to have elected officials make decisions on behalf of the people or should citizens be permitted to make policy decisions themselves?

are made up of atoms that move and combine in perfectly random and accidental ways. The *theory of becoming* camp did not believe that a preexisting plan or sacred objective guides our material world. They speculated that our universe is rather simply what it *becomes* as a result of random configurations established when matter in our universe collides into other forms of mass, setting that material form into motion against another. They conjectured that our universe is simply the by-product of a long series of perfectly random and accidental collisions. This camp also claimed that reality is best understood by examining things that we can measure in our universe, rather than in attaching religious, mystical, and/or metaphysical explanations to our material world. The *theory of becoming* school of thought prescribed to the view that we can best understand our universe, and our role in it, by gaining a deeper scientific understanding of our physical world.

Theory of Being

In contrast, those associated with the *theory of being* school of thought believed that underlying our ever-changing material world is a preexisting and permanent design. Pythagoras, for example, posited that a permanent invisible and unchanging structure underpins our world of appearances.[4] Pythagoras argued that the key that unlocked all of the mysteries of the universe could be found in mathematical formulas that represent a deeper reality than the reality ascertained through our physical senses.

The question of whether the universe is in a constant state of random change (i.e., *state of becoming*) or whether a permanent deeper reality exists beyond our world of appearances (i.e., *state of being*) eventually gets incorporated into political theory. Pythagoras, for example, incorporated the *theory of being* into political theory by conjecturing that we instill within the human soul the same principles that exist in our physical world by intellectualizing mathematical principles.[5] By linking mathematical concepts found in our universe to human consciousness we transform our conception of ourselves and the way we ought to interact with each other. The important point is these discussions reflect the emergence of Greek rationality, or the preference for using human reasoning powers to discover objective truths rather than relying on conventional mythologies to explain important questions of the day.[6] Plato adopts Greek rationality in his classic text *The Republic* through the style of the dialogue approach, where the weaknesses of commonly held misconceptions are exposed through public discourse.

Do you believe our universe is in a perpetual state of random change or do you believe a guiding life force underpins our universe?

THE SOPHISTS

Athens became the world's primary cultural gathering place after the Greek military victory over the Persians in 448 BCE. It was during this period that Greek culture became strongly influenced by a group of political thinkers called the *sophists*. The sophists were primarily responsible for shifting the focus of Greek philosophy from the universe to the individual. They were skeptical (hence the name *skeptics*) about whether we can ever truly come to understand our ultimate reality or acquaint ourselves with the mysteries of our universe.[7]

Skeptics: *Philosophers who generally agree that nothing can be known with absolute certainty.*

They were instead primarily concerned with questions surrounding human behavior. The sophists shared a common worldview called *sophia,* which viewed the study of man, as opposed to the study of the universe, as the most important unit of analysis.[8] Protagoras reflected this view when he said *"Man is the measure of all things, of the reality of those which are, and the reality of those which are not.*[9] The sophists were primarily concerned with how Greek citizens ought to conduct their lives.

One of the primary subjects taught by the sophists was rhetoric and the art of public debate. Their emphasis on teaching debate (or sophistry) opened them up to criticism that they were more interested in teaching the power of persuasion than in establishing a strong intellectual framework. The sophists broadly assumed that human beings are naturally power seeking and predisposed to the pursuit of self-interest. In addition, they did not believe in the existence of a universal truth and viewed such concepts as "justice" or "truth" as social conventions rather than natural constructs.[10] Many of the teachings of Socrates and Plato directly challenged the sophist view of human nature.

SOCRATES

Socrates was born in 470 BCE and was sentenced to death by the democratic Greek Senate for "corrupting the youth" and "religious impiety" in 399 BCE. Socrates's life and influence over ancient Western political thought is in many respects analogous to the life and influence of Jesus in Christianity. Both men were excellent teachers, both threatened the political status quo, both were put on trial for their teachings, and both were unjustifiably put to death for their beliefs.[11] Another similarity is that neither Socrates nor Jesus ever transcribed their teachings to the written word. We came to learn what we know about Socrates through the writings of his greatest student

© NICK PAVLAKIS/SHUTTERSTOCK.COM

▲ THE GREEK PHILOSOPHER SOCRATES

Normative Theory: *Any theory that examines the way something "should" or "ought" to be rather than focusing on the way something actually "is."*

Plato, who was approximately 50 years his junior, just as we came to know Jesus through the writings of his devotees.

Socrates was an unimpressive physical specimen in an era when attractive appearances were held in very high regard, much like today. He had bulging eyes, a potbelly, long hair, was unclean, and typically carried a stick as he walked without footwear.[12]

One of Socrates's greatest contributions to Western civilization was his introduction of the inductive method in the teaching profession. The Socratic teaching method (see "Why Politics Matters to YOU!" on page 31), in fact, is still the primary teaching technique used in American law schools today. Socrates agreed with the sophists on a number of points, including the notion that more can be learned by the study of human behavior than by the study of the universe. He also employed the **normative theory** approach to philosophy, in that he was most interested in uncovering the purpose of our human existence, and how the "good life" can be achieved if humans interact with each other in a just and ethical manner.

He emphasized that we must first agree on the definitions of words before we can adopt universal principles. He was a controversial teacher because he asked his students to question the intellectual rationale behind society's guiding principles. For instance, students were asked to define such terms as justice or courage, and when their definitions fell short, it highlighted the shortcomings of their conventional views. His incessant questioning of students shook their confidence and caused them to question everything they held as true, including societal norms and the motivations of the Greek ruling class. Socrates never claimed to possess the truth and held that we can only come to knowledge by first recognizing our own ignorance. Yet he came to believe that he was wiser than the political leaders of Greek society because he was at least aware of his ignorance, whereas most Greek political figures held convictions that were simply untrue, as well as self-serving.[13]

Socrates and the sophists were also in agreement that the purpose of life is to find happiness. However, Socrates and the sophists profoundly disagreed on how humans ought to conduct their lives in order to obtain it. The measure for human happiness offered by both the sophists and Socrates was inextricably linked with the concept of virtue, which in today's parlance can be used somewhat interchangeably with the concept of excellence.

The sophists lectured that people find happiness by pursuing virtue or excellence in their human activities. A shoemaker, for example, can find happiness through

The Socratic Teaching Method

The Socratic teaching method fosters critical thinking in students by probing their minds with questions, rather than by providing them with answers. Responses from students frequently generate additional questions that foster a deeper analytic discussion. The purpose of the Socratic method is to help students process course material and to engage "students in dialogue and discussion that is collaborative and open-minded as opposed to debate, which is often competitive and individualized."[14] The professor guides students to a deeper understanding of the material and to respect the viewpoints of others. The Socratic method of questioning does not always bring the students to a definitive answer, but more frequently reveals weaknesses in hypotheses.

The Socratic teaching method was brought to prominence in *The Paper Chase,* a film and later a television show appearing from 1978 to 1979 about a Harvard law school class. The strictness of the Socratic method in law school was captured in one scene when Professor Charles W. Kingsfield Jr. portrayed by John Houseman, summoned an unprepared student to the front of the class, handed him a dime, and then told him to call his mother for a ride home because he would never make it through law school. The Socratic method intimidates some law students because professors randomly call on them regardless of whether they are prepared to answer. Performing poorly in this setting is embarrassing because it

▲ John Houseman as Professor Charles W. Kingsfield in *The Paper Chase* in 1973. The Professor used the Socratic Method as his primary teaching tool in his law school class. The Socratic teaching method is still widely used in law school classes today.

continued

causes classmates to think less of one's legal abilities. The questions posed typically assume the student has read and is familiar with the legal nuances of the case. The professor will sometimes juxtapose the facts of a case in order to test the critical thinking skills of students.

> Do any of your professors use the Socratic teaching method and/or stimulate critical thinking at your college or university?
>
> Do you believe the Socratic teaching method should be used more widely in undergraduate classes? Why or why not?

the virtue of making excellent shoes, just as a painter can find happiness through the virtue of painting first-rate pictures, and a carpenter can find happiness through the virtue of building a secure and attractive house. The sophists link happiness to a person's capacity to excel at a particular skill and/or occupation.

Additionally, the sophists taught their mostly privileged and affluent students that human happiness is also established through the virtue of acquiring objects that give most people pleasure, such as "wealth, honor, and status."[15] They considered material success and the acquisition of power to be the standard fare in attaining human happiness, which was consistent with their overarching belief that humans are primarily self-interested creatures. The sophists lectured on moral relativism and that laws formulated by the polis (or state) were merely conventional prescriptions drafted for the purpose of protecting the weak from the strong.[16] They taught that this was an unusual arrangement, absent from the laws of nature, where the powerful customarily dominate over the feeble. This was a very popular critique with the privileged students in that it encouraged them to leverage their advanced standing into greater material and political gains and served as a prevailing justification for exploiting the downtrodden. The sophists taught that the laws of the state were unnatural in that they inhibited great leaders, thereby stunting their human development and their probability of attaining happiness.

It was this widely accepted view of "might makes right" that Socrates, and later Plato and Aristotle sought to debunk. Socrates was a unique and important thinker because he was one of the first to associate the concept of virtue or excellence to ethical human behavior. For Socrates there was an important distinction between exhibiting brilliance in a particular activity or occupation and demonstrating excellence in ethical conduct.

The great tragedy for Socrates was that the vast majority of Greeks were destined to lead discontented lives because they were exceedingly unaware and disinterested in the highest form of human happiness: *the cultivation of the human soul*.[17] True happiness for Socrates meant pursuing the "good life," which is attained when humans conduct their lives in accordance to ethical principles derived from reason. Life in and of itself is not important for Socrates, it is only the "good life" that matters:

> I say that it is the greatest good for a man to discuss virtue every day and those other things about which you hear me *conversing and testing myself and others, for the unexamined life is not worth living for man*.[18]

Socrates transformed the concept of happiness by emphasizing the significance of nurturing the human soul. While he does not necessarily renounce worldly possessions, he does consider materialism an inferior form of happiness.[19] Because Socrates believed the soul is connected to our intellectual senses, he reasoned that it is the responsibility of all humans to examine their lives by pursuing knowledge and truth, particularly on issues involving individual ethics. This view represented a fundamental theoretical shift away from materialism and toward ethical reflection. For Socrates the essential variable in promoting harmony within the soul, and in realizing the highest form of happiness, occurs when we pursue justice at all levels and at all times. His views are colorfully described in Plato's classic text *The Republic*.

Socrates believed that individual behavior must, above all else, be guided by reasoned ethical standards, even if that behavior violates state laws. He also believed that one should accept willingly the negative consequences for violating public laws. In his own life Socrates refused to cease teaching his philosophy to the youth, even after it became apparent that he would be arrested (and ultimately sentenced to death) for "corrupting" them. He engaged in an early form of **civil disobedience** by defying a court order to stop teaching because he believed his teaching was just and ethical.[20] To Socrates, one's personal ethical code represents a higher value than the customs and laws of the state.

His conformist view of citizenship, however, is characterized in Plato's Crito dialogue. During his incarceration, a friend of Socrates named Crito visited him in jail and revealed a plan for his escape. Socrates explained to Crito that escaping from his jail cell would be unjust because he had an obligation as a citizen to accept his punishment, even if the punishment was excessive.[21] Socrates accepted his death sentence and ultimately drank the poisonous hemlock rather than take flight from his unjust sentence. His decision is instructive because it highlighted Socrates's view that *it is better to be the recipient of a major injustice (i.e., death sentence) than to commit even a minor injustice yourself*. Or, put another way, it underscores Socrates's observation that death is preferable to an unjust existence.

Civil Disobedience: *The refusal to obey governmental demands or commands especially as a nonviolent and usually collective means of forcing concessions from the government.*

Socrates's refusal to stop teaching Athenian youth represented one of the earliest accounts of civil disobedience. The virtues of civil disobedience was later championed by Henry David Thoreau (1817–1862), whose essay *On the Duty of Civil Disobedience* in 1849 argued that citizens should not allow government policy to take precedence over individual core beliefs. Thoreau engaged in civil disobedience by refusing to pay taxes over his objection to slavery and the Mexican-American War. He paid a highway tax because he viewed it as beneficial to neighbors but refused to pay any tax that went to the government itself. Thoreau said he felt freer in jail than he did outside of prison walls when he was briefly incarcerated for his beliefs.

Mohandas Gandhi (1869–1948) once claimed that Thoreau was one of the greatest men America ever produced. Gandhi employed an active form of nonviolent civil disobedience in successfully gaining Indian Independence from Great Britain in 1947. Some of Gandhi's principles of civil disobedience included nonviolence (ahimsa), truth (satya), and boycotts (swadishi policy), and his leadership style inspired civil rights movements across the globe.

Martin Luther King Jr. (1929–1968) borrowed Gandhi's rules on civil disobedience when leading the civil rights movement in the United States. He counseled civil rights protesters to actively resist segregationist policies without expressing anger, and that protesters should never submit, yet never retaliate. Martin Luther King's leadership played a key role in the passage of the Civil Rights Act in 1964 and in the passage of the Voting Rights Act in 1965 (see Chapter 4 for fuller discussion).

Socrates, Gandhi, and King were each executed for their convictions. Socrates was forced to drink poisonous hemlock by his government, Mohandas Gandhi was assassinated while taking his nightly walk on January 30, 1948, in Delhi, India, and Martin Luther King was assassinated outside a Memphis hotel by segregationist James Earl Ray on April 4, 1968.

> Can you think of other historical figures who engaged in a form of civil disobedience? Have you ever engaged in civil disobedience?

© ISTOCKPHOTO.COM/LORENZO COLLORETA

Socrates held that individuals can only find true happiness by remaining removed and distant from the affairs of the state. He taught that one could not pursue the good life and politics simultaneously because he believed a successful political career required one to surrender core ethical principles. This is why Socrates is considered a moral philosopher and not a political philosopher. He counseled his students to avoid the corrupting influences associated with politics, to shun the glare and false praise of public life, and to instead quietly follow a just ethical code. The first Western political philosopher is actually Plato, a student of Socrates.

In Figure 2.1 we provide a timeline highlighting ancient political theorists.

PLATO

The first written work considered political science is Plato's classic text *The Republic.* In *The Republic,* Plato introduces the teachings of Socrates through the method of the dialogue. As a result, it is sometimes difficult to discern where the views of Socrates end and where the observations of Plato begin. Plato was born in Athens in 427 BCE and died in 347 BCE at the age of 81. While little is known of his personal history, most scholars suspect that he was never married, that he traveled extensively, including trips to Sicily and Egypt, and that he was greatly influenced by his teacher and mentor Socrates.[22] Plato's veneration for Socrates was no doubt enhanced by the tragic circumstances surrounding Socrates's life, particularly his willingness to die for his philosophy.

Plato was born into a prominent political family. Members of Plato's family, in fact, seized power in Athens and established control in 404 BCE, only to be overthrown

FIGURE 2.1. Meet the Ancients: Greek Philosophers and Schools of Thought

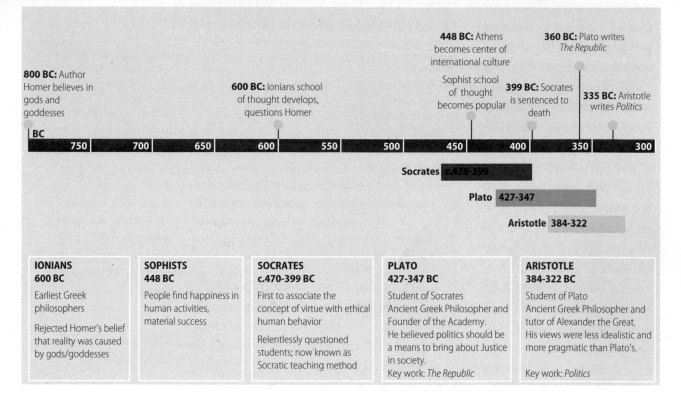

800 BC: Author Homer believes in gods and goddesses

600 BC: Ionians school of thought develops, questions Homer

448 BC: Athens becomes center of international culture

Sophist school of thought becomes popular

399 BC: Socrates is sentenced to death

360 BC: Plato writes *The Republic*

335 BC: Aristotle writes *Politics*

BC
750 | 700 | 650 | 600 | 550 | 500 | 450 | 400 | 350 | 300

Socrates c.470-399

Plato 427-347

Aristotle 384-322

IONIANS 600 BC	SOPHISTS 448 BC	SOCRATES c.470-399 BC	PLATO 427-347 BC	ARISTOTLE 384-322 BC
Earliest Greek philosophers. Rejected Homer's belief that reality was caused by gods/goddesses	People find happiness in human activities, material success	First to associate the concept of virtue with ethical human behavior. Relentlessly questioned students; now known as Socratic teaching method	Student of Socrates. Ancient Greek Philosopher and Founder of the Academy. He believed politics should be a means to bring about Justice in society. Key work: *The Republic*	Student of Plato. Ancient Greek Philosopher and tutor of Alexander the Great. His views were less idealistic and more pragmatic than Plato's. Key work: *Politics*

FIGURE 2.2. Beyond the Greeks: Eastern, Roman, and Christian Theorists

600 BC | 400 BC | 200 BC | 0 | 200 | 400 | 600 | 800 | 1000 | 1200 | 1400

Siddhartha Guatama 563-483 BC

Confucius 551-479 BC

Sun Tzu c.544-496 BC

Cicero 106-43 BC

St. Augustine 354-430 AD

St. Thomas Aquinas 1225-1274 AD

SIDDHARTHA GUATAMA circa 563-483 BC	CONFUCIUS 551-479 BC	SUN TZU c.544-496 BC	CICERO 106-43 BC	ST. AUGUSTINE 354-430 AD	ST. THOMAS AQUINAS 1225-1274 AD
Founder of Buddhism Born in what is now modern Nepal. He advocated "The Middle Way", or a lifestyle that balances the influences of worldly and ascetic values.	Ancient Chinese philosopher. His teachings serve as the foundation of Chinese philosophy. Some compare his influence in China to the influence of Socrates in the West.	Ancient Chinese Military philosopher. His writings offer advice on the best strategies for winning military battles. Key work: *The Art of War*	Roman statesman and philosopher. He was executed in 43 B.C. in his defense of the Roman Republic. Key work: *The Republic (or Commonwealth) and The Laws*	Catholic theorist. Fused the teachings of Plato with Catholic thought. Key work: *The City of God*	Catholic theorist. Reconciled Aristotle's theories with Catholic Doctrine by incorporating both "faith" and "reason". Key work: *Summa Theolgiae*

a year later by the democrats. It was this democratic government that ultimately sentenced and executed Socrates a few years later. Plato also grew up during the **Peloponnesian War**, a decisive war between the Greek city-states of Athens and Sparta, which was launched because of Spartan insecurities over a growing Athenian maritime threat and ended in a humiliating Athenian defeat in 404 BCE.

Plato was left jaded and dejected by these two experiences. He grew disillusioned over the willingness of Athenian leaders to place self-interest over the public interest, and blamed the irrational impulses emanating from the democratic government for both the execution of Socrates and the haunting Athenian defeat to Sparta in the Peloponnesian War.

These two experiences left Plato very distrustful of democracy and popular government. They also explain Plato's detour from a life in politics, an expected path for someone of his stature, and why he was inspired to explore the perceived higher vocation he found in philosophy. Plato was enthused and passionate about revising and expanding upon the teachings of his martyred teacher Socrates.

In this pursuit Plato founded the first Western university called The Academy, which was built to carry on Socrates's legacy of teaching moral philosophy to young intellectuals. But Plato's initial foray into philosophical teaching was met with misfortune and humiliation. The most degrading moment occurred when Plato traveled to Sicily to counsel the despot Dionysius I. The autocrat eventually grew tired of Plato's moral counseling and sold Plato into slavery rather than heed his advice to reform the political system.[23] Unlike his mentor Socrates, however, Plato accepted the support of friends and escaped a life of slavery.

The Republic

In *The Republic*, Plato recounts Socrates's conversation about justice that took place in the home of the sophist Polymarchus, which included Polymarchus, his father Cephalus, the famous sophist Thrasymachus, and other prominent thinkers of the day. The discussion revolved around the proper definition of *justice*. Cephalus, a man of great wealth, stated that a just person is one who repays his debts and always tells the truth.[24] Socrates was unsatisfied with this definition and asked whether it would be just to return a borrowed weapon to a companion who had grown unstable and violent. Cephalus agreed that it would not be just to return the weapon if you believed the companion would use it for an unjust purpose. This exchange pointed out that while it is important to repay debts, there are scenarios where individuals might have a larger social responsibility not to repay them. Thrasymachus, a leading sophist, argued that justice is simply what is in the best interest of the stronger party.[25] Through his inquisitive questioning of Thrasymachus, Socrates gets him to acknowledge that some leaders make mistakes in their decisions. That is an important concession because Socrates is now able to establish through his relentless questioning that knowledge is a higher value than power and that might does not always make right.[26]

Peloponnesian War:
The war between Athens and Sparta from 431–404 BCE. Sparta, with the assistance of Persia (now Iran), built a massive fleet that destroyed the Athenian navy at Aegospotami in 405 BCE. The war destroyed Athens.

The purpose of Plato's *Republic* is to highlight Socrates's contention that knowledge goes well beyond simply understanding individual self-interest and is needed in order to understand a larger objective truth: *that the highest form of happiness is attained when we nurture the human soul by pursuing justice rather than self-interest.* Ultimately Socrates attempts to establish that just behavior is innately superior to unjust behavior, and the only way he can substantiate this theory is to convince prominent thinkers that *a just person perceived to be unjust is happier than an unjust person perceived to be just.*[27] *The Republic* is Plato's attempt to establish the correctness of Socrates's theory that the purpose of our existence is to realize happiness by leading a just life. The next section explains Plato's suppositions on why a just existence facilitates a higher level of human happiness than an unjust existence.

Happiness in the Republic and the Human Soul

Plato theorized that the polis (or state) is a natural configuration emanating from our inability to function efficiently in a solitary existence. He taught that we are social creatures requiring assistance from others in order to survive, and that the state represents a natural extension of human activity. In order to illustrate that a just person perceived to be unjust is happier than an unjust person perceived to be just, Plato incorporated the model of the state. Plato considered the ideal polis and the ideal human soul to be one and the same. Because the small size of the human soul makes it difficult to scrutinize justice, Plato opted to distinguish it on the larger tableau of the state. The rationale is that one can discover justice in the human soul by first discerning it on the larger canvass of the republic.[28]

Plato believed the ideal republic and the human soul comprise three critical parts respectively:

1. craftspeople/appetites
2. auxiliaries/spirit
3. guardians/rational

Table 2.1 provides a brief summary of how Plato linked the ideal republic to the human soul.

TABLE 2.1. The Three Parts of the Republic and the Human Soul

The Republic	The Human Soul
Craftspeople–Citizens engage in economic activity (businesspeople, farmers, merchants)–Taught restraint	Appetites–Behavior guided by impulses stemming from our desires and urges, without regard for consequences
Auxiliaries–Citizens defend the Republic (military)–Taught courage and restraint	Spirit–Behavior guided by impulses stemming from feelings of pity, compassion, and/or remorse
Guardians–Rule the Republic–(Political leaders)–Taught wisdom, courage, and restraint	Rational–Behavior guided by knowledge and our intellect

The Republic divides the citizenry into three functioning groups, partitioned by a division of labor that accentuates the skill sets of the community, thus producing social harmony. These three communities include: the *craftspeople, the auxiliaries, and the guardians*.[29] Plato then associates these three social groupings to three parts of the human soul, which he argued consists of *the appetite, the spirit,* and *the rational*. He further theorized that the ideal forms of both the state and the human soul function harmoniously when the guardians (i.e., rational part of soul) rules over the craftspeople (i.e., appetite part of soul).

Craftspeople and Appetite

The craftspeople represent society's working class and include farmers, shopkeepers, and merchants. Their function is to produce economic activity and to ensure social sustenance. Plato understood that basic human needs, such as food and shelter must be secured before humans can follow higher needs, such as philosophy and the good life. The requisite skills required to succeed in economic life, specifically the pursuit of self-interest and profit, do not translate well to traits essential to the furtherance of the public good. That is why Plato associated the craftspeople with the appetite portion of the human soul. Our appetites urge us to satisfy base desires without any regard for the consequences of our actions. Plato believed our appetites, as well as the craftspeople, need to be checked by higher impulses. The craftspeople, therefore, should be taught *temperance or restraint* so they do not attempt to rise from the economic life into the political life.

Auxiliaries and the Spirit

The auxiliaries' primary function is to enforce the laws of the state and defend the state from foreign invasion (i.e., serve as the military). The auxiliaries are taught both *courage* and *temperance*. They require a more sophisticated training because they need to be taught courage in order to ensure the polis (or state) is bravely defended, yet they also need to be taught temperance so they do not attempt to rule the state. Plato argued that just as a watchdog requires both the courage to attack intruders and the temperance not to bite the master, so too does the military need to possess the courage to fiercely defend the homeland and the temperance not to turn their weapons on the domestic population.[31] Plato links the auxiliaries with the *spirit* portion of the human soul. The spirit for Plato is a positive energy force in our soul that checks the negative energy emanating from our urges and appetites. Feelings of remorse, compassion, or empathy, for example, originate from our spirit and serve to check our base desires.

Guardians and the Rational

The guardians represent the ruling class and require intensive training in order to ensure the pursuance of the public good and justice. The guardians must possess "wisdom, courage, and temperance." Guardians require the most sophisticated

THEORY AND PRACTICE

Wealth of U.S. Members of Congress

In *The Republic*, Plato argues that those who excel in the business world should not rule the polis because the skills needed to secure profits do not necessarily translate well to the skills required to lead the Republic. Yet according to the Center for Responsive Politics, the median net worth of U.S. senators is approximately $1.7 million. While roughly only 1 percent of Americans are classified as millionaires, 61 percent of U.S. senators and 39 percent of the members of the House of Representatives are millionaires. Below find the 10 wealthiest members of Congress.[30]

1. Rep. Darrell Issa (R-CA) $251 million
2. Rep. Jane Harman (D-CA) $244.8 million
3. Sen. Herb Kohl (D-WI) $214.6 million
4. Sen. Mark Warner (D-VA) $209.7 million
5. Sen. John Kerry (D-MA) $208.8 million
6. Rep. Jared Polis (D-CO) $158.1 million
7. Rep. Vern Buchanan (R-FL) $142.4 million
8. Sen. Jay Rockefeller (D-WV) $94.3 million
9. Sen. Frank Lautenberg (D-NJ) $74.7 million
10. Sen. Diane Feinstein (D-CA) $72.4 million

Do you believe the personal wealth of a member of Congress impacts his/her legislative behavior in Congress? Why or why not?

educational training. Only those who demonstrate excellence in mathematics, dialectic argument, military matters, and philosophy are permitted to rule *The Republic*.[32] It is important to remember that Plato believed that an objective permanent truth (i.e., theory of being) undergirds our physical world. He further believed that only those possessing perfect knowledge should rule the Republic because perfect knowledge is required in order to fully understand the full dimension of justice. Plato's three divisions of society is perhaps analogous to the caste system in ancient India whereby society was divided into four hierarchal social groupings including: (1) Brahmins (priests and scholars); (2) Kshatriyas (ruling nobility and soldiers); (3) Vaishyas (merchants); and (4) Shudras (laborers and servants).

THEORY AND PRACTICE

The Greek Influence on Early Christian Thought:
St Augustine and St. Thomas Aquinas

One of the most important developments in Western civilization is the extent to which theories associated with early Greek thinkers eventually joined together with Judeo-Christian religious traditions. Plato's theory of forms, for example, which distinguished between the world of appearances and the intelligible world influenced early Christian thinker Saint Augustine (354–430 CE). In his work *City of God*, Augustine also created a dualistic vision of the universe that distinguished between the earthly city and the heavenly city. Whereas Plato argued happiness is attained when we pursue a just existence by placing the public good over individual self-interest, Augustine similarly asserted that happiness is attained when we place the love of God over the pursuit of earthly self-interest.[33] Augustine was also influenced by Plato's contention that the human soul is divided into three parts (rational, spirit, desire) in his view that conflict between good and evil not only occurs throughout society at large, but also within the confines of the individual soul. Augustine differed from Plato in his belief that justice in the "earthly city" is not an end unto itself, but rather a necessary condition to enable people to practice their faith in God, which facilitates the ultimate goal of gaining entry into the "heavenly city" after death.[34]

Centuries later, Saint Thomas Aquinas (1225–1274 CE) incorporated theories associated with Aristotle while addressing an emerging conflict between religious and political thought in the West. Academics challenged the Church's emphasis on faith rather than reason in the Middle Ages as universities emerged as intellectual centers of society. Aquinas incorporated Aristotle's theories in successfully bridging the gap between

continued

religion and philosophy in his classic work *Summa Theologiae*. Here Aquinas makes the case that reason and faith can both be used to bring about a greater understanding of God. Through the power of reason, Aquinas provided five arguments to "prove the existence of God."[35] It was in part because Aquinas was able to link philosophical reason with religious faith that Christianity has grown to where approximately one in every three people on earth (i.e., 2.1 billion) is identified as a Christian.

> **In what ways are modern religious teachings similar and/or different from the theories associated with the ancient Greeks?**

© ISTOCKPHOTO.COM/LORENZO COLLORETA

Plato's Theory of Forms

For Plato only those with a perfect understanding of justice should lead the Republic because only they will truly appreciate the need to pursue the public good. His rationale for this is best explained in his frequently misunderstood and somewhat mystical view outlined in his theory of forms. Plato's theory of forms reveals his dualistic vision of the universe that distinguishes between:

1. the *world of appearances* (i.e., things we can see) and
2. the *intelligible world* (i.e., things beyond our physical senses).

For Plato the world of appearances is nonpermanent and ever changing (i.e., state of becoming) and the intelligible world includes a more permanent design that transcends our material world (i.e., state of being). Plato's theory of forms is difficult to grasp because of its mystical and transcendental components. He speculated that there is an ideal form of everything in the world of appearances and the intelligible world, a way things "ought to be." Only those (women included) who have reached "the good," defined by Plato as possessing perfect knowledge of everything in the world of appearances and the intelligible world, are qualified to rule because only they can be counted on to place the public interest of society over individual self-interest. As we learned in the previous section, Plato associated the guardians with the rational part of the human soul. Acquiring perfect knowledge helps to inform our spirit, which, once empowered by knowledge will dominate over our base appetites; producing happiness and harmony in both the Republic and the human soul.

For Plato, the things most of us see in the world of appearances are actually imperfect representations of their ideal form.[36] So when we view a chair in a room, we are actually viewing an imperfect representation of an ideal form of *chairness*. There is such a thing as a perfect chair for Plato, just as there is a perfect form of every item in our world of appearances. There is also an ideal form of everything in the intelligible world for Plato, such as the concept of justice or "justiceness." But when we experience a variant of justice in our physical world we are actually experiencing an imperfect representation of justiceness, or the ideal form of justice. The important point is that Plato employs the theory of forms to demonstrate a larger belief that there is such a thing as an ultimate objective truth, or a way we ought to be. And only those who have reached "the good" should rule our society because only these select few possess a comprehensive understanding of the ideal form of justice. Plato's theory of forms is later challenged and amended by his most famous student, Aristotle.

Allegory of the Cave

This point is further developed in his renowned *Allegory of the Cave*. The allegory underscores the need for philosophical rule by revealing how some forms of judgment (or opinions) are more valuable than others. Through a dialogue between Socrates and Glaucon in Book VII of *The Republic*, we are asked to imagine "human beings living in an underground cave" from childhood who have their "legs and necks chained so that they cannot move," and spend their entire lives staring endlessly at the back of the cave wall. He then asks us to imagine there is a fire behind them, with men "carrying all sorts of vessels, and statues and figures of animals made of wood and stone," but because they are chained, they are only able to view the objects indirectly as shadows reflecting against the cave wall. If they spent their entire lives in this condition, they would ultimately come to view the shadow of a wooden cat, for example, as their reality of an actual cat. Plato refers to this level of recognition as "*imagining*" and argued it constitutes the lowest form of human comprehension. Suppose now they were freed from their chains and able to turn around and view the objects directly. This represents a higher form of comprehension that Plato referred to as a "*belief*." Imagine now they were pulled from the cave and out into the blazing sun. They would now possess the advanced form of understanding that Plato referred to as "*knowledge*." The cave for Plato represents the world of appearances and the sun represents "the good," or the perfect understanding of everything in the world of appearances and the intelligible world.[37] This allegory is instrumental in highlighting why Plato believed only those with the highest forms of knowledge should rule the republic. The vast majority of citizens are unqualified to rule because most never leave the cave. Most citizens confuse shadows for reality, or come to mistakenly accept their opinion as truth.

Plato viewed democracies as a substandard political system because it is a system premised on the fact that all opinions are equally legitimate. He believed a political system based on majority rule made little sense since those possessing mediocre levels of knowledge will vastly outnumber enlightened members of society. Democracies are destined to fail, he argued, because the masses lack the intellectual training required to promote justice in society. They will confuse "shadows" for truth and inevitably pursue their own self-interest rather than the public good. Democracies will then eventually degenerate into mob rule and crumble under the weight of competing self-interested groups.

Critics sometimes dismissively refer to this as Plato's "the masses are asses" theory of politics. It is because of these concerns, however, that James Madison did not incorporate the word *democracy* into the U.S. Constitution, opting instead for the term *republic*, not coincidentally the title of Plato's classic text. In our original system of government only 5 percent of the population (i.e., 150,000 out of 3 million people) were eligible to vote in U.S. elections. Moreover, it is in part because of the influence of Plato that the only federal officials that were originally elected into office were members of the U.S. House of Representatives. In Chapters 5 and 6 we will discuss at length how U.S. senators were originally appointed by state legislatures (until the seventeenth amendment in 1913) and how the original electoral college system did not allow citizens any voice in the selection of the American president. So, in short, it is in part because of Plato that popular elections were not very popular with our Founding Fathers.

Staying in the theoretical realm, would you support a political system that gave "enlightened citizens" two votes and "unenlightened citizens" only one vote if there was an objective way to accurately distinguish between the two? Why or why not?

© ISTOCKPHOTO.COM/LORENZO COLLORETA

Opinion is the opposite of truth for Plato, representing a mere starting point on the long and arduous road to knowledge.

Achieving "the good" makes it virtually impossible for a Guardian to commit an unjust act. For Plato people do not engage in unjust behavior because they are inherently unjust, but rather because they simply do not have a full understanding as to why their behavior is unjust in the first place. Nearly everyone in society, after all, resides in the cave confusing shadows for truth. But the Guardians would be incapable of participating in selfish or unjust behavior because they possess a perfect understanding of justice. For example, if a person had perfect knowledge of the injustice associated with committing the violent crime of rape, it would be out of the question for that person ever to commit this crime. Those possessing this knowledge would sooner surrender their own life than commit such an egregious act. This principle is intensified with Guardians because they would sooner surrender their life than engage in any form of injustice.

Gradations of Happiness in the Republic and the Human Soul

So how does Plato establish that a just person perceived to be unjust is happier than an unjust person perceived to be just? The definitive argument is provided at the end of *The Republic* in the section linking the gradations of happiness in the state with the human soul.

Plato writes that the ideal philosophical **aristocracy** depicted in *The Republic* will eventually decline, as all things in the world of appearances are in a perpetual state of change and transformation. The decline of the just republic will begin in the leadership selection process, where future leaders stray from the pursuit of justice and instead begin to favor the lower values of courage and honor. The state will initially devolve from a philosophical *aristocracy* to a republic ruled by warriors, referred to as a **timocracy**, where society values courage and honor over the higher value of justice. The children of the ruling warrior class will then establish an **oligarchy** as they grow to prefer economic prosperity and private property over the value of courage and honor. The republic will then further disintegrate when the spoiled children of the oligarchs continue to value possessions and paltry pleasures, but lack the discipline and work ethic to accumulate them. This group will demand independence and the freedom to pursue trivial delights.[38] They will form a democracy that values liberty and freedom over economic prosperity and work ethic. As the political order descends, there will be a progressive relaxation of discipline.

Plato distinguishes between types of desires by highlighting differences between necessary desires and unnecessary desires. Moderate consumption of food and drink, for example, represent necessary desires in that the nourishment they provide make it possible to live. Unnecessary desires, such as the desire to consume

Aristocracy: *A government in which power is vested in a minority, consisting of those believed to be best qualified.*

Timocracy: *A government in which the love of honor is the ruling principle.*

Oligarchy: *A government in which a small group exercises control over the masses.*

junk food, on the other hand, can be eliminated if we resist surrendering to base urges. Democracy ranks second to last in Plato's gradations of happiness in the state because it encourages the pursuit of all desires, both necessary and unnecessary. It is founded on the erroneous premise that all opinions are equally valid. He viewed it as an inferior system because it is ruled by the masses, whom, for Plato, reside in the cave and habitually confuse their opinions (or shadows) with reality (or truth). It is a system that invites the ignorant majority to rule over the enlightened minority.

Table 2.2 features Plato's rankings of political systems from his preferred form of government to his least favorite form of government.

Finally, this democratic system of government will eventually collapse into a tyrannical system of government, the lowest form of political order for Plato. The impoverished democratic majority will blame the affluent for their plight and will select a leader to oppress the wealthy. This leader will come to tyrannize over the poor as well as the rich and will consolidate all political power in the regime. The entire Republic will become enslaved to the tyrant's whims and desires. The **tyrant** represents the lowest form of justice because tyrants pursue both *lawful unnecessary desires* and *unlawful unnecessary desires*. The tyrant will be immune to the appeals of reason and will carry through on desires that occur only in nightmares, such as committing heinous murders or having sexual relations with a parent. The appetite part of the despot's soul will dominate over the spirit and intellect, which in the end will drive the tyrant to depression and madness. While the tyrannical despot and Plato's Guardians both impose their judgment on the body politic, they differ in that Guardians are guided by a perfect knowledge of justice, while the tyrant is guided by base desires, urges, and appetites. It is here that Plato establishes the correctness of Socrates's theory that a just person perceived to be unjust is happier than an unjust person perceived to be just. Plato asserts that the tyrant's immoral behavior stems from the desire to fill a void in the soul by seeking the love of followers. But Plato

Tyrant: *An absolute ruler unrestrained by law or constitution.*

TABLE 2.2. Gradations of Happiness in the Republic and the Human Soul

Type of Political System	The Valued Concept
Philosophical Monarch/Aristocracy	Justice and Knowledge
Timocracy	Courage
Oligarchy	Work Ethic and Wealth
Democracy	Freedom to Pursue Necessary and Unnecessary Desires
Tyrant or Despot	Freedom to Pursue Lawful and Unlawful Unnecessary Desires

contends that the tyrant's pursuit of love will not lead to happiness because love offers only finite pleasures, rather than the infinite pleasures attained through knowledge and the pursuit of justice. The tyrant's frustration will ultimately culminate in the destruction of everything in the tyrant's path that brings displeasure, all in a pathetic attempt to fill the emptiness in the soul created by an unjust existence.[39] The tyrant's self-centered existence coupled with unbridled power to satisfy all urges and appetites leads the tyrant down a path to insanity. The psychosis will intensify as the masses applaud the tyrant's increased callousness. Plato's description of the tyrant as a lonely, discontented figure brings to mind public images of Adolph Hitler, Josef Stalin, Saddam Hussein, and other renowned despots. This portrayal of the tyrant is offered as evidence that a just person perceived to be unjust (i.e., Socrates) is happier than the unjust person perceived to be just (i.e., tyrant).

The Republic is not only the first political science book ever written, it is also quite possibly Western civilization's most noteworthy and influential text. Plato was the first to initiate the premise that the government and its leaders have a special responsibility to promote an ethical and just society. That, of course, does not mean that The Republic is flawless. The mostly widely criticized section involves Plato's idea to partition the Republic according to craftspeople, auxiliaries, and guardians. Why would craftspeople ever agree to harmoniously contribute when they are not permitted to assume leadership positions? Plato answers this question with his controversial myth of the metals explanation.[40] The population will be told that they were created by god with dissimilar amounts of metals in their souls. Those meant to rule will have gold mixed in their soul; those meant to be auxiliaries will have silver; and those meant to be craftspeople will have bronze. People will also be told that the metal distribution is not hereditary, thereby holding out the possibility that those born with bronze in their souls (i.e. craftspeople) could produce guardian children, born with gold in their souls. Craftspeople and auxiliaries will therefore likely accept their station in life rather than risk offending the gods, fearing their unbefitting behavior might destroy any chance of god granting them a guardian child or grandchild. The Republic is in the end then fastened together by a noble lie, which is naturally difficult to reconcile with the text's primary emphasis on the virtues of truth and justice. Ironically, some of the most incisive challenges to Plato's theories came from his most famous student, Aristotle, regarded by many as the greatest thinker in the history of Western civilization.

ARISTOTLE

Plato's most gifted student Aristotle lived from 384 to 322 BCE. Aristotle became Plato's student at the age of seventeen and remained under his tutelage until Plato's death, approximately twenty years later. He then traveled extensively over the next twelve years and even served a stint tutoring Alexander the Great, the son of the then Macedonian King Philip II.

Aristotle returned to Athens and founded the Lyceum, his own academy designed to include a full range of academic departments. He strayed from some of the major theories associated with Plato and went on to develop original perspectives on human nature, the attainment of human happiness, personal and public ethics, idyllic leadership traits, and the relative strengths of a variety of political systems.

Unlike Plato, whose idealistic theories sometimes necessitated transcendence into the metaphysical sphere, Aristotle pursued a much more pragmatic, empirical, and/or scientific approach to the major questions of the day. This is probably because of the influence of his father, Nicomachus, who served as the chief physician to the Macedonian King Amyntas III. Aristotle relied heavily on scientific knowledge and inherited an aptitude for the natural sciences from his father, excelling in biology, medicine, and physics.[41]

Aristotle also borrowed heavily from the political philosophy associated with Plato, particularly in the principle of an objective truth and the need to fuse politics and ethics. Whereas Plato divided the human soul into three parts (rational, spirit, and appetite), Aristotle similarly separates the soul into a higher rational section guided by reason and a lower irrational part dominated by our appetites and urges. Aristotle also agreed with Plato that happiness is attained in both the republic and the human soul when rationality governs over our appetites and urges. Where Aristotle and Plato drastically differ is in their approach to studying politics. Aristotle adopted a more practical systematic approach.

▲ In this painting Plato (left) counsels Aristotle, his most prominent student. Plato's hand pointing to the sky represents his transcendental view of politics, while Aristotle's hand gesture symbolizes his more pragmatic and empirical approach to politics. It is entitled "School of Athens" and is regarded by many as Italian artist Raphael's greatest work. Raphael painted "School of Athens" in the Vatican around 1510 as Michelangelo worked on the Sistine Chapel.

The Natural State

Aristotle's most important contribution to political science is his volume *Politics*, which can be read alongside his other classic text *Nicomachean Ethics*, believed to be named after either his father or son, both named Nicomachus. The meticulousness of the rationality established in these texts prompted the Roman statesman Cicero to refer to them as "a river of gold" centuries later. Aristotle also agreed with Plato that the polis (or state) is a natural outgrowth of human development, reasoning that man is above all else a "political animal."[42] He theorized that there are three distinct forms of human communities that naturally evolve into more complex political arrangements:

1. The family unit
2. The village
3. The polis (state)

Natural Law: *A body of law or a special principle held to be derived from nature and binding upon human society.*

Positive Law: *A body of law established or recognized by a governmental authority.*

THEORY AND PRACTICE

The Greeks, the Roman Empire, and the Incorporation of Law into the State

The power of Aristotle's works prompted the Roman statesman Marcus Tullius Cicero (106–43 BCE) to refer to them as "a river of gold" centuries later. Cicero was a Roman statesman and philosopher who was an important link in the Greco-Roman tradition in that it was in part through Cicero that Greek philosophy came to play a role in the governing structure of the Roman Empire. In the *Republic* and *Laws*, Cicero advocated for a mixed constitution in the Roman Republic, consisting of the (1) consuls as the regional power; (2) the senate as the aristocratic power; and (3) the popular assembly.[43] Cicero's call for an aristocratic republic also influenced many of the American Founding Fathers.

Whereas Plato argued that justice in the Republic should be maintained through the leadership of the philosopher-king, Cicero instead argued that law, not philosophers, should guide the behavior of government. Cicero argued that leaders of society should be above all else knowledgeable in the realm of natural and positive law. He called for a unity between law and politics so that the political leader "is a speaking law, and the law a silent magistrate."[44] It is in part because of Cicero's emphasis on incorporating law into the State that many of the American Framers advocated creating a nation based on natural law.

Can you think of any existing law that places the well-being of special interests groups over the public good? If so, how would you change this law and how would this change improve our society?

To Aristotle, the most divine-like power humans possess is the ability for two people to come together to create another person. The natural desire to procreate and to form a family corresponds to the first type of community: *the family unit*. But because the family unit is not self-sufficient, it requires families to organize into more complex communities called *villages*. Villages provide greater efficiency, in that families with distinct skill sets can specialize in particular occupations for the betterment of all families.

Greater efficiency is generated when families concentrate on specific occupations such as farming or carpentry and establish a trading community, where families can exchange goods and services. However, the village on its own is not self-sufficient either. Because individual villages are vulnerable to foreign attacks, they naturally join together and establish a more complex community called the *polis*. The polis brings greater efficiency to the economic system and provides the requisite organizational infrastructure to more skillfully deter and repel foreign invasions. Self-sufficiency is consequently achieved in the polis because basic human needs are met, which helps to facilitate the pursuit of the "good life."[45]

Aristotle then compares this evolution of the three communities with the development of human beings. The family household represents the lowest form of community and is compared with the embryonic stage of human development. The village is a higher form of community and is compared to the childhood stage of human development. The polis is the highest form of community and is put side by side with the adulthood stage of human maturity.

Table 2.3 highlights how Aristotle made the linkage between human and political development.

TABLE 2.3. Aristotle's Human Communities and Stages of Development

Family Unit	Village	Polis (State)
↓	↓	↓
Embryonic Stage	Childhood	Adulthood

Aristotle's Theory of Forms and Happiness

In his theory of forms, Plato offered a dualistic approach to the universe. He speculated that the highest form of human happiness is achieved when an individual attains perfect knowledge (i.e., the good) about everything in the world of appearances and the intelligible world. Aristotle's *Politics* challenged Plato's assertion that happiness can be found in the pursuit of knowledge alone. He drifts from Plato's mystical approach and offers a more practical formula for happiness. Unlike Plato, Aristotle does not bring his theory of forms into the transcendental, but rather incorporates a naturalistic perspective by positing that all living forms have an ideal fate or a preexisting purpose within them. Rather than viewing forms in a supernatural manner, he instead concentrated on the progression of forms as they biologically transition from potentiality to actualization.[46] His theory of forms theorizes that all living things have a preexisting design or an ideal form of the way they are supposed to be. Happiness for Aristotle is achieved when we actualize our potential by achieving our preexisting purpose. Just as a tiny acorn has the potential to become a great oak tree, humans too have an ideal form or preexisting purpose. Where Plato looked for ethics and justice in the transcendental world, Aristotle searched for it in the human condition. He began his investigation of our "purpose" by reexamining Plato's concept of "the good." He similarly concluded that "the good," or that toward which all good things aim, is human happiness.

But then what makes for human happiness? The key to happiness for Aristotle, like Plato, is found in the one attribute that separates humans from other animals: *the ability to reason.* The power to reason is unique to humans because unlike other animals, humans are capable of moving beyond a biological or instinctive existence through our reasoning powers. While other social creatures exist in nature, such as bees and ants, only humans possess the power to think in the philosophical abstract. This prompts Aristotle to conclude that the key to our purpose is found when we pursue virtue (or excellence) in our reasoning powers.[47] This, of course, is quite similar to the conclusion reached by Plato, that happiness is attained when our intellect dominates over our appetites, leading us to a just existence. The critical difference is that Aristotle's *Politics* challenged Plato's assertion that happiness can be found in the pursuit of knowledge alone.

To Aristotle, the acquisition of knowledge only takes us so far. In order to attain the highest form of happiness, those possessing knowledge must take the next step by carrying reason into action through politics.[48] The immersion into politics represents the highest form of happiness because the community of the polis offers the highest plane of reasoning. The community of the family, on the other hand, represents the lowest form of community because life within the family embodies a largely biological and instinctive existence, free from abstract philosophical thinking. In the community of family, we engage in procreation, seek nourishment and other provisions, and exist in a manner quite similar to other creatures found in nature. The highest form of happiness therefore occurs when we fully immerse ourselves in politics because it is here in the community of the polis that our thinking is elevated to the peak form of reasoning, where discussions are most abstract and decisions have the greatest consequence. Moral virtue is therefore not identical to knowledge as Plato contended, but instead requires the coupling of knowledge with political action. This is significant because it underscores the distinction behind the favored leadership selection process for each theorist.

Distinct from Plato's philosopher king, who reluctantly assumes leadership after acquiring perfect knowledge, Aristotle believed leaders need to possess the requisite political skills to govern. The ability to reason about politics must be matched with vital political skills in order to affect positive change in society. And Aristotle's *Politics* informs us that the ability to debate is the highest valued political skill because it is through debate that we are able to carry reason into action. Reason and Debate represent two sides of the same political coin. Debate is the public vehicle by which we come to know the *truth*.

Aristotle believed that the existence of virtue is located in the means between the extremes, and that the nature of debate exposes extreme positions, enabling us to find happiness in the virtue of the middle ground. The virtue of the concept of courage, for instance, is found between the extremes of cowardly behavior on the one hand and foolhardy behavior on the other.[49] Courage requires the ability to associate appropriate levels of apprehension with dissimilar types of risks. The important point is that Aristotle believed that leaders should possess both the wisdom to know what is right and the political skills to be able to carry that wisdom into action in the polis in order to promote justice for all. Asking who should lead the polis for Aristotle is thus akin to asking who should sing soprano in a prominent chorus; naturally, the person who would function best in the role.

Theory of Mixed Constitutions

Another major difference between Plato and Aristotle can be found in Aristotle's theory of mixed constitutions, which greatly influenced many of the American Founding Fathers.

Aristotle's theory of mixed constitutions is at variance with Plato in that Aristotle does not advocate as vigorously for any one particular political system over another.

TABLE 2.4. Aristotle's Theory of Mixed Constitutions

Type of Government	Just Constitutions–Leaders Pursue Justice	Perverted Constitutions–Leaders Pursue Self-Interest
Government by One	Monarchy	Tyrant
Government by Few	Aristocracy	Oligarch
Government by Many	Polity	Democracy

Does Democracy Require a Strong Middle Class?

Aristotle was the first political theorist to assert that a state's economic system serves as the foundation for a state's political system. Aristotle argued that a democracy requires a strong middle class to help balance the interests of the wealthy and the poor. The field of international relations has since incorporated this view, and modern society is now replete with examples of how a nation's economic downturn can lead to political instability, which sometimes leads to war. The implosion of the German middle class during the interwar period, for instance, created an environment that led to Adolph Hitler's rise to power. It is also partially for this reason that most modern conflict occurs in the developing world. Some of the world's poorest countries (i.e., the Sudan and Afghanistan) have recently suffered from large-scale civil and/or transnational violence.

> How can Aristotle's theory that a strong middle class is required for a democracy to flourish help to inform American foreign policy decision makers on U.S. policy in Afghanistan?

He asserts instead that all political systems can be either excellent or dreadful depending on the ultimate value pursued by those managing the political system. He categorized all political systems according to the number of leaders ruling over the state and the ultimate value pursued by those leaders. He identifies six types of political systems (or constitutions) and weighs the value of each according to the "purpose" of their leaders.

1. A *monarchy*, where the political system is led by a single individual, is a good constitution if that particular monarch pursues justice.
2. This same political structure could be perverted if the monarch becomes a *tyrant* and pursues self-interest rather than justice.
3. Similarly, an *aristocracy*, where the political system is managed by a small number of leaders, could be a good constitution if these leaders pursue justice.

4. However, this same system could also degenerate into a perverted constitution if it devolves into an *oligarchy*, where a few wealthy leaders follow economic self-interest over the public good.

5. Similarly, a *polity,* where many leaders administer the political system, could be first-rate if leaders pursue justice.

6. But it can also deteriorate into a *democracy*, where the majority pursue their self-interest and behave unjustly to minority factions.

Aristotle was also one of the first theorists to examine the extent to which economics undergirds politics. Aristotle's primary concern with democracies is the potential for an impoverished majority to seek revenge against a wealthy minority. It is because of this that Aristotle hypothesized that democracy requires a strong middle class in order to balance the extreme interests of the wealthy and the poor.[50] We should remember that virtue is found in the means between the extremes for Aristotle. This is a remarkably advanced concept that continues to inform discussions on 21st century statecraft. The important point here is that Aristotle's theories are just as relevant today as they were in his day.

© JON HICKS/CORBIS

SUMMARY

Whereas Plato seeks the ideal form of government in the Republic, Aristotle searches for the best possible government given the situation as it exists on the ground. The major contribution of Socrates, Plato, and Aristotle is their imperturbable call for the fusion of politics and ethics. They transformed Western civilization by revising the purpose of politics. Politics for Plato and Aristotle is a higher calling, where leaders have a special responsibility to serve the public by promoting the public good over self-interest. In Chapter 4 we will examine how this view of politics was shared by many of the delegates at the American Constitutional Convention as they constructed the three branches of government.

While the American Framers were directly influenced by their experiences with the British, key points associated with Aristotle's theory of mixed constitutions were also incorporated into the American Constitution. The Framers learned from Aristotle not to fixate on any particular political system, but to combine the strengths of dissimilar forms of governments into one. The American system of government, after all, includes a President (government of one), a Supreme Court (government of a few), and Congress (government of many). It is also not a coincidence that the Framers did not insert the term *democracy* into the American Constitution, instead describing our system of government as a "republic" in deference to Plato's and Aristotle's conviction that only those enlightened on the virtues of justice should lead society. The Founding Fathers, after all, created a representative democracy that consisted of a president who was initially appointed directly by an electoral college (see Chapter 6), a judiciary appointed by the president and confirmed by the Senate (see Chapter 7), and a Senate originally appointed by their respective state legislatures (see Chapter 5). Members of the House of Representatives were the only federal officials popularly elected by citizens in part because of Greek concerns that democracies are likely to degenerate into mob rule because most citizens are not trained to place the public good over their own petty self-interests. The Framers were quite intentional in their efforts to structure the American government to ensure that those perceived to be wise would check the self-interested impulses of the majority. This tyranny of the majority concern is addressed directly in Chapter 4's examination of James Madison's *Federalist Paper No. 10*, widely regarded as America's greatest contribution to political theory. In Chapter 8 we highlight how this Greek view of government also influenced the design and purpose of European parliamentary systems of government by comparing the U.S. political system to European democracy and other forms of government across the globe. But first, in the next chapter we will explore how Niccolo Machiavelli and Thomas Hobbes advocate for nondemocratic forms of government in their assertion that "power" rather than "justice" is the key unit of analysis in politics.

KEY TERMS

Aristocracy p. 45

Civil Disobedience p. 33

Democracy p. 26

Ionians p. 26

Natural Law p. 49

Normative Theory p. 30

Oligarchy p. 45

Peloponnesian War p. 37

Positive Law p. 49

Republican p. 26

Skeptics p. 29

Timocracy p. 45

Tyrant p. 46

KEY PEOPLE

3

MODERN POLITICAL THEORY

▲ Female Activists In Pakistan Celebrate Their Political Party's Submission Of Nomination Papers For An Upcoming General Election In Lahore, Pakistan.

INTRODUCTION: THE ORIGINS OF MODERN POLITICAL THOUGHT

The previous chapter reviewed early political thought by highlighting some of the most important theories associated with leading ancient political theorists. These ancient thinkers pursued a normative approach to political theory in that they were primarily interested in the study of individual ethics and ideal forms of government. Normative theorists speculate about what is right or wrong in society and typically investigate how we "ought" to behave in order to reach an ideal standard of public conduct. In the previous chapter we learned from Plato's *Republic* that leaders should acquire perfect knowledge before assuming power because those possessing wisdom are most likely to advocate for justice and the public good. But you may be asking yourself if it is realistic to expect or even possible for leaders to acquire perfect knowledge. How do these ideals factor into today's political reality? And isn't it important to understand how leaders and governments actually operate if we are going to assess their effectiveness and try to improve them? These are some of the same questions many modern political theorists considered as they confronted the challenges of their times, marking a shift away from the *normative approach* and toward an *empirical approach* to studying politics. Those advocating a more empirical method were less interested in the way politics "ought" to be and more interested in the way it "is" actually practiced.

In this chapter we examine how the empirical approach strays from the normative tradition by asserting that an understanding of power is more important that an understanding of justice in helping to explain politics. This chapter places special emphasis on Machiavelli's *The Prince*, Thomas Hobbes's *Leviathan*, John Locke's *The Two Treatises of Government*, and other classic works associated with modern political thought.

Machiavelli called for a powerful monarch, but warned that using executive power unwisely could lead to political instability and civil insurrections. He is one of the first to wander from the Greek tradition by asserting that power rather than justice is the

Questions to Consider Before Reading this Chapter

1. Is it more important to understand the way politics "ought" to be or to understand the way it "is" actually practiced?

2. Is it more important for a leader to be feared or loved?

3. Are you by nature more cooperative or competitive?

4. What is a social contract theory?

5. What influence did John Locke have on American independence?

6. What role did the Declaration of Independence have on the expansion of political rights for women?

© ARIF ALI/AFP/GETTY IMAGES

most important variable in understanding politics. Thomas Hobbes, John Locke, and Jean-Jacques Rousseau are three of the leading *social contract theorists* whose collective work serves as the philosophical underpinning for both authoritarian and democratic forms of government in the 21st century.

Thomas Hobbes employed a scientific method in his attempt to bear out Machiavelli's contention that power is the key unit of analysis in politics. John Locke, known as the father of liberalism, challenged Hobbes's social contract by calling for individual liberties and a very limited form of government. Rousseau's social contract advocates for a more direct form of democracy. It was their writings that ultimately inspired subsequent ideologies such as classical liberalism, **traditional conservatism**, **modern liberalism**, Marxism, feminism, and **environmentalism**.

NICCOLO MACHIAVELLI

Niccolo Machiavelli (1469–1527) was born in Florence, Italy. Little is known about Machiavelli's early years beyond the speculation that he attended the University of Florence.[1] The public record of his life begins when he was appointed the Second Chancellor of Florence in 1498. Machiavelli thrived in the Florentine democratic government installed after the French King Charles VIII toppled the ruling Medici family in 1494. His fortunes, however, took a turn for the worse when the Medici family regained power in Florence in 1512.[2] Machiavelli was tortured and temporarily imprisoned under the suspicion that he plotted with the French against the family.

In what turned out to be a failed attempt at recapturing a prominent place in Florentine government, Machiavelli sought to curry favor with the Medici family by dedicating his most famous literary work entitled

▲ **LORENZO DE'MEDICI (1449–1492):**
Florentine statesman and ruler of Florence during the Italian Renaissance. Also known as Lorenzo the Magnificent, he is credited with maintaining a fragile yet peaceful balance of power with the other Italian city-states, a balance that collapsed into conflict shortly after his death.

© CLASSIC IMAGE/ALAMY

The Prince to **Lorenzo de' Medici** (also called Lorenzo the Magnificent). We are perhaps fortunate the family never trusted Machiavelli to serve in their authoritarian government because it afforded him the time to write his most sophisticated text entitled *The Discourses on the First Ten Books of Titus Livius* (1521). While *The Discourses* provided wider and deeper analysis on the nuances of republican government, *The Prince*'s straightforward, forceful, and uncompromising theories on executive leadership made it one of the most controversial yet widely read texts in the history of western civilization. We can safely assume that most leaders and political advisers in the 21st century have both read and been influenced by the political advice offered by Machiavelli 500 years ago. Beginning with Machiavelli, Figure 3.1 provides an important timeline of important modern theorists and/or social activists below.

Machiavelli lived during the European Renaissance, an era that sparked a cultural rebirth in Europe that stretched from the late 14th century into the 17th century. It was also a period that bridged the Middle Ages with our modern world. The Renaissance brought with it a new intellectual vision that transformed the culture, economy, and political life of Europe. It was during this era that the political order in Europe transitioned from the **feudal system** to the **nation-state system**. The form of feudalism that existed in Europe was a complicated arrangement that included a host of towns and principalities kept largely in check by the authority of the Catholic Church. The Protestant Reformation led by Martin Luther in 1517 weakened both the authority of the Catholic Church and the feudal system in Europe. Feudalism was eventually replaced by the nation-state system with the signing of the Treaty of Westphalia in 1648, which ended the Thirty Years' War in Europe. The nation-state system is defined as a collection of sovereign territories that give its allegiance to a recognized government, as is discussed in greater detail in Chapter 11. There are now 195 nation-states recognized by the United Nations in the modern international system.

It is important to understand the political context that served as the backdrop to Machiavelli's writing of *The Prince*. The transition from the feudal to the nation-state system was not a peaceful one. What is now the nation-state of Italy was in the 15th century divided into five separate states, including Florence, Naples, Venice, Milan, and the Vatican. These five states were involved in a series of conflicts that thwarted Italian unification. Machiavelli believed the merger of the five states was necessary in order for Italy to compete against Spain, Britain, France, and other major European powers.[3] Machiavelli was a political **realist** who was one of the first theorists to divorce the study of politics from religious and ethical viewpoints. This is in part because Machiavelli believed the Catholic Church was too weak to bring about Italian unification. The primary purpose of *The Prince* was to offer the ruling Medici family needed analysis on how to gain and maintain political power. Consolidating the five Italian city-states would require a strong and skillful prince capable of navigating through the diplomatic landmines associated with the emerging nation-state system.

Early on in *The Prince* Machiavelli explained his reasoning behind employing an empirical approach to studying politics. In a not-so-veiled attack on Plato's depiction of the ideal state in *The Republic*, Machiavelli asserted that it is

Feudal System: *System of economic, political, and social organization that flourished in Europe during the Middle Ages. It was based on the relationship of lord to vassal and the holding of land in feud.*

Nation-state System: *A sovereign state inhabited by people who share political and cultural traditions.*

Realist: *A school of thought in international relations that emphasizes the furtherance of national interests and military security. Realists primarily believe nations exist within an anarchic international political system, and because of a tendency to distrust international organizations, believe nations must be prepared to militarily defend themselves at all times.*

FIGURE 3.1. Timeline of Important Modern Political Thinkers and Social Activists

1450	1500	1550	1600	1650	1700	1750	1800	1850	1900

1469–1527
Niccolo Machiavelli

Thomas Hobbes **1588–1679**

John Locke **1632–1704**

David Hume **1711–1776**

Jean-Jacques Rousseau **1712–1778**

Adam Smith **1723–1790**

Immanuel Kant **1724–1804**

Edmund Burke **1729-1797**

Jeremy Bentham **1748-1832**

Alexis de Tocqueville **1805-1859**

John Stuart Mill **1806-1873**

Elizabeth Cady Stanton **1815-1902**

Karl Marx **1818-1883**

Friedrich Nietzsche **1844-1900**

Niccolo Machiavelli	Thomas Hobbes	John Locke	David Hume	Jean-Jacques Rousseau	Adam Smith	Immanuel Kant
1469–1527	1588–1679	1632–1704	1711–1776	1712–1778	1723–1790	1724–1804
Machiavelli author of *The Prince* argues power is key unit of analysis in politics	Author of *The Leviathan* Attempts to prove the correctness of Machiavelli that power, and not justice, is the key unit of analysis in politics.	The Enlightenment John Locke – His Two Treatises of Government influenced the American Declaration of Independence and the US Constitution	The Enlightenment - Scottish Philosopher and author of *A Treatise of Human Nature*	The Enlightenment A Social Contract Theorist who advocated Direct Democracy. He authored *Discourses on the Origins of Inequality* in 1755	The Enlightenment Published *The Wealth of Nations* in 1776	The Enlightenment Kant made major discoveries in the areas of ethics and human nature. He authored *Critique of Pure Reason* in 1781

Edmund Burke	Jeremy Bentham	Alexis de Tocqueville	John Stuart Mill	Elizabeth Cady Stanton	Karl Marx	Friedrich Nietzsche
1729-1797	1748-1832	1805-1859	1806-1873	1815-1902	1818-1883	1844-1900
Political Theorist, Stateman, and Author	Modern Liberalism Regarded as Father of Utilitarianism.	French Political Theorist	Political Theorists	American Feminist Social Activist And Author	German Theorists	German Nihilist
Father of Modern Conservatism	Author of *An Introduction to the Principles of Morals and Legislation*	Author of *Democracy in America* in 1835	Author of *On liberty* Utilitarianist who distinguished between qualitative and quantitative pleasures	Authored *Declaration Of Sentiments* Read at Seneca Falls Convention in 1884	Author of *Communist Manifesto and Das Kapital*	Author of *Beyond Good and Evil* Christian critic and advocate of self deification (ubermansch)
Opponent of the French Revolution	Expansion of political rights and advocate of Adam Smith	Leading democratic theorist who critiqued American democracy		Advocate for Equal Rights for Women	One of the Founders of modern Communism	

▲ Painting entitled "Cesare Borgia and Niccolo Machiavelli in Conversation."
Some speculate that Machiavelli used Borgia as a model of leadership when
writing *The Prince*. Borgia (1475–1507) was the son of Pope Alexander VI and was
widely regarded as a skillful yet ruthless military general.

more proper to go to the real truth of the matter than to its imagination; *and many
have imagined republics and principalities which have never been seen or known to exist in reality;
for how we live is so far removed from how we ought to live, that he who abandons what is done for
what ought to be done, will rather learn to bring about his own ruin than his preservation.*[4]

His thinking evolved somewhat in *The Discourses,* where he advocated for a republican
form of government.

Machiavelli is regarded as a modern political thinker because he is one of the first
to assert that **power**, and not justice, is the key unit of analysis in politics.[5] He instructed
the prince to think about politics in new ways and to reject notions of morality and
ethics that blind leaders to the truth about effective leadership. Leaders must be
logical and single-mindedly employ tactics that will enhance their power. *The Prince* is
a straightforward text that provides practical yet amoral advice on how to attain and
maintain political power. Machiavelli makes use of "instrument rationality," which emphasizes how to find the most efficient means for achieving a particular political goal.[6]

Power: *The ability to
persuade others to do what
they would not do on their
own. Machiavelli asserts that
power can be exercised through
the use of force, by making
threats, and/or by enticing
desired behavior by providing
gifts.*

The Prince as Lion and Fox

What makes Machiavelli truly unique is that he applies his theory of human nature
to the rough and tumble world of politics. Unlike the ancient Catholic philosopher
St. Augustine, Machiavelli does not view self-interested and power-seeking behavior

as sinful or wicked; it is simply human nature. In his view it is no more sinful for people to seek power and pursue self-interest than it is sinful for the earth to orbit the sun.[7] The new empirical prince must understand that people will only follow if they perceive it to be in their best interest to do so. The prince must consequently have a firm grasp on power in order to prevent insurrections and a clear understanding of the power ramifications of every decision he makes. He can best do this by adopting some of the finest traits associated with members of the animal kingdom. Machiavelli advised that a successful prince should be as strong as a *lion* and as cunning as a *fox* when leading the state. As the excerpt below reveals, he should possess the attributes of both animals since the lion alone cannot defend against snares, just as the fox alone cannot defend against wolves. However, the prince who possesses the strength of a lion and the slyness of the fox will be able to control the governed through the use of (1) force; (2) threats; and/or (3) gifts. The prince must exercise power with an innate sense about when it is best to use force, make threats, and/or give gifts in order to enhance his political power.

You must know there are two methods of fighting, the one by the law, *the other by force; the first method is of men, the second of beasts; but because the first is frequently not sufficient, one must have recourse to the second. Therefore it is necessary for a prince to understand how to use the methods of the beast and the man . . . A prince . . . ought to choose the fox and the lion; because the lion cannot defend himself against traps and the fox cannot defend himself against wolves. Therefore, it is necessary to be a fox to discover the traps and a lion to terrify the wolves. Those who rely simply on the lion do not understand this.*[8]

The Prince as the Lion

By defining power as the ability to control the masses, Machiavelli implies the prince has at his disposal a range of options for managing the public mood. Perhaps Machiavelli's greatest contribution in *The Prince* is that he offers specific guidelines as to the types of activities that have historically attracted the prince's praise or blame. For Machiavelli, being a prince is no job for the squeamish, as he must be prepared to use overwhelming force if necessary to repel invasions and/or suppress domestic insurrections. Because the prince should view the military and personal advisors as both a source as well as a threat to political power, he must know when to *caress* and when to *annihilate* them in order to maintain control.[9] To ensure loyalty he should manipulate impressionable subjects and in extreme cases kill political challengers that prove difficult to manage.

For Machiavelli, using violence is simply another instrument for the prince to use to enhance political power. Machiavelli is not *immoral* in that he does not advocate bad behavior for its own sake, but is rather *amoral,* in that he instead advocates removing morality from political equations altogether. It is largely because of this that Machiavelli's writings were banned by the Catholic Church for promoting

Modern Leaders and the Use of Violence: *Kim Jong Il and Saddam Hussein*

Machiavelli advises leaders to use force against political opponents when necessary to maintain political power. Some modern leaders have been merciless against domestic populations perceived as political threats. For instance, North Korean leader Kim Jong Il currently has approximately 200,000 political prisoners detained in North Korean gulags. According to a report published by the Korean Bar Association, prisoners in the gulag are forced to work 12 to 15 hour days, until they generally die of malnutrition. Detainees in the gulag mostly eat a diet of corn and salt, lose their teeth, have their gums turn black, "their bones weaken and, as they age, they hunch over at the waist."[10] It is estimated that hundreds of thousands of North Korean detainees have already perished in these camps.

Some scholars have also drawn parallels between Machiavelli's *economy of violence theory* and the conduct of former Iraqi president Saddam Hussein, who systematically killed and tortured political prisoners and used chemical weapons to kill thousands of Iraqis during his reign. Hussein used fear to control Iraqi factions and was quick to execute domestic critics. He issued a decree in 1978 that called for the execution of any Iraqi citizen opposing the leadership of the Baath political party. After Iraqi Shiite militants tried to assassinate Hussein in 1982, Hussein ordered the murder of approximately 150 local residents, including dozens of women and children. He also pursued a policy of ethnic cleansing against Iraqi Kurds in northern Iraq and killed between 60,000 and 182,000 Kurds in the al-Anfal campaign from 1986 to 1989.[11]

Are leaders ever justified in using violence against domestic populations?

anti-Christian beliefs, and why the Prussian leader Frederick the Great in 1739 referred to him as a "criminal, a monster, and an enemy of humanity."[12] This is also why the term *Machiavellian* is today used as a pejorative to describe someone who is untrustworthy and prone to bending rules and breaking promises in order to achieve personal goals.

Do you agree with Machiavelli that the ends justify the means in politics? Why or why not?

Machiavelli urged the prince to be empirical and to use the power of reason to assess whether the use of violence will enhance political power over the long haul. In what has been referred to as his *economy of violence* theory, he counseled that force should only be used when necessary because violence wrongfully implemented can diminish the prince's power.[13] Violence used judiciously, on the other hand, can prevent larger insurrections that could result in more deaths. Here he cited the example of Cesar Borgia, whose ruthless military campaign effectively put down a revolt and brought political stability to the Italian region of Romagna in 1502:

A Prince, therefore, must not mind incurring the charge of cruelty for the purpose of keeping his subjects united and faithful; *for, with a very few examples, he will be more merciful than those who, for excess of tenderness, allow disorder to arise, from whence spring bloodshed and rapine, for these as a rule injure the whole community, while the executions carried out by the prince injure only individuals.*[14]

He also cited the example of the Carthaginian General Hannibal, who in 200 BCE successfully maintained a large multinational army over a long period of time because of his reputation for cruelty.

The prince, like the lion, should be constantly preparing and ready to engage in warfare because when "princes think more of luxury than of arms, they lose their state."[15] He should never let his mind wander from warfare and should instead voraciously read history and study how "eminent men" acted in warfare and "examine the causes of their victories and defeats in order to imitate the former and avoid the latter."[16] Aside from keeping the troops well-disciplined, the prince should also "engage continually in hunting, and thus accustom his body to hardships; and meanwhile learn the nature of the land."[17]

Is It Better for the Prince to Be Loved or Feared?

In Machiavelli's ideal world it is best for the prince to be both loved and feared. However, he maintained that if this is not possible, it is preferable for a prince to be feared rather than loved, which is the opposite view of the ancient Roman statesman Cicero who asserted it is better to be loved. Machiavelli contended it is better to be feared because the prince is better able to control those who fear him than those who love him since "men love at their own free will, but fear at the will of the prince . . . a wise prince must rely on what is in his power and not on what is in the powers of others."[18] Fear for Machiavelli is a strong and long-lasting emotion, whereas the love emotion is occasionally fickle, here today and at times gone tomorrow. But it is here where the prince must walk a very fine line between being feared without being hated by the public. The prince should avoid being hated because it is harder to manipulate those in this irrational state. Remember Machiavelli's theory of human nature

Do you believe it is more important for a leader to be loved or feared?

TABLE 3.1. Some of Machiavelli's Tips on How Best to Maintain Political Power

1. The Prince should be as strong as the lion and as cunning as the fox.
2. It is best for the Prince to be feared and loved, but it is better to be feared than loved.
3. The Prince should avoid being hated because it is harder to control those in this emotional state.
4. The Prince should inflict all necessary injury early and at once but give benefits slowly.
5. The Prince should be decisive and strong.
6. The Prince should build religion into the state but not actually be religious.
7. The Prince should appear to be trustworthy but willing to break commitments when necessary.

holds that people at their core are motivated by self-interest. The prince should avoid being hated because people in this emotional state exhibit unpredictable behavior. They are harder to control because their natural reasoning powers are substituted with vengeful emotions that cause them to behave in ways that run counter to their self-interest. When people are blinded with hatred they are more likely to engage in thoughtless and/or violent behavior they later come to regret. People in a state of hatred are sometimes even willing to risk their lives in an attempt to overthrow rulers. The prince "need trouble little about conspiracies when the people are well disposed, but when they are hostile and hold him in hatred, then he must fear everything and everybody." We provide a summary of Machiavelli's advice on how to acquire and maintain political power in Table 3.1.[19]

The Prince as the Fox: How to Avoid Being Hated

So how can a prince engender fear without it evolving into hatred? Machiavelli directs the prince to only "take the life" of someone when there is "proper justification and manifest reason for it" and when using violence to do so swiftly and brutally because people "will revenge themselves for small injuries, but cannot do so for great ones." He further warns the prince against "taking the property of others, for men forget more easily the death of their father."[20]

A wise prince should furthermore impose all necessary pain early in his tenure and in one fell swoop, rather than spread small doses of pain over a long period of time. Just as slowly removing a Band-Aid from a wound is more excruciating than hastily peeling it from the skin, inflicting necessary injury on subjects is better applied with swift and overpowering force. If unpleasant acts are implemented properly, injured parties will come to respect and fear the prince while those free from the imposition of harm will show gratitude for being spared. People will grow tired and come to hate the prince, on the other hand, if he inflicts injury in a slow and tedious fashion over an extended time period. Conversely, the prince should spread benefits

THEORY AND PRACTICE

Karl Rove:
The Mayberry Machiavelli

Machiavelli warned the prince against appearing indecisive to the general public. He counseled that the public will lose respect for leaders who waver on important policy positions. Former President Bill Clinton struck a similar chord when advising Democrats after the 2002 mid-term congressional elections. Reflecting the American inclination toward strong leadership in the aftermath of Al Qaeda's attack on the United States in 2001, he counseled Democrats that "when people are insecure, they'd rather have somebody who is strong and wrong than someone's who's weak and right."[23] This was perhaps sage advice at the time considering the 2004 presidential election turned almost entirely on the theme of indecisiveness. You might recall that President George W. Bush's chief political strategist Karl Rove, referred to as the "Mayberry Machiavelli" by other White House advisors, coordinated President Bush's campaign around the premise that the Democratic nominee was an indecisive leader.[24] Mayberry is a fictional town that served as the setting for the TV sitcom *The Andy Griffith Show* (1960–1968). Perhaps borrowing from Machiavelli's playbook, the Bush campaign, rightly or wrongly, labeled Senator John Kerry (D-MA) as an ineffectual "flip-flopper" after Kerry asserted that he voted for the war in Iraq before voting against it, when explaining his vote on an $87 billion Iraqi appropriations bill. Kerry's nuanced approach to the Iraq war in retrospect was not a particularly effective strategy.

The Kerry campaign could have arguably benefitted from Machiavelli's counsel in the passage urging princes to state positions clearly rather than straddle political fences on important issues. Leaders, he claimed, who try to be on both sides of the same issue are viewed as irresolute and weak by the public. It is better for the prince to be seen as a "true friend or true enemy" because irresolute princes who "follow the way of neutrality are mostly ruined by it." Barack Obama avoided this pitfall in the 2008 presidential election by more decisively opposing the decision to invade Iraq.

Do you agree with President Clinton that voters prefer candidates who are "strong and wrong" over candidates who are "right but indecisive" on the issues?

to the population in measured and deliberate ways in order to better control the public mood. He specifically directs that "injuries should be committed all at once, that the last being the less . . . but benefits should be distilled in drops."[21]

Leaders Must Be Decisive

What was most interesting to Machiavelli was why some leaders were successful while other leaders who pursued similar policies failed. For Machiavelli, what separates successful leaders from ineffective leaders is their leadership style. And one of the most important traits a prince must possess is self-assuredness. He cautioned that leaders who appear "frivolous, indecisive and effeminate" will become despised by citizens. Princes should instead show signs of "seriousness, strength, and decisiveness" when leading the state.[22] Machiavelli also advised the prince not to delegate important powers to subordinates and to choose good ministers rather than be surrounded by flatterers.

Leaders Must Appear to be Religious, but Not Actually be Religious

Because Machiavelli was generally critical of the Vatican, some are initially surprised by his call to incorporate religion into the state. For Machiavelli the benefits of religion are not found in the spiritual realm, but rather in our political world. He believed adherence to religion was an essential contrivance to help the prince enforce state codified laws. It is here where Machiavelli distinguished between the concept of "power" and "authority" in government. We discussed earlier that Machiavelli defined power as the ability to control the governed. A prince who is loved and/or feared will be better able to exercise power because people fear the repercussions of challenging him. Obedience to religion is different in that religious devotees obey what they perceive to be the authority of God out of a conviction that it is morally correct to do so.[25] He explained that "no institution is firm or lasting if it rests on man's strength alone. History and reason combine to show that the roots of all great institutions are to be found outside this world . . . sovereignties, in particular, possess strength, unity, stability only to the degree to which they are sanctified by religion." The authority inherent in a state religion should consequently serve to undergird the power of the prince. People are more likely to obey the laws of the state if an omnipresent God is watching and judging their behavior. Political power is likewise greatly fortified when the power of the prince and the authority of a state religion become so entwined that citizens can no longer decipher between the two. The prince will be better able to manipulate civilians if noncompliance of state laws becomes comparable to disobeying the rules set forth by God. The authority provided by a state religion will moreover diminish the prince's need to use force to coerce public obedience and diminish the likelihood of domestic insurrections.

The Fusion of Politics and Religion in Iran

Machiavelli advised the prince to strengthen his political power by linking his powers to the authority of a state religion. History is replete with examples of political figures cloaking themselves in a state religion in order to maintain political power. There is also some evidence that political instability can emerge when politics and religion disentangle. For example, the authority of the religious cleric and Iran's Supreme Leader Ayatollah Ali Khamenei was tarnished with his perceived mishandling of the Iranian presidential election in June of 2009. The Supreme Leader's authority was challenged by street protestors who contested the integrity of the presidential election results between President Mahmoud Ahmadininejad and his two main challengers Mir-Hossein Mousavi and Mehdi Karobi. The religious leader drew the ire of reform minded Iranians by hastily endorsing the electoral victory of incumbent President Ahmadinejad even though many in Iran and around the globe suspected corruption in the electoral process. Some Iranians were later killed and hundreds detained for continuing to protest the Iranian elections after being warned by the Supreme Leader against taking to the streets.

Did the Iranian leader correctly balance the traits of the lion and the fox during this crisis in Iran?

Can you think of another example of political leaders using religion to further political goals?

The Prince Must Keep Up Appearances

In order to maintain political power, it is essential for the prince to uphold certain customs and traditions. It is in fact in some cases more important for the prince to appear to possess certain qualities than to actually possess them. Machiavelli's view that public perception quickly cements into political reality was well ahead of its time and is actually quite similar to the type of advice candidates today receive from media consultants. Since the prince's power is buttressed by the authority of religion, it is very important for the public to believe the prince worships at the same altar. This became an issue during the 2008 U.S. presidential campaign when political opponents challenged Barack Obama's Christian credentials by either portraying his Chicago minister as an extremist or by giving emphasis to his father's Muslim heritage. The Obama campaign eventually overcame these perceived politically unhelpful obstacles by stressing Obama's adherence to mainstream Christian values. His campaign's approach, in fact, paralleled Machiavelli's admonition for the prince to always appear to be "faithful, humane, sincere," and "religious" and never allow himself to be depicted in any other way.

While it is important to foster the perception that the prince is religious, it is perhaps even more important that the prince not actually be religious. The prince must instead always be logical and empirical and not allow his decision making to be influenced by religious mythologies. Besides appearing to be religious, the prince should also appear to be trustworthy. But once again, Machiavelli contends the appearance of being trustworthy is more important than actually being trustworthy. Princes must be prepared to break their word when it is in their political interest to do so. He directs that "a prudent ruler ought not to keep faith when by so doing it would work against his interest, and the reasons which made him bind himself no longer exist."[26] Lastly, Machiavelli warned while it is desirable to create the appearance of generosity, leaders are better served to engage in miserly behavior when expending state funds. Leaders who are preoccupied with appearing to be generous will soon become hated by the public as the prince will be required to "tax the people very heavily" and raise money "by all possible means." It is therefore preferable in the long run for the prince to "worry little" about a miserly reputation.

Which attributes of leadership do you most admire and why?

Machiavelli's *The Prince* is viewed as a depraved and unprincipled examination of politics by some because of its amoral focus on power rather than the public good. Whereas Plato and Aristotle stressed the need for leaders to be both ethical and competent in order to promote harmony in the state, Machiavelli instead instructs leaders to do whatever is necessary to enhance individual power. Some critics of Machiavelli go further by asserting that the advice offered in *The Prince* more closely resembles the work of a political consultant than a political theorist in that it offers very specific advice on how aspiring leaders can acquire and maintain political power. His defenders, however, argue *The Prince* must be viewed in the context of the chaotic times in which it was written and serve as a reminder that tyrannical power is sometimes required to preserve republics.[27] Abraham Lincoln made a similar case when he asserted the U.S. Constitution was not meant to be viewed as a suicide pact when defending his decision to suspend *habeas corpus* during the U.S. Civil War. *The Prince* is now just as controversial and provocative as it was when it was written 500 years ago.

THOMAS HOBBES

One hundred years later, Thomas Hobbes (1588–1679) delved much more deeply into the scientific approach to politics than Machiavelli. In his seminal text *Leviathan* Hobbes set out to empirically test Machiavelli's assertion that power rather than justice is the most important variable in politics. And he attempted to do this by offering what was at that time Western civilization's most scientific analysis of human nature and politics. This section explores how Hobbes adopted the scientific method in (1) his denial of objective truth; (2) his negative view of human nature; and (3) his **social contract theory**.

Hobbes once remarked that "fear and I were born twins" after his mother prematurely gave birth to him upon learning the Spanish Armada was within sight of the English coastline.[28] It was in the year of his birth in 1588 that Britain's Queen Elizabeth routed the fleet of over 100 naval ships deployed by Spain's King Phillip II. Hobbes also supported the Royalists during the English Civil War against the more radical Puritans, who favored a parliamentary system of government. The Puritans were ultimately victorious in the Glorious Revolution of 1688 in establishing the supremacy of the British parliament over the British monarch. But Hobbes was more greatly influenced by the scientific revolution that was raging through Europe at the time.[29]

Hobbes agreed with the philosopher Francis Bacon (1561–1626) who argued that only through the scientific method can we liberate our minds from the widely accepted mythologies (i.e., idols) inherent in all societies. Bacon argued that we should leave behind old ways of thinking and adopt a new scientific approach to understanding our universe. Hobbes opposed Plato's normative approach and instead held a high regard for Galileo and the scientific method of inquiry. The term *political science* itself originated from the belief that we can, in fact, study politics scientifically.

Galileo (1564–1642) was one of the first scientists to argue that we can understand our physical world by applying mathematical principles, just as we can understand

Social Contract Theory:
A wide range of theories linked most closely with Thomas Hobbes, John Locke, and Jean-Jacques Rousseau on the most appropriate relationship between the state and the individual. Social contract theorists typically provide an (1) observation on human nature; (2) observation on problems that arise in the absence of government (i.e., precontract state); and (3) a recommendation on a form of government best able to solve these problems.

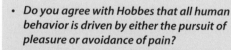

CourseReader ASSIGNMENT

Log in to **www.cengagebrain.com** and open CourseReader to access the reading:

Leviathan **by Thomas Hobbes**

Thomas Hobbes's (1588–1679) was an English philosopher who developed a political theory based on the assumption that all humans are primarily self-interested. In his book *Leviathan* (1651) he wrote that all human behavior is primarily motivated by the pursuit of pleasure and the avoidance of pain. In this excerpt from *Leviathan*, you will gain a deeper understanding of Hobbes's social contract theory and why he believed our existence would be "solitary, poor, nasty, brutish, and short" without a strong government to enforce rules. He reasoned that in order to escape this violent state of nature, people will willingly surrender freedoms to a strong sovereign in order to acquire security. His social contract theory continues to serve as the philosophical justification for monarchs and/or authoritarian governments.

- *Do you agree with Hobbes that all human behavior is driven by either the pursuit of pleasure or avoidance of pain?*
- *Have you ever behaved in a manner that was not in your self-interest?*

modern machinery by studying the functioning of its parts.[30] Hobbes drew similar comparisons between the inner workings of a watch and our ability to understand human nature and politics. Through empirical research, Galileo established the correctness of **Copernicus's** controversial theory that the sun, rather than the earth, was at the center of our galaxy. Galileo was later charged with heresy during the Inquisition and spent the latter part of his life under house arrest for undermining the teachings of the Church, which at the time incorrectly held that the earth was at the center of our solar system. At the time, the Church argued against the scientific method because it believed the supreme powers of God were beyond human comprehension. Hobbes, nonetheless, set out to prove the correctness of Machiavelli's theory on power by using the scientific approach, just as Galileo used science to prove Copernicus's theory accurate years before.[31]

Hobbes versus the Greeks: Is There an Objective Truth?

The ancient Greeks believed that the primary purpose of government is to promote social harmony. Political power for the Greeks was merely a means to promote the ends of justice. For Hobbes, political power was not viewed as a means to promote social justice, but rather a means toward the more limited aim of preventing chaos and warfare. Hobbes, like Machiavelli, broke from the Greek tradition by denying the existence of a universal objective truth. Hobbes was instead a nominalist, a concept that originated in the 12th century by French philosopher Peter Abelard. He did not believe that a permanent objective truth lies beneath our world of appearances, but rather held that humans instead construct a perception of "truth" through the filter of self-interest and the syllogisms of language. Nominalists believe language is necessary in part to help us make sense of the world as the complexities of the universe far surpass the limits of our reasoning powers. Hobbes believed we can only come to know the truth indirectly through the boundaries of self-interest and language. From a nominalist's perspective, people are neither physically attractive nor unsightly, they simply appear as they do. There is no universal objective standard for beauty, as good looks are instead determined by cultural constructs that evolve over time. Similarly, human behavior for Hobbes is not objectively good or bad, it is simply human behavior. What makes us interpret some behavior as good and some as bad is simply the extent to which the behavior

▲ The book cover of Hobbes's *Leviathan*, which was published in 1651. In the *Leviathan*, Hobbes's argues for the necessity of a strong sovereign to prevent society from degenerating into civil war and death. This book serves as the theoretical rationale for monarchs.

facilitates our self-interest. We tend to label behavior that promotes our self-interest as good and brand behavior that works against our self-interest as bad. Or as Hobbes puts it: *"whatsoever is the object of any man's appetites or desire, that is which he for his part calleth good; and the object of hate, evil."*[32] There is then for Hobbes no such thing as a real objective truth toward justice, but only the truth we make up through our self-interest and through the limits of language.

Hobbes's View of Human Nature

Hobbes also challenged Plato's major assumptions about human nature and the purpose of government. In the previous chapter we examined Plato's contention that just behavior is innately superior to unjust behavior. The *Republic* was his attempt to establish the correctness of Socrates's view that a just person perceived to be unjust is happier than an unjust person perceived to be just. He did this at the end of the *Republic* in his theory on the gradations of happiness in the republic and the human soul. Here Plato argued the highest form of happiness occurs when the guardian reaches "the good" (or perfect knowledge) because it is in this state that our intellect dominates over our appetites and urges and steers us toward justice. The worst form of government for Plato was a tyrannical system of government because tyrants instead follow their appetites and urges rather than pursue the public good.

The theories of Plato and Hobbes conform in the sense that both agree human nature is divided between the rational part of our intellect and the self-interested impulses of our appetites. Where they differ is in Plato's assertion that human happiness is best achieved when our intellect is trained to dominate over our desires. For Hobbes it is not possible for our intellect to dominate over our natural urges. He instead examined human nature in the same manner that physicists study our natural world. Scientists established that most things in the universe can be best explained by exploring the concept of matter and motion. Modern science observes our physical world by studying how matter when set into motion hits upon other forms of matter that then unleashes a long chain of random events. Hobbes incorporated this view from science to explain human behavior. He counseled that within the matter of the human body exists the "vital motion" of the circulation of blood and breathing patterns. Human behavior similarly is best explained by studying the "voluntary motion" (i.e., psychology) that controls physical movement and the way we speak.[33] So for Hobbes the study of politics first requires an in-depth understanding of human psychology. Human behavior is best understood by examining how the sensations associated with sight, hearing, touch, taste, and smell interact with the mind.[34] Hobbes argued that humans have natural "appetites" (e.g., hunger and thirst) and natural "aversions" that explain the way we behave. He differs from Plato in that he believed all human behavior is principally driven by our natural pursuit of pleasures and our natural aversion to pain.

He reasoned that our intellect plays a secondary role to our natural urges and merely serves to determine what we perceive to be pleasurable or painful. And it is in this finding that Hobbes declared he is able to substantiate Machiavelli's contention that power is the most important variable in the study of politics.

Human Nature and Our Lust for Power

So what if all human behavior is driven by our pursuit of pleasure and the avoidance of pain? How does this help us make generalizations about human nature and/or the study of politics? What is pleasurable for one person, after all, might be painful to another and vice versa. It is from Hobbes's explanation of human behavior that he is able to assert that all human beings possess a natural lust for power. While it is true that what is pleasurable for one might be painful to another, he argued we all must possess a natural inclination toward power because it is through the possession of power that we are able to pursue whatever it is we perceive to be pleasurable. This does not mean that we all secretly wish to be president of the United States. Remember, it is our intellect that determines our perceptions of pleasure and pain. But even those who prefer to pursue life's simpler pleasures, such as gardening or spending time with family, still require a certain amount of power to pursue these pleasures.

The chief problem for Hobbes is that satisfying one's desire in the state of nature provides only temporary pleasure and results in a continued struggle to ensure that pleasure is maintained into the future. He stated that "the object of man's desire is not to enjoy once only and for one instant of time, but to assure forever the way of his future desire. And therefore the voluntary actions and inclinations of all men tend not only to the procuring but also to the assuring of a contented life."[35] It is because of this natural lust for power for Hobbes that people will inevitably come into conflict with one another in the state of nature. Since resources in nature are in limited supply, quarrels will occur when "two men desire the same thing, which nevertheless they cannot both enjoy, they become enemies."[36] He extended on this point by asserting that in nature "we find three principal causes of quarrels:" (1) competition; (2) diffidence; and (3) glory. In the first case, people will violently compete against each other for possessions; whereas in the second, conflict will ensue out of a sense of fear and insecurity; and in the third, fighting will be caused by our desire to enhance personal reputations.

People in the state of nature live in a persistent state of warfare and fear as "every human being is capable of killing any other." Hobbes's view of the state of nature is consequently in direct odds with John Locke's assertion that society is guided and structured by an imperceptible natural law. Because Hobbes instead views the world through the scientific lens of matter and motion, concepts such as natural law, which will be discussed in greater detail in the next section, serves as an imaginary solution to a genuine human predicament. Hobbes concludes our existence in the

Realism and Liberalism in International Relations

This discussion on whether conflict and violence is inherent in human nature is carried on today in the field of international relations. In Chapter 11 we examine and contrast theories associated with realism and liberalism. Realists argue that the international system is in a state of chaos and that states should maximize their own power in order to deter foreign aggression. Thucydides (400 BCE), Machiavelli (1469–1527), and Thomas Hobbes (1588–1679) are regarded as renowned realist theorists. Former president Ronald Reagan is generally considered a modern realist, in that he relied heavily on American military power to expand America's sphere of influence.

Liberalism, on the other hand, is more optimistic about our ability to bring structure and order to the international system. Immanuel Kant (1724–1804) and John Locke (1632–1704) are liberal theorists who believed humans can exist in nonviolent and cooperative political structures. Former American president Woodrow Wilson's attempt to build a collective security system by way of the League of Nations is consistent with the liberal approach to problem solving. The liberal approach relies more heavily on involving international organizations such as the United Nations to solve problems in the international system.

Do you believe the United Nations is effective in solving global problems?

unstructured and unmanaged environment of the precontract state (i.e. life before government) is "solitary, poor, nasty, brutish, and short." Society will inevitably degenerate into total war "of every man against every man" where "notions of right and wrong, justice and injustice have no place."[37]

Hobbes's Social Contract Theory

This does not mean to suggest that Hobbes believed we are by nature wicked and depraved. His view on human nature does not mirror the Christian doctrine of original sin that asserts people are born sinful as a result of Adam and Even eating forbidden fruit in the Garden of Eden. He additionally does not subscribe to the view that

Prisoner's Dilemma:
Are you more competitive than cooperative?

Hobbes argued that civil society will inevitably degenerate into civil war and death because people in the precontract state will not cooperate with each other out of a fear that placing trust in an untrustworthy person could have disastrous impacts. It is based on this finding that Hobbes argued we are by nature more competitive than cooperative. In 1950, Merrill Flood and Melvin Dresher from the Rand Corporation developed the prisoner's dilemma game theory to illustrate that people sometimes will not cooperate with each other even when it is their best interest to do so. Prisoner's Dilemma has been widely applied in the field of international relations and is highlighted again in Chapter 11.

Are you by nature a competitive or cooperative person? Pretend you and a classmate joined forces in robbing a bank. The two of you are later apprehended and brought to the police station for questioning. Because the police officers only have circumstantial evidence against you, they need to solicit a confession in order to ensure a conviction. One police officer takes you into an interrogation room while another police officer takes your classmate into an adjoining room. You are then each informed that it is in your best interest to cooperate with the investigation by admitting that you and your classmate were involved in the robbery. You then learn that if both you and your classmate remain quiet you will each do one year in prison. If you and your classmate both confess, you will each do five years in prison. If one confesses and the other remains quiet, the one who confesses will go free while the one who remains quiet will get 10 years in prison.

		Student A	
		Talk	Quiet
Student B	Talk	5 years each	A = 10 years B = 0 years
	Quiet	A = 0 years B = 10 years	1 year each

What would you choose to do?

people take joy in the suffering of others: "For, that any man should take pleasure in other men's great harms without other end of his own, I do not conceive it possible."[38] Instead he argued people behave quite rationally in the precontract state considering the absence of government. In some respects, his views parallel the *tragedy of the commons* effect depicted by Garrett Hardin (1968), who argued resources will become depleted whenever high demand meets a limited resource in an unregulated environment. Because of the intense competition for resources, people are unlikely to trust others out of a fear that placing one's trust in an untrustworthy person could have devastating effects.[39] Here Hobbes was perhaps influenced by Machiavelli's advice to the prince on the necessity to break promises when it is in the best interest of the prince to do so: "If men were all good, this precept would not be a good one; but as they Are Bad, and not observe the faith with you, so you are not bound to keep faith with them."[40] So while Hobbes believed we are primarily motivated by self-interest, he also recognized that we are in fact vulnerable creatures who must rely on faulty logic and are susceptible to the self-interested behavior of others.

Hobbes is regarded as the first social contract theorist because he recommended a specific form of government that is best suited to address the problems associated with his vision of the precontract state. Social contract theorists accordingly analyze three distinct components of political theory including (1) an observation of human nature; (2) an observation of the problems that arise in the absence of government; and (3) a recommendation on a form of government best able to solve the problem.[41]

Because conditions in the precontract state are so abhorrent, people will voluntarily leave it in favor of the more secure environment provided by government, or commonwealth as Hobbes refers to it. For Hobbes a commonwealth is created when all associated with it are willing to surrender all freedoms to a governing authority that consists of either one person or assembly of people. In so doing, all members of the commonwealth make the following pledge: I Authorize and give my Right of Governing myself, to this man, or to this Assembly of men, on this condition, that thou give thy Right to him, and Authorize all his Actions in like manner."[42] For Hobbes, members of the commonwealth must surrender almost all of their rights to either a ruler or a ruling assembly in exchange for personal security. Later in *Leviathan*, Hobbes stated his preference for an individual monarch out of a belief that governing assemblies are more likely to be filled with those more interested in pursuing personal wealth than the public's business. As opposed to the American system of federalism which is discussed in great detail in the next chapter, Hobbes instead advocated a unitary form of government where the sovereign is responsible for making, executing, and interpreting the law. The most controversial aspect associated with Hobbes's commonwealth is the sovereign stands above the law and is answerable to no one. Hobbes asserted that people will willingly surrender almost all rights to the sovereign because the alternative is life in the precontract state which inevitably leads to civil war and death. The purpose of government for Hobbes is consequently not to promote justice as the ancient Greeks asserted, but rather to provide security.

When looking at Hobbes and all political thinkers you'll encounter in this book, think about how their historical surroundings and circumstances influenced their theories. How were their thoughts shaped by the cultural, political, religious, and scientific beliefs of their time? How might their theories differ if they lived in the 21st century? Or would they?

TABLE 3.2. Hobbes, Locke, and Rousseau: The Major Social Contract Theorists[43]

View of Nature and Government	Thomas Hobbes (1588–1679)	John Locke (1632–1704)	Jean-Jacques Rousseau (1712–1778)
Human Nature	Humans have an inherent lust for power.	Humans are by nature cooperative and defensive.	Humans are naturally good, driven primarily by a natural aversion to suffering. Men are noble savages.
State of Nature	Life in the State of Nature is solitary, poor, nasty, brutish, and short. The state of nature is in constant state of war, where everyone is capable of killing everyone else.	The State of Nature is largely cooperative and guided by natural laws.	The state of nature is naturally a peaceful place where people live uncomplicated lives until they are corrupted by the introduction of private property.
Social Contract Theory	People should surrender all rights to the sovereign in order to avoid civil war and death.	Favors limited representative democracy and believes government should merely do what is not provided for in the state of nature in order to promote the right to life, liberty, and the protection of private property.	Favors a system of direct democracy.

The political theory espoused by Hobbes has served as the theoretical rationale for monarchs and authoritarian governments. In Table 3.2 we provide a brief comparison of Thomas Hobbes's social contract theory against the social contract theories of John Locke and Jean-Jacques Rousseau.

JOHN LOCKE

Hobbes's view of human nature as self-interested and his call for an authoritarian government to prevent society from degenerating into chaos and civil war was directly challenged by John Locke in his classic work entitled the *Two Treatises of Government* in 1690. Locke was a British political philosopher who both influenced and was influenced by England's Glorious Revolution of 1688. While considered a "bloodless" revolution, the insurrection was successful in driving England's King James II into exile in France, thereby officially ending the dominance of the English monarch. King James II was a polarizing figure who, through the use of force, undermined the laws of Parliament and sought to convert England to Catholicism. The British Parliament in 1689 offered the vacant throne to Prince William and his wife Mary. But this authority was conferred under conditions set forth in a new British Bill of Rights that stripped from the throne considerable fiscal and military powers. The British monarch was no longer empowered to appropriate funds or to raise armies during peaceful times without the consent of the British Parliament. A new English era of Parliamentary government (see Chapter 9) had begun.

It was in this context that Locke founded a new trend of thinking under the banner of **classical liberalism,** which viewed human beings as innately principled,

Do you agree with Hobbes that people should surrender basic rights to government in order to maintain security in society? Do you believe Americans have too few or too many rights in the 21st century?

Classical Liberalism:
Classical liberalism advocates for a limited government and for greater individual liberties at the political, social, and economic levels of society. John Locke (1632–1704) and Adam Smith (1732–1790) are generally regarded as two leading classical liberals. This movement inspired the American and French Revolutions, and the economic system of capitalism.

Log in to **www.cengagebrain.com** and open CourseReader to access the reading:

The Second Treatise of Civil Government, Chapter II: Of the State of Nature **by John Locke**

John Locke is one of the most important philosophers to influence the thinking of America's founders. In chapter two of his *Second Treatise*, you will read how Locke's depiction of the state of nature vastly differs from Thomas Hobbes's view. In this section Locke explains how a limited government can preserve our natural state of cooperation while maintaining political order. His social contract theory asserts that a limited government can maintain order and equality in society by legislating and judging against the minority that violate popular laws.

- *Why did Locke believe it is better to elect Representatives to make decisions on behalf of the people (i.e. Representative Democracy) than it is to have people make decisions for themselves (i.e. Direct Democracy)? Do you agree with Locke? Why or Why Not?*

mentally gifted, and capable of self-rule. It was this political doctrine more than any other that influenced the American uprising against the British in the American Revolution. Classical liberalism stresses individual liberty, the importance of natural rights, personal privacy, and the need for limited democratic government.

Locke depicted the pre-contract state as a primitive society where human beings are free, autonomous, and rational creatures who are first and foremost motivated to acquire private property.[44] Thomas Jefferson borrowed liberally from Locke when drafting the Declaration of Independence, and Locke's instruction that it is better to rise up in arms against oppressive governments than to live under their tyranny gave courage to American patriots during the Revolutionary War. The power of Locke's theory is long-lasting and far reaching, as today approximately sixty-four percent (i.e., 122 nations) of the world's governments operate under some form of a democratic system.[45] This section compares John Locke's view of human nature, life in the precontract state, and his social contract theory against the positions held by Thomas Hobbes.

Locke and Human Nature

The difference between Hobbes's view of human nature and Locke's view of human nature is sometimes simplified to suggest that Hobbes considered humans to be naturally evil, while Locke considered our nature to be innately good. But just as the previous section pointed out that Hobbes did not believe humans were naturally wicked, neither did Locke believe we were naturally virtuous. Though Locke believed in God, whereas Hobbes most likely did not, he did not view humans as divine beings born into the world with pre-existing notions of right and wrong. In his work entitled *An Essay Concerning*

THEORY AND PRACTICE

John Locke and the U.S. Declaration of Independence

Thomas Jefferson and other Founding Fathers were strongly influenced by Locke's notion of natural rights and natural law. In what is likely the most celebrated sentence ever written in American history, Jefferson wrote in the Declaration of Independence that: "We hold these truths to be self-evident that all men are created equal, that they are endowed by their Creator with certain unalienable Rights, that among these are life, liberty, and the pursuit of Happiness." Jefferson's assertion that we have a natural right to life was borrowed from Locke's notion that we are the owners of our own bodies. If we have a natural right to life, then a government is required to enforce the corresponding natural law against taking the life of another. As for the natural right of liberty, Locke explained since we are the owners of our bodies then we are also in possession of our limbs, and our mouth, and by extension the words that come out of it. We therefore have a natural right of free expression. Jefferson interestingly detours somewhat from Locke on the third natural right listed in the Declaration of Independence. Rather than give emphasis to the natural right to pursue private property as Locke counseled, Jefferson instead cited a natural right to pursue happiness. On this point Jefferson was more influenced by the writings of Plato and Aristotle, whom you might recall from the previous chapter defined happiness as the right to pursue knowledge and justice.

Do you believe people have unalienable (or natural) rights? Why or why not? How would Hobbes argue against Locke's view of natural rights?

Human Understanding he instead supported the principle of *tabula rasa*, (translates to "blank slate"), which stated that we come into the world without any preconceived notions about anything. Here he rejects René Descartes "doctrine of innate principles" that avowed we are born with a priori knowledge of the existence of God. For Locke our sense of right and wrong is rather developed through the knowledge we gain from our five senses and our powers of

▲ A portrait of John Locke (1632–1704) painted by Sir Godfrey Kneller in 1697. Locke's writings helped inspire the writing of the U.S. Declaration of Independence and the American Revolution. At the time of this portrait, Locke was largely removed from public life, opting instead to spend his remaining years in the quiet company of close friends.

reflection. We cannot hold any principles, according to Locke, until we are either first taught them or are able to acquire them by converting our experiences into knowledge.

Locke, like Hobbes, was an empiricist, and subscribed to the scientific approach to the study of human nature and politics. Hobbes and Locke also agreed that human nature is divided between the rational part of our intellect and the self-interested impulses of our desires. But where Locke and Hobbes disagreed on human nature is on the emphasis each placed on the importance of our intellect, or rational side of our nature. In the previous section we examined Hobbes's assertion that all humans have a natural lust for power because power is required in order for us to pursue pleasure and avoid pain. Hobbes also asserted that human behavior is largely driven by our natural appetites and that the rational side of our nature merely serves to determine our perception of pleasure and pain. Though Locke never mentioned Hobbes by name, he challenged his contention that human nature is principally driven by our urges and desires. He instead argued that the rational side of our nature can dominate over our appetites. Our reasoning abilities, Locke counseled, is gained from "external experiences" where information received from our five senses is converted into knowledge. You might recall that Hobbes also believed that our behavior is influenced by how we interpret information that flows to our brain from our five senses. But Locke differs from Hobbes in that he also highlights a second type of knowledge that comes from our "internal experiences," which emphasizes how our reasoning abilities are enhanced through the power of reflection. This power of reflection is unique to humans and enables us to process complicated and abstract thoughts about the potential repercussions of future behavior. Locke believed that our human nature is largely peaceful and cooperative because our natural reasoning powers point us in this direction. It is through our power of reason that we will come to learn "that no one ought to harm another in his life, liberty, or possessions."[46] So whereas Hobbes believed our behavior is driven by our desires, Locke believed that our behavior is largely controlled by our reasoning powers.

John Locke, Mary Wollstonecraft, and the Expansion of Women's Rights

John Locke's belief in individual rights helped pave the theoretical path for the expansion of women's rights. While Locke was not a feminist in the modern sense, he did advocate property rights for women, and his influence on the writing of the American Declaration of Independence forever changed the course of history. Mary Wollstonecraft (1759–1797), regarded by some as the founder of feminism, expanded on some of Locke's writings in her critique of the treatment of women in the 18th century entitled *Vindication of the Rights of Women* (1792). Wollstonecraft criticized the role played by women in 18th century marriages and argued for equal education and equal rights for women.

Elizabeth Cady Stanton later used the Declaration of Independence as a template when drafting the Declaration of Sentiments for the historic Women's Rights Convention in Seneca Falls in 1848. The Declaration of Sentiments read, "We hold these truths to be self-evident, that all men and women are created equal, that they are endowed by their creator with certain inalienable rights that among these are life, liberty, and the pursuit of happiness." Stanton went on to list 18 "injuries and usurpations" committed against women by men, which is the equal number of grievances Thomas Jefferson filed against King George III.[47] Stanton later went on to work with Susan B. Anthony in the struggle for women's suffrage. Charlotte Woodward, a young worker in a glove factory, was the only signer of the Declaration of Sentiments that was still alive when all women received the right to vote over 70 years later in the Constitution's 19th Amendment in 1920.[48] Women voters now vote in much higher numbers than their male counterparts. Of the 131 million voters casting a ballot in the 2008 U.S. presidential election, 70.4 million were women and only 60.7 million were men. Recent voting trends also reveal a growing gender gap in American politics. For instance, 56 percent of women voted for Barack Obama and 43 percent of women voted for John McCain in the 2008 presidential election. This compares to only 49 percent of men voting for Barack Obama and 48 percent of men voting for John McCain.

Why do you believe women were more likely to vote for Barack Obama than men?

Property Rights in the State of Nature

The chief principle associated with John Locke is that of a "fundamental respect for the integrity of the autonomous individual."[49] In the *Second Treatise*, Locke portrayed the state of nature and the social contract in an opposing light from the views depicted by Hobbes. Locke believed that we are born free and exist naturally in a "state of liberty."[50] In this state of perfect freedom, we will naturally come to possess private property. For Locke owning private property is considered one of the most important natural rights bestowed upon man by God. He argued that since "man has property in his own person . . . the labor of his body and the work of his hands, we may say are properly his." It is a matter of simple fairness then for Locke that only those who are "industrious and rational" should benefit from the fruits of their labor.[51] He also contended that those who are not industrious yet attempt to benefit from the labor of others violate the natural rights of productive members of society. The leading capitalist thinker Adam Smith incorporated this view into his theory of the invisible hand, which stressed that economies run more efficiently when guided by the invisible hand of supply and demand rather than by regulations set forth by government. Locke's view of property is also based on his belief that individual liberty brings with it the right of individuals to "make choices about the direction of one's life."[52] Whereas Hobbes argued that the competition for property will inevitably lead to chaos and violence, Locke insisted that the laws of nature as expressed through human reasoning will provide the necessary structure to ensure a peaceful existence.

This does not mean to suggest that Locke believed our reasoning powers make certain that everyone in the precontract state will at all times behave in a defensive

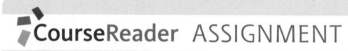

CourseReader ASSIGNMENT

Log in to **www.cengagebrain.com** and open CourseReader to access the reading:

"Declaration of Sentiments." History of Woman Suffrage. Ed. Elizabeth Cady Stanton, Susan B. Anthony, and Matilda Joslyn Gage. Vol. 1. 1881. 70–71.

A bold extension of the logic and wording of Thomas Jefferson's Declaration of Independence to women, the Declaration of Sentiments shocked Victorian America with its challenge to accepted gender relations. The Declaration was the product of the Seneca Falls Convention organized by Lucretia Mott and Elizabeth Cady Stanton. Already famous as Abolitionists, Mott and Stanton felt that the same logic that drove the American Revolution and the antislavery crusade should extend equality to women. This Declaration of Sentiments was approved by the convention on July 20, 1848.

- *The Equal Rights Amendment was first proposed in 1923 and called for women and men to have equal rights under the law. While the ERA received a two-third vote from the House and Senate, it was never officially ratified by the states. Do you believe the Equal Rights Amendment should be ratified as a constitutional amendment? Why or Why not? Do you consider yourself a feminist? Why or why not?*

Karl Marx and Communism

Adam Smith incorporated some of John Locke's views on private property in his theories on capitalism in his classic text *The Wealth of Nations* (1776). Karl Marx (1818–1883) challenged the tradition of modern political theory by arguing that private property should no longer serve as the foundation of western civil society, as John Locke and Adam Smith argued. Marx emerged as a leading force against the economic system of capitalism. He argued that the capitalist system was inherently flawed because the capitalist producer's (i.e., bourgeoisie) single-minded pursuit of "profit" causes him/her to exploit the working class (i.e., proletariat). Society under a capitalistic economic system is thus transformed into two hostile camps, the Bourgeoisie versus the Proletariat. He also railed against organized religion by referring to it as "the opium of the people." Marx counseled that social misery and human alienation is the by-product of the bourgeoisie exploitation of the proletariat, and urged the proletariat to revolt against capitalism. Marx's critique of capitalism was bolstered by the deplorable working conditions that existed during the industrial revolution.

Marx called for a workers revolution against capitalism and advocated that capitalism be replaced by universal socialism. He co-authored his most famous work, *The Communist Manifesto,* with Friedrich Engels in 1848. Marx borrowed from Hegel's theory on the dialectic that espoused that truth evolves out of a long series of opposing forces, referred to as the synthesis, the antithesis, and the synthesis. He amends Hegel's "dialectic" in his analysis on "historical materialism" by arguing humankind evolves "through successive modes of production: from feudalism to capitalism and eventually to communism.[53] Marx speculated that socialism will naturally evolve from the system of capitalism. Marxism inspired the Russian Revolution of 1917 and the founding of the Soviet Union. There are also many modern nations, such as Cuba, the People's Republic of China, and Vietnam, that are guided at least in part by socialistic principles. Marxism is discussed in greater detail in the discussion in Chapter 11 on dependency theory.

Do you believe developing nations are more likely to follow the Chinese model of economic development or the American model of economic development?

and cooperative manner. There will be some who stray from the norm and engage in uncivilized behavior. But Locke believed that because we are by nature social creatures with advanced reasoning powers, we will naturally develop rules to punish those who violate them. We will realize that freedom must be coupled with responsible behavior to ensure one's freedom of action does not bring harm to another. The state of nature for Locke benefits from a thriving and fully functioning civil society. He further counseled that while we have a right to private property, we do not necessarily have a right to horde so much of it that we could not "make use to any advantage of life before it spoils." Our natural condition in the state of nature is then not a state of war of every man against every man as Hobbes suggested, but is rather described by Locke as "a state of peace, good-will, mutual assistance, and preservation."

THEORY AND PRACTICE

Jean-Jacques Rousseau: *The Last Great Social Contract Theorist*

© ISTOCKPHOTO.COM/DIEGO CERVO

Jean Jacques Rousseau (1712–1778) is regarded as the father of the French Revolution and by some as the last great social contract theorist. Rousseau caused a stir when he stated that "Man is born free, and yet we see him everywhere in chains" in his most famous work, *The Social Contract*. This statement was at odds with other major works during the Enlightenment in that most theorists of the day argued the "light of reason" was for the first time guiding public behavior.[54] Rousseau believed people are born in liberty with a natural aversion to seeing others suffer in the precontract state. He counseled we behave as "noble savages" up until the introduction of private property. Private property transforms the state of nature by creating social classes that are based on the inequalities stemming from property rights. And it is this competition for property that ultimately destroys our inherent goodness. The inequality associated with property rights later corrupts "reason" itself. Rousseau attacked Locke and other theorists during the Enlightenment by arguing their theories do more to advance the interests of the "enlightened" than in empowering people. He is critical of Locke's call for a representative democracy because he believed that political power in republics is simply used to exploit the uneducated and advance the interests of political elites. Rousseau instead advocated for a more direct form of democracy.

continued ➤

continued

Rousseau differs from Locke in that his social contract calls for greater equality under law. Rather than have a select few make decisions on behalf of the population, Rousseau instead believes each individual should play a role in government. Rousseau argues we ourselves are transformed from a primitive being into a civilized being when we enter the social contract. The highest form of civil society is established when our natural "feelings" of pity and compassion are linked with ethical reasoned "thought" so that the public interest and the private interests of individuals become one and the same.[55] Rousseau proposed a new social contract whereby individuals surrender all rights to a general will in exchange for having an equal voice in what that general will should be. In Rousseau's social contract, all members of the contract are required to abide by the general will, and those who object to societal rules will be forced to comply. In Rousseau's social contract, individuals both serve under the authority of the general will while serving as equal members of the general will.

> Do you agree with Rousseau that direct democracy political systems are preferable to representative democracies? Why did the American Framers warn against direct democracies?

Locke's Social Contract

So the obvious question is if life in the state of nature is as serene as Locke will have us believe, why would we want to leave it for a new life under government? Why depart from this wonderful existence in nature? He answers this by stating that while people enjoy the benefits of freedom in the state of nature, this liberty is vulnerable to the "invasions of others." Through our power of reason we will come to realize that the gifts associated with the state of nature are best protected by forming a government to make certain of its preservation. And the primary reason for establishing a commonwealth is to ensure the preservation of private property. The purpose of government is to uphold our natural rights and to do for us what is not provided for in the state of nature. Locke believed that every natural right had a corresponding natural law that needed to be enforced by government. If we have a natural right to property than there must be a corresponding natural law that tells us it is wrong to seize the property of others. Locke's social contract theory called for a very limited representative government whose purpose is to protect private property and to uphold natural law.

Hobbes argued that an all powerful sovereign was required in order to prevent civil war and death in his social contract theory. People must surrender almost all freedoms to the sovereign in exchange for a peaceful existence since individual liberty would simply be used to gain more power. Locke turned Hobbes's argument here by asserting that living under a tyrannical government will cause, rather than prevent, violence because people will inevitably revolt against the unnatural environment of oppression. Locke's social contract instead called for a limited government to perform two basic functions. The first role of government is to pass laws that protect the preservation of citizens and are aligned with the laws of nature. The second purpose of government is to punish those who violate these laws. It is for these reasons that Locke's first order of business is to establish a legislative branch of government in order to enact just laws. An executive should also be created in order to help enforce these laws. And lastly, an impartial arbiter must be established in order to fairly determine the guilt or innocence of the accused. Locke's social contract was quite radical in that he also counseled that people have the right to revolt if the government violates the social contract. It was this view that, of course, helped motivate American colonists to take up arms against the British in the American Revolution.

© ARIF ALI/AFP/GETTY IMAGES

SUMMARY

This chapter examined the major theories associated with many of the important modern political theorists. These modern political thinkers are distinct from the early political thinkers highlighted in the previous chapter in that modern thinkers adopted the empirical method of examining politics. Machiavelli's *The Prince*, Thomas Hobbes's *Leviathan*, and John Locke's *The Second Treatise of Government* are three of the most important political texts written in Western civilization. Machiavelli was the first to stray from the premises of early theorists by stressing that "power" rather than "justice" is the most important variable in understanding politics. Thomas Hobbes attempted to validate Machiavelli's theory on power and politics and developed the philosophical rationale for monarchs and authoritarian governments. John Locke and Jean-Jacques Rousseau challenged Hobbes's social contract by asserting a limited government that allows us to remain as close to our original state of nature as possible is the best form of government. These thinkers also laid the theoretical foundation for the development of democratic systems of government and the expansion of individual rights. In the next section we will explore how John Locke's social contract theory influenced the American Framers and the creation of the American government. Here we will explore how American democracy has evolved and the process by which political rights for African Americans and women were expanded.

KEY TERMS

KEY PEOPLE

4

THE AMERICAN GOVERNMENT

Some say the U.S. Constitution is America's greatest export. The Constitution was adopted at the constitutional convention in Philadelphia on September 17, 1787. It is the oldest living federal constitution in the world today.

INTRODUCTION: THE ORIGINS OF AMERICAN DEMOCRACY

American democracy was born in Philadelphia in 1787 at the Constitutional Convention. For that reason it is somewhat ironic that the term *democracy* itself was not included in the American Constitution. This is because democracy was a loaded term in the late eighteenth century, and conjured up images in the minds of the framers of mob rule and political anarchy. Our system of government was instead referred to as a **republic** in order to steer clear of long-established attacks on *direct democracies*. We learned in Chapter 2 that Plato (427–347 BCE) viewed democracies as inferior systems of government because they are founded on the premise that all opinions are equally valid. A political system based on majority rule was thought to be unwise because communities typically include more ordinary than enlightened thinkers. Plato reasoned that since the overwhelming majority of citizens lacked the necessary training in the virtues of justice, most would place their own selfish desires over the interests of the nation.

Because of this many of the delegates at the Constitutional Convention believed the new government might fail if majority groups were permitted to impose their will on unreceptive political minorities. Some argued that a political system based on majority rule would degenerate into a "mobocracy," where self-interested groups would struggle to dominate over less organized interests. Thomas Jefferson made the point more clearly when he stated, "[A] democracy is nothing more than mob rule, where 51 percent of the people may take away the rights of the other forty-nine."[1] The manner in which the American framers addressed this **tyranny of the majority** concern is highlighted later in the chapter in the review of James Madison's *Federalist Paper No. 10,* arguably America's greatest contribution to political theory. Today, however, approximately 123 of the 195 nations across the globe have adopted some form of popular government, making it hard to imagine what our modern world would be like without democratic systems of government. Perhaps former British prime minister Winston Churchill said it best when he remarked that "democracy is the worst form of government, except all others that have been tried."[2]

Questions to Consider Before Reading this Chapter

1. Why is the term *democracy* not included in the U.S. Constitution?

2. Which British Acts inspired the American colonists to rise up against British rule?

3. Why did the Articles of Confederation (1781–1787) system of government fail?

4. What role did the Voting Rights Act of 1965 play in Barack Obama's presidential electoral victory in 2008?

5. Who wrote the *Federalist Papers* and why?

6. How did the Supreme Court expand federal powers over the states in the *McCulloch v. Maryland* (1819) decision?

7. How has *Federalist Paper No. 10* contributed to democratic theory?

8. Should we in the 21st century be guided by a Constitution written in the 18th century?

Republic: *A system of government where power lies with the body of citizens who elect representatives to make decisions on their behalf*

Tyranny of the Majority: *A chief criticism of democratic systems of government where those in the political majority violate the rights of those in the political minority*

THE ARTICLES OF CONFEDERATION: THE FAILED EXPERIMENT

The American system of government that existed during the Constitutional Convention was the Articles of Confederation (1781–1787). As we discussed in Chapter 3, the framers were heavily influenced by John Locke's *Two Treatises of Government,* which called for a very limited form of government.

THEORY AND PRACTICE — The Tea Party Then and Now

"We hold these truths to be self-evident, that all men are created equal, that they are endowed by their Creator with certain unalienable rights, that among these are life, liberty, and the pursuit of happiness." No sentence ever penned has been more widely cited or has had such a transforming effect on American political culture than this second sentence of the Declaration of Independence. The 56 signers of the Declaration of Independence sacrificed their lives when they publicly declared independence from Britain on July 4, 1776. The document drafted by Thomas Jefferson, John Adams, Benjamin Franklin, Roger Sherman, and Robert Livingston highlighted the "repeated injuries and usurpations" of King George III, and proclaimed the birth of a new nation to the international community.

The Declaration of Independence was inspired by a series of British Acts that sought to regulate American political and economic life in a manner beneficial to the British Empire. The British Stamp Act of 1765, for instance, placed a three pence stamp tax on the colonies to help offset the staggering British national debt incurred from the Seven Years War (1756–1763). This Act represented the British Parliament's first attempt at asserting economic control over the colonies. The Townshend Acts (1767) then exacerbated tensions by placing British tariffs on a host of other commodities, including glass, lead, paper, paint, and tea. The Massachusetts legislature was later disbanded by the British for refusing to enforce the collection of new taxes. One of the Townshend Acts also abolished New York's legislature for failing to abide by the Quartering Act (1765), which required colonists to accept British troops into their homes.

British troops were later dispatched to Boston, where opposition to the Townshend Acts was most vociferous. It was here on March 5, 1770, that British troops shot and killed five protesting American colonists, an event that later came to be known as

continued ➤

continued

the Boston Massacre. In 1773, a group of American colonists, some of whom were disguised as Mohawk Indians, protested the Tea Act (1773) by dumping 90,000 pounds of tea from three ships into the Boston Harbor. This act of civil disobedience helped spark the passage of the Declaration of Independence and the American Revolution. When the residents of Boston refused to compensate Britain for the costs of the tea, Britain responded by passing what colonists referred to as the Intolerable Acts, which among other things closed Boston's port to commerce, encroached on the powers of the Massachusetts Assembly, and gave legal immunity to British officials.

Beginning in 2009, images of the Boston Tea Party were evoked by a conservative citizen group protesting the increase of deficit spending during the Bush and early Obama years. This Tea Party movement, informally led in part by former vice presidential candidate Sarah Palin, opposed the $700 billion bailout of the American banking system, better known as the Troubled Asset Relief Program (TARP), the $800 billion spent on the American Recovery and Reinvestment Act of 2009, also known as the stimulus bill, the Health Care Bill of 2010, and the size of the national debt.

© CHERYL CASEY/SHUTTERSTOCK.COM

▲ Tea Party protesters in Pensacola, Florida, attending a nationwide rally on tax day against increased federal spending.

Do you believe there are any similarities between the modern tea party movement and the tea protests associated with early American colonists? Why or why not?

©ISTOCKPHOTO.COM/LORENZO COLLORETA

The American framers by and large shared Locke's optimistic view of human nature. Most believed that humans are inherently cooperative and defensive in nature, and are not above all else the power-seeking creatures described by Thomas Hobbes. As the previous chapter highlighted, Locke believed that authoritarian governments are unworkable because they create oppressive living conditions that are far removed from the way we were intended to live in nature. He argued that living under the tyranny of monarchs takes us away from our natural cooperative state and toward an unnatural state of conflict and violence. Limited governments, Locke argued, are therefore preferred because they more closely resemble the way we lived in nature before governments were created (i.e., pre-contract state).

It is in part because of this view that America's first system of government was made extraordinarily weak. The Articles of Confederation lacked both an executive and judicial branch of government. It granted most powers to the original thirteen state governments. Because the national government did not have the power to tax, it was frequently criticized for not sending needed supplies to American troops during the Revolutionary War (1775–1783) with Britain. It soon became apparent that the Articles of Confederation was not a workable form of government.

In Table 4.1 we provide a list of the signers of the Declaration of Independence and the state each represented.

Some state delegations did not take the Articles of Confederation very seriously and many delegates only sporadically attended meetings. Thomas Jefferson expressed his frustration over this in a letter to James Madison in 1784:

We cannot make up a congress at all. There are eight states in town, *six of which are represented by two members only. Of these, two members of different states are confined by gout, so that we cannot make a house, i.e., a quorum. We have not sat above three days, I believe, in as many weeks. Admonition after admonition has been sent to the states to no effect, We have sent one today. If it fails, it seems as well we should all retire.*[4]

The Articles of Confederation was also unable to produce an enforceable peace treaty with Britain, create a national currency that had any meaningful value, or establish reasoned public policy in either domestic or foreign affairs. The final two fatal blows for the Articles occurred in the fall of 1786, with the disappointing Annapolis Convention and in the bedlam created by Shays's Rebellion.[5]

Annapolis Convention:
An interstate convention called in 1786 to discuss issues of commerce. The meeting was largely seen as a failure because only 5 of the 13 states sent delegations.

The **Annapolis Convention** (1786) was called to resolve interstate trade disputes between the original 13 states. The three-day meeting was a

TABLE 4.1. Signers of the Declaration of Independence

The first to sign the Declaration of Independence was John Hancock, the president of the Continental Congress, who later served as the governor of Massachusetts. According to American folklore, Hancock stated, "There, I guess King George will be able to read that!" after signing his name in a bold and flamboyant manner. John Adams and Thomas Jefferson, future American presidents, also signed the document. The youngest to sign was Edward Rutledge from South Carolina at 26 years of age, and Benjamin Franklin from Pennsylvania, at 70, was the oldest signer of the Declaration of Independence.[3]

Connecticut	Samuel Huntington	Roger Sherman
	William Williams	Oliver Wolcott
Delaware	George Read	Caesar Rodney
	Thomas McKean	
Georgia	Button Gwinnett	Lyman Hall
	George Walton	
Maryland	Charles Carroll	Samuel Chase
	Thomas Stone	William Paca
Massachusetts	John Adams	Samuel Adams
	John Hancock	Robert Treat Paine
	Elbridge Gerry	
New Hampshire	Josiah Bartlett	William Whipple
	Matthew Thornton	
New Jersey	Abraham Clark	John Hart
	Francis Hopkinson	Richard Stockton
	John Witherspoon	
New York	Lewis Morris	Philip Livingston
	Francis Lewis	William Floyd
North Carolina	William Hooper	John Penn
	Joseph Hewes	
Pennsylvania	George Clymer	Benjamin Franklin
	Robert Morris	John Morton
	Benjamin Rush	George Ross
	James Smith	James Wilson
	George Taylor	
Rhode Island	Stephen Hopkins	William Ellery
South Carolina	Edward Rutledge	Arthur Middleton
	Thomas Lynch Jr.	Thomas Heyward, Jr.
Virginia	Richard Henry Lee	Francis Lightfoot Lee
	Carter Braxton	Benjamin Harrison
	Thomas Jefferson	George Wythe
	Thomas Nelson Jr.	

major disappointment in that 8 of the 13 states did not even send delegates. Delaware, New Jersey, New York, Pennsylvania, and Virginia were the only five states to participate in the meeting. This poor showing prompted those who did attend, most notably Alexander Hamilton and James Madison, to issue a report urging all states to participate in a subsequent meeting the following May in Philadelphia. The purpose for calling the Philadelphia meeting was to tinker with some of the obvious weaknesses of the Articles of Confederation. This subsequent Philadelphia meeting came to be known as the Constitutional Convention. And it was at this convention that our current system of government was born.

Shays's Rebellion:
An armed insurrection in Massachusetts led by Revolutionary war hero Daniel Shays. The rebellion targeted attacks on courthouses in an attempt to prevent farm foreclosures.

The second episode to cause a deliberate nudge toward the Constitutional Convention was **Shays's Rebellion.** The Revolutionary War caused economic hardships and most states were in serious debt in the war's aftermath. These economic conditions made it difficult for many small farmers to pay back loans. In Concord, Massachusetts, in 1786, for instance, there were three times as many people "in prison for debt as there were for all other crimes combined."[6] Daniel Shays, a Revolutionary war hero who served at the Battle of Lexington and who distinguished himself during the Battle at Bunker Hill, led a farmers' insurrection against Massachusetts. Angry farmers stormed the Springfield courthouse in order to prevent the foreclosure of additional farms. While the insurrection was ultimately put down, it revealed in clear terms that most states were not willing to help Massachusetts in its moments of crisis. The Articles of Confederation failed again.

Fearing that Shays's Rebellion might prove the correctness of Thomas Hobbes's pessimistic view that democracies were unworkable and invariably degenerate into civil war and death, George Washington remarked:

I am mortified beyond expression when I view the clouds that have spread over the brightest morn that ever dawned in any country . . . *What a triumph for the advocates of despotism, to find that we are incapable of governing ourselves and that systems founded on the basis of equal liberty are merely ideal and fallacious."*[7]

Others, however, viewed Shays's Rebellion through a more optimistic lens. Thomas Jefferson, for instance, reacted by saying, "A little rebellion now and then is a good thing. It is a medicine necessary for the sound health of government. God forbid that we should ever be twenty years without such a rebellion."[8]

Jefferson, however, was in the minority in this view. The experiences from the Annapolis Convention and Shays's Rebellion caused many American colonists to conclude a stronger national government was required. In Figure 4.1 we provide a timeline of important events leading up to the Constitutional Convention.

THE CONSTITUTIONAL CONVENTION

Many of the architects of the Articles of Confederation were selected to represent their states at the Constitutional Convention in May of 1787. While 74 delegates were selected to participate in the Convention, only 55 actually made the long and arduous trip to Philadelphia.[9] The delegates came from elite society, which was perhaps predictable considering that less than 5 percent of the population (i.e., 150,000 out of 3.9 million) were eligible to vote as free, property-owning white males over the age of 21.[10] By today's standards, the delegates were very young. The youngest delegate was New Jersey's Jonathan Dayton at 26 years of age, Alexander Hamilton of New York was 32, and James Madison, the primary author of the Constitution, was only 36 at the time of the Constitutional Convention. More than half (i.e., 33) of the delegates were trained in the legal profession, and seven were former governors.[11] Unlike the Annapolis Convention, the Philadelphia Convention took on an air of importance, especially after the revered George Washington agreed to attend.

Historian Charles Beard's classic work portrays the Founding Fathers as wealthy property owners who were primarily interested in protecting property rights.[12] Beard's analysis concludes that delegates had an economic interest in either supporting or opposing ratification. His study concludes that delegates in favor of ratifying the Constitution represented elite society and were primarily motivated by a governmental pledge to pay off defaulted loans to well-heeled lenders of the day. Other research, however, disputes Beard's finding and argues the delegates were

CourseReader ASSIGNMENT

Log in to **www.cengagebrain.com** and open CourseReader to access the reading:

An Economic Interpretation of the Constitution
by Charles A. Beard

In 1913 the historian Charles A. Beard published his *Economic Interpretation of the United States*. Beard, a founder of the economic determinist method of history—meaning that he took economic data and constructed historical arguments from them—provided a controversial account of what he believed motivated the American framers when they drafted the U.S. Constitution. In an *Economic Interpretation of the Constitution*, Beard analyzed the property and other wealth of the framers of the Constitution. The Constitution, Beard concluded, was a document designed to ensure the continued stability of government—one crafted not for idealistic or democratic principles but for the safeguarding of wealth and private property. Although many modern historians rejected his analysis, his work remains important in showing how one generation of scholars viewed the origins of the U.S. Constitution.

- *Do you agree with Beard that the drafters of the U.S. Constitution were most likely more interested in promoting their own economic well-being rather than in creating an enlightened government? Why or why not?*

- *Do you believe the U.S. Constitution generally protects the interests of ordinary citizens or the well-connected and wealthy segments of society? What arguments can you provide to support your point of view?*

FIGURE 4.1. Confederation to Constitution Timeline

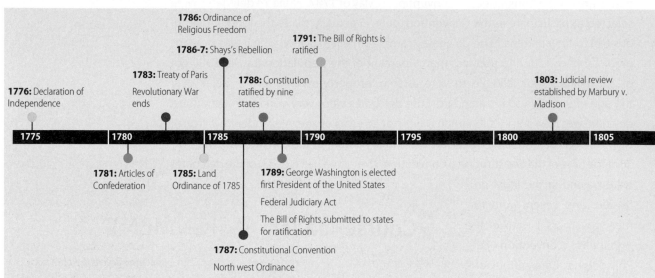

1776: Declaration of Independence.
1781: Articles of Confederation officially "in force" after ratification by the colonies.
1783: Treaty of Paris is signed by Great Britain and the United States, ending the Revolutionary War. Senate ratifies in 1784.
1785: Land Ordinance of 1785 passed by Congress provides for rectangular survey dividing northwestern territories into townships, which are in turn divided into lots of 640 acres, with one lot set aside for the public.
1786: Ordinance of Religious Freedom adopted by Virginia legislature written by Thomas Jefferson, this statute would later become the model for the first amendment to the Constitution.
1786-7: Daniel Shays leads a rebellion of 1,200 men in an attack against a federal arsenal in Springfield, MA, an important incident in influencing the creation of a new Constitution.
1787: Constitutional Convention assembles in Philadelphia.

Northwest Ordinance enacted by Congress provides for the eventual incorporation of three to five new states in the Northwest Territories, with the establishment of a bicameral assembly, freedom of religion, the right to trial by jury, public education, and a ban on slavery.

The Great Compromise (Connecticut Compromise) is presented by Roger Sherman, reconciling the Virginia and New Jersey Plans. This compromise advocated for proportional representation in the House of Representatives and equal representation in the Senate.

Constitution is endorsed by Congress and sent to state legislatures for ratification.

Federalist Papers begin to be published.
1788: The Constitution is in effect after receiving the approval of the requisite nine states.
1789: George Washington is elected first President of the United States. John Adams is Vice President.

War and Treasury Departments are established by Congress. Henry Knox named Secretary of War; Alexander Hamilton named Secretary of the Treasury.
Federal Judiciary Act is passed by Congress creates a six-man Supreme Court with a Chief Justice and five Associate Justices. Also provides for an Attorney General, and for a judicial system of 13 district courts and three circuit courts.

The Bill of Rights is submitted by Congress to the states for ratification.

Thomas Jefferson is officially named Secretary of State; John Jay is named Chief Justice of the Supreme Court.
1791: The Bill of Rights is ratified.
1803: The principle of judicial review is established by the Supreme Court in Marbury v. Madison.

motivated by more than economic self-interest.[13] Nonetheless, each of the framers came to the Constitutional Convention with state-centric political constraints and distinct worldviews. Alexander Hamilton (New York) was arguably a monarchist, George Washington (Virginia) and Benjamin Franklin (Pennsylvania) stopped short of that in their call for a strong national government, James Madison (Virginia) and James Wilson (Pennsylvania) advocated a more democratic form of government, while Edmund Randolph (Virginia), George Mason (Virginia), Elbridge Gerry (Massachusetts), and Luther Martin (Maryland) were altogether distrustful of national power as fierce states' rights advocates.[14] Perhaps the real genius of the U.S. Constitution is that delegates were able to compromise on many topics that appeared to have no middle ground.

Congress and Representation: Large versus Small States

These diverse worldviews clashed on almost every issue addressed at the Convention. A major rift soon emerged between delegates from the large and small states over the creation of Congress. Delegates from Virginia offered the **Virginia Plan,** which called for a strong central government. Virginia represented the interests of the large states by calling for a **bicameral legislature** with membership in the lower house determined by population and members from the upper house selected from members of the lower house. This plan benefited the more populated states such as New York, Pennsylvania, Virginia, and Massachusetts because they would gain more representatives in Congress.

The less populated states objected to the Virginia Plan because they believed they would lose political influence. The Articles of Confederation had an equal representation system, whereby each state was given one vote regardless of population. Smaller states were thus reluctant to form a Congress based on population because they would be giving up the voting strength they enjoyed in the Articles of Confederation system.

William Paterson of New Jersey, representing the interests of the small states, proposed the **New Jersey Plan.** The New Jersey Plan called for a **unicameral legislature** with each state given an equal number of representatives regardless of population. A Committee of Eleven was formed with the hope of finding a compromise over the structure of the national congress.

This committee was successful in creating the **Connecticut Compromise,** so named because several Connecticut delegates served on the committee. The Connecticut Compromise, or the *Great Compromise* as it is sometimes known, called for a bicameral legislature comprised of the House of Representatives, with membership determined by each state's population, and the Senate, where each state was allocated two senators, thus benefiting the smaller states by adhering to the principle of equal representation.[15]

Virginia Plan: *Primarily drafted by James Madison and Edmund Randolph of Virginia. It was proposed at the Constitutional Convention and called for representation in Congress to be apportioned according to the state's population.*

Bicameral Legislature: *A legislature that consists of a two-house body. The U.S. Congress and every state legislature except Nebraska's are bicameral.*

New Jersey Plan: *Proposed by William Paterson at the Constitutional Convention and called for a one-house chamber apportioned according to equal representation of each state.*

Unicameral Legislature: *A legislature that consists of a one-house chamber.*

Connecticut Compromise: *The Great Compromise between the large and small states at the Constitutional Convention that called for the U.S. House of Representatives to be apportioned according to the state's population and the U.S. Senate comprised of two senators per state.*

Representation and Slavery: The North–South Dispute and the Three-Fifths Compromise

All of the great accomplishments of the Constitutional Convention sometimes overshadow the major failure of the meeting, and that is leaving the Convention with the institution of slavery intact. The issue of slavery arose when southern states proposed counting slaves as part of their population when determining representation in Congress. The Constitution stipulates that each state is permitted one representative for every 30,000 residents. (This method was later altered and is explained in Chapter 5.) The southern states wanted to count slaves as part of their population because this would give them greater representation in Congress. In what was perhaps the low moment of the Convention, the framers agreed to count each slave as three-fifths of a person, thus strengthening southern power in Congress. The outcome of this controversy significantly impacted the regional balance of power in the new nation as some southern states were inhabited by more slaves than nonslaves at the time. Approximately 65 percent of the residents of South Carolina, for example, were enslaved in the early 18th century. Northern states were opposed to counting slaves as part of the population because slaves were not given any rights typically associated with citizenship, and because this would strengthen southern power in Congress. Southern slave states were apportioned 47 members of Congress in 1793, whereas they would have been apportioned only 33 members of Congress if slaves were not counted in the Three-Fifths Compromise. Table 4.2 draws attention to Federalist Paper #54, which reveals the thinking of some of the framers when they settled on the Three-Fifths Compromise.

TABLE 4.2. Three-Fifths Compromise: *Federalist Paper No. 54*

Federalist Paper No. 54–The Apportionment of Members Among the States as It Relates to the Issue of Slavery, authored by Alexander Hamilton or James Madison

Slaves are considered as property, not as persons. They ought therefore to be comprehended in estimates of taxation which are founded as property, and to be excluded from representation which is regulated by a census of persons. This is the objection, as I understand it, stated in its full force. I shall be equally candid in stating the reasoning which may be offered on the opposite side. "We subscribe to the doctrine," might one of our Southern brethren observe, "that representation relates more immediately to persons, and taxation more immediately to property and we join in the application of this distinction to the case of our slaves. But we must deny the fact, that slaves are considered merely as property, and in no respect whatever as persons. The true state of the case is, that they partake of both these qualities: being considered by our laws, in some respects, as persons, and in other respects as property. In being compelled to labor, not for himself, but for a master; in being vendible by one master to another master; and in being subject at all times to be restrained in his liberty and chastised in his body, by the capricious will of another, the slave may appear to be degraded from the human rank, and classed with those irrational animals which fall under the legal denomination of property. In being protected, on the other hand, in his life and limbs, against the violence of all others, even the master of his labor and liberty; and in being punishable himself for all violence committed against others, the slave is no less evidently regarded by the law as a member of society, not as part of the irrational creation; as a moral person, not as a mere article of property. The federal Constitution, therefore, decides with great propriety on the case of our slaves, when it views them in the mixed character of persons and property . . . Let the compromising expedient of the Constitution be mutually adopted, which regards them as inhabitants, but as debased by servitude below the equal level of free inhabitants, which regards the SLAVE as divested of two fifths of the MAN.

The Expansion of Poltical Rights:
The Voting Rights Act of 1965

© ISTOCKPHOTO.COM/
CARACTERDESIGN

One of the reasons why it is now hard to imagine that African Americans were originally counted as only three-fifths of a person is because of the passage of the Voting Rights Act of 1965. President Lyndon B. Johnson signed the Voting Rights Act into law on August 6, 1965. He referred to the Act as his greatest accomplishment as president during his final news conference, comparing it with President Abraham Lincoln's Emancipation Proclamation. The original purpose of the Act was to provide an enforcement mechanism to the Fifteenth Amendment by securing for African Americans the most basic of all rights—the right to vote.

What is not widely known is the extent to which African Americans flourished politically after the ratification of the Fifteenth Amendment in 1870. Their political power was protected by federal troops dispatched to the South after the U.S. Civil War and bolstered by the fact that 90 percent of all African Americans resided in the South during this period. Extending voting rights to freed slaves met with heavy resistance from white segregationists for a variety of reasons, not the least of which was the fact that whites were a numerical minority in five southern states.

African Americans were politically energized during the post–Civil War Reconstruction era and soon came to represent nearly one-half of the state house delegate seats in Mississippi, Louisiana, and South Carolina, and 16 African Americans were elected to Congress.[16] A political arrangement, however, crafted by Republicans and Democrats during the controversial 1876 presidential election set off a segregationist backlash against the Fifteenth Amendment. The leaders agreed to award 20 contested electoral votes from Florida, Louisiana, and South Carolina to Republican candidate Rutherford B. Hayes in exchange for his pledge to remove federal troops from the South, effectively ending Reconstruction. This post–Reconstruction period (1877–1901) is regarded by scholars as the nadir or the "Dark Ages" of African American political life, and it is here that the southern strategy to once again disenfranchise African American voters took root.[17]

Southern states effectively nullified the Fifteenth Amendment by implementing disenfranchising measures such as literacy tests, which sometimes included

continued

"grandfather clauses," exempting from the test those eligible to vote before Reconstruction, or "understanding clauses," which granted broad discretionary powers to segregationist registrars to enroll white illiterates "who could understand constitutional provisions read to them."[18] Every southern state adopted poll taxes, where payments were required months in advance in the hope that the few African Americans able to pay might misplace the tax receipt by election day. African Americans were excluded from "white primaries" with the blessing of the U.S. Supreme Court, who upheld the notion that political parties were private associations until the *Smith v. Allwright* decision in 1944. It was also common for southern county poll officials to place registration offices and polling stations in Ku Klux Klan strongholds, where African Americans were routinely brutally beaten and sometimes killed for attempting to exercise their right to vote.

These measures proved successful. In Louisiana, African American voter registration fell from its peak of 95.6 percent in 1896 to 1.1 percent in 1904. South Carolina, which had an African American majority in the lower House during Reconstruction, did not elect one African American to the body from 1896 until the 1970s. Congress and the executive branch largely deferred to southern home rule, and the Supreme Court routinely sided with southern state governments on substantive challenges to literacy tests, poll taxes, white primaries, and other disenfranchising measures into the mid-20th century. The political tide began to turn after World War II, however, when the more than 1 million African American soldiers sent off to defeat Hitler's racist ideology in Europe returned determined to challenge racism in their own hometowns.[19] Leaders such as Atlanta's Martin Luther King Jr. and Mississippi's Medgar Evars organized a civil rights movement across the region that brought northern volunteers and national attention to white supremacy in the South. It was in this climate that Congress enacted the groundbreaking Civil Rights Act of 1964, which outlawed segregation in places of public accommodations, but failed to address voter disenfranchisement.

One of the most prominent features of the Voting Rights Act (1965) is found in Section 2 of the provision, which prohibits all states from imposing literacy tests and poll taxes, and other voting prerequisites resulting in the disenfranchisement of voters on the basis of race. The Voting Rights Act is distinct from the Civil Rights Act in that it contains permanent and nonpermanent features. The two most controversial

continued

nonpermanent provisions are found in Sections 4 and 5. Section 4 outlines the "triggering formula," describing the conditions "that would bring a jurisdiction under the protection of the act."[20] This provision was controversial because it meant that the Act would target only states with a history of discriminatory practices, defined as those jurisdictions that had a voter turnout rate of less than 50 percent and a "voting test" in place during the 1964 presidential election. The covered jurisdictions included the states of Alabama, Alaska, Georgia, Louisiana, Mississippi, South Carolina, Virginia, and certain counties in Arizona, Hawaii, Idaho, and North Carolina.

Section 5 of the Act prohibits all covered jurisdictions from implementing any electoral changes without first receiving permission from either the U.S. Attorney General's office or a D.C. district court. This "preclearance" provision shifts the legal burden of proof away from protected groups to the government entity proposing electoral reform.

The Voting Rights Act has been either substantively amended and/or reauthorized in 1970, 1975, 1982, 1992, and 2006. In 1975, Rep. Barbara Jordan (D-TX) sponsored a bill that extended the provisions of the Act to non-English speaking minorities, requiring local jurisdictions to "provide bilingual voting registration and materials and ballots" if a particular language minority constituted more than 5 percent of the population and if that jurisdiction's voter turnout was less than 50 percent in the 1972 national election, thereby extending the Act to Arizona, Texas, California, Florida, New York, and South Dakota.[21] Barack Obama was victorious in several states (e.g., Virginia, North Carolina) that were placed in the original "penalty box" because of a history of discriminatory voting practices as defined by the Voting Rights Act of 1965.

> **What role did the Voting Rights Act (1965) play in Barack Obama winning the presidency in 2008?**

The Three Principles of the U.S. Constitution

The major lesson learned from living under the weak Articles of Confederation was that government needs to do more than simply not tyrannize over states. Governments also need to solve problems. This is the central point of James Madison's

Federalist Paper No. 51 where he asserted that the Constitution "must first enable the government to control the governed; and in the next phase oblige it to control itself."[22] In order to construct a government that is strong enough to solve national problems, but not so strong that it dominates over states, the framers established three basic Constitutional principles that include: (1) the separation of powers; (2) the system of checks and balances; and (3) the system of federalism.

Separation of Powers

You might remember from Chapter 2 that the American framers were strongly influenced by Aristotle's theory of mixed constitutions. Aristotle did not strongly advocate for one particular political system over another. For him political systems were not ends in and of themselves, but rather the means toward the ends of justice. Aristotle believed that governments ruled by one (i.e., monarchy), by the few (i.e., aristocracy), or by many (i.e., polity) can all be effective if leaders of these particular governments pursue justice. He also asserted that each of these systems could be perverted if those leaders instead pursue self-interest over the public good. The framers learned from Aristotle not to become preoccupied with any particular system, but to instead merge the best attributes of different types of government into one. The Founders looked to Aristotle's theory of mixed constitutions as a guide to reconcile "democratic and aristocratic values."[23] The American system of government thus heeds Aristotle's advice by mixing three constitutions into one with the establishment of a President (rule of one), a Supreme Court (rule of few), and a Congress (rule of many).

Table 4.3. underscores how Aristotle's Theory of Mixed Constitutions influenced the thinking of the American framers at the Constitutional Convention.

Separation of Powers:
A system of government that is divided between a legislative branch, an executive branch, and a judicial branch of government.

While the **separation of powers** concept is not expressly articulated in the Constitution, the basic principle is outlined in the structure and powers of the legislative, executive, and judicial branches of government.[25] It was believed that the national government can be restrained by making each branch of government

---

TABLE 4.3. Aristotle's Theory of Mixed Constitutions and Its Influence on Separation of Powers

For the addition of its weight to either side will turn the balance and prevent excess at the opposing extremes. For this reason it is a most happy state of affairs when those who take part in the constitution have a middling, adequate amount of property; since where one set of people possess a great deal and the other nothing, the result is either extreme democracy or unmixed oligarchy, or a tyranny due to the excess of either. For tyranny often emerges from an over-enthusiastic democracy or from an oligarchy, but much more rarely from intermediate constitutions or from those close to them … most states are either democratic or oligarchic; for the middle being frequently small, whichever of the two extremes is on top, those with possessions or the common people, abandons the middle and conducts the constitution according to its own notions, and so the result is either democracy or oligarchy … Also, those who came to exercise leadership among the Greek states installed democracies or oligarchies in them according to the constitution which each had at home, looking entirely to their own advantage, not to that of the states themselves. So for these reasons the middle constitution has never occurred anywhere, or only seldom and sporadically … Wherever the middle people outweigh a combination of the two extremes, or even one only, then there is a good chance of permanence for the constitution. There is no danger of the rich and poor making common cause against them; for neither will want to be slaves to the other, and if they are looking for a constitution more acceptable to both, they will not find any better than this … The better mixed a constitution is, the longer it will last.[24]

independent of each other in the first phase, and then assigning overlapping tasks to each branch of government. The legislative branch was thus created to make the law, the executive was created to enforce the law, and the federal judiciary was formed to interpret the law.

The Genius of the Constitution: The System of Checks and Balances

While there were many major disagreements at the Constitutional Convention, the framers did share one basic conviction: that power in one branch of government must be used to counterbalance power in the other branches of government. The real genius of the Constitution is found in the system of **checks and balances.** It is here where Thomas Hobbes's view of human nature is incorporated into our system of government. In Chapter 3 we discussed Hobbes's belief that all human behavior is driven by a lust for power and his view that individual freedoms should be surrendered to the state in order to maintain security. James Madison extends on these concerns in *Federalist Paper No. 51* when he asserted that "ambition must be made to counteract ambition" and that "if men were angels, no government would be necessary. If angels were to govern men, neither external or internal controls on government would be necessary."[26] By making each branch of government independent, and by structuring the government so that each branch is checked by another, one branch of government is prevented from becoming dominant.

Here Madison was also heavily influenced by Baron de Montesquieu's (1689–1755) *The Spirit of the Laws*, which argued that tyranny could be prevented by having the branches of government check each other. Montesquieu warned that tyranny is likely to reign when law making and law enforcement powers are placed in the same branch of government. However, it was not enough to simply separate branches of the federal government. Who is to say there will not be collusion amongst the branches? In order to ensure that the "ambition" of one branch of government is checked by the "ambition" of another branch, the framers created a political mechanism whereby each branch of government checks the behavior of the others.

Montesquieu, like Aristotle, advocated for a system of government that blends democratic and aristocratic values. His ideal structure of government sought the middle ground between the political extremes of democratic anarchy and oppressive monarchies. Montesquieu coined the term *checks and balances* in his description of three political classes of French society labeled as the monarchy, the aristocracy, and the commons. He promoted the division of powers between these three groups in France in order to prevent one class from becoming too dominant. The Founding Fathers were influenced by Montesquieu's writings when they incorporated the system of checks and balances into our government.

The legislative branch checks the executive through (1) its impeachment powers; (2) its ability to overturn a presidential veto with a two-thirds vote; (3) the power of the purse; and (4) through the Senate's power to ratify presidential treaties and

Checks and Balances:
A system of government where each branch of government can limit, amend, and/or nullify the acts of another branch of government.

▲ Howard Chandler Christy's painting entitled *Scene at the Signing of the Constitution of the United States*. Only 39 of the 55 delegates attending the Philadelphia convention are included in the painting. George Washington, as President of the convention, is prominently standing in front of the flags. This painting is currently on display in the United States Capitol building.

Unitary System of Government: *A system of government where all powers are located in the central government. In this system, regional and local government derive power from the central government. Approximately 150 nations currently have a unitary system of government including Britain, China, France, and Japan.*

Confederate Form of Government: *A system of government that gives little power to the central government and instead gives power to smaller state governments. The United States adopted a confederate system when it operated under the Article of Confederation system from 1781 to 1787.*

Federalist System of Government: *A system of government that divides power between the national and state governments. The system is in place in a number of countries including the United States, Canada, and India.*

confirm presidential appointments. The legislature can also check the judiciary through its impeachment powers and the senate's power to confirm judicial appointments. The executive branch checks the legislative branch with veto powers and checks the judiciary with the power to appoint federal judges. The judiciary checks the executive and legislative branches of government with the power to declare legislative and/or executive acts unconstitutional.

Figure 4.2 illustrates how each branch of government can check the other branches of government.

Federalism

All nations in the world can be classified as possessing either a (1) unitary government; (2) confederate government; or (3) federalist government.[27]

A **unitary system of government** grants all governmental control and power to one central government. Most nations around the world are classified as unitary governments. A **confederate form of government** gives weak authority to the central government and grants most powers to the smaller state governments. The Articles of Confederation, which vested most powers to the original 13 states, is an example of a confederacy. A **federalist system of government** is unique in that power is shared between the national and state governments.

FIGURE 4.2. Checks and Balances

The Supreme Court can declare presidential actions unconstitutional.

The president nominates federal judges; the president can refuse to enforce the Court's decisions; the president grants pardons.

THE JUDICIARY

The Supreme Court can declare congressional laws unconstitutional.

Congress can rewrite legislation to circumvent the Court's decisions; the Senate confirms federal judges; Congress determines the number of judges.

The president proposes laws and can veto congressional legislation; the president makes treaties, executive agreements, and executive orders; the president can refuse, and has refused, to enforce congressional legislation; the president can call special sessions of Congress.

Congress makes legislation and can override a presidential veto of its legislation; Congress can impeach and remove a president; the Senate must confirm presidential appointments and consent to the president's treaties based on a two-thirds concurrence; Congress has the power of the purse and provides funds for the president's programs.

THE PRESIDENCY

THE CONGRESS

Why do we have a federalist system? The Founding Fathers created a system of federalism in order to prevent the national government from dominating over the original 13 state governments. Because states were in existence (i.e., colonies) for approximately 180 years prior to the Constitutional Convention, most delegates had greater loyalty to their respective state governments and were fearful that the new national government would rule over the states. For this reason they created a federalist system of government that divided power between the national and state governments.

Dividing power between the national and state government served as the perfect compromise between those who advocated for a stronger national government and those who were primarily interested in preserving states' rights. The primary advantage of federalism is that states can check against abuses of federal powers and vice versa. The previously cited Voting Rights Act (1965) is a clear example of the federal government preventing southern states from disenfranchising African Americans during the civil rights struggle in the mid-1960s. Another benefit of federalism is that it allows for "unity without uniformity" in that local customs can be incorporated into government.[28] People living in Salt Lake City, Utah, for instance, are free to live under different laws than people in New York City. Federalism also allows for creativity in government in that states can be viewed as social laboratories, free to experiment in the realm of public policy. Massachusetts, for instance, was the first state in the Union to permit same-sex marriages in 2004. Seven other states have since

TABLE 4.4. Articles of Confederation versus the Constitution

	Articles of Confederation	Constitution
Tax powers	No power to tax	The U.S. Congress has authority to tax individuals
Federal courts	No federal courts	Created Supreme Court and allows Congress to create other federal courts
Bill of Rights	No Bill of Rights	Bill of Rights added as the first 10 amendments to the Constitution
President	No president	Created executive branch—Individual executive to serve as commander-in-chief and given special powers in foreign policy
Amendment Process	All 13 states need to approve amending the Articles	Constitution can be amended by two-thirds vote in Congress if ratified by three-fourths of states
Representation in Congress	Each state receives one vote	House of Representative determined by population. Each state sends two senators to Senate.
Military	No power—militia formed by states	Congress authorized to raise armies
Trade	No involvement in regulating trade	Interstate Commerce clause authorizes Congress to regulate trade between states
Passing Laws	Needs approval of 9 of 13 States	Requires majority vote in House and Senate and presidential signature

legalized same-sex marriages including Connecticut, California* (since repealed), Iowa, Maine, Vermont, New York, and New Hampshire.[29] In a federalist system, states can benefit from the experiences gained when similar policies are implemented in other states.

In Table 4.4 we highlight key differences between the Articles of Confederation system of government and the system of government created at the Constitutional Convention.

THE GROWTH OF FEDERAL POWER

Enumerated Powers:
Expressly granted to the government in the U.S. Constitution. The power to declare war, for example, is an enumerated power of Congress that can be found in Article 1, Section 8 of the U.S. Constitution.

The distribution of power between the state and national government is addressed in the Tenth Amendment to the U.S. Constitution. The Tenth Amendment states that "the powers not delegated by the Constitution, nor prohibited by it to the States, are reserved to the States respectively, or to the people."[30] The **enumerated powers** of the federal government are found in Article 1, Section 8 of the U.S. Constitution. These powers include the power to declare war, to coin money, to regulate foreign commerce, to raise and support armies, and to establish a federal court system. The Constitution also prohibits states from engaging in certain activities such as entering into treaties with foreign nations and placing taxes on foreign imports. Initially, state governments assumed all powers except those that were expressly assigned to the federal government or explicitly denied to them by the Constitution.

McCulloch vs. Maryland: The Elastic Clause and the Expansion of Federal Power

Federal powers were soon greatly enhanced in the landmark Supreme Court case *McCulloch vs. Maryland* **(1819).** The controversy surrounding the *McCulloch* case can be traced back to George Washington's administration.

Alexander Hamilton, the nation's first secretary of treasury, persuaded President Washington to form a central bank in 1791. Thomas Jefferson, Washington's secretary of state and a strong states' rights advocate, forcefully objected to Hamilton's plan on the grounds that he did not believe the Constitution granted the national government the power to create a central banking system. This power, after all, was not specifically granted to the national government in the Constitution. Jefferson believed a national banking system would be dangerous because it would allow the national government to encroach on the economic powers of states. Jefferson later resigned as Washington's secretary of state in 1793 for this and other reasons.

One of these federal banks was placed in Baltimore, Maryland. The issue came to a head when the state of Maryland taxed the federal bank $15,000. The federal cashier, James McCulloch, refused to pay the tax because he did not believe Maryland had the legal authority to tax the federal government. This case raised two important constitutional questions: (1) Does the federal government have the constitutional authority to create a federal banking system? and (2) Do states have the constitutional authority to tax the federal government?

Regarding the first question, the Supreme Court substantially expanded federal powers by asserting the national government was permitted to create a banking system because the national government had "implied powers" beyond those expressly stated in the Constitution. The Court located this power in the Constitution's **necessary and proper clause** (or elastic clause).

Chief Justice Marshall expanded federal powers by claiming the national government has additional implied powers when these powers are "necessary and proper" in carrying out enumerated powers, or those expressly granted to the federal government in Article 1, Section 8 of the Constitution. New Hampshire's Daniel Webster, arguably America's greatest orator, made the case that creating a banking system was "necessary and proper" in order to carry out expressed constitutional powers, such as the power to coin money and raise armies.

On the second question, the Supreme Court grappled with whether Maryland was empowered to tax the federal government. Luther Martin, Maryland's attorney general, argued the case on behalf of the state. Martin was a leading states' rights advocate who refused to sign the Constitution, opting instead to storm out

McCulloch versus Maryland (1819): *The landmark Supreme Court case that expanded the powers of the national government by finding the government had "implied powers" in addition to the expressed powers found in Article 1, Section 8 of the U.S. Constitution.*

Necessary and Proper Clause: *Also known as the elastic clause, it is found in the last paragraph of Article 1, Section 8 of the Constitution and expands federal power by granting the federal government all powers that are "necessary" and "proper" to carry out the enumerated powers of Congress.*

CourseReader ASSIGNMENT

Log in to **www.cengagebrain.com** and open CourseReader to access the reading:

McCulloch v. Maryland **by John Marshall**

McCulloch v. Maryland (1819) was an important Supreme Court case that helped to expand federal powers over the states. The case involved the constitutionality of whether: 1) the U.S. government was empowered by the Constitution to create a federal bank; and 2) whether the states were empowered to tax the federal government. In his majority opinion, Chief Justice John Marshall borrowed heavily from Alexander Hamilton's writings in *The Federalist* to the effect that the national government had powers beyond those specified in the Constitution. Marshall highlighted the "necessary and proper clause", also known as the "elastic clause", in his ruling that the national government also has "implied" powers provided they are necessary to carry out the enumerated powers granted to the federal government in Article 1, Section 8 of the Constitution. Marshall also ruled that states are not permitted to tax the federal government since "*the power to tax involves the power to destroy.*"

- ***Do you agree with Chief Justice John Marshall's interpretation of the necessary and proper clause in this case? Why or why not?***

- ***Do you believe the federal government now has too much power over the states? Why or why not?***

Concurrent Power: *Powers that are granted to both the national and state government in the U.S. Constitution. The power to tax is an example of a concurrent power.*

Supremacy Clause: *Found in Article VI of the U.S. Constitution, the supremacy clause asserts that the Constitution, national laws, and treaties are supreme over state laws when national laws are in compliance with the U.S. Constitution.*

of the Convention in protest of what he perceived to be the granting of excessive federal powers. He also successfully defended the former vice president Aaron Burr in his treason case in 1807. Martin argued that Maryland was within its Constitutional authority to tax the federal government because taxing powers represented a **concurrent power**, in that both the federal and state governments are assigned this power in the Constitution. States, after all, are permitted to levy income and sales taxes on residents. Daniel Webster, on behalf of the national government, argued that Maryland does not have the authority to tax the federal government because the state's taxing power is limited in the Constitution. States, for example, are prohibited from taxing foreign governments and/or imports. The Supreme Court again sided with the federal government in stating that because "the power to tax involves the power to destroy," the Founding Fathers never intended to give state governments the power to tax the federal government.[31] Allowing state governments to tax the national government would place the national government at the feet of the states, a scenario never envisioned by the Framers. The Court supported this view by pointing to the Constitution's **supremacy clause**, which asserts that all federal laws that further the Constitution are the supreme laws of the land. In the end, the *McCulloch* case substantially increased federal power in relation to the state by linking additional implied powers to the national government and by denying the state the right to tax the federal government. In Chapter 7 we provide a more thorough review on the important role played by the U.S. Supreme Court in expanding federal powers over states.

In Table 4.5 we highlight national, state, and concurrent powers as outlined in the U.S. Constitution.

TABLE 4.5. The Constitution's Division of Power

National Powers	State Powers	Concurrent Powers—Shared by national and state government
Right to raise armies, declare war, coin money, regulate foreign and interstate commerce, and other powers prescribed in Article 1, Section 8	Power to create county and municipal governments	Power to tax
Implied powers (elastic clause) when required to carry out enumerated powers	Power to regulate elections	Power to pass laws
Treaty-making powers	Right to all powers not granted to national government or denied to states	Power to borrow and spend

The Constitution and Interstate Relations

Federalism is complicated because it involves more than a simple understanding of national–state relations, but also includes relations between the states themselves. What responsibilities do states have toward each other? Article IV of the U.S. Constitution addresses the theme of interstate relations.

Is a citizen with a North Carolina driver's license permitted to drive through Wisconsin? Is your birth certificate recognized as a legal document in all 50 states? The answer to both questions is yes. And that is because of Article IV's **full faith and credit clause**. The full faith and credit clause stipulates that "Full Faith and Credit shall be given in each state to the public Acts, records, and Judicial Proceedings of every other State."[32] The primary purpose of this clause was to ensure that legal judgments rendered in one state would be recognized by all states. Without this clause, citizens might be able to avoid the enforcement of legal contracts by simply moving to another state. Or a person might be prevented from driving through another state without first securing a driver's license from that state. All of this is avoided by the full faith and credit clause's requirement that all states recognize the public and legal records of other states.

Full Faith and Credit Clause: *A clause found in Article IV of the U.S. Constitution that requires each state to recognize the civil judgments and public records of other states.*

The full faith and credit clause is currently at the center of a major controversy in American politics. The state of Massachusetts became the first state to allow same-sex marriages in 2004. Does this mean that the other 49 states must recognize a same-sex marriage performed in Massachusetts? A marriage certificate, after all, is a public record that is recorded and filed by a state or county clerk. The issue is made more complicated by the **Defense of Marriage Act,** a federal law signed by President Clinton in 1996 that permits states to refuse recognition of same-sex marriages performed in other states. The Defense of Marriage Act also defines marriage as the union between a man and a woman as it relates to federal matters. States, therefore, are not required to recognize same-sex marriages. However, in 2010, the state of Maryland joined New York and Rhode Island in recognizing same-sex marriages performed in other states.

Defense of Marriage Act: *A federal law enacted in 1996 that allows states to not recognize same-sex marriages performed in other states.*

Since same-sex marriage was made legal in Massachusetts in 2004, 27 states have adopted state constitutional amendments defining marriage as a union between a man and woman. Does the Defense of Marriage Act violate the Constitution's full faith and credit clause? A federal court in 2005 found it did not.[33] The U.S. Supreme Court, however, has not weighed in on the issue and the question remains a major controversy in political and legal environments. In 2011, the Obama administration asserted that the federal government would no longer oppose legal challenges to the Defense of Marriage Act because it believes the law violates the constitutional rights of same sex couples.

WHY POLITICS MATTERS TO YOU!

The Constitution:
College Tuition and Child Custody Cases

© ISTOCKPHOTO.COM/ CARACTERDESIGN

Article IV of the U.S. Constitution emphasizes three major clauses that help guide the relationship between states including the privileges and immunities clause, the full faith and credit clause, and the extradition clause. The purpose of the privileges and immunities clause was to make certain that citizens traveling across the states would not be unfairly treated. This clause generally prohibits states from preventing nonresidents from purchasing property and conducting business, and requires equal treatment in tax policy. One of the major controversies in the privilege and immunities clause was whether states can have separate tuition rates for out-of-state and in-state students. The courts determined that states are permitted to charge higher tuition rates for out-of-state residents because states are permitted to subsidize the education costs of residents.

The full faith and credit clause requires states within the United States to respect the "public acts, records, and judicial ruling of other states." The Supreme Court has interpreted this provision to mean that legal judgments are generally more binding than state laws across states. The Supreme Court has been reluctant to require states to recognize laws enacted in other states. It has, however, applied the full faith and credit clause more strictly on matters of legal judgments. This clause has been particularly important in the modern era in child custody cases. Congress passed the Parental Kidnapping Prevention Act in 1980, which required custody decrees to receive full faith

continued

continued

and credit across states. This Act was passed to stop parents from kidnapping their own children and moving them to another state in order to avoid a custody judgment benefiting the other parent.

> Do you believe states should be permitted to charge higher tuition rates for out-of-state residents? Why or why not?
>
> Do you believe states should also be required to recognize same-sex marriages performed in other states?

RATIFYING THE CONSTITUTION

The Constitution was not officially approved after it was signed by the delegates at the Constitutional Convention on September 17, 1787. The next hurdle was getting the individual state governments to support this new form of government. One of the important decisions made at the Convention stipulated that 9 of the 13 state legislatures must ratify the Constitution before the new government could begin. Ratifying the Constitution was an intensely political process that divided the nation into two political camps. The **Federalists** believed a strong national government was necessary to address national problems and to promote a sense of national unity. Federalists were mostly wealthy property owners who primarily resided in the Northeast and Middle Atlantic states. George Washington, Alexander Hamilton, and Benjamin Franklin gave a major boost to the Federalist movement when they endorsed the Constitution. The **Anti-Federalists** were strong states' rights advocates who largely opposed the Constitution because they believed the new government would dominate over the states. Anti-Federalists were mostly farmers and merchants who advocated local control, frequent elections, and were distrustful of the motives of the Federalists. The Anti-Federalists were disadvantaged, however, by not having an alternative plan to the Constitution. This early split between the Federalists and Anti-Federalists set the stage for the subsequent emergence of political parties in the nation.[34]

The Federalists had the upper hand early on when some states' rights advocates boycotted the Constitutional Convention. Patrick Henry said that he "smelt a rat" when he declined his invitation, and Samuel Adams and other leading states' rights advocates also made the mistake of not attending. It is perhaps because of the

Federalists: *Persons supportive of ratifying the U.S. Constitution. Federalists such as Alexander Hamilton and George Washington generally favored a stronger central government. A Federalist Party later emerged under Alexander Hamilton's leadership.*

Anti-Federalists: *Persons who were generally opposed to both a stronger central government and the ratification of the U.S. Constitution.*

THEORY AND PRACTICE

From Factions to Party:
The Evolution of the American Political Party System

The U.S. Constitution makes no mention of political parties and many of the American Founding Fathers argued against parties on the grounds that they would divide rather than unite the nation. The American political party system has evolved throughout American history. The first political party system emerged in 1796 between the Federalist Party and the Democratic-Republican Party. The Federalist Party was led by Alexander Hamilton and favored a stronger central government, advocated for banking and commercial interests, and was most popular in the Northeastern and Middle Atlantic states. The Democratic-Republican Party was led by Thomas Jefferson and appealed primarily to southern agricultural interests and states' rights advocates.

The second and third political party system was heavily influenced by the era of Jacksonian democracy. Andrew Jackson helped transform the Democratic-Republican Party into the Democratic Party, which continues as one of the two major parties in the modern era. This movement called on incorporating the masses into the political process. Later the Whig Party included Henry Clay and Daniel Webster and included a coalition of northern industrialists and southern farmers. The issue of slavery caused the downfall of the Whig Party. The fourth political party system included the pro-slavery and/or pro-states' rights Democratic Party and the antislavery Republican Party. President Abraham Lincoln was the first president elected under the Republican banner. The Democratic and the Republican parties have served as the two leading American political parties since 1860.

Since 1860 the nation has witnessed several **political realignments** where one political party dominates over the other for an extended period of time. Famed political scientist V. O. Key argued that political realignments frequently occur after a critical presidential election.[35] Abraham Lincoln's election in 1860 started a Republican realignment that lasted for over 20 years. Similarly, the election of Franklin D. Roosevelt in 1932 started a 20-year Democratic realignment.

> **Do you believe another political realignment is likely to emerge in the modern era? Why or why not?**

continued

In Table 4.6 we provide a brief summary of the evolution of the political party system in the United States.

TABLE 4.6. American Political Parties

THE FIRST PARTY SYSTEM 1796–1820		
FEDERALIST	**vs.**	**DEMOCRATIC-REPUBLICAN**
1796	John Adams	
1800		Thomas Jefferson
1804		Thomas Jefferson
1808		James Madison
1812		James Madison
1816		James Monroe
1820		James Monroe

THE SECOND PARTY SYSTEM 1824–1836		
NATIONAL REPUBLICAN	**vs.**	**DEMOCRAT**
1824	John Quincy Adams	
1828		Andrew Jackson
1832		Andrew Jackson
1836		Martin Van Buren

THE THIRD PARTY SYSTEM 1840–1856		
WHIG	**vs.**	**DEMOCRATS**
1840	William Henry Harrison	
1844		James Polk
1848	Zachary Taylor	
1852		Franklin Pierce
1856		James Buchanan

THE MODERN POLITICAL PARTY SYSTEM 1860–?		
REPUBLICAN	**vs.**	**DEMOCRAT**
1860	Abraham Lincoln	
1864	Abraham Lincoln	
1868	Ulysses S. Grant	
1872	Ulysses S. Grant	
1876	Rutherford B. Hayes	
1880	James A. Garfield	
1884		Grover Cleveland

THE MODERN POLITICAL PARTY SYSTEM 1860–?		
REPUBLICAN	**vs.**	**DEMOCRAT**
1888	Benjamin Harrison	
1892		Grover Cleveland
1896	William McKinley	
1900	William McKinley	
1904	Theodore Roosevelt	
1908	William H. Taft	
1912		Woodrow Wilson
1916		Woodrow Wilson
1920	Warren Harding	
1924	Calvin Coolidge	
1928	Herbert Hoover	
1932		Franklin D. Roosevelt
1936		Franklin D. Roosevelt
1940		Franklin D. Roosevelt
1944		Franklin D. Roosevelt
1948		Harry S. Truman
1952	Dwight D. Eisenhower	
1956	Dwight D. Eisenhower	
1960		John F. Kennedy
1964		Lyndon B. Johnson
1968	Richard M. Nixon	
1972	Richard M. Nixon	
1976		Jimmy Carter
1980	Ronald Reagan	
1984	Ronald Reagan	
1988	George H. W. Bush	
1992		Bill Clinton
1996		Bill Clinton
2000	George W. Bush	
2004	George W. Bush	
2008		Barack Obama

shortage of states' rights advocates at the Convention that the Federalists were able to advance their agenda.

Table 4.7 chronicles the timeline associated with the ratification process across states.

TABLE 4.7. Ratification of the U.S. Constitution: The process for ratifying the U.S. Constitution was as contentious as it was long

State	Date
Delaware	December 7, 1787
Pennsylvania	December 12, 1787
New Jersey	December 19, 1787
Georgia	January 2, 1788
Connecticut	January 9, 1788
Massachusetts	February 6, 1788
Maryland	April 28, 1788
South Carolina	May 23, 1788
New Hampshire	June 21, 1788
Virginia	June 25, 1788
New York	July 26, 1788
North Carolina	November 21, 1789
Rhode Island	May 29, 1790

Do you believe it would be easier or more difficult for states to come to agreement on controversial issues today?

The *Federalist Papers:* Madison, Hamilton, and Jay

Newspapers played a particularly important role during the ratification process. The entire Constitution was printed in the *Pennsylvania Packet* two days after the end of the Convention.[36] Written editorials in support and opposition to the Constitution soon flooded into every major newspaper around the country. From October 1787 to May 1788, James Madison, Alexander Hamilton, and John Jay submitted 85 essays to New York newspapers under the pseudonym "Publius," a Latin term translated to mean "the people." These articles are now referred to as the *Federalist Papers*. The *Federalist Papers* are significant because they provide insight into the original intent of those who drafted the Constitution. The delegates voted to conduct the meeting in secrecy in order to encourage frank discussion away from editorial writers and other curious onlookers. Guards were placed outside the Convention's doors, and George Washington assigned a chaperone to Benjamin Franklin, who had a reputation for being rather loose lipped. The *Federalist Papers* give a deeper meaning to the brief passages included in the text of the Constitution. The Constitution's Article II, Section IV, for instance, informs us that a president can be impeached for "treason,

The Impeachment of President Bill Clinton and President Andrew Johnson

Former President Bill Clinton was impeached by the House of Representatives on December 19, 1998, on charges of perjury and obstruction of justice on issues relating to his extramarital affair with White House intern Monica Lewinsky. The only other American president to be impeached was President Andrew Johnson who was impeached for violating the Office of Tenure Act in 1868. The U.S. Senate did not convict either American president with the necessary two-thirds vote required for expulsion. In 1974, the House Judiciary Committee voted to impeach Richard Nixon for his involvement in the Watergate Scandal, but President Nixon resigned from office before an impeachment vote was scheduled in Congress.

Should presidents be impeached only if they commit a crime or should a president also be impeached if the public believes he/she is incompetent?

bribery, or other high crimes and misdemeanors." Does this mean a president must commit a crime in order to be impeached? It is a debatable point, but an informed discussion can take place by a closer reading of the *Federalist Papers*.

The *Federalist Papers* are also significant in that they played a key role in persuading states to ratify the Constitution. Delaware was the first state to ratify the Constitution on December 7, 1787, followed within two weeks by Pennsylvania and New Jersey. The Constitution was officially ratified when New Hampshire as the ninth state ratified the Constitution on June 21, 1788. Virginia and New York, however, two states that included approximately 40 percent of the nation's population, still had not ratified. James Madison, Alexander Hamilton, and John Jay published the *Federalist Papers* in New York newspapers as a way to thwart New York Governor George Clinton's efforts to block ratification. Strong sentiments existed against the Constitution. The state of Rhode Island, in fact, did not even send delegates to the Constitutional Convention, and North Carolina and Rhode Island did not ratify the Constitution until months after George Washington was sworn into office.[37]

▲ Portraits of James Madison, Alexander Hamilton, and John Jay, authors of the Federalist Papers. James Madison (1751-1836) was also the chief author of the U.S. Constitution and went on to serve as the fourth President of the United States (1809-1817). Alexander Hamilton (circa 1755-1804) served as a top aid to George Washington during the Revolutionary War and went on to become the nation's first Secretary of Treasury. John Jay (1745-1829) was particularly influential on matters of foreign affairs. The Jay Treaty (1794), for example, played a large role in preventing another war with Britain. He also served as the nation's first Chief Justice of the U.S. Supreme Court.

Federalist Paper No. 17 and *Federalist Paper No. 39*

States' rights advocates argued against the Constitution because they feared that the national government would dominate over the states. They also believed that the powers granted to the American president too closely resembled the powers assigned to European monarchs, which is discussed in greater detail in Chapter 6.

Two of the most significant *Federalist Papers* on the issue of national-state relations can be found in Alexander Hamilton's *Federalist Paper No. 17* and James Madison's *Federalist Paper No. 39*. In these papers, Hamilton and Madison attempt to assure the Anti-Federalists that the national government will not dominate over the states.

In *Federalist Paper No. 17* Hamilton rebuts the attacks of Patrick Henry, Samuel Adams, and other states' rights advocates by asserting the federal government will have no interest in encroaching on state powers. Hamilton argued that because the federal government will be preoccupied with issues of war and peace, interstate commerce, and foreign relations, the national government will not become entangled with the responsibilities of states. Specifically, Hamilton informs the Anti-Federalists that "the regulation of the mere domestic police of a state appears to me to hold out slender allurements to ambition."[38] He also calms some states' rights advocates by arguing that it is actually more likely that state government will encroach on the powers of the national government because citizens have greater loyalty to their state than to the national government. He claims that because . . . "a man is more attached to his family than to his neighborhood, to his neighborhood than to the community at large, the people of each State would be apt to feel a stronger bias towards their local governments than towards the government of the Union."[39]

Madison's *Federalist Paper No. 39* eased some Anti-Federalist fears by pointing out the state's role in selecting federal officials. He argued that if states do not want the national government to have authority over states then state legislatures should appoint states' rights advocates to the U.S. Senate. Remember, immediately following the ratification of the Constitution, most federal officials were appointed by state legislatures. Members of the House of Representatives were initially the only federal officials elected through popular elections. He also pointed out that states' rights are further protected in the process of amending the U.S. Constitution, where a three-fourth's super majority across states is required to ratify amendments.

Do you think this is still true in the 21st century? Do you feel greater loyalty to your national or state government?

America Meets the Greeks: *Federalist Paper No. 10*

Perhaps America's greatest contribution to political theory is found in James Madison's *Federalist Paper No. 10*. It is here where Madison confronts long-standing criticisms of democracies. We began the chapter by emphasizing how great thinkers from Plato to Hobbes opposed democratic forms of government. Remember Plato argued the Republic should be ruled by leaders who first acquire perfect knowledge in order to promote harmony and justice in society. He disliked democratic systems and blamed the Athenian democracy for killing his mentor Socrates and for losing the Peloponnesian War with Sparta. Also, Thomas Hobbes believed that all human behavior is driven by our lust for power. He therefore concluded society would degenerate into war and that life would become "solitary, poor, nasty, brutish, and short" if people are left to govern themselves.

The reason that *Federalist Paper No. 10* is considered by some to be America's greatest contribution to Western political thought is because it is here that Madison explains how it is possible to simultaneously have a system of government that allows for majority rule while safeguarding minority rights and the national interest. Madison was most worried about whether the new government would be durable enough to stand the test of time. He witnessed first-hand the failures of the rickety Articles of Confederation and was now principally concerned with preventing another governmental collapse. His chief concern was that citizens in the political minority might grow resentful living under the rules set by the majority. Those frequently in the minority view might become sufficiently motivated to secede and bring about the downfall of the government.

Madison addressed this theme in his discussions on factions. A faction is a group of citizens who share a common interest or impulse adverse to the interests of others. American society is replete with competing factions, such as the wealthy versus the poor, men versus women, competing ethnic and special interest groups, and Democratic versus Republican Party members. A faction could be a minority or a majority faction. A minority faction is considered less dangerous by Madison because its behavior can be checked by the majority. A majority faction is more precarious because it is difficult to check its behavior in a system that allows for majority rule. Madison asserted that majority factions have two cures: (1) government can remove the cause of factions; or (2) government can control the effects of factions.[40]

In the end, Madison concluded that we cannot remove the cause of factions without abolishing the major principles underlying our Constitution. Madison cited liberty as the cause of factions since people in open societies are free to form groups or associations. He draws the analogy that "air is to fire as liberty is to faction" in order to illustrate that just as eliminating air to prevent fire would be too drastic and cause our physical death, eliminating liberty in order to prevent majority factions would also cause our political death. We accordingly have to accept that we will not be able to eliminate factions from our political life.

Controlling the Effects of Factions

The brilliance of *Federalist Paper No. 10* is on display when Madison instructed on how best to control the effects of majority factions. How can you have a system of majority rule that is sensitive to those in the political minority? Madison explained that this could be accomplished by first dividing power between the national and state governments (i.e., federalism) because this structure makes it difficult for a majority faction to form in the first place. A federalist system of government is hierarchal in that it includes local governments, county governments, state governments, and a national government. He explained that because factions take shape locally, where people first meet and interact with each other, they can be contained by this hierarchal structure of government. Let's imagine a group in your town emerges that is adverse to the rights of Irish Americans. It is possible that this group could become quite influential in your town and might influence local officials to work against the interests of Irish Americans. In order for this anti-Irish movement to become a majority faction, it will have to climb the political ladder of federalism. This local group (or faction) would then have to persuade county and state officials to advance their unfair and unconstitutional agenda before ultimately persuading the national government to do the same. Madison contends this will be very difficult to do because factions (or groups) will likely grow weaker every time they take a step up the political ladder. In the above example, Irish Americans and other sympathizers will likely organize and blunt the effectiveness of this anti-Irish faction as they attempt to grow from town to county, county to state, and state to national government. This is because it is much easier to derail a movement than it is to grow one. Former Speaker of the House Sam Rayburn once remarked in another context that even a jackass can kick down a barn, but it takes a carpenter to build one.[42] The system of federalism thus makes it difficult for particular groups to dominate the national agenda because they will be weakened by opposing groups as they attempt their ascendancy to majority status.

WHY POLITICS MATTERS TO YOU!

Do You Belong to a Political Party?

In *Federalist Paper No. 10* James Madison warned that political factions could cause disunity and threaten the long-term survival of popular governments. For this reason George Washington advised against the establishment of political parties in his Farewell Address to the nation in 1796. He believed political parties would divide our nation into quarreling political factions. Washington warned that political parties would lead to geographic rivalries between the North and South and could negatively impact U.S. foreign relations with European powers.

On the other hand renowned political scientist David R. Mayhew argues that political parties play a positive role in American democracy.[41] The theory behind political parties is perhaps best outlined in the Responsible Party Model. The Responsible Party Model emphasizes that parties play an important role in democracies when parties: (1) offer voters a clear choice between competing political platforms; (2) parties effectively educate voters on the differences between political platforms; and when (3) party members are effective in implementing their party's platform once elected.

Many Americans in the 21st century are politically dealigning from both the Republican and Democratic parties. In 1952, only 23% of Americans identified themselves as political Independents, compared with 47 percent registered Democrats and 28 percent registered Republicans. In 2010, 40 percent of Americans identified themselves as Independents, compared with 31 percent registered Democrats and 24 percent registered Republicans. College-age students are also increasingly identifying themselves as Independents. Approximately 41 percent of college-age students identify themselves as Independents.

Do you believe political parties are good for American democracy?

Do you belong to a political party? Why or why not?

Log in to **www.cengagebrain.com** and open CourseReader to access the reading:

Federalist Paper No. 10

Federalist Paper # 10 is regarded by some as America's greatest contribution to political theory because it is here that James Madison reveals how it is possible for a political system to allow for majority rule while remaining sensitive to those in the political minority. Writing under the pseudonym Publius, James Madison, Alexander Hamilton, and John Jay published 85 essays in New York newspapers from October 1787 through August 1788. These essays became known as the *Federalist Papers*, and earned the reputation as the basic texts for an understanding of the intentions of the framers of the Constitution. These papers sought to counter the arguments of critics of the Constitution by demonstrating that republican institutions could work in a nation as large as the United States, and that some central government was necessary to bring order to the new nation. *Federalist Paper # 10* is considered to be the centerpiece of this explanation of the Constitution and the primary document in the development of American pluralism.

- *Do you believe the majority population tyrannizes over the minority population here in the 21st Century? If so, can you think of an example of this?*

- *Should the U.S. move away from a representative democracy and toward a direct democracy? Why would James Madison likely argue against that?*

Direct Democracy: *A system of democracy whereby citizens directly participate in the decision-making process of government*

Do you believe members of Congress have historically represented the best and brightest in society given that women and African Americans were initially barred from participating in the political process?

There is no guarantee, however, that federalism will prevent majority factions from tyrannizing over those in the political minority. African Americans, for instance, were enslaved and/or disenfranchised by the majority for most of our history. Madison's second method for controlling the destructive effects of majority factions is to institute a representative democracy (i.e., republic) rather than a **direct democracy**. He argued that the effects of tyranny of the majority can be softened by selecting the best and brightest to represent citizens in government. Because enlightened members of society would be more likely to do what is right, rather than what is popular, a representative democracy will be more effective than a direct democracy in guarding against the potentially destructive impulses of the majority. Madison stressed that enlightened representatives will be more sensitive to the views of the political minority because they will more likely be educated on the virtues of justice and the national interests. *Federalist Paper No. 10* makes a major contribution to political theory by asserting the negative impacts associated with the tyranny of the majority can be weakened by creating a federalist system of government and by having the most enlightened members of society make decisions on behalf of the general population. This is why the Framers did not use the term *democracy* in any of the 4,400 words penned in the Constitution (7,500 words with 27 amendments) opting instead to use the term *republic* to emphasize the need to have the best and brightest assume leadership positions in government.

ADOPTING THE CONSTITUION

The 85 essays that came to be known as the *Federalist Papers* were mostly effective in calming Anti-Federalist fears that the national government would dominate over the state governments. On June 25, 1788, the populous state of Virginia ratified the U.S. Constitution in a narrow vote and New York followed suit a month later. The Anti-Federalists were also concerned, however, that the Constitution did not include a Bill of Rights. North Carolina still refused to ratify the Constitution over this issue. They argued that the Constitution should not be ratified until the natural rights of individuals were protected. The Anti-Federalists wondered why it was necessary to have a Bill of Rights in state constitutions but not in the national Constitution. They were worried that if natural rights were not specifically protected, there would be nothing to prevent the national government from restricting free speech, encroaching on the freedom of the press, and infringing on the free exercise of religion. The Federalists, on the other hand, were opposed to including a Bill of Rights for two reasons. They believed the main text of the Constitution already prohibited the national government from violating the natural rights of citizens. Including a Bill of Rights could become a slippery slope by creating the impression that the national government was authorized to violate any individual right not listed in a Bill of Rights. The Federalists were also concerned that a call for a Bill of Rights would require a second Constitutional Convention. The Federalists believed a second Constitutional Convention could cause the unraveling of all of the progress made in the first Constitutional Convention. The rules of the Constitutional Convention permitted any delegate to revisit any previously approved measure. A second Constitutional Convention might therefore be used by Anti-Federalists to rescind other provisions that were already agreed upon in the first Constitutional Convention.

The Federalists and the Anti-Federalists again found

CourseReader ASSIGNMENT

Log in to **www.cengagebrain.com** and open CourseReader to access the reading:

Excerpt of *Democracy in America* **by Alexis de Tocqueville**

Alexis de Tocqueville visited the United States from France in the early 1830s to study American prison reform. After the visit, he published a lengthy work of observations and analyses of American society. Nothing impressed him more than the young nation's democratic institutions and apparent lack of aristocracy, especially in New England. While Tocqueville praises the United States for its equality and freedom, he also perceptively identifies many of the problems associated with the republic's form of government, observing that popular governments did not always elect the best leaders or produce the best laws. Moreover, a government based on the will of the majority did not guarantee the rights of the minority.

- *Do you agree with Tocqueville that Americans favor equality over liberty?*

- *Why did Tocqueville believe it was important for citizens of democracies to belong to group associations. Do you belong to any groups? If so, has that group affiliation influenced the way you think about the government?*

compromise by agreeing to add a Bill of Rights by attaching them as amendments to the Constitution. This satisfied the Anti-Federalist demand for a Bill of Rights and was ultimately agreeable to the Federalists because the process would not require a second Constitutional Convention. Thomas Jefferson was one of the strongest advocates for the inclusion of a Bill of Rights and pledged to voters in Virginia that if he was elected to Congress he would "prepare and recommend to the states for ratification, the most satisfactory provisions for all essential rights."[43]

James Madison was then assigned the difficult task of sifting through the hundreds of potential amendments that came flooding in from across the 13 states. Madison ultimately recommended that the Bill of Rights should consist of 17 amendments. Congress later did away with five of the amendments, and two of the amendments that dealt with the apportionments of members of Congress and congressional salaries were not ratified by the states.[44] The Bill of Rights was ratified on December 15, 1791, as the first 10 amendments to the Constitution.

Table 4.8 highlights the Bill of Rights, the First 10 Amendments to the Constitution.

TABLE 4.8. The Bill of Rights: The First Ten Amendments to the Constitution

First Amendment—Protects Freedom of Speech, Press and Religion, and Right to Assemble
Second Amendment—Protects the Right to Bear Arms
Third Amendment—Prevents Quartering of Soldiers
Fourth Amendment—Prevents Illegal Searches and Seizures
Fifth Amendment—Grand Juries, Self-Incrimination, Double Jeopardy, Due Process, and Eminent Domain
Sixth Amendment—Right to Speedy Trial
Seventh Amendment—Right to Trial by Jury
Eighth Amendment—Prevents Cruel and Unusual Punishment
Ninth Amendment—Broadly Protects Individual Civil Rights
Tenth Amendment—Divides Power between National and State Government

AMENDING THE CONSTITUTION

The U.S. Constitution is a natural law constitution meant to address enduring principles. Thomas Jefferson argued that because the "Constitution belongs to the living and not the dead," it must be altered periodically in order to reflect the wishes of those living under it. The formal process for amending the Constitution is found in Article V. Amending the Constitution is a two-step process that requires a proposal and a ratification stage. Although there have been more than 10,000 constitutional amendments proposed in Congress, the Constitution has only been officially amended 27 times. The first step of the amendment process is the proposal stage. The Constitution stipulates that a proposal to amend the Constitution must be approved by either a two-thirds vote in the House and Senate, or by two-thirds of the states at a national convention. All proposals to date have come from a two-thirds vote in the House and Senate.

The Constitution also provides two possible methods for ratifying constitutional amendments. An amendment can either be ratified by a majority vote in three-fourths of the state legislatures (i.e., 38 states) or by the approval of special state conventions called in at least three-fourths of the states. The Twenty-first Amendment, which repealed the Eighteenth Amendment's prohibition of alcohol in 1933, is the only amendment to be ratified by state conventions. All others were ratified by state legislatures. The Founding Fathers made it very difficult to amend the Constitution by requiring a supermajority vote in both the proposal and ratification stage of the amendment process. Most constitutional amendments fail at the proposal stage. Of the more than 10,000 constitutional amendments proposed to the House and Senate, only 33 have passed the proposal stage with a two-thirds vote in Congress. Most of the 17 amendments passed since the ratification of the Bill of Rights (i.e., the first 10 amendments) have either expanded political rights of citizens (i.e., Thirteenth, Fourteenth, Fifteenth, Seventeenth, Nineteenth, Twenty-fourth, and Twenty-sixth) and/or altered the presidential selection process (i.e., Twelfth, Twentieth, Twenty-second, Twenty-third, and Twenty-fifth).

Table 4.9 reveals the two methods prescribed by the U.S. Constition for proposing and ratifying Constitutional Amendments

One of the few amendments to clear the proposal stage but not the ratification stage is the Equal Rights Amendment. The Equal Rights Amendment stipulated that "equality of rights under the law shall not be denied or abridged by the United States or by any State on account of sex." While this amendment is widely popular with the majority of Americans, several southern states voiced opposition and successfully blocked ratification of the ERA.

Why do you believe the Equal Rights Amendment for women has never been ratified?

TABLE 4.9. **How to Amend the Constitution**

Proposing amendment	Two-thirds vote in both houses of Congress	Congress convenes national convention and two-thirds of state legislatures support proposal
Ratifying amendments	Majority vote in three-fourths of state legislatures	Three-fourths of states approving at national convention

© STEVE MCALISTER/GETTY IMAGES

SUMMARY

The American Constitution is the oldest and most revered national constitution in the world today. The core of the Constitution rests on the assumption that a tyrannical system of government can be avoided by adopting a federalist system of government that includes a system of checks and balances and a Bill of Rights. This chapter highlighted the weaknesses of the Articles of Confederation, the major principles underlying the American Constitution, and the politics associated with the ratification of the Constitution. It also revealed that the system of government created by the American Founding Fathers is quite different from the government we have here in the 21st century. The American Framers were well aware of Plato's and Hobbes's critique that democracies left to their own devices will eventually degenerate into a "mobocracy." James Madison and the other delegates at the Constitutional Convention sought to build a system of government that blended both democratic and aristocratic values into a new type of government.

The U.S. Constitution has since emerged as America's "most important export" in both promoting democratic values and in setting the international trend on establishing a Constitution to guide the relationship between the government and the people. The power of the ideas expressed in the U.S. Constitution inspired a Belgian revolution in 1789, influenced Poland and France to adopt a Constitution in 1791, caused Spain to follow suit in 1812, with other nations following until we now have only a handful of democratic nations (e.g., United Kingdom, Israel, and New Zealand) and a few nondemocratic nations (Saudi Arabia, Oman, and Libya) that still do not have a guiding Constitution.[45]

In the next three chapters we will concentrate on the expansion of American democracy as it relates to individual rights and the structure and powers of our three branches of government. Since the Constitutional Convention, the electoral college has been democratized, judicial elections are in place in most states, and Americans now directly elect U.S. Senators. This democratic movement in the United States, in conjunction with advances in mass communications and a more informed electorate, has also helped to change the political landscape across the globe. In the next chapter we will examine how the expansion of American democracy has impacted and been impacted by the American Congress.

KEY TERMS

KEY PEOPLE

5

THE AMERICAN CONGRESS

The United States Capitol building in Washington, D.C. The Capitol has housed the U.S. House of Representatives and the U.S. Senate for approximately 200 years. It stands as a monument to American democracy.

INTRODUCTION: THE ORIGINS OF THE AMERICAN CONGRESS

The American Congress serves as the centerpiece of our republican form of government. It is the citizens' most powerful link to our national government. In this chapter on the American Congress we first explore the original intent of the Founding Fathers by highlighting the structure and constitutional powers of Congress. We then examine the electoral process by focusing on the expansion of voting rights in the United States. Because the House of Representatives is viewed as the "people's body" it is important to review the impact of landmark measures, such as the Fifteenth Amendment, the Nineteenth Amendment, and the Voting Rights Act (1965), on helping to make Congress a truly representative body. The third section explores the importance of this electoral connection to the behavior of members of congress. Why does your member of Congress vote the way he or she does? Lastly, it is important to remember the significance placed on public ethics by Socrates, Plato, and Aristotle covered in the first chapter. The final section will highlight historic shortcomings of congressional ethics and recent progress made to restore the public trust in Congress.

The American System of Government

As we learned in Chapter 4, the delegates to the Constitutional Convention were distrustful of federal power. They accordingly structured the government in a manner that made it difficult for the federal government to encroach on either state or individual rights by doing the following:

1. They created a **federalist system** of government that divided power between the state and national government.
2. The Framers then established a **separation of powers** in the federal government by creating a legislative body to make the law, an executive body to enforce the law, and a judicial body to interpret the law.

Questions to Consider Before Reading This Chapter

1. Are modern congressional districts too large? If so, should we increase the size of the House of Representatives so that fewer people reside in each district?

2. Is the coffee still hot? Do we still need a two-house chamber now that members in both houses are elected to office?

3. Why do congressional incumbents win reelection approximately 95 percent of the time?

4. Do women legislate differently than men?

5. How can we make congressional elections more competitive?

6. Should it be unconstitutional for states to deny voting rights to felons after they are released from prison?

7. How will the Health Care Act of 2010 impact college-age students?

8. What steps, if any, should be taken to ensure ethical behavior in Congress?

Federalist System:
A national system of government that divides power between the federal and state government.

Separation of Powers:
The U.S. Constitution divides federal powers among three branches of government: the legislative, the executive, and the judiciary.

© RENA SCHILD/SHUTTERSTOCK.COM

Checks and Balances:
The U.S. Constitution limits each of the three federal branches of government by giving each branch the right to change the acts of another branch on matters that fall within its jurisdiction.

Does the system of checks and balances cause political gridlock, thus making it difficult for the government to solve problems in the twenty-first century?

3. The delegates then created a system of **checks and balances** to prevent any of these branches from dominating over another.

THE CREATION OF CONGRESS

The drafters of the Constitution improvised in the creation of Congress. While Congress is typically viewed as a single institution, it is divided into two self-ruling legislative chambers. The Framers created a **bicameral legislature** (i.e., two-chamber legislature) consisting of the House of Representatives and the Senate. Each was intended to serve a very specific function. The House of Representatives is viewed as the *people's body* and is responsible for incorporating the views of the masses into government. In Chapter 4 we highlighted how the *Connecticut Compromise* established that the number of representatives per state is based on a state's population and that each state is equally represented with two senators. The House was created in part to establish a social contract between the government and the people. This linkage was ensured first by allowing citizens to select their representatives directly, and strengthened by requiring frequent elections every two years.

Senators, on the other hand, were not viewed as representatives of the people by the Framers. Instead, senators were viewed as guardians of the public trust and the protectors of states' rights. It is because of this that senators were initially appointed to the chamber by their respective state legislatures. Giving state legislatures the authority to appoint senators was viewed as a compromise to the **Anti-Federalists** who were fearful that the national government would come to dominate over the states. As Madison pointed out in *Federalist Paper No. 39*, it is far less likely that the national government would dictate terms to states if state legislatures were directly responsible for selecting U.S. senators.[1]

Congressional Powers

The structure and powers of Congress were established at the Constitutional Convention in 1787. Article I of the U.S. Constitution established strong congressional powers and allowed members of Congress enormous discretion in arranging both legislative chambers. It was important to the drafters of the Constitution that Congress remain independent of the influence of the executive branch. Article I, Section 6, for instance, established that members are immune from arrest (except for treason, felony, and breach of peace) while "going to and returning from" congressional sessions. This is to prevent the president from arresting members on their way to casting an important vote, as some European monarchs were known to do. This section also ensures that no member of Congress may be "questioned in any other Place" for their speech on the floor of either chamber, thereby ensuring free speech in each assembly. [2]

John Locke's belief that the legislative branch is both the "supreme power" and the "sacred" institution in the Republic was incorporated into the U.S. Constitution (see Chapter 3).[3] Article I, Section 8 of the Constitution established the broad and expansive powers of Congress. Congress was expressly granted authority over the two most important powers of government: (1) the power to declare war; and (2) the power of the purse. Convention delegate James Wilson remarked that the decision to go to war should "not be in the power of a single man, or a single body of men to involve us in such distress, for the important power of declaring war is vested in the legislature at large."[4] Congress is also constitutionally empowered to "lay and collect taxes," to "borrow money," to "regulate foreign commerce," and to "coin money." These powers ensure that Congress maintains control over economic policy and also buttresses Congress's oversight powers by enabling the body to cut off funding of any unpopular governmental program. In foreign policy, congressional powers overlap with executive authority, thereby facilitating an "invitation to struggle" between the executive and legislative branches.[5]

THEORY AND PRACTICE

The War Powers Act:
Drone and Warfare in Pakistan

The Constitution does not specifically prescribe the daily routine of congressional or executive behavior in foreign affairs. It is instead written so that Congress and the president are required to share foreign policy powers without providing specificity as to how the relationship should function on war powers. Was President Harry Truman authorized to send troops into the Korean conflict without congressional authorization? Was Congress authorized to enact the War Powers Act over a presidential veto in 1973? The War Powers Act requires the president to "consult" with Congress before deploying troops into hostile regions and requires the president to return troops from hostile areas within 60 days unless Congress issues a declaration of war. Congress and the President have historically battled over war powers in part because of the vague language in the Constitution that guides the two branches in foreign affairs. Others believe the War Powers Act is merely a symbolic gesture of congressional power, pointing out that Congress has never seriously invoked the Act to curb presidential power.

Modern warfare poses some particularly challenging legal questions. President Barack Obama has aggressively gone on the offensive against the al-Qaeda terrorist network by authorizing more missile strikes from unmanned aerial vehicles (i.e., drones) in Pakistan and Afghanistan in his first two years than his predecessor had in the previous eight years. The United States currently has in place two separate drone programs in the Afghanistan–Pakistani region, one administered by

continued

the U.S. military and the other run by the Central Intelligence Agency (CIA). Some drones operating in this region are piloted from within the United States. While Congress has been largely deferential to President Obama's controversial drone programs in the region, Pakistan's foreign minister argued the strikes violate Pakistani sovereignty.[6] In May of 2011, the Pakistani parliament also condemned the successful U.S. raid against Osama bin-Laden's compound in northwestern Pakistan and criticized U.S. drone attacks in the country. Supporters of the drone program point to the successful targeting of Mustafa Abu al-Yazid and other leading al-Qaeda members, while detractors emphasize that approximately one-third of the 1,400 casualties of drone warfare since 2004 have been civilians.[7]

Should Congress place a greater check on the use of drone warfare in Pakistan?

Why or why not?

Congress is constitutionally authorized to "regulate Commerce with foreign nations," to punish "Felonies committed on the high Seas," "*to raise and support armies,*" and given the power to "declare war."[8] The Framers initially granted Congress the power to "make war" but later amended the language to "declare war" in order to enable the executive branch to defend the nation if attacked when Congress is not in session.

As discussed in the previous chapter, the expressed constitutional powers of Congress (see Table 5.1) were also greatly enhanced in the landmark Supreme Court decision *McCulloch v. Maryland* (1819). In *McCulloch,* the Supreme Court extended *implied powers* (i.e., the Elastic Clause) to Congress through their interpretation of the *necessary and proper clause,* granting Congress additional implied powers if needed to carry out the expressed powers listed in Article 1, Section 8 of the U.S. Constitution.

The Structure of Congress:
The House and the Senate

The first American Congress consisted of 65 members in the House of Representatives and 26 members in the Senate. The institution has grown dramatically since then to 435 members in the House of Representatives and 100 members

TABLE 5.1. Major Powers of Congress, Found in Article 1, Section 8 of the U.S. Constitution

- To lay and collect taxes and duties
- Power to borrow money
- Regulate commerce with foreign nations and between states
- Establish rules of naturalization (how to become a citizen)
- Coin money
- Punish counterfeiting
- Establish post offices and roads
- To promote science and establish patents and copyrights
- To establish a federal court system
- May punish piracies and felonies committed on high seas
- To declare war
- May raise and support armies
- May provide and maintain a navy
- May regulate land and naval forces
- Necessary and Proper Clause (Elastic Clause)—May make any law necessary and proper for carrying into execution the powers listed above

in the Senate today. Members of the House of Representatives serve two-year terms and Senators serve six-year terms without term limits. Article I, Section 2 of the Constitution spells out the needed qualifications of House members and specifies how members are to be apportioned across states. The Constitution stipulates that House members must be American citizens for at least seven years, at least 25 years of age, and a resident of the state that he or she represents.[9] Article I, Section 3 instructs that the Senate "shall be composed of two Senators from each state" and that each senator must be an American citizen for at least nine years, at least 30 years of age, and a resident of the state he or she represents.[10]

All 435 House seats and 37 of the 100 Senate seats were in play in the 2010 congressional mid-term election. This was an historic election in that the Republican Party picked up 63 seats in the House of Representatives and six seats in the Senate (see Table 5.2). Having the Republican Party in control of the House meant a changing of the guard in House leadership positions. In 2011, the Speaker of the

▲ House Speaker John Boehner receives the gavel from the previous Speaker of the House, Nancy Pelosi, as the 112th Congress convenes in the U.S. Capitol on January 5, 2010. Boehner became the 53rd Speaker of the House on this day.

House John Boehner (R-OH) assumed the mantle of power from Nancy Pelosi, the previous Speaker, and Republicans assumed leadership positions on all House committees. Republicans generally ran their campaigns against government spending and the Affordable Health Care Act of 2010, which is discussed later in this chapter. Mid-term elections take place every two years after a presidential election and sometimes serve as a snapshot of the popularity of the sitting president. Table 5.3 reveals that the 2010 election represented the largest swing away from the president's party since Democrats lost 71 seats during Franklin D. Roosevelt's presidency in 1938.

Should we still require that members of the House be at least 25 years of age and Senators be at least 30 years of age? Why or why not?

TABLE 5.2. Congressional Mid-term Election Results

House of Representatives	111th Congress 2009–2010	112th Congress 2011–2012
Democrats	256 members	193 members
Republicans	179 members	242 members
Independents	0	0
Republican Net Gain +63		
United States Senate		
Democrats	57	51
Republicans	41	47
Independents	2	2
Republican Net Gain +6		

TABLE 5.3. 2010 Congressional Election in Historical Perspective: Presidential Mid-term Losses in the House of Representatives

President	Year	No. of Seats Lost by President's Party
Grover Cleveland (Dem.)	1894	−116 seats
Warren G. Harding (Rep.)	1922	−75 seats
Franklin D. Roosevelt (Dem.)	1938	−71 seats
Barack Obama (Dem.)	2010	−63 seats
Woodrow Wilson (Dem.)	1914	−59 seats
William H. Taft (Rep.)	1910	−57 seats
Harry S. Truman (Dem.)	1946	−55 seats
Bill Clinton (Dem.)	1994	−54 seats
Dwight Eisenhower (Rep.)	1958	−48 seats
Richard Nixon (Rep.)	1974	−48 seats
Lyndon B. Johnson (Dem.)	1966	−47 seats
George W. Bush (Rep.)	2006	−28 seats

THEORY AND PRACTICE

Term Limits, the American Congress, and the U.S. Supreme Court:

The concept of limiting the terms of elective officials extends all the way back to ancient Greece. The Athenian council, for instance, replaced all 500 incumbent members with new members each year. The Founding Fathers were well aware of this Athenian practice, yet decided against placing term limits on either members of Congress or the American President in the U.S. Constitution. Thomas Jefferson and George Mason argued forcefully for term limits on senators and the president during the ratification process, but they were unsuccessful. Term limits were subsequently placed on the American president in the Twenty-second Amendment to the Constitution in 1951.

Residents of the state of Arkansas voted to place term limits on Arkansas officials serving in the U.S. Congress in 1992. Shortly thereafter, the League of Women Voters took the state to court asserting that it was unconstitutional for the state to place term limits on federal legislators. Congressman Ray Thornton, a sitting member of Congress from Arkansas at the time, joined the League of Women Voters in the suit. In *U.S. Term Limits v. Thornton* (1995), the U.S. Supreme Court decided in a 5 to 4 vote that states are not permitted to place term limits on U.S. Members of Congress. In the decision, Justice John Paul Stevens (see profile of Justice Stevens in Chapter 7) wrote, "Permitting Individual States to formulate diverse qualifications for their congressional representatives would result in a patchwork that would be inconsistent with the Framers' vision of a uniform National Legislature representing the people of the United States." Since the U.S. Constitution specifically addresses the area of congressional qualifications, any changes to this arrangement would need to come from a constitutional amendment, rather than statutory law.

Do you support a constitutional amendment limiting the terms of members of Congress?

Why or why not?

Structuring the House of Representatives

The original constitutional formula for determining the size of the House was based strictly on the population of the state. Each state was originally assigned one representative for every 30,000 residents living in that state. Critics arguing against the ratification of the U.S. Constitution wrangled over the size of the first House of Representatives. The Anti-Federalists speculated that the small size of the House of Representatives (65 members) prevented it from serving as a "people's body" and conjectured that the House would instead serve only the interests of the powerful and well-connected. In *Federalist Paper No. 55*, Madison recognized the need for the House to be large enough to incorporate the views of the masses, but not so large that it would degenerate into an unruly mob.

Sixty or seventy men may be more properly trusted with a given degree of power than six or seven. *But it does not follow that six or seven hundred would be proportionably a better depository . . . In all very numerous assemblies, of whatever character composed, passion never fails to wrest the scepter from reason. Had every Athenian citizen been a Socrates, every Athenian assembly would still have been a mob.*[11]

Madison then attempted to calm the concerns of the Anti-Federalists by reassuring them that the size of the House of Representatives would expand over time. Because the Constitution requires that a national census be conducted every 10 years, and given the constitutional formula requiring one Representative for every 30,000 inhabitants, the size of the House was designed to grow in direct proportion to the U.S. population. House membership, for instance, increased from 65 members to 104 members after the 1790 census.

The Permanent Apportionment Act of 1929 capped the number of representatives at 435 and created a procedure for reapportioning members according to population growth across states. Each member of Congress on average now represents more than 700,000 people, which causes some scholars to worry that congressional districts have grown too large. Only India has larger legislative districts in their lower legislative chamber. The modern House of Representatives, however, would have more than 10,000 members today if it continued to apportion membership according to the original constitutional formula of one representative for every 30,000 citizens.

Federalist Paper No. 57 provides other arguments against the Anti-federalist charge that the small size of the House of Representative prevents it from serving as a people's body. Written by either James Madison or Alexander Hamilton, still a matter of historical dispute, the author provides a broader rationale as to why the House of Representatives "will have sympathy with the mass of the people" and not degenerate into an elitist body. *Federalist Paper No. 57* speculates that the linkage between the people and the House will be facilitated by frequent elections every two years. Frequent elections are thus meant to serve as an important check on the behavior of House members.[12] It also emphasized that House members will have

Should the U.S. House of Representative increase the number of representatives beyond 435 in order to have less populated congressional districts?

Do you know the name of your member of Congress?

TABLE 5.4. Major Differences Between the House of Representatives and the Senate

House of Representatives	Senate
Structure	**Structure**
Total of 435 members	Total of 100 members
Number per state varies according to the state's population	Two senators per state
Members serve two-year terms	Members serve six-year terms
Member Qualifications	**Member Qualifications**
Must be at least 25 years old	Must be at least 30 years old
Must be American citizen for at least seven years	Must be American citizen for at least nine years
Differences in Constitutional Role	**Differences in Constitutional Role**
Initiates all revenue bills Initiates all impeachment procedures	Ratifies foreign treaties Confirms presidential appointments Tries impeached officials

gratitude to those who elected them and would possess a natural proclivity to serve their interests in federal government. We highlight some of the major differences between the House and Senate in Table 5.4.

Structuring the U.S. Senate

Thomas Jefferson, an advocate for *unicameral legislatures* (i.e., single legislative chambers), initiated a conversation with George Washington over the philosophical underpinnings of bicameralism (i.e., two legislative chambers) in 1787. As they spoke over coffee, Washington sidestepped Jefferson's questioning of the need for a bicameral legislature by inquiring why Jefferson poured his coffee into a saucer before drinking. Jefferson responded that he was allowing his coffee to cool. Washington replied, "And so the senate is the saucer into which we pour legislation to cool."[13]

The Framers were responsive to Plato's and Aristotle's warnings against the excesses of self-interest and popular government. They were well versed in the teachings of political philosophy and carefully designed the Senate so that it would remain impervious to the whims of the electorate. The House of Representative was viewed as the people's body, but the Senate was structured to prevent the popular and fickle sentiments of mass society from dominating the national agenda. Legislation enacted in the House of Representatives was meant to "cool" in the U.S. Senate, where senators were originally insulated from political pressure. Senators originally did not face the electorate and were instead appointed to six-year terms by members of their respective state legislatures. Remember from Chapter 2 that Plato categorized the democratic political system as one of the worst forms of government. Plato argued that democracy was a flawed system because the majority of citizens would advocate for their self-interest rather than pursue the national interest and the public good. It is because of this that popular elections were not very popular with the delegates at the

Senator Robert C. Byrd (1917–2010)

America lost a legendary statesman when Senator Robert C. Byrd (D-WV) died on June 28, 2010, at the age of 92. Senator Byrd (D-WV) took his final senatorial oath in January 2009, marking his 56th anniversary as a member of Congress. Byrd took office during the Truman administration and went on to serve with (not under) 12 American presidents. Approximately 12,000 men and women have served in the American Congress throughout our history, and Senator Byrd served longer than all of them.

▲ Sen. Robert Byrd (D-WV) spoke on the Senate floor on Wednesday, November 18, 2009. He became the longest serving member of Congress on this day. He served in the U.S. Congress for 57 years before passing away while in office on June 28, 2010.

He was a renowned defender of Congress's constitutional role in the American system of checks and balances and routinely challenged executive encroachments on these powers. He was openly critical of the modern Congress's tendency "to regard a chief executive in a role more elevated than the Framers intended."[18] Accordingly, the *Almanac of American Politics* noted that Robert Byrd may have come closer to the kind of senator the Founding Fathers had in mind than any other.

Senator Byrd was also widely regarded as a Senate historian and the master of Senate rules and procedures. He gained this reputation by authoring two books, *The Senate 1789–1989* and *The Senate of the Roman Republic*, and from his eloquent orations on the Senate floor. His floor speeches were typically filled with references to the classics, including Greek and Roman Philosophers, Shakespeare, and the Founding Fathers. He also had an uncanny ability of linking the classics with modern policy issues, such as the line item veto and tax policy.

Senator Byrd was born on November 20, 1917, in North Wilkesboro, North Carolina with the name Cornelius Calvin Sale Jr. His father sent him to live with his aunt and uncle in Stotesbury, West Virginia, after his mother died in the flu epidemic of 1918–1919. They adopted him and renamed him Robert Carlyle Byrd. He only learned of his real name at the age of 16. His foster father was a coal miner, roaming from town to town for employment. His meager beginnings sometimes resulted in suppers "with only lettuce and a little butter . . . and sugar on the table" and Christmases without presents.[19]

continued ➤

These impoverished beginnings shaped Senator Byrd's self-image. In a fiery exchange at a Senate Budget Committee hearing with former Treasury secretary Paul O'Neill, Senator Byrd declared, "Well, Mr. Secretary, I lived in a house without electricity too. No running water, no telephone, a little wooden outhouse. I started out in life without any rungs in the bottom ladder. I can stand toe to toe with you."

Byrd started his political career as a charismatic campaigner, entertaining crowds with fiddle renditions of such blue grass classics as "Cripple Creek" and "Rye Whiskey."[20] Byrd ran for the U.S. House of Representatives in West Virginia's sixth congressional district in 1952. During the primary, H. D. Ragland, one of Byrd's opponents, disclosed that Byrd had been an organizer for the Ku Klux Klan in 1942 and 1943. Byrd took the offensive and purchased radio and television advertisements attributing the membership to a mistake of youth. However, during the general election, his Republican challenger produced a sympathetic letter Byrd had written to the Imperial Wizard of the Ku Klux Klan in 1946, three years after he allegedly left the organization. In the letter, Byrd stated, "The Klan is needed today as never before and I am anxious to see its rebirth in West Virginia." Although the letter cost him the support of the governor, Byrd went on to win with 57.4 percent of the vote and was reelected by greater margins in 1954 and 1956. During a television interview in 2001, Byrd said, "We all make mistakes, I made a mistake when I was a young man. It's always been an albatross around my neck, joining the Ku Klux Klan." The race issue reemerged in the U.S. Senate when Byrd filibustered the Civil Rights Act of 1964 with a 14-hour speech, which is still one of the longest Senate speeches on record. Again, Byrd expressed regret for this chapter of his career. He went on to establish strong ties with African American organizations in the last few decades of life.

Byrd was elected to the U.S. Senate in 1958 at the age of 40. He earned his law degree from American University in 1963, and had his diploma presented to him by President John F. Kennedy, who delivered the commencement speech. He went on to assume the Majority Leader position after Mike Mansfield retired in 1976. He served in more leadership positions than any other senator in the history of the United States.

Byrd also became chairman of the Appropriations Committee in 1989. While he was generally regarded as a loyal Democrat, he tended to place greater emphasis on the powers of the Senate and the economic welfare of West Virginia. In 1990, Byrd proudly stated that he wanted "to be West Virginia's billion-dollar industry." He

continued

realized his dream 10 years later with the 2000 appropriations bill, which earmarked more than $1 billion of federal funds for West Virginia.

On the legislative front, he cast more than 18,000 roll call votes, more than any other senator in the history of the United States. He also surprised some by casting the deciding vote against a constitutional amendment banning flag desecration in 2000. He explained his vote by stating, "The foolish and the dead alone never change their minds." During the Bush administration, Byrd admonished the Senate for its unwillingness to debate the decision to invade Iraq. "We stand passively mute in the United States Senate, paralyzed by our own uncertainty, seemingly stunned by the sheer turmoil of events."

Byrd once stated that people in West Virginia believe in four things: "God Almighty; Sears and Roebuck; Carter's Little Liver Pills; and Robert C. Byrd."[21] He came to personify both the U.S. Senate and the state of West Virginia, though, he once stated that he preferred the company of his wife and children over that of political colleagues. He remained married to his high-school sweetheart Erma, and was the father of two daughters, and grandfather to six grandchildren. In a reflective moment he once said, "One of these days, I'll be over in a hospital somewhere with four walls around me and the only people who'll be with me will be my family. The rest will be pretty busy with their responsibilities. It's pretty easy to be fast forgotten."[22]

Constitutional Convention. The only federal officials, in fact, to face voters in popular elections were members of the House of Representatives. Senators, Justices, and the American president were all originally appointed to their position by political elites.

Federalist Paper No. 62 postulated that granting state legislatures control over the Senate selection process served as a "convenient link" between the state and federal governments.[14] The Framers envisioned an upper chamber where Senators grappled with salient state, national, and international issues, free of electoral considerations. The Senate would remain above the political fray and serve a quasi-presidential advisory role in foreign affairs, which is why it was granted the joint power to declare war and the sole power to ratify treaties and confirm foreign appointments. *Federalist Paper No. 63* highlights the Framers' interest in the Senate paying particular "attention to the judgment of other nations" and the need to serve as a stable counterweight to the democratic impulses emanating from the House.[15] The Senate was designed to direct its attention to national and state interests rather than facilitate the interests of well-connected political groups.

The Origins of the Seventeenth Amendment (1913): Direct Election of Senators

This all changed 126 years later when the Seventeenth Amendment (1913) to the Constitution transformed the Senate selection process from an appointive to an elective position. Senator Robert C. Byrd (D-WV) once stated that the passage of the Seventeenth Amendment represents the most significant reform in the history of the U.S. Senate.

The ratification of the Seventeenth Amendment was the result of a decades-long movement to democratize the Senate selection process. The Senate selection process was amended for three fundamentally distinct reasons.

1. First, the process itself was substantially flawed. Most states required senatorial candidates to win approval in both houses of the state legislature.[16] Legislative chambers often disagreed and sometimes remained **gridlocked** for substantial periods of time. The state of Delaware, for instance, was without any Senate representation from 1901 to 1903 because of this form of legislative infighting.

2. Second, some state legislatures were vulnerable to corrupting influences. Rather than serving as the protectors of state and national interests, senators were increasingly viewed as the protectors of party bosses and corporate elites.[17]

3. Third, the American political culture changed dramatically during the latter half of the nineteenth century. The **Jacksonian Democracy** era fueled democratic fires in the United States. The movement sparked the decentralization of the Electoral College (discussed at great length in Chapter 6), judicial elections in many western states, and a fundamental belief that government should be accountable to the people. This movement, in conjunction with advances in mass communications and a more informed electorate, sounded the drumbeat for change.

Gridlock: *A lack of progress on enacting legislation typically caused by partisan and/or institutional infighting.*

Jacksonian Democracy: *Jacksonian democracy refers to the political philosophy and influence of President Andrew Jackson. The era (1824–1854) was marked with the expansion of democratic rights and started the trend away from political appointments and toward the use of elections to select public officials.*

The Senate ultimately passed the proposed amendment on June 12, 1911, by a vote of 64 to 24, and the House followed suit 11 months later by a vote of 238 to 39. The amendment was made official when it was ratified by 36 of the then 48 states on May 31, 1913.

One Person, One Vote? The Malapportioned Senate

Because each state is equally represented with two U.S. Senators, smaller states have a disproportionate amount of influence. This causes some to criticize the Senate as going against the principle of one person, one vote. The term *malapportionment* refers to the underrepresentation of the population that arises when one legislative district is considerably more populated than another. The nine most populated states, for instance, represent more than one-half of the U.S. population yet account

Filibuster: *A formal method used in the Senate in order to stop a bill from coming to a vote. Senators can prevent a vote by making long speeches or by engaging in unlimited debate.*

Cloture: *A rule in the Senate that requires 60 senators to vote to stop a filibuster.*

for only 18 percent of the Senate vote.[23] Smaller states also have a disproportionate amount of influence by being able to bring the legislative process to a halt through a **filibuster**, where senators can engage in unlimited debate in order to prevent a bill from coming to the Senate floor for a vote. The only way to end a filibuster is for 60 senators to support a **cloture** vote, which means that senators representing the 21 least populated states (i.e., 11 percent of the U.S. population) can prevent legislation from moving forward to a vote. Senators representing the least populated 13 states (i.e., 4.5 percent of the U.S. population) can also prevent a constitutional amendment from passing the Senate.

THEORY AND PRACTICE

The Filibuster and the Nuclear Option

© ISTOCKPHOTO.COM/DIEGO CERVO

South Carolina senator Strom Thurmond delivered the longest filibuster in U.S. history when he spoke for over 24 hours against the 1957 Civil Rights Act. He began his speech on the Senate floor at 8:45 p.m. on August 28th, 1957 by saying the Civil Rights Act was a form of cruel and unusual punishment to southern states, and concluded his remarks the following evening at 9:12 p.m. California senator William Knowland later complained that Thurmond's speech was a form of cruel and unusual punishment to Senate supporters of the act who were required to remain in the chamber in order to maintain a quorum. The term *filibuster* derives from the Spanish term *filibustero* which loosely translates to "pirate" in the English language.

The purpose of the filibuster is to prevent the Senate majority from running roughshod over the Senate minority on important legislative matters. Senators in the minority party can prevent this from happening by making lengthy speeches in order to thwart those in the majority from proposing a particular bill. There is no specific Senate rule on the filibuster; there is simply no rule prohibiting senators from engaging in one. In 1806, the Senate dropped a provision from Roberts Rules permitting the majority to call for a vote with a majority vote.

Senate Rule 19 empowers senators with the "right to debate" where each senator has the right to speak without being interrupted by another senator without his or her consent. In 1917, the Senate adopted Rule 22, which permitted senators from ending debate with a two-thirds Senate vote. This provision was amended in 1975 to allow senators to stop a debate in a cloture vote with the approval of 60 senators.[24]

continued ➡

continued

The filibuster has become very controversial in the modern era because it is now used much more frequently than in the past. For example, the Senate engaged in only one cloture vote from 1927 to 1936, two cloture votes from 1951 to 1960, and 367 cloture votes from 2001 to 2010.[25]

Republican senators during the Bush administration were frustrated by the frequency by which Democratic senators were willing to use the filibuster to prevent confirmation votes on President George W. Bush's judicial appointees. Senator Bill Frist (R-TN), the Republican Senate Majority Leader at the time, caused a stir when he threatened to end the practice of filibusters in the Senate, a threat that came to be known as his "nuclear option." A bipartisan group of fourteen U.S. Senators then reached a compromise that limited the use of the filibuster against Bush appointees and maintained the viability of the filibuster in the Senate. In a strange twist of fate, it was Democratic senators who later threatened the "nuclear option" in retaliation to the frequency of Republican threats of filibusters in 2009–2010. Several Democratic senators grew frustrated by the threat of a Republican filibuster against some procedural matters relating to the Health Care Bill of 2010. Senator Tom Harkin (D-IA) is currently attempting to reform the filibuster practice in the Senate. Senator Harkin believes that the requirement of a 60-vote super-majority to pass legislation makes it too difficult to enact substantive legislation.

Do you believe the filibuster serves a positive role in American democracy?

Why or why not?

Although it does not affect the structure of the U.S. Senate, the *Baker v. Carr* (1962) decision was a landmark case credited with legally establishing the noted principle of "one person, one vote" by paving the way for the prohibition of malapportionment in state legislative districts.[26] The setting that catapulted this issue to the Supreme Court's doorstep came about in Tennessee. The disparity in the state house district population ranged from 2,340 citizens in one county to 42,298 citizens in another county.[27] Mr. Charles Baker, a voter along with other Tennessee voters, filed a lawsuit in federal district court against the state, naming Joe Carr, the state official in charge of elections, as the defendant. Mr. Baker claimed that malapportionment violated the equal protection clause of the Fourteenth

Amendment to the U.S. Constitution. The federal district court applied the precedent from *Colgrove v. Green* (1946) and dismissed the complaint finding that it was powerless to make a determination of the issue as it was a *political question*.

In the *Colgrove* case the Illinois legislature failed to reapportion districts based upon population growth as documented in prior census data. In the Supreme Court opinion, Justice Frankfurter invoked the Political Question Doctrine. The Political Question Doctrine conceptualizes the Court's perception that a political issue, even one with constitutional questions, is best resolved by the legislative branch. Thereafter, Baker appealed to the Supreme Court, which decided to rule on the case, noting that the Political Question Doctrine is "a tool of maintenance of government order," and should not be used as a constraint upon the judiciary to examine the legislature's actions. The plaintiffs in *Baker* also sorted through implementation issues surrounding the redistricting of legislative districts to ensure that the Court would not bog down in minutiae, as was the case when the Court desegregated public education in *Brown v. Board of Education* (1954).[28]

The most significant impact of the Court's ruling in favor of Baker was it established that states should possess population equality across legislative districts, thus protecting the concept of one person, one vote. The *Baker* decision also motivated a sweeping reapportionment movement across the nation that culminated in the redrawing of legislative districts in every state and greater representation for both urban areas and African Americans.

Should the U.S. Senate be forced to comply with the standard set in Baker v. Carr?

The Composition of Congress and the Expansion of Democratic Rights

▲ Former Lieutenant Dan Choi, an Iraq combat veteran who was discharged from the military because of his sexual orientation under the controversial "don't ask, don't tell" policy. This policy was lifted in September of 2011, thus enabling openly gay soldiers to now serve in the U.S. military.

© AP PHOTO/GARY KAZANJIAN, FILE

Congress did not always include members from all segments of our society. It was not until the Fifteenth Amendment (1870) that states were prohibited from denying voting rights on the basis of race, marking the first time the U.S. Constitution granted the right to vote upon any demographic group. There are now 44 African Americans serving in the 112th Congress (2011–2012), all of whom serve in the U.S. House of Representatives. The Nineteenth Amendment, ratified in 1920, made it unlawful for states to deny voting rights on the basis of gender. There are now 91 women serving in the 112th Congress, including 74 women in the House of Representatives and 17 women in the U.S. Senate, which is less than the 93 women who served in the 111th Congress (see Table 5.5). The first female elected to Congress was Representative Jeanette Rankin of Montana in 1917, and approximately 250 other women have since been sworn in as members of Congress. There are also 28 Hispanic or Latino members now serving in the 112th Congress (not including delegates), including two members in the U.S. Senate. The 112th Congress also consists of 13 Asian or Native

TABLE 5.5. Does the U.S. House of Representatives look like America?[30]

Ethnic and Gender Groupings	Numbers of House Members if Prorated to the Larger American Society	Numbers of Representatives in the 112th Congress (2011–2012)
Men	184	344
Women	226	91
African Americans	52	44
Hispanic	30	28

Hawaiian members, and one Native American member of Congress. The average age of members of the 112th Congress is 62.2 years of age, and approximately 400 of the 535 members of Congress cite either business or the law as their previous profession.[29]

Congress became a much more representative body during the twentieth century, evidenced by Congresswoman Nancy Pelosi's (D-CA) swearing-in as the first female Speaker of the House of Representatives in 2007, and the 2008 Democratic presidential contest between two leading U.S. senators, Hillary Clinton (D-NY) and Barack Obama (D-IL), a female and an African American senator respectively. Much of the progress on making the American Congress a more representative body came through congressional action over the last 50 years. And no piece of congressional legislation did more to promote the political rights of African Americans and non-English-speaking minorities than the Voting Rights Act of 1965, which is discussed at length in the previous chapter.

There have been some underlying tensions in the modern voting rights movement. Should voting rights be viewed as a positive or a negative right? Should government take affirmative steps to enhance the political position of historically disenfranchised groups (i.e., positive right), or should government merely prohibit local jurisdictions from obstructing voter access (i.e., negative right)? By the 1990s, voting rights issues had become more subtle, and the Supreme Court was asked to address the philosophical question inherent in racial gerrymandering, in such cases as *Shaw v. Reno* (1993), *Miller v. Johnson* (1995) and *Easley v. Cromartie* (2001). If it is illegal to draw congressional district lines "at the expense of one political group, can we justify manipulating it for their benefit?"[31] The upshot to these decisions is that while race or ethnicity may be considered when drawing congressional district lines, race cannot be the dominant factor in how congressional districts are drawn. Some also question whether political influence might be greater in ethnic communities if minority populations were dispersed more broadly across more congressional districts than for ethnic constituencies to be concentrated in fewer **majority-minority concentrated districts.**

Majority-minority District: *A congressional district that includes a majority of minority voters that increases the probability of electing a minority representative.*

THEORY AND PRACTICE

Are Female Legislators More Productive than Male Legislators?

Table 5.5 reveals that women are still vastly underrepresented in the U.S. Congress. While the majority of the U.S. population is female, women only comprise 17 percent of the membership in Congress. Would American political culture be different if gender roles in Congress were reversed? Most of the research on female legislators has been conducted on the state and local levels of government. Karen O'Connor integrated research on female legislators at the state and local level over the past 30 years and reached some interesting conclusions. From a public policy perspective, she found women are more likely than men to pursue a legislative agenda that includes "children, education, and health care." Women legislators with some seniority also sponsor more legislation and are more likely to have their bills enacted into law than their male counterparts. In terms of their legislative style, some studies find female legislators are also more likely to work in a collegial and collaborative fashion than male legislators.[32]

> Do you think our public policy would be different if 83 percent of the members of Congress were female rather than male?

The 2008 presidential race witnessed historic turnout rates in the African American community when 66.8 percent of voter-eligible African Americans cast ballots in overwhelming numbers for candidate Barack Obama. Advocates of the Voting Rights Act assert, however, that remnants of efforts to disenfranchise protected groups might still be with us today. In 2006, a Georgia voter identification law requiring voters to possess one of six preapproved photo identifications was approved by the Chief of the Department of Justice's Voting Rights section after Department of Justice staff members recommended blocking the law. There were 675,000 registered voters in Georgia, many of whom were African American, who did not possess a photo identification driver's license. The measure banned the previous practice of accepting birth certificates, Social Security cards, or utility bills as 1 of 17 types of identification previously accepted at polling stations in Georgia. The Voting Rights Act played a pivotal role in helping to make Congress a much more representative body in the twenty-first century.

CONGRESSIONAL DECISION MAKING

Have you ever wondered why your member of Congress votes the way he or she does? The field of congressional decision making currently has several long-standing theoretical models that seek to explain the voting behavior of members of Congress. Most research on congressional decision making can be divided according to "electoral" or "nonelectoral" explanations on congressional voting behavior.

The Electoral Connection

Perhaps the most influential text on the American Congress is David Mayhew's *Congress: The Electoral Connection*.[33] His portrayal of members as single-minded reelection seekers precipitated an avalanche of research on electorally beneficial activities. Members of Congress might be able to fortify the advantages of *incumbency* by engaging in three activities:

1. *"Advertising,"* where members attempt to gain an electoral advantage by increasing their name recognition through the franking privilege (i.e., free mailing) in Congress and in making frequent weekend trips to the district.
2. *"Credit-claiming,"* where members build goodwill with constituents by making use of a professional staff to work on behalf of voters. This activity also involves steering federal revenue to the district which enables candidates at election time to claim credit for securing federal dollars for local projects.
3. "Position taking," where members create the impression that they are taking action on a particular issue when in fact they are simply stating a supportive public position to a targeted audience. Members, for instance, might highlight their support of a federal college loan program when addressing college students, creating the false impression that they are taking action on the matter.

The institution itself is also structured to facilitate reelection concerns. The committee system creates specialized groups that empower members to gain expertise on issues that are electorally beneficial. A congresswoman from Kansas, for instance, could benefit politically from serving on the Agricultural Committee, given the importance of agriculture on the Kansas economy.

Should congressional elections use public financing in order to reduce the influence of private campaign contributions?

Congress and Home Style

Building on Mayhew's research, Richard Fenno (1978) argues that members of Congress have two goals: (1) to enact meaningful public policy (i.e., *Washington style*); and (2) reelection concerns (i.e., *Home style*).[34] He puts forward that legislators are as interested in policy goals as they are in reelection ambitions. Members of Congress thus need to balance their professional life in Washington against the need to maintain strong ties to the home district. Members spending too much time in Washington could pay the price on election day if voters come to believe they are out of touch with the concerns of the district. An example of this is when Senate Majority Leader Tom Daschle (D-SD) was defeated by John Thune in his reelection bid in 2004 in part because of the perception that Daschle was spending too much time in Washington and not enough time in his home state of South Dakota. Conversely, members of Congress will lose the respect of their Washington colleagues if they spend an inordinate amount of time engaging in district political matters rather than engaging in the important policy matters in Washington. Members of Congress thus need to balance their "Washington style" against their "Home style" because too much emphasis placed in one area might hurt them in the other.

Fenno, like Mayhew, views the electoral goal as the primary objective of most members of Congress. Because the electoral goal is critical, members tend to alter their behavior in a manner that best ingratiates them to their constituency. This is accomplished through "resource allocation, presentation of self, and their explanation of Washington activities." Fenno finds that legislators routinely place distance between themselves and other legislators, and are inclined to campaign as outsiders against the Washington establishment. This occurrence might reveal why the institution of Congress traditionally suffers from low public approval ratings while individual members are frequently held in high regard by their respective constituencies.

Is it more important for a member of Congress to focus on public policy (Washington style) or constituent casework (Home style)?

The Electoral Connection and Partisan Gerrymandering

The attention paid to the goal of reelection has also caused some to focus on the manner by which congressional districts are drawn by state legislatures. **Partisan gerrymandering** refers to the state legislative practice of drawing congressional districts to benefit one political party over the other. The redistricting of congressional districts within states occurs every 10 years following the constitutionally mandated national census. The methods employed in partisan gerrymandering include "cracking" (dividing) a legislative district to dilute the influence of one party, or "packing" a legislative

Partisan Gerrymandering: *The act of dividing congressional districts to give one political party an unfair advantage in congressional elections.*

district in order to strengthen the influence of a particular party. The state of Texas, for example, redrew their congressional district in a manner that benefited the Republican Party in 2003. Democrats held 17 of the 32 congressional districts in Texas before the 2003 redistricting plan. After the redistricting plan, Republicans in Texas went on to win 21 of the 32 congressional districts in the 2004 election. The congressional redistricting process became so overtly political that Texas Democrats in the state legislature fled to Oklahoma in order to prevent Texas Republicans from having a legislative **quorum** on the vote. The Texas Democrats eventually returned to the state and were defeated in their attempt to stop the controversial redistricting plan.

CourseReader ASSIGNMENT

Log in to **www.cengagebrain.com** and open CourseReader to access the reading:

Home Style **by Richard Fenno.**

In this article Richard Fenno distinguishes between the behavior of members of Congress in Washington (e.g. Washington style) and in their home districts (e.g. home style). He points out that members of Congress are interested in getting reelected and in making good public policy. Members thus need to balance time between Washington and home because those who spend too much time in Washington will become vulnerable at home, and members who spend too much time with constituents will not gain the respect of peers in Washington.

- *Do you think it is more important for members of Congress to sponsor legislation or to do constituent casework?*

Quorum: *A legislative rule that requires a minimum number of legislators to be present in order for a bill to be voted on.*

It is in part because of these practices that the average margin of victory for incumbents was 40 percentage points in 2004 and is why members of Congress enjoyed a 98.8 percent reelection rate in 2002 and 2004, and a 96 percent reelection rate in 2008. In *Vieth v. Jubelirer* (2004), the Supreme Court ruled that the practice of partisan gerrymandering is constitutional, and the practice continues in most state legislatures. Some states, however, such as the state of Iowa, have made great strides in taking partisan politics out of the congressional redistricting process and might serve as a model for the future.

Other Explanations of Congressional Voting Behavior

Others contend that congressional voting behavior is instead primarily motivated by "internal" considerations, such as the influence of congressional leaders, the congressional committee system, or a member's personal ideology. Mann and Ornstein's (2006) seminal work highlights how congressional rules and party leaders impact the congressional agenda and the political climate in Congress.[38] Other studies highlight the extent to which members

© 1812, GILBERT STUART, PUBLIC DOMAIN

▲ The term "gerrymander" stems from this Gilbert Stuart cartoon from 1812 of a Massachusetts electoral district twisted beyond all reason. Stuart thought the shape of the district resembled a salamander, but his friend who showed him the original map called it a "Gerry-mander" after then Massachusetts Governor Elbridge Gerry approved rearranging legislative districts for partisan advantage.

There are now approximately 2.2 million people (i.e., 724 per 100,000) behind bars in the United States. The United States has more people in its prisons than any other country in the world. China, whose population is more than three times that of the United States, currently has the second largest prison population, with approximately 1.5 million people imprisoned.[35] Today 48 American states prohibit prisoners from voting in elections (only Maine and Vermont allow inmates to vote), and 11 states in some form or fashion deny voting rights to ex-convicts who have reintegrated back into society. Some of these states permanently deny voting to those convicted of certain types of crimes, others require an appeals process (many quite cumbersome) before restoring voting rights, and some place a permanent voting ban on all ex-felons.[36]

The process for purging state voting rolls to ensure ex-felons are not eligible to vote was a matter of great controversy in the 2000 presidential election between George W. Bush and Al Gore. The state of Florida hired out a private company from Texas to purge the voting rolls. This company erroneously purged approximately 8,000 names, mainly from African American strongholds (90 percent of African American Floridians voted for Gore) in the days leading up to the 2000 election. These 8,000 Florida residents were wrongfully prohibited from voting in the 2000 election. This was particularly controversial because the 2000 presidential election was ultimately decided in the state of Florida, which George W. Bush won by 537 votes, and because the brother of George W. Bush was the Florida governor at the time.

Nicholas Thompson's article entitled "Locking Up the Vote" reveals that there are now approximately 1 million ex-felons who have rejoined American society and are ineligible to vote by state law. The article further points out that nationally "one out of seven adult black men will never again get to vote. In Alabama, which permanently denies felons the right to vote, about one out of three adult black men is barred for life."[37] In *Farrakhan v. Gregoire* (2010), the U.S. Court of Appeals for the Ninth Circuit ruled that Washington State's law banning ex-felons from voting violates the Voting Rights Act because it has the effect of disproportionally

continued ▶

disenfranchising African American voters. The Ninth Circuit found that because of racial discrimination in the state's criminal justice system, denying voter access to ex-felons disproportionately impacts the state's African American voters.

Do you believe ex-felons should be forever stripped of their voting rights or should ex-felons be permitted to vote upon their release from prison?

of Congress are influenced by each other. Some members engage in institutional "**cue-taking**" and vote with the herd when an issue is perceived to be noncontroversial. Members are most likely to take political cues from congressional leaders in the House and Senate and colleagues from their state delegation. The **Speaker of the House**, the **majority** and **minority leaders**, and the Republican and Democratic **Whips** play an especially important role in influencing members on how to vote in the House of Representatives. The **Senate Majority Leader** and the **Senate Minority Leader** also have an inordinate amount of influence on the voting behavior of senators.

Some legislators also engage in **logrolling**, where members make agreements with each other to trade their vote on a particular bill in exchange for a member's pledge to support or oppose an upcoming bill. If, however, an issue is surrounded by controversy, legislators tend to isolate the principal actors in their "perceptual field of forces," namely their constituency, political party, relevant political action committees (PACs), and vote with the majority opinion of this group.

Others contend that congressional voting behavior is motivated by the committee assignments of individual members of Congress. Congress institutionalized the committee system in 1816, and a number of committees have been created since then. There are four distinct types of committees in Congress, including:

1. *Standing committees:* the Committees that "stand" from one Congress to the next. These committees receive proposed legislation from members. The U.S. House of Representatives is organized around 20 standing committees. The U.S. Senate currently has 16 standing committees (see Table 5.6).
2. *Conference committees:* A committee of members of the House and Senate formed to merge differences between Senate and House versions of the same bill.

Do you agree with the Supreme Court's decision in Vieth v. Jubelirer (2004)? Why or why not?

Cue-taking: *Taking a political cue from a respected colleague or party leader when determining how to vote on a particular bill.*

Speaker of the House: *The presiding officer of the House of Representatives. The Speaker is the highest-ranking official in the House of Representative. He or she is third in line of succession to the presidency, and is responsible for establishing the political agenda of the body.*

House Majority Leader: *The second-most important person in the House of Representatives. The majority leader assists the speaker in establishing the political agenda in the House.*

House Minority Leader: *The elected leader of the party with minority status in the House of Representatives.*

Whip: *Party leaders who work closely with rank-and-file members to ensure individual members vote in accordance with the wishes of party leaders.*

Senate Majority Leader: *The elected leader of the majority party in the U.S. Senate. The majority leader is responsible for setting the agenda in the U.S. Senate and plays a role in selecting committee assignments.*

Senate Minority Leader: *The elected leader of the minority party in the U.S. Senate.*

Logrolling: *Trading influence or votes among legislators to achieve passage of projects that are of interest to one another.*

What factors would influence your voting behavior if you were a member of Congress?

3. *Joint committees:* Include members of both the House and Senate. Joint committees are typically formed to investigate a particular matter or concern.

4. *Select committees:* Special committee in each house created to investigate a particular matter.

Senate committees are generally less significant than House committees in the extent to which they dominate a legislator's role in that body. The smaller, more elite nature of the Senate extends greater stature on senators and more flexibility to vote in accordance with their personal belief systems. There is little question, however, that a member's committee assignments play a significant role in why members of Congress vote the way they do.

Still others point to a member's political *ideology* as explaining why members of Congress vote the way they do. Most issues by their very nature can be viewed through a liberal or conservative prism. The congruity between a legislator's ideology and the partisan leaning of a legislator's constituency makes it difficult to extrapolate the extent to which the constituency influences a legislator's belief system.

TABLE 5.6. Committees in the 112th Congress

House of Representatives	Senate
Agriculture	Agriculture, Nutrition, and Forestry
Appropriations	Appropriations
Armed Services	Armed Services
Budget	Banking, Housing, and Urban Affairs
Education and Labor	Budget
Energy and Commerce	Commerce, Science, and Transportation
Financial Services	Energy and Natural Resources
Foreign Affairs	Environment and Public Works
Homeland Security	Finance
House Administration	Foreign Relations
Judiciary	Health, Education, Labor, and Pensions
Natural Resources	Homeland Security
Oversight and Government Reform	Judiciary
Rules	Rules and Administration
Science and Technology	Small Business and Entrepreneurship
Small Business	Veterans' Affairs
Standards of Officials Conduct	
Transportation	
Veterans' Affairs	
Ways and Means	

How a Bill Becomes a Law

There are roughly 14,000 bills proposed in the modern two-year legislative sessions. However, the overwhelming majority of these bills will never make it to a full vote on the floor of the House or Senate.[39] Only 442 of these 14,000 bills (3.3 percent) were actually signed into law in the previous election cycle.[40] Many of these enacted bills were merely symbolic in nature. For instance, 144 of the 442 pieces of recently enacted legislation (32 percent) simply renamed federal buildings.[41] The number of bills enacted into law has sharply dropped in the modern era in large part because of the rise in **omnibus legislation**, where dozens of smaller bills are collapsed into one very large bill.

The process by which a congressional bill becomes a law is a long and difficult road (see Figure 5.1). A successful bill must secure a majority vote in the House of Representatives and the Senate before it is signed into law by the president. Once introduced by a member of Congress, a bill is first assigned to an appropriate congressional committee by either the Speaker of the House or the Senate Majority Leader. The committee chair will then assign the bill to the appropriate subcommittee where public hearings are held in order to allow for expert testimony in either favor or opposition to the bill.[42] Committee members can then "mark up" or alter the original bill by receiving a majority committee vote to amend the bill. Committees will then vote on whether to report the bill to the full chamber. Once a bill is approved at the committee level it is sent on to the Rules Committee. The Rules Committee then establishes the rules guiding the floor debate in each chamber. The Rules Committee plays an important role in that they can vote to prohibit motions to amend the bill during the full session on the floor of each chamber. If the House and Senate vote on different versions of the same bill, a conference committee of House and Senate members convenes to iron out discrepancies in the bills.

Once the bill passes the House and the Senate it is forwarded to the executive branch, where the president can do one of three things including: (1) sign the bill into law; (2) veto the bill, thus returning it to Congress where the veto could potentially be overridden with a two-third **super-majority vote** in both chambers; or (3) the president can simply ignore the bill. If the president takes no action on the bill it will become law within 10 days if Congress remains in session. If no action is taken by the president and Congress adjourns within this 10-day period, the bill will be defeated by a **pocket veto**.

Omnibus Legislation: *A large bill that contains several smaller bills.*

Super-Majority Vote: *A congressional vote requiring more than a simple majority vote. The Constitution requires a two-thirds super-majority vote in Congress in five instances: (1) when overriding a presidential veto; (2) when impeaching federal officials; (3) on Senate treaty ratification votes; (4) when removing fellow members for misconduct; and (5) when proposing constitutional amendments.*

Pocket Veto: *An indirect presidential veto occurs when a president takes no action on a bill for 10 days and Congress has adjourned.*

Congressional Ethics

We learned in Chapter 2 that political ethics was the most important value in ancient political thought. Socrates, Plato, and Aristotle stressed the need to remain vigilant in maintaining public trust in government. It is therefore important to point out the

FIGURE 5.1. How a Bill Becomes a Law

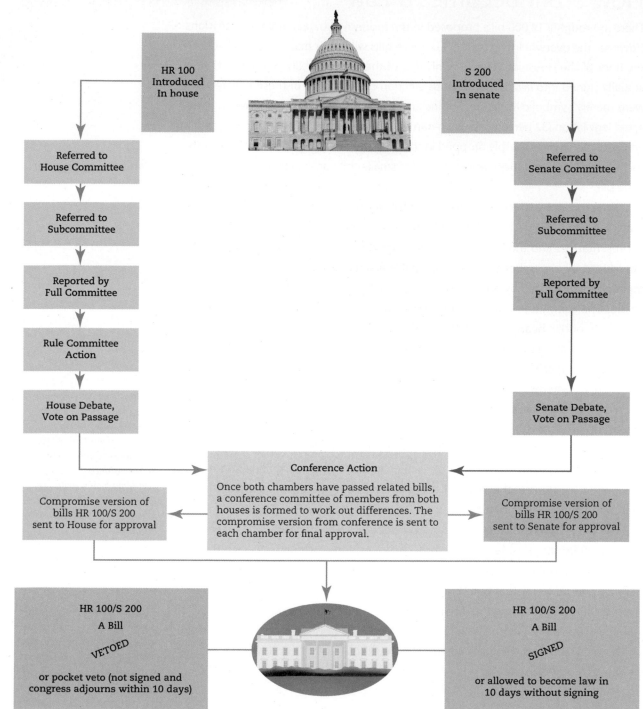

HR 100
Introduced
In house

S 200
Introduced
In senate

Referred to
House Committee

Referred to
Senate Committee

Referred to
Subcommittee

Referred to
Subcommittee

Reported by
Full Committee

Reported by
Full Committee

Rule Committee
Action

House Debate,
Vote on Passage

Senate Debate,
Vote on Passage

Conference Action

Once both chambers have passed related bills, a conference committee of members from both houses is formed to work out differences. The compromise version from conference is sent to each chamber for final approval.

Compromise version of
bills HR 100/S 200
sent to House for approval

Compromise version of
bills HR 100/S 200
sent to Senate for approval

HR 100/S 200

A Bill

VETOED

or pocket veto (not signed and
congress adjourns within 10 days)

HR 100/S 200

A Bill

SIGNED

or allowed to become law in
10 days without signing

Congress and the Affordable Health Care Act of 2010:
What Does it Mean for College-Age Students?

In 2010, there were approximately 46 million Americans without health care. Over 30 percent of those without health insurance were in the 18 to 29-year-old age bracket, a bracket that includes only 17 percent of the U.S. population. So why do so many young people lack health insurance? Many recent college graduates were required to leave their parents' insurance policies or "age off" of other Children Health Insurance Programs.[43] Compounding the problem is the fact that unemployment rates have skyrocketed in the youth demographic, now at 17.2 percent in the 20 to 24–year-old age group. A study in 2009 found that 76 percent of the uninsured youth did not get needed medical treatment and 46 percent of uninsured youth with a chronic health issue claimed their condition worsened because of an inability to afford health costs.[44] In order to address this problem and others, Congress enacted the "Affordable Care Act of 2010," sometimes dubbed "Obama care" by critics. This is the most sweeping piece of health care legislation since Congress enacted Medicare and Medicaid in 1965.

Lyndon B. Johnson signed Medicare and Medicaid into law on July 31, 1965, at a signing ceremony at the Truman Library in Missouri, a site selected to pay tribute to President Truman's efforts to bring about universal health care. Medicare was first drafted in the House Ways and Means Committee by then Chairman Wilbur Mills (D-AR) and primarily focused on providing health care to retirees.[45] Medicare paralleled the Social Security system in that a trust fund was established and funded through employer/employee deductions. Once retired, Medicare recipients receive coverage for hospital stays, other health care, and nursing-home reimbursements. The third part of Medicare was entitled "Medicaid," a federal-state program that provides access to care to the impoverished and disabled. Medicare and Medicaid together then provide access to care to the elderly and poor.

The Affordable Care Act of 2010 endured a bruising battle in Congress before ultimately passing in the House by a razor-slim margin of 219 to 212, with all Republicans and 34 Democrats voting against it. Recognizing that the success of his presidency was on the line, President Obama invoked Abraham Lincoln in a speech to House Democrats the day before the vote. In what might be his most memorable speech

continued

in his first few years of office, Obama called on House Democrats to have the courage of their convictions and twice recited Lincoln's line that "I am not bound to win, but I am bound to be true."

The passage of the Affordable Care Act of 2010 means that approximately 32 million new people will receive health insurance over the next 10 years, including most young adults. The act most specifically targets young Americans by: (1) requiring insurance carriers to expand dependant coverage until the dependant is 26 years of age. This became effective in September 2010 and expanded coverage for 1.2 million young adults; (2) banning the current practice of placing lifetime limits on how much insurance companies will pay for any individual throughout their life, effective 2014; (3) expanding Medicaid to adults at 133 percent of the federal poverty level. This is likely to have the greatest impact on the young. More than half of the uninsured youth live in families that earn less than 133 percent of the poverty level.[46] One of the more controversial aspects of the act is it requires those able to buy health insurance to do so. It also requires each state to establish health care exchanges where individuals and small businesses can purchase insurance more efficiently by purchasing insurance in bulk. The act also prohibits insurance companies from discriminating against those with preexisting conditions.

Would you have voted for the Affordable Care Act if you were a Member of Congress in 2010?

Why or why not?

instances when this trust has been violated in order to ensure that the American Congress is able to recapture its reputation as one of the most well-respected legislative assemblies in the world. Of serious concern is the fact that congressional job approval rates are currently at historic lows with only 18 percent of Americans voicing approval of Congress.[47] What's worse, half of the public now believes that *most* members of Congress are corrupt.[48] This is not exactly what James Madison had in mind when he integrated the theories of Aristotle, Montesquieu, and Locke into the design of our representative government. Corruption is now a highly salient political issue with 55 percent of voters professing it was either the "most important" or a "very important" issue when they went to the polls in recent elections.[49]

The public distrust of Congress comes on the heels of a steady accumulation of congressional corruption cases over the past 30 years. These cases include the investigation of Sen. Ted Stevens (R-AK), Rep. William Jefferson (D-LA), the recent conviction of congressional lobbyist Jack Abramoff, the Duke Cunningham (R-CA) bribery case in 2005, James Traficant's (D-OH) expulsion in 2002, Speaker Newt Gingrich's (R-GA) financial impropriety case in 1997, the House Banking scandal in 1992, the Keating Five scandal in 1989, the resignation of Speaker Jim Wright (D-TX) in 1987, the Abscam scandal in 1980, and Koreagate in 1976 to name but a few.

Who Checks Bad Behavior in Congress?

The delegates at the Constitutional Convention empowered Congress with the authority to impeach and remove from office executive officers and federal judges. The Framers borrowed the concept of impeachment from the British in order to curb abuses of power in the executive and judicial branches of government. But who checks abuses of power in Congress? The Framers authorized Congress to establish and impose its *own* ethical standards. Article I, Section 5 of the Constitution states "each house shall be the judge of the elections, returns and qualifications of its own members" and may "punish its members for disorderly behavior, and, with the concurrence of two thirds, expel a member." Congressional sanctions of unprincipled members come in one of three forms:

1. A written reprimand from the Ethics Committee.
2. A censure, where members are publicly rebuked on the floor of Congress.
3. Congressional expulsion.[50]

Only two members of Congress have been expelled over the last 140 years—Rep. Traficant (D-OH) in 2002 and Rep. Myers (D-PA) in 1980. The uncommonness of expulsions leads one to question whether asking Congress to impose its own ethical standards is equivalent to asking the fox to guard the proverbial henhouse.

In fairness, political corruption in Congress is sometimes difficult to discern, not to mention prove, in part because there can be a fine line between successful legislative behavior and unethical conduct. Members of Congress are now spending a significant amount of time raising campaign funds and assisting constituents through constituent **casework**, leaving less time for policy enactment and oversight responsibilities.

Casework: *When members of Congress use their staff or intervene personally in order to do favors for constituents.*

The ethical boundaries surrounding these activities are vaguely defined, while the necessity of mastering these political skills is critical to the success of modern legislators. Cases of political corruption are sometimes shadowy because there is frequently no bright line as to when a legislator's conduct in constituent case work and fundraising takes them through the beaded curtain of political corruption. Members of Congress, after all, have conflicting responsibilities between advancing the public's interest while advocating for the private interests of constituents.

Sunshine Laws: *Laws that require public agencies to open meetings up to the public and to make public information available to the citizens.*

Some contend that institutional **sunshine laws** and tougher campaign finance disclosure rules might simply reveal indiscretions that went largely unnoticed in gone by eras.

There is perhaps an association between political corruption and the increased devotion to constituent casework and electoral goals. It might be helpful therefore to distinguish between personal-gain types of corruption and career-advancing forms of corruption. A personal gain variety of corruption typically involves the violation of the existing bribery standard. A career-advancing form of corruption, on the other hand, highlights how ethical conflicts can emerge in the course of raising campaign revenue and in the delivery of constituent services, the standard fare in the daily activities of today's legislators. These dimensions can then combine to give rise to two types of congressional corruption, illuminated through brief descriptions of the Duke Cunningham Scandal and the Keating Five scandal. It is also important to note that the vast majority of our members of Congress are highly principled and ethical public servants.

Personal Gain Corruption: The Duke Cunningham Scandal

Randall "Duke" Cunningham was sentenced to eight years and four months in prison after pleading guilty to one count of bribery and one count of tax evasion in November 2005. The scope of legislative malfeasance in the Cunningham case is unparalleled in the sordid history of congressional corruption. Cunningham was convicted of accepting $2.4 million in bribes from two defense contractors in exchange for securing $240 million worth of government contracts. What is most astounding is the degree to which the illegal activity unfolded in plain view. The investigation was initiated after newspaper reporters wondered how Congressman Cunningham was able to afford a mansion, a yacht, and a Rolls Royce on a congressional salary.

Cunningham had a distinguished career as a naval fighter pilot and openly boasted in campaigns that many of his flying maneuvers were depicted by Tom Cruise in the 1986 film *Top Gun*. His proficiencies in military affairs landed him a prestigious committee assignment on the Defense Appropriation Subcommittee, which provides oversight on military funding allotments. This committee assignment made him a natural target of defense industry lobbyists. Cunningham accepted bribes from two defense contractors named Brent Wilkes and Mitchell Wade. Cunningham intervened with the Pentagon in order to secure government contracts to convert government documents into digital form for Wilkes and Wade. The most notable example is a $9.7 million contract to scan "engineering drawings from the 1870s and images of boats from the 1910s" in the Panama Canal Zone even though Pentagon procurement officers requested the funds be used for more pressing needs at the Army's Missile Command.[51] The Assistant Undersecretary of Defense Louis Kratz later disclosed he never encountered anything close to the level of political pressure exerted by Cunningham to go forward on the superfluous project.[52] It was later revealed that Cunningham even prepared a "bribe memo" on congressional stationary that detailed how much he expected to be paid for each government contract **earmarked** to one of the two defense contractors. The Cunningham scandal is classified as personal-gain form of corruption because it involved a clear violation of existing bribery standards.

Corruption motivated by career advancement, on the other hand, is vaguely defined and rarely enforced. The bribery standard has never been applied to campaign contributions and fund-raising activities. The Keating Five case, in fact, represents the first time members of Congress were sanctioned for going too far in advancing the interests of private citizens. The Keating Five case highlights how ethical conflicts can emerge in the course of raising campaign revenue and in the delivery of constituent services.

Career-Advancing Corruption: The Keating Five Scandal

The Keating Five scandal made headlines during the 2008 presidential election because of Sen. John McCain's involvement in the controversy years before. Parallels have also been made between this scandal and the **2008 bailout of America's financial industry**.

The Keating Five scandal was linked directly to the Savings and Loan debacle of the late 1980s. The name itself is derived from Charles H. Keating Jr., a Phoenix construction company owner and anti-pornography advocate, who went on to become the poster child for the corrupt practices that resulted in the $300 billion taxpayer bailout of mismanaged banks. This case represents the most expensive political scandal in American history. The saga behind the Keating Five scandal began when Keating made an application to purchase the Lincoln Savings and Loan in Irvine, California. Lincoln had a strong reputation for sound fiscal administration and boasted the lowest delinquent mortgage rates in California while demonstrating a "commitment to mortgage-deprived areas."[53] The savings and loan industry was substantially deregulated during the Reagan era in the 1980s. Keating early on played a leading role in lobbying against regulations that barred thrifts from making commercial investments. He also raised regulatory eyebrows by investing Lincoln's federally insured funds into risky commercial investments, including the purchase of "junk" bonds from controversial financier Michael Milken.

The plot thickened when the San Francisco branch of the Federal Home Loan Bank (FHLB) initiated a standard audit of Keating's Lincoln Savings. It was in this context that Keating solicited assistance from his friends in the U.S. Senate. He was rightfully concerned that auditors might recommend seizing Lincoln for irregular lending practices of federally insured funds. Keating first contacted Sen. Dennis Deconcini (D-AZ), his strongest ally in Washington. An infamous meeting was then arranged between Senators Deconcini (D-AZ), Alan Cranston (D-CA), John Glenn (D-OH), John McCain (R-AZ), Donald Riegle (D-MI), later known as the Keating Five, and federal bank regulators.

The meeting with the federal bank regulators lasted a little over two hours. The senators interrogated the regulators with great vigor on Keating's behalf. One of the federal regulators, William Black, later commented on how he felt intimidated in the meeting and remarked, "You really did have one-twentieth of the Senate in one room, called by one guy, who was the biggest crook in the S&L debacle.[54] The tables were quickly turned, however, when the bank examiners defiantly stated they were about to issue a criminal referral against Keating for violating lending laws at Lincoln. The senators were visibly shaken by the news, and the meeting ended shortly thereafter.

Did the senators violate federal law or Senate ethics with this meeting? It was not clear. The Senate Ethics Committee investigated the matter for 14 months, which included 26 days of televised hearings on C-SPAN. Over 25 million Americans tuned in to hear the committee's verdict. No member of Congress throughout history had to this point been reprimanded for intervening on behalf of a constituent. The findings of the Ethics Committee did little in the way of clarifying the matter. The committee ultimately determined that four of the senators, namely Deconcini, McCain, Riegle, and Glenn, were guilty of expressing poor judgment for interfering with a federal audit, but concluded that punishments were not in order for the four because it would be "setting the standard after the fact."[55] Senator Alan Cranston received the harshest treatment and was censured by the Senate because he approached bank regulators six more times after learning that the Board was issuing a criminal referral against Keating. Cranston also received almost $1 million from Keating over a two-year period, with the money going primarily to voter registration groups directed by Cranston's son.

The case highlights the tendency of the Ethics Committee to "individualize" institutional corruption in an effort to "exonerate" the institution.[56] Conversely, accused members typically justify misconduct by "institutionalizing" their behavior, discounting the importance of accusations by claiming other members engage in similar activities. Senator Cranston, for instance, in his defiant censure speech in front of 95 senators stated that "my behavior did not violate established norms. . . . Here, but for the grace of God stands you."[57]

Recent cases reveal how "important" constituents are able to procure services from members as they simultaneously contribute to campaigns, organize fund-raising venues, sponsor travel junkets, funnel large sums of money into member-affiliated nonprofit organizations, and hire congressional spouses and family members. The Duke Cunningham case also showcased the proclivity of members to curry favor by earmarking projects to their clients. We need to be vigilant against political corruption because it undermines important democratic principles by fostering public cynicism and the erosion of public trust in government. It is therefore our responsibility to remain active in government in order to ensure that government promotes the public good. The good news is that these congressional scandals have led to significant reforms in ethics in Congress. The Honest Leadership and Open Government Act of 2007, for instance, brought greater transparency to both the lobbying industry and the earmarking process, and bans members of Congress from participating in lobbyist-sponsored travel junkets. In 2008 Congress also created the Office of Congressional Ethics (OCE) to provide independent oversight over the ethical behavior of members of Congress.

SUMMARY

© RENA SCHILD/SHUTTERSTOCK.COM

The American Congress was addressed in the first Article of the U.S. Constitution because the Framers believed it to be the most important branch of our government. This chapter examined the original intent of the Framers in creating our legislative branch. It also discussed Congress's evolution into one of the most representative legislative bodies in the free world. The second half of the chapter revealed the motivations behind congressional behavior, and the need for Congress to remain vigilant in the realm of congressional ethics. In the next chapter we will address important themes relating to a second branch of American government: The American presidency. This chapter will concentrate on the creation of the presidency at the Constitutional Convention, the presidential selection process, presidential powers, and the character of modern presidents.

KEY TERMS

2008 Bailout of financial industry p. 159

Anti-Federalists p. 130

Casework p. 157

Checks and balances p. 130

Cloture p. 142

Cue-taking p. 151

Earmarks p. 159

Federalist system p. 129

Filibuster p. 142

Gridlock p. 141

6

THE AMERICAN PRESIDENCY

▲ U.S. President Barack Obama walks on the red carpet while inspecting the guard of honor during a ceremonial reception at Rashtrapati Bhavan in New Delhi, India, on November 8, 2010. On the trip, President Obama was accompanied by over 200 U.S. corporate leaders interested in expanding U.S. exports to Asian markets. Presidential powers are particularly strong in the realm of foreign affairs.

INTRODUCTION: THE AMERICAN PRESIDENCY

The 2008 presidential election between Barack Obama and John McCain was one of the most electrifying presidential elections in recent history. It was historic in that President Barack Obama became the first African American elected president of the United States, a mere 43 years after the Voting Rights Act (1965) made it illegal for states to disenfranchise African American voters. It was also historic because Senator Hillary Clinton (D-NY) became the first major female presidential candidate before losing an astonishingly close race to Obama in the 2008 Democratic primary. The Obama campaign transformed the way presidential campaigns are conducted by aggressively using technology to raise campaign funds and to reach young voters. It is in part because of this that he was able to garner 66 percent of the 18- to 29-year-old vote, and raise $745 million, shattering previous presidential fund-raising records.[1] Table 6.1 reveals that 132 million voters participated in the election, and voter turnout as a percentage was higher than it had been since the 1968 presidential election.

This chapter highlights five major themes associated with the American presidency, including: (1) the creation of the American presidency; (2) presidential qualifications; (3) the presidential selection process; (4) presidential powers; and (5) presidential–congressional relations in the realm of foreign affairs.

THE CREATION OF THE AMERICAN PRESIDENCY

When the Articles of Confederation (1781–1787) was formed most Americans equated executive leadership with the tyranny associated with Britain's King George III, the British monarch at the time. Reflecting the prevailing disdain for strong executive leadership, the Articles made no stipulation for an executive branch, and the

Questions to Consider Before Reading this Chapter

1. Why did the Founding Fathers prefer an individual executive rather than an executive council?

2. Should foreign-born American citizens be permitted to serve as president?

3. Does the American president possess imperial powers?

4. How is the electoral college system that selected Barack Obama different from the electoral college system that selected George Washington?

5. Why were young voters such a major force in the 2008 presidential election?

6. Which principles should be included in a future American foreign policy doctrine?

NAVEEN JORA / INDIA TODAY GROUP / GETTY IMAGES.

TABLE 6.1. National Voter Turnout in Presidential Elections: 1960–2008[2]

Year	Candidates	Total Vote	Turnout of Voting as a percentage (percentage includes those ineligible to vote because of incarceration and other reasons)
2008	Obama vs. McCain	132,618,580	56.8
2004	Bush vs. Kerry	122,294,978	55.3
2000	Bush vs. Gore	105,586,274	51.3
1996	Clinton vs. Dole vs. Perot	96,456,345	49.1
1992	Clinton vs. Bush vs. Perot	104,405,155	55.1
1988	Bush vs. Dukakis	91,594,693	50.1
1984	Reagan vs. Mondale	92,652,680	53.1
1980	Reagan vs. Carter	86,515,221	52.6
1976	Carter vs. Ford	81,555,789	53.6
1972	Nixon vs. McGovern	77,718,554	55.2
1968	Nixon vs. Humphrey vs. Wallace	73,211,875	60.8

leaders of Congress were not given any substantive executive powers. It was also during this period that the United States was in the throes of fighting the Revolutionary War with Britain. Some blamed the lack of executive leadership for the difficulty in getting needed provisions to the troops on the battlefield during the Revolutionary War. This coupled with the crisis caused by Shays's Rebellion (see Chapter 4) caused many of the American Framers to conclude the system was not a workable form of government.

Another perceived weakness of the Articles of Confederation was that it did not project a unified voice to foreign nations. Some of the Framers complained that the states were conducting 13 separate and sometimes conflicting foreign policies. Alexander Hamilton, for example, wrote in 1782 "There is something . . . diminutive and contemptible in the prospect of a number of petty states, with the appearance only of union, jarring, jealous and perverse, without any determined direction, fluctuating and unhappy at home, weak and insignificant by their dissensions in the eyes of other nations."[3]

Many of the delegates at the Constitutional Convention turned ambivalent about executive leadership after witnessing the ineptitude associated with the Articles of Confederation. It is because of this that many of the most controversial issues at the Convention revolved around the creation of the American presidency. The three most contentious issues were: (1) whether the executive branch should consist of an individual executive or an executive council; (2) the presidential selection process; and (3) the scope of presidential powers. By the time the Constitutional Convention was called in 1787 the delegates were largely divided between those who were fearful of creating a budding monarchy and those who believed a strong executive was necessary to keep the fledgling nation intact.[4] Their distrust of executive leadership also ran alongside a hidden desire to make George Washington king.

Individual Executive or Executive Council?

James Madison, the principal author of the U.S. Constitution, expressed his uncertainty about the formation of the executive branch in a letter to fellow Virginia delegate Edmund Randolph. Madison revealed that he had yet to form his own opinion on either "the manner in which the executive ought to be constituted or of the authorities with which it ought to be clothed."[5] In other words, Madison was uncertain as to whether the executive branch should take the form of an individual executive or an executive council and was unsure of the types of powers the office should be granted. The chief problem for Madison was that neither political theorists nor history provided any desirable executive models from which to draw. Blackstone's influential *Commentaries on the Laws of England (1765–1769)*, which advocated for supreme executive powers, was largely viewed with contempt by most delegates at the Convention. Alexander Hamilton drew comparisons between the powers of the presidency and the powers of New York's governor in *Federalist Paper No. 69*. This comparison drew the ire of New York governor George Clinton, a leading opponent of both strong executive powers and the U.S. Constitution during the ratification process.

The initial discussion on the executive branch was also made awkward by the fact that George Washington served as the chair of the Constitutional Convention. It was clear to almost everyone that Washington would serve a leading role in the first administration. Debate on the presidency was initially stifled because delegates went to great lengths to avoid offending the revered Washington. Benjamin Franklin brought a needed perspective to the discussion by stating, "[T]he first man at the helm will be a good one," but what after?[6]

The Virginia Plan called for an executive branch, but was silent on whether the executive should take the form of an individual or council. The delegate who had the greatest influence on the design of the executive office was James Wilson from Carlisle, Pennsylvania. Wilson argued for a strong single executive because he believed a single executive would bring the "most energy, dispatch, and responsibility to the office." Virginia delegates George Mason and Edmund Randolph argued against a single executive believing the office would degenerate into a monarchy.[7] Delegates were thus largely split on how the office should be structured and in the amount of power the office should be granted. Connecticut delegate Roger Sherman advocated for a weak executive council that would be selected by Congress and granted the mere authority to execute the will of Congress. New York delegate Alexander Hamilton, on the other hand, made a five-hour speech at the Convention on June 18, 1787, where he called for a strong individual executive.

Hamilton advocated for a life term and extraordinary executive powers.[8] He called for a British-style government and argued the president should be equipped with war powers, appointment powers, an absolute veto, and executive pardon powers. It is debatable as to whether Hamilton truly advocated imperial executive powers or whether his speech was an attempt to shift the parameters of the debate away from the weak presidential models offered by the Virginia and New Jersey plans. In an attempt to break the impasse, James Madison proposed suspending the debate on whether the office should consist of an individual executive or an executive council in order to first clarify the powers of the office. He reasoned delegates might be in a better position to advocate for either an individual executive or an executive council once the body came to an agreement on the purpose of the office. The Framers then settled on an individual executive after deciding that the executive should play a critical role in foreign affairs. An individual executive was preferred because it was believed a council might bog down in debate and appear irresolute to foreign nations. Alexander Hamilton argued in *Federalist Paper No. 70* that a single executive was preferable because the executive branch requires "energy" to repel foreign attacks, to protect property, and to oversee the "steady administration of laws."[9]

THE CONSTITUTION AND PRESIDENTIAL QUALIFICATIONS

The American Constitution spells out the qualifications required for serving in the office. Article II, Section 1 reads "No person except a natural born Citizen, or a Citizen of the United States, at the time of the Adoption of this Constitution, shall be eligible to the Office of the President; neither shall any Person be eligible to that Office who shall not have attained the Age of thirty five Years, and been fourteen Years a Resident within the United States." The Constitution thus mandates three presidential qualifications: (1) an age requirement; (2) a residency requirement; and (3) a citizenship requirement. These qualifications are mostly extended and modified from the qualifications outlined for members of Congress in Article I of the U.S. Constitution.

Why a Presidential Age Requirement?

Much was made of the age difference between Barack Obama and John McCain during the 2008 presidential election. The 25-year age difference between Obama and McCain was the largest age gap between presidential candidates in U.S. history (McCain 72 and Obama 47). Barack Obama's youthful persona helped attract throngs of college-age voters to his campaign, which played a vital role in helping Obama win both the Democratic nomination and the 2008 general election.

The Young and the Restless:
The Emergence of Young Voters as a Force in the 2008 Presidential Election

While much attention has focused on the role of gender and race in the 2008 presidential election, one of the most exciting and underreported stories was the extent to which voter turnout rates soared in the youth vote. This reversed trends in voter turnout rates among college-age students, which have been faint since the ratification of the Twenty-first Amendment (1971) of the U.S. Constitution. The Twenty-first Amendment made it illegal for any state to deny voting rights to those who are 18 years old or older. Most states prior to the ratification of the Twenty-first Amendment required voters to be at least 21 years old.

The historic battle between Senator Barack Obama (D-IL) and Senator Hillary Clinton (D-NY) in the Democratic primary in some ways mirrored the 1968 Democratic race between Robert F. Kennedy, Eugene McCarthy, and Hubert Humphrey. Barack Obama, akin to Robert Kennedy, ran as the insurgency candidate, challenging Bill and Hillary Clinton's nearly two-decade-old predominance over the Democratic Party. Obama emphasized the need for "change" and a renewed sense of "hope," while Clinton contrasted by accentuating her experience and reminding voters that she will be "ready on day one." Another important similarity to the 1968 campaign was the extent to which the 2008 campaign enlisted college-age students to the cause.

Barack Obama was the largest benefactor of this youthful political resurgence. Obama won by large margins in the youth demographic, even in states won by Clinton. Obama won the youth vote 59 percent to 39 percent in New Jersey, while losing the state by 10 percentage points. Young voters, however, put Obama over the top in several key states, including Missouri, where Obama won by a razor-thin margin after winning the youth vote 59 percent to 33 percent. The youth vote also went overwhelmingly for Barack Obama in the general election. Young people came out in record numbers in the 2008 general election. Obama received 66 percent of the 22 million 18- to 29-year-old voters participating in the 2008 election between Obama and McCain.

This reverses the trend of young people disconnecting from the political process since the 1968 election. A vicious cycle developed where presidential candidates stopped targeting young voters in serious ways because the young stopped voting, prompting

continued

© ISTOCKPHOTO.COM/ CARACTERDESIGN

the young to claim that they were not voting because campaigns were not speaking to them. While political participation takes shape in many forms and can be expressed through many channels, the primary variable for measuring political participation has always been voter turnout. The voter turnout rate among 18 to 29 year olds since 1968 has been faint, slipping to an all-time presidential election low of 43 percent in the 2000 presidential race. The good news is this trend reversed dramatically in 2004 and in 2008.

Prior to 2004, most blamed disappointing voting trends among the youth on structural and societal factors. The structural explanation posits the young tended to vote in lower percentages because of voter registration guidelines and rules governing voter access across states. Nearly one-third of the nation relocates every two years, mostly from the youth demographic. Rigid registration laws requiring voters to register weeks in advance of an election disproportionately disenfranchises college-age voters because of their transient lifestyle. States allowing same-day registration, such as Minnesota, Wisconsin, and Maine, can rightfully brag of significantly higher voter turnout rates. Others argue that societal factors explain low voter turnout rates. Low voter turnout in college-age students might represent a lifestyle choice that rises in time with the strengthening of community ties, suggesting the young are simply preoccupied with more immediate concerns than voting, such as finding a suitable mate and/or career.

Efforts to reverse college-age voting trends are working. We caught a glimpse of this in the 2008 presidential election. More than 22 million 18 to 29 year olds voted in the 2008 presidential election, which is up from 20 million young voters in 2004, and 16.2 million in 2000. Approximately 53 percent of 18 to 29 year olds voted in 2008, a 10-percentage point jump from 2000.[10] The young are turning their restlessness into political action, and that is a very good thing for American democracy.

Why do you believe young voters came out to vote in such high numbers in the 2008 presidential election?

© ISTOCKPHOTO.COM/SABLAMEK

Do you agree with the constitutional age requirement that presidents must be at least 35 years of age when taking office? Why or why not?

Table 6.2 reveals that President Obama is the fourth-youngest president in American history. The youngest American president was Theodore Roosevelt who was only 42 years of age when he assumed the office after President McKinley was assassinated in 1901. President John F. Kennedy was the youngest president ever elected to the office at 43 years of age.

TABLE 6.2. **Age of Presidents upon Entering Office**

Youngest American Presidents	Oldest American Presidents
Theodore Roosevelt (1901–1909) 42 years and 10 months old	Ronald Reagan (1981–1989) 73 years and 11 months
John F. Kennedy (1961–1963) 43 years and 7 months	William Henry Harrison (1841–1841) 68 years
Bill Clinton (1993–2001) 46 years and 5 months	James Buchanan (1857–1861) 65 years and 10 months
Barack Obama (2009–current) 47 years and 5 months	Zachary Taylor (1849–1850) 64 years and 3 months

The Constitution requires that the president be at least 35 years of age, which extends on the 25-year-old age requirement for members of the House of Representatives and the 30-year-old age requirement for U.S. senators. There are primarily two reasons for the presidential age requirement. The first is that delegates wanted the American president to possess wisdom and to have political experience. Chapter 2 highlighted Plato and Aristotle's belief that leaders should pursue and acquire knowledge before assuming leadership positions in the state. The Framers reasoned that wisdom is acquired from both intellectual pursuits and the lessons learned from worldly experiences. They believed that it was important for the chief executive to possess the type of wisdom that comes from experiencing life lessons over an extended period of time. The second reason for the age requirement is highlighted by New York delegate John Jay in *Federalist Paper No. 64.* Jay argued that presidential aspirants who are at least 35 years of age will also likely have assembled a public record for electoral college members to assess during the presidential selection process.

Why a Presidential Residency Requirement?

The presidential residency requirement stipulates that the American president must live on U.S. soil for at least 14 years. A residency requirement of 21 years was originally proposed but was amended after discovering that three of the delegates (Alexander Hamilton, Pierce Butler, and James McHenry) would be ineligible to serve as president because of this requirement. The residency requirement was later amended to 14 years to accommodate these three delegates. This was a long enough time period to eliminate most British sympathizers who fled to England during the Revolutionary War from serving as president. It was also a long enough period to prevent distrusted foreign officials, such as Prussian Army general Baron Von Steuben, who served under George Washington at Valley Forge during the Revolutionary War, from assuming the office.

The residency requirement became a source of controversy in the early twentieth century when political critics claimed Herbert Hoover was ineligible to serve in the

TABLE 6.3. The Best and Worst Presidents

Who do you believe was the best president? Who do you believe was the worst? C-SPAN ranked the 42 presidents from George Washington to George W. Bush by surveying historians across the nation. The historians rated Abraham Lincoln as America's greatest president and James Buchanan as the worst American president.[12]

PRESIDENTIAL RANKINGS: THE C-SPAN SURVEY OF HISTORIANS, FEBRUARY 2009

The 10 Best American Presidents	The 10 Worst American Presidents
1. Abraham Lincoln	42. James Buchanan
2. George Washington	41. Andrew Johnson
3. Franklin D. Roosevelt	40. Franklin D. Pierce
4. Theodore Roosevelt	39. William Henry Harrison
5. Harry S Truman	38. Warren G. Harding
6. John F. Kennedy	37. Millard Fillmore
7. Thomas Jefferson	36. George W. Bush
8. Dwight D. Eisenhower	35. John Tyler
9. Woodrow Wilson	34. Herbert Hoover
10. Ronald Reagan	33. Rutherford B. Hayes

office because he did not live on U.S. soil for 14 consecutive years leading up to the 1928 presidential election.[11] Hoover was sent to Europe to lead relief efforts in the aftermath of World War I by President Woodrow Wilson. It was later determined that the 14-year residency requirement merely requires candidates to live in the United States for 14 years over the course of a lifetime, not consecutively in the years leading up to an election. In Table 6.3 we highlight how political historians have ranked American presidents.

Why a Citizenship Requirement?

The constitutional citizenship requirement has been a source of some controversy as well. There is some dispute about exactly what the delegates had in mind when they stated that "no person except a natural born citizen, or a Citizen of the United States, at the time of the Adoption of this Constitution" shall be eligible to serve as president. Though the citizenship requirement was never openly debated at the Constitutional Convention, it was most likely a sensitive topic given that eight of the delegates were foreign born (see Table 6.4). There is scarce information on the topic except for a letter sent by New York delegate John Jay to George Washington where Jay asks "whether it would be wise and seasonable to provide a strong check to the admission of Foreigners into the administration of our national Government; and to declare expressly that the Commander in Chief of the American army shall not be given to nor devolve on, any but a natural born Citizen."[13] The primary purpose of the provision was to prevent foreign monarchs from appointing someone to the

The Citizenship Requirement and the "Birther Movement" in the 2008 Presidential Election

There has been some controversy over whether presidential candidates must be born on American soil or whether children born to American parents abroad also meet the citizenship requirement. The issue was raised against Barry Goldwater, who was born in the Arizona territory before it achieved statehood, when he ran for the office against Lyndon Johnson in 1964. Some also questioned whether Senator John McCain was eligible to run for the presidency in 2008, as he was born in the Panama Canal Zone to American parents serving in the U.S. military. The U.S. Senate even passed a resolution in April 2008 declaring that Senator McCain was a natural-born citizen and thus eligible to serve in the oval office.[14] Others belonging to the "birther movement" challenged Obama's citizenship status in the blogosphere. The birther movement was given national attention from conservative talk show host Rush Limbaugh and former CNN commentator Lou Dobbs. Those in the birther movement claimed that President Obama did not meet the natural-born citizen standard because he had dual citizenships at the time of his birth (his father was Kenyan) and/or challenged the authenticity of his Hawaiian birth certificate. Obama's Hawaiian birth certificate has since been authenticated by experts and his birth announcement was published in a Hawaii newspaper. The U.S. Supreme Court effectively ended the controversy when it refused to hear a lawsuit challenging Obama's citizenship in the days leading up to the election in November 2008.

Do you believe American presidents should be required to be natural born citizens? Why or why not?

position. There was some concern, for instance, that the reigning British monarch King George III might appoint his son to the office.

Congress addressed the citizenship issue when it declared that children born to American parents abroad are recognized as American citizens in our nation's first naturalization law in 1790. Accordingly, those born on American soil or those born abroad to American parents are eligible to run and serve in the office. There has also been a recent call to amend this provision of the Constitution. Some complained that

TABLE 6.4. Eight Foreign-Born Delegates to the Constitutional Convention

Foreign-Born Delegates	Place of Birth
Pierce Butler (SC)	Ireland
William Richardson Davie (NC)	England
Thomas Fitzsimons (PA)	Ireland
Alexander Hamilton (NY)	West Indies
James McHenry (MD)	Ireland
Robert Morris (PA)	England
William Paterson (NJ)	Ireland
James Wilson (PA)	Scotland

the citizenship requirement prevents some like Canadian-born former Michigan governor Jennifer Granholm and/or Austrian-born former California governor Arnold Schwarzenegger from ever serving in the office. Senator Orrin Hatch (R-UT) proposed a constitutional amendment to allow foreign-born citizens to serve as president after living in the United States for an extended period of time. However, as discussed in Chapter 4, it is exceptionally difficult to amend the Constitution and it is unlikely the amendment will be ratified anytime soon. It is also interesting to remember that the Framers added an often overlooked provision to the Constitution that enabled the eight foreign-born delegates to serve as president as long as they became American citizens prior to the ratification of the U.S. Constitution. Alexander Hamilton, for instance, who was born on the island of Nevis in the Caribbean was eligible to become president because he became a U.S. citizen prior to ratification.

THE PRESIDENTIAL SELECTION PROCESS

One of the greatest challenges faced by the Founding Fathers was determining how the chief executive should be selected. The issue of presidential selection was initially raised during the first week of the Constitutional Convention (May 29, 1787) and was not settled until September of that same year, a mere 11 days before the end of the Convention.[15] The Virginia Plan proposed having the president selected by Congress. This was a logical proposal considering that 8 of the 13 state governors were selected by their respective state legislatures at the time. Members of Congress were also in the best position to know the qualifications and shortcomings of candidates for the office. Pennsylvania delegate James Wilson opposed this method because he believed it gave Congress too much power over the executive branch and undermined the spirit of a separation of powers system. Wilson instead argued for allowing citizens to select the president through a direct popular vote. This proposal was not taken very seriously by delegates as many did not trust ordinary citizens to make this important decision, given that most citizens lived in distant communities and possessed little information on the strengths and weaknesses of potential candidates. Merging the concerns of those who wanted to maintain the sanctity of the separation of powers system, and those who wanted state officials to dominate the process, the electoral college system was proposed on September 4, 1787, by the Committee on Postponed Matters.[16] The concept behind the electoral college was not borrowed from European political theorists. It is for better or worse a uniquely American system that in its original form allowed political elites across the states to control the presidential selection process.

The Electoral College

The method used to select Barack Obama here in the twenty-first century varied greatly from the system used to select President George Washington in the late eighteenth century. The modern Electoral College system is different from the original system in: (1) how Electoral College members are selected; (2) the transition to a presidential–vice-presidential ticket; and (3) the shift toward the winner-take-all system of counting electoral votes.

The Original Method

The number of electoral votes each state is assigned is determined by the number of U.S. representatives and senators apportioned to that particular state. This method for determining the number of electoral votes per state has not changed since Washington's time. The state of Iowa, for instance, currently has six electoral votes because Iowa has four members representing them in the U.S. House of Representative and two senators in the U.S. Senate. The manner by which Electoral College members are selected, however, has evolved quite a bit since Washington's day. State legislatures originally appointed individual Electoral College members to select the American president The U.S. Constitution stipulates that Electoral College members cannot be federal officials in order to prevent members of Congress from serving, as this would violate the separation of powers rationale. The original method also stipulated that each elector is permitted two votes (later amended by the Twelfth Amendment) and required that each elector use at least one of these votes for an out-of-state candidate.

There was some concern that electors might simply vote for candidates from their respective state, which would result in biases toward home-grown candidates. The Framers hoped that a national candidate with broad appeal would emerge if electoral college members were required to vote for one out-of-state candidate. The Constitution also requires that in order to win the presidency, candidates must secure a majority of the electoral votes. The candidate with the majority of electoral votes then became president, and the runner-up candidate assumed the vice presidency. The vice presidency was simply awarded to the election's second-place finisher as the original system did not designate anyone as either the presidential or vice-presidential candidate. In the 1796 presidential election, for instance, Thomas Jefferson assumed the vice presidency after coming in second place to John Adams. The fact that candidates were not originally designated as the presidential or vice-presidential nominees caused a major crisis in the election of 1800, and motivated the passage of the Twelfth Amendment in 1804.

The Election of 1800 and the Impact of the Twelfth Amendment

The flaws of the electoral college soon became apparent in the election of 1800. In this election, Thomas Jefferson, the sitting vice president, challenged President John Adams in his reelection bid. Jefferson started a grass-roots effort to defeat Adams, and in the process established the Democratic-Republican political party, which later evolved into the modern Democratic Party. Jefferson, as a Virginian, sought a regional balance by asking New Yorker Aaron Burr to run as his vice-presidential candidate. They ran against another regionally balanced team in President John Adams from Massachusetts and Charles Pinckney from South Carolina.

Thomas Jefferson and Aaron Burr defeated Adams and Pinckney in the election of 1800. A national debacle ensued, however, as Jefferson and his running mate Burr tied for the lead, each receiving 73 electoral college votes. This was a problem because the Constitution stipulates that the House of Representatives selects the president when no candidate receives a majority of electoral college votes. Because electoral college members were required to cast two votes, and because candidates were not clearly designated as either the presidential or vice-presidential candidate, the Federalist House of Representatives was called upon to break the tie. Many Federalist House members slighted Jefferson by casting their vote for Burr.

The House of Representative remained deadlocked for six days on the matter until Delaware representative James A. Baynard switched his vote on the 36th ballot, giving the election to Thomas Jefferson.[17] Alexander Hamilton was very influential in persuading some House members away from Burr. Burr later exacted revenge by killing Hamilton in a duel in Weehawkin, New Jersey, in 1803. The Twelfth Amendment (1804) altered the presidential selection process by having presidential and vice-presidential candidates designated as such on a single ticket.

The Modern Electoral College

It was the emergence of political parties that helped spark the democratization of the Electoral College system. In the modern Electoral College, electors are appointed by political parties rather than state legislatures. The state of Iowa, for instance, currently has six electoral votes. This means that the Republican Party and the Democratic Party in Iowa each appoints six party loyalists to serve as members of the Electoral College in the event that their party's candidate wins the state. Iowa, like all states, except Maine and Nebraska, adopts a winner-take-all system, which means their candidate will receive all six electoral votes if their candidate wins the popular vote in the state.

There are now 538 possible electoral votes since the number of electors is determined by the number of U.S. Representatives (435) and Senators (100), plus the three electoral votes granted to the District of Columbia by the Twenty-third Amendment (1961). Candidates need 270 Electoral College votes in order to win the presidency because this number represents the majority of all possible electoral votes. Because the winner-takes-all system grants all of the states' electoral votes to the candidate who wins the popular vote of that state, it is now possible for a candidate to win the presidency by winning the popular vote in the 11 most populated states, even if that candidate does not receive even one vote in the other 39 states. If a candidate were to win the popular vote in California (55), Texas (38), New York (29), Florida (29), Pennsylvania (20), Illinois (20), Ohio (18), Michigan (16), Georgia (16), North Carolina (15), and New Jersey (14), that candidate would have 270 electoral votes and would become the next president of the United States. In Table 6.5 and Figure 6.1 we highlight the number of electoral college votes apportioned to each state and how each state voted in the 2008 presidential election.

One of the most controversial aspects of the electoral college is that it is possible for a candidate to win the national popular vote and still lose the election. That is because the presidential selection process is not determined by a national popular vote, but rather by winning the popular vote in enough individual states to amass the needed 270 electoral votes. In fact, there have been

TABLE 6.5. U.S. Electoral College in 2012

LIST OF STATES AND VOTES			
TOTAL VOTES: 538			
Majority Needed to Elect: 270			
Alabama—9	Illinois—20	Montana—3	Rhode Island—4
Alaska—3	Indiana—11	Nebraska—5	South Carolina—9
Arizona—11	Iowa—6	Nevada—6	South Dakota—3
Arkansas—6	Kansas—6	New Hampshire—4	Tennessee—11
California—55	Kentucky—8	New Jersey—14	Texas—38
Colorado—9	Louisiana—8	New Mexico—5	Utah—6
Connecticut—7	Maine—4	New York—29	Vermont—3
Delaware—3	Maryland—10	North Carolina—15	Virginia—13
District of Columbia—3	Massachusetts—11	North Dakota—3	Washington—12
Florida—29	Michigan—16	Ohio—18	West Virginia—5
Georgia—16	Minnesota—10	Oklahoma—7	Wisconsin—10
Hawaii—4	Mississippi—6	Oregon—7	Wyoming—3
Idaho—4	Missouri—10	Pennsylvania—20	

FIGURE 6.1. State Electoral Votes in 2012

Blue states voted for Barack Obama in 2008 and red states voted for the Republican challenger John McCain.

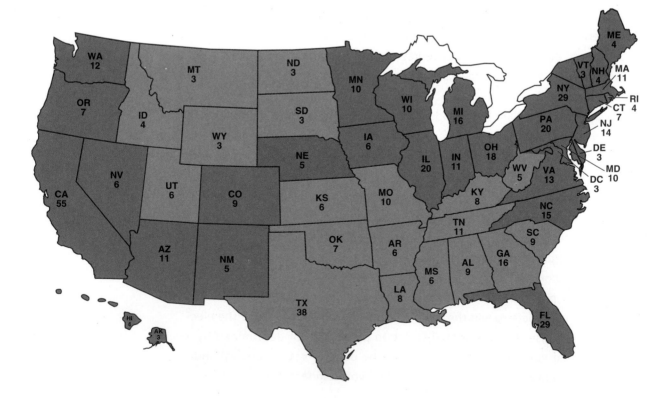

three examples in American history where a candidate ascended to the presidency after losing the national popular vote: Rutherford B. Hayes (Republican) in 1876; Benjamin Harrison (Republican) in 1888; and George W. Bush (Republican) in 2000 (see Table 6.6). In Table 6.7 and Table 6.8 we highlight the 2008 presidential election results and President Obama's public approval ratings across states two years later.

TABLE 6.6. Presidents Winning the White House While Losing the National Popular Vote

1876 Presidential Election	Popular Vote	Electoral Vote
Rutherford B. Hayes (R)	4,036,298	185 (winner)
Samuel J. Tilden (D)	4,300,590	184
1888 Presidential Election		
Benjamin Harrison (R)	5,439,853	233 (winner)
Grover Cleveland (D)	5,540,309	168
2000 Presidential Election		
George W. Bush (R)	50,456,002	271 (winner)
Al Gore (D)	50,999,897	266[18]

TABLE 6.7. 2008 Presidential Election Results

2008 Presidential Election	Popular Vote	Electoral College Vote
Barack Obama	69,492,376 (53%)	365
John McCain	59,946,378 (46%)	173

TABLE 6.8. President Obama's Highest and Lowest Approval Ratings Across States as of July 2010[19]

Top 10 Obama Job Approval by State	Bottom 10 Obama Job Approval by State
1. District of Columbia—85%	50. Wyoming—29%
2. Hawaii—68%	49. Utah—34%
3. Delaware—62%	48. West Virginia—34%
4. Maryland—60%	47. Idaho—34%
5. New York—57%	46. Oklahoma—37%
6. Connecticut—57%	45. Alaska—38%
7. California—56%	44. Montana—38%
8. Rhode Island—56%	43. Arkansas—40%
9. Massachusetts—56%	42. Kentucky—40%
10. Illinois—54%	41. Tennessee—41%

THE CONSTITUTION AND PRESIDENTIAL POWERS

The powers of the presidency are vaguely defined in Article II of the U.S. Constitution. Unlike congressional powers, which are explicitly stated in Article I, Section 8 of the U.S. Constitution, some presidential powers are ambiguous and imprecise. Article II, Section 1, for instance, established that the "executive Power shall be vested in a President of the United States of America." This language was borrowed from a modified version of the Virginia Plan offered at the Constitutional Convention. There is some debate amongst constitutional scholars as to precisely what delegates had in mind when they stated that all executive powers shall be vested in the office.

"Vested" Executive Powers and the President's Cabinet

The executive branch was certainly created in part to execute laws passed by Congress. The president was viewed as the chief executive officer of the nation by the American Framers. This point is reinforced in Article II, Section 3, where it reads that the president "shall take care that laws be faithfully executed." Executive departments were created in order to help the executive branch carry out these laws. There are now approximately 3 million civilian federal employees, and the president serves as the chief executive over the duties of all federal employees. President Harry Truman

▲ Harry S. Truman sitting at a desk in a reproduction of the Oval Office in the Harry S. Truman Library in Independence, Missouri. The "buck stops here" sign was sent by a personal friend who came upon a similar sign in a federal reformatory in Oklahoma. Truman referred to the sign in his farewell address to the nation when he said "The President—whoever he is—has to decide. He can't pass the buck to anybody. No one can do the deciding for him. That is his job."

famously placed a placard on his desk in the Oval Office declaring that "the Buck Stops Here" as a reminder that his desk was the final destination for all executive decisions.

While the U.S. Constitution did not explicitly create presidential cabinets, Article II, Section 2 of the Constitution states that the president may require "the opinion, in writing of the principal officer in each of the executive departments," which signals that the delegates expected the president to lead executive departments. Congress created executive departments in its first session in 1789 when it created the Departments of Treasury, State, and War.[20] These three executive departments were initially responsible for all federal business. The Department of Homeland Security became the 15th executive department in 2003 when it was created in response to the al-Qaeda terrorist attacks on New York, Washington, and Pennsylvania on September 11, 2001.

The president's cabinet includes the secretaries of each of these 15 executive departments. President Warren Harding expanded the president's cabinet to include his vice president Calvin Coolidge in 1921, and subsequent presidents have assigned a "cabinet rank," a special "status not recognized in law" to other federal officials.[21] President Eisenhower, President Nixon, and other twentieth-century presidents have assigned cabinet ranking to the director of the Office of Management and Budget (OMB) and other high-ranking ambassadors. Each of the 15 executive department secretaries is confirmed by a majority vote in the U.S. Senate. Table 6.9 reveals that the

TABLE 6.9. The Presidential Line of Succession and President Barack Obama's Department Secretaries as of 2011

1. Vice President Joseph Biden
2. Speaker of the House John Boehner (R-OH)
3. President pro tempore of the Senate Daniel Inouye (D-HI)
4. Secretary of State Hillary Rodham Clinton (Department of State, 1789)
5. Secretary of the Treasury Timothy F. Geithner (Department of the Treasury, 1789)
6. Secretary of Defense Leon Panetta (Department of Defense, 1947, 1789)
7. Attorney General Eric Holder Jr. (Department of Justice, 1870; attorney general created in 1789)
8. Secretary of the Interior Ken L. Salazar (Department of the Interior, 1849)
9. Secretary of Agriculture Thomas J. Vilsack (Department of Agriculture, 1862)
10. Secretary of Commerce Gary F. Locke (Department of Commerce, 1903)
11. Secretary of Labor Hilda L. Solis (Department of Labor, 1903)
12. Secretary of Health and Human Services Kathleen Sebelius (Department of Health and Human Services, 1953)
13. Secretary of Housing and Urban Development Shaun L. S. Donovan (Department of Housing and Urban Development, 1966)
14. Secretary of Transportation Ray LaHood (Department of Transportation, 1966)
15. Secretary of Energy Steven Chu (Department of Energy, 1977)
16. Secretary of Education Arne Duncan (Department of Education, 1979)
17. Secretary of Veteran Affairs Eric K. Shinseki (Department of Veteran Affairs, 1988)
18. Secretary of Homeland Security Janet A. Napolitano (Department of Homeland Security, 2003)

creation date of the executive departments was used to determine the presidential line of succession in the Presidential Succession Act of 1947.

Presidential Prerogative Powers

Some speculate that the enumerated executive power that is "vested" in the executive branch might also authorize the president to exercise a wider range of implied executive powers. John Locke's *Second Treatise on Government*, for instance, advocated allowing executives to use *prerogative powers* when leaders in times of crisis are compelled to "do things of their own free choice, where the law was silent, or sometimes, too, against the direct letter of the law, for the public good, and their acquiescing in it when so done."[22] In Chapter 4 we highlighted how President Abraham Lincoln asserted these types of prerogative powers by suspending habeas corpus during the U.S. Civil War, claiming the Founding Fathers did not intend for the Constitution to serve as a national "suicide pact." Some constitutional scholars believe presidents possess prerogative powers to take extreme and sometimes illegal action if faced with a national crisis. However, prerogative powers are very controversial, and many critics claim that prerogative powers are sometimes inappropriately asserted in an attempt to mask abuses of power in the executive branch.

THEORY AND PRACTICE

Should Presidents Be Permitted to Wiretap Phones?

President George W. Bush issued an order in 2001 that permitted the National Security Agency to wiretap phone conversations and review e-mail accounts of U.S. citizens without first receiving court warrants as required by the Foreign Intelligence Surveillance Act (FISA). President Bush claimed that the threat of terrorism required him to bypass the FISA law. Critics of the policy argued that this policy was both a violation of the privacy rights of Americans and an abuse of presidential power. The American Civil Liberties Union (ACLU) took the administration to court over the wiretap issue. The Supreme Court dismissed the ACLU's challenge in February 2008.

Do you believe the wiretap issue represents a permissible prerogative power or does it represent an abuse of presidential power?

Commander in Chief Powers

Article II, Section 2 also asserts that the "President shall be Commander in Chief of the Army and Navy of the United States, and of the Militia of the several States, when called into the actual Service of the United States." It is here where the Framers invite a struggle between the executive branch and Congress by asking both branches of government to share similar powers.[23] As discussed at greater length in Chapter 5, the president's commander-in-chief powers are substantially checked by Congress's constitutional authority to "declare war," "regulate commerce with foreign nations," "raise and support armies," and punish "Felonies committed on the high Seas." Whereas most constitutional scholars agree that most of the constitutional war-making power rests with Congress, modern presidents have assumed a much greater role in this area since the end of World War II in 1945.

Treaty Powers

Article II, Section 2 of the U.S. Constitution also confers on the American president the power to make treaties with foreign nations. It is clear from this provision that the Framers wanted the chief executive to play a particularly important role in foreign policy. It is in part because the delegates wanted the nation to speak with one voice that they ultimately structured the office to consist of a single executive. The Framers were careful, however, to check presidential treaty-making powers by mandating a two-thirds Senate ratification vote.

THEORY AND PRACTICE

Treaty Powers, the League of Nations, and Executive Agreements

A clash between the executive and the U.S. Senate occurred when President Woodrow Wilson (1913–1921) proposed the Treaty of Versailles to the U.S. Senate in the aftermath of World War I. President Wilson broke with the tradition of isolation from Europe that was established with the Monroe doctrine of 1823. While U.S. foreign policy was expansive in Asia and the Western Hemisphere, each president prior to Wilson heeded George Washington's warning about forming "entangling alliances" with European powers. President Wilson's conviction that the European balance-of-power system was responsible for frequent eruptions of war in Europe drove him to push for U.S. involvement in World War I. It was clear to President Wilson that in order for the United States to play a pivotal role in constructing the post-war international

continued

system, it would have to first involve itself in the fighting in Europe. The Senate's refusal to ratify the Treaty of Versailles prohibited the United States from becoming a member of the League of Nations. Presidents have increasingly used **executive agreements** instead of treaties in order to bypass Senate ratification. While executive agreements are technically only binding throughout the president's term, they are frequently adhered to by subsequent administrations. From 2001 to 2006 President George W. Bush successfully negotiated 45 treaties and entered into 612 executive agreements with foreign nations.[24]

> **Should the U.S. Congress play a larger role in foreign affairs? Why or why not?**

Executive Agreements: *Agreements initiated by the president that involve the United States and a foreign nation that do not require the advice and consent of the Senate.*

The Pardon Powers

Article II, Section 2 also gives the president the "Power to grant Reprieves and Pardons for Offenses against the United States, except in Cases of Impeachment." Most governors of the original 13 states possessed the pardon power during the time of the Articles of Confederation.[25] Pardon powers for the American president were officially offered at the Constitutional Convention on May 29, 1787, by South Carolina delegate Charles Pinckney. Alexander Hamilton discussed pardon powers in *Federalist Paper No. 74,* asserting their usefulness in "seasons of insurrections or rebellions." Hamilton stressed there are "critical moments when a well-timed offer of pardon to the insurgents or rebels may restore the tranquility of the commonwealth." The pardon power permits the president to grant immunity from punishment to someone convicted of a crime. Presidential pardon powers, however, became very controversial over the last 20 years (see Theory and Practice box).

The Appointment Power

The Constitution also authorizes the president to appoint "Ambassadors, other public Ministers and Consuls, judges of the supreme Court, and all other Officers of the United States, whose Appointments are not herein otherwise provided for, and which shall be established by Law." The presidential appointment power requires a majority vote approval in the U.S. Senate. Presidential appointments of federal justices and the tradition of senatorial courtesy are discussed at great length in Chapter 7.

THEORY AND PRACTICE

Presidential Pardon Powers in the Modern Era:
Ford, Clinton, Bush, and Obama

Presidential clemency typically comes in two forms: (1) full pardon; and (2) commutation of sentence. Presidential pardons immediately end all punishment for those convicted (or stop prosecutions) and clear the record of those receiving the pardon. Presidential commutations, on the other hand, simply reduce the severity of the punishment (e.g., death sentence to life term) without clearing the record of the person receiving a commutation.

The most controversial presidential pardon occurred when President Ford pardoned former President Nixon in 1974 "for all offenses against the United States which he, Richard Nixon, has committed or may have committed or taken part in during the period from January 20, 1969, through August 9, 1974." President Ford's pardon of Nixon for his involvement with the Watergate scandal was controversial because some believed it placed the former president above the law and others raised concerns that Nixon might have agreed to resign on the condition that he receive a presidential pardon. Others argued that Ford's presidential pardon of Nixon helped to bring closure to the Watergate scandal.

The wisdom of presidential pardon powers was called into question once again when former President Bill Clinton pardoned Mark Rich a few hours before leaving office in 2001. Mark Rich was imprisoned in 1983 for failure to pay $48 million in taxes and for engaging in illegal oil sales with Iran. His wife, Denise, was a Democratic Party fund-raiser who perhaps not coincidentally donated $400,000 to the Clinton library around the time of the pardon. Another controversy emerged when President George W. Bush commuted Scooter Libby's prison sentence in 2007. Scooter Libby, a former chief of staff for Vice President Dick Cheney, was found guilty of perjury and obstruction of justice in the Valerie Plame federal investigation. This investigation sought to determine whether White House officials illegally revealed the covert identity of CIA official Valerie Plame, in an effort to discredit her husband Joe Wilson, who asserted in a *New York Times* editorial that President Bush intentionally misled the nation in his State of the Union address on the need to remove Iraqi leader Saddam Hussein from power.

continued

continued

President Obama used his pardon power for the first time in December 2010 when he pardoned nine individuals convicted of either drug possession, counterfeiting, or coin mutilation years ago. These pardons were not particularly controversial. President Obama reviewed approximately 5,000 new and pending pardon requests in 2010.

Many of the presidential powers (e.g., treaty powers, appointment powers) require Senate approval. Should the Constitution be amended to require Senate approval of presidential pardons? Why or why not?

© ISTOCKPHOTO.COM/LORENZO COLLORETA

The president makes approximately 3,000 appointments to the federal government and roughly 1,000 of these appointments require a confirmation vote in the Senate.[26]

The Veto Power

The Constitution also confers upon the president the power to veto congressional legislation. The presidential veto power is a limited power in that Congress can override a presidential veto with a two-thirds vote in both houses of Congress. As of 2009, there have been 2,562 presidential vetoes and only 110 (4 percent) were overridden by Congress. President Franklin D. Roosevelt vetoed 372 pieces of legislation and was overridden only on nine occasions. Conversely, President George W. Bush only vetoed 11 bills but was overridden by Congress four times.[27]

In 2010, President Obama asked Congress to grant him a variation of the line-item veto. The line-item veto authorizes the executive to veto only certain provisions of a bill while signing into law other provisions. Today, 43 out of the 50 governors in the United States are empowered with the line-item veto. President Bill Clinton was the first president granted the line-item veto power with the passage of the Line Item Veto Act of 1996. However, the U.S. Supreme Court struck down this Act as unconstitutional in *Clinton v. City of New York* (1998), on the grounds that it violated the presentment clause of the Constitution which stipulates the range of presidential options available once Congress "presents" the bill to the executive branch. Presidents can also use an **executive signing statement** in lieu of a presidential veto. President George W. Bush issued 125 signing statements during his two terms in office, which impacted 750 federal statutes.

Executive Signing Statements: *Written remarks on congressional legislation made by the president that enable the president to express displeasure with a particular provision of a bill and/or impact the way bills are implemented.*

Presidential Powers and *Federalist Paper No. 69*

After the Constitutional Convention, many of the Anti-Federalists who were opposed to the ratification of the U.S. Constitution pointed to the scope of executive powers to make their case. Patrick Henry argued that the executive branch "squinted toward monarchy," while James Monroe of Virginia protested that the lack of term limits on the executive would result in life terms. Presidential terms limits were later placed on the American president when the **Twenty-Second amendment** was ratified in 1951.

Perhaps the greatest critic of the newly created presidency was George Clinton, New York's governor and later vice president for Thomas Jefferson (1805–1809) and James Madison (1809-1812). Governor Clinton wanted term limits on the office and believed the delegates granted the president too much power. Clinton argued that the power of the presidency "must be compensated by brevity of duration and longer than a year would be dangerous." He went on to say that a four-year "term was ample time to ruin a country." Alexander Hamilton responded to these attacks in *Federalist Paper No. 69*.

In *Federalist Paper No. 69* Hamilton challenged Governor Clinton's assertion that the powers assigned to the American president resembled the powers granted to the British monarch. Hamilton chides Governor Clinton by comparing presidential powers to the powers of New York's governor. He also refuted Clinton by pointing out that the powers of the president are dissimilar from the British monarch in that: (1) the king serves a life term, whereas the American president serves four-year terms; (2) the king has an absolute veto, whereas the American president has a limited veto that can be overturned by a two-thirds vote in Congress; (3) the king declares war and raises armies, whereas Congress possesses these powers; and (4) the king cannot be impeached, whereas the American president can be impeached and removed from office by Congress.

New York governor George Clinton reacted to Hamilton by warning against comparisons between the powers of the American president and New York's governor by claiming the two no more resemble each other than the "angels of darkness resemble the angels of light."[28] Under the pen name "Cato," in honor of the Roman statesman who fought against Julius Caesar's encroachments on liberty, Clinton pointed out that unlike the American president, New York's governor is selected by the people, rather than appointed by an electoral college, does not make foreign treaties, and does not influence war-making decisions.

Twenty-Second Amendment:
A constitutional amendment ratified in 1951 that prohibits a president from serving more than two full terms in office (president may serve up to 10 years if he/she inherits the office as a result of impeachment or death of the previous president).

Presidential Powers in the Modern Era: An Imperial Presidency?

Some modern presidential scholars have concluded that we have witnessed the emergence of an *imperial presidency* with the recent ascendancy of executive powers in foreign affairs that might represent a dangerous departure from the original intentions of the Founding Fathers.[29] President Truman's deployment of troops in the Korean War, President Nixon's secret bombings of Cambodia and Laos during the Vietnam War, and President George W. Bush's decision to secretly wiretap citizens in the fight against terrorism are illustrated as prime examples of *imperial* tendencies in modern presidents. Contrary to the depiction of an imperial presidency, others examine presidential leadership from the perspective that presidents are constitutionally weak and have been imperiled by Congress, the bureaucracy in Washington, and the modern media. Renowned presidential scholar Richard Neustadt argues that presidents need to be especially skillful at "persuading" Congress and the Washington bureaucracy to take action on their agenda. Neustadt contends that presidents have two sources of power that stem from both their professional reputation within Washington's beltway and their level of public support across the nation.[30] He warns that constitutional powers ascribed to the presidency will not go very far if presidents are unable to persuade the Washington establishment to act on their agenda. Neustadt, sometimes known as the American Machiavelli, posits that presidents need to understand the power ramifications of every decision they make. Presidential power is diminished if presidents make unwise decisions or are involved in executive blunders, and presidential power is enhanced if presidents are perceived as politically skillful by the Washington establishment.

Others argue that presidents can no longer govern simply through bargaining, but now must also exercise leadership through direct appeals to the public. Presidents are now increasingly bypassing the bargaining process with Congress and the federal bureaucracy, choosing instead to make direct appeals by "going public" to the American people.[31] The growing tendency among modern presidents to make direct appeals to the public is facilitated by the power of television and the computer age, the decline of party loyalty, and the modern presidential selection process that is no longer dominated by political elites.

CourseReader ASSIGNMENT

Log in to **www.cengagebrain.com** and open CourseReader to access the reading:

Presidential Power **excerpt by Richard Neustadt**

Richard Neustadt is sometimes referred to as the "American Machiavelli" because of his emphasis on how presidential decision making can strengthen or weaken presidential power. Neustadt's primary point is that presidential power links directly with the president's ability to persuade. He argues that the president's main sources of power come from from his/her reputation inside Washington and in the president's level of public support. Neustadt advises that presidential power will grow if the president exercises excellent judgment but will grow weak if the president is prone to executive blunders.

- *Can you think of an example of how President Obama's power has been either strengthened or weakend by a decision he made while in office?*

- *How is the advice offered by Machiavelli in* **The Prince** *similar to the advice offered by Neustadt? How are they different?*

Nonconstitutional Powers in the Modern Era

Clinton Rossiter views presidential powers through the metaphor of the many "hats" a president must wear while in office. The president serves as the nation's chief executive, commander in chief, and chief foreign diplomat. The president is also the chief legislator, responsible for submitting annual budgets, setting the national agenda, and possesses the power of the veto. Modern presidents also wear many nonconstitutional hats as president. The president serves as the "chief of state" and is responsible for managing the general mood of the nation through national crises and ceremonial functions. President George W. Bush received high marks for managing the national mood following the September 11 attack, but was widely criticized during the Hurricane Katrina crisis, which devastated New Orleans in 2005. Modern presidents are also the de facto leaders of their respective political party and spend a significant amount of time helping to raise campaign funds and campaigning for gubernatorial and congressional candidates across the nation. The president also plays a large role in international affairs and is responsible for helping to manage the international system.[32]

PRESIDENTIAL–CONGRESSIONAL RELATIONS IN FOREIGN AFFAIRS

The president and Congress have throughout history struggled for control over foreign policy. While George Washington and Thomas Jefferson were both relatively sympathetic to James Madison's notion of a congressional-centered foreign policy, subsequent presidents challenged this arrangement. One of the first major challenges to congressional dominance over foreign policy occurred during President James Polk's term in 1846. President Polk (1845–1849), recognizing that Congress, not to mention Mexico, stood in the way of America actualizing its manifest destiny by having the nation stretch from sea to shining sea, provoked a skirmish with Mexican soldiers along the Rio Grande border. By igniting the Mexican-American War, President Polk demonstrated that although Congress had the constitutional authority to declare war, presidents can easily manipulate events so that Congress has little alternative but to declare one.[33]

After the Spanish-American War in 1898, the nature of presidential–congressional relations changed dramatically. By acquiring Spanish colonies, namely Guam, Puerto Rico, and the Philippines, the American president "can never again be the mere domestic figure he had been throughout" U.S. history.[34] Theodore Roosevelt (1901–1909), believing Congress was too disorganized and public opinion "the voice of a fool," was quick to test the limits of this new foreign policy presidency. When Congress refused to ratify a treaty he proposed dealing with Latin America, he by-passed the treaty-making process by signing an executive agreement. As previously mentioned, while an executive agreement is technically only binding until the end of the signing president's tenure, Roosevelt correctly assumed that future presidents would be reluctant to nullify the arrangement.

Subsequent to World War I, the pendulum began to swing back to a congressional-centered foreign policy. The Senate's refusal to ratify the Versailles Treaty, which called for the creation of the League of Nations, highlighted a new and stronger wave of **isolationism** in the U.S. Congress. Foreign policy throughout much of the 1920s and 1930s, in fact, was largely dominated by an isolationist Congress. Perhaps the crowning moment of this period came with the passage of the Neutrality Act in 1935. Members of Congress reasoned that because U.S. entry in past wars were precipitated by the death of Americans on the high seas (e.g., the **USS *Maine*** 1898; **RMS *Lusitania*** 1915), the United States could stay out of harm's way by prohibiting the president from transferring arms to any belligerent nation.[35] The pendulum be-gan to swing back to the president, however, in 1937, when the Neutrality Act was amended to include a "cash and carry" provision. Nations involved in war could now purchase weapons from the United States provided they pay promptly and carry the weapons away in their own ships.[36] Because Britain was no longer able to comply with the cash provision of the Neutrality Act, Congress approved the Lend Lease Act in March 1941, which gave the president authority to "manufacture additional muni-tions and war supplies to be turned over to the democratic powers."[37]

The Cold War Consensus and the Emergence of the Imperial Presidency

The second half of the twentieth century witnessed flagrant executive encroach-ments on the powers of Congress.[38] The general perception of congressional inepti-tude during the 1930s, fostered largely by an isolationist Congress that failed to check Adolf Hitler and Nazi Germany, led to the ascendancy of executive power on matters of foreign affairs. Presidents were essentially given carte blanche in foreign affairs during the **cold war.** Immediately following World War II, President Harry Truman (1945–1953) worked feverishly to ensure that the United States did not return to its policies of isolationism.

It was generally agreed that because the United States did not assert world lead-ership after World War I, the interwar period was wrought with economic and politi-cal instability. It was clear to President Truman that the United States would have to play a leadership role in order to promote stability in the international system. The **Truman doctrine** speech and the **Marshall Plan** both reflected a U.S. commitment to remain in Europe, and the new U.S.-designed United Nations, World Bank, and

International Monetary Fund represented a U.S. pledge to manage the international system.[39] Congress willingly took a back seat to President Truman in large part because of the new international role assumed by the United States.

The North Korean invasion of South Korea (1950) confirmed in President Truman's mind the wisdom of this new approach as it was demonstrated that the perceived monolithic communist movement was prepared to use force to expand its base. The emergence of the imperial presidency came into view in 1950 when Truman, in his haste to repel the North Korean invasion of South Korea, dispatched troops into Korea without a congressional declaration of war and without even having consulted Congress.[40]

Eisenhower's "New Look" Approach

U.S. foreign policy was shrouded in secrecy throughout the 1950s and mid-1960s. Eisenhower's "New Look" approach, also called the **Eisenhower doctrine,** relied heavily on the CIA and covert operations to contain Soviet influence. The special emphasis on covert operations, stemming largely from Eisenhower's budgetary concern brought about by the financial costs of the Korean War, were made even more cozy by the fact that Eisenhower's secretary of state (John Foster Dulles) and his director of the Central Intelligence Agency (Allen Dulles) were brothers. Covert operations were relatively inexpensive when compared to the costs of troop deployments, and they enabled the president to manipulate the internal working of foreign governments without the knowledge of Congress and the American public.[41] Eisenhower also relied on his Policy of Massive Retaliation, the threat of using nuclear weapons against China, to bring the Korean War to an end in 1953.

Eisenhower Doctrine: *The plan announced in 1957 in the aftermath of the Suez Crisis between Egypt, Britain, France, and Israel. Primarily concerned with the Middle East, Eisenhower declared the United States would provide economic aid and/or military support to nations threatened by armed forces of belligerent states.*

Kennedy's Policy of Flexible Response

President John F. Kennedy was critical of Eisenhower's "New Look" approach to containing the Soviet Union. He believed that Eisenhower's policy of massive retaliation and his reliance of nuclear weapons limited the range of options for U.S. foreign policy decision makers. He opted instead for a more flexible approach to containing Soviet power that included increasing troop strength in Europe, the development of intercontinental ballistic missiles (ICBMs), the expansion of special forces, such as the Green Berets and the Navy SEALs, and a proactive approach of reaching out to the developing world with the Peace Corps and other foreign programs.[42] Some speculated that because of President Kennedy's relative inexperience in foreign affairs and because of his role in the **Bay of Pigs** fiasco, Congress might reassert itself against the imperial presidency model launched during the Truman administration. Congress, however, remained extraordinarily deferential in matters of foreign affairs.

The **Cuban missile crisis** enabled President Kennedy to project his power in foreign affairs with little congressional interference.[43] Kennedy never consulted with Congress about his decision to implement a naval blockade of Cuba during

Bay of Pigs: *A bay in South Cuba and the site of an unsuccessful invasion by anti-Castro exiles secretly supported by the U.S. government in 1961.*

Cuban Missile Crisis: *Crisis between the United States and the Soviet Union as a result of Cuban leader Fidel Castro's decision to allow the Soviet Union to place Soviet nuclear missiles in Cuba in 1961.*

the Cuban missile confrontation. Gaining confidence from his triumph in the Cuban missile crisis, President Kennedy then bolstered the number of U.S. military advisors in Vietnam from the 1,000 sent by President Eisenhower to 16,000 military advisors, again with little congressional involvement.[44]

WHY POLITICS MATTERS TO YOU!

Does a President's Personality Impact Whether We Go to War?

Presidential behavior is largely influenced by the character of the person sitting in the oval office. James David Barber's *Presidential Character: Predicting Performance in the White House* argues that we should understand the character of presidential candidates before casting our vote. Rather than accept media or campaign-driven biographical narratives, we can instead research the true: (1) character; (2) worldview; and (3) style of those seeking our highest office. Barber's controversial text classifies each of the twentieth-century presidents as one of four personality types. These four personality types are derived from two basic orientations toward life including: (1) an active–passive dimension, determined by presidential energy level; and the (2) positive–negative dimension, determined by a president's high or low self-esteem. Active-positive presidents are more likely to be successful than active-negative presidents because they expend a great deal of energy and find enjoyment in their work. Active-negative personality types have a lower self-esteem and tend to be preoccupied with whether they are succeeding or failing. Active-negatives are also more likely to engage in questionable behavior in order to prevent a perceived failure because failure might cause further damage to their sense of self-worth.

PRESIDENTIAL PERSONALITY TYPES		
	Active	**Passive**
Positive	F. D. Roosevelt, Truman, Kennedy, Ford, Carter, G. H. W. Bush	Taft, Harding, Reagan
Negative	Wilson, Hoover, L. B. Johnson, Nixon	Coolidge, Eisenhower

Do you agree with Barber's classification of twentieth-century presidents?

How would you categorize Barack Obama?

President Lyndon B. Johnson (1963–1969), a former majority leader of the U.S. Senate, was extremely skilled in building consensus in Congress. The Gulf of Tonkin Resolutions, which passed unanimously in the House and with only two dissents in the Senate in 1964, gave President Johnson congressional authorization to deploy troops in Vietnam.

Nixon's Policy of Détente and Beyond

During President Richard M. Nixon's administration (1969–1974), Congress began to take a more active role in U.S. policy in Vietnam. Congress, for instance, repealed the Gulf of Tonkin Resolution in 1971. Then, in 1973, the House and Senate prohibited President Nixon from bombing "Indochina after July 1 of that year."[45] The War Powers Resolution (1973) came to symbolize a transition away from the imperial presidency and toward a resurgent Congress on foreign policy decision making. The War Powers Resolutions had two main components: (1) it required the president "to consult with Congress before committing troops to combat areas," and (2) it required the president to withdraw troops within 90 days of entering hostilities "unless Congress expressly approved the commitment."[46] This resolution was passed over President Nixon's veto. Nixon's policy of détente (the **Nixon doctrine**) sought to ease tensions with the Soviet Union by integrating the Soviet economy into the international economic system and to end the arms race between the two countries. Nixon's controversial "linkage" policy incorporated the "carrot and stick" approach to diplomacy by attempting first to lure the Soviet Union into a "web of incentives" by agreeing to trade computer technology and wheat to the Soviet Union in return for an arms agreement at the negotiating table.[47] This policy reduced the communist threat by placing a greater emphasis on economic rather than military concerns.[48] These factors, along with the Watergate scandal, which seriously weakened the office of the presidency, caused the pendulum to temporarily swing back to a congressional-centered foreign policy.

Nixon Doctrine: *Nixon sought to "Vietnamize" the Vietnam War by supplanting American troops with Vietnamese troops. The Nixon doctrine (1969) sought to extricate American forces from the fighting in Vietnam. All U.S. troops were withdrawn four years later in 1973.*

CourseReader ASSIGNMENT

Log in to **www.cengagebrain.com** and open CourseReader to access the reading:

Presidential Character **excerpt by James David Barber**

James David Barber's *Presidential Character: Predicting Performance in the White House* argues that we can do a better job predicting whether a president will thrive in office by having a deeper understanding of the character of the person in the office. Barber believes a president's personality stems from his/her character, worldview, and style. He further categorizes personalites into four distinct types including: 1) active-positive presidents; 2) active-negative presidents; 3) passive-positive presidents; and 4) passive negative presidents. He advises that active-postive presidents are likely to perform more successfully in office than active-negative personality types.

- *Why does Barber believe active-positive presidents are likely to have more success than active-negative presidents? How can personal insecurities propel some people to positions of power?*

Neither President Ford (1974–1977) nor President Carter (1977–1981) was very successful in seizing foreign policy control from Congress. The little credibility President Ford had in foreign policy was lost when in a televised presidential debate he made the bewildering remark that "no Soviet domination of Poland existed."[49] The **Carter doctrine** was equally criticized in the realm of foreign affairs. The era of détente came to a close after the Soviet invasion of Afghanistan in 1979. The cold war became "chilly" once again, causing President Carter to stop all technology and grain exports to the Soviet Union, to increase military spending, and to boycott the Moscow Olympic Games in 1980. President Carter's leadership in foreign affairs was weakened after the failed Iranian hostage rescue, which caused 82 percent of Americans to disapprove of Carter's handling of foreign affairs.

Although President Ronald Reagan (1981–1989) also lacked experience in foreign affairs he was advantaged by an unshakable belief that the Soviet Union was solely responsible for all of the world's political turmoil. In contrast to President Carter, who made European leaders nervous that the United States might not defend them in the event of a Soviet invasion, the **Reagan doctrine** made leaders throughout the world worried that he might be a little too eager to defend them. By refocusing America's attention to the cold war with the Soviet Union, Reagan successfully captured, albeit temporarily, the foreign policy initiative from Congress.

Presidential–Congressional Relations in the Post–Cold War Era

The end of the cold war in the early 1990s drove the international system into a state of flux. Within a matter of years the Soviet Union disbanded, Germany was unified, ideological conflicts subsided, and a peaceful transition of power in South Africa took place.[50] The world, before everyone's eyes, became a fundamentally different place. While almost everyone agreed that there was a "new world order," scarcely anyone, including President George Herbert Walker Bush (1989–1993), knew what that meant. The first major test of the new world order occurred in the Persian Gulf where the absence of "a superpower rivalry left a power vacuum" that Iraqi President Saddam Hussein tried to fill by invading Kuwait.[51] The Bush administration, fearful that Hussein would invade Saudi Arabia after finishing with Kuwait, deployed 250,000 U.S. troops to the region. While President Bush skillfully cultivated a strong international coalition against Hussein, he faced stiff opposition in the Democrat-controlled Congress. Congress, however, narrowly supported the resolution to use force against Iraq.

While President Bill Clinton (1993–2001) campaigned as a domestic policy president, he had more success with Congress in the realm of foreign affairs, including successes in Haiti, Ireland, and the Middle East. Senator Jesse Helms, the former chairman of the Senate Foreign Relations Committee, however, derailed the ratification of the Nuclear Non-Proliferation Treaty in 1999 over President Clinton's public support for the treaty.

Members of the al-Qaeda terrorist organization hijacked American passenger planes on September 11, 2001, and crashed them into the heart of the American financial district, bringing down both the World Trade Center and old ways of thinking about American foreign policy. The landscape was officially transformed when President George W. Bush (2001–2009) declared that America's new foreign policy mission would not be actualized until "every terrorist group of global reach has been found, stopped, and defeated."[52]

The **Bush doctrine** was premised on the fact that the world is a fundamentally more dangerous place because of the threat of terrorism. In his State of the Union speech in 2002, President Bush argued that an "axis of evil" existed in the world that included Iraq, Iran, and North Korea. He argued that the United States should disengage from international organizations that shackled America's ability to act against the "Three T's" that threaten American national security: (1) tyrants; (2) terrorists; and (3) technologies of mass destruction.[53] President Bush therefore commenced the invasion of Iraq and toppled the Iraqi president Saddam Hussein in 2003. While Congress approved a resolution authorizing the presidential use of force in Iraq, President Bush has been criticized for relying on faulty intelligence in making the decision to deploy troops. Congress, however, had been largely deferential to President Bush in the realm of foreign affairs throughout his presidency.

President Barack Obama's foreign policy has to this point been both a reaction against the Bush doctrine and a continuation of it. His 2010 National Security Strategy asserts greater emphasis on a policy of "global engagement" over President Bush's unilateral approach. Obama seeks to build closer alliances with European nations and has more publicly reached out to Arab leaders in the Middle East. His policies against international terrorism have also been viewed as a continuation of the Bush doctrine in that his administration raised U.S. troops levels in Afghanistan and has to this point more aggressively moved against al-Qaeda in counterinsurgency offensives in Pakistan, including the successful raid on Osama bin Laden's compound in 2011. The Obama administration has more aggressively targeted leaders of al-Qaeda with hellfire missiles launched from MQ-1 unmanned predator drones in the Pakistani border region. In 2010 it was estimated that drone attacks were responsible for 1,400 deaths in the region since 2004. Drone attacks have successfully targeted high-ranking al-Qaeda officials, but ethical issues have also been raised about this form of warfare because approximately one-third of all drone casualties have been civilian.[54]

Bush Doctrine: *The policy formulated by President George W. Bush after the 2001 terrorist attacks on the United States. The doctrine was codified in 2002. The policy marks a break from the decades-old foreign policy of "containment" and asserts that the United States will act unilaterally to "preempt" any threat against the United States.*

SUMMARY

Opinions on the American presidency have varied widely over the last 50 years. Some political observers believe that the modern presidency has taken on an "imperial" character that threatens the American system of checks and balances. Others, however, argue that the office has been "imperiled" by Congress, the bureaucracy, the media, and the blogosphere. The Founding Fathers spent a significant amount of time at the Constitutional Convention debating: (1) whether the executive should take the forms of an executive council or a single individual; (2) the extent of presidential powers; and (3) the method by which the chief executive should be selected. There is little doubt that the American government has transformed from a congressional-centered government in the eighteenth century to a presidential-centered government in the twenty-first century. The American president now personifies the American government.

This chapter highlighted the American presidency by focusing on five major themes that included: (1) the creation of the American presidency; (2) the Constitution and presidential qualifications; (3) the presidential selection process; (4) presidential powers; and (5) presidential–congressional relations in foreign affairs. In the next chapter we will examine the role that our judicial branch of government plays in our system of government.

KEY TERMS

Bay of Pigs p. 191

Bush Doctrine p. 195

Carter Doctrine p. 194

Cold War p. 190

Cuban Missile Crisis p. 191

Eisenhower Doctrine p. 191

Executive Agreements p. 184

Executive Signing Statements p. 186

Isolationism p. 190

Marshall Plan p. 190

Nixon Doctrine p. 193

Reagan Doctrine p. 194

RMS *Lusitania* p. 190

Truman Doctrine p. 190

Twenty-second Amendment p. 187

USS *Maine* p. 190

KEY PEOPLE

THE AMERICAN JUDICIARY

▲ Though the judiciary has always been a coequal branch of government, it did not have its own building until 1935 (shown here). The Supreme Court initially met in the Merchants Exchange Building in New York City before moving to Philadelphia's Independence Hall and City Hall. The Supreme Court heard cases in the U.S. Capitol Building from 1800-1935 after the national capital moved to Washington, D.C. In 1929, Chief Justice William Taft, who also served as President of the United States from 1909-1913, convinced Congress to build the Supreme Court a permanent home.

INTRODUCTION: HOW THE SUPREME COURT IMPACTS OUR SOCIETY

James Dale served in a leadership position with the lesbian/gay student alliance as a Rutgers University student in 1990. In July of that year he discussed his sexual orientation with a member of the press while attending a lecture on the health needs of gay teenagers. Dale is a former Eagle Scout who also served as an assistant scoutmaster for a New Jersey chapter of the Boy Scouts of America. Boy Scout officials learned of Dale's sexual orientation when the article was published in a local newspaper. In reaction to the article Boy Scout officials notified Dale that he was no longer permitted to serve as a scoutmaster because his homosexual lifestyle was inconsistent with the values the organization was attempting to instill in young boys.

In 1992 Dale filed suit in a New Jersey state court alleging that his dismissal from the Boy Scouts violated New Jersey's public accommodation law, which prohibits organizations from discriminating on the basis of sexual orientation. The New Jersey Supreme Court sided with the student, ruling that the Boy Scouts violated New Jersey's public accommodation law by ordering Dale's expulsion. The Boy Scouts then appealed this decision to the U.S. Supreme Court claiming that as a private organization they are within their First Amendment rights to set standards and place conditions on members of their organization. Dale countered that the Boy Scouts are actually a de facto public organization in that their meetings are frequently held in public schools, and because they regularly make use of public parks. In *Boy Scouts v. Dale* (2000), the U.S. Supreme Court in a 5–4 vote overturned the New Jersey Supreme Court by finding that "applying New Jersey's public accommodation law to require the Boy Scouts to admit Dale violates the Boy Scouts' First Amendment right of expressive association."[1] The *Boy Scouts v. Dale* (2000) case is instructive because it highlights how our federalist system governs the relationship between state and federal courts.

The American legal system operates within a dual court system that includes a federal court system and 50 individual state

Questions to Consider Before Reading this Chapter

1. Why did the Founding Fathers view the judiciary as the "least dangerous branch" of government?

2. Why do many consider the *Marbury v. Madison* (1803) case the most important Supreme Court decision ever rendered?

3. What is the best method for selecting judges at the federal and state level?

4. How did the Interstate Commerce Clause help expand civil rights for African Americans and the disabled?

5. How did the Bill of Rights become nationalized into the states?

6. Should justices practice "judicial activism" or "judicial restraint"?

▲ Members of the Westboro Baptist Church picket in front of the Supreme Court on October 6, 2010 for what they argued was their right to protest at military funerals. The group, among other things, is opposed to homosexuals serving in the military. Many believed that the group went too far in expressing their viewpoints in a public protest during Marine Lance Corporal Matthew Snyder's funeral, who was killed in Iraq in 2006. In *Snyder v. Phelps* (2011), the Supreme Court sided with the controversial group by ruling in an 8-1 vote that Westboro Baptist Church was protected by the First Amendment to protest at military funerals.

court systems. The *Boy Scouts v. Dale* (2000) case is useful because it brings to light legal issues and political nuances associated with the roles and responsibilities of state and federal courts today. While the New Jersey Supreme Court and the U.S. Supreme Court were both directly involved in the Boy Scouts dispute, each court applied the same set of facts to entirely separate legal questions. The New Jersey Supreme Court ruled against the Boy Scouts because it determined that its membership policies violated New Jersey's public accommodation law, which prohibits private businesses in the state from denying accommodation to anyone because of their race, gender, national origin, and sexual orientation. The Boy Scouts appealed this state decision to the U.S. Supreme Court on the grounds that it violated their First Amendment freedom of expression rights. They argued that because they are not a "place of public accommodation" like a restaurant or movie theater, but rather a private organization, they are empowered by the U.S. Constitution to determine membership guidelines. The U.S. Supreme Court agreed with the Boy Scouts and overturned the New Jersey Supreme Court by asserting that private organizations are protected by the U.S. Constitution's First Amendment rights of expressive association. You might remember from Chapter 4 that the U.S. Supreme Court is authorized to overturn state supreme court rulings on federal issues by the U.S. Constitution's **supremacy clause**, located in Article VI of the Constitution. The supremacy clause states that:

Supremacy Clause: The provision of the Constitution that stipulates that the Constitution, and the Laws of the United States, represent the supreme law of the nation.

This Constitution, and the Laws of the United States which shall be made in pursuance thereof; *and all Treaties made, or which shall be made, under the Authority of the United States, shall be the supreme Law of the Land; and the Judges in every State shall be bound thereby, any Thing in the Constitution or Laws of any State to the Contrary notwithstanding.*

Building on the example provided in the *Boy Scouts v. Dale* (2000) case, this chapter examines the evolving relationship between federal and state courts in our federalist system by highlighting: (1) differences between federal and state court systems; (2) the power of judicial review; (3) the Supreme Court's role in expanding civil and political rights; (4) judicial selection at the federal and state levels; and (5) theories on judicial decision making in the modern era.

DIFFERENCES BETWEEN FEDERAL AND STATE COURTS

It is important to remember that no federal judiciary existed when the American states originally organized under the Articles of Confederation from 1781 to 1787. We learned in Chapter 4 that the ratification of the U.S. Constitution transformed our political system by dividing powers between the national and state government and by creating a system of checks and balances within the federal government's legislative, executive, and judicial branches of government. Unlike the controversial executive branch, the judiciary was not hotly debated at the Constitutional Convention, probably because 35 of the 55 delegates were either legally trained or serving as practicing attorneys in their respective state court systems. Reflecting the strong comfort level with the judiciary, Alexander Hamilton in *Federalist Paper No. 78* asserted the judiciary is the *least dangerous branch* of government because it possesses neither the presidential "sword" nor the congressional "purse," and must rely instead on its mere "judgment" to interpret legal disputes.

> The Judiciary . . . has no influence over either the sword or the purse; *no direction either of the strength or of the wealth of society; and can take no active resolution whatever. It may truly be said to have neither force nor will, but merely judgment; and must ultimately depend upon the aid of the executive arm even for the efficacy of its judgments.*[2]

There was widespread agreement at the Constitutional Convention on the need for a national judiciary. However, the Framers were split on the scope of federal judicial power. William Randolph of Virginia offered the first proposal for the judiciary by calling for a Supreme Court and additional lower federal courts. William Paterson of New Jersey opposed this plan and instead proposed only a single national Supreme Court.[3] Paterson's chief objection to Randolph's plan, also known as the Virginia Plan, was his inclusion of lower federal courts. States' rights advocates argued that state courts should play a dominant role on judicial matters by serving as courts of **original jurisdiction** and that the national Supreme Court should have only **appellate jurisdiction** on cases involving the U.S. Constitution or federal law.

The delegates at the Constitutional Convention were in agreement on the need for a national Supreme Court, but disagreed on whether the federal court system should include lower federal district courts. This dispute was ultimately resolved by one of the many compromises made at the Constitutional Convention.[4] Article III, Section 1 of the Constitution stipulates that the judicial power of the United States "shall be vested in one Supreme Court and in such inferior Courts as the Congress may from time to time ordain and establish."[5] The Framers thus resolved the disagreement over whether to include lower federal courts by placing the controversy on the doorsteps of Congress. Congress later created our federal court system in the Judiciary Act of 1789, which is highlighted later in the chapter in our discussion of the *Marbury v. Madison* (1803) case.

Original Jurisdiction: *Courts that hear cases for the first time. These court decide on guilt or innocence or resolve civil disputes on the merits of the facts of the case.*

Appellate Jurisdiction: *Courts that hear cases on appeal from a lower court. These courts primarily determine whether a legal mistake was made at trial.*

Log in to **www.cengagebrain.com** and open CourseReader to access the reading:

Federalist Paper #78

The Federalist 78 is the first of Alexander Hamilton's great essays on the judiciary. Here Hamilton presents in detail his argument for judges holding their office "during good behavior," as the Constitution specifies they should. He says the judiciary is the least dangerous branch of government because it "can never attack" without the assistance of the other two branches of government. It is because of this that Hamilton argued judges need to be secure in their position through a life appointment. In this document Hamilton also asserts his belief in judicial review, the power of the court to declare legislative and executive acts unconstitutional. The court first exercised this power in the case of *Marbury v. Madison* in 1803.

- *Do you believe the Supreme Court is still the "least dangerous branch" of government? Why or why not?*

- *Why does Hamilton believe the judiciary is an essential branch of government? Does his rationale still apply today?*

Article III, Section 2 of the U.S. Constitution specifies which types of court cases are heard in federal courts. Cases that involve (1) the U.S. Constitution; (2) laws of the United States; (3) foreign policy; (4) maritime jurisdiction; (5) a state and citizen of another state (modified by Eleventh Amendment); and (6) litigants from different states are almost always tried in federal courts. The structure of the modern federal court system is quite straightforward. It consists of a three-tiered system that includes: (1) 94 district courts; (2) 12 regional courts of appeal and one Court of Appeals for the Federal Circuit; and (3) one U.S. Supreme Court. Most federal cases originate at the district court level. Each state has at least one district court and some larger states, such as California, Texas, and New York have four district courts. These courts primarily hear cases that involve disputes over federal laws, issues emanating from the U.S. Constitution, or diversity of citizenship cases, where a resident of one state files suit against a resident of another on an issue worth over $75,000. Rules granting federal jurisdiction over diversity of citizenship cases took shape during the Constitutional Convention when most residents felt greater loyalty to their respective states than to the federal government. We provide a visual representation of the federal court structure and highlight the number of federal case filings in Figure 7.1 and Table 7.1.

Having federal courts settle diversity of citizenship cases prevented either petitioners or respondents from having a home court advantage, and might have also encouraged some to invest in other regions of the nation, armed with the knowledge that any potential lawsuit would be heard in a neutral federal court. The number of diversity of citizenship filings has sharply increased from 48,626 in 2000 to 88,457 filings in 2008.[7] Congressional legislation enacted in the 1960s, such as the Civil Rights Act of 1964, the Voting Rights Act of 1965, and the Fair Housing Act of 1968 also sparked a rise in the number of cases filed in the federal courts. The number of civil rights cases, for instance, rose from approximately 300 in 1960 to almost

FIGURE 7.1. Federal Court System

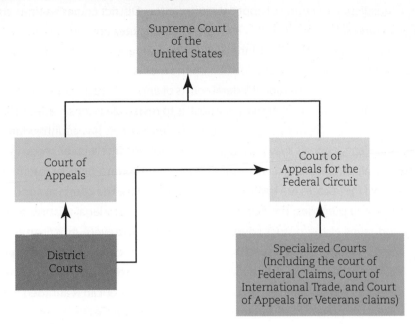

TABLE 7.1. Number of Civil and Criminal Cases Filed in U.S. District Courts[6]

Year	Criminal Cases Filed in Federal District Court	Civil Cases Filed in Federal District Court
1995	63,986	248,335
2000	83,303	259,519
2008	91,866	267,257

TABLE 7.2. Differences Between Federal and State Courts

	State Courts	Federal Courts
Court structure	Every state has its own court system. Some states have as many as 50 different types of courts. All states have at least three courts including a district court, a court of appeals, and a state supreme court.	Includes 94 district courts, 12 circuit court of appeals, one court of appeals for the federal circuit, and one U.S. Supreme Court. It also includes bankruptcy courts, federal claims courts, and the Court of International Trade.
Types of cases	Jurisdiction includes all cases that fall under state law including traffic violations, divorce and child custody, creditor–debtor disputes, personal injury cases, probate and inheritance matters, medical malpractice suits, and most criminal matters.	Jurisdiction includes cases involving the U.S. Constitution, federal laws, interstate disputes, issues involving foreign nations, or civil suits involving citizens from two different states when damages exceed $75,000.

25,000 filings by the late 1980s.[8] Federal district courts also include specialized courts, including bankruptcy courts, federals claims courts, and the Court of International Trade. In 2009, there were approximately 1.4 million filings in bankruptcy court, a 35 percent increase from the number of bankruptcy filings in 2008.[9]

Courts at the federal level are divided according to whether they are courts of original jurisdiction or courts of appellate jurisdiction. District courts serve as courts of original jurisdiction because this is where legal disputes are first heard. It is here where determinations of guilt or innocence are made, and it is in these courts that legal disputes of a civil nature are decided on the merits.

There are currently 12 regional federal courts of appeals and one Court of Appeals for the Federal Circuit, whose primary purpose is to review decisions made at the district court level. The Court of Appeals for the Federal Circuit has countrywide jurisdiction and hears appeals in specialized cases involving intellectual property (e.g., patents), administrative law, claims against the federal government, or international trade. Most of these cases are heard by three-judge panels. The courts of appeals primarily serve two purposes. The first purpose is to correct any legal mistake made by judges and juries at the district court level to ensure that every American receives due process under the law. A district court judge, for instance, might incorrectly interpret a legal procedure at trial that might call into question the integrity of the verdict. Appellate courts were established in part because every American is afforded the due process right to appeal a decision made at the district court level. One study found that federal appellate courts uphold federal district court decisions 88 percent of the time when reviewing cases on the merits.[10] The second purpose of the courts of appeals is to remove ambiguity and inconsistency in the way law is carried out. Decisions at the courts of appeals help to ensure that laws are applied in a similar manner across the nation.[11] Many appeals are not at all based on issues of due process, but rather highlight disputes involving legislative statutes or rules guiding administrative agencies. Appellate courts thus frequently settle disputes and set the standard for future cases by interpreting and setting guidelines on vague statutes or ambiguous administrative rules. The U.S. Court of Appeals also serves as the court of last resort for the vast majority of federal cases that do not make it to the U.S. Supreme Court. In Table 7.3 we provide an overview of the number of case filings in the U.S. Court of Appeals.

Almost all cases heard by the U.S. Supreme Court arrive on appeal from either the federal court of appeals or a state supreme court. The U.S. Supreme Court, however, will only hear an appeal from the state courts when a federal issue arises. A criminal defendant might appeal to the U.S. Supreme Court if he or she believes an existing state law violates a provision in the U.S. Constitution. There are currently nine justices on the U.S. Supreme Court as established by Congress in 1869.

TABLE 7.3. Appeals Filed to U.S. Court of Appeals[12]

ADMINISTRATIVE AGENCY				
Year	**Criminal**	**Civil**	**Prisoner Petitions**	**Bankruptcy**
1990	9,642	16,977	10,003	3,665
2000	10,707	18,528	17,252	4,244
2008	13,667	14,601	16,853	12,356

Double Jeopardy—From Ancient Greece to Hollywood

While all Americans have a right to appeal the lower court's decision, The U.S. Constitution's Fifth Amendment provision against double jeopardy prohibits federal prosecutors from charging the same person twice for the same crime. The concept of double jeopardy was used as a central theme in a Hollywood thriller starring Tommie Lee Jones and Ashley Judd in 1999. In the movie *Double Jeopardy* a woman was wrongfully imprisoned for the murder of her husband. It was later learned that her husband was actually still alive. After researching the double jeopardy provision, the Ashley Judd character reasoned that she could kill her husband once paroled because the government would be constitutionally prohibited from charging her once again for the murder of her husband. Would the double jeopardy provision allow this character to get away with such a murder in real life?

The Fifth Amendment to the U.S. Constitution bars the federal government from prosecuting individuals more than once for the same crime. The Constitution reads that no person shall be "subject for the same offence to be twice put in Jeopardy of life or limb." The theory behind double jeopardy extends all the way back to the Ancient Greek philosopher Demosthenes who in 355 BCE stated that "laws forbid the same man to be tried twice on the same issue."[13] St. Jerome in 391 CE interpreted the Old Testament to read that not even God passes judgment on man twice for a single act, and Roman law codified double jeopardy in the Digest of Justinian in 533 CE. The concept of double jeopardy is also found in British common law, albeit more narrowly tailored to defendants acquitted of felony charges.

The theory behind double jeopardy is, of course, to impede the government from using its immense power to unjustly convict the innocent, and to spare citizens the economic and emotional drain of never-ending prosecutions. In the United States, the concept of double jeopardy attaches to all criminal proceedings, both felonies and misdemeanors. The U.S. Supreme Court also expanded individual rights in its interpretation that double jeopardy should attach once a jury is convened, rather than once a defendant is acquitted. This means that prosecutors cannot charge a defendant for the same crime even if charges are dismissed before a verdict is rendered. Defendants, however, may be charged with the same crime when a mistrial is granted

continued ▶

in instances when juries are unable to reach unanimous verdicts. In *Blockburger v. United States* (1932), the Supreme Court established that the government may "prosecute an individual for more than one offense stemming from a single course of conduct only when each offense requires proof of a fact the other does not."[14] In other words, double jeopardy does not attach if two separate criminal codes are violated in a single act. The courts have also established that since the state and federal governments are separately sovereign, double jeopardy does not attach to the federal government in state proceedings, and vice versa.

While the movie *Double Jeopardy* received mixed reviews from film critics, it was universally panned by legal scholars who pointed out that double jeopardy only prevents prosecutors from bringing charges on the same set of facts twice. The double jeopardy provision would thus not attach in the scenario played out in this Hollywood movie.

Do you believe the double jeopardy provision is an important civil right or do you believe the government should be able to try a person more than once for the same crime?

State courts were established by individual state governments. Most Americans enter the American legal system through the state and local court level where approximately 96 percent of all cases are filed in the United States. The state and local courts are much more active than federal courts because the reach of their jurisdiction spans into areas involving traffic violations, divorce and child custody battles, creditor–debtor disputes, contract disputes, personal injury cases, and criminal matters involving such issues as illegal possession of drugs, theft, rape, and murder. Justice William Brennan once remarked that the "work of the courts in the 50 states probably has greater significance (than that of the U.S. Supreme Court) in measuring how well America attains the ideal of equal justice for all."[15] The state of Texas alone, for instance, had 9.4 million residents become more acquainted with municipal traffic courts than they probably cared to be from 1997 to 2006.[16]

Each state has established civil and criminal laws to regulate the conduct of its residents. While some cases at the state level are occasionally reviewed by federal courts, most begin and end at the state and local court level. Although there are some similarities in the way state courts are structured in that most include a supreme court, a court of appeals, and a trial court, state court systems are similar

TABLE 7.4. Types of Law[18]

Statutory Law	Law that comes from authoritative and specific law-making sources, primarily legislatures, but also includes treaties and executive orders.
Common Law	Judge-made law that originated in England in the twelfth century, when royal judges traveled around the country settling disputes in each locality according to prevailing custom. The common law continues to develop according to the rule of *stare decisis*, which means "let the decision stand."
Constitutional Law	Statements interpreting the U.S. Constitution that have been either given approval by Lower Courts or the Supreme Courts, or practiced without being tested in the courts.
Administrative Law	Law relating to the authority and procedures of administrative agencies as well as to the rules and regulations issued by those agencies.
Criminal Law	Law that defines crimes against the public order and provides for punishment. Government is responsible for enforcing criminal law, the great body of which is enacted by states and enforced by state officials in state courts. However, the criminal caseload of federal judges is growing.
Civil Law	Noncriminal forms of law that guide social relationships between residents. Civil law includes contract law, tort law, or property disputes that typically are settled through financial settlements.

to fingerprints in that no two are exactly the same. This is largely because states have continued to tinker with their respective court systems in order to address the changing nature of the legal system in that state. States have largely responded to particular challenges by creating additional and more specialized courts which some believe has resulted in a "complex" and rather "incoherent" court system in many states.[17] Some have called for standardizing court systems in order to streamline the way cases are handled across states. Table 7.4 provides an overview of the types of laws reviewed in state and federal courts.

THE POWER OF JUDICIAL REVIEW

So, how do judges at the federal and state level play a role in our system of government? Is the Supreme Court a coequal branch of government in name only? This section examines how through the power of judicial review our courts came to play a critical role in our system of government. The U.S. Supreme Court first gathered on February 1, 1790, in the Wall Street section of New York City, the nation's capital at the time. John Jay, one of the authors of the *Federalist Papers,* was appointed the first chief justice. The Court did not hear a case during the first year and it was still unclear as to how exactly the Court would operate in our system of checks and balances. Some of the justices were critical of the "limited stature" of the Court and the hardships associated with having to "ride circuit" under "primitive travel conditions."[19] The Supreme Court only heard approximately 50 cases from 1790 to 1799, and it was not originally viewed as the revered institution it is today. Chief Justice John Jay resigned from the position in order to run for governor of New York in 1795, and Robert H. Harrison declined his nomination to the U.S. Supreme Court during this period, opting instead to serve in the more prestigious state court system.[20]

▲ John Marshall served as the Chief Justice of the U.S. Supreme Court from 1801-1835. The Supreme Court was not highly regarded when Marshall was appointed Chief Justice by President Adams in 1801. However, his landmark decisions, such as Marbury v. Madison (1803), McCulloch v. Maryland (1819), Gibbons v. Ogden (1824), and others, helped transform the Court into the co equal branch of government it is today. The Liberty Bell in Philadelphia cracked while being rung to honor his death in 1835.

During this period there was still uncertainty as to where the authority of the state court ended and where the jurisdiction of the federal court began. In *Chisholm v. Georgia* (1793), a controversy erupted when the Supreme Court ruled that federal courts have jurisdiction when a citizen of one state brings a suit against another state. In this case two citizens from South Carolina sued the state of Georgia in an attempt to recover property acquired by the state of Georgia during the Revolutionary War. The South Carolina residents filed suit in federal court because the U.S. Constitution granted jurisdiction to federal courts when controversies arise "between a state and citizens of another state."[21] The state of Georgia refused to appear in federal court and enacted legislation barring participation because they believed this "would effectively destroy the retained sovereignty of the states."[22] The Supreme Court ruled against the state of Georgia in a 4–1 vote and temporarily broadened the scope of the federal court's jurisdiction on state matters. This decision, however, galvanized states' rights advocates and inspired the **Eleventh Amendment** to the U.S. Constitution, which overturned the *Chisholm* decision by stipulating that federal courts are prohibited from hearing cases when a resident brings a suit against a state.

Chief Justice John Marshall is widely heralded as the nation's finest chief justice because it was during his 34-year tenure that the Supreme Court became a coequal branch of government, and it is during this era that the Supreme Court defined its role in our system of checks and balances. John Marshall was born in Virginia as the eldest member of his 15 siblings. He fought in the Revolutionary Was against Britain and, unlike his cousin Thomas Jefferson, generally favored a stronger national government. He also authored more than 500 legal opinions over his career as chief justice, including such landmark decisions as *Marbury v. Madison* (1803), *McCulloch v. Maryland* (1819), and *Gibbons v. Ogden* (1824).

Without question the Supreme Court decision that had the most impact on the U.S. system of government occurred in *Marbury v. Madison* in 1803. This case transformed the role of the Supreme Court in our system of checks

Eleventh Amendment: *The judicial power of the United States shall not be construed to extend to any suit in law or equity, commenced or prosecuted against one of the United States by citizens of another State, or by citizens or subjects of any foreign State.*

Judicial Review: *The court's power to strike laws that violate the U.S. Constitution.*

and balances by establishing the court's power of **judicial review.** The term *judicial review* refers to the judiciary's power to declare legislative and presidential acts unconstitutional. It was initially unclear what role the Supreme Court would play in our system of government. The *Marbury v. Madison* (1803) case was a landmark decision because it represented the first time the Supreme Court asserted the power of judicial review. By striking down a congressional statute as unconstitutional, the Marshall Court defined the role the Supreme Court would come to play in our system of checks and balances. This decision established that the primary purpose of the Supreme Court is to verify that state and federal governmental behavior is consistent with the principles outlined in the U.S. Constitution.

THEORY AND PRACTICE

Federal-State Powers and the Regulation of Sexual Activity in the Twenty-first Century

Many states throughout American history restricted certain forms of sexual activity by enacting sodomy laws. The concept of sodomy originally arose in biblical descriptions associated with the perceived depraved behavior of the residents of Sodom and Gomorrah. Sodomy was initially defined as "anal intercourse between two men or a man and a woman," or sexual intercourse between a human and nonhuman.[23] Greek mythology prominently featured centaurs, creatures that were half-man and half-horse, and during the Middle Ages some in the science community believed it was possible for humans to procreate with members of the animal kingdom. By 1900, 13 states expanded their definition of sodomy to include fellatio, or oral sex.

The first federal privacy challenge against state sodomy laws did not occur until 1944. An Arizona man unsuccessfully argued his privacy rights were violated after he was arrested for "consensual fellatio" with another man in his home. In *Griswold v. Connecticut* (1965), the Supreme Court for the first time recognized the right to privacy by striking down a Connecticut law that prohibited the distribution of contraceptives to married couples. This newly established constitutional right of privacy influenced approximately 20 states to repeal their sodomy laws during the 1970s. The momentum against sodomy laws continued into the early 1980s when New York, Pennsylvania,

continued

© ISTOCKPHOTO.COM/DIEGO CERVO

continued

Alaska, and Wisconsin revoked sodomy laws.[24] However, the U.S. Supreme Court upheld Georgia's sodomy law in the *Bowers v. Hardwick* case in 1986. Justice Byron White's majority opinion affirmed a previous standard that only recognized a right to "engage in procreative sexual activity" and argued that the Founding Fathers would not support a "right" to engage in sodomy. The Georgia sodomy law banned the practice of sodomy to heterosexual and same-sex couples.

The Supreme Court heard another sodomy case almost 20 years later in the *Lawrence v. Texas* (2003) case. In this case John Geddes Lawrence and Tyrone Garner were arrested for engaging in consensual anal sex. Police observed the sexual encounter when they entered the home after receiving a false report of a weapons disturbance. The Texas sodomy law differed from the Georgia sodomy law in that it targeted only same-sex couples. This is significant because it enabled Lawrence to argue that because the Texas law did not apply to heterosexual couples the statute violated both his constitutional right to privacy and the equal protection clause of the Fourteenth Amendment. The Supreme Court ruled in favor of Lawrence and struck sodomy laws as unconstitutional, marking the first time same-sex behavior has been afforded constitutional protection by the U.S. Supreme Court.

Do you believe states are within their rights to prohibit same-sex couples from marrying?

Why or why not?

© ISTOCKPHOTO.COM/LORENZO COLLORETA

The facts of the *Marbury v. Madison* case have their roots in the infamous presidential election of 1800. Some of the controversial aspects of this election were reviewed in the American presidency chapter. This election was ultimately decided by the House of Representatives after Thomas Jefferson and his running mate Aaron Burr were deadlocked with 73 electoral votes, surpassing the vote totals of then president John Adams and his running mate Charles Pinckney. In the original version of the Electoral College candidates were not designated as presidential or vice presidential candidates. Candidates with the majority of electoral votes became president and the second-place vote getter became vice president. This election prompted the Twelfth Amendment, which established that candidates must run on a ticket that designates the presidential and vice presidential candidate. The House of Representatives eventually broke the tie in Thomas Jefferson's favor after Delaware representative James A. Baynard switched his vote on the 36th ballot.

John Adams did not take losing the presidency well. He was so humiliated by the defeat to his long-time rival that he did not even attend Jefferson's presidential inauguration, opting instead to get an early start on his journey home to Braintree, Massachusetts. On the eve of Jefferson's inauguration President Adams made

CourseReader ASSIGNMENT

Log in to **www.cengagebrain.com** and open CourseReader to access the reading:

Lawrence v. Texas

In *Lawrence v. Texas (2003),* the U.S. Supreme Court ruled that the Texas statute that made it illegal for same-sex couples to engage in sodomy violated the constitutional rights of same-sex couples on privacy and equal protection grounds. This decision overturned the precedent in *Bowers v. Hardwick (1986),* which upheld Georgia's sodomy law that applied to both heterosexual and same-sex couples. This is the first time the U.S. Supreme Court extended constitutional protection to same-sex behavior.

- *Should the state be permitted to regulate any type of sexual activity between consenting adults?*
- *How are sodomy laws different than laws against prostitution or incest?*

a flurry of **"midnight appointments"** to the federal judiciary. This was a particularly provocative thing to do because Jefferson, as a states' rights advocate, campaigned against the growth of the federal court system. In what was perhaps a partisan act against Jeffersonian Republicans, Adams appointed 16 federalist judges and 42 federalist justices of the peace to the federal court system before leaving the White House. These appointments were all approved the following day in the U.S. Senate. The nominating commissions, however, needed to be delivered to the appointed justices in order to make the appointments official. The responsibility to deliver these commissions fell to Adams's secretary of state, who ironically happened to be none other than John Marshall, who carried on as Adams's Secretary of State even after being appointed chief justice of the U.S. Supreme Court. In the haste to leave the White House, Marshall neglected to deliver some of the commissions to the newly appointed justices. It was wrongfully assumed that James Madison as President Jefferson's new secretary of state would deliver the remaining commissions upon entering office.

However, one of President Jefferson's first official acts was to order his staff not to deliver the remaining judicial commissions, which in his view rendered those judicial appointments null and void. William Marbury, an enthusiastic supporter of John Adams, was one of the justices denied his judgeship by President Jefferson. Marbury sued Jefferson's secretary of state James Madison, who was also the principal author of the U.S. Constitution. The drama reached a fever pitch when President Jefferson suggested that he might not follow through on Marbury's nomination even if ordered to do so by the court. This potential scenario concerned Chief Justice Marshall because it could create a constitutional crisis that might forever weaken the Supreme Court. What would happen, after all, if the president simply ignored a Supreme Court ruling? In this one decision Chief Justice Marshall managed to write an opinion that avoided a constitutional showdown with the executive branch, politically embarrassed his cousin President Jefferson, and elevated the stature of the Supreme Court to a coequal branch of government by establishing the power of judicial review.

Marshall decided the case by reasoning through three legal questions. The first was whether Marbury was legally entitled to the judgeship. Here, Marshall answered in the affirmative by declaring Marbury's appointment was valid because he was appointed by a sitting president and confirmed by the U.S. Senate, thus meeting the judicial appointment standard outlined in the Constitution. The fact that Marbury's commission was never delivered (by Marshall) was a mere technicality that did not invalidate Marbury's appointment. The second question was whether the Supreme Court was equipped with a remedy to facilitate Marbury's appointment. On this point the Court again answered in the affirmative. The **Judiciary Act of 1789** granted the Court the authority to issue a writ of mandamus. The writ of mandamus authorizes the Court to order public officials to perform a particular act. Chief Justice Marshall thus reasoned that the Court is authorized to order President Jefferson to seat Marbury. The third and most critical question grappled with whether asking the Supreme Court for a writ of mandamus was an acceptable legal remedy. It is on this question that Marshall found a legal loophole that enabled him to avoid a political showdown with Jefferson. The Court ruled that Section 13 of the Judiciary Act was invalid because it stipulated that petitioners requesting a writ of mandamus may bring the matter directly to the Supreme Court.

This was problematic for Marshall because Article III, Section 2 of the Constitution expressly stipulates that only cases "affecting Ambassadors, other public Ministers and Consuls, and those in which a State shall be a Party" may bring their case directly to the Supreme Court.[25] All other cases must be appealed to the Supreme Court. Marshall contended that Congress was not authorized to stipulate that the Supreme Court will have original jurisdiction on cases involving a writ of mandamus because this would in effect amend the language in Article III, Section 2 of the U.S. Constitution. And the only legal way to alter the language of the U.S. Constitution, he reasoned, is through a constitutional amendment.

Marshall avoided the showdown with President Jefferson by declaring the original jurisdiction provision of the judiciary act unconstitutional. The Court's assertion of judicial review in this case was never seriously challenged, and eventually cemented into legal precedent. This is probably because Marshall did not assert the power of judicial review to challenge President Jefferson's executive authority, but was rather used to avoid a confrontation with him. Marshall's decision was also masterful because judicial review was first used on an issue involving the judicial process, rather than on a question involving the constitutional authority of one of the other

Judiciary Act of 1789:
Principally written by Senators Oliver Ellsworth of Connecticut and New Jersey's William Paterson, the Judiciary Act of 1789 established the federal court system that originally included one federal district court per state. Section 13 of the Judiciary Act also granted the Supreme Court the authority to issue a "writ of mandamus" loosely translated to mean "we order," which played a key role in the legal battle associated with the landmark Marbury v. Madison (1803) case.

Do you believe it was unethical for Chief Justice Marshall to rule in the case of Marbury v. Madison considering he was personally involved in the matter?

two branches of government.[26] Marshall did not use the power of judicial review to strike down any other congressional statute after the Marbury case. The Court did, however, use the power of judicial review to strike down state laws in the landmark cases of *McCulloch v. Maryland* (1819) and *Gibbons v. Ogden* (1824).

THE SUPREME COURT'S ROLE IN EXPANDING CIVIL AND POLITICAL RIGHTS

In Chapter 4, we reviewed how federal powers were greatly enhanced because of the Marshall Court's decision in *McCulloch v. Maryland* (1819). You might remember that it was this decision that established the federal government was permitted to create a national banking system because the national government had "implied powers" (also known as the elastic clause) that went beyond the enumerated powers of the national government. The Marshall Court established that the national government has additional implied powers when these powers are *"necessary and proper"* in order to carry out the enumerated powers outlined in Article I, Section 8 of the U.S. Constitution. Marshall also angered states' rights advocates in *McCulloch* by ruling state governments are not permitted to tax the federal government because the "power to tax involves the power to destroy." The Marshall Court expanded federal power once again in the landmark *Gibbons v. Ogden* (1824) decision. This case involved a dispute between the state of New York and the federal government. In this case a steamboat operator named Aaron Ogden was issued a license to ferry passengers from New Jersey to New York City and back by the state of New York. Thomas Gibbons, one of Ogden's competitors in the ferry business, received a similar license from the U.S. Congress to operate his ferry along a similar route. The constitutional issue in this case revolved around whether New York's practice of licensing business permits to steamboat carriers conflicted with Congress's enumerated power to regulate interstate commerce. Marshall once again expanded federal power by ruling against the state of New York by asserting that the navigation of interstate waterways falls under the authority of the national government because it is expressly authorized to regulate interstate commerce in Article I, Section 8 of the Constitution.

Similar to *Marbury v. Madison* (1803) and *McCulloch v. Maryland* (1819), Marshall's ruling in *Gibbons v. Ogden* (1824) was a transforming legal decision whose importance has grown with each passing decade.[27] An expansive interpretation of the Interstate Commerce Clause, for instance, was used to uphold sections of the Civil Rights Act of 1964 when the Supreme Court found racially restrictive practices, such as barring African Americans from hotels or restaurants could be made illegal by Congress because a substantial number of potential customers could come from other states.[28] The Gibbons decision expanded federal power by broadening federal regulatory control over business transactions that cross state lines. The Interstate Commerce Clause now serves as the rationale for federal regulatory control over the environment, the public airwaves, and major financial institutions. It is because of the Interstate Commerce Clause that the federal government had strong regulatory control over the recent financial crisis in the United States that led to the $800 billion dollar bailout of the U.S. banking system in 2008.

Marshall's opinions in *Marbury v. Madison* (1803), *McCulloch v. Maryland* (1819), and *Gibbons v. Ogden* (1824) significantly strengthened the power of the national government in the early decades of the nineteenth century. Some southern states strongly opposed Marshall's legacy of favoring the supremacy of the national government. John C. Calhoun, for instance, was a strong states' rights advocate who argued on behalf of the institution of slavery. Calhoun advocated for the "**doctrine of nullification,**" arguing that states were empowered to veto any federal policy

Doctrine of Nullification: *The doctrine associated with John Calhoun and other states rights advocates in the late 1820s and 1830s asserting that states were within their rights to declare null and void any federal law they believed violated the constitutional rights of states.*

WHY POLITICS MATTERS TO YOU!

Federal-State Powers, the Interstate Commerce Clause, and the Americans with Disabilities Act of 1990

The Interstate Commerce Clause has been successfully used by the federal government to assert authority over the states in the realm of civil rights. Article 1, Section 8 of the Constitution stipulates that the "Congress shall have Power . . . to regulate Commerce with foreign Nations, and among the several States. . . ." In the 1930s, constitutional law professor Edward S. Corwin stated that the "most important source of national power touching private conduct is, in ordinary times, the power of Congress to regulate commerce among the states."[29] It is because of this that Supreme Court Justice Sonia Sotomayor was asked about her interpretation of the Interstate Commerce Clause in her Senate confirmation hearing in 2009.

While the Fourteenth Amendment prohibits states from denying residents the due process of law, the equal protection of the law, and privileges and immunities, it did not ban the private sector from discriminating on the basis of race, gender, or religion. It was not until the Civil Rights Act of 1964 that public and private businesses were forbidden from discriminating against targeted communities. Congress enacted the Civil Rights Act in 1964 on the premise that it was authorized to do so by the Interstate Commerce Clause. The Civil Rights Act barred "private business owners from discriminating based

continued

on race, sex, or religion" on the premise that most businesses have customers who at least occasionally come from across state lines.[30] In *Katzenbach v. McClung* (1964) the Supreme Court upheld Congress's right to prohibit restaurants from denying food service on the basis of race. In *Heart of Atlanta Motel v. Atlanta* (1964) the Supreme Court used the same rationale to uphold laws prohibiting hotel owners from denying accommodations on the basis of race.

Congress also used the Interstate Commerce Clause (and the Fourteenth Amendment) to extend the basic features of the Civil Rights Act to the disabled when they enacted the Americans with Disabilities Act (ADA) in 1990. The Americans with Disabilities Act is one of the most significant pieces of legislation ever enacted into American law. The Act transformed American society by putting in place the necessary infrastructure that made it possible for the disabled to leave the confines of their homes and become full-fledged members of American society. The Act affords extensive federal protection to the disabled in the workplace, in public restaurants, on public transportation, and in telecommunications.[31] Title 1 of the Act prohibits employers from discriminating against qualified disabled people, who may or may not require "reasonable accommodation," in private hiring or promotion practices. The Act defines the disabled as those who possess a "physical or mental impairment that substantially limits one or more of the major life activities."[32]

Title III of the ADA prohibits members of the public or private sector from discriminating against the disabled by denying them public accommodation in hotels, restaurants, theaters, schools, private offices, museums, parks, and other public and private facilities. This provision among other things required these facilities to build ramps and retrofit bathrooms to accommodate wheelchair access. In *Martin v. PGA Tour* (2001) the Supreme Court ruled that the ADA public accommodation requirement required the PGA Tour to make a reasonable accommodation to a disabled professional golfer by allowing him to use a golf cart on the PGA tour.

> **Do you believe the Supreme Court's interpretation of the Interstate Commerce Clause in the area of civil rights has given the federal government too much authority over the states? Why or why not?**

that it perceived to be unconstitutional. The nullification issue came to a head after the South Carolina legislature nullified a federal tariff that it found objectionable. President Andrew Jackson eventually persuaded South Carolina to refrain from pursuing its nullification strategy, but states' rights passions later instigated the U.S. Civil War that resulted in 600,000 American deaths.[33] Echoes of the nullification movement can be heard in the debate about how best to implement the recently enacted Health Care Reform Act of 2010 (see Chapter 5). The Act expands health care coverage to 32 million Americans in part by requiring those who can afford health care to purchase it. In 2010, 26 states filed suit against the federal government asserting that this provision and others go beyond the constitutional authority of the federal government. In 2011, a Florida district judge ruled that the federal government did not have the constitutional authority to require individuals to purchase health care. This matter will ultimately be decided by the U.S. Supreme Court.

During the Civil War era, states' rights advocates received a boost when Roger Taney ascended to chief justice in 1835. Taney chaired Andrew Jackson's presidential campaign in Maryland and went on to serve as Jackson's attorney general before becoming chief justice. Taney is most widely known for his role in the *Dred Scott v. Sanford* (1857) decision. This decision is frequently pointed to as the low point in the history of the U.S. Supreme Court because it lent legitimacy to the institution of slavery and played a role in polarizing North–South tensions.

Dred Scott was a slave "owned" by Missouri army surgeon Dr. John Emerson. Scott was taken by Emerson into the free Louisiana territory. Dred Scott filed suit claiming that Emerson's wife "beat, bruised, and ill-treated him" and that he should no longer be considered "the property" of the Emerson's because they relocated to "free" territory.[34] In the suit Scott and his national supporters claimed a "once free, always free" legal strategy by asserting Scott was legally a free man since he resided for seven years in "free" territory. The first question addressed by the Taney court was whether Dred Scott had legal standing to bring a case to the Supreme Court. The Court ruled Dred Scott did not have legal standing because as a slave he did not possess any of the rights associated with citizenship.

Abolitionists: *Members of a political movement that sought to abolish the institution of slavery. The movement in the United States was largely led by William Lloyd Garrison and Frederick Douglas.*

Missouri Compromise (1820): *A political compromise whereby Missouri was admitted into the Union as a slave state and Maine as a free state. The remaining states in the Louisiana territory were divided as slave states in the south and free states in the north.*

They [African Americans] are not included, and were not intended to be included, under the word "citizens" in the Constitution, and can therefore claim none of the rights and privileges which that instrument provides for and secures to citizens of the United States. On the contrary, they were at that time [1787] considered as a subordinate and inferior class of beings, who had been subjugated by the dominant race, and, whether emancipated or not, yet remained subject to their authority, and had no rights or privileges but such as those who held the power and the Government might choose to grant them.[35]

The case should have concluded on the legal standing issue alone. The Taney Court, however, infuriated northern **abolitionists** by further declaring a portion of the **Missouri Compromise (1820)** unconstitutional. One of the provisions of the

Missouri Compromise prohibited slave owners from bringing slaves into free territories. The Taney court ruled Congress did not have the constitutional authority to prohibit slave owners from bringing slaves into free territories. This decision enraged northern abolitionists who feared slavery would expand into western territories. The *Dred Scott* decision accelerated the forces that led to the Civil War and seriously damaged the reputation and stature of the Court. This decision was later made moot with the passage of the Thirteenth Amendment which abolished the institution of slavery.

The Incorporation of the Bill of Rights into the States

The Civil War resulted in the passage of three constitutional amendments that granted all rights of citizenship to African Americans. The **Thirteenth Amendment (1865)** outlawed slavery, the **Fourteenth Amendment (1868)** broadly prohibited states from denying rights of citizenship, and the **Fifteenth Amendment (1870)** made it illegal for states to deny voting rights on the basis of race. These amendments transformed federal–state relations because the Constitution for the first time stipulated parameters on how states are to treat its residents. It is important to remember that the Bill of Rights, highlighted in the first 10 amendments of the U.S. Constitution, were ratified for the purpose of restricting only the behavior of the national government. In *Barron v. Baltimore* (1833) Chief Justice Marshall ruled that states were not bound by the just compensation provision of the Fifth Amendment because the Bill of Rights were written to limit the powers of the federal government, not limit the powers of the states. The Fourteenth Amendment modified this arrangement. The Fourteenth Amendment states that "no state shall make or enforce any law which shall abridge the privileges or immunities of citizens of the United States, nor shall any State deprive any person of life, liberty, or property, without due process of law, nor deny to any person within its jurisdiction the equal protection of the laws.[36] Did this mean that states were now required to abide by the Bill of Rights? This was answered over the next few decades when the Court adopted the process of **selective incorporation.**

In *Gitlow v. New York* (1925) the Court ruled that the freedom of speech and the freedom of press provisions of the First Amendment can be applied to the states, thereby setting in motion the principle of selective incorporation. In the *Gitlow* case, the Supreme Court nationalized the rights associated with freedom of speech and freedom of the press because it ruled these rights were of a "fundamental value."[37] Selective incorporation meant that the Court would require the states to abide by any of the Bill of Rights that it perceived to be a "fundamental value." Later in the *Palko v. Connecticut* (1937) double jeopardy case, the term *fundamental value* is defined as any right that is vital in order for liberty to exist in the state.[38] In 2008, the Supreme Court nationalized the individual right to own and carry a gun by striking down gun control legislation in *D.C. v. Heller* (2008). Table 7.5 reveals that most, but

Thirteenth Amendment: *An amendment to the Constitution that abolished the institution of slavery in the United States*

Fourteenth Amendment: *The post civil war amendment that guaranteed all Americans the rights of due process of law, equal protection of law, and equal privileges and immunites.*

Fifteenth Amendment: *The amendment that made it illegal to deny voting rights on the basis of race.*

Selective Incorporation: *The process by which many of the bill of rights were nationalized into the states.*

TABLE 7.5. The Nationalization of the Bill of Rights—Selective Incorporation[39]

First Amendment
Speech and press—*Gitlow v. New York* (1925)
Free exercise of religion—*Cantwell v. Connecticut* (1940)
Establishment clause—*Everson v. Board of Education* (1947)

Second Amendment
Individual right to own a gun—*D. C. v. Heller* (2008)

Fourth Amendment
Search and seizure—*Wolf v. Colorado* (1949)
Exclusionary rule—*Mapp v. Ohio* (1961)

Fifth Amendment
Just compensation (eminent domain)—*Burlington and Quincy v. Chicago* (1897)
Self-incrimination—*Molloy v. Hogan* (1964)
Double jeopardy—*Benton v. Maryland* (1969)

Sixth Amendment
Right to counsel (felony)—*Gideon v. Wainwright* (1963)
Speedy trial—*Klopfer v. North Carolina* (1967)
Jury trial—*Duncan v. Louisiana* (1968)

Eighth Amendment
Cruel and unusual punishment—*Louisiana v. Resweber* (1947)

Ninth Amendment
Privacy—*Griswold v. Connecticut* (1965)

Rights That Have Never Been Incorporated into the States

Third Amendment
Quartering soldiers

Fifth Amendment
Right to grand jury

Seventh Amendment
Right to jury trial in civil cases

not all, of the major provisions in the Bill of Rights have since been incorporated into the states through the process of selective incorporation.

President Dwight Eisenhower appointed Earl Warren to the U.S. Supreme Court in 1953. Warren served as governor of the state of California after running for the vice presidency with presidential candidate Thomas Dewey in 1948. Dewey lost in a close election to Harry Truman that year. President Eisenhower was disappointed with Warren's liberal interpretations on the Court and later remarked that nominating Warren was "the biggest-damn-fool mistake I ever made."[40] Perhaps the most important decision rendered by the Warren Court was the *Brown v. Board of Education* (1954) case, which was responsible for asserting federal power by desegregating public school systems across all states. In that case Linda Carol Brown, an eight-year-old African American girl from Topeka, Kansas, was denied access to a neighborhood school because of the color of her skin. The girl's father was a pastor in a local church in what was a mostly white neighborhood. Schools in Topeka were segregated by race at the time, which was permissible under Kansas law. The Brown family believed that the school designated for black students was inferior to the all-white school. The all-black school was also a much longer distance from their home. The Brown family thus filed suit challenging the school segregation policy as a violation of their daughter's rights guaranteed under the Equal Protection Clause of the Fourteenth Amendment.[41]

In order to win the case the Browns needed to overturn the long-standing **"separate but equal"** precedent established in the *Plessy v. Ferguson* case of 1896. The *Plessy* case involved a Louisiana law that made it illegal for African Americans to commingle with whites in railroad cars. In the *Plessy* case the Court ruled that segregating train travel did not violate the equal protection clause of the Fourteenth Amendment. This ruling established that segregation was permissible as long as the races had access to similar public facilities. It was because of the *Plessy* ruling that states were permitted to segregate rest rooms, water fountains, schools, hospitals, restaurants, hotels, cemeteries, and other places of public accommodation.

"Separate but equal doctrine": *The legal doctrine established in the Plessy v. Ferguson (1896) case that upheld racial segregation laws in the south.*

The *Brown v. Board of Education* (1954) decision overturned the legal precedent of separate but equal. Chief Justice Warren concluded in the *Brown* decision "that in the field of public education the doctrine of 'separate but equal' had no place." The Court was particularly persuaded that public segregation was in fact not equal because one race was preventing another race access to superior public schools. This was psychologically damaging and harmful to the self-esteem of African American children who were brought up believing they were inferior to white children. The Warren Court expanded on the rationale of *Brown* in the **Loving v. Virginia (1967)** case by striking down a Virginia law that prohibited interracial marriages. It is now hard to imagine that these types of discriminatory laws were carried out in some states only a few short decades ago.

The Warren court also expanded democratic rights in the landmark *Baker v. Carr* (1962) case discussed in Chapter 5 on the American Congress. The *Baker* decision was a landmark case credited with legally establishing the noted principle of "one person, one vote," by prohibiting malapportionment in state legislative districts.[42] The setting that catapulted this issue to the Supreme Court's doorstep came about in Tennessee. The disparity in the state house district population ranged from 2,340 citizens in one county to 42,298 citizens in another county.[43] Charles Baker, a voter along with other Tennessee voters, filed a lawsuit in federal district court against the state, naming Joe Carr, the state official in charge of elections, as the

▲ Sisters Linda and Terry Lynn Brown sit on a fence outside of their school, the racially segregated Monroe Elementary School, Topeka, Kansas, in March of 1953. The Brown family initiated the landmark civil rights lawsuit Brown v. Board of Education, which ruled it was unconstitutional to racially segregate students in public schools.

© CARL IWASAKI/TIME & LIFE PICTURES/GETTY IMAGES

▲ The nine U.S. Supreme Court Justices gather for a group portrait at the Supreme Court building in Washington, D.C., in October of 2010. The Justices include (sitting from left to right) Clarence Thomas, Antonin Scalia, John G. Roberts (Chief Justice), Anthony Kennedy, and Ruth Bader Ginsburg. Standing (from left to right) is Sonia Sotomayor, Stephen Breyer, Samuel Alito, and Elena Kagan. The Court now, for the first time, includes three female Justices.

defendant. Baker claimed that malapportionment violated the equal protection clause of the Fourteenth Amendment to the U.S. Constitution because it had the effect of weakening the political clout of minority groups. The most significant impact of the Court's ruling in favor of Baker was it established that states must possess population equality across legislative districts, thus protecting the concept of one person, one vote, and expanding political power for urban areas. The *Baker* decision also motivated a sweeping reapportionment movement across the nation that culminated in the redrawing of legislative districts in every state and greater representation for both urban areas and ethnic minorities.

THE FEDERAL JUDICIAL SELECTION PROCESS

The judicial selection process has also caused great controversy throughout our history. This is largely because our desire to have a judiciary that is insulated from political pressures runs alongside our desire to hold judges accountable for decisions that negatively impact our society. The problem is that the goal of "judicial independence" is somewhat mutually exclusive from the objective of "judicial accountability."[44] In order to have an independent judiciary it is necessary to remove judges from the political process, and in order to hold justices accountable it becomes necessary to include justices in our political process. It is naturally equally important to devise a judicial selection process that produces the most capable justices. The great debate revolving around our judicial selection process largely involves whether it is preferable to appoint or elect justices to the bench.

The Framers at the Constitutional Convention were primarily interested in creating an independent federal judiciary that would remain above the political fray. It is because of this they opted for an appointive process that granted a life term for federal justices. Some of the Framers pointed to problems in the British judicial system where it was somewhat common for British monarchs to punish British justices by lowering their salary when they disagreed with judicial decisions. They sought to prevent this from happing in American courts by stipulating in Article III of the

Constitution that federal justices will serve life terms and "shall hold their Offices during good Behaviour" and receive "Compensation which shall not be diminished."[45] While Congress can use its budgetary powers to voice its discontentment with judicial decisions, the primary political check on the behavior of federal justices is the threat of impeachment. Although the judicial branch was initially viewed as a weak and ineffective branch of government, the executive and legislative branches came into conflict with the Court only a few years after the Constitution's ratification. President Thomas Jefferson convinced members of Congress to impeach Supreme Court Justice Samuel Chase in 1805 mostly because the justice sometimes went on tirades against Jefferson and his policies from the bench. Chase was later acquitted by the Senate and no Supreme Court justice has since been impeached, although Justice Abe Fortas was pressured to resign in 1969 for accepting a secret retainer from a Wall Street financier. Table 7.6 highlights the number of state and federal judges across the nation.

The federal judicial selection process is in most respects quite straightforward. All federal justices are appointed by the president and confirmed by a majority vote in the U.S. Senate. Alexander Hamilton in *Federalist Paper No. 76* argued that it is better to have a single individual appoint federal justices because "there would be fewer personal attachments to gratify."[46] Presidents are typically actively involved in the selection process of Supreme Court justices because of the potential impact it could have on the president's agenda and political legacy. The confirmation process typically includes input from vocal special-interest groups and can be an intensely political affair, as witnessed by the Senate rejection of Robert Bork in 1987 and controversies surrounding the successful confirmation of Justice Clarence Thomas in 1991. The Senate has confirmed 27 of the 31 nominees appointed to the U.S. Supreme Court since 1949.[47]

Hundreds of federal justices are appointed at the district and court of appeals level during each presidential term, which makes it difficult for the president to be directly involved in these appointments. At this level the Department of Justice and the U.S. Senate play a particularly important role. During the mid-nineteenth century a system of **senatorial courtesy** developed. Senatorial courtesy empowers senators of the same political party as the president and representing states with a judicial vacancy to play a significant role in the process. These senators frequently recommend nominees to the Justice Department, and the Senate will typically reject nominees that do not meet with the approval of the senator from that state. Presidents are likely to select another justice if a home state senator threatens to invoke senatorial courtesy.

Senatorial Courtesy: *The unofficial U.S. Senate custom of rejecting presidential judicial appointees when the nominee from the Senator's state is not supported by that state's senior Senator of the President's party.*

TABLE 7.6. Number of Federal and State Court Judges[48]

	State Court	Federal Court
Number of judges	17,108	874

The Senate Confirmation of Justice Sonia Sotomayor

In August 2009 the U.S. Senate confirmed Justice Sonia Sotomayor to the U.S. Supreme Court on a 68–31 vote. Justice Sotomayor was only the third female justice to sit on the U.S. Supreme Court since the founding of our nation. Supreme Court Justice Sandra Day O'Connor was the first woman to serve after being nominated by President Reagan in 1981 and Justice Ruth Bader Ginsberg was later appointed to the Court by President Bill Clinton in 1993. Justice Sotomayor is also the first Hispanic American to serve on the nation's highest Court, making her confirmation an especially proud moment for 47 million Hispanic Americans. President Barack Obama welcomed her confirmation as "breaking yet another barrier and moving us yet another step closer to a more perfect union."[49]

Justice Sonia Sotomayor spoke mostly in Spanish as a child growing up in a Bronx, New York public housing development. Her parents immigrated to New York City from Puerto Rico during World War II. She was diagnosed with juvenile diabetes when she was eight years old, and her father, who worked as a tool and die maker, died a year later.[50] Her mother raised Justice Sotomayor and her younger brother while working as a nurse in a New York City methadone clinic. On a single income, her mother struggled to purchase an encyclopedia set, which was used as the major resource for homework assignments throughout her childhood. Inspired by her mother's strict emphasis on education and the positive example set by her high school debate coach, Justice Sotomayor went on to graduate from Princeton University in 1976. At Princeton she honed her writing skills, and later went on to graduate from Yale Law School in 1979, where she served as the editor of the *Yale University Law Review*. Justice Sotomayor was originally appointed to the federal bench by President George H. W. Bush in 1991 and was later appointed by President Bill Clinton to serve on the U.S. Court of Appeals in 1997.[51]

While Justice Sotomayor's confirmation was never seriously in doubt, some conservative special-interest groups attempted to delay it. During her confirmation debate on the Senate floor some Republican senators labeled her a "judicial activist" and criticized her judicial opinion on a "racial discrimination case brought by white firefighters" in Connecticut.[52] Other Republican senators were reluctant to oppose her nomination, however, fearing that it might result in a political backlash from Hispanic women voters in subsequent elections. The future direction of the Court is not likely

continued

continued

to be changed significantly by her presence on the bench as her moderate-to-liberal judicial record does not widely deviate from Justice David Souter, the justice whose vacancy she has filled.

What criteria do you believe presidents should use when selecting Supreme Court Justices?

JUDICIAL SELECTION ACROSS STATES

At the beginning of this chapter, we gave emphasis to the fact that no two state court systems are exactly alike. Accordingly, states use a variety of methods for selecting judges at the state level. There are four distinct methods used at the state level including: (1) gubernatorial/legislative appointment; (2) partisan elections; (3) nonpartisan elections; and (4) the merit system. Some states use one process for selecting Supreme Court justices and another approach for selecting lower level judges. The gubernatorial appointment approach closely mirrors the approach used at the federal level. In this system the governor of the state appoints the justice and the state senate confirms the appointment. As Table 7.7 reveals, three of the four states that use this approach were in existence at the time of the Constitutional Convention. Virginia is somewhat unique in that they have their state legislature appoint judges. Approximately 75 percent of justices selected using this approach are former state legislators.[53]

Most state courts across the nation select judges through the electoral process. These states are perhaps more concerned with holding judges politically accountable than they are in ensuring judicial independence. There are currently twenty-one states who select judges at the ballot box. Eight states use a partisan election approach whereby judges run under a political party affiliation (i.e. Republican or Democratic candidates). Many states select judges through a non-partisan election approach. Judges in these states run in an election but do not attach themselves to a particular political party. Critics of judicial elections warn against the potential corrupting influences of campaign contributions and potential conflicts of interests, particularly after the *Citizens United* (2010) Supreme Court decision, which overturned a 100 year old ban on the use of corporate and union funds in political campaigns. Some also point to the non-competitive nature of judicial elections and problems associated with low name recognition of judges with voters.

TABLE 7.7. Judicial Selection Methods at the State Level[54]

Merit System	Appointment by Governor or Legislature	Partisan Election	Nonpartisan	Multiple Methods
Alaska	California (G)	Alabama	Georgia	Arizona
Colorado	Maine (G)	Arkansas	Idaho	Florida
Connecticut	New Jersey (G)	Illinois	Kentucky	Indiana
Delaware	Virginia (L)	Louisiana	Michigan	Kansas
District of Columbia		North Carolina	Minnesota	Missouri
Hawaii		Pennsylvania	Mississippi	New York
Iowa		Texas	Montana	Oklahoma
Maryland		West Virginia	Nevada	South Dakota
Massachusetts			North Dakota	Tennessee
Nebraska			Ohio	
New Hampshire			Oregon	
New Mexico			Washington	
Rhode Island			Wisconsin	
South Carolina				
Utah				
Vermont				
Wyoming				

Do you believe judges should be selected via an election, an appointment, or the merit system and why?

Reformers to the state judicial selection process developed the merit system, also known as the Missouri Plan in 1940. The merit system uses a combination of appointments and elections and incorporates the views of the legal community into the process. In this system the governor appoints a judge from a pool of several potential nominees selected by a committee that includes members of the state bar association and gubernatorial appointments.[55] Appointed justices are then required to face a special election after serving as justice for a specified period of time. Advocates of this approach believe this system allows for a high degree of judicial independence while giving voters an opportunity to hold judges accountable if they disapprove of judicial interpretations.

JUDICIAL DECISION MAKING

Prior to 1925, the Supreme Court was obligated to hear almost all cases that came to it on appeal. Chief Justice Taft was vocal in his concern that the Supreme Court was no longer able to keep up with the number of cases coming before the court. Congress heeded these concerns by passing the Judiciary Act of 1925, which empowered the Court to determine which cases it wanted to hear. The Supreme Court is now unique in that it has total discretion over which cases it will hear. The Court thus now engages in

The Retirement of Justice John Paul Stevens: Profile of a Supreme Court Justice

Justice John Paul Stevens became the 101st justice of the Supreme Court, serving from 1975 until his retirement in 2010. Justice Stevens was nominated by President Gerald Ford and was unanimously confirmed by the U.S. Senate in 1975. Ford's selection of Stevens to succeed Justice William O. Douglas surprised most political pundits because he was not very well known beyond the Illinois borders. He was selected because Ford wanted to nominate a justice of "unquestioned integrity and talent"[57] in the aftermath of Watergate and because Stevens had admirers in high places, including then U.S. attorney general Edward Levi and former senator Charles Percy (R-IL). This admiration was earned during Stevens's investigation of two Illinois Supreme Court justices who were accused of judicial malfeasance in 1969. It was this investigation that catapulted Stevens from relative obscurity to the nation's highest bench.

Leading the investigation against the two Illinois Supreme Court justices, Stevens proved to be as feisty in the investigative hearings as he was meticulous in his research. He was able to weave the truth through testimony that was at times combative, evasive, and even perjurious. His fair-minded but relentless search for the truth even won him praise from the opposing counsel. The sheer volume of corroborating facts presented by Stevens left little doubt that there was at the very least an appearance of impropriety in the conduct of the two Illinois Supreme Court justices. The two justices were forced to resign from their positions because it was believed they had received corporate gifts in return for favorable judicial rulings. It was during this investigation that Stevens became a local hero in Chicago and was featured on front-page stories across the state as a tenacious fighter for truth and integrity in the Illinois judicial system. A year later, he was nominated by President Richard Nixon to serve on the U.S. Court of Appeals, where he served until he was nominated to the U.S. Supreme Court in 1975.

Regarded as a liberal by some judicial observers, Justice Stevens employed a "logical reasoning" approach to judicial decision making, preferring to examine the facts of each case separately and deciding on the specifics of the case. This approach can be found in *Federal Communications Commission v. Pacifica Foundation* (1978) and in the landmark *Bush v. Gore* (2000) decision. In *Pacifica,* where a father filed a complaint

continued ➤

against a radio station for airing George Carlin's "filthy words" routine, Stevens grappled with the specifics of the case rather than on freedom of speech as a legal abstraction. He ultimately voted with the majority of the court in concluding the FCC had a compelling government interest in regulating indecent language during times children are most likely to be listening, specifically 6:00 am until 10:00 pm. In *Bush v. Gore* (2000) Stevens deferred to the sanctity of state institutions by voting again Bush's challenge to overturn the Florida Supreme Court decision to recount the votes in Florida. The predisposition toward logical reasoning and deferring to state institutions can be traced back to the lessons learned from his role as an independent counselor investigating public corruption at the state level in Illinois.[58]

> **Do you agree with Justice Stevens's opinion in *FCC v. Pacifica* (1978) and *Bush v. Gore* (2000)? Why or why not?**

two forms of decision making. The first type involves its role as the legal "gatekeeper," where it determines which cases are worthy of the court's attention. The second form of decision making is where the court is asked to resolve legal disputes before it.[56] People who feel they have been treated unfairly in American courts are sometimes quick to announce their plans to appeal their case all the way to the Supreme Court. The reality is that since the Supreme Court has almost total discretion over which cases it will hear, the overwhelming majority of cases are never heard by our top court.

The Supreme Court receives approximately 7,500 appeals each year, but agrees to hear only approximately 60 cases per year, which is less than 1 percent of the cases appealed to our highest court. Almost all cases brought to the Supreme Court are appeals of a decision from a lower court. Congress established the rules guiding how the Supreme Court decides which cases to hear. The first step is for a party to appeal to the Court by filing a writ of certiorari, a Latin term which translates to "make more certain." The Court typically only hears cases when it is interested in weighing in on an important issue facing society. The Supreme Court is more likely to decide to hear a case when a lower court employs judicial review in striking down an existing law as unconstitutional, or when the U.S. government is directly involved in the case. Because Supreme Court justices are unable to personally sift through the merits of approximately 7,500 appeals, they rely on their law clerks to help narrow the field to a more manageable number. The law clerks play an important role in helping to establish a *discuss list,* whereby a case will receive further consideration if at least one

THEORY AND PRACTICE — Judicial Activism versus Judicial Restraint

Since the nation's founding, judicial philosophy has been largely divided into the two distinct camps of "judicial activism" and "judicial restraint." Those advocating a judicial activist approach believe judicial decision making should play a role in the policy-making process, whereas justices subscribing to judicial restraint typically defer to the legislature in policy making and characteristically adopt a strict constructionist view of the U.S. Constitution. Strict constructionists believe justices should "strictly construe" the original intent of the wording put forth by the Founding Fathers in the U.S. Constitution when making decisions.

The term *judicial activist* was first coined by the famed political historian Arthur Schlesinger Jr., who labeled the judicial philosophy of Supreme Court justices as either "judicial activistic" or as "self-restrained" in 1947.[61] What makes the terms somewhat confounding is that they do not neatly align with conservative and/or liberal ideologies because judicial activism can take either form. Opponents of judicial activism argue that rather than simply interpreting the law, judicial activists tend to make law from the bench and to base legal decisions on their own political viewpoints. Some cite the *Roe v. Wade* (1973) case as an example of judicial activism favoring the liberal perspective because, in this case, the Supreme Court not only extended a woman's right to privacy in prohibiting states from banning abortions, but also set different standards of governmental intrusion depending on how far along (i.e., which trimester) the woman was in the pregnancy. Others point to the decision in *U.S. v. Lopez* (1995) as an example of judicial activism favoring the conservative worldview. In this case the Supreme Court ruled in favor of states' rights by striking down the federal Gun-Free School Zone Act, which banned the carrying of weapons in local school zones. The federal law was successfully challenged after a 12th-grade student brought a concealed .38 caliber gun to school. Chief Justice Rehnquist wrote the majority opinion where the Court for the first time in decades asserted that the federal government went beyond its constitutional authority in applying the Interstate Commerce Clause as a means to regulate state behavior. Opponents of judicial restraint argue that justices adopting this judicial philosophy are sometime reactionary in their thinking and allow injustices to fester for too long in society.

continued ▶

> **Do you believe justices should follow a judicial activist approach or a judicial restraint approach when making decisions and why?**

of the justices has an interest in hearing it. Approximately 75 percent of the cases appealed to the Supreme Court do not make it to the discuss list and are instead placed on the *dead list,* where the appeal is dismissed without further consideration.[59] The Court then gives greater scrutiny to the cases placed on the discuss list.

In order for a case to be placed on the Court's docket it must pass the *rule of four* stage of the process. The case will be placed on the docket of the Court if at least four of the nine justices express an interest in hearing it. Because the Court deliberates behind closed doors it is difficult to determine why the Supreme Court decides to accept or reject a particular case. Some research has shown that the Court is more likely to hear cases that: (1) have conflicting rulings between the district court and the court of appeals; (2) involve petitions from the *solicitor general,* who represents the federal government at the Supreme Court; or when special-interest groups lobby the Court by filing amicus curiae briefs.[60]

Legal and Extralegal Approaches to Judicial Decision Making

Legal scholars also group approaches to judicial decision making into the separate camps of *legal* and *extralegal* judicial behavior. The legal model of decision making concentrates on the rule of law whereas the extralegal approach contends justices mostly incorporate political, sociological, and psychological factors into decision making.[62] From the legal approach, some justices employ the **doctrine of original intent** by basing their decision on what they believe to be the original intentions of the Founding Fathers or on a "literalist" interpretation of the Constitution.[63] Some justices adopt a **logical reasoning** approach to judicial decision making. Justice Marshall in the *Marbury v. Madison* (1803) case, for example, adopted this approach by reasoning through three legal questions before deciding the case. The advantage of this approach is it ensures the facts of the case under review are given considerable weight. The potential downside is cases might ultimately be decided according to the political ideology of the judges. Another approach to judicial decision making is referred to as **stare decisis,** a Latin term translated to mean "let the decision stand." Justices employing a stare decisis approach rely heavily on legal precedent

Doctrine of Original Intent: *The view that judicial decisions should be based on what justices believe to be the original intention of the Founding Fathers when they drafted the U.S. Constitution.*

Logical Reasoning: *The belief that justices should use logical reasoning on a case by case basis as it relates to the facts of a particular case.*

Stare Decisis: *A latin term translated to mean "let the decision stand" that relies heavily on legal precedents established in previous cases.*

from previous cases of a similar nature. These judges believe that case precedent is the most important factor when deciding cases.

Others employ an **attitudinal model** or **rational choice theory** in shedding light on judicial decision making. Research focusing on the attitudinal model highlights how judicial behavior can largely be understood by analyzing the political ideology of justices. Some speculate that the ideology of justices plays a role in how they frame legal issues when legal issues can be viewed through an ideological prism. Some studies even incorporate theories associated with psychologist Sigmund Freud in attempting to explain judicial opinions of members of the Supreme Court.[64] The rational choice approach emphasizes how justices are constrained from basing decisions entirely on ideology because of institutional rules and coalitions that sometimes form among the justices. The **institutionalist approach** is an extralegal approach to decision making that examines how Supreme Court rules and norms influence judicial opinions. Research in this area focuses primarily on the process by which the Supreme Court decides on which cases to hear. The **separation of powers model** also examines judicial decision making by analyzing the extent to which justices are willing to challenge the executive and legislative branches of government. Justices who are reticent about challenging other branches are more likely to adhere to the political question doctrine. The **political question doctrine** conceptualizes the Court's perception that a political issue, even one with constitutional questions, is best resolved by the legislative branch.

Judicial Decision Making in the Twenty-first Century

Chief Justice William Rehnquist presided over the Supreme Court until he died at the age of 80 in 2005. Rehnquist was nominated chief justice in 1986 by Ronald Reagan. He presided over the landmark *Hamdi v. Rumsfeld* (2004) case where the Supreme Court ruled it was not within the executive branch's authority to deny due process rights to U.S. citizen Yaser Hamdi, even though he was captured fighting alongside the Taliban in Afghanistan against American forces. However, Chief Justice Rehnquist will most likely be remembered for presiding over President Clinton's impeachment trial and for his role in the *Bush v. Gore* (2000) decision that awarded the presidency to George W. Bush. He dissented in many of the landmark cases associated with his era. He voted in the minority in the *Texas v. Johnson* (1989) case, which struck down a state law banning the burning of the U.S. flag as a violation of free speech; the *Planned Parenthood v. Casey* (1992) case, where the Court declined to eliminate abortion rights; and the *Kelo v. City of New London* (2005) case, where the Court allowed local governments a wider range of eminent domain powers.

Justice John G. Roberts Jr. was confirmed as the 17th chief justice of the United States on September 29, 2005. Roberts, at 50 years old, was the youngest chief justice sworn in since John Marshall became chief justice at the age of 45 in 1801.

Rational Choice Theory: *The view that judicial decisions are best understood by analyzing the political ideology of justices.*

Institutionalist Approach: *An extralegal approach to judicial decision making that examines how the rules and norms of the court help shape judicial decisions.*

Separation of Powers Model: *The approach to judicial decision making that explores the extent to which justices are willing to challenge the executive and legislative branches of government.*

Political Question Doctrine: *The legal view that some political matters should be addressed by the legislative rather than the judicial branch of government.*

TABLE 7.8. Some Landmark Supreme Court Cases (1989–2011)

Snyder v. Phelps (2011) Found that a controversial anti-gay group has freedom of speech rights to protest at military funerals.

Citizens United v. Federal Election Committee (2010) Overturns law banning corporate contributions in federal elections.

District of Columbia v. Heller (2008) Right to bear arms is an individual right.

Kelo v. City of New London (2005) Expands eminent domain powers by asserting that economic development can be deemed a public purpose.

Roper v. Simmons (2005) Found that executing minors violates cruel and unusual punishment standard of Eighth Amendment.

Hamdi v. Rumsfeld (2004) Ruled that those detained as enemy combatants at Guantanamo had a right to challenge their classification as enemy combatants.

Lawrence v. Texas (2003) Supreme Court case that struck down a Texas sodomy law as unconstitutional.

Grutter v. Bollinger (2003) The Court upheld an affirmative action policy used for enrollment at the University of Michigan.

Boy Scouts v. Dale (2000) Ruled that the Boy Scouts were within their First Amendment rights to expel a scoutmaster because of his sexual orientation.

Bush v. Gore (2000) The Court voted to stop the recount in Florida, effectively granting the presidency to George W. Bush in the 2000 presidential election against Al Gore.

United States v. Virginia (1996) Found that Virginia violated equal protection for women by providing inferior education to women enrolled at Virginia Military Institute.

Planned Parenthood v. Casey (1992) Upheld that women have a right to an abortion.

Lee v. Weisman (1992) Found that high school principal violated establishment clause for inviting clergy to offer prayer at middle school graduation.

Employment v. Smith (1990) Denied free exercise of religion claim of a Native American denied unemployment benefits for failing a drug test.

Texas v. Johnson (1989) Court ruled that laws banning the burning of the flag violate speech rights.

Chief Justice Roberts and President Barack Obama both graduated from Harvard Law School. Their first face-to-face encounter was made a little awkward when the nation witnessed a botched swearing-in ceremony during President Obama's inauguration in 2009. He privately readministered the presidential oath the next day at the White House because it was misstated at the inaugural. As a senator, Obama voted against Roberts during Roberts's confirmation process. In his confirmation hearing, Roberts stressed the importance of judicial temperance by stating "It's a jolt to the legal system when you overrule a precedent." However, he sided with the 5–4 majority in the landmark *Citizens United v. Federal Election Commission* (2010) case which overturned two previous Supreme Court cases by ruling the government may no longer ban corporate or union campaign contributions in elections. President Obama criticized the ruling calling it "a major victory for big oil, Wall Street banks, health insurance companies and the other powerful interests that marshal their power every day in Washington to drown out the voices of everyday Americans."[65] The impact of the *Citizens United* decision was felt in the 2010 congressional midterm elections. Approximately $3.7 billion was spent in the 2010 congressional elections and hundreds of millions of dollars were contributed by previously prohibited corporate and union sources, much of it undisclosed and given to private organizations to fund negative television advertisements.[66]

© AP PHOTO/SUSAN WALSH

▲ Barack Obama, right, joined by his wife Michelle and daughters Sasha and Malia, takes the oath of office from Chief Justice John Roberts to become the 44th President of the United States at the U.S. Capitol in Washington, D.C., on Tuesday, Jan. 20, 2009. The Constitution requires incoming presidents to pledge: "I do solemnly swear (or affirm) that I will faithfully execute the Office of President of the United States, and will to the best of my ability, preserve, protect, and defend the Constitution of the United States." The presidential oath was re administered in a private White House ceremony because Chief Justice Roberts rearranged some of the wording by reciting, "That I will execute the Office of President to the United States *faithfully*" while administering the presidential oath. President Calvin Coolidge also did two presidential oath ceremonies after some questioned whether the oath administered by his father was valid.

In 2006, Chief Justice Roberts expressed concern that his colleagues in "issuing 5–4 opinions divided along predictable lines, were acting more like professors than members of a collegial court."[67] He expressed his desire to have the Court more frequently reach consensus and to draft more unanimous opinions as the Marshall Court frequently did 200 years ago. However, recent trends show that the Court is issuing even more 5–4 decisions than it did in 2006. Chief Justice Roberts completed his fifth year at the end of June 2010. Most

CourseReader ASSIGNMENT

Log in to **www.cengagebrain.com** and open CourseReader to access the reading:

Citizens United v. Federal Election Commission **(2010)**

During the 2008 presidential primary season an organization named Citizens United released an unflattering documentary about Hillary Clinton and wanted to have it air on cable television. The organization used its general treasury to pay for the distribution of the documentary. The Federal Election Commission (FEC) ruled this would violate the federal law prohibiting corporations from making independent expenditures in federal elections. In *Citizens United v. Federal Election Commission* (2010), the Supreme Court overturned precedent by asserting the government was violating free speech rights by banning corporate and union campaign contributions in elections.

- *Do you believe corporations and unions should be permitted to contribute to federal elections?*

- *Should individual freedom of speech rights be extended to corporations? Why or why not?*

FIGURE 7.2. The American Judiciary Timeline

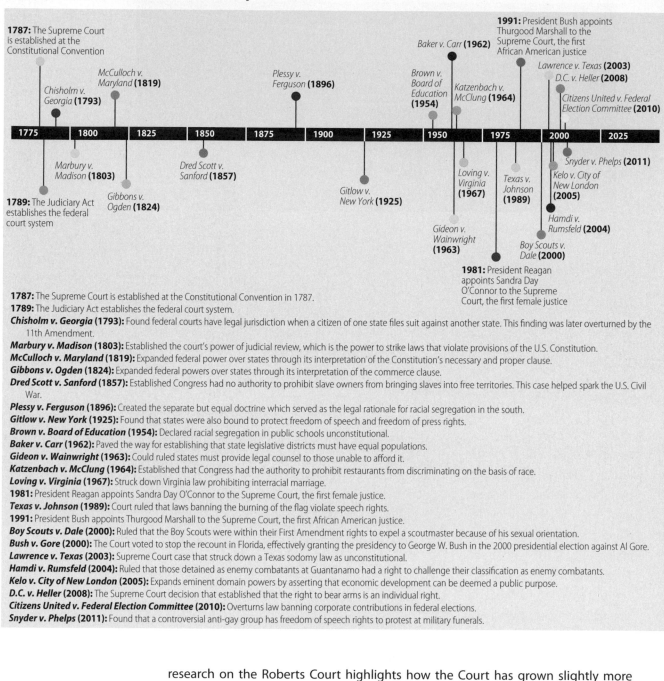

1787: The Supreme Court is established at the Constitutional Convention

Chisholm v. Georgia **(1793)**

McCulloch v. Maryland **(1819)**

Plessy v. Ferguson **(1896)**

Baker v. Carr **(1962)**

Brown v. Board of Education **(1954)**

Katzenbach v. McClung **(1964)**

1991: President Bush appoints Thurgood Marshall to the Supreme Court, the first African American justice

Lawrence v. Texas **(2003)**

D.C. v. Heller **(2008)**

Citizens United v. Federal Election Committee **(2010)**

1775　1800　1825　1850　1875　1900　1925　1950　1975　2000　2025

1789: The Judiciary Act establishes the federal court system

Marbury v. Madison **(1803)**

Gibbons v. Ogden **(1824)**

Dred Scott v. Sanford **(1857)**

Gitlow v. New York **(1925)**

Gideon v. Wainwright **(1963)**

Loving v. Virginia **(1967)**

Texas v. Johnson **(1989)**

1981: President Reagan appoints Sandra Day O'Connor to the Supreme Court, the first female justice

Boy Scouts v. Dale **(2000)**

Hamdi v. Rumsfeld **(2004)**

Kelo v. City of New London **(2005)**

Snyder v. Phelps **(2011)**

1787: The Supreme Court is established at the Constitutional Convention in 1787.

1789: The Judiciary Act establishes the federal court system.

***Chisholm v. Georgia* (1793):** Found federal courts have legal jurisdiction when a citizen of one state files suit against another state. This finding was later overturned by the 11th Amendment.

***Marbury v. Madison* (1803):** Established the court's power of judicial review, which is the power to strike laws that violate provisions of the U.S. Constitution.

***McCulloch v. Maryland* (1819):** Expanded federal power over states through its interpretation of the Constitution's necessary and proper clause.

***Gibbons v. Ogden* (1824):** Expanded federal powers over states through its interpretation of the commerce clause.

***Dred Scott v. Sanford* (1857):** Established Congress had no authority to prohibit slave owners from bringing slaves into free territories. This case helped spark the U.S. Civil War.

***Plessy v. Ferguson* (1896):** Created the separate but equal doctrine which served as the legal rationale for racial segregation in the south.

***Gitlow v. New York* (1925):** Found that states were also bound to protect freedom of speech and freedom of press rights.

***Brown v. Board of Education* (1954):** Declared racial segregation in public schools unconstitutional.

***Baker v. Carr* (1962):** Paved the way for establishing that state legislative districts must have equal populations.

***Gideon v. Wainwright* (1963):** Could ruled states must provide legal counsel to those unable to afford it.

***Katzenbach v. McClung* (1964):** Established that Congress had the authority to prohibit restaurants from discriminating on the basis of race.

***Loving v. Virginia* (1967):** Struck down Virginia law prohibiting interracial marriage.

1981: President Reagan appoints Sandra Day O'Connor to the Supreme Court, the first female justice.

***Texas v. Johnson* (1989):** Court ruled that laws banning the burning of the flag violate speech rights.

1991: President Bush appoints Thurgood Marshall to the Supreme Court, the first African American justice.

***Boy Scouts v. Dale* (2000):** Ruled that the Boy Scouts were within their First Amendment rights to expel a scoutmaster because of his sexual orientation.

***Bush v. Gore* (2000):** The Court voted to stop the recount in Florida, effectively granting the presidency to George W. Bush in the 2000 presidential election against Al Gore.

***Lawrence v. Texas* (2003):** Supreme Court case that struck down a Texas sodomy law as unconstitutional.

***Hamdi v. Rumsfeld* (2004):** Ruled that those detained as enemy combatants at Guantanamo had a right to challenge their classification as enemy combatants.

***Kelo v. City of New London* (2005):** Expands eminent domain powers by asserting that economic development can be deemed a public purpose.

***D.C. v. Heller* (2008):** The Supreme Court decision that established that the right to bear arms is an individual right.

***Citizens United v. Federal Election Committee* (2010):** Overturns law banning corporate contributions in federal elections.

***Snyder v. Phelps* (2011):** Found that a controversial anti-gay group has freedom of speech rights to protest at military funerals.

research on the Roberts Court highlights how the Court has grown slightly more conservative since 2005. One recent study revealed that the Roberts Court issued conservative opinions 65 percent of the time in 2009, the highest conservative rating since 1953.[68] By comparison, the Burger Court (1969–1986) issued conservative opinions only 34 percent of the time, and the Rehnquist Court (1986–2005) issued conservative opinions 55 percent of the time. Even with the recent appointees of President Obama, most legal experts do not expect the Court to make a significant ideological shift over the next few years.

SUMMARY

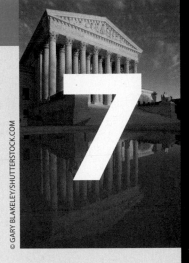

© GARY BLAKELEY/SHUTTERSTOCK.COM

It is perhaps somewhat ironic that the branch of government responsible for interpreting the U.S. Constitution is actually the least democratic of our three branches of government. The Supreme Court, after all, consists of nine unelected jurists with life terms who deliberate behind closed doors checked only by the threat of impeachment.[69] This is in part because the judiciary was viewed as the least controversial branch of government. States had in place deeply rooted court systems at the time of the Constitutional Convention in 1787, and nearly half of the Founding Fathers were well-acquainted with legal systems as practicing attorneys in their respective states. The Framers were thus far more at ease creating our judicial system than in creating our legislative and executive branches of government.[70] Accordingly, very little attention was paid to the judiciary at the Constitutional Convention which explains why James Madison devoted only 369 words to this branch of government in the U.S. Constitution.

In this chapter the American judiciary was reviewed through the prism of federalism by highlighting the creation of the federal judiciary, distinctions between state and federal court systems, the impact of the Supreme Court federalism on the evolving nature of federal–state relations, and judicial decision making. The judicial system unfolds in the context of the federalist system of government. While the U.S. Supreme Court sits at the top of the judicial system, most Americans enter the legal system through state and local courts. The Supreme Court, however, has played a critical role in expanding the powers of the national government and in expanding political and legal rights to all citizens.

KEY TERMS

Abolitionists p. 216

Administrative law p. 207

Appellate jurisdiction p. 201

Attitudinal model p. 229

Civil law p. 207

Common law p. 207

Constitutional law p. 207

Criminal law p. 207

Doctrine of Nullification p. 214

Doctrine of original intent p. 228

Eleventh Amendment p. 208

KEY PEOPLE

KEY CASES

8

COMPARATIVE POLITICS:
UNDERSTANDING THE BASICS

Iranians take to the streets to show their disapproval of the outcome of the 2009 presidential election. Scholars have indicated that the election was rife with fraud.

INTRODUCTION: COMPARATIVE POLITICS

Comparative politics is the subfield of political science that evaluates political issues and trends according to the ways different states set political agendas, formulate and implement policies, and create laws within established government institutions. Comparative politics therefore is a two-tiered enterprise. While on the one hand, it compares and contrasts the issues and trends present in different states (e.g., the voting behavior of 18–24 year olds in the United States, Great Britain, and France) it also seeks to explain them within the framework of government institutions, such as executives, legislatures, judiciaries, bureaucracies, militaries, and the like. Since governing styles rely on the cultural, social, and political histories of the people within the confines of states, most of which were not created equally, it is important to understand the ways in which similar issues are handled across a wide range of states.

In this chapter, we will introduce you to two types of states: **authoritarian states** and **democracies**. Although these terms are broad descriptions of the states of the world, they will provide you with an important starting point for an understanding of the work of comparative political scientists. In addition to looking at the differences between the two types of states, it also seeks to answer a number of fundamental questions. For instance, are all authoritarian states the same? Or conversely, is there a formal model of democracy? What are the characteristics of authoritarian states? How can Iran, North Korea, and Saudi Arabia be considered authoritarian, yet have different economic systems, allies, and levels of wealth? How can the United States, United Kingdom, and France be considered democracies but have different types of constitutions and institutions? By trying to find answers to these questions we hope to shed greater light on the reasons behind policies chosen by different countries around the world. We will begin with our examination of authoritarian states.

Questions to Consider Before Reading this Chapter

1. Why is it important to understand the characteristics of different states?
2. What are the major characteristics of authoritarian states?
3. What are the major characteristics of democratic states?
4. What did Alexis de Tocqueville and John Stuart Mill contribute to democratic theory?
5. What is a "civil society" and why is it an important component to democracy?

Comparative Politics: *The subfield of political science that evaluates political issues and trends according to the ways different states set political agendas, formulate and implement policies, and create laws within established government institutions.*

Authoritarian States: *Countries that are characterized by the rule of one person or a few people and tend to prohibit a great many rights and privileges.*

Democracies: *States that are based on political representation, fair and free elections, personal freedom, and civil rights.*

AUTHORITARIAN STATES

Since the end of World War II, the world has witnessed what can only be described as an explosion of democracy as both an ideology (i.e., belief system) and an instrument of governance. With the end of **colonialism** in Africa, Asia, and the Middle East, the democratization of Germany (West Germany until 1989) and Japan, and the dissolution of the Soviet Union (1991), it appears that traditional authoritarianism as a governing style is in its twilight years. However, this recent wave of democratization must be placed within a proper perspective. The success that democracy has been experiencing is unprecedented, which has made it somewhat more difficult to define since it varies drastically from one place to another. (For example, certain states in the former Soviet Union are considered to have components of democracy and authoritarianism; thus making a clear-cut distinction more difficult.) What has been easier to define is the more traditional nature of authoritarian states because they follow a set of characteristics that go back to the earliest points in human history.

As we learned in Chapters 2 and 3, authoritarianism has been praised and justified by political theorists from Plato to Machiavelli, by theologians from St. Augustine to Averroes, and by the numerous kings, queens, caliphs, and emperors who instituted authoritarian rule at every point in time and every corner of the globe. King Henry VIII of England (sixteenth century), King Louis XIV of France (seventeenth to eighteenth centuries), Adolph Hitler of Germany (twentieth century) and Saddam Hussein of Iraq (twentieth century) are all examples of authoritarian rulers. The authoritarian state is not confined to a particular region or a single ideology. It can be a government run by a **regime** that provides well for its people, or one that deprives them of basic necessities.

Still, as political science students it is important that you are able to identify some of the most common characteristics shared by authoritarian states. The following section will provide you with a brief overview of what authoritarian states look like.

Characteristics of Authoritarian Regimes

Characteristic 1: *Authoritarian Leaders are the Primary Source of Laws and Policy Choices within their State's Borders*

Authoritarian states are designed to give all legislative priorities and policy choices to either one person (**autocracy**) or a small group of people (**oligarchy**). Depending on time, place, and tradition, autocrats have been referred to by a number of names: king, queen, caliph, pharaoh, and more recently, president (Hosni Mubarak, the former head of Egypt, was referred to as the president of Egypt). The leader or leaders of an authoritarian state do not need the consent of their people. Whether the regime is considered a benevolent monarchy like that of Queen Elizabeth I or a tyrannical

Colonialism: *The practice of conquering and incorporating states/territories within the political control of one state; with the "mother country" serving as the core and the colonies as "peripheries." For example, throughout most of the nineteenth and twentieth centuries, Great Britain practiced colonialism because it had controlled a number of states beyond its borders in places as diverse as Ireland, Egypt, and India. Great Britain could be understood as the "core" while its colonies could be understood as the "peripheries"; those groups serving the "mother country" with resources, services, and labor.*

Regime: *The ruling government in a given country.*

Autocracy: *A type of authoritarian regime where one person is in control of the laws and policies of the state.*

Oligarchy: *A type of authoritarian state in which the laws and policies are in the hands of a small group of people.*

dictatorship like that of Josef Stalin, the one feature that binds all authoritarian states is that they deny their citizens the right to freely participate. Although most authoritarian states promise to provide their citizens with rights and freedom, few ever deliver on these promises. Instead, citizens have few guarantees and even under the most decent of rulers, the citizens still serve at the whims of the leader(s). Constitutional freedoms are not guaranteed and are by definition, subject to the demands and expectations of each regime.

In some unique circumstances, autocratic regimes have been characterized as being *totalitarian*. **Totalitarian states** are defined as those that desire to maintain power (as all authoritarian states do) but more importantly, to create a **utopian society** that is powerful enough to change the political mindset of its citizens. You are probably already familiar with some totalitarian states and their leaders. Can you think of any? The most common answer is probably Nazi Germany under the reign of Adolf Hitler or the Soviet Union under Josef Stalin. But what others can you think of? Remember, these rulers did not only desire power for themselves, but also an ideological change in the very fabric of their citizens.

Totalitarian rulers, whether **fascist** (Adolf Hitler) or **communist** (Josef Stalin) require a full mobilization of the people. Where apathy is seen as an acceptable form of citizenship in most authoritarian states, it is entirely *unacceptable* in the totalitarian model. The typical, nontotalitarian authoritarian state is mainly concerned with maintaining political power. The totalitarian state, on the other hand, requires all of the political, economic, and social institutions of the state to *create* individuals who can reinforce the utopian vision.

The totalitarian state alone (and its leader and ideologically driven, single political party) is defined as the only solution to the perceived problems of the political status quo. Thus, the actions of the state, whether they take the form of the construction of communes (China under Mao's communist party), nationalization of industrial output (Germany under Hitler's Nazi Party, Italy under Mussolini), and/or ethnic cleansing of those considered "undesirable" (Cambodia under Pol Pot's Khmer Rouge, Germany under Hitler's Nazi Party) are justified as necessary. For more information on the differences between totalitarianism and authoritarianism check out *Theory and Practice: The Cult of Personality and Promise of a Future Paradise*.

Characteristic 2: *The Transition of Power in an Authoritarian State is Determined by Means Other than Free and Open Elections*

Because authoritarian states do not ask for the consent of the people, the transitioning of power from one ruler to the next can be a difficult undertaking. This is one of the most important and obvious differences between authoritarian and democratic states. Democratic states (as we will see) have what are known as constitutional guarantees protecting everything from fair and free elections to the right to free speech. This mechanism translates into trust. Citizens in a democracy have the trust of the

Totalitarian States: *States that employ policies and strategies that attempt to completely transform the attitudes and beliefs of the citizens by placing commitment to "the state" as their highest duty*

Utopian Society: *Defined as a "perfect place" and a "place that does not exist."*

Fascist: *A type of totalitarian state in which power is tightly controlled by the government and is derived from extreme nationalist policies. The beliefs of the state are held above those of the individual and each individual is forced into working for the success of the entire state. The concept emerged in Italy in the 1920s under the leadership of Benito Mussolini as an antidemocratic and antisocialist ideology.*

Communist: *A type of totalitarian state is one in which power is controlled by the government and whose policies are based on the suppression of religion, nationalism, and private property. In communist states, the economy is said to be centrally planned, that is, prices and salaries are controlled and regulated by the state.*

The Cult of Personality and Promise of a Future Paradise

© DIEGO CERVO

What has always been a point of fascination for scholars of totalitarianism is the power of the political leader and/or party to indoctrinate the masses into political action. Hannah Arendt in her famous account on the subject spent a considerable amount of time on the ways "the disaffected masses" become "the devout followers" of a totalitarian ideology.[1] The leaders develop what has become known as a "cult of personality." Although the phrase "cult of personality" can be attributed to former Soviet leader Nikita Khrushchev when describing his predecessor Josef Stalin, the term has now become synonymous with any leader whose infectious personality and utopian vision amongst a largely disaffected population can transform political society.

When a revolutionary leader takes control of a state whether through legitimate means (as is the case of Adolf Hitler's democratic ascent) or by force (Mao Tse-Tung in China), he or she will have a vision for future greatness. Take for example Mao's revolution in China. Mao's version of communism was predominantly an agrarian version of Marxian economics and land redistribution. Found within the pages of Mao's *Red Book* one will find his critique of the status quo and how his vision of a classless society of Chinese peasants must replace the status quo. His political programs (One Hundred Flowers Bloom and Cultural Revolution) and economic programs (establishment of communes, land redistribution, forced labor) were designed to change the very nature of Chinese society at the time. It is this feature that makes totalitarian leaders distinct from their authoritarian cousins: They have an ideological vision of a future glory that requires large-scale mobilization of the people. It is therefore important that the leader and/or political party constantly use propaganda, censorship, or force to achieve their goals because they are the only ways to ensure movement toward future glory.

Why do you think that most totalitarian leaders came to power in the middle of the twentieth century? Does it have something to do with modern society?

What are the differences between a traditional authoritarian state and a totalitarian one?

© LORENZO COLLORETA

Fascism by the Ballot Box

©EVA SERRABASSA

Although many of you are somewhat familiar with the atrocities committed by Adolf Hitler and Benito Mussolini in the name of fascism, most of you probably did not know how popular fascism was in the United States during the same time. In fact, during the presidency of Franklin Delano Roosevelt, fascism was hailed as a possible solution to the economic woes brought on by the Great Depression. In his book, *The Defining Moment: FDR's First Hundred Days and the Triumph of Hope*, journalist Jonathan Alter recounts just how close the American people were to embracing this particular ideology. Alter writes: "The famous broadcaster Lowell Thomas narrated a film called, *Mussolini Speaks* in 1933 that featured an ad campaign calling it "A Hit" . . . because it appeals to all 'red-blooded Americans' because it might be the answer to America's needs.'"[2]

Even acclaimed aviator and pop-culture icon Charles Lindbergh was a devotee of fascism and committed to prevent American involvement in Western Europe. As Wallace noted:

> *On May 19, 1940, Charles Lindbergh took to the airwaves and delivered a national radio address urging America not to interfere with the internal affairs of Western Europe . . . The next day President Roosevelt was having lunch . . . with his most trusted Cabinet official and declared,* "If I should die tomorrow I want you to know this. I am absolutely convinced that Charles Lindbergh is a Nazi."[3]

Yes, that's right. During the 1930s, fascism and its European leaders were hailed by certain members of the American establishment as heroes. Now why should this matter to you? Because it appears that many Americans view themselves and their government as exceptions

▲ Two of the warlords of World War II: Adolf Hilter of Germany and Benito Mussolini of Italy.

continued

to many political rules. Americans have a great tendency to view the political system as something constant and undoubtedly democratic. What few Americans realize is how precious and fragile *all* governments are. Not just those countries in parts of the developing world, rife with civil war and poverty, but countries everywhere.

It would be good to remember that following World War I, the Weimar Republic was established in Germany. The Weimar Republic was hailed as one of the most democratic societies on earth. It even provided women with the right to vote several years before the United States did. What does this mean to you? Well, after a series of severe international agreements and a wave of economic recessions, Adolf Hitler assumed power *legally*. In other words, Hitler became dictator after the sitting German president was unable to assume his role as head of state. Thus, Hitler was constitutionally and legally given the leadership of Germany. If there is one thing then, that you should never take for granted in any democracy, it is the possibility that it could degenerate into something authoritarian.

> **What is significant about the fact that Adolf Hitler rose to power democratically?**
>
> **Why do you think fascism was so popular in the United States before World War II?**

© KEMAL BAŞ

government to transition from one regime to the next without fear of revolution or bloodshed. Those in a democracy might not always be pleased with the results of an election or the policy choices of those in office, but at least they are guaranteed that their system is guided by a process and a tradition of transition. Citizens in an authoritarian state do not have this guarantee.

Absolutist Monarchy:
A rule by one person who is the creator and enforcer of all legislation. This is in contrast to a "constitutional monarchy," which can be said to describe the governments of Great Britain, the Netherlands, and Spain: all of which have limited monarchical authority and strong representative traditions.

Take for example the present-day government of Saudi Arabia. The Kingdom of Saudi Arabia (official name) is a modern-day example of an **absolutist monarchy**. Saudi Arabia is governed by a royal family (Al Saud) with a king. When Saudi Arabia was founded, it was decided through law (constitution of Saudi Arabia is known as the Basic Law) "that the throne shall remain in the hands of the sons and grandsons of the kingdom's founder."[4] Although we refer to the Basic Law of Saudi Arabia as its *constitution*, we must realize that its constitutional authority is solely based on the whims of the royal family. In an authoritarian state like Saudi Arabia the citizens have to depend entirely on the attitudes and interests of the royal family to create change or answer public requests. This is not to say that the citizens of Saudi Arabia are unhappy or discontented with their government. It only means that their rights are interpreted and protected by the royal Saud family.

In other authoritarian states, governments have come to power by means of a **coup d'etat** (violent overthrow of the state). Usually instigated by members of the military establishment, most coup d'etats resulted in what are commonly referred to as **military dictatorships**. At the most basic level, military dictatorships fuse the political institutions with those of the military. Just as democracies tend to separate the civilian government from that of the military and provide constitutional guarantees limiting domestic military initiatives, many authoritarian states see the military as a means of dominating the entire political system and maintaining order.

Even though the era of the military dictatorship is slowly coming to an end, it is by no means a relic of the distant past. Military dictatorships were common in Latin America (where they are referred to as *juntas*) and Africa throughout most of what is referred to as the **Cold War**: the period from the end of World War II until the end of the Soviet Union in the early 1990s. During this time, the whims of the two superpowers perpetuated strict adherence to policy choices. Both the United States and the Soviet Union required their **proxy states** in Latin America, Africa, and Asia to adhere to their political objectives. For example, after the Soviet Union entered Afghanistan in 1979, the United States gave neighboring Pakistan billions of dollars as a means of supporting the anti-Soviet forces there.

Characteristic 3: *Authoritarian States Limit Free Speech and Control the Press in an Attempt to Maintain Political Power*

In authoritarian states, all forms of traditional media are controlled by the government in order to maintain control. For centuries, the traditional media (newspapers, magazines, books, plays, radio, and television) have served as a major source of political upheaval and change. From Thomas Paine's *Common Sense*[8] to Vaclav Havel's *The Memorandum*,[9] members of the literary and journalistic communities have been successful in promoting discussions that attack the practices of authoritarianism. Silencing opposition groups is therefore a major priority of most authoritarian regimes.

Since the French Revolution, the media have been referred to as the **Fourth Estate**: a pillar of society that projects its voice amidst a chorus of government institutions and public demands. In authoritarian states, it has been common to imprison activists and journalists in an attempt to suppress antigovernment speech. Take for example the actions of the elected Venezuelan president, Hugo Chavez.

Coup d'etat: *The violent overthrow of an existing regime.*

Military Dictatorship: *An authoritarian government in which political power is controlled and employed by the military. Sometimes it is within the control of the highest ranking official in the military, other times it may be in the hands of a few high-ranking officials.*

Cold War: *The period that began following the end of World War II and was defined by the ideological and political struggle between the United States and the Soviet Union. Both sides made economic and military commitments to states around the world willing to ally themselves to either country. In addition, this era was defined by the prospect of nuclear war, as both sides possessed vast arsenals of nuclear missiles. The era (which will be covered to a greater degree in the following part) ended with the formal dissolution of the Soviet Union in 1991.*

Proxy State: *A state that is under some indirect control of another country. It is not a colony per se, but an ally due to economic or military reasons. For example, if a country during times of war gains military or financial assistance, they can be considered to be a proxy state. During the Cold War it was very common for the United States to financially and/or militarily support countries that were opposed to the Soviet Union.*

Fourth Estate: *The members of the media. Its roots are found in the days of the French Revolution where society was divided into three groups or estates: the clergy, the nobility, and the masses. The term fourth estate was therefore applied to the members of the press who provided commentary on the other official three estates.*

Religion and Politics at Home and Abroad

Should religion have a public voice? Should all religions be protected under the law? Should religious leaders be given the protection by the state to influence the masses? These are all important questions when one discusses the differences between authoritarian and democratic states. Unfortunately, answers to all or any of these questions are problematic. Why? Because religion can serve as the basis of some of the world's strongest democracies and most powerful authoritarian states.

Alexis de Tocqueville in what many have considered the greatest appraisal of the norms and mores of the United States, *Democracy in America*, stated that religion was not only one of the most important features of American political culture, but the "first of their political institutions."[5] In addition Tocqueville proclaimed that "America is still the (only) country in the world where the Christian religion has retained the greatest real power over people's souls and nothing shows better how useful and natural religion is to man, since the country where it exerts the greatest sway is also the most enlightened and free."[6] Thus, the United States was (and is) a tremendous paradox. While it is considered one of the freest countries on earth, it is also one that seems to have its populism stem from its religiosity. Yet, how can this be? Isn't religious devotion contrary to individual liberty and democracy?

In the Islamic Republic of Iran, as noted in Chapter 3, religion serves as the guiding force for legislation and civic participation. Yet, it is hardly a shining symbol of democracy. Although the Iranian Constitution sounds democratic in that it calls for the election of a president for a four-year term (with one additional four-year term if reelected), it mandates that each candidate be a Muslim man, "of political and religious distinction."[7] Thus, one is *free* to seek the presidency in Iran as long as the person is a male and is considered by the Supreme Religious leader to be accordance with Islam's holy book, the Koran.

So, why bring this up? And more importantly, how does this impact you? Well, if you are an American you are seen by many in the world as not only a citizen of the most powerful democratic country on earth, but also one of the most religiously

continued

continued

oriented. In fact, according to a Pew Research Center Poll from 2006, 42 percent of Christian Americans identify themselves as "Christian" first and "American" second; a comparatively high number when compared with other democratic states.

> **What does this do to American power?**
>
> **Does religion make American power stronger or weaker?**
>
> **How does it impact decisions that relate to the rest of the world?**

© KEMAL BAŞ

In December 2004, Chavez created a new media censorship policy for his citizens. Article 147 of the Venezuelan constitution now stipulates that "Anyone who offends with his words or in writing or in any other way disrespects the President of the Republic or whomever is fulfilling his duties will be punished with prison of 6 to 30 months if the offense is serious and half of that if it is light."[10] In addition to Article 147, Chavez has created additional articles outlining his commitment to halting opposing viewpoints.

> "Article 444 says that comments that "expose another person to contempt or public hatred" can bring a prison sentence of one to three years; Article 297a says that someone who "causes public panic or anxiety" with inaccurate reports can receive five years. Prosecutors are authorized to track down allegedly criminal inaccuracies not only in newspapers and electronic media, but also in e-mail and telephone communications.
>
> The new code reserves the toughest sanctions for journalists or others who receive foreign funding. . . . Persons accused of conspiring against the government with a foreign country can get 20 to 30 years in prison. The new code specifies that anyone charged with these crimes will not be entitled to legal due process."[11]

These measures are commonplace in authoritarian states. In order to maintain political control, authoritarian regimes enact policies designed to stifle opposition. Although Chavez's policies appear repressive, they are by no means uncommon. Similar tactics have been used by dictatorial regimes around the world for centuries.

Characteristic 4: *Authoritarian States Lack Representative Political Parties*

One of the defining features of democratic governments is the presence of a multitude of political parties. In democracies, political parties are useful in organizing viewpoints and electing individuals to public office. They provide

How Free is American Media?

©EVA SERRABASSA

Hunter fair do you think your news is? How fair is its presentation? Does it do a good job of delivering important stories to you on a wide range of policy and social issues? If not, there may be a reason why. Currently in the United States, five (yes, that's right, five) giant corporations control all of the media: AOL/Time Warner, Disney, News Corporation, Bertelsmann of Germany, and Viacom (formerly CBS). According to the Media Reform Information Center (www.corporations .org/media/) that number has dropped severely in recent years. In 1983, for example, there were 50 corporations in the news business. Since then, the corporate world in the words of Ben Bagdikian has monopolized the industry.[12]

Yet, the United States is obviously not an authoritarian state. So how can this occur? Well, the answer seems to be a combination of deregulation and free market principles.

In the United States, we have an independent commission known as the Federal Communication Commission (FCC). The FCC has five members all of whom are appointed by the president and approved by Congress.[13] In recent years it has been

FIGURE 8.1. **The Number of Corporations that Control a Majority of U.S. Media**

Number of corporations that control a majority of U.S. media:

(newspapers, magazines, TV and radio stations, books, music, movies, videos, wire services, and photo agencies)

Source: Media Reform Information Center. Found at http://www .corporations.org/media/media. Accessed on October 12, 2009.

continued

continued

argued that the FCC has deregulated the system so severely that media consolidation is unavoidable. In fact, most experts point to the Telecommunications Act of 1996 (an amendment to the Communications Act of 1934, which created the FCC) as the point at which media consolidation became set in stone. Without going into too much detail, the Telecommunications Act of 1996 allowed for a system in which private ownership of the different forms of media became much easier. According to Common Cause:

The Telecommunications Act of 1996:

- Lifted the limit on how many radio stations one company could own. The cap had been set at 40 stations.
- Lifted from 12 the number of local TV stations any one corporation could own, and expanded the limit on audience reach. One company had been allowed to own stations that reached up to a quarter of U.S. TV households. The Act raised that national cap to 35 percent. These changes spurred huge media mergers and greatly increased media concentration. Together, just five companies—Viacom, the parent of CBS, Disney, owner of ABC, News Corp, NBC, and AOL, owner of Time Warner, now control 75 percent of all prime-time viewing.[14]

So, as you can see, the media in the United States are controlled by a handful of corporations. Is this good or bad? And more importantly perhaps, is it democratic?

At the very least, we can agree that corporations are designed to sell products. Therefore, it is not difficult to assert that media consolidation has serious consequences. This is why this idea should matter to you. On the whole, Americans have become equal consumers of both information and products.

> **Should the presentation of news be treated differently than other types of television programs?**
>
> **Is media consolidation always a negative phenomenon?**

democracies with differing opinions and viewpoints, and offer citizens a variety of political choices. Although political parties have different levels of membership and platform appeal, they serve to add legitimacy to the system.

Authoritarian states, on the other hand, lack this diversity in organized political viewpoints. In fact, some authoritarian states have only one political party that serves to provide a veil of legitimacy to an otherwise illegitimate government. The Ba'ath Party of Iraq under Saddam Hussein serves as an important example.

In 1940, the Arab Socialist Ba'ath Party was founded in Damascus, Syria, by Michel Aflaq and Salah al-Bitar. Largely a political party founded on the popular, postwar Arab beliefs of anticolonialism, socialism, and Arab nationalism, which had gained ideological momentum in response to the creation of the state of Israel (1948), Ba'athism would not gain major political momentum in Syria until the 1960s.

Since the Ba'ath Party was originally designed as a vehicle for Arab and thus regional unity, it was deemed by its advocates as the most powerful force for political change in the Middle East. However, this would not be the case. As the Ba'ath Party gained political power in nearby Iraq, its "regional" vision was replaced by an "Iraqi" vision by the new leadership there.[15] This changed the nature of its power in the region and allowed Iraq under the direction of Saddam Hussein to introduce measures that pertained exclusively to his own beliefs.

Since taking control of the Ba'ath party in 1979, Hussein used it to eliminate opposing viewpoints and political opponents. Once widely regarded as a party of intellectuals calling for **pan-Arab secularism,** it degenerated into one of the harshest vehicles of repression in the Middle East. "In one display of his brutality, Saddam stood in front of an audience of party members where he named several high-ranking Ba'athists who were quickly ushered out of the auditorium and executed for allegedly planning a coup. The infamous speech was videotaped and used to strike fear in anyone who dared consider challenging Saddam's authority."[16]

The Ba'ath Party, like all authoritarian single parties, necessitates political control in the hands of a few individuals whose positions ultimately depend on the whims of the individual in power. Differing political views and platforms are restricted in authoritarian states because they could lead to an undermining of political control. Therefore, *legitimacy* is defined by the ruling political party. If the one-party system determines legitimacy, all other parties are by definition, *illegitimate* and criminally punishable.

▲ Former "president" of Iraq Saddam Hussein.

DEMOCRACIES

Historically, democracies have been defined by degenerative rather than progressive means. As we saw in Chapter 2, political thinkers like Plato and

Russia: Part Democratic, Part Authoritarian

Is Russia authoritarian or democratic? That is a major point of contention among scholars who focus on the recent developments there. Following the dissolution of the Soviet Union (formally on December 25, 1991), the Russian people elected a new president, Boris Yeltsin, all the members of the Duma (the Russian legislature), witnessed the explosion of free media outlets, and ushered in a system of free markets. Russia's transition from a centrally planned economy to a free market–oriented one was based on the notion that capitalism and democracy were not just coincidentally linked, but that the former helped the latter to develop.

Unfortunately, however, Russian society in the 1990s did not fare as well as its leaders had hoped. Unemployment rates and inflation (the weakening of the Russian currency) soared, while the quality of life of many Russian citizens plummeted. The Russia that Boris Yeltsin and his advisors helped move from one dominated by the state to one dominated by the people emerged too quickly for the people to handle. In essence, the idea of a mature and thriving democracy (and capitalism for that matter) was unleashed on a public not ready for it. It must be remembered that the capitalist system that had evolved in Western Europe and North America took centuries. In Russia, this fact was either forgotten or overlooked. Thus, when Vladimir Putin won the Russian presidency in 2000 (he actually first took over from the then-ailing president Yeltsin on December 31, 1999, before winning an election in 2000), he had inherited what many Russians believed to be a society in free fall that needed greater structure and stability, when in fact it just needed more time.

Nevertheless, in the early 2000s Putin benefited from a perfect political storm. As the

▲ Prime Minister (and former president) Vladimir Putin with current President Dmitri Medvedev. Many suggest that Putin is still directing policy in Russia.

continued

1990s were described as politically chaotic and financially unstructured, the 2000s became to be understood as an era of political strength and economic growth. As oil prices soared and the overall economy grew, Putin's job approval went through the roof, allowing him the opportunity to create a political system that eliminated political opponents and restricted many freedoms. Viewing the leadership of the Russian media with disdain because of the manner in which many of them had received their fortunes in the days following the collapse of the Soviet Union, Putin began a campaign of censorship and forced exile. As Michael McFaul and Kathryn Stoner-Weiss have noted, "Today, the Kremlin controls all the major national television networks . . . (and Russia) now ranks as the third-most dangerous place in the world to be a journalist behind only Iraq and Colombia."[17] This is not exactly what many scholars would consider a move in the name of democracy.

Thus, the new Russian leadership has been successful in taking credit for economic development which has translated into electoral victories while creating a state that is reminiscent of the Soviet Union. A case in point is its policy of combating terrorism. Wars in the separatist region of Chechnya which have spilled over into a number of terrorist attacks inside Russia (one including a school in Beslan) have allowed Putin and now Medvedev (the current president) to suggest that *security* is more important in the short term than anything else. And it appears to be working as Putin's and Medvedev's popularity continue to grow. They have been able to weave a narrative (as McFaul and Stoner-Weiss suggested) that proclaims the virtues of Russian identity and the necessity of control as a means to achieving greater Russian strength in the world.

What does this do to our understanding of the terms *democracy* and *authoritarian*?

Russia's leadership is elected and most of the people have little objections to the limitations on their freedom. So is it democratic? Or is it authoritarian? What do you think?

Aristotle spoke of *democracy* when referring to a form of government that had resulted from a revolution or at the very least, a severe breakdown of civil society. To these Greek philosophers, democratic governments were defined by the uneducated and economically deprived masses. It was argued that successful governance—achieving the common good—required either intellectual expertise (Plato) and/or a mixed constitution (Aristotle). According to both standards at the time, most democracies were incapable of such statecraft. Over time, however, the understanding of what constituted proper governance began to change. With the publication of John Locke's *Two Treatises of Government* (1689), which created the ideology of classic liberalism, and Adam Smith's *The Wealth of Nations* (1776), which argued in favor of a **free market system of economics**, *good* government became synonymous with *limited* government. Classical liberalism, the ideology mentioned in Chapter 3, that prompted some of the arguments about the role of the government of the United States, was defined by the belief that because natural rights predate the concept of government, the only legitimate constitution was one that allowed the citizens the greatest opportunity to pursue life, liberty, and wealth. To this day, democracies are often defined by the manner in which they define government involvement and protect individual liberties. Some have chosen a parliamentary model, others a presidential model. Some have included principles of socialism, while others have espoused more laissez-faire practices, that is, economic practices that keep the economic and political spheres separate.

Before we can examine some of the characteristics of modern democratic states, it is important that we examine the ways in which democracy as a concept has changed over time. We'll begin with a look at two political theorists who challenged the very basis of liberty and freedom as it related to democratic states: Alexis de Tocqueville and John Stuart Mill.

Free Market System of Economics: *The belief that the market, i.e., the way goods are bought and sold, can and will regulate itself. Adam Smith believed that consumers ultimately control the prices of goods by forcing sellers into competition. Because consumers shop comparatively, businesses that maintain higher prices will be forced out of business. This coincides with the beliefs espoused by classic liberals because the government provides no influence on the price of the goods for sale; it remains limited.*

The Evolution of Modern Democracy: Majority Rules?

In 1831, a young French traveler named Alexis de Tocqueville was commissioned by the French government to study the American prison system. While in the United States, Tocqueville witnessed a new nation defined by its representative government, unique decentralization of authority (federalism), and its claims of individual freedom. In roughly 40 years, the United States had become recognized as a champion of democracy and a land of opportunity.

Tocqueville evaluated the manner in which democratic institutions provided equality for its citizens. If the *common good* was defined by natural rights, and the cornerstone of such rights was based on the ability of the individual to participate in elections, speak freely about government actions, and protest policy choices, how could the American democracy allow the interests of the majority to trample the interests of the minority? It was this question that created a watershed in democratic political thought and a reformulation of the role that democratic governments play in the lives of its citizens: the tyranny of the majority. In *Democracy in America* (1835), Tocqueville argued that democracy must not only be defined by the rights of those in the majority, but by those in the minority as well.

A majority taken collectively is only an individual, whose opinions, and frequently whose interests, *are opposed to those of another individual, who is styled a minority. If it be admitted that a man possessing absolute power may misuse that power by wronging his adversaries, why should not a majority be liable to the same reproach? Men do not change their characters by uniting with each other; nor does their patience in the presence of obstacles increase with their strength.*

. . . Unlimited power is in itself a bad and dangerous thing. . . . When I see the right and the means of absolute command are conferred on any power whatever, be it called a people or a king, an aristocracy or a democracy, a monarchy or a republic, I say there is the germ of tyranny, and I seek to live elsewhere, under other laws.[18]

This attack against democracy led to a reconceptualization of the notion of "majority rule." While it is true that democracies require the consent of the majority in terms of electoral participation, laws that are derived in the same spirit must also consider the interests of those in the *minority*. The thrust of Tocqueville's critique is that "majority rule" can be just as sinister as authoritarian rule, because it is still depriving a segment of the population of its equality.

Tocqueville's critique is important because it recognized the weaknesses of previous classic liberal thinkers on the nature of democratic rule. Before Tocqueville's concept of the tyranny of the majority, the main arguments related to freedom and liberty emerged from theorists committed to the principle of **utilitarianism**: the greatest good for the greatest number. Theorists like Jeremy Bentham and James Mill examined liberty in terms of majority happiness.[19] As long as the greatest number of

Utilitarianism: *The belief that the greatest good for the greatest number is the most justifiable course of action.*

people experienced the greatest amount of happiness, the democratic government would be justified and its legislation deemed legitimate.

Tocqueville raised the standards by which democracies should be judged. Yet his critique is only one necessary component on the road toward the characteristics of modern liberal democracy. The other is provided by the British philosopher, John Stuart Mill. John Stuart Mill, in his famous work *On Liberty* (1869), provided an argument similar in nature to that of de Tocqueville. While Mill agreed that majority-driven institutions will deteriorate into tyrannies, he suggested that the solution must be based on an application of two primary virtues: justice and liberty. Justice is valued as the *higher* virtue because it yields a higher degree of happiness and liberty and allows one the ability to express one's self. It is the preservation of these virtues that will save liberal democracy.

> Like Tocqueville, Mill recognizes that liberty, particularly liberty of opinion, is crucial in a democratic society, *for it is the one virtue that prevents the tyranny of the majority . . . (and) it is the necessary precondition for human development, for without it we would have no way to determine the values that do constitute the higher qualitative pleasures of human experience. It is precisely in debating our values and ideals that we arrive at the truth of the matter. . . . Thus any attempt by the majority to prevent dissent actually prevents the truth from being expressed.*[20]

Mill therefore balanced the whims of the classic liberal theorists with those of Tocqueville. The principle of utility (greatest good for the greatest number) is not defeated, but simply reorganized. The tyranny of the majority would always be a constant threat, yet its organization could be *redesigned*. The power of the government would be diffused amongst different institutions and a system of checks and balances applied. "And to Mill's mind there are really only two possibilities: Either an intellectually and morally superior elite must be given special roles within government, or the intellectual and moral level of the mass of people must be raised."[21] Mill suggested that the constraints of liberty imposed by a tyrannical majority must be weakened by a mass pursuit of intellectualism. This will avoid the pitfalls of a restrictive majority.

Characteristics of Modern Democracies

The modern era's democratic explosion has challenged the ways political scientists have historically defined the term *democracy*. States that at one time had been under the control of a colonial power or a totalitarian regime have taken certain strides toward democracy. While longstanding democracies like the United States and Great Britain may have served as models for newer democracies, it must be understood that not all democracies look and behave the same.

We must be clear in stating that democracies vary by size, geography, and governmental procedure. Nevertheless, while we recognize that modern democracies do not all take the same form, students in an introductory course in political science need a place to begin. As such, the following section will address some of the general

Containing Tyranny:
Checks and Balances or Parliamentary Supremacy?

© DIEGO CERVO

According to both John Stuart Mill and Alexis de Tocqueville, democracies rely on the belief that tyranny will prevail if the people allow it. For instance, most democracies have a certain level of checks and balances to contain the potential for tyranny. The United States has a strong system of federalism as well as a number of checks and balances. In the United Kingdom (UK), a system has developed that places the real authority of government in the House of Commons. Both states are democratic, but both handle the division of power differently. As we will see in the next chapter, the British legislature is the final word on legislation; there is no judicial review process to determine if a law is constitutional or not. In the United States, the division of governmental authority is valued as the greatest check against tyranny.

Still, Mill asserted that democracy is best understood by an educated populace that is both informed about and connected to the political processes. If members of a democratic society forget those rules or are led astray, there is a great potential that the government will collapse. Therefore, Mill argued in favor of a unique representative model for new democracies: proportional representation.

Although this will be covered in Chapter 9 in greater detail, it is worth mentioning now. A system of proportional representation is designed to allow a number of political parties to have a voice in the political process. The theory goes like this: If a society has the ability to articulate a number of issues that it deems important, it is best represented by a number of political parties. Why? Because this will ensure that a greater number of voices are heard which will most likely keep a greater number of people interested in politics. In short, an enlightened society is a great way to ensure that a society remains democratic and free.

In the United States, we have two dominant political parties and a winner-take-all system. Would our system be improved by making it a multiparty, proportional system of government?

Is there a downside of a multiparty system? What do you think?

© LORENZO COLLORETA

characteristics of the democratic tradition. Think of this section as a starting point to a better understanding of terms that political scientists and public officials use when describing the political world. Although we realize that the "one-size-fits-all" description is insufficient, it can provide an important service to the person who is new to the field.

Characteristic 1: Democracies Enumerate Citizens' Rights and Government Structures, Procedures, and Limitations by Means of a Constitution

Although democracies vary by population, electoral procedures, representation, and numbers of political parties, they all possess a legal framework based on the understanding that the citizenry possesses rights that require protection. In fact, the concept of rights defines most legal institutions in democratic governments. Constitutional democracies place guarantees on these rights and have executive, legislative, and judicial branches to enforce such guarantees.

Constitutions also enumerate the powers, duties, and limitations of each branch of government. As you may recall, the U.S. Constitution divides governmental authority among three branches of government: the legislative (Article I), executive (Article II), and judicial (Article III), and provides the American public with a system of checks and balances to ensure these separated powers. In the absence of such protections, it is believed that authoritarianism would prevail.

Characteristic 2: Democracies Rely on the Presence of a Civil Society

The existence of a **civil society** perpetuates the advancement of democracy. States that are ravaged by war, economic dislocation, extreme poverty, and corruption are not only unstable, but are also unable to maintain the necessary level of security to create a civil society. In essence, civil society exists when a section of the population is able to live (and live well) within a particular state without being dependant on that state. Civil society depends on economic freedom and an overall acceptance of the legitimacy of the government. The Center for Civil Society (CCS) at the London School of Economics provides a good definition intended to help students understand its importance in democratic governance.

Civil Society: *An indicator of political stability that has been used as a characteristic of democracies. Within a civil society, individuals and organizations promote a diversity of interests and a respect for civil liberties.*

Civil society refers to the arena of un-coerced collective action around shared interests, purposes and values. *In theory, its institutional forms are distinct from those of the state, family and market, though in practice, the boundaries between state, civil society, family and market are often complex, blurred and negotiated. Civil society commonly embraces a diversity of spaces, actors and institutional forms, varying in their degree of formality, autonomy and power. Civil societies are often populated by organisations such as registered charities, development non-governmental organisations, community groups, women's organisations, faith-based organisations, professional associations, trades unions, self-help groups, social movements, business associations, coalitions and advocacy groups.*[22]

It must be remembered that civil society relies on the actions of "uncoerced" individuals. Because authoritarian states rely on the maintenance of the regime in power, it is unlikely that they allow the level of unrestrained individualism that democracies do.

Characteristic 3: Fair, Free, Open Elections

In addition to constitutional guarantees and the presence of civil society, it has been the presence of fair, free, and open elections that have historically best characterized democratic governments. Amongst the duties of citizenship, very few are as important to the functioning of modern democracies as voting. Voting provides citizens with the ability to cause change, and more importantly, to force legislators to govern on their behalf. Essentially, free and open elections give legitimacy to the processes of government.

Democratic elections are based on the notion of a strong connection between the government and the citizenry. Since the government is determined by the voters, the results legitimate the entire system. If a candidate was not successful in his or her election race, there might be disappointment, but there is not disapproval of the entire system. When democracies are successful, they are usually successful in terms of their electoral behavior. When democracies fail, they usually fail because the citizens have lost faith in the legitimacy of government. Fair, free, and open elections are defined as those that allow citizens regardless of sex, race, economic level, or religion the right to vote. While not every democracy is insulated from occasional electoral mishaps, they are by no means the norm. In fact, there is usually a mechanism in place that allows recounts or investigations to take place.

Characteristic 4: Free Political Parties

One of the major features of liberal democracies is the presence of free political parties. Political parties serve several important functions. First, they express the beliefs of a wide spectrum of people. Although the number and power of political parties vary from country to country, all define themselves by their **platforms**, or the key issues that they stand for as parties.

Platform: *The ways that political parties articulate their stances on economic, political, and social issues.*

For example, in the United Kingdom, there are two dominant political parties: Conservative and Labour. These parties have historically been based on the different social classes in Great Britain. The Conservatives, or Tories, have typically represented the interests of the wealthy classes and have adopted an ideology largely based on private rather than public control of the economy. The Labour party, by contrast, has been the *voice* of the working classes calling for greater government involvement in social problems.

Each of these dominant political parties has broad platforms that define its memberships. This is not to say that countries with two dominant political parties force their citizens into choosing one or the other. Most countries have a wide array of political parties. Some are based on local interests, some on state or provincial interests, and some on federal interests.

THEORY AND PRACTICE

Equality:
The Key to Democracy

Political scientist Robert A. Dahl is recognized as one of the most important thinkers when it comes to understanding the appropriate characteristics of democratic governance. In his book, *On Democracy,* Dahl tried to determine the fundamental characteristics upon which democratic society must rest. After some argument, Dahl comes to the conclusion that *equality* is the dominant feature of democratic society because without it, citizens lack the ability to implement legitimate laws. "To Dahl, a state is only a democracy when it widens suffrage to include everyone in the decision-making process."[23]

There are, however, problems with this understanding. "For example, Dahl argues that if everyone's votes count equally, but a few elites control what goes on the agenda (in essence, what the government should do) democracy has not been fully realized. And equal access to decision making by itself is not enough—all must have enough information to make competent choices."[24] Therefore, the *idea* of democracy is much more difficult than the *practice* of democracy. This chapter and the next provide you with a good starting point. But according to Dahl, we fall way short of the goal. But that is okay. As long as you are thinking about the broad differences between democratic and authoritarian states, we have done our job.

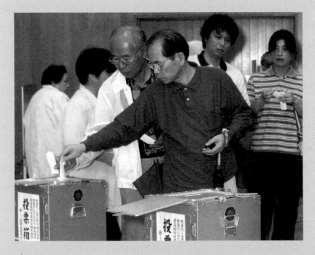

▲ Voters take part in a Japanese election for their lower house of parliament.

Do you think that we live in an equal society? Do men and women have equal rights?

Why do you think Dahl places such an emphasis on equality?

Secondly, all political parties are designed to select candidates for public office. For instance, while the Green Party of the United States is not considered one of the two dominant political parties in the American landscape, its environmentally driven platform still functions like the two dominant parties: the Republican and Democratic. The Green Party's purpose is to provide environmentally conscious citizens with a candidate who can get elected and represent their interests. It is this necessary cycle of platform issues, party memberships, and candidate selection which makes political parties a necessary feature of modern democracies.

Characteristic 5: Democracies Accept the Basic Freedoms of Speech, Press, Religion, Protest, and Economy

One of the most important contributions of the democratic model of governance is its acceptance and toleration of certain basic freedoms, such as the freedoms of speech, the press, religion, protest, and economy (the ability to freely make a living without government intrusion). Freedoms such as these allow individuals the ability to openly question the policy choices of their elected officials. This openness gives greater strength to the system by providing another check on the power of the government. In fact, one of the telltale signs of democratic erosion is the weakening of such freedoms. Whereas voting continues to provide citizens with the most direct form of political participation, it is the acceptance of basic freedoms that allows individuals to make the best choices when determining candidates. Open political debate over the major issues of the day provides individuals with a sense of ownership over the entire system. These freedoms are interdependent and allow progress in the form of social and economic mobility to occur.

This sense of freedom is what permeates democratic society. The freedoms presented reflect the belief that humans possess certain rights that must be protected. Freedoms of speech, press, religion, protest, and economy are understood as those rights which humans possess due to our very nature as human beings. Therefore, as those in the liberal tradition have argued, no state (government) has the right to limit such freedoms because in doing so the state would be acting against the law of human nature itself. This is the underlying notion of civil society and democracy itself.

DEMOCRACY AND AUTHORITARIANISM: CONTEMPORARY ANALYSIS

At the beginning of the 1950s, only 22 countries were considered democratic, and today there are over 120.[25] What factors led to this explosion? First of all, it must be

Will Third Parties Enhance Democracy?

©EVA SERRABASSA

Did you realize that the number of independents in the United States has matched the number of Democrats and Republicans?[26] Why do you think that is the case? As a college student, you may see signs on campus to join the College Democrats or the College Republicans? Have you done so? If not, you are probably not alone.

In recent years it appears that many "lifelong" Republicans and Democrats have left their traditional parties on the basis that each party's platform is too ideologically rigid. For instance, there are many people who have historically identified with the Republican Party who feel strongly that *Roe v. Wade* should not be overturned. They believe that abortion should be a viable option for pregnant women. So where do these former party members go?

Well, in recent years they have declared themselves independent and have attempted to find smaller third parties that better suit their ideological beliefs. The only problem is, however, that around election time, it is the Democratic and Republican candidates who seem to be the only ones with a realistic chance of winning. Is that fair? Should we have a system that promotes more parties? If so, what will that do to elections in general?

We must remember that although third parties sound great (and are great in democracies that tend to be parliamentary), they can create an election result in which the winner only receives a small percentage of the total vote. For instance, suppose we have an election with six parties: Republican, Democrat, Green, Independent, Reform, and Workers. Suppose the election results show that the Republican candidate received 18 percent of the vote, the Democratic candidate received 22 percent of the vote, the Green party candidate received 16 percent of the vote, the Independent candidate received 14 percent, the Reform candidate received 14 percent, and the Workers Party candidate received 16 percent of the vote. Who won the election? Well, clearly it was the Democrat who received 22 percent of the vote. What are the problems with this outcome? The winner in this election style (known as a winner-take-all system, which you will learn about in Chapter 9) has only 22 percent of the vote, yet has to represent all 100 percent of the voters. I know that this probably will not convince you that the

continued

continued

United States needs to maintain its two-party system, but it was a shot. (It is also worth noting that in the United States "independent voters" usually lean toward one of the two dominant parties when it comes to elections. So, the above is definitely a hypothetical situation that was provided to start you on the road toward thinking comparatively and outside the box.)

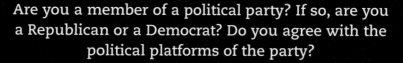

> Are you a member of a political party? If so, are you a Republican or a Democrat? Do you agree with the political platforms of the party?
>
> Do you think that third parties enhance or weaken democratic values? Can third parties undercut major political initiatives?

CourseReader ASSIGNMENT

Log in to **www.cengagebrain.com** and open CourseReader to access the reading:

"How did Europe democratize?" **by Daniel Ziblatt**

In this book review, Daniel Ziblatt addresses the patterns of democracy that took place across Europe over the past 150 years and attempts to understand the factors involved in their development. In doing so, Ziblatt (and the authors he reviews) sees democracy as a process that balances elements of authoritarianism with those more commonly thought of as democratic. This analysis is therefore useful as you think about the development of democracy in non-democratic places in the world today.

- *If democratic development is a process that is not always as revolutionary or successful as we believe, what does this say about its development in the Arab world?*

- *What are the major factors mentioned that led to the creation of successful democratic regimes?*

understood that World War II not only ended the military and political establishments of Germany and Japan, but also European colonialism in general. The rebuilding of Europe meant the reprioritization of the colonial powers. Colonialism was no longer a viable option for the once great powers of Europe, which had experienced an unthinkable level of destruction.

One by one, the states of Western Europe lost their colonies in Africa, the Middle East, and Asia. As a result, the number of independent states tripled and quadrupled over the next two decades. Although most of the newly independent states had desired a democratic system of rule at the time of their independence, certain problems related to poverty and historical differences prevented a smooth transition from colonial status to democracy. It is this rocky transition that best defines our understanding of those states we define as newly democratic.

A second event that caused a major explosion in the number of states and the way political scientists examine the concept of *democracy* was the collapse of communism. Embodied in the disintegration of Yugoslavia and the Soviet Union, the end of communism meant the emergence of a whole host of newly independent states in Eastern Europe and Central Asia. States that had been centrally planned and occupied were now able to exert their own sovereignty. This has led to a great transformation in the terms *democratic* and *authoritarian*. Do democracies require *all* of the major characteristics previously mentioned, or only some? If they require only *some,*

CourseReader ASSIGNMENT

Log in to **www.cengagebrain.com** and open CourseReader to access the reading:

"Quantifying Arab Democracy: Democracy in the Middle East"
by Saliba Sarsar

In this article, Saliba Sarsar attempts to place a numeric value on the levels of freedom of the states of the Middle East. Taking into consideration a number of standard democratic values like media freedom, the presence of fair/free elections, the protection of women's rights, etc., Sarsar tries to determine if the Middle East is becoming more or less democratic.

- *What is the least democratic state in the Middle East?*
- *Are the numerous factors provided fair indicators of a state's level of democracy? If not, what other factors do you think are relevant?*

THEORY AND PRACTICE

It's the Oil Stupid:
*Getting to the Bottom
of Authoritarianism*

© DIEGO CERVO

Did you ever wonder why most oil-producing states are authoritarian? If you were to perform a rudimentary analysis of the states of the world that produce oil, you will notice that they tend to be run by dictators. Why? Well, according to some economists the answer has less to do with leadership and more to do with oil.

Paul Collier, an Oxford economist and author of the book *The Bottom Billion: Why the Poorest Countries Are Failing and What Can Be Done About It*, has discussed an economic belief known as "Dutch Disease" (named because of the negative impact that the discovery of natural gas in the North Sea had on the Dutch economy) argues that countries that have only one strong commodity (say oil, or diamonds), are far more likely to have undemocratic regimes in power. Why? Because when a country has just one commodity from which it profits, it will usually neglect other products to trade. Its research and development programs therefore will only be used to establish better ways of refining and transporting oil. But you still may be wondering why the country is authoritarian.

Let us put it this way, democracies tend to grow bureaucracies, or in other words, they tend to develop a number of different agencies that employ hundreds and thousands of people to work in these government jobs. If an economy is linked to only one source of international wealth, it is ultimately reliant on the price that the international community has set for it. When the price is good, democratic bureaucracies grow and the citizens and government workers are happy because there is money present. When the price drops and people can't get paid as they once had, they tend to get unhappy. If this large-scale discontent lasts weeks, let alone months, a revolution may occur. When the dust settles and a new government is established, nine out of ten times, it will be authoritarian.

To illustrate this point further, we will use an example that Collier uses in *The Bottom Billion*: Nigeria in the 1970s.

> As oil revenues built up, the country's other exports—such as peanuts and cocoa—became unprofitable, and production rapidly collapsed. The loss of these agricultural activities

continued

continued

hurt the farmers who had produced them, but it probably didn't itself curtail the growth process because traditional export agriculture (fruits and vegetable traded) was generally not a very dynamic sector with many opportunities for technical progress and productivity growth.

However, Dutch disease can damage the growth process by crowding out export activities that otherwise have the potential to grow rapidly . . . the key activities are labor-intensive manufactures and services, the sort of exporting now done by China and India. **A low-income country with abundant natural resources is unlikely to be able to break into these markets because the foreign exchange they generate is not sufficiently valuable within the society.**[27]

If Paul Collier (and others) are correct, what will happen when the natural resources disappear?

Is this the best way to understand why certain states remain authoritarian? Or are there other factors at play?

which ones are essential for our classification? It is these questions that make defining democracy so difficult.

While the previous section defined the general characteristics of democracy, they are by no means uniform to all democracies. If this is confusing, let us put it another way. Democracy and authoritarianism are best defined as features on either side of a large pendulum. Sometimes the pendulum swings to the left (democratic), while at other times it swings to the right (authoritarian). Sometimes governments that are democratic behave in authoritarian ways. Quite often the job of the comparative political scientist is to examine the movement of the pendulum and the factors that have caused it to move in one direction or the other.

SUMMARY

©PHOTO CREDIT HERE

While it appears that democracy as a concept contains certain general character-istics, there is by no means a standard model of what is considered a democratic government. The general characteristics of authoritarianism and democracy have provided us an introduction to the ways in which different governments make poli-cies, create legislation, and maintain order. The specific institutions of both types of states will be discussed in the next two chapters. Remember that the best way to evaluate states in the modern world is to examine them according to their protection of rights and freedoms. If a country has open, fair, and free elections, but prevents a segment of its population from expressing itself in the media, it might not be the greatest example of what we would consider a democracy. On the other hand, it really cannot be considered *authoritarian* either. The following chapters will attempt to provide you with a better understanding of democratic and authoritarian states by letting you evaluate examples of each.

KEY TERMS

Absolutist monarchy p. 242

Authoritarian states p. 237

Autocracy p. 238

Civil society p. 255

Cold War p. 243

Colonialism p. 238

Communist p. 239

Comparative politics p. 237

Coup d'etat p. 243

Democracies p. 237

Fascist p. 239

Fourth Estate p. 243

Free market system of economics p. 251

Military dictatorships p. 243

Oligarchy p. 238

Pan-Arab secularism p. 248

Platform p. 256

Proxy state p. 243

Regime p. 238

KEY PEOPLE

UNDERSTANDING DEMOCRACIES

▲ People watch fireworks during the inauguration celebrations of Ukrainian President Viktor Yushchenko, the 50-year-old hero of the Orange Revolution, in Maidan Nezalezhnosti square (Independence Square) in Kiev on January 23, 2005. Yushchenko became the third president of an independent Ukraine, taking over after a decade of authoritarian-leaning rule.

INTRODUCTION: ONE SIZE DOES NOT ALWAYS FIT ALL

By now you should feel more confident in your knowledge of some of the differences between authoritarian and democratic states. You should realize that democracies and authoritarian states are not bound to any specific region or culture and that their differences are ultimately based on power and control. If there is one feature that distinguishes the two types of rule, it is representation. Authoritarian states are defined by their unwillingness to allow their citizens the opportunity to exact change in society.

While there is no perfect model of democracy, the idea of allowing people to take an active role in their collective destiny is a democracy's strongest characteristic. In this capacity, democracies are governed by the people. If the citizens of a particular state object to the policies or initiatives taken by the existing government, they have the opportunity to make their voices heard. They can protest and, more pragmatically, they can vote elected officials out of office.

Yet amidst all of the apparent similarities between democracies, they too have different structures and institutions. Take the United Kingdom and the United States for example. The United Kingdom and the United States are both considered democracies, however the United Kingdom is known as a parliamentary democracy, while the United States is defined as a presidential one. They both place a high level of protection on individual rights, but they have developed different institutions that they believe best serve their people.

This analysis of democracies and their institutions will be the focus of the following chapter. We will begin by looking at the distinctions between the different operating systems (federal and unitary), then move onto different branches of government (executive, legislative, and judicial), and finally conclude with the nature of different political parties, electoral systems, and interpretations of freedoms and liberties.

YURI KADOBNOV/AFP/GETTY IMAGES

Questions to Consider Before Reading this Chapter

1. **What are the differences between unitary and federal states?**

2. **What are the major differences between parliamentary and presidential systems?**

3. **What are the differences between the United Kingdom and the United States?**

4. **What is parliamentary sovereignty? How does it impact a country's decision to have judicial review?**

5. **What are the different electoral systems? Which promote two-party systems? Which promote multiparty systems?**

REPRESENTING THE PEOPLE: UNDERSTANDING FEDERAL AND UNITARY SYSTEMS

Before we begin to examine some of the institutional differences that exist between different democracies, it is important to look at how power is diffused within them. In Chapter 4, we learned that power in the United States is divided among municipal or local governments, state governments, and the national government. This decentralized approach to governance is known as *federalism*—or rather, a system that divides authority between a national government and local/regional governments. Federal systems rely on the belief that limited governmental authority is the best type of governmental authority. The thinking goes, if the regions or provinces have constitutionally defined powers, and the federal government also has its own constitutionally defined power (even if it is superior), in theory there is a lesser chance of tyranny because neither will have *absolute* authority. Those in favor of federalism have argued that provinces or regions should have the constitutional authority to create and pass legislation within their own regions because the local or regional governments are best suited to understand their own region's policies, problems, and people. Examples of such federal systems are the United States, Australia, and Switzerland.

While proponents of federalism praise the representative and provincial merits of a decentralized system, the overwhelming majority of states in the world have favored a more centralized role for the federal government. In fact, only 25 of the world's 194 countries are federal states.[1] Most states opt for a **unitary system** where the national government is not only superior to the regional or provincial governments but also has absolute authority because it adds to the general stability of the state. In unitary states, the national parliament serves as the sole repository of legislation. Unitary systems have both the constitutional authority to create all of the state's legislation and also the ability to overrule the legislation of smaller provinces or regions. The classic example of the unitary system of rule was France, where it was once joked that all of the school bells in France ring simultaneously, underlining the notion that the seat of the national government in Paris ruled all lesser provinces and regions.

In summary, it must be understood that whether the political system of choice is decentralized (federal) or centralized (unitary), they both remain representative of the people. The reasons that a country opts for one system instead of another has to do with its particular history, culture, and size. For the United States, it made (and still makes) a great deal of sense to allow the states and local governments to determine many of their own policies. In France, for example, the situation was obviously different. Deep cultural and political divisions had caused previous French governments to crumble. Therefore, the writers of its present constitution have created a much more uniform, unitary type of system.

Unitary System:
The central government has absolute authority and is the sole repository of legislation.

DEMOCRATIC INSTITUTIONS: UNDERSTANDING THE DIFFERENCES

Although an understanding of the differences between unitary and federal systems is important when discussing democracies, it is only our starting point. To best understand the behavior of government, we must also examine institutions.

Each democracy has its own unique constitution, culture, and history, but all have similar divisions of rule, namely executive, legislative, and judicial branches of some kind. These branches help to reinforce the freedoms and liberties outlined in Chapter 8. In the first of the sections that follow, we will explain some of the institutional differences between the executives of parliamentary and presidential systems of government. (In the meantime, take a look at the first CourseReader selection by Larry Diamond. It is a good place to think about the nature of different democracies.)

CourseReader ASSIGNMENT

Log in to **www.cengagebrain.com** and open CourseReader to access the reading:

The Spirit of Democracy by **Larry Diamond.**

In his book *The Spirit of Democracy*, Larry Diamond questions the universal claims of democracy and determines that in the modern era there has emerged a number of 'thresholds' or standards by which democratic countries are to be judged. The first threshold looks at political institutions and elections. For example, if a country has fair and free elections, it is technically democratic. However, for Diamond, democratic states also require the protection of universal freedoms and the protection of minority claims. It is this second threshold that makes defining democracies so difficult. Some states may claim to be democratic but lack the necessary guarantees. While reading this selection, try to think about what the word 'democracy' means to you.

- *Why is democracy absent in certain parts of the world?*
- *Is democracy a universal value? Or is it a Western construct that is only applicable in Western societies?*

EXECUTIVES: PRESIDENTS OR PRIME MINISTERS

The most obvious distinction between presidential and parliamentary systems is the manner in which the head of government is elected. In **presidential systems,** like Argentina, Mexico, Ukraine, and the United States, the head of government, the president, is elected by the citizens by means of a separate election. This means that the people themselves, rather than the parliament or congress, decide on the chief executive. In most presidential systems, the president (and his/her cabinet) commands the direction of the entire executive branch. Although there are some nuances

Presidential System:
A system in which the executive branch is separate from that of the legislature.

▲ Prime Minister David Cameron of the United Kingdom (left) and President Barack Obama of the United States represent the differences between the executive branch of a parliamentary system and the executive of a presidential system.

between presidential democracies, such as term limits and presidential powers, most presidents (in presidential systems) have the unique capacity of serving as commander in chief of the military, leader of his/her respective political party, and the most visible person in government.

Presidential visibility has allowed contemporary presidents to have the unique distinction of being the face of the entire government. In a globalized world the presidency as an institution has gained a great deal of power through the president's heightened visibility. Members of a state's legislature are important to the everyday functioning of government, but they lack the visibility of the president. It is this distinction that has proved to be both an asset and a weakness. Since the president is not only the head of the executive branch, but (in most cases) also the head of his/her particular political party, he/she has the unique ability to either greatly strengthen or weaken the positions of other elected government officials. In the media frenzy of the twenty-first century, presidential popularity (or unpopularity) has the capacity to determine the outcomes of elections in which he/she is not even running.

While presidential systems are defined by the presence of an independent executive branch, determined by the citizens directly, **parliamentary systems** are defined by the fusion of their legislative and executive branches. The head of the government in a parliamentary system—the prime minister—serves as head of both the executive and legislative branches. Prime ministers come to power through their party and are elected to their position by their colleagues in parliament. In this way, parliamentary systems are designed to allow their elected officials, and not the citizens, the opportunity of choosing the head of government.

Another interesting feature of the executive branch of some parliamentary systems is the presence of a symbolic head of state. In addition to the prime minister, who is considered the head of government, most parliamentary systems have a symbolic leader serving as head of state. Although the manner in which these heads of state come to power varies, they are usually present in order to show continuity with and serve as the embodiment of the cultural history of the people of the state. Examples of such symbolic heads of state are the queen of England, the emperor of Japan, and the president of Germany. Each serves his/her respective people by representing the traditions of the state while balancing the obligations of government.

Parliamentary System:
A system in which the executive branch is part of the legislature.

LEGISLATURES: THE REPRESENTATION OF THE PEOPLE'S WILL

Within the three branches of government, the legislature is considered the most representative agent of the people. Legislatures allow local interests to permeate national debates and best reflect the political beliefs of the population at large. Although the president or prime minister may "put a face" on the entire government, it is the local/national representatives that allow modern citizens to have their own unique interests served. The following section will examine the nature of the modern democratic legislature. Modern democracies are structured to avoid centralized authority (one branch of government gaining too much authority) and to best represent the interests of their citizens. Therefore, the size, strength, and configuration of the national legislature are important features of the life of the state. In contemporary politics, democracies have opted for one of two legislative models; legislatures with one house (known as **unicameral legislatures**) or those with two houses (known as **bicameral legislatures**). The strengths and weaknesses of each type will be examined, along with several examples of each. We will begin with the type of legislature most common to students in the United States, the bicameral system.

Unicameral Legislatures: *Legislatures that have only one house.*

Bicameral Legislatures: *Legislatures that have two houses; an upper house and a lower house.*

Bicameral Legislatures: An Introduction

The belief that there exists the need for a two-chambered legislature comes from both British and American understandings of proper governance. In order to unite and better represent the different interests in British society, the British parliament was divided between an upper-class, conservative House of Lords, and a working/middle-class House of Commons. The houses were designed to lessen the legislative ability of the monarch and to balance the power of the competing socioeconomic interests of Great Britain. It was believed that two houses, each reflecting the citizens' particular interests, would provide the British people with the greatest ability to have their voices heard.

For the American James Madison, proper representation was only part of his defense of bicameralism. Madison's main argument concerned his fear of tyranny. He argued that in addition to a separation of powers among the three branches of government, there must also be a division within the legislature. In *Federalist Paper No. 51*, Madison wrote:

> In republican government, the legislative authority necessarily predominates. The remedy for this inconveniency is to divide the legislature into different branches; *and to render them, by different modes of election and different principles of action, as little connected with each other as the nature of their common functions and their common dependence on the society will admit.*

▲ Members of the United Kingdom's House of Commons, right in dark suits, enter the House of Lords to hear Queen Elizabeth II deliver her speech during the State Opening of Parliament in London.

© AP PHOTO/ ADRIAN DENNIS, POOL

Madison's solution was therefore to create two houses, designed with different powers and electoral procedures that could not only balance the authority of the executive, but also limit the power of factions that could develop within the legislature itself. In many ways, it has been this understanding of the potential weaknesses of governance that has contributed to the modern divisions of national parliaments.

Since the late eighteenth and early nineteenth centuries, most bicameral systems have been based on a combination of Madisonian logic and expansion of rights. What has resulted is a trend in bicameralism that not only divides authority between two houses, but grants more authority to the house that more directly represents the people—the house commonly referred to as the *lower* house.[2] Serving as the model for how political scientists examine legislatures, it was the British system that allowed us to refer to the house nearer to the people as the **lower house** and the house somewhat removed from the general public as the **upper house**. Therefore in contemporary politics, the house with more political power is not only more representative of the people, but also universally referred to as the *lower* house.

Lower House: *A lower house, like the British House of Commons, is designed to best represent the will of the people. Thus, its members are elected directly by the people and their representation is based on population.*

Upper House: *An upper house is intended to be removed from the day-to-day activities of the legislature. Thus, it promotes the national interest and provides consultation on serious issues.*

Lower houses, like the British House of Commons or the Japanese House of Representatives are designed to represent local interests from across the entire country. Although Madison had envisioned the creation of two houses with *different* areas of authority, most democracies have interpreted this distinction to mean that the house that best represents the "will of the people" must be given more power than the house that does not. Thus, most of the lower houses not only have the authority to name the prime minister (in the case of a parliamentary system) but also the authority to propose, pass, and implement important policy choices.

In contrast most upper houses in today's world have been designed to provide a national focus to the concerns of the people and to allow a more removed segment of the government the opportunity to evaluate potential legislation.[3] For example, the upper houses in Japan and the United Kingdom are limited to delaying legislation and/or making recommendations on legislation rather than actually having the authority to change it themselves. (The United States is a unique exception in that its upper house, the Senate, and lower house, House of Representatives, have a greater degree of equity in the making of legislation.)

TABLE 9.1. Comparing Democracies

Country	Executive Model	Legislative Model	Judicial Review	Parties
United States	presidential	bicameral	yes	two party
United Kingdom	parliamentary	bicameral	no	two party*
Japan	parliamentary	bicameral	yes**	multiparty
Germany	parliamentary	bicameral	yes	multiparty
Denmark	parliamentary	unicameral	yes	multiparty
Israel	parliamentary	unicameral	no	multiparty
Ukraine	presidential	unicameral	yes	multiparty
Costa Rica	parliamentary	unicameral	yes	multiparty

*In the UK, there is a third, smaller party that is known as the Liberal Democrats. The Liberal Democratic Party is usually considered a "half" party that rarely directly influences the outcome of public policy. However, at times it may be able to add a stronger voice to one of the two dominant parties.

** The Japanese Constitution allows for judicial review; however, it is rarely used.

Bicameral Systems: The United Kingdom and Japan

In order to best understand the bicameral legislative framework, we will now proceed with a look at the basics of two specific bicameral systems: The United Kingdom and Japan. We will begin first with the United Kingdom.

The United Kingdom

The United Kingdom is considered by many as the model of the modern parliamentary state. Although its election process is considered unique by modern parliamentary standards (as will be discussed later) and its dominant two parties are a European exception, its influence in terms of legislative structuring is unsurpassed. Centering the prime minister as head of government within the lower house of parliament has served as a model for most contemporary democracies. Even the terms *parliament* and *upper* and *lower houses* emerged from the British style of governance.[4]

For two and a half centuries, the United Kingdom (which includes Britain, Scotland, Wales, and Northern Ireland) possessed an empire that brought its domination, people, goods, and services to every corner of the globe. Following World War II, the British government lost its colonial empire but sealed its reputation as the democratic model of choice. Since the end of World War II, the bicameral, parliamentary model of democracy has been the choice of most new states. The bicameral system, with its two houses, has allowed many burgeoning democracies the opportunity to balance tradition and cultural distinctiveness with local representation and national interests. The British system in many ways has been the model for this particular mindset.

The British legislature consists of the **House of Lords** and the **House of Commons.** Although traditionally both chambers represented the different socioeconomic interests in British society, they no longer have this distinction.

House of Lords: *The upper house in the British parliament. The House of Lords reflects the history and traditions of British society. Today it serves as a deliberative body that can no longer prevent the passage of legislation, but simply delay it.*

House of Commons: *The lower house in the British parliament. Members of the House of Commons (known as members of Parliament or MPs) are directly elected by the people and therefore are charged with the duty of passing legislation.*

THEORY AND PRACTICE — How the Past can Impact Policy

One of the more interesting questions related to representation in governments around the world relates to the idea of the influence of history on the political system. We tend to think that the founding of the United States played a major role on the nature of American federalism and the systems of checks and balances and separation of powers. We tend to see the American system as one based on constitutionality and juris prudence. When we look to times in our past that were less than democratic (eradication of Native Americans, the institution of slavery, limitations placed on women, Japanese and German American internments during World War II, etc.), we rarely let them influence our present state of affairs. For example, women received the right to vote in 1920. Although women are rarely given equal treatment in terms of pay to their male counterparts, they technically, have equal protection under the law. Once again, it is the *law* to the rescue.

In Germany however, its past (and in particular its actions toward minorities during World War II) is very much alive in its present political affairs. According to David P. Conradt, the placement of the Bundestag, the German lower house, is an example of this. It is literally right across the street from the Holocaust Museum in Berlin. Why? Was this accidental? No, absolutely not. It was deliberately placed there as a constant reminder of the threat of fascism to those currently holding office there. It was designed to keep the memory of the Holocaust alive for not only ordinary Germans, but also for those entrusted with the passage of law. The memory of the Holocaust in many ways still dictates contemporary German policies toward minorities and its limitations on what is known as "hate speech."[5]

Do you think that the past should play a role in the making of public policy?

Should groups that have been the targets of racial or religious discrimination be given fair compensation? If so, how could this be accomplished?

© ISTOCKPHOTO.COM/LORENZO COLLORETA

Today, the House of Lords (the upper house in the British parliament), is to a large degree an ineffectual institution; it comprises members of the Anglican Church and landed nobles who up until 1999 had maintained their seats on the basis of heredity and ancestry.[6] As Peters concludes, "[T]oday the House of Lords may not delay money bills longer than one month—nor can it vote them down and prevent their implementation—and any legislation passed by the House of Commons in two successive sessions of Parliament, provided one calendar year has passed, goes into effect without approval by the Lords."[7] The House of Lords is mainly used as a forum for discussion. Because democracies are designed to provide individuals with the greatest opportunity for debate and protest, it is best to value the House of Lords as a place where debates are continued and tradition is maintained.

In Britain, it is the House of Commons that represents a truer expression of the will of the people and is therefore responsible for passing legislation. It must be stated that the British system is designed to be adversarial. In Great Britain, there are two dominant political parties, the Conservative and Labour, and what is referred to as a half-party, the Liberal Democratic Party. Though their election system and political affiliations will be discussed later, it is important to know that political debates in the House of Commons are made by the prime minister (head of government and leader of his/her political party) and waged against political opponents, namely the members of his/her opposition party and its leader.

Because policies are generated within the prime minister's cabinet, the prime minister of the United Kingdom is mandated to discuss policy choices within the House of Commons at a weekly, half-hour session called Question Time. During this time, the prime minister is required to answer all of the questions related to policy decisions and argue in front of a televised audience all of the policies he/she has chosen.[8] Many have argued that this requirement has added to the strength of the British system by keeping a "leash" on the otherwise dominant power of the prime minister and allowing those in the loyal opposition a fair chance to raise objections.

While the British system, with its largely ineffectual House of Lords and its dominant House of Commons, may appear strange to an American it is a division that reflects the history and culture of the United Kingdom. Just as the British people value the importance of the monarch as part of the dual executive branch, so too do they value the legislative branch. The House of Lords and House of Commons are important reminders of both democracy and tradition. We must remember that democracies allow governments to change peacefully to meet the needs of the people in such a way that recognized traditions are still maintained.

Parliamentary Supremacy or Judicial Review?

© ISTOCKPHOTO.COM/ CARACTERDESIGN

What has always confused (and probably amazed) American college students is the fact that the United Kingdom lacks a written constitution but is still considered a functioning democracy with a long legal tradition. How can this be? How do the British people survive knowing that their laws are decided exclusively by the House of Commons and to a lesser degree, the House of Lords? Where is the British Supreme Court? What if laws are passed that are seemingly unconstitutional? How can a British citizen appeal a law as being unconstitutional, when there is not even a constitution?

These questions are easily answered by means of parliamentary procedure. In the United Kingdom, the political agenda is set and policies are formulated and enacted by the prime minister and his/her political party. So, once a law is formalized, it is seen as a mark on the ruling party. If over time, that law or a particular policy choice becomes perceived as something negative to the British people, and as a defining feature of the prime minister's agenda, the opposition party may win the next election and change the law.

> Is this fair? The British system allows the government (and only the government) to determine the laws. Is this a good idea or not?
>
> Is judicial review a positive feature of democratic life?

© ISTOCKPHOTO.COM/SABLAMEK

Japan

National Diet: *The formal name of the Japanese legislature composing the House of Councilors and the House of Representatives.*

In Japan, where the legislature is referred to as the **National Diet**, there too is a bicameral legislature composed of the **House of Councilors** (upper house) and the **House of Representatives** (lower house). Following World War II, the Japanese constitution created a parliamentary democracy that required legislative approval from both houses. However, when one examines the power between the two houses, it becomes clear that the House of Representatives has the upper hand in shaping and passing legislation.

The Japanese House of Representatives has a constitutional mandate to serve as the ultimate voice in choosing the prime minister as well as the ability to sign international treaties and to create and approve the final budget. Although both houses have the authority to name potential candidates for prime minister, it is the House of Representatives that has the final say. In fact, the House of Representatives also has the ability to pass legislation voted down by the House of Councilors. For example, suppose a legislative bill is created in and approved by the House of Representatives. The rules require that the bill must go to the House of Councilors for approval. However, even if the House of Councilors rejects the bill, it still goes back to the House of Representatives for another vote.[9] If the bill then receives a two-thirds majority in the House of Representatives, it becomes law. Thus, even if a potential piece of legislation arises in the upper house, it can become law only upon its acceptance in the lower house.

While this may sound a great deal like the British parliamentary system, the Japanese Diet does have several unique characteristics. First, the members of both the upper and lower house in Japan are elected by the people. Although the upper house operates according to a proportional representation of the people based on party affiliation, they are elected nonetheless.

Second, Japan is a **multiparty parliamentary democracy**. Even though the Liberal Democratic Party (LDP) dominated the government from the mid 1950s until the early 1990s, it now has to operate amongst a group of contending parties such as the Democratic Party of Japan (DPJ), the Clean Government Party (CGP), the Liberal Party (LP), the Social Democratic Party (SDP), and the Japan Communist Party (JCP). The presence of a multiparty system is an important feature of many modern parliamentary democracies. In fact, most of the democracies in the world today have a number of different political parties that allow each constituency to feel that they have some voice in the shaping of national policies.

Unicameral Legislatures: One Voice, One House

Although most democracies seem to have adopted the Madisonian theory of bicameralism and the practice of the British parliament, there are several states that have opted for one-chambered national legislatures. Proponents of unicameralism, like Jeremy Bentham and Louis Rockow, have argued that a one-house system offers its people three superior options: greater efficiency, greater accountability, and fewer expenses. These three arguments will serve as the focus of the following section.

Efficiency

Most proponents of a unicameral system claim that it is a more efficient system of conducting the people's business. Why? Because the policy and legislative processes of most states revolve around the ability to place important issues/problems on the agenda, formulate appropriate measures to handle these problems, and lastly, implement programs that actually solve them. One of the strongest arguments against bicameralism is that it is an inherently slow process *by design*. While deliberation is a

House of Councilors: *The upper house in the Japanese parliament. It is designed to approve proposed legislation that has already been passed in the lower House of Representatives. However, if it chooses to reject the proposed law, its ruling can be overturned in the House of Representatives by a two-thirds majority vote.*

House of Representatives: *The lower house in the Japanese parliament. Its members are voted on directly by the people and it is the ultimate source of authority in the legislative process.*

Multiparty Parliamentary Democracy: *A democratic state that has more than two active political parties in the legislature.*

necessary part of the passage of productive legislation and the overall functioning of democracy, it can sometimes cause problems that ultimately hurt the citizens.

In today's world, many states have opted for unicameralism because of the arguments made by Louis Rockow. They underline the belief that an efficient legislature is one that creates and implements *effective* policies and that a two-house system potentially prevents such levels of efficiency. As Tom Todd writes, "Because its decision-making process is relatively simple and efficient, a unicameral legislature has the time to provide a fuller and fairer hearing to all interests and points of view."[10]

THEORY AND PRACTICE

Two Houses Might Not be Better than One

In 1928, Lewis Rockow published an article entitled "Bentham on the Theory of Second Chambers." In addition to summarizing Bentham's beliefs on two-chambered houses, Rockow argued that second legislative chambers are impediments to good legislation because they are largely redundant.[11] In the article, Rockow writes:

> "The existence of two chambers, each sharing in legislation, will, [according to Bentham] involve useless delay in the process of legislation. To pass a law will then cost double the amount of effort. The same documents, witnesses, and most of the arguments will have to be presented in both chambers. In fact, the delay which the existence of a second chamber will produce may be infinite, for in addition to the double amount of work there will also arise deadlocks due to mutual jealousies and conflict of authority. Thus wholesome legislation will be retarded and the people derived of its benefit, while those who are opposed to all reform will have additional opportunities to conceal their selfish interests behind parliamentary guile and craft."[12]

So for Bentham, slower deliberation is not good for democracy. In fact, he argued that a faster, leaner legislature will ensure that the people's immediate interests are met.

What do you think? Are two chambers better than one?

Can you think of any other benefits to a one-chambered legislature?

Greater Accountability

While efficiency in passing legislation is a necessary feature of any legislature, democratic rule also requires an accurate representation of the people's will. As redundant and obvious as this appears, an argument has been made by those in favor of unicameralism suggesting that upper houses lack an appropriate level of accountability necessary to democratic governance. We must remember that most upper houses are designed to be removed from local interests and that in many countries their ministers are elected as representatives of political parties rather than as representatives of the people themselves.[13] Thus, those in favor of unicameralism have suggested that if anything, upper houses are less representative than lower houses and bicameral systems are less democratic.

Fewer Expenses

Lastly, those in favor of unicameralism also argue that it is more cost-effective. To put it in plain economic terms, two houses cost more money and also generate more waste than one. As government responsibilities have grown, so too has the number of individuals who work for the elected members of the legislature.

Consider the example of the state of Nebraska. Although the national government of the United States is bicameral, because it is a federal system, it allows its states to have their own types of legislatures. Nebraska is the only state in the United States that has a unicameral legislature. This example is important for the "fewer expenses" argument because it demonstrates the amount of money that Nebraska has saved since changing from a bicameral structure to a unicameral one. As Zanotelli writes, "the difference between the last bicameral session of the (Nebraska) legislature ($202,593) and the first unicameral session ($103,445) yielded a savings of nearly $100,000—almost a fifty percent savings in this instance.[14]

Although political systems must be chosen on merit and ability to legislate rather than financial expenditures, those systems that yield fewer costs are still important to examine. The case of Nebraska is important because it has operated within a sea of bicameralism, and it has largely been successful. If citizens have kept it alive in the heartland of the United States for almost 70 years, it must have certain popular traits; one of which is that it has allowed Nebraskans to lower the cost of government and limit the amount of waste.

Unicameral Systems: Ukraine and Costa Rica

The previous section examined the general merits of a unicameral system. It focused on both its strengths as a system and its strength in relation to bicameralism. The following case studies will briefly outline the basic structures of two specific unicameral systems: Ukraine, a former part of the Soviet Union, and Costa Rica, the most democratically stable state in Latin America. These analyses are designed to shed greater light on both the general theory of unicameralism and the more specific characteristics of each state. We will begin with Ukraine, a unitary, presidential democracy in Eastern Europe.

Ukraine

Today, Ukraine is classified as a unitary, presidential democracy. However, this is a very recent designation. Like many other states in Eastern Europe, Ukraine's history, people, and culture have largely been shaped by its relationship with Russia. While its current political borders were established at the end of World War II, the Russo-Ukrainian story began with the earliest founding of the city of Kiev, the current capital of Ukraine. Established in the ninth century as a political unit known as Kievan Rus', the founders of Kiev served as the historical basis for the modern states of Belarus, Ukraine, and Russia: three peoples who have claimed Kievan ancestry. For centuries, it has been this claim that has perpetuated the tension between Russia and Ukraine.

Since Ukraine is situated between Western Europe and Russia, its population has historically been divided: individuals in the East favored a Russian viewpoint and those in the West, a more European one. Once Russia began to grow in influence over a segment of the Ukrainian population and made claims of common ancestry, it

▲ As you can see, Ukraine is situated in between two worlds. Will its leaders look to the West or to the East? Only time will tell.

was not long before Ukraine was conquered and placed under its control. Although Ukraine experienced a brief period of independence following World War I, it eventually fell under the domain of the Soviet Union where it remained until 1991.[15]

It is this historical connection with Russia that has formed many of the contemporary opinions of Ukrainian society as well as certain features of the Ukrainian government. Today, culturally, Ukraine is still a divided nation with its Western populations favoring a more European existence and its Eastern population favoring a more Russian one.[16] Divisions like these are hard to mend. Yet, the establishment of a free Ukraine in the early 1990s has attempted to mend these differences through democratic institutions and a unitary system of authority.

In 1991, the government created a unitary, unicameral, presidential democracy: one that divides power between a president and a one house legislature. It was decided that a country that had operated as part of the Soviet Union for so long needed a form of rule that was democratic, yet still powerful enough to pass necessary legislation in the face of a culturally divided people and that a bicameral legislature would only serve as an impediment to the proper functioning of government.

In Ukraine, proposed legislation is seen as a direct debate between the one-chambered legislature known as the *Verkhovna Rada* (national parliament) and the country's president, who is elected by the people in a separate election (as is the case in all presidential democracies), who serves five years (with a limit of two terms). The Ukraine president also has a number of constitutional powers relating to parliament. Once legislation is approved in the Rada, it is signed by the chairman of the Verkhovna Rada; it then goes on to the president for approval. Given the relatively recent creation of the independent state of Ukraine and its long history with Russia, its constitution has attempted to place a relative balance between its different branches. Although the president is the most visible person in government, entitled to a great many powers over the Rada, including the constitutional right of naming/dismissing the prime minister, the constitution of Ukraine operates by a unique separation of powers.

⟨image⟩ CourseReader ASSIGNMENT

Log in to **www.cengagebrain.com** and open CourseReader to access the reading:

Viktor Yushchenko's *Inaugural Address, January 25, 2005.*

Yushchenko's inaugural address is in many ways a reflection of the events of the Orange Revolution (which brought him to power) and an appraisal of the past glories of the Ukrainian people. However, it was also a call for reform and modernization. When Yushchenko addressed his hope that Ukraine must become an active participant in the European Union, he was underlining his belief that democracy requires a modern economy and an advanced culture. His dreams about Ukraine producing "high culture" echo his beliefs that although he will continue to have a "stable" relationship with countries in both the East and West, it is in Ukraine's democratic interest to become a firm member of the European Union.

- *Why is European inclusion a top priority for Ukraine?*
- *What role has history played in the development of democracy in Ukraine?*

According to Chapter 4, Article 76 of the Ukrainian constitution, "The constitutional composition of the Verkhovna Rada of Ukraine consists of 450 National Deputies of Ukraine who are elected for a four-year term on the basis of universal, equal and direct suffrage, by secret ballot." Each deputy has the right to propose legislation and when the piece of legislation is approved after review by special committees (mostly by majority vote), it is sent to the president for final passage.

THEORY AND PRACTICE

Ukraine:
Look to the East or to the West?

© ISTOCKPHOTO.COM/DIEGO CERVO

In Ukraine, most arguments against both bicameralism and federalism center on its ethnic configuration. Ukraine, which has been dominated by hundreds of years of Russian and later Soviet dominance, still shows the signs of what Ukrainians characterize as "occupation" and Russians call "incorporation."[17] To look at the ethnic configuration of Ukraine, one might be shocked to see how divided it is. The western part of Ukraine values itself as primarily Ukrainian and has a strong allegiance to the member states of the European Union (EU). The eastern part, on the other hand, comprises a combination of Ukrainians and ethnic Russians, many of whom still speak the Russian language and identify their future as being inextricably linked with that of Russia.

If the Ukrainian government and people decide, in the spirit of democracy, that a federal system would be more appropriate for them, it could be problematic. Why? Because of the strongly divergent interests of the East and West. While most Americans view federalism and bicameralism as safeguards against tyranny and government expansion, Ukrainians view them differently. Ukraine is on the verge of major change and its future is still quite uncertain. How its legislature acts is largely dependant on how its history and its different ethnic groups view each other. If the system gets broken down and it becomes a federal system, it could mean the refusal of certain territories to participate. If this happens, it will take the government and all of its resources (including the courts) to prevent the collapse of the country.

How can ethnic differences impact decisionmaking?

Is it in Ukraine's best interest to look to the East (Russia) or the West (European Union)?

© ISTOCKPHOTO.COM/LORENZO COLLORETA

Once the bill is received by the president, he/she has 15 days to either pass it or send it back for further changes. According to Article 94,

> In the event that the President of Ukraine has not returned a law for repeat consideration within the established term, *the law is deemed to be approved by the President of Ukraine and shall be signed and officially promulgated. If a law, during its repeat consideration, is again adopted by the Verkhovna Rada of Ukraine by no less than two-thirds of its constitutional composition, the President of Ukraine is obliged to sign and to officially promulgate it within ten days. A law enters into force in ten days from the day of its official promulgation, unless otherwise envisaged by the law itself, but not prior to the day of its publication.*

The Ukrainian legislature was designed to create legislation that both properly serves the peoples' interests and serves them in a reasonable amount of time. The unicameral legislature within this unitary democracy was designed to promote political freedoms while also creating a sense of stability. Although there are many arguments that concern presidential power and the different segments of society who favor either a more Euro-centric Ukraine or a Russo-centric one, it has been the one-chambered house balanced by a separate and powerful executive that has quite possibly created the stability the world has recently witnessed.

While there have been recent attempts and arguments made in favor of creating a federal, bicameral legislature, this is most likely years away from happening. Many segments of Ukrainian society are still divided on the issue concerning its role in the world. Most of those who favor unicameralism in Ukraine would argue that if power is decentralized (like the federal states of the world) and "bicameralized," political debate would become too polarized for any successful democracy. The results could be catastrophic.

Costa Rica

Like Ukraine, Costa Rica is classified as a unitary, presidential democracy. Situated between Nicaragua and Panama, Costa Rica stands as one of the most stable states in Central America. In fact, since its independence from Spain in 1821, Costa Rica has had only two brief periods of nondemocratic rule.[18]

So what has caused this stability? How has Costa Rica been able to maintain a legitimate electoral system and a valid government? The most significant answer seems to be the creation of government agencies committed to protecting the sanctity of the electoral process. As Booth suggests, it has been this protection which has made all the difference in Costa Rica.

> [L]iberal democracy in Costa Rica could not have survived without something "most untypical of Latin America: *honest elections. . . . The establishment of liberal democracies . . . included the creation of powerful, independent agencies to administer the electoral process, agencies carefully structured to assure that neither the government nor any party could covertly control an election."*[19]

The agency known as the Tribunal Supremo de Elecciones (TSE) monitors the election process from the distribution of voter identification cards to the management and organization of procedures. "The TSE normally consists of three magistrates and six *suplentes* (substitutes) who are appointed to staggered six-year terms by the Supreme Court of Justice."[20] It has been successful in "keeping tabs" on the tendencies of political parties and presidential candidates toward fraud.

Because Costa Rica is a unitary, unicameral, presidential democracy, its system is based on a direct division of legislative authority between its president and its Asamblea Legislativa (Legislative Assembly). Unlike the decentralized nature of federal systems, Costa Rican policies are made at the national level on behalf of its seven provinces. The seven provinces, however, do not constitute seven different local governments. Provinces are divided into smaller political units known as *cantons,* whose size is determined by population. The configuration of each canton's municipal government is usually determined by the success or failure of the national political elections (held on the same day as the local elections) and in particular the success or failure of the two dominant political parties, the *Partido Unidad Social Cristiana* and the *Partido Liberacion Nacional*.

Costa Rica's Asamblea Legislativa has 57 seats and they are directly elected by the people in proportion to the state's population from the seven provinces. According to Title IX of the Costa Rican Constitution, the "Assembly's powers include the following: to amend the Constitution; legislate; declare war and peace; approve the national budget; levy taxes; ratify treaties; authorize the suspension of civil liberties; appoint magistrates to the Supreme Court of Justice and the TSE; and many similar tasks."[21] This is what has made Costa Rica a well-balanced democracy. It has created a system that effectively monitors elections and affords it legislature with the type of authority not often found in one-chambered systems.

Unfortunately, however, this authority has recently been challenged by a growth in presidential power related to economic mismanagement by the Assembly and a series of economic crises.[22] Because the government of Costa Rica and in particular the Assembly controls a great many of

▲ Situated in the heart of Latin America, Costa Rica has always been valued as one of the most stable states in the region.

the nation's major industries, they have been associated with causing many of the recent economic crises. As a result, the presidency has grown in authority and popularity.

Are Two Houses Better Than One?

Based on the factors involved, it appears that the answer to this question is based on each state's history, culture, and interpretation of democracy—namely, how the power should be distributed. Since the majority of federal states are bicameral, it would appear that the two designations seem to imply some coordination. In federal states, where power is decentralized to lesser regional/provincial governments—as in the United States, Canada, and Australia—the concept of democracy is based on the concept of diffusion as a remedy against tyranny. However, in unitary, bicameral states such as France, the United Kingdom, and Japan, the two-house structure is employed as a way of continuing debate while maintaining historical traditions of *removed* representation.

Although unitary, unicameral states are found in diverse locations around the world, they do possess some similar features. First, unitary, unicameral states are usually more culturally and linguistically homogeneous than federal, bicameral states. It is believed that one-chambered houses are designed to concentrate the beliefs of individuals and/or political parties, yet also reflect the nation as a whole. Ideological differences are valued as necessary to democracies but should never be powerful enough to destroy the entire system; one-chambered houses like Ukraine and Costa Rica reflect this attitude.

Second, unitary unicameral states are the most common form of government in the world today. With the end of the colonial era and a rise in those who believe in direct representation, most newly created states have opted for unitary, unicameral systems. As was previously stated, many of the new states do not see the need for a two-chambered legislature. Therefore, most new states that share a common culture and history have opted for unicameralism.

JUDICIARIES: INTERPRETERS OF THE LAW

We now come to the third branch of government: the judiciary. Judiciaries are essential to the functioning of democratic life because simply put, they are entrusted with the law. The courts interpret established laws or policies and attempt to determine whether or not they are in line with legal traditions. What makes comparing judicial systems a difficult endeavor is that each state has its own legal traditions, methods of interpretation, values and norms, and institutional power structure. Therefore, this section will evaluate different "high courts" within the greater institutional structure of government. It will focus on a comparative assessment of a topic previously discussed in Chapter 7 on American politics: judicial review.

Judicial Review: Aid or Impediment to Democracy

Simply put, **judicial review** is the power granted to certain supreme courts to declare acts and laws passed by legislatures and executives to be invalid if they are in conflict with the state's constitution. Although judicial review has already been discussed within the American context, it exists in other democracies as well. The judiciary is unique in the modern context because it is generally considered the least representative branch of government. Thus, the *practice* of judicial review is not necessarily determined by its presence in a state's constitution. Some states value its presence as a necessary feature of democracy, but choose to use it only in certain circumstances.

In Japan, for example, judicial review is constitutionally granted to its Supreme Court; however, it has rarely been used. Chapter VII, Article 81 of the Japanese Constitution clearly articulates the power entrusted to the Supreme Court of Japan: "The Supreme Court is the court of last resort with power to *determine the constitutionality of any law, order, regulation or official act.*" Since 1947, however, "(Japan's) Supreme Court (has) upheld lower court verdicts on the unconstitutionality of existing laws in only *five* cases, none of which involved a controversial political issue."[23] According to Fukai and Fukui, the Court's unwillingness to use its power is due to both practical and cultural reasons. They write:

First, there is an influential legal culture in Japan that holds that the Judiciary should not intervene in decisions of the legislative or executive branches of government. . . . *Second, Japan has a much weaker case law tradition than either the United States or Great Britain. . . . Third, judicial passivity may reflect the traditional reluctance of Japanese people to resort to litigation to settle disputes . . . (and) finally, Japan lacks a tradition of judicial review: under the Meiji Constitution, the emperor was above the law, and the courts did not have the power to deny the legality of any executive act taken in his name.*[24]

In Japan, therefore, judicial review is seen as a legal practice lacking both the modern necessity of representation and cultural traditions of litigation. It has been this combination that has made judicial review a limited practice in Japan.

Even in the United Kingdom, a state that prides itself on a rich legal tradition, judicial review does not exist. The United Kingdom bases its legal tradition on what is referred to as the Common Law—a collection of laws based on past cases, precedents, and judicial interpretations. The unique quality of the United Kingdom is that it has always based its democratic values in its legislature. As was previously noted, it is the British Parliament that serves as the most powerful branch in the British system. Therefore, it is the principle of **parliamentary sovereignty** that best defines the manner in which British laws are created and defined.

British jurists suggest that parliamentary sovereignty best serves the interests of British citizens because it has to a large degree kept the courts out of the political fray. Since it is the members of parliament and, in particular, the prime minister, who determine the policy choices of the government, the courts have been able to remain above (or below) the dirty nature of modern politics. Unlike United States's Supreme Court justices who have become notoriously associated with political agendas and ideologies, British tradition allows its Parliament to legislate, and its courts to officiate.

While it is clear that the British tradition has precipitated a denial of judicial review and the Japanese are reluctant to use it, there are certain states that have utilized it as a useful check on governmental power. Since the end of World War II, the German Constitutional Court has been given a mandate by the German people to act as a strong voice in the political system. In fact, "surveys generally find that Germans have more trust in the Court than in any other public institution."[25] The Constitutional Court serves as an active voice in the political arena, the conscience of what is valued as right for Germany.

For instance, it was the Constitutional Court, not the Bundestag (lower house) that made it illegal for anyone to deny the existence of the Holocaust and to form any neo-Nazi parties. The German Constitutional Court is easily considered one of the strongest federal courts in the world because it has actively taken advantage of its constitutional right of judicial review. The Court has impacted public policies across a wide spectrum of issues including education, religion, taxes, abortion, and immigration.[26]

In 1999, for example, a legal case came before the Constitutional Court that had a major impact on both the income levels of families and the overall economic well-being of the German economy. Conradt writes:

> The decision ruled that the existing tax laws for child care expenses were unconstitutional because they allowed single parents to deduct more than married parents. *The existing law assumed that "intact" families would spend less for child care than single parents. The Court ruled that the law violated the equal protection provisions of the Constitution as well as Article 6, which obligates the state to protect and promote the family. The decision, however, (will) cost the federal treasury about $13.5 billion in reduced revenues and would wreak havoc on the government's plan to reduce taxes."[27]*

A ruling of this kind is even beyond the scope of the United States Supreme Court. While American justices are at times ideologically motivated and have been labeled at different times as "activist judges," the American people would most likely never support this level of involvement.

Parliamentary Sovereignty: *A distinction that holds that the legislature is the most powerful source of law making and interpretation.*

Free Speech:
How Political Culture can Influence Speech

Do you think judicial review is an asset to democratic stability? Do you think that it is good for a Supreme Court (known elsewhere as a Constitutional Court) to have the power to deem certain laws unconstitutional? Or should it be up to the legislature to make such determinations? What do you think?

Why do you think that the Constitutional Court has outlawed the formation of neo-Nazi groups in Germany? And maybe more importantly, why hasn't the U.S. Supreme Court done the same? The answer to these questions, of course, relies on a combination of history and the states' interpretation of what constitutes free speech.

In Germany, the memory of the Holocaust continues to define attitudes on what is considered acceptable or unacceptable political behavior. Since the end of World War II, the German educational system, media, and political community have made a concerted effort to remind Germans of their responsibility in one of the worst acts of violence in human history.[28] Although German society is free and open, the German courts have made it quite clear that there are serious limits to speech that invokes memories of the Holocaust in any way.

In the United States, political history has dictated that speech is a much more fluid term. As long as one doesn't yell "fire" in a crowded theater or personally threaten the lives of fellow Americans or the president, he/she can form any kind of group he/she likes. In fact, the United States even has a legal group committed to upholding such type of behavior: the American Civil Liberties Union (ACLU). In its storied history the ACLU has defended some of the most unsavory hate groups including some neo-Nazi groups and members of the Ku Klux Klan (KKK). It is therefore important for you to remember that freedom of speech is not a universal right and that it is based on each state's historical context of what is thought of as acceptable and/or unacceptable.

What are other limitations placed on speech in the United States?

Why do neo-Nazis have greater protection under the law in the United States than in Germany?

POLITICAL PARTIES AND ELECTIONS

Political parties have become major players in modern democracies because of their ability to choose candidates, express united viewpoints of particular constituencies, and ultimately, win elections. Simply put, "political parties are a major 'inputting' device, allowing citizens to get their needs and wishes heard by government."[29] Defined by a set of political issues, commonly referred to as the party *platform* (see Chapter 8), political parties are designed to take the beliefs of a certain group of people to the seat of government. Just as there exist a number of nuances among the different democracies of the world, so too are there a number of different political parties and election systems. Although not entirely inclusive, the following section will examine the relationship between political parties and electoral systems. Since modern democracies rely on representation rather than the direct participation of the citizenry, the following section will focus on the ways in which different electoral systems have perpetuated the number, power, and types of different political parties.

Winner-Take-All or First Past the Post Systems

In the United States, there are two dominant political parties: Republicans and Democrats. Although there are a number of lesser political parties, the American political landscape is largely governed by these two. Why? Well, because the established electoral system dictates the predominance of two dominant parties. The United States operates according to an electoral system known as a **winner-take-all system**, or as it is referred to in the United Kingdom, a first-past-the-post system.

Winner-take-all System: *An electoral system that grants victory to the candidate who receives the majority of votes in his/her district.*

Winner-take-all systems are the simplest model to understand. This is not because they are more familiar to the American student, but because they operate according to the simple principle of "first past the post." The candidate that receives the majority of votes (51 percent) in his/her particular district wins the seat. There are no seats for second, third, or fourth place. The only candidate who represents the district is the candidate that wins the majority of the people's votes. So each seat in government corresponds to a particular district. In the U.S. House of Representatives, we have 435 members that correspond to the 435 districts in the 50 states. In the United Kingdom, there are currently 650 seats, which means that there are 650 districts represented in the House of Commons.

This also means that winner-take-all systems tend to create a two-tiered representative dilemma. On the one hand, winner-take-all systems perpetuate the predominance of the two dominant parties. They force both parties to create broad ideological platforms in order to inspire the largest segment of the voters. In doing so, they also put an end to the hopes of smaller, third parties. Many individuals who consider themselves "independents" will continue to vote for one of the two dominant parties because they feel that otherwise they will be wasting their vote. Thus, winner-take-all systems are much more suited to a two-party dominant system.

WHY POLITICS MATTERS TO **YOU!**

Underrepresented and for What Reason?

Do you know who your representative in the U.S. House of Representatives is? Well, that's OK because he/she doesn't know you either. He or she is a member of the House of Representatives of the United States, one of the least representative bodies in the Western world. If you don't believe me, think about these facts and figures.

In the U.S. House of Representatives, there are 435 members. That means that each congressman and congresswoman on average represents roughly 700,000 Americans! If that seems like a lot of people to represent, you are right. In fact, Americans are so greatly underrepresented, it is ridiculous. "The average British MP (member of parliament) represents 90,000 people . . . and the average member of the French National Assembly represents more than 100,000 people."[30] In each institution, there are more than 600 people representing the law-making interests of the people. Democracies are designed to represent the interests of the people. So what is wrong here? Why are we stuck on 435 members of Congress and 100 members in the Senate?

Well, it is not in the Constitution (although the constitutional standard is one representative for every 30,000 people) and it was not even determined by the Framers. It emerged from a bill introduced in 1911, following the 1910 census, and finally passed in 1929, that fateful year often associated with the beginning of the Great Depression.[31] In 1929, Congress passed a law that guaranteed the number of representatives in the House at 435. Yes, that is the reason. So, although much has changed since 1929, the scale of representation has not.

Should we try to have greater representation?

What would this do to the number of congressmen? Is increasing the size of government the solution?

Elections in the United Kingdom

To best understand this system, let's take a look at the United Kingdom. In the United Kingdom there are two dominant parties, the Labour Party (representing the interests of organized labor and the overall belief that government involvement is necessary to democracy) and the Conservative Party (representing the business interests and the overall belief in free market economics). Although there is a smaller third party, the Liberal Democratic Party, most decisions and elections revolve around the measures of the two dominant ones.

As we learned on page 275, the leader of the House of Commons, and in fact, the leader of the entire government is the prime minister. The prime minister of Great Britain, like every other member of the House of Commons, serves an **indefinite term** of five years. This means that the prime minister is given the authority to call for new elections at any point he/she chooses within a five-year period. If, however, the five-year period is about to expire and the prime minister has not called for an election, then an election is held at a predetermined date.

To an American student, this process of indefinite election terms may seem strange. Yet when taken in a comparative perspective, it is seen as the system that is preferred by British citizens because it has lasted for centuries. The British system, like all parliamentary systems, fuses the authority of the executive (prime minister) with that of the legislature. After an election is held, the winning party (majority party) in the House of Commons names the prime minister.

Indefinite Term: *Term that is defined by the head of government, not by a constitutional decree. For example, the prime minister of the United Kingdom must call for general elections at some point before a five-year period expires, but its timing is up to his/her discretion.*

Disciplined versus Undisciplined Political Parties

Before we examine other types of electoral systems, something must be said about **disciplined** versus **undisciplined political parties.** For the most part, the United States is unique in that its elected Republicans and Democrats are allowed to be much more fluid than their European, Latin American, Asian, or African democratic counterparts. In the United States, there is a long history of elected officials acting against their own party's interests when they think that a particular policy is one that their consciences will not allow. For instance, while there are certain issues that are defined as in line with the national Republican platform, there are some senators and congressmen/women who deviate from this trend. New York City Mayor Michael Bloomberg and former NYC Mayor Rudolph Giuliani fit this model, as they are both pro-choice, and yet are still considered to be strong members of the Republican Party. The fact that elected officials are allowed to vote according to their consciences rather than according to their party platform, describes the parties as *undisciplined*.

In the United Kingdom, by contrast, political parties are considered *disciplined*. Simply put, disciplined political parties strictly conform to the platform issues and

Disciplined Political Parties: *Political parties whose members vote according to the established party platform and rarely vote according to their own consciences.*

Undisciplined Political Parties: *Political parties whose members are free to vote according to their own personal beliefs.*

will usually vote in favor of the party leadership's position. For example, when the House of Commons is in session, rarely, if ever, will a member of Her Majesty's Loyal Opposition (the minority party) side with the reigning prime minister's party. It might be helpful for disciplined political parties to be thought of as great pyramids, with the leader of the party at the top and the party faithful at the bottom. Each elected representative must maintain loyalty to the party because his/her future depends on it. If a particular *rogue* party member begins to deviate too strongly from the platform, the head of the party will make sure that he/she is taken off the ballot in the next election (This is another important component of the British party system: The party leader has the power to remove party members.). Disciplined political parties stress platform loyalty and ultimately determine the candidates for each election.

Proportional Representation Systems

Proportional Representation Systems:
An electoral system that is designed to send a number of different party representatives to the national legislature.

As Alexis de Tocqueville noted, there is more to democratic life than majority rule (see Chapter 8). Those in a democracy must make sure that all voices are taken into consideration—even the weakest. This is the spirit in which **proportional representation (PR) systems** operate. They are electoral systems that are designed to ensure that even the smallest parties are represented (based on their proportion) in government. Thus, PR systems usually promote the interests and involvement of smaller third parties to a much larger degree than winner-take-all systems, who because of their "first past the post" mentality help the dominance of two, large, broadly based parties.

Proportional representation systems are designed to send a number of different party representatives to the national legislature. Sometimes the representation is determined by the representation of parties in a particular district/province; sometimes it is determined by the representation of parties across the entire country. To begin, let us look at a hypothetical election.

Suppose it has been determined that our district will send one party candidate for every 5 percent of the vote that the party receives. Before the election, we find out that there are five political parties in our district: Party A, Party B, Party C, Party D, and Party E, and each party has its own list of 10 candidates. So then what happens? Well, after the vote was calculated it was determined that Party A received 35 percent, Party B received 32 percent, Party C received 18 percent, Party D received 10 percent, and Party E received 5 percent. So, who goes to the national legislature?

In this particular example, Party A will send its top seven candidates; Party B will send its top six candidates; Party C will send its top three candidates; Party D will send its top two candidates; and Party E will send just one candidate to the national legislature. PR systems are designed to best represent the voice of the people. If this

Republican, Democrat, or Independent?

D o the two dominant parties in the United States represent your interests? If you answered no, you are not alone. In fact, in the U.S. today there are as many independent voters as there are Republicans and Democrats. Many people have argued that the two parties and the winner-take-all electoral system provide stability to the United States. The thinking goes like this: In the United States, voters have to choose between two large parties. In order to receive enough votes to win, each party has to expand its platform to meet the needs of many, many people. So, when members of either party are elected they are forced to consider the interests of all those who voted for them and those who did not.

What do you think? Are you happy to vote for either party, or would you rather vote for a party that is more narrowly defined to serve your particular interests? Those that support the idea of proportional representation favor the latter. They (like John Stuart Mill) argue that the best method of ensuring a well-functioning democracy is to ensure that all ideas are heard even if it is only 5 percent of the voting public.

What do you think? Should the United States consider such a concept or should we continue to have only two parties decide the fate of the republic?

election were held in a single-member, winner-take-all-system, can you see the difference? Because Party A received the most votes, it would represent the entire district. This type of system is known as the Party List PR system.

Personalized Proportional Representation System

Another type of PR system commonly employed is referred to as a **personalized proportional representation system.** In this system, a hybrid approach to selecting

Personalized Proportional Representation System: *A hybrid approach to selecting party representation that combines elements of the winner-take-all and proportional representation systems.*

party representation is employed, one that combines both the winner-take-all and the proportional representation systems. Germany employs a good example of this hybrid system in elections for the Bundestag, its lower house. Citizens vote for half of the Bundestag by means of a winner-take-all election and the other half by proportional representation.

Each voter votes twice, once in the winner-take-all election and once in the proportional representation election. *The former is called the voter's first vote; the latter, his or her second vote. Both votes are cast the same day, on the same ballot. For the first, or winner-take-all vote, the country is divided into smaller electoral districts that correspond in number to half of the parliamentary seats. In each district the candidate with the most votes is elected. For the proportional part of the election, the Germans use party list PR, with the candidate ranking done by the parties. . . .*

Voters are allowed to split their two votes. In the winner-take-all election, they may vote for one party and in the party list PR election, for another. This provision creates the opportunity for some highly sophisticated voting behavior. Supporters of the small Free Democratic Party might cast their first vote for a candidate of one of the two large parties, knowing that their own candidate has virtually no chance of winning the winner-take-all election but they can still cast their second vote for their own party list.[32]

SUMMARY

This chapter focused on democratic institutions and the ways in which different systems operate, giving the reader a general understanding of the basic principles of life in a democracy. By examining the different branches of government within the context of different systems of rule, we hope to have shed a greater light on the ways in which other democracies function.

In an era of globalization, every American student should know how some of the world's democracies work. Americans need to be reminded that change in a democracy is a positive force and can lead to greater accomplishments. The sections on unitary versus federal systems and the theoretical differences between bicameralism and unicameralism were intended to stimulate debate—the one important function of every open society. Since the focus of this chapter was to provide you with an institutional analysis of contemporary democracies, the following chapter will examine some of the authoritarian states of the world and some of the issues that define their political systems.

KEY TERMS

KEY PEOPLE

10 AUTHORITARIAN STATES

▲ Saudi women and girls wear the black abaya, worn by some Muslim women, as they walk in public through the marketplace in Dammam, Saudi Arabia. There is effectively a ban on women driving. The World Economic Forum 2010 Global Gender Gap Report ranks Saudi Arabia 129th out of 134 countries for gender equality.

INTRODUCTION: AUTHORITARIANISM, POWER TO THE . . . RULERS!

Authoritarianism is a concept as old as humanity itself. Its endurance can be attributed to both simplicity and tradition, while its justification has been derived by both the sword and the pen. Until the middle of the twentieth century, **authoritarian states**, those states whose governance is not based on popular consent, had dominated world politics. Although authoritarian states have used different titles for their leaders (king, queen, caliph, sultan, czar, president) and different rationales to govern (tradition, religion, security), they all define their political power in absolute terms; justice as something the rulers define and something the people must follow.

This chapter will attempt to place the idea of authoritarianism within a historical perspective. It will begin with a brief look at some of the major arguments that have justified authoritarian rule as a method of governance. Although today, arguments of this nature are largely dismissed, they are still worthy of discussion considering that several states continue to base their authoritarian claims on similar conclusions. Following this predominantly theoretical and historical examination, the chapter will then focus on the development of contemporary authoritarian states—those states that are still ruled by monarchs, military leaders, and presidents—who continue to make headlines in today's world.

AUTHORITARIANISM: INTELLECTUAL AND RELIGIOUS JUSTIFICATIONS

Some of the strongest arguments in favor of authoritarianism can be found in some of the most famous works of political and theological literature, for example, the works of the Greek philosopher

Questions to Consider Before Reading This Chapter

1. What is authoritarianism and how has it been justified?
2. What do Niccolo Machiavelli and Thomas Hobbes say about human nature in relation to authoritarianism?
3. Why is authoritarianism still present in the world today?
4. What are the similarities among the three authoritarian states mentioned in this chapter?
5. Does economic development in China mean more or less government intervention in the lives of its citizens?

Authoritarian States: *States that continue to lack principles such as due process of the law, free and open elections, legitimate political parties, human rights, and so forth.*

AP PHOTO

Plato, the medieval works of both Christian and Islamic scholars, and the modern writings of Machiavelli and Hobbes. As you may recall in Chapter 2, Plato's *guardians* were leaders willing to get rid of their personal wealth for the benefit of the community. This idea highlights some of the earliest understandings of the need for a system in which the *best* leaders rule on behalf of those unable and unwilling to do so. It was believed that leadership was a quality that only the most intelligent could understand. For Plato, the king had to be a philosopher, one who both understood the nuances of justice and was committed to its fair application. For the ancient Greeks, understanding justice was not a quality possessed by the masses. It required years of training in both academic and ethical pursuits. Although Plato in no way should be considered as someone that favored a malicious dictatorial type of rule, he did set an academic precedent for "enlightened or benevolent" monarchy.

Following Plato's assessment of the necessity of just rule were the Christian and Islamic scholars of the medieval period. For the Christian scholars, St. Augustine and St. Thomas Aquinas, and the Islamic scholars, Al-Farabi and Ibn Rushd, the classic Greek model of enlightened monarchy was translated into a new, religious model. Both Christian and Islamic scholars argued that issues of governance were best decided by those with the capabilities to understand what is in the best interests of their people. For the Christian intellectuals, it was the Pope's infallibility and his status as Jesus's representative on earth that dictated his authority over the masses. For the Islamic thinkers, the *guardians* (to use Plato's terms) also had to be religious leaders, those individuals capable of understanding and properly interpreting Islam's holy book, the Koran.

Although both ancient and medieval scholars decided that proper governance is within the grasp of the few, religion has always played a major role in the history of authoritarianism. Prior to the intellectual justification of authoritarian rule, religiously defined legal documents such as Hammurabi's Code and the Ten Commandments had been relied on to create legal standards. The Epilogue to Hammurabi's Code (written by the emperor Hammurabi himself (1792–1750 BCE), suggested that the gods called on Hammurabi to lead the people.

I, Hammurabi, the perfect king, was not careless (or) neglectful of the black-headed (people), *whom Enlil had presented to me, (and) whose shepherding Marduk had committed to me; I sought out peaceful regions for them; I overcame grievous difficulties; With the mighty weapon which Zababa and Inanna entrusted to me, with the insight Enki allotted to me, with the ability that Marduk gave me, I rooted out the enemy above and below; I made an end of war; I promoted the welfare of the land; I made the people rest in friendly habitations; . . . The great god called me, so I became the beneficent shepherd whose scepter is righteous. . . .*[1]

Thus, Hammurabi's role was not only defined in human terms but also in divine terms. His authority emerged from the will of the gods, which obviously trumped the will of the people.

Religious justification has proven to be one of the strongest rationales for authoritarian leaders, whether they are referred to as emperors, queens, or caliphs. What we have witnessed is that this justification has been based on both the interpretation of religious texts and the understanding of the role of governments. In the ancient and medieval worlds, religion and politics provided a similar function: to create the best laws in order to create the greatest amount of order, which will, in turn, create the greatest level of happiness and virtue. Scholars of the ancient and medieval worlds decided that universal laws—those laws that apply to all humans—were out of humanity's reach because they were divine in origin.

While we have categorized this particular type of justification as "ancient" and "medieval," religion continues to play a major role in contemporary authoritarian states. This is not to say that states that continue to define power in religious terms are ancient or medieval, but that they have continued in and developed a tradition of authority that dates back several hundred years. We must remember that it is democracy, not authoritarianism, that has a very brief history. Religion is as old as humanity itself. It has served societies for centuries and most likely will continue to serve it in the future. It is best to analyze the several states that continue to opt for the fusion of religion and politics with this perspective in mind.

THEORY AND PRACTICE

Justice:
In the Interest of the Stronger Party

As you have already seen in Chapter 2, Plato's *Republic* is concerned with justice. He began from the individual perspective (what makes a just individual?) and then moved on to justice in the community (what makes a just community?). By the end of the *Republic* Plato determined that those who have both the greatest capacity for knowledge and have the greatest desire to seek the truth are most fit to rule. Unfortunately, he never got around to answering one of the strongest arguments of Book One of *Republic*: the idea that "justice is only in the interest of the stronger party," or in other words, "justice is always defined by those groups in positions of power."

This argument (made by the character Thrasymachus) has resonated down through the ages and can still be considered one of the greatest philosophical dilemmas of modern politics because it eliminates the moral arguments that surround justice.

continued ➤

For example, can you disagree about what is right and what is wrong? Yes. Can you change the law yourself? No. The law has been decided by a number of people in positions of political power. Therefore, even if you believe that a law is justified (or good), you must also accept the fact that it is only justified because the people in power accept it as justified.

What distinguishes democratic states from authoritarian states is that democracies allow their citizens to argue over what they see as just and unjust. What unites them is that age-old issue addressed first by Plato, that at the end of the day, justice still remains in the interest of the stronger party.

> **Is Plato's character Thrasymachus correct in his assumption that "justice is in the interest of the stronger party"?**
>
> **What do you think are the best defenses against ruling parties from creating unjust laws?**

MODERN JUSTIFICATIONS: POWER AND SECURITY
Machiavelli and Hobbes

At the end of the medieval period, political science witnessed the beginning of a new rationale for authoritarianism; one that argued that security and power, on their own, are strong enough to provide justification to ruling parties. With the publication of *The Prince* by Niccolo Machiavelli (first introduced to you in Chapter 3), leaders were given a manual on how best to secure power for themselves and to create security for their people. While students today may not consider the fifteenth and sixteenth centuries as "modern," in the scheme of political thought, they are. *The Prince* articulated a major shift in how intellectuals viewed humanity. Machiavelli's firm insistence that "how men actually behave is so far removed from how we ought to behave," ended the dominant position that normative claims had over governance.[2]

As we discussed in Chapter 3, Machiavelli created the argument that ruthless-ness and deceitfulness are essential ingredients in attaining and maintaining author-ity. Machiavelli argues that the best leaders are those who behave according to a calculus that defines *virtue* as effectiveness. Machiavelli's *Prince* therefore only needs to *appear* virtuous, without ever having to actually *be* virtuous. This is a distinction that earlier scholars would never have dreamed of. In fact, it is a distinction that places the authoritarian state on a path of destruction.

Machiavelli's insistence on the utilization of "force and fraud" as a means of ensuring peace and security was grounded in two interrelated ideas: first his unwavering belief in the immorality of human nature; and second, his desire to see the unification of the competing Italian city-states under the rule of one strong leader. For Machiavelli and later, Thomas Hobbes, competing interests are the sources of conflict and war. In the fifteenth century, Italy was a frag-mented peninsula composed of city-states more interested in their own survival than the survival of all. *The Prince*, in many ways, is both a plea and a plan on how best to bring competing Italian interests together, a concept that reflects his overall negative view of humanity.[3]

Yet, just as Machiavelli's negative view yielded his belief in the installation of one powerful leader to provide both national unity and security, it was Thomas Hobbes who made the process a "natural" consequence. Hobbes's *Leviathan* argues that man's *natural* level of selfishness and greed perpetuated the desire for authoritarian-ism. Hobbes in effect argues that the reason authoritarian states exist is because the people allow them to exist.

Think back to Chapter 3 and the development of Hobbes's state of nature. Hobbes argued that authoritarian states are socially constructed for reasons of security and stability. Since humanity's existence in this *time before govern-ment* was so bleak, at some point its members decided that they must turn complete authority over to a strong, central government; hence, the creation of the *Leviathan*. Authoritarian rule was therefore justified because it eliminated the death and destruction of the state of nature. For Hobbes, authoritarian rule eliminates absolute freedom and replaces it with a different type of freedom, one that stresses security and justice.

By basing their authoritarian claims on security rather than religion, Machiavelli and Hobbes reinterpreted the classic relationship between the gov-ernor and the governed. In this reinterpretation, security replaces salvation as the goal of the government. For both Hobbes and Machiavelli, leaders cannot be as concerned with the "good life." The "good life" is impossible to discover and there-fore deemed irrelevant. "Good" leaders are those evaluated on the basis of their ability to maintain power and national security; in other words, they are those able to provide their subjects with a feeling of safety and power in relation to oth-ers in the international community.

Give Me Liberty or Give Me . . . More Security?

Are we self-seeking, self-motivated, selfish creatures? Most authoritarian leaders would say that Hobbes and Machiavelli are right when they argue that human nature is essentially self-serving. Machiavelli goes so far as to say that the effective leader will realize that people are more easily swayed by fear (or the threat of fear) than by love and exploit this quality. Was he right? Are we willing to give up personal freedom for heightened security?

As Americans, these questions might offend you. After all, you have been taught from a very early age that the United States stands for freedom and personal liberty and that nothing (especially no government we elect) can take that away. But what about responses to terrorism? Uh oh, now I have released the cat from the bag. Let's start over. Are you willing to give up some level of freedom for more security? Yes or no?

Think about airport security. Should airports install full-body x-ray type scanners as a security measure? What about personal liberties? Is it right to force airline passengers to endure a full-body scan? What about racial profiling? Do you think that it is alright to allow airport security personnel to target certain individuals they deem as potential security risks?

Answers to these questions are important because they are vital to discussions of authoritarianism and democracy. How far are Americans willing to go for the sake of security? Remember, authoritarian states do not have trouble making these types of determinations because they place security and maintenance of political authority as their top priorities.

> In light of the tragic events of September 11, 2001, are you willing to give up some freedom for greater security? Are you willing to wait in long lines at the airport and then be subjected to full-body scans?
>
> Are you willing to have a government agency examine your library records or your e-mail messages?

CONTEMPORARY AUTHORITARIANISM: SAUDI ARABIA, NORTH KOREA, AND CHINA

In Chapter 8, we discussed some of the general characteristics of authoritarian states. Focusing on issues of human-rights abuses, media censorship, lack of due process, arbitrary arrests and seizure, and the lack of fair and open elections, we attempted to provide a basic framework from which to progress. Fortunately, in today's world there are only a few states that continue to behave in an absolutely undemocratic, authoritarian fashion. We have chosen three states that we believe best exemplify modern authoritarianism: the Kingdom of Saudi Arabia, the Democratic People's Republic of North Korea, and the People's Republic of China. All three are classic examples of authoritarianism and will hopefully allow the reader the opportunity to see how authoritarian states deny their people certain freedoms. The section will begin with Saudi Arabia, one of the wealthiest countries in the world and one of the last remaining monarchies.

The Kingdom of Saudi Arabia

Situated in the heart of the Middle East, Saudi Arabia is a state of incredible contradictions. With an estimated gross domestic product (GDP) of $310 billion, an annual economic growth of 6.6 percent, and an economic sector dominated by its vast oil reserves, the Kingdom of Saudi Arabia is one of the wealthiest countries in the Middle East.[4] On the other hand, Saudi Arabia is also the birthplace of Islam, a religion known for its modesty and shunning of materialism. So how does Saudi Arabia balance the opulence of capitalism with the piety of Islam? The answer seems to lie with the configuration of its government and the application of its law.

Constitutional Provisions and Political Powers

Maintaining its role as the birthplace of Islam and the custodian of two of Islam's holiest sites, Mecca and Medina, the Kingdom of Saudi Arabia (as seen in the following map) is governed by a traditional, royal family committed to the legal application and interpretation of **Wahabbism**, a variation of Sunni Islam known for its strict teachings and literal interpretations of the Koran. To suggest that Islam plays a large role in the establishment of Saudi law would be a gross understatement. The Saudi constitution, known as the Basic Law, is based entirely on three sources: the Koran (Islam's Holy Book), Shari'a Law (Islamic law), and the cultural traditions of

Constitutional Provisions: *Constitutional provisions refer to the specific arrangement of the law in any particular country. It refers to exactly what protections individuals have and how the government is able to act.*

Wahabbism: *A form of Sunni Islam established in the 18th century by Muhammed Ibn Abdul-ahl-Wahhab. It is considered by most scholars as one of the most conservative interpretations of the Muslim holy book, the Koran.*

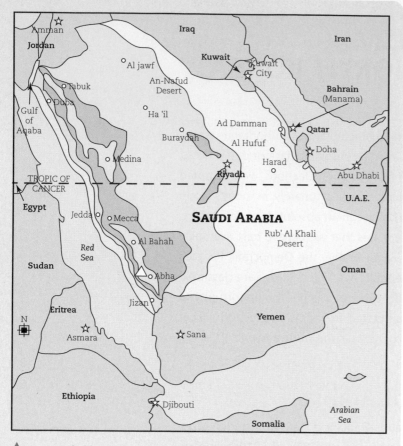

▲ Surrounded by many states in North Africa and the Middle East, Saudi Arabia is home to two of Islam's holiest sites: Mecca and Medina.

the region.[5] In fact, Chapter 2, Article 6 of the Saudi constitution defines the role of the citizens as having "to pay allegiance to the King, in obedience to the Holy Koran, and in the tradition of the Prophet."[6] Islam, and in particular Wahabbism, is therefore much more than simply the state religion of Saudi Arabia. It is the source of all legal and social legitimacy. It serves as both the glue that binds Saudi society together and the wedge that drives it apart.

In much the same way that legal authority flows from Islam, *political* authority flows from the monarch. The king of Saudi Arabia along with an appointed Council of Ministers, Shura Council, and Consultative Council determine all of the constitutional provisions and form the entire political system. Formally proclaimed in Chapter 2 of the Saudi constitution, "Rule passes to the sons of the founding king, Abd al-Aziz Bin Abd al-Rahman al-Faysal Al Sa'ud, and to their children's children. [In practice] the king chooses the heir apparent and relieves him of duties by Royal order."[7] Since its formal unification as a state in 1932, the Kingdom of Saudi Arabia has been ruled by six kings, the founder of the kingdom and the five subsequent kings, the founder's sons.

Like other contemporary authoritarian states, the recent wave of democratization has forced Saudi Arabia to create some semblance of a legislative system. In addition to the king, who serves as both head of state and head of government, there are three advisory bodies: the aforementioned Council of Ministers, Shura Council, and Consultative Council. Although these institutions lack the electoral and legislative features of their democratic counterparts, they each perform certain functions. Because Wahhabi Islam is both the unifying legal and social feature, all potential political legislation must proceed through a process of religious justification. Since the early 1950s, the Council of Ministers and the Shura Council (Islamic council) have been given the authority to determine if potential legislation is in accordance with

Shari'a law.[8] If the legislation is deemed appropriate, it is then passed onto the king for his final approval.

The most recently created legislative body, the Consultative Council, was established in 1993 as one of the late King Fahd's reform initiatives. Designed to provide the king with an understanding of issues at the local and provincial levels, the Consultative Council serves as a way of prioritizing issues before the Saudi bureaucracy.[9] In essence, the Consultative Council was created as an attempt to balance the streamlined federal monarchy with that of the 13 provinces. Its 150 appointed members provide the people of Saudi Arabia with a sense that their local interests are being considered. While it is a far cry from that of a democratically elected legislative body, it seems to have given the citizens a greater level of transparency in the policy-making domain of their government.

Recently the kingdom has seen a rise on the number of critics who claim that this recent move toward greater governmental transparency is merely an attempt by King Abdullah to maintain power. In 2004, international observers were shocked when the king announced that Saudi citizens would be allowed to vote for their local municipal councils. While it appeared at the time to be a positive move, it turned out to be something quite different. According to Amr Hamzawy, a senior associate at the Carnegie Endowment and an expert in Middle Eastern politics, the 2005 municipal elections were merely a way of distracting international observers and continuing the king's authoritarian rule. Hamzawy stated:

> [The elections witnessed] the exclusion of women as [both] voters and candidates, *low levels of citizens' participation, trivial competencies assigned to elected local councilors who were kept away from high politics and supposed to primarily discuss urban planning and street lighting and finally dominance of tribal loyalties and religious inclinations in determining voters' preferences.*[10]

In many respects, the 2005 municipal elections highlight the difficulties that continue to plague Saudi Arabia: strict governmental control, a poor human and women's rights record, a lack of political parties, and an overall lack of political freedoms. The royal family of Saudi Arabia continues to dominate all political debate. Like all authoritarian states, the Saudi regime has successfully exploited its own unique social characteristics that have allowed it to stay in control.

Like elsewhere in the Middle East, Saudi society is defined by the twin pillars of **patriarchy** and Islam. The patriarchal arrangement that prevents women from even the most basic rights (for example, women are denied the right to drive an automobile or appear in public without a related male escort) is reinforced by a misinterpretation of Islam that predominates all social life. Patriarchy by definition is a system designed to keep power in the hands of the male population. It must be remembered that Islam in its truest form, is not patriarchal.[11] Unfortunately, what has occurred in Saudi Arabia is that Islam, and in particular Wahabbism, has become an excuse for the royal family to maintain this patriarchal view of life.

Patriarchy: *A concept that is used to define societies that places men in positions of power over women.*

▲ King Abdullah of Saudi Arabia is an example of a present day monarch.

According to Islam's holy book, *The Koran*, women and men are supposed to be treated as equals. In fact, one famous passage condemns those who are unwilling to maintain this equality. Chapter 4, Verse 19 (which speaks specifically to men) states, "You are forbidden to inherit women against their will. Nor should you treat them with harshness . . . [and that you must] live with them on a footing of kindness and equity."[12] This passage and others like it reinforce the notion that Islam is a religion that values the equality of human life. Even the prophet Muhammad "often stated that, 'all people are equal . . . [and] that there is no merit of an Arab over a non-Arab, or of a white over a black person, or of a male over a female.'"[13] Thus, what must be understood is that it is the *application*

WHY POLITICS MATTERS TO **YOU!**

Saudi Arabia: *American Ally?*

I am sure that most of you reading this book have grown up in the United States. I am also almost certain that 51 percent of you are females. If this is correct, I can also be assured that most of you look at Saudi Arabia with anger, outrage, shock, and a whole host of other negative emotions. What you probably have not considered, however, is how Saudi Arabia may affect you in your lifetime or has already affected you.

Saudi Arabia possesses major oil reserves that have formed the basis of most of its wealth since they were discovered there in the early part of the twentieth century. They supply most of the oil for Europe and have produced such an abundance of oil that it literally pays off its people. Saudi Arabia is known as a rentier state. Since the oil revenues (money coming in) are so vast, they can provide their citizens with money.[14] This can be compared to a bribe. In Saudi Arabia, a citizen might not have political rights or freedoms (especially if female) but at least each month the government sends a check in the mail.

You still may wonder, however, what this has to do with you. Good question. The answer has to do with the fact that 15 of the 19 hijackers on September 11, 2001, were

continued

Saudi nationals. In Saudi Arabia, it is difficult to see who is really being held hostage: the citizens who have limited rights or the royal family that has to pay off its religious leaders and citizens so that they do not overthrow the regime. The people of Saudi Arabia have discovered the pretty obvious fact that their government is a favorite of the United States. Although most American officials will tell you that Israel is our greatest ally in the Middle East, it is fair to say that the Saudis are number two.

Still how does this affect you? Let's answer that question in simple terms. Since public-opinion polls place American popularity in Saudi Arabia in single digits, the government has to make sure that its people and in particular its children (the next generation of Saudis) are taught things that suggest they feel the same way. Take, for example, Nina Shea's article in the *Washington Post* entitled, "This is a Saudi textbook. (After the intolerance was removed)." Shea discovered that first-graders (six year olds) were taught, "Fill in the blanks with the appropriate words (Islam, hellfire): Every religion other than _____ is false. Whoever dies outside of Islam enters _____."[15] While eighth-graders were taught: "The apes are Jews, the people of the Sabbath; while the swine are the Christians, the infidels of the communion of Jesus."[16] The article continues with a litany of other despicable attacks on other religious groups and an array of international innuendo directed at American foreign policy with Israel and American foreign policy in general.

So why should you be concerned? Because we now live in a global community, where individuals are able to communicate and travel with ease. This means both those with good and bad intentions. It also means that you as a member of the global community may have to take a trip to Saudi Arabia or to another authoritarian country for business. Keep these things in mind, and remember that while you may possess a high level of freedom at home, you do not when you are traveling abroad.

Do you think that your education is free of bias?

We all realize that the Kingdom of Saudi Arabia is not a democratic country, yet it has been an ally of the United States. Why do you think that this is the case? Should oil determine political relationships? Are there problems with this?

and not the beliefs of Islam that seem to perpetuate division. The Saudi regime has simply co-opted Islam as a way of maintaining its authority.

This response, however, has serious consequences. It has led to a treatment of women, non-Muslims, and foreigners that is unconscionable. These groups have few rights in Saudi Arabia and continue to be subjected to harsh treatment from religious police and other government agents. The misuse of Islam as a political weapon is at the heart of the debate, as is the rise in government-sanctioned Wahabbism.[17]

The Democratic People's Republic of North Korea

In 2002, in his State of the Union address, former U.S. President George W. Bush labeled North Korea as part of an "Axis of Evil," one of three authoritarian states "arming to threaten the peace of the world" by furthering the development of nuclear weapons.[18] However, North Korea's authoritarianism goes well beyond its nuclear ambitions and capabilities. It is a country that has been described as a massive prison, where many of its people, including its children, live in forced labor camps. Although the world has little concrete evidence of the policy-making apparatus and exact nature of "the hermit kingdom," one report estimates that between "150,000 and 200,000 political criminals are incarcerated in five large labor camps."[19] And what does it take to be labeled a "political criminal"? Apparently, not that much. According to *The Economist*, North Korea ranks the population based on its loyalty to (its leader) Kim Jong II and more than half of those incarcerated are labeled as "wavering"; a term that suggests that their support is not as strong as it should be."[20] If this sounds absurd, it is not. It is a logical outcome of an authoritarian state that lacks independent institutions based on the rule of law. In order to best understand this system, we must understand its origins. The following section does just that.

The origins of the Democratic People's Republic of Korea (North Korea's official name) can be found amidst the ruins of World War II. Following Japan's defeat in 1945, the Korean peninsula was divided into two parts: a communist north that was eventually propped up by the Soviet Union and a south that was placed under the protection of the United States. By 1948, Kim Il-Sung had risen to prominence within North Korea's communist party. By 1950, armed with Soviet military support, Kim's North Korean army invaded the south, making Korea the first battlefield of the Cold War.

Although never formally recognized by the United States as a war, the Korean conflict encapsulated and formalized the essence of the Cold War. It proved to be a microcosm of

▲ North Korea's Kim Jong Il attends a meeting with Chinese President Hu Jintao in 2010.

the struggle between the Soviet Union and the United States, communism versus capitalism. When a cease-fire agreement was reached in July 1953, the division of the Korean peninsula became cemented. The 38th parallel, the land that divides North and South Korea, became the symbol of the ideological divide between the two superpowers. The South was placed on the road to free-market capitalism as the North suffered under its leader Kim Il-Sung and the military abandonment of the Soviet Union, which viewed North Korea as a losing battle.

This sense of abandonment forced Kim to take on a new dimension of leadership. The anti-Japanese, communist revolutionary had begun to transform the ideology according to his own visions of statecraft. Labeling this new form of governance *juche* (self-reliance), Kim began to deliberately isolate his country from all things associated with the West.

What resulted from this dual policy of isolationism and self-reliance was the creation of a centrally planned economy. Trade from Western countries dwindled and private initiatives within North Korea disappeared. Kim's Public Distribution System (PDS), which rationed everything from rice to televisions, became the centerpiece of the North Korean bureaucracy. Determining the exact amount of food and other goods became one of the government's top priorities. In fact, the PDS took the rationing of grain to unbelievable heights. Different socioeconomic classes were given different amounts of foodstuffs. According to Andrei Lankov, an expert in North Korean politics:

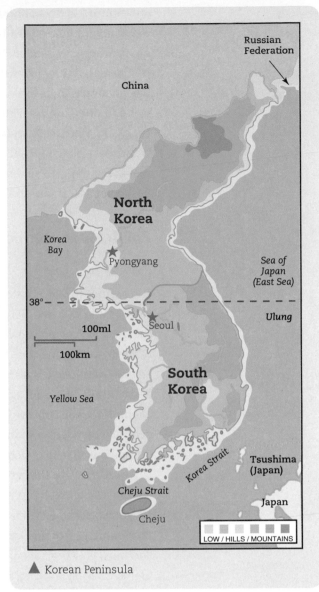

▲ Korean Peninsula

The largest amount, *900g daily, was reserved for workers engaged in hard manual labor: steelworkers, miners, loggers and others. A majority of the population was entitled to a daily ration of 700g. College and high-school students were given 600g and younger students received 300–400g, depending on their age. Retirees were also entitled to 300g of cereals. The North Koreans were given some other foodstuffs—cabbage, soy sauce and other products—but in terms of nutrition almost all calories in their diet came from rice and other cereals."*[21]

Throughout most of the Cold War this system of rationing worked pretty well. This success was partly because of traditional Korean eating habits and partly because of Kim's tightly controlled propaganda machine, which kept North Koreans from comparing their lifestyles with those of their neighbors.

Yet how is North Korea actually governed? This question is essential to an understanding of North Korea's current role in the world. Its answer, however, is based on its historical situation. North Korea (along with China, Cuba, Laos, and Vietnam) is considered a remnant of the communist world. However, in today's world, this designation is quite misleading. When one realizes that China's economy continues to be flooded with private investors and that most of the people living in Cuba, Laos, and Vietnam have forgotten the reasons for their government's ideological views, it is safe to say that North Korea is an archaic reminder of a time gone by. This makes North Korea all the more interesting (and dangerous) because it still continues to act as a closed society, largely shut off from the rest of the world.

Political, Economic, and Social Structure

Politics

Today, the government of North Korea is best classified as a one-man dictatorship.[22] Although the actual structure of the government remains unclear, one thing *is* clear: all policies, domestic and foreign, emerge from Kim Jong Il, the son of North Korea's founder, Kim Il-Sung. In addition to being referred to as "the Great Leader," Kim Jong Il is also considered the General Secretary of the Korean Workers Party (KWP), Supreme Commander of the People's Armed Forces, and Chairman of the National Defense Commission.[23] Because North Korea is still technically a centrally planned, communist state, the KWP remains the only official state party. This means that all government officials are required to be members of the KWP.

In addition to the executive branch, there is a unicameral legislature (Supreme People's Assembly) and a supreme court (Central Court). Unfortunately, both institutions lack any of the typical roles of their democratic counterparts. All of the representatives of the Supreme People's Assembly have to be members of the KWP and must vow their allegiance to Kim. As in many other authoritarian states, these "democratically looking" institutions are designed to give the international community (and the North Korean people) the sense that Kim is a legitimate leader. However, Kim's combined practices of propaganda and forced allegiance tactics are the very antithesis of an open and free society.

According to Kongdon Oh, a nonresident senior fellow at the Center for Northeast Asian Policy Studies, North Korean society has been divided into three categories of people based upon loyalty to the Kim regime: a loyal *core* class, a suspect *wavering* class, and a politically unreliable *hostile* class.[24] These designations were created so that Kim would be able to distinguish his political friends from his political foes. "As of the most recent Party Congress . . . approximately 25 percent of the population fell into the *core* class, 50 percent fell into the *wavering* class, and the remaining unfortunate 25 percent were relegated to the *hostile* class."[25] While the exact placement procedures are unknown, Oh has suggested that most people have been placed into one category or another because of their family history. For example, if one's parents were loyal party members, then he or she will most likely be placed in the *core* class. If, however, one's parents or grandparents were of a noble or upper class before Kim Il-Sung's consolidation of power, then that individual will likely never escape the confines of the hostile class—a class that has faced the worst kinds of criminal treatment over the past 60 years.

Economy

Today, in much the same way that North Korea's political power structure is unclear, and the treatment of its citizens arbitrary and harsh, so is its economy. According to the *CIA World Fact* book, "North Korea does not publish any reliable National Income Accounts."[26] Its estimated gross domestic product (GDP) of $10 billion clearly indicates that its people are living well below the poverty level. (To put this in perspective, even Haiti, which has undergone some of the worst dictators and natural disasters in recent history, has a GDP of around $11 billion.)[27] In fact, the people of North Korea experienced a famine in the 1990s that resulted in the deaths of at least 600,000 people.[28] Why was there such devastation? Because when the Soviet Union collapsed, so too did its aid to many of its client states. According to Marcus Noland, "The Soviets had supplied North Korea with most of its coal and refined oil and one-third of its steel . . . the fall from imports from Russia in 1991 was equivalent to 40 percent of all imports, and by 1993 imports from Russia were only 10 percent of their 1987–1990 average."[29] Thus, the implosion of the Soviet economy sent shockwaves throughout North Korean society. To this day, its economy still experiences major food shortages and is still dependent on the economic aid packages it receives from the World Food Programme, a privately funded organization that operates within the structure of the United Nations that is committed to the eradication of hunger in the poorest parts of the world.

But how can this kind of state continue in this interconnected, technologically driven era of globalization? In essence, how is a state like North Korea able to isolate itself and its people from the outside world? Unfortunately, the answer is all too simple. It appears that Kim Jong Il has relied on the most basic, traditional, authoritarian measure: a tightly controlled media with a strong propensity toward propaganda. The most notable example of North Korean propaganda is its Korean Central News Agency, which is the only source for news about North Korea. It can be accessed online at http://www.kcna.co.jp/index-e.htm. This is as "globalized" as North Korea gets. Since this virtual newspaper is owned and operated by those loyal to Kim Jong Il, it is only allowed to print stories deemed acceptable to the "Great Leader." For example, readers will never find any editorials critical of Kim Jong Il or the practices of his party members. Instead, one usually finds sensational stories depicting Kim as a demi-god. One story went so far as

CourseReader ASSIGNMENT

Log in to **www.cengagebrain.com** and open CourseReader to access the reading:

"Authoritarianism in Pakistan" by Zoltan Barany.

From the moment of its creation in 1947, Pakistan has been plagued by ethnic tensions, mismanagement, and corruption. The Pakistani experience outlined in this essay supports the argument that the fate of political transitions is frequently determined in the first few years after the fall of the old regime.

Soon after independence, a political system began to take shape in Pakistan in which army generals would hold the ultimate levers of power. Several historical circumstances have played important roles in perpetuating instability in Pakistan, including the following: (1) The movement of millions of migrants to the new state created instability and social upheaval, and the imposition of the Urdu-speaking political and intellectual elite, alien to the larger population of Pakistan, generated resentment and mistrust. (2) Pakistan started out with extremely weak political institutions; its bureaucracy was small, disorganized, and incompetent. In fact, the only functioning state institution Pakistan inherited was the armed forces. (3) Through illness and assassination, Pakistan became rudderless soon after independence, at a time when political direction, constancy, and steadfastness were most needed. This pattern has continued to play out ever since. (4) From the beginning, Pakistani elites believed that India was an adversary, out to harm their country, and therefore believed that turning Pakistan into a fortress against India was essential.

- *How has history shaped the governance structure in Pakistan?*
- *How does India impact policymaking in Pakistan?*
- *Why are states more vulnerable to authoritarian regimes in the immediate aftermath of revolutions?*

to claim that during his first attempt at golf, Kim produced 11 holes-in-one, a feat even the greatest golfers could never achieve.[30]

But what will happen to North Korea, and more importantly, why does it matter to you? In addition to its long and brutal history of human-rights violations, labor camps, and food shortages, the government of North Korea possesses a nuclear weapons program. This fact makes North Korea a regional concern. However, what makes its nuclear weapons program even more dangerous and global in scope is the belief that it has been selling secrets to other authoritarian regimes. A number of experts have suggested that North Korea played a major role in the production and sale of uranium hexafluoride—a necessary ingredient in the development of nuclear material.[31] It seems that nuclear power has given North Korea a level of international significance much in the same way that oil has provided power to a number of states in the Middle East. What makes North Korea even more dangerous, however, is the fact that its bargaining chip is nuclear, and its leader is determined to continue to ignore international pressure.

Another state that has nuclear arms and an overwhelmingly poor population is Pakistan. See the CourseReader selection for a detailed analysis of the role that poverty plays in the development of a militarily controlled authoritarian state.

WHY POLITICS MATTERS TO YOU!

What if Deterrence Does Not Apply?

The Democratic People's Republic of North Korea, which is neither democratic nor a republic, seems as if it is stuck in the past. You can almost think of North Korea as a relic of a previous era, one that is trapped by a maniacal leader and a vanquished ideology. However, it is still a member of the nuclear club, which gives it special status in the global community. But why should this matter to you? Because traditional threats and economic sanctions might not work on North Korea.

As we will see in the next few chapters, the United States had several benefits over most countries on earth. First of all, it possesses nuclear arms. The United States had the ability to launch a nuclear weapon and to deliver it to any place on earth. This meant that during the early years of the Cold War, the United States only had to worry about the nuclear arsenal of the Soviet Union, the only other member of the nuclear club. Second, and probably more important than the first reason, since the Soviets had their own nuclear arsenal, a policy known as deterrence emerged which many have argued protected the world from a nuclear holocaust. What deterrence argued was that neither side had the will to launch a "first strike" because each side realized that retaliation would mean the end of the world. Therefore, deterrence created a type of logic that maintained the stability of the global order for almost 50 years.

The point of this story (which we will go into greater detail in the next section) is that North Korea may not operate according to these standard "rules of engagement." If in fact the reports are true that Kim Jong Il is dying, then what are his incentives for maintaining peace (or at the least, not launching a nuclear weapon)?[32] Was the logic of deterrence only useful to explain Cold War relations? If so, North Korea may operate outside the realm of traditional power politics and bring a tremendous amount of disorder to the world.

> Is the logic of deterrence still useful?
>
> Is North Korea a unique case? If it is, does this mean that it should be dealt with differently?

The People's Republic of China

On April 14, 1989, as a result of the death of former Communist Party general secretary Hu Yaobang, a number of Chinese activists, college students, and intellectuals took to Tiananmen Square in downtown Beijing to protest decades of nondemocratic rule. Over time, hundreds of thousands of individuals joined the protests and expanded it to other parts of the country. "On May 4, a student declaration was read in Tiananmen Square calling on the government to accelerate political and economic reform, guarantee constitutional freedoms, fight corruption, adopt a press law, and to allow the establishment of privately run newspapers."[33] One month later, on June 4, the military stepped in and violently put an end to the protest. Although the death toll still remains unclear because of the Chinese government's refusal to take responsibility for its actions, Nicholas D. Kristof of *The New York Times* stated, "It seems plausible that about a dozen soldiers and policemen were killed, along with 400 to 800 civilians."[34]

One of the protesters that survived the June 4th military crackdown was a college professor named Liu Xiaobo, who was so inspired by the events in Tiananmen Square that he dedicated his life to protesting China's human-rights violations. In 2008, Liu released a document entitled, "Charter 08" that called for a massive change in China's government policies. It was subsequently signed by hundreds of Chinese intellectuals. Unfortunately, this did not go over well with the Chinese authorities who went to his house, placed him under arrest, and subsequently sentenced him to 11 years in prison.[35] On October 8, 2010, Liu Xiaobo was awarded the prestigious Nobel Peace Prize, an award that he was unable to receive. For many international observers and Chinese citizens, Liu's incarceration symbolizes the authoritarian nature of the People's Republic of China.

Today, China remains a paradox of power in the international arena. On the one hand, its repressive policies make it seem similar to other authoritarian states we have already discussed. On the other hand, however,

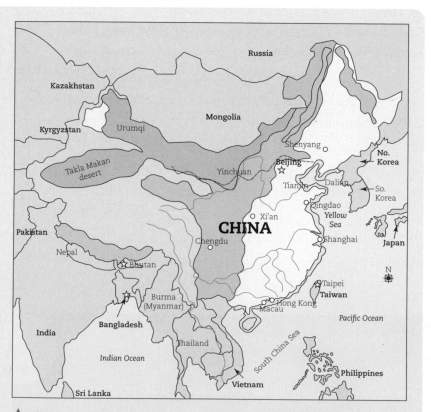

▲ With a population of more than 1.3 billion and an ever-expanding economy, China will continue its dominance in the twenty-first century.

it has emerged as one of the world's strongest powers with a vibrant and increasingly diversified economy. This paradox makes China's future unclear. Will it remain mired in authoritarianism? Or will it seek to grow into a more liberal democratic state? While we cannot answer these questions, we can provide you with a look into the nature of Chinese politics today and some of the issues the country has to address. (The previous account may make you think about the ways in which states use media to their advantage. The CourseReader selection is a classic examination of the way Adolf Hitler and his chief propagandist, Joseph Goebbels, used the media to bring the Nazi party from obscurity into dominance. It is provided to show you how the behavior of one totalitarian state is usually very similar to all totalitarian states.)

Executive and Legislative Institutions of the Communist Party

On October 1, 1949, Mao Zedong established the People's Republic of China (PRC). Mao was considered by many Chinese citizens at the time as a symbol of opposition and strength because of his commitment to the defeat of the Japanese in World War II and to the overthrow of the corrupt government of Chiang Kai-Shek. Mao developed a theory of governing that incorporated elements of Marxism-Leninism (see Chapter 11) into a

---

CourseReader ASSIGNMENT

Log in to **www.cengagebrain.com** and open CourseReader to access the reading:

"Hitler's Propaganda Machine" by Roger Nelson.

The National Socialist German Workers' Party (or Nazi Party) of Adolf Hitler (1889–1945) began with a handful of followers shortly after World War I. Hitler's ruthlessly brilliant leadership differentiated the Nazis from the many other racist-nationalist groups of the era. Hitler had tried to grasp power in 1923 at the Beer Hall Putsch, but Germany's electoral democracy had prevailed. By the time of the 1928 elections, the Nazis were a minor party of the radical right. Their ideology of ultranationalism, anti-Marxism, anti-Semitism, anti-big business "socialism," and militarism, coupled with bold oratory, resulted in less than 3 percent of the popular vote. Yet by 1933 Hitler was chancellor of Germany, placing such key men as Hermann Göring (1893–1946) and Joseph Goebbels (1897–1945) in charge of key state institutions. By August 1934 Hitler had totalitarian control of the state.

Historians have noted a number of causes for the Nazi rise. Some argue German intellectual traditions venerated the authority of the state, lauded military virtues, and praised the greatness of the German people, thus making Hitler's victory inevitable. The Nazis deftly manipulated this authoritarian political culture. The Great Depression (1929–1940) gave Hitler's movement its greatest boost. As business indicators fell and the unemployment lines grew, the Nazis scored impressive electoral gains. It was not primarily the unemployed who voted for Hitler; most of the unemployed were working-class people devoted to Marxism. If moderate, they voted Social Democrat; if radical, they voted Communist. The Nazi voters came largely from the ranks of the middle classes: shopkeepers, managers, small farmers, white-collar workers, and civil servants. They feared the rhetoric of the Marxists and abandoned the traditional bourgeois parties in frustration. The Nazis, with their vigor, toughness, and aggressive (if somewhat ill-defined) program, stood out in stark contrast to the modesty and fatigue of other middle-class parties. Hitler's leadership, amplified by Goebbels's public relations genius, brought many solid German burghers to his side. This selection from 1933 examines the effectiveness of National Socialist German Workers' Party propaganda.

- *What role did the Great Depression play in the rise of Nazi Party?*

- *Why was propaganda so effective in Germany in the 1930s? What role did nationalism play in Hitler's success?*

largely peasant-based society. Between 1949 and his death in 1976, Mao created a political system that transformed Chinese society into a totalitarian state that was driven by the power of the Chinese Communist Party (CCP).

In the first few lines of his *Little Red Book*, Mao stated, "The force at the core leading our cause is the Chinese Communist Party . . . [and that] without the efforts of the Chinese Communist Party . . . China can never achieve independence and liberation, or industrialization and the modernization of her agriculture."[36] In many ways, this attitude toward the CCP remains true to its leadership today. The CCP is still the dominant force in Chinese political life and maintains a membership of approximately 70 million members.[37]

According to William A. Joseph, "to fully understand governance and policy making in China, it is necessary to look at the structure of both the CCP and the government of the PRC (the 'state') and the relationship between the two."[38] This is the case because the PRC operates at the will of the CCP. Since both the PRC and the CCP have their own "constitutions" and elections that are not considered fair, free, or open, political mobility remains undefined. In essence, there is no definite path to the general secretary of the Communist Party, no Electoral College, no winner-take all system, etc.

So how does one become general secretary of the Communist Party? Although most Chinese leaders have emerged from a lifetime of service to the Communist Party, rising to its highest offices (the Politburo and the Standing Committee), this is not always the case. Take, for example, Deng Xiaoping who served as general secretary from 1978 to 1998. "The sources of Deng's immense power came from informal factors, such as his seniority as one of the founders of the regime, his *guanxi* (personnel connections) with key military and political leaders, and his long advocacy of now widely supported ideas about how China should develop into a strong and modern nation."[39] In many ways, the general secretary of the Communist Party with consultation with the Politburo and Standing Committee sets and enforces the agenda for Chinese politics reinforcing the fact that political power in China is now and has always been a "behind-the-scenes" operation.

Nevertheless, there are also a number of "legislative institutions" of varying levels of influence and power within the CCP. The two most important, the National Party Congress and the Central Committee, are representative in name only and really serve only to underline the policies already made by the party leadership. For example, the National Party Congress "meets for one week, every five years" is composed of "more than 2,100 members," and serves symbolically to demonstrate to China (and others around the world) its commitment to unity and its leadership.[40] Even the more *representative* Central Committee holds elections for its members from across China, but in a tightly controlled manner. Only those members of the party who gain approval from the highest levels are allowed to have their names listed on political ballots.

Facebook and Change in the Middle East and North Africa

© ISTOCKPHOTO.COM/ CARACTERDESIGN

By 2011, Egyptian president Hosni Mubarak had been president of Egypt for almost 30 years. Consistently criticized by human-rights group for his authoritarian policies which included the outlawing of opposition parties and the jailing and executions of political dissidents, Mubarak's reign of terror came to an abrupt end in February 2011 after only 18 days of protests and riots. What caused such a speedy revolution? Although the factors of any revolution are vast, some people have argued that the online social networking site *Facebook* played a large role. According to the *Huffington Post*,

> Shortly after . . . Mubarak stepped down . . . activist Wael Ghonim spoke with CNN's Wolf Blitzer and credited *Facebook* with the success of the Egyptian people's uprising. Ghonim, a marketing manager for *Google*, played a key role in organizing the January 25, 2011, protest by reaching out to Egyptian youths by *Facebook*. Shortly after that protest, Ghonim was arrested in Cairo and imprisoned for twelve days."[41]

Following his release from prison and the collapse of the Mubarak regime, Ghonim was quoted as saying that "he wants to meet Mark Zuckerberg and to thank him" because *Facebook* allowed him and others to "post videos . . . that would be shared by 60,000 people . . . within a few hours."[42]

In this particular instance, it appears that *Facebook* helped gain support for a revolution. We realize that this is most likely *not* the reason most of you use *Facebook*, but it is an interesting reminder to the power of this new social medium.

Do you think that social networking sites like Facebook enhance the spread of democracy? Or is this a unique case?

What are your overall impressions of Facebook? Can you think of ways that Facebook might allow you to become more active in your communities?

© ISTOCKPHOTO.COM/SABLAMEK

Domestic Issues and Concerns: Media Censorship and Energy Consumption/Environmental Devastation

Since Chinese politics is controlled by an ideologically driven, authoritarian political party (CCP), life in China for the average citizen is quite demanding. Over the past few decades, however, in large part to the Tiananmen Square protests and the rise of information technology, a number of domestic and international activists and scholars have attempted to shed light on China's human-rights violations. These revelations, coupled with China's rise as a financial superpower, have made Chinese society a unique paradox. Although there are countless issues affecting the livelihoods of the Chinese people, we will briefly address two that we believe best exemplify this modern authoritarian state as it attempts to wrestle with the new demands placed on it by its financial success: media censorship and environmental devastation.

Media Censorship and the Slow Crawl Toward Openness

Today the biggest threat to the status quo power of the CCP is the ever-increasing influence of new forms of media. Over the past few years, China has attempted to maintain its tight grip on information in a number of authoritarian ways. In 2010, China went to "war" with Google by eliminating its people's access to the popular search engine and, in February 2011, in response to the uprisings that took place across parts of the Middle East and North Africa, it banned foreign journalists from certain parts of the country. In fact, after a number of Chinese citizens indicated that they too wanted to openly protest their government's policies, "Foreign media who tried to take photos or shoot video on Beijing's Wangfujing shopping street . . . were told they needed special permission to work there."[43] The effects of such policies have allowed the Communist Party to maintain its dominance in the delivery of news and information.

In China, the media have always been directly controlled by the state and monitored by the Communist Party's Central Propaganda Department (CPD). This means that the state information agencies are only allowed to produce information that gains approval from the CPD. According to Isabella Bennett, a research associate on the Council on Foreign Relations, the Chinese government "revised its existing *Law on Guarding State Secrets* to tighten control over information flows . . . (which) extended requirements to Internet companies and telecommunications operators to cooperate with Chinese authorities in investigations into leaks of state secrets."[44] In China (like any country), the media are considered the avenues by which information is given to the public. However, unlike its democratic counterparts, the CCP views the media not as a source of freedom, but as a threat to its security. Since policy making in China is couched in secrecy, the only acceptable vehicle of information is the Communist Party itself, which has developed a series of state-controlled agencies to oversee "acceptable" news sources.

This, however, may be changing. As China continues to experience large-scale financial growth because of the size of its economy, and more and more people have the means to acquire access to new forms of technology, the media are slowly becoming at least *partly* privatized. Although "only state agencies can *own* media in China . . . the Chinese News Network Corporation (CNNC), a 24-hour global news network launched in July 2010 . . . is reportedly half-privately financed."[45] This means that the Chinese media may be on their way to increased openness. It may also suggest that the future of freedom in China is dependent on its continued economic development. For example, as the rest of the world suffered (and continues to suffer) from large deficits as a result of the economic decline of 2008, the Chinese government experienced a huge surplus, which allowed it "to launch a 4 trillion yuan ($586 billion) stimulus that pumped money into the economy through public works spending, tax cuts, subsidies to car buyers and aid to industries."[46] Thus, China might be witnessing the growth of a sizeable middle class. If a large middle class continues to grow in China, it will most likely demand greater protection of its assets and therefore make greater demands on the government to expand its political voice. In practical terms, this means that the current level of Chinese media censorship will continue to weaken and be replaced by a more privately controlled group of competing media outlets. This, of course, may be perceived as wishful thinking, but typically, financial growth equals democratic growth and a weakening of state control.

Energy Use and Environmental Devastation

According to the World Bank, "demographic trends in China indicate that the urban population of about 430 million people (assessed in 2001) will reach 850 million by 2015, and the number of cities with over 100,000 people will increase from 630 (2001) to over 1,000 by 2015."[47] Because urban centers require greater energy usage than their rural counterparts and are valued as the primary sources of a nation's wealth, the Chinese government states that it must remain committed to acquiring fossil fuels at a reasonable rate. This is why it is no accident that China has scoured the globe to acquire oil. Currently the Chinese government has focused its efforts on "overseas oil projects in Sudan, Iran, Kazakhstan, and many other countries."[48]

This international campaign has made oil consumption in China skyrocket. In fact, over the past few years, oil consumption in China "has been . . . close to 40 percent of the total world oil demand."[49] And it is not even near its economic growth potential. While China continues to primarily rely on coal for the majority of

▲ City dwellers in China's new urban centers battle unprecedented levels of air pollution.

its energy needs (see Figure 10.1), oil consumption is creeping up toward the demand currently employed by the world's largest consumer of oil, the United States. As its population centers continue to grow and its industries become more and more reliant on energy, its hunger for petroleum will continue to expand and its reliance on coal will decline. Either way, however, we must stop and think about what this is doing to the well-being of the planet. China might be emerging as one of the dominant states of the twenty-first century, but at what cost to the health and safety of its people? To put this in proper perspective, we should stop and demonstrate the numbers. Look at Figures 10.1 and 10.2. Both indicate that China is heavily invested in the procurement of **fossil fuels.**

Fossil fuels: *Coal, oil, and natural gas.*

Fossil fuels (which are coal, oil, and natural gas) take millions of years to form and are the by-products of animal and plant remains.[50] They also must be burned in order to produce energy. This is what has led to what climate scientists refer to as the **greenhouse effect.** As fossil fuels are burned they release carbon dioxide (CO_2) and water (H_2O), which are then trapped in the atmosphere. When sunlight shines through to the earth's surface, it reflects back through the atmosphere but is trapped by the accumulated carbon dioxide. Thus, it is the burning of large amounts of fossil fuels that many scientists suggest causes **climate change.** As the earth gets warmer, the weather becomes more erratic.

Greenhouse effect: *The burning of fossil fuels that results in CO2 and H20 being trapped in the atmosphere.*

Climate change: *The result of many years of burning high levels of fossil fuels which has caused the earth to heat up.*

Although climate change is a hotly debated topic in many political circles, to a rapidly expanding economy like China, it can often be overlooked. Why? Because such a debate over an issue like climate change has the potential to slow down China's massive industrial base. In simple terms, China believes that it needs to continue its industrial path even at the expense of its environment and the health of its citizens. According to its own Ministry of Health, "pollution has made cancer China's leading cause of death . . . [as] ambient air pollution alone is blamed for hundreds of thousands of deaths each year."[51] To put this in a better perspective, "only 1 percent of the country's 560 million city-dwellers breathe air considered safe by the European Union."[52] In fact there are "industrial cities where people rarely see the sun; children [are] killed or sickened by lead poisoning or other types of local pollution; [and] a coastline so swamped by algal red tides that large sections of the ocean no longer sustain marine life."[53] One may ask why? But the answer appears to be simple: for the ability to compete in and dominate the global economy of the twenty-first century.

However, if China continues to pollute on such an elaborate scale, its economic power will have to be used to correct domestic environmental problems. In fact, it is this assessment that was recently mentioned by both China's Ministry of Environmental Protection and its premier Wen Xiabao. Zhou Shengxian, China's chief environmental minister, said that "if China meant to quadruple the size of its economy over 20 years without more damage, it would have to become more efficient in resource use."[54] Zhou continued by saying that "the depletion, deterioration, and exhaustion of resources and the deterioration

FIGURE 10.1. Total Energy Consumption in China, by Type (2006)

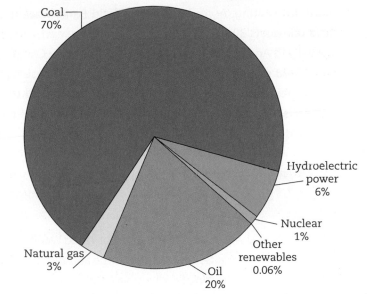

Accessed online from: http://www.eia.doe.gov/iea/overview.html

FIGURE 10.2. Oil Consumption in China

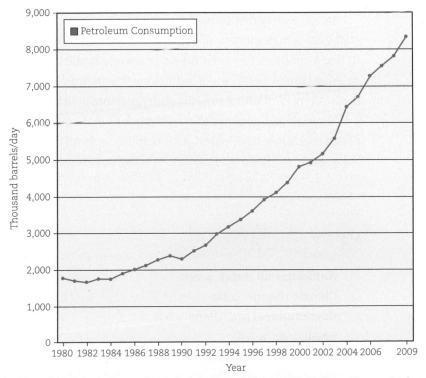

Source: The U.S. Energy Information Administration. Accessed from http://www.eia.doe.gov/countries/country-data.cfm?fips=CH#data

of the environment have become serious bottlenecks constraining economic and social development."[55]

To put a financial total on such "bottlenecks" makes their statements even more devastating. According to the World Bank, water pollution in the form of "acid rain costs 30 billion yuan in crop damage and 7 billion in material damage annually."[56] And in 2003, overall "water pollution in China was 362 billion yuan, or about 2.68 percent of GDP for that same year."[57] These figures highlight the true cost of development and argue that unless China (and the United States for that matter) is serious about placing limits on its energy consumption, it will be fueling its own demise.

© AP PHOTO

SUMMARY

Although many have argued that the end of World War II brought an end to the traditional authoritarian state, it is clear that some authoritarian states continue to play an active role in world politics. Saudi Arabia continues to dictate international oil prices, North Korea continues to develop its nuclear program, and China continues to expand its economy at the expense of its population. Authoritarian states therefore pose an interesting dilemma to the international community. Their continued denial of their own people's rights places them at philosophical odds with their democratic counterparts, but their power (economic or military) keeps them at the bargaining table.

In the twenty-first century it will be interesting to see how long authoritarian states can last. Has the era of authoritarianism ended? Or are they going to continue to find justifications for their power. In a world that is constantly changing with the development of new forms of technology (Internet, iPod, Blackberry), those that suppress information will face much greater pressure than those who do not. We will see.

The next part attempts to answer some of these questions from the international perspective. As we have looked at the domestic realm of both democracies and authoritarian states, it is now necessary to look at the ways these states interact in the world.

KEY TERMS

Authoritarian states p. 297
Climate change p. 320
Constitutional provisions p. 303
Fossil fuels p. 320
Greenhouse effect p. 320
Patriarchy p. 305
Wahabbism p. 303

KEY PEOPLE

11 UNDERSTANDING INTERNATIONAL RELATIONS: TERMS AND THEORIES

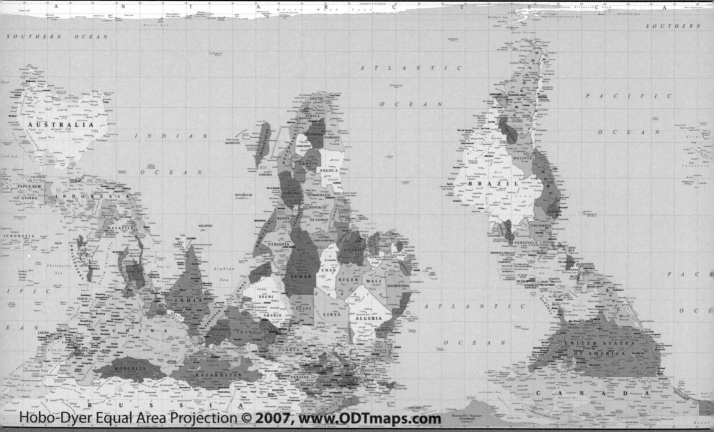

Hobo-Dyer Equal Area Projection © 2007, www.ODTmaps.com

For maps and other related teaching materials contact: ODT, Inc., PO Box 134, Amherst MA 01004 USA; 800-736-1293; Fax: 413-549-3503; Skype: ODTInc; E-mail: odtstore@odt.org; Web: www.ODTmaps.com

▲ The famous "upside down" map of the world is designed to give you a different perspective on both geography and power.

INTRODUCTION : INTERNATIONAL RELATIONS

For more than 3,000 years scholars have attempted to explain international relations (IR). Although the *state* as a governing unit is a relatively modern creation, investigations into the cross-border activities of political units is not. Since at least the fifth century BC, scholars have attempted to understand what makes people go to war and what makes them cooperate. In the process, a number of theories have been developed that have attempted to provide society with a better understanding of human nature as it relates to issues of conflict and peace.

Beginning with some of the classic arguments of realism, liberalism, radicalism, and constructivism, this chapter will introduce you to the different theories and concepts that have been developed to evaluate the subfield known as international relations. In this chapter we seek to explain some of the reasons states at certain times opt for war and, at other times, opt for cooperation. Since subsequent chapters are designed to provide you with an appropriate background on the evolution of the international system, this chapter is designed to provide you with an array of appropriate theoretical perspectives. It must be remembered that the international system is a multifaceted domain in which a wide array of actors (both governmental and nongovernmental) operate with one another. Sometimes the actors' intentions conflict, sometimes they do not. The purpose of this chapter is to demonstrate how the different schools of thought have developed to evaluate international behavior.

In addition to the different schools of thought, this chapter will also introduce you to the three levels of analysis as an approach developed by esteemed IR scholar Kenneth Waltz. The *three levels of analysis* is a useful tool when explaining international behavior (within the realist perspective) because it lends itself to a more complete understanding of state behavior. According to Waltz, international activity is best explained by an examination of three

Questions to Consider Before Reading this Chapter

1. What is power? What is the difference between hard power and soft power?

2. What are the three main assumptions of classical realism?

3. How can the three levels of analysis be useful to understanding issues of international conflict?

4. What are the main arguments of Marx pertaining to the inequalities of the international system? How have the neo-Marxists elevated the arguments to explain globalization?

5. What is dependency theory? Does it accurately explain poverty in certain parts of the world?

FIGURE 11.1. Timeline of International Relations Theory

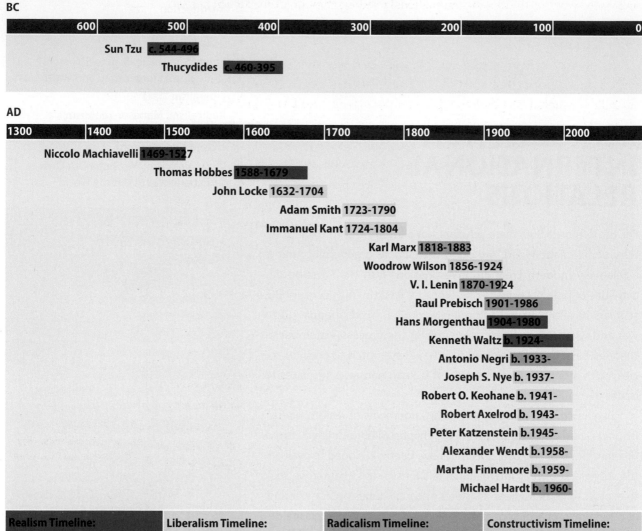

BC

| 600 | 500 | 400 | 300 | 200 | 100 | 0 |

Sun Tzu c. 544-496

Thucydides c. 460-395

AD

| 1300 | 1400 | 1500 | 1600 | 1700 | 1800 | 1900 | 2000 |

Niccolo Machiavelli 1469-1527

Thomas Hobbes 1588-1679

John Locke 1632-1704

Adam Smith 1723-1790

Immanuel Kant 1724-1804

Karl Marx 1818-1883

Woodrow Wilson 1856-1924

V. I. Lenin 1870-1924

Raul Prebisch 1901-1986

Hans Morgenthau 1904-1980

Kenneth Waltz b. 1924-

Antonio Negri b. 1933-

Joseph S. Nye b. 1937-

Robert O. Keohane b. 1941-

Robert Axelrod b. 1943-

Peter Katzenstein b.1945-

Alexander Wendt b.1958-

Martha Finnemore b.1959-

Michael Hardt b. 1960-

Realism Timeline:
Sun Tzu (writes the *Art of War* 5th century BC) and Thucydides (5th century BC) help define classical realism.

Reinforced by Niccolo Machiavelli (15th century), Thomas Hobbes (17th century), and Hans Morgenthau (20th century).

Kenneth Waltz (20th century) develops structural realism.

Liberalism Timeline:
Classic Liberalism: John Locke (17th century), Adam Smith (18th century).

Development of idealism by Immanuel Kant (18th century) and Woodrow Wilson (20th century).

Development of neoliberal institutionalism Robert Axelrod, Robert O. Keohane, and Joseph S. Nye (late 20th century).

Radicalism Timeline:
Marxism and Revolutionary Communism: Karl Marx (19th century) and V. I. Lenin (20th century).

Development of dependency theory, Raul Prebisch (20th century).

Rise of neo-marxism, Michael Hardt and Antonio Negri (late 20th century).

Constructivism Timeline:
Social Constructivism: Alexander Wendt, Martha Finnemore, Peter Katzenstein (Late 20th century).

levels of actors: individuals within states whose personalities dictate cross-border behavior; domestic pressure groups within states whose influence or interaction motivate international events; and the international system itself whose structure may change as a result of a refiguring of the balance of power. To bring this approach to light, we will be investigating the Rwandan genocide. The *three levels of analysis* approach allows us to examine international relations through domestic and international prisms, realizing that the complexity of the system is so vast that it requires complex explanations.

By the way, before we move on, have you ever seen a map like the one at the beginning of this chapter? How does it make you feel? Do you think that there is something wrong with it or does it just seem strange to you? If you think that there is something fundamentally wrong with it, you are incorrect. There is nothing inaccurate about it whatsoever. However, if you think that the map seems strange, you must ask yourself why that is? Have you ever considered that your own beliefs and ideologies about international politics might have been shaped in a similar fashion? Perhaps, a lot of the "facts" about international politics that you have taken for granted are not really facts at all, but only opinions. Take a few minutes to consider these questions, but not too long, because we are about ready to dive into our section on international relations theory.

CLASSIC REALISM: POWER IN INTERNATIONAL RELATIONS

As you'll recall from Chapter 3, realism flows from the ideas of those scholars that saw politics as the ability of one to achieve and secure power. Therefore, at the heart of realism lies **power** and the ways in which states gain and maintain it. Therefore, to best understand realism you first must have a basic understanding of the term *power* itself. For purposes here, we can define power as one's ability to make others (persons or states) do something they would not have otherwise done on their own. Sometimes it may take the form of force, that is, an act of violence. Other times it might be the *threat* of force coming from one who is recognized as having both the ability and the will to back up such statements. For example, if you do not do *x*, then we will resort to the use of force. Nevertheless, power is a major theme in the school of thought known as realism. As we will see, for realists, power is the primary determinant of political behavior and therefore the only measure by which international relations should be evaluated.

In discussions of international relations two types of power have emerged: hard power and soft power. **Hard power** refers to the type of power we have just defined. When one state either directly utilizes or at least threatens force (military or economic), scholars in international relations refer to it as *hard* power. **Soft power**, on the other hand, is best defined by those agents in the international system that bring about change through the use of diplomacy or ideology. Coined by IR scholar Joseph Nye in his book *Bound to Lead: The Changing Nature of American Power*, Nye argued that American interests are best served in a post–Cold War world through diplomacy

Power: *The ability to make others do something that they would otherwise not have done.*

Hard power: *Using military and/or economic pressure in a way that allows one state to force another to do something it might not have wanted to do.*

Soft power: *Using methods other than military/economic coercion to receive desired outcomes. For example, getting another country to "want" the things we want can create a system of security.*

© ISTOCKPHOTO.COM/ DIEGO CERVO

Force is one of the most obvious understandings of power. Simply put, force is the physical expression of power. It was force that was employed when you got in a fight with your brother over what television show to watch, and force that was used by the U.S. military to punish the Taliban for supporting Al Qaeda in Afghanistan. But does force have to be *violent*?

For Mohandas Gandhi, force was an effective tool against an oppressor, but one that did not require violence. While Gandhi understood that persuasion (another form of power) was the most preferred choice of conflict resolution, he also understood that sometimes rational arguments fall on deaf ears. Thus, he created a policy called *satyagraha* (from the Sanskrit meaning "truth" and "insistence") in order to achieve desired demands (Indian independence from Great Britain). *Satyagraha* is based on the assumption that those who are being oppressed have a right to be free and that the only justifiable way of achieving freedom is through nonviolent means. In doing so, the oppressed oppose those in power, but do so in a way that elevates their moral position while forcing the oppressor to resort to violence, solidifying their reputation as an unjust entity.

Gandhi's policy of *satyagraha* led to Indian independence in 1947 and inspired Dr. Martin Luther King Jr.'s nonviolent, civil disobedient campaign against racial injustice in the United States.

Have you ever considered nonviolence as a way of achieving political goals?

Do you think that the policymakers in the United States see it as a viable alternative?

If not, why not? Are American policymakers realists?

© ISTOCKPHOTO.COM/LORENZO COLLORETA

and perception.[1] For Nye, the power of the United States will be enhanced if the United States behaves in ways that increase its positive standing in the eyes of the international community. Instead of using the "carrot and stick" approach (rewards versus punishment), Nye argued for a third way that American foreign policy can be perceived. In other words, it is in the best interest of the United States to behave in a manner that makes it look good to other states and peoples.

According to Nye, soft power "arises from the attractiveness of a country's culture, political ideals and policies."[2] Because, of course, "attractiveness" like "beauty" is in the eye of the beholder, soft power is based on perception. Thus, "sometimes we can get the outcomes we want by affecting behavior without commanding it. If you believe that my objectives are legitimate, I may be able to persuade you to do something for me without using threats or inducements."[3] This in many ways is much more common than you may think.

Take, for example (one in fact that Nye examined), the simple issue of one's view of morality (the notion of what is right or what is wrong) in relation to action. What motivated members of Al Qaeda to attack the World Trade Center and the Pentagon on 9/11? For Nye, it is "not because of payments or threats (hard power) but because they believe bin Laden's views are legitimate."[4] Numerous terrorist attacks occur in which neither money nor threats of retribution are employed. Al Qaeda has been very successful using persuasion when recruiting potential terrorists. Radical Islamic fundamentalists wanted to act for bin Laden because they believed his views were legitimate. The same applies for traditional state actors whose politicians at times employ persuasion to get certain laws passed and policies agreed upon.

Power, whether hard or soft, is necessary in any discussion of realism because it defines states as simply as possible: governmental actors act out for themselves. Take, for example, the current rise of the BRIC countries in the international system: Brazil, Russia, India, and China. What type of power will they likely employ in the twenty-first century as they seek to enhance their influence and maintain their security?

In recent years, certain scholars have examined the economic growth rates of Brazil, Russia, India, and China and have decided that these four economies possess the greatest ability to influence international relations in the twenty-first century. Why? Because they are heavily populated countries that have experienced a massive amount of development over the past decade. This means that over the next fifteen to twenty years, the BRICs will attempt to maintain their growth trajectory by attempting to alter the framework of the international system.

According to Harold James, the greatest threats to the current international system are the ways in which the BRICs handle internal, domestic pressures. His brief analysis follows:

1. Highly populous countries must integrate their poor and ill-educated underclass (in China and India, mostly rural) as they engage with world markets.
2. China and Russia have financial systems that lack transparency, while Brazil and India are financially underdeveloped, putting further integration in the world economy at risk and increasing prospects for a financial crisis.

3. Russia is already facing massive demographic decline and an aging and sickening population; China faces the near certainty of a Japanese-style demographic downturn from the 2040s onward, a belated legacy of its one-child policy.

The potential result: Flawed geopolitical giants have in the past been a source of instability (Germany before World War I), and there are good reasons to see them presenting an increased risk in the twenty-first century. The result is that BRICs will look for compensating power and military prestige, as a way to solve internal problems.[5]

So here is the question. How will the BRICs attempt to change the international system? Will they use military and economic might (hard power) or will they attempt to influence the behavior of the international community by crafting a system that gives them high regard in their region (soft power) such as a new commitment to the environment (China) or the export and development of technology to the developing world (India)? Only time will tell.

It is this concept of **national interest** that best defines the overall understanding and development of realism as a school of thought. The following section will provide you with some of the core assumptions of **classic realism**. Be aware, however, that little attention, if any, is paid to moral determinations of foreign policy. If anything can be said of the classic realists, it is that they tend to be amoral beings—those who understand international affairs exclusively through power relationships.

Core Assumptions of Classic Realism

Because of this understanding of power relations, classic realists have asserted that the international system is based on three core assumptions. First, classic realists have maintained that the *state* is the dominant actor in international affairs. The evolution of the international system has given states the primary task of conducting international affairs. Why? Because states have sovereignty, the ability to collect taxes, and to wage war. Other actors in the international system do not. It is from this initial premise that classic realism flows.

Second, classic realists assert that states are rational, unitary actors. This means that states are assumed to behave like rational individuals with the ability to evaluate certain strengths and weaknesses as they relate to their own security. For instance, when a particular state determines that it must go to war, it does so as a unitary actor. Thus, when scholars evaluate international relations and say that the United States invaded Iraq, they are evaluating the action as if both were rational individuals.

Finally, classic realists claim that the international system is anarchical and chaotic. This determination is based on the fact that the international system does not have a world government capable of stifling conflict and war. It is this absence that has placed the state as the only legitimate actor capable of creating stability on an international level. International institutions have helped to avoid certain international

National interest: *For realists, states (countries) will always behave in ways that expand their security and protect what they deem as essential to their well-being.*

Classic realism: *The school of thought in international relations that sees power as the main goal of each state. In addition, classic realists claim that the state is the main actor in international relations, that it is to be thought of as a unitary actor, and that international politics is inherently chaotic.*

Are classic realists correct in their assessment of the international system? Is it always best to assume that states are acting in their own self-interest?

FIGURE 11.2. Classic realism asserts that these components are best suited to explain international relations

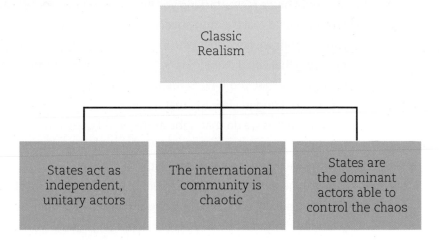

conflicts, but their ultimate successes or failures are determined by the distribution of power. In a world of powerful and less powerful states, the powerful make the rules and the less powerful follow. This may translate into inequalities, but classic realists assert that it also creates a **balance of power** capable of preventing gross instability.

Classic Realists: The Thinkers

Realism's roots can be found within both the Eastern and Western traditions. In fact, one of the first books ever written on state behavior in warfare was written in China in the fifth century BC. Sun Tzu's *The Art of War* was and is considered one of the earliest accounts of classic realism.[6] Arguing that individual state power is the only reliable indicator of international behavior, Sun Tzu used his book as a manual for future leaders in the art of trickery and deception. We will find that Sun Tzu's placement of morality as secondary to national security is one of the cornerstones of realist thought.

Writing in the Western tradition at roughly the same time as Sun Tzu was the Athenian historian Thucydides. Though his *History of the Peloponnesian War* is credited as one of the first written histories, Thucydides's discussions on "power politics" bring to light his unique contribution to the field of international relations. In one of the most famous scenes in the *History*, the reader is presented with "The Melian Dialogue," a debate between representatives from the powerful Athenian delegation and the tiny, much-weaker island of Melos.

The Melian Dialogue is a demonstration of classical realism in action. Read how the Athenians provide the tiny island of Melos with the ultimatum of choosing either death or slavery. This is a classic example of how "might makes right" and that the powerful will do what is in their interest and the weak can only accept the consequences.

Balance of power: *A term that has historically referred to the ways in which great political powers have attempted to maintain security and to avoid international conflicts. The balance of power concept originated in Europe during the early part of the nineteenth century when five great powers (Great Britain, France, Austria, Russia, and Prussia) dominated international politics and were committed to avoiding war and maintaining each state's position as a dominant power.*

Athenians: "For ourselves, we shall not trouble you with specious pretences—either of how we have a right to our empire because we overthrew the Mede, or are now attacking you because of wrong that you have done us—and make a long speech which would not be believed; and in return we hope that you, instead of thinking to influence us by saying that you did not join the Lacedaemonians, although their colonists, or that you have done us no wrong, will aim at what is feasible, holding in view the real sentiments of us both; since you know as well as we do that right, as the world goes, is only in question between equals in power, while the strong do what they can and the weak suffer what they must."

Melians: "As we think, at any rate, it is expedient—we speak as we are obliged, since you enjoin us to let right alone and talk only of interest—that you should not destroy what is our common protection, the privilege of being allowed in danger to invoke what is fair and right, and even to profit by arguments not strictly valid if they can be got to pass current. And you are as much interested in this as any, as your fall would be a signal for the heaviest vengeance and an example for the world to meditate upon."

Athenians: "The end of our empire, if end it should, does not frighten us: a rival empire like Lacedaemon, even if Lacedaemon was our real antagonist, is not so terrible to the vanquished as subjects who by themselves attack and overpower their rulers. This, however, is a risk that we are content to take. We will now proceed to show you that we come here in the interest of our empire, and that we shall say what we are now going to say, for the preservation of your country; as we would fain exercise that empire over you without trouble, and see you preserved for the good of us both."

Melians: "And how, pray, could it turn out as good for us to serve as for you to rule?"

Athenians: "Because you would have the advantage of submitting before suffering the worst, and we should gain by not destroying you."

Melians: "So that you would not consent to our being neutral, friends instead of enemies, but allies of neither side."

Athenians: "No; for your hostility cannot so much hurt us as your friendship will be an argument to our subjects of our weakness, and your enmity of our power."

Melians: "Is that your subjects' idea of equity, to put those who have nothing to do with you in the same category with peoples that are most of them your own colonists, and some conquered rebels?"

Athenians: "As far as right goes they think one has as much of it as the other, and that if any maintain their independence it is because they are strong, and that if we do not molest them it is because we are afraid; so that besides extending our empire we should gain in security by your subjection; the fact that you are islanders and weaker than others rendering it all the more important that you should not succeed in baffling the masters of the sea."[7]

In this scene, the Athenians provided the Melians with a bleak ultimatum: death or slavery. In other words, if the Melians made the decision to fight the much stronger Athenian army, they would die. However, if the Melians chose submission, they would be spared but would face enslavement. Although this is hardly a fair choice (as the Melian delegation provides), Thucydides's depiction conveys one of the major tenets of classic realism, that "might makes right." In essence, the powerful make the laws that the weak must follow. Following in this tradition are two theorists you have already encountered: Niccolo Machiavelli and Thomas Hobbes. Though their works were written two centuries apart, both began with similar premises and conclusions about order and power in the international system. For Machiavelli, the greatest impediment to effective rule is morality. Writing at a time when the Italian city-states were competing with one another instead of unifying their collective efforts, Machiavelli argued that the survival of the Italian state as a whole was dependant upon the willingness of the many city-states to create *effective* policies, rather than those considered moral, ideological, or religious. The worldview that Machiavelli created was solidified by Thomas Hobbes. Previously introduced as one of the social contract theorists, Hobbes's distinction within classic realism has more to do with his negative understanding of human nature than strictly his powerful, all-enforcing government. For Hobbes, human nature is selfish and, ultimately, self-destructive; a condition that in the "state of nature" creates an environment where everyone is involved in war with one another, that is, a "war of all against all." For Hobbes, chaos ensued until a social contract was designed to empower a strong centralized government. It is with Hobbes that we are presented with the third component of classic realism: Without a strong, powerful government, the world will continue to be determined by anarchy and chaos.

FROM CLASSIC REALISM TO STRUCTURAL REALISM: MORGENTHAU TO WALTZ

In the aftermath of World War II, many scholars reevaluated their attitudes toward international relations. The Wilsonian idealism of the previous era was regarded as not only naïve, but also as a reckless response to a more practical understanding of international affairs. Scholars and policymakers alike viewed

Hard or Soft Power? The United States and Defense Spending

How do you think the United States is handling international relations in this post-9/11 world? Is it continuing to rely on traditional hard power tactics like economic sanctions (monetary punishments) and/or military force (or threats), or is it trying more of a soft power approach when facing its adversaries in the twenty-first century?

Well, here is a statistic that might help you to answer this question. Consider this: The defense budget of the United States for fiscal year 2009 (the amount of federal dollars that goes to defense-oriented projects and personnel) was $663.8 billion![8] Yes, your eyes have not deceived you; that number is correct. It is over half a trillion dollars. To put this in perspective, the United States spends more money on defense programs, projects, and personnel than almost all other countries in the world spend on defense *combined*! The United States therefore does not simply spend more on defense than the next country; it spends more on defense than almost the remainder of the list put together. So, do you think the United States is trying to use hard power or soft power?

Why does this matter to you? Because as a taxpayer and an American citizen, you should be aware of the programs on which your country is spending money and exactly how much of your taxes they are using to finance them. It should also matter to you because in this era of globalization, more and more people (and leaders) have the ability to see what U.S. priorities are and how they can copy them in their own countries.

Is it an accident that the Chinese government in late 2010 developed a stealth fighter jet?

Or is it a consequence of the ways in which other emerging powers are modeling American power?

idealism as one of the root causes of the appeasement policy that had led to the outbreak of World War II. Idealists were likened to ostriches, tending to value isolation and appeasement to preemptive aggression aimed at combating a real threat.

Hans Morgenthau: Classical Realism for the Modern Era

One of the first scholars to employ a reactionary understanding of postwar power politics was the classical realist Hans Morgenthau. In his book *Politics Among Nations*, Morgenthau transformed one of the major assumptions concerning the nature of *power* in classic realism. For centuries, classic realists had argued that *power* itself was the desired goal and, therefore, sole determinant of state behavior. Morgenthau, on the other hand, asserted that power was not the goal but simply a *means* to achieving the dual objectives of national security and survival. According to this repositioning, it could be argued that Hitler did not invade his neighbors for the sake of political power, but for the sake of acquiring greater security and influence within the international system; a fear that the German people had felt since the end of World War I.

Maintaining the core principles of classic realism, Morgenthau argued that there is little room for morality or legality in issues of war and peace and that there has been a great deal of misunderstanding when it comes to the essential claims of realism's arguments. As Morgenthau wrote:

Intellectually, the political realist maintains the autonomy of the political sphere, as the economist, the lawyer, the moralist maintain theirs. *He thinks in terms of interest defined as power, as the economist thinks in terms of interest defined as wealth; the lawyer, of the conformity of action with legal rules; the moralist, of the conformity of action with moral principles. The economist asks: "How does this policy affect the wealth of society, or a segment of it?" The lawyer asks: "Is this policy in accord with the rules of law?" The moralist asks: "Is this policy in accord with moral principles?" And the political realist asks: "How does this policy affect the power of the nation?" (Or of the federal government, of Congress, of the party, of agriculture, as the case may be.)*

The political realist is not unaware of the existence and relevance of standards of thought other than political ones. As a political realist, he cannot but subordinate these other standards to those of politics. And he parts company with other schools when they impose standards of thought appropriate to other spheres upon the political sphere. It is here that political realism takes issue with the "legalistic-moralistic approach" to international politics. That this issue is not, as has been contended, a mere figment of the imagination, but goes to the very core of the controversy, can be shown from many historical examples.[9]

▲ Hans Morgenthau was one of the first scholars following World War II to restate some of the major features of classic realism.

As far as Morgenthau was concerned, realism is the ideology best suited for the explanation of international behavior. Although he is not asserting that the fields of economics, law, or morality are useless, Morgenthau is asserting that they are hampered by idealistic principles of behavior, rather than the *real* issues of national security aimed primarily at state survival.

Kenneth Waltz: Structural Realism

Following Morgenthau in the realist tradition was Kenneth Waltz, a pioneer in international relations theory who created a new school of thought that reinterpreted some of classic realism's core beliefs. Waltz, in his famous book *Man, the State, and War,* expanded the scope of classic realism by arguing that although power politics helps to determine state behavior, it is the *structure* of the international system that best determines it. Agreeing with the primary assumptions of classic realism in that the international system is anarchic and unstable because it lacks a global sovereign, Waltz added that it is the system *itself* that needs to be understood when explaining or predicting state behavior. For Waltz and other structural realists (or neorealists), it is the international system that determines the level of power within each state, not the states themselves. In short, Waltz concluded that while states matter, it is the system that matters more.

For structural or neorealists, state power is determined by the prospect of the balance of power within the international system. Sometimes the balance of power within the international system motivates states to pursue aggressive policies; sometimes it stifles them. Because all realists assert that states will pursue what is in their own national interests, structural realists argue that it is only plausible to assume that certain states have limited potential within the existing international system. We must remember that **structural realism** is not an attack on classic realism; it is just an addition or specification of it. The following section will highlight Kenneth Waltz's three levels of analysis and its role in explaining international relations.

Structural realism:
The international system that determines the level of power within each state. State power is determined by the prospect of the balance of power within the international system. Sometimes the balance of power within the international system motivates states to pursue aggressive policies; sometimes it stifles them.

Three Levels of Analysis

According to Kenneth Waltz in his book, *Man, the State, and War,* there are three ways of investigating the causes of war.[10] A first level examines the certain personality traits of leaders involved in conflict, a second level examines the internal composition of the states, and a third level examines the structures that exist at the international level. Through this investigation you may be able to perform a more thorough study of a particular conflict. For example, suppose you would like to examine the causes of World War II. Where would you begin? By using the **three levels of analysis**, you can examine the outbreak of World War II from three different perspectives.

Level One: The Individual

At the first level, Waltz suggested that scholars should try to understand the relationship between leaders and their roles in perpetuating war. For example, you may ask, "What are some of the psychological forces that shape presidential decision making in terms of foreign policy?" Or "Can a leader's personal obsession(s) be translated into rallying cries for war?" Are there certain leadership traits that make some leaders more likely to seek violent confrontations? The individual level seeks to establish some of the personal dynamics that go into international decision making.

Let's stay with the example of World War II for the time being. Who were the important leaders in this conflict? Obviously, there is Adolf Hitler. But what about the prime minister of Great Britain, Winston Churchill, and the American president, Franklin D. Roosevelt? Did Adolf Hitler's hatred of Jews and foreigners translate into an aggressive array of policy choices? Did the personal relationship between Churchill and Roosevelt make the American president more likely to engage in war? The individual level of analysis seeks answers to these questions and argues that personal traits strongly affect policy choices.

Level Two: The State

At the second level, Waltz examined those forces that exist within the state itself. How strong are lobbyists in calling for war? What about competitive ethnic or religious groups? How powerful are members of the business community in relation to the government

Three levels of analysis:
The three levels of analysis were developed by political scientist Kenneth Waltz as a way to better understand the reasons for conflict. The "three levels" refers to three difference actors involved in warfare: the individual (political leaders, terrorists, etc.), the state (domestic level actors like interest groups, political parties, ethnic or religious groups), and the international community (international tensions that spill over and cause conditions ripe for wars to occur).

FIGURE 11.3. The Three Levels of Analysis was designed by IR scholar Kenneth Waltz as a way of explaining the reasons why states go to war

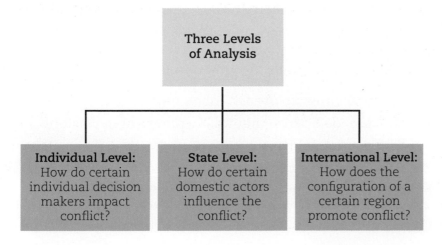

in power. The second level seeks to examine certain *substate actors* that might contribute to violence. For example, what were the forces within Nazi Germany itself that led to say, the Holocaust or the invasion of Poland? Were there groups who helped fuel the state's aggressive policies? The state level of analysis would try to determine that there are pressure groups in certain societies that perpetuate international violence.

Level Three: The International Setting

At the third level, Waltz decided to examine the effect of the configuration of the international community on international violence. Does the configuration of a particular region make it more volatile? If state A begins to dominate the trade (and therefore the wealth) of state B and state C, does the region itself become unstable? Was Nazi Germany's position in Europe detrimental to the ways in which Europe had functioned for centuries? Did the weaknesses of the League of Nations prevent an international system from being strong enough to contain Germany? The international level of analysis attempts to look at particular regions and determine if the very structure of the region makes it vulnerable to war.

THEORY AND PRACTICE

Using the Three Levels of Analysis: The Case of the Rwandan Genocide

Let's see if we can use the three levels of analysis to better understand the complexity of the Rwandan genocide.

Background: Colonialism and the Ethnic Divide

- Traditionally, diversity in Rwanda was based on the presence of three ethnic communities: Hutus (about 90 percent of the population), Tutsis (between 8 percent and 10 percent of the population), and the Twa (less than 1 percent of the population). While little is known about Rwandan political and social life before its experience with Europeans, the one item that is known is that the Tutsis served as the ruling elite and the Hutus served as a slave class. When Belgium acquired Rwanda (from Germany following World War I), they assumed that this political structure was based upon each tribe's physical features and level of civility. *Eugenics* the pseudo-science that was so prevalent in Western Europe at the dawn of the twentieth century demonstrated to the Belgians that Tutsis were in control of the monarchy because they *looked* more refined and therefore had much more in common with Europeans. You see, Tutsis tended to

continued ➡

continued

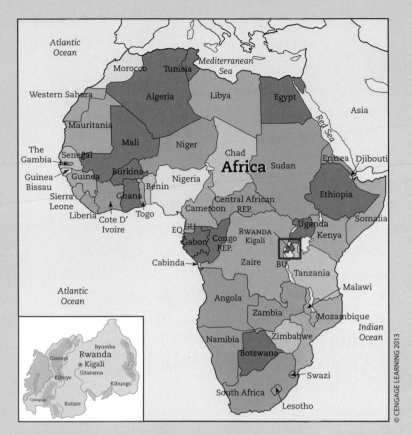

The continent of Africa was largely colonized by the European powers in the 19th century. In addition, they drew the borders of African states to their liking; not taking into account pre-existing borders or ethnic differences.

be tall and thin (more civilized, to the European that believed in the unsavory practice of eugenics) while Hutus tended to be short and stout (more primitive).

- 1933: The Belgian government conducted a census where they issued identification cards that forced Rwandans to demonstrate not only who they were or where they lived, but to what tribe they belonged. It was this census that paved the way for the divided society that would become modern Rwanda.

- 1962: The Belgians realized that they were no longer able or willing to maintain its colonial rule over the people of Rwanda. Since democracy was the political ideology of the day, the Belgians decided that Rwanda needed to institute a republican style government that would allow the true will and expression of Rwandan society. What occurred was quite dramatic. Rwanda, for the first time in the modern era, became a Hutu-dominated country because of the outpouring of support from Hutu voters.

continued

continued

- 1963: Disenfranchised Tutsi rebel groups from outside of Rwanda began to challenge the legitimacy of the ruling Hutu party known as the Party of the Hutu Emancipation Movement or PARMEHUTU.
- 1970s–1980s: A civil/regional war ensued for the better part of the 1970s and 1980s which required the international community under the auspices of the United Nations to attempt to end the violence.
- 1986: Paul Kagame becomes head of the newly formed Tutsi rebel group known as the Rwandan Patriotic Front (RPF). It is formed in neighboring Uganda and begins plans to invade Rwanda on behalf of the Tutsi people.
- 1990: The RPF invades Rwanda. Large-scale violence ensues between the Hutu military under Rwandan president Juvenal Habyarimana.
- 1993: Government-controlled radio stations begin to call for attacks against all Tutsis, referring to them as "cockroaches." Nevertheless, after three years of violence, a cease-fire agreement known as the Arusha Accords is signed between the leadership of the RPF and President Habyarimana. The United Nations Assistance Mission in Rwanda (UNAMIR) was deployed as a way of maintaining the cease-fire.
- 1994: On April 6, 1994, Hutu President Habyarimana's plane was shot down; speculation ensued as to who carried out the attack. Many have argued that it was a group of Hutus who had lost faith in Habyarimana's ability to secure Rwanda. Many Hutus believed that the Arusha Accords demonstrated a weakness on the part of the Rwandan president and was unacceptable.

Between April and July of 1994 approximately 800,000 to 1,000,000 ethnic Tutsis and moderate Hutus were killed by the Hutu paramilitary group known as the Interahamwe. Most victims were killed with the use of machetes.

It is within this context that we may proceed to examine what became known as the Rwandan genocide within Waltz's *three levels of analysis*. You now have the basic facts of the conflict surrounding the Rwandan genocide. Try to determine why the genocide occurred.

Who were the individuals involved?

Who were the actors within Rwandan society?

What role did the international community play?

LIBERALISM

At the core of **liberalism** is the belief that human beings are generally good and that our ability to reason allows us to make economic, political, and social progress. For liberals, acts of war, terrorism, or genocide are not the result of human nature, but are flaws in the social, economic, or political infrastructure at a particular time and place. Liberals argue that state cooperation is essential to our survival because it is only through cooperation that conflict is avoided.

For liberals, an institution that promotes individual freedom (and in particular the freedom to buy and sell goods in an open market and the freedom that allows individuals a voice in the political system) creates the best chance of reducing the instances of conflict. Therefore, liberals would argue that a democratically arranged international system would be the best way to limit international hostilities. If state A is democratic (in that it is representative of its people) and states B, C, D, and E are also democratic, they are less likely to engage in conflict.

In the eighteenth century, it was Immanuel Kant (1724–1804) who provided us with one of the earliest prescriptions for achieving this type of peace in the international system. According to Kant:

> A state of peace among men living together is not the same as a state of nature, which is rather a state of war. *For even if it does not involve active hostilities, it involves a constant threat of their breaking out. Thus, the state of peace must be formally instituted, for a suspension of hostilities is not in itself a guarantor of peace. And unless one neighbor gives a guarantee to the other at his request (which can happen only in a lawful state), the latter might treat him as an enemy.*[11]

For Kant, peace is only possible through the establishment of republican states that value the necessity of the *system* in equal proportion to that of its own. In other words, although I may be a citizen and live in state A, I equally value the merits of the entire system to which my state belongs. Thus, creating the belief that my well-being is dependant on the state, the system, and the democratic laws upon which both rest. This model creates what Kant refers to as the *perpetual peace* theory because national legislation will become international law and will therefore not only have to protect domestic, *civil* rights, but also those at the international level, namely cosmopolitan or universal rights.[12]

It was this interpretation of liberalism that led to the development in the late nineteenth and early twentieth centuries of the theory of *idealism*. Idealism is best defined as an expansion of some of the core beliefs of liberalism. Personified by the American president Woodrow Wilson, idealism is based on the notion of ethical determinations in foreign policy and the spreading of democratic principles, including the right of self-determination, free speech, fair and free elections. Wilson's major contribution to the understanding of idealism is embodied in his famous Fourteen Points. A list of necessary principles written at the end of World War I, the Fourteen Points

Liberalism: *The school of thought that is centered on the creation of international institutions designed to enhance the natural tendencies of cooperation found in human nature.*

CourseReader ASSIGNMENT

Log in to **www.cengagebrain.com** and open CourseReader to access the reading:

Barack Obama's *Speech upon acceptance of the Nobel Peace Prize, Oslo, Norway, 2009.*

In President Obama's 2009 Nobel Peace Prize acceptance speech, he outlined some of the current challenges facing the global community and his commitment to balance the ideological aspirations of idealism with the grave realities of human conflict. In the process, President Obama presented the world with a vision of human nature that is hopeful and optimistic, yet at the same time, realistic in its understanding of the corrupting effects of power.

- *Is President Obama proclaiming a commitment to realism, idealism, or something in between?*
- *Can you see any similarities between President Obama's speech and any other thinker(s) you have encountered so far?*
- *Is an international legal framework powerful enough to protect human rights? If not, should states be allowed to violate another state's sovereignty if it is denying its people's human rights?*

Collective Security:
The idea that an attack on one particular state by another, should be understood as an attack against all states.

Neoliberalism: *The school of thought that says because states are constantly interacting with each other they value cooperation as part of their own self-interest.*

outlined Wilson's beliefs that through proper education, democratic governance, the promotion of equality, and most importantly, an international relations agenda committed to **collective security**, peace was possible.

In Chapter 12, we will be reminded of the failure of the League of Nations, Wilson's testament to collective security. Although many scholars have associated its problems with its reliance on the hopefulness of states to combat aggressors to peace, its failure was also related to its founders' lack of consensus and economic and political support. At the end of World War I, both the United States and the Soviet Union refused to join, placing an ever-increasing burden on states less suited to handle the challenges of the day, namely, the aggressive power politics of Adolf Hitler.

Neoliberalism: Cooperation may come from self interest

During the 1970s, liberalism received a scholarly revival and a repackaging. Political scientists Robert Axelrod, Robert O. Keohane, and Joseph S. Nye began to reexamine the factors responsible for international cooperation.[13] They felt that the answers given by realist and neorealist scholars were not sufficient. These scholars, who eventually became known as **neoliberals** (or neoliberal institutionalists) decided that state cooperation is not always based on realist assumptions and that international cooperation is a highly complex enterprise. So they decided to seek out alternatives and discovered that cooperation sometimes occurs when states see that it is in their own interests to cooperate within an established system. Still, how did they illustrate their views? One of the most basic ways was the *prisoner's dilemma*, a game that we introduced to you back in Chapter 3 that argues that rational decision making will force states (and in this case prisoners) to cooperate with one another because it is in each state's self-interest to do so.

Suppose that two criminals are arrested for burglary. After they are booked, they are placed in two different jail cells with no means of communication. The detectives tell both prisoners that if one confesses to the crime and the other remains silent, the one who confesses will be released and the other will have a lengthy prison sentence, say ten years. However, if they both decide to confess to the crime each will get a reduced sentence, say five years. If neither of the prisoners confesses, both will receive a light sentence (say six months) because of a lack of evidence and testimony. So what will they do? They will both confess to the crime of burglary and therefore serve a five-year term.

Why didn't the prisoners cooperate with each other and keep quiet about the crime? The simplest answer is because the situation required a one-time choice. They are not given time to repeat the process. If they were, they would most likely cooperate with the other, keep quiet, and receive a short prison sentence. Keep in mind that if the prisoners had the ability to understand and familiarize themselves with the process, they would choose the optimal payoff in the given situation, which in this case would be to stay silent. The prisoner's dilemma argues that in certain circumstances, it is actually in the best interest of each person or state to cooperate. In the international arena there are certain factors that could emerge that change the ways states view cooperation. This change may come as a result of a certain technological innovation or economic development. Over the next few decades, for example, China and India will most likely see their cooperation grow with the

FIGURE 11.4. The Prisoner's Dilemma

Prisoner A

		Remain Silent (Cooperate)	Confess (Defect)
Prisoner B	Remain Silent (Cooperate)	Six months sentence/Six months sentence	Ten Years Sentence/Released
	Confess (Defect)	Released/Ten years sentence	Five Years Sentence/Five Years Sentence

So Who Is Right, Realists or Liberals?

Is the international community as chaotic and reliant upon self-seeking states to bring security to the world as the realists say? Or is it a world that wants to work together to ensure greater progress for the common good and the enhancement of freedom as the liberals say? Which one is it? The answer is probably not as simple as who has the best answers or the wrong ones, but who has the power to dictate an international agenda.

If the United States continues to have the loudest voice in international affairs because of the size of its defense budget (equal to every other country's defense

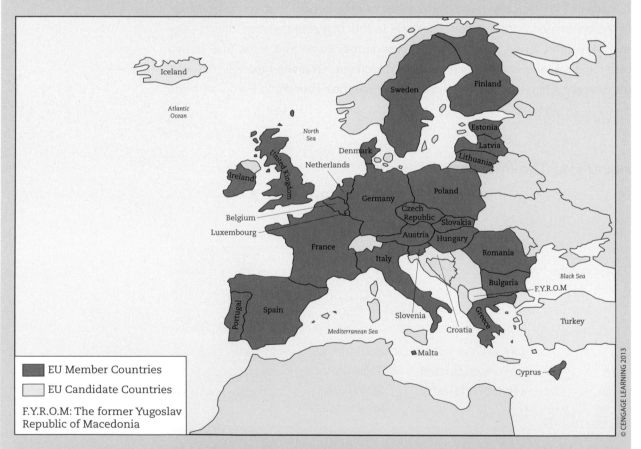

EU Member Countries

EU Candidate Countries

F.Y.R.O.M: The former Yugoslav Republic of Macedonia

The European Union, which came into force officially in 1993, has a common currency (the Euro) and a developing, symmetrical legal system.

continued ➡

budget combined) and its economy, then most will continue to argue that the realists have the upper hand. On the other hand, if another state comes to rival American power in nontraditional ways, then perhaps the fundamental arguments of idealists/ neoliberals will win out.

Let's take for example the European Union (EU). Currently it is composed of 27 European states that have all agreed to share currency (the euro) and begin the long process of aligning state laws with those established at its headquarters in Brussels, Belgium. If the EU is a model for the future in terms of how regions come together for common economic and legal policies, then perhaps liberal arguments will gain greater attention. If, on the other hand, the EU is a unique experiment doomed to fail, then once again perhaps the reasons for its dissolution will be based on realism. Only time will tell.

Will military power continue to play a major role in what makes states strong or weak?

Or can economic power and the development of a large array of trading partners bring greater stability to the international system?

United States on number of foreign policy initiatives because of the ways the global economy has changed their statuses. They (and the United States) will realize that cooperation will be the best way of achieving long term growth.

So, what distinguishes liberalism from neoliberalism is centered on the reasons why states cooperate in an international system. For classic liberals, states cooperate in international institutions because they argue that humans are generally good natured and have the capacity to better the human experience by constantly reforming the ills of existing institutions. Neoliberals, on the other hand, argue that because states are constantly interacting with one another they value cooperation as a part of their self-interest. So, why do you think states will cooperate with one another? Is it because states desire cooperation, or is it because states feel that cooperation is in their best interest? Are there examples in today's world where it appears that states are cooperating out of self interest?

RADICALISM: MARXISM-LENINISM, DEPENDENCY THEORY, AND NEO-MARXISM

Marxism

For scholars in international relations, Karl Marx (1818–1883) is the predominant force in what has become known as the radical perspective. Living at the dawn of the European industrial revolution, Marx created a unique model of understanding economic, political, and social life that opposed the existing order's understanding of capitalism and classical liberalism. This approach has been considered "radical" because of the ways it seeks to challenge the dominant views held by most. According to Marx, history is best understood as a constant and long-term class struggle between those who control the modes of production (bourgeoisie) and those who work within the confines of such a system (proletariat). The bourgeoisie consists of the wealthy "owners" and the proletariat consists of the impoverished "workers." The bourgeoisie *own* the factories, the proletariat *work* and are exploited in the factories. The bourgeoisie *own* the tenements and are the landlords, whereas the proletariat live in the tenements and are the tenants.

Basing much of his preliminary logic on the works of G. W. F. Hegel, Marx argued that history unfolded according to a logical progression. Whereas Hegel argued that issues of morality or what is considered right and wrong (which Hegel called "spirit") was passed down from generation to generation based on the ability of the state to preserve such morality, for Marx, only the people themselves could protect such values and judgments. Humans have always realized that there are certain obstacles in life. For Hegel it was the state that should and could eliminate such obstacles. For Marx, it was the state that *created* most of the obstacles. Still, Marx utilized Hegel's concept of spirit to argue that history flows according to a plan. However, in Marx's view, history was really a history of class struggle between those with wealth (private property) and those who work to ensure that the wealthy maintain their property. In essence, the wealthy from subsequent generations seemed to learn from previous generations about how best to control power and wealth. The Roman Empire witnessed a certain type of exploitation that had created categories of wealth, as did the Medieval period. But what was unique about the nineteenth century for Marx was the intensity of the exploitation that had developed and the setting in which the exploitation took place.

It must be understood that the feudal period (the time before the emergence of capitalism), which had dominated economic, political, and social lives (and provided much of the framework for Marx's analysis) was largely based on a dependant relationship between a Lord (who owned the land) and a Serf (who worked and lived on the land). Although the Lord, had a great deal more political power than the Serfs, he still relied on the health and well-being of his workers. The landowners during the feudal era were therefore somewhat dependant on their workers. The workers' lives might not have been as pleasant as those of the Lords, but at least they were provided shelter and food on the land. By the nineteenth century in Western Europe, the feudal era was largely dead, replaced by an economic system that relied more on factory than farm and a preference for specialization over craftsmanship.

In his greatest work, *Das Kapital (Capital),* Marx examined the economic system known as capitalism and argued that it perpetuates a negative environment based on the dual forces of efficiency and exploitation. Efficiency, which allowed factories to specialize in how goods are produced, led to a continued cycle of exploitation for the workers. A simple illustration will bring Marx's view of capitalism to light. Let's pretend that you are the owner of a shoe factory in the nineteenth century. How do you produce shoes that are at both a competitive price and a good quality? We have at our disposal several options. Should we force each worker to make his/her own pair of shoes? Or should we force each worker to perform a simple and limited task in the creation of the shoes? Of course, in the name of efficiency you would prefer the latter. Why? Because it is far more efficient to have each worker contribute to a small part in the production of the shoes. It saves time and, more importantly, money. Workers can produce hundreds of shoes collectively in the time it would take one skilled shoemaker to produce one pair of extremely expensive shoes. For Marx, it is this process that created the highest level of exploitation. To the factory owner, the workers are valued as parts of a production machine, but are easily replaced and cheap.

Within this context, the factory worker is forced to sell his/her own labor and is denied any gratification that comes from the production of the shoes. Why? Because each factory worker is unable to experience the joy of his creation from start to finish. For Marx, it is the **alienation of labor** that allows the owners to continue to exploit the workforce. Since workers cannot experience the joy of creation and only the results of their labor, they also become commodities for the employer. And as the tasks of the production grow in simplicity, the numbers of workers grow, and the wages for the number of potential workers declines. For Marx, this is why both wages and working conditions will continue to deteriorate.[14]

Bu why does the government allow such practices in the workplace? According to Marx it is because the bourgeoisie (owners) and the government are one and the same. Since the government benefits from the wealth it can accumulate in the form of taxes, it refuses to pass laws that could possibly jeopardize economic growth. Thus, we see in Marx a critique of not only the economic structure, but the political structure as well.

▲ Karl Marx is known as the father of revolutionary communism. His works directly inspired revolutions in Russia, China, Cuba, and other parts of the developing world during the 20th century.

Alienation of labor: *The concept developed by Karl Marx that explained the ways in which modern life removes the worker from the product he/she is creating.*

Communist Manifesto **by Marx and Engels** (excerpt), 1848.

Marx and Engels are the most influential socialist thinkers and activists in history. Born in Germany, they wrote *The Communist Manifesto* for the Communist League (1847–1852), the first international working-class communist party. The *Manifesto* was released on the eve of the 1848 revolutions in Europe for democratic rights, national unification, independence, and constitutional reform. This selection from Part 1, "Bourgeois and Proletarians," examines the rise, role, impacts, and conflicts of the two social classes that define the modern era—the capitalists and the wage laborers.

- *Why do Marx and Engels discuss the relationships between oppressor and oppressed to begin the* Communist Manifesto?

- *What are the differences between the feudal period and that of the capitalist?*

- *In today's world, we see a great deal of manufacturing taking place in some of the poorest places on earth. Does this mean that Marx was right when he discusses the nature of colonialism?*

When one takes Marxism and applies it to the international community, his theory takes on another dimension. States that have succeeded in terms of economic development have done so through the exploitation of the developing world. For Marx, it was not an accident that Great Britain had the largest empire during the late nineteenth and early twentieth centuries. It was a simple fact born out of what it viewed as political necessity. The British government realized that it needed a constant supply of resources in order that it might remain as one of Europe's dominant powers.

As the British Empire grew, so too did its wealth and security. For Marx, this was the pinnacle of capitalist exploitation: once the capitalist government realized that it was unable to create the kinds of profits necessary for development, it searched out new lands in possession of natural resources and/or labor. After the colonials (say in India) had been conquered, the British created a political system that kept the people from revolting, kept its resources growing, strengthened international laws that protected trade policies and routes, and lastly, brought colonial elites to London to be educated and then transferred them back to the colony. Therefore, the perpetuation and protection of private property is what drove **colonialism**.

Colonialism: *A form of state domination in which one state controls the political system of another or several others for its own gain.*

Imperialism: *The highest stage of capitalism according to V. I. Lenin. It was the stage at which industrial growth and the banking system become monopolized by a wealthy group of state and industry leaders. For Lenin, it was the stage immediately before the worldwide communist revolution.*

V. I. Lenin and Imperialism

It is within this context of exploitation that the radical perspective grew. Following Marx, came V. I. Lenin, the person most responsible for the expansion of the idea of colonialism into the idea known as *imperialism* and the first leader of the Soviet Union.

For Lenin, **imperialism** was the highest stage of capitalism: the stage that witnessed the defense of the state (by capitalists), the monopolization of industrial

THEORY AND PRACTICE

The Rwandan Genocide from the Marxist Perspective

How would a Marxist view the genocide in Rwanda? Well, first of all, one would argue that the colonial structure that had placed Rwanda under the control of first the Germans and then the Belgians was designed to advance only the interests of the European state system. Since Rwandans were denied economic mobility and political representation, their labor was the only real commodity designed to impede development of any kind.

Secondly, Marxists would point to the deliberate destruction of Rwandan culture on the basis of race. As the map of Africa was drawn without any regard to tribal differences or existing boundaries, the Europeans transformed a continent from one that was poor and underdeveloped into one that was still poor but artificially fragmented as well. As the colonial period ended and the African states gained their freedoms, they attempted to enact policies designed to enhance their stability. But because the levels of poverty were so extreme, violence and warfare persisted. Marxists would suggest that the civil wars and genocides in Rwanda resulted from the inequalities that were developed during the colonial period and exacerbated during the postcolonial period.

Lastly, Marxists would argue that the Rwandan genocide occurred because the powerful states of the world did not value a Rwandan's life worthy of protection. Remember, for Marxists, laborers are defined as expendable commodities. Thus, the international community turned a blind eye to the atrocities in Rwanda because of the fact that Rwandans were seen as expendable, and because their land did not provide the industrialized world with anything of monetary value.

Would the international community have gotten involved to stop the civil war and genocide if Rwanda possessed oil?

Can genocides be stopped only when it is in the national interest of the world's powerful countries?

Is exploitation of the
developing world by those
in the industrialized world
unavoidable? If so, does this
mean that Marx and Lenin
were correct?

production, and an international system based on exploitation. Imperialism was no longer to be understood as the practice by which Empire A conquered Colony A for the benefit of Empire A, but as a practice that required a violent revolution of all workers committed to its destruction. In many ways, Lenin restated Marx's arguments about exploitation, but emphasized the "irreconcilability of class antagonisms."[15] Imperialism was therefore the vehicle by which the exploited gain power and a greater understanding of the inequalities of the international system. It was also the agent for revolution and the violent overthrow of not only the state, but of the entire system of imperialism and the entire ideology of capitalism.

Dependency Theory

Modernization theorists: *The most famous is Walt Whitman Rostow. Rostow argued that there is a formula for economic growth and development. Prosperity is based on the ability of certain states to assume an economic formula that will move them from "traditional life" to "mass consumption."[26]*

Third world countries: *Sometimes referred to as countries in the developing world. They received this distinction during the Cold War when the world was thought to be divided between a First World (most industrialized states), a Second World (the communist states), and a Third World, the poorest states located everywhere from Africa, to Latin America, Central, South and South East Asia. (See Theory and Practice Box on page 356–357.)*

First world countries: *Countries that receive this distinction are the wealthiest, most industrialized states. The states in this category have the highest levels of wealth and middle classes, highest levels of technology, lowest infant mortality rates (number of children per 1,000 that die before age five), highest life expectancies, and the like.*

Following the end of World War II, certain scholars attempted to explain economic development and global inequalities. What emerged were two competing schools of thought. On the one hand were the **modernization (development) theorists**, who argued that economic development was based on an evolutionary pattern of growth and that **third world countries** (states defined as poor, largely agriculturally based, former colonies of major European powers in parts of Latin American, South Asia, and Sub-Saharan Africa (such as India, Rwanda, Kenya, and Uruguay) had the ability to become **first world countries** (the most industrialized states such as the United States, Great Britain, France, Germany, and Japan) if they adhered to certain principles of growth, namely free market principles and capitalism.[16] On the other hand were the *dependency theorists* who argued that economic development was based on the exploitation of the poor by the wealthy: a relationship based on unfair trade policies that benefited the first world at the expense of the third world. At this point, you should have no problem determining which theoretical perspective is considered part of the radical perspective and why it is considered as such.

In 1948, world-renowned Argentine economist Raul Prebisch became director of the Economic Commission for Latin America (ECLA). Two years later he published a study entitled "The Economic Development of Latin America and Its Principal Problems." In the study, Prebisch proposed a radical understanding of the economic relationship between the world's wealthiest and poorest states. First, Prebisch stated that the world was best understood as one that was divided between "core" and "peripheral" states: the core referring to the wealthy states and the peripheral referring to the poorer states. Second, Prebisch stated that because peripheral states produced primary goods (agricultural goods that are easy to produce) for export to the core states and core states produced secondary goods (manufactured goods) for export to the periphery, technology took off in the core but remained underdeveloped in the periphery. Third, the core states gained wealth because they were able to save their money through the development expansion of trade unions and strong financial institutions. Fourth, because the peripheral

Sweatshop Labor in Bangladesh:
Development or Disaster?

Have you ever imagined what it would be like to grow up in another society? We have already asked you to think about life in a restrictive authoritarian state, but what about life in a country whose people survive on less than $2.00 a day. How would you make ends meet? How would you view the world?

Your first reaction might be one of anger toward those parts of the world that have higher levels of wealth whose governments may be responsible for your economic and political plight. But as economist Jeffrey Sachs tells us, you might be wrong.

In Sachs's book *The End of Poverty*, he discusses the controversial issue of sweatshop labor from a unique perspective. Instead of making the traditional argument that sweatshop labor of all kinds is demeaning and a violation of human rights, he approached it from a development perspective. In Bangladesh, many young female garment workers "already have a foothold in the modern economy that is a critical, measurable step up . . .

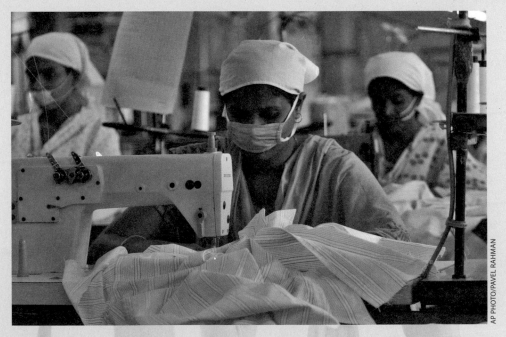

Sweatshop workers in Bangladesh provide a great deal of the world's clothing. Bangladesh and other parts of Asia have become a prime destination for many multinational corporations.

continued

continued

from their lives in the villages where they grew up."[17] Sachs goes on to say that although the garment industry does not receive high marks in terms of women's rights, it is at least a viable path toward economic and political growth. Today's women of Bangladesh are far better off than their mothers and grandmothers who had limited opportunities.

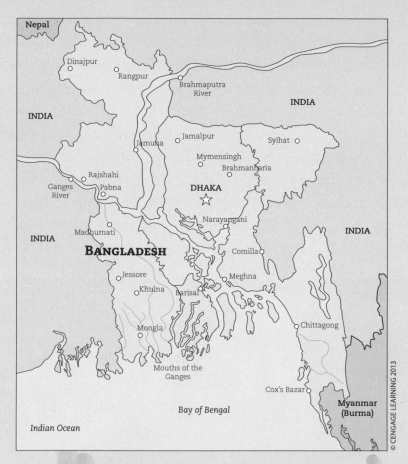

Bangladesh broke away from neighboring Pakistan and gained independence in 1971.

How does the practice of sweatshop labor tie into the discussion of neo-Marxism and dependency theory?

Is sweatshop labor unjust or is it a necessary evil? Your perspective will most likely be based on your understanding of some of the schools of thought we've just presented.

THEORY AND PRACTICE

Dependency Theory and the Latin American Debt Crisis of the 1980s

In the 1970s and 1980s, the world experienced a massive economic recession. As the economies of the world weakened, the price of oil went through the roof. What resulted was an economic disaster in Latin America and an economic boom for the oil-producing countries. Rising oil prices had serious consequences. As citizens in

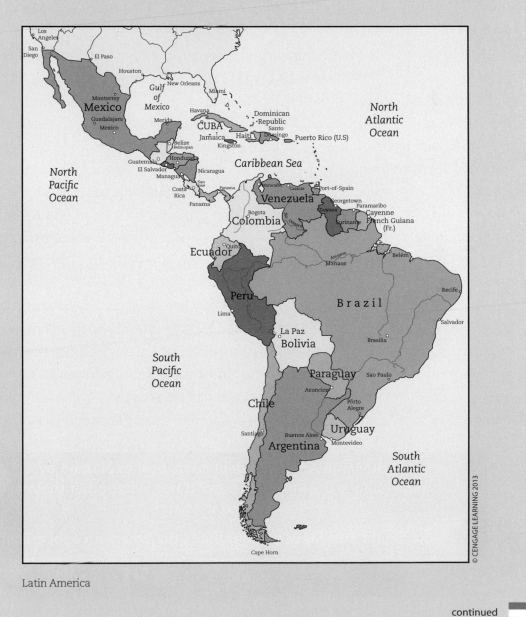

Latin America

continued ➤

Latin America had to spend more of their incomes on oil (which meant that they had less money to spend on items like food, education, health, and social services), the oil-rich countries could invest their money in international banks, which, in turn, gave loans to the countries of Latin America.

By the end of the 1970s, interest rates in the industrialized world (namely the United States and its European allies) went up. This meant that it became increasingly difficult for the Latin American states to repay their debts. According to Thomas J. D'Agostino, "Latin America's total foreign debt surpassed $400 billion during the 1980s with Brazil, followed by Mexico and Argentina, incurring the largest national debts."[18]

So what did the Latin American countries do? First they attempted to take out new loans so they might be able to pay off (defer) some of the loans that were due while at the same time continuing to spend more money than they took in.[19] What resulted were immense budget deficits. If a country refuses to raise taxes out of fear of revolution and it simply keeps spending money that it does not have, the value of the currency will plummet. That is exactly what happened in Latin America in the 1980s.

"By 1990, Argentina, Brazil, Nicaragua, and Peru had annual inflation rates in excess of 10,000 percent."[20] Inflation and rising deficits will usually scare away potential investors. So it is no surprise that "as a whole investment spending fell from 25 percent of GDP (Gross domestic product) in the late 1970s to 17 percent by the late 1980s."[21]

The states of Latin America had seen already low wages fall, its investors flee or dry up, and its economies crash and devalue at alarming rates. For dependency theorists, much of this catastrophe was based on the initial state of dependency that the agriculturally based continent was to the industrialized continent to the north. Since the Latin American states were largely dependent on what had become necessities to growth, they were unable to secure their economies during economic downturns.

Is the Latin American debt crisis best explained by dependency theory? If so, how? If not, what other theory explained it better?

How would Karl Marx explain the Latin American debt crisis?

states did not need technology to produce items for export, its goods remained cheap and uncompetitive, and their governments could not save money and grow wealth. Thus, the peripheral became dependent on the core states. In the 1960s and 1970s, Prebisch's thesis developed into the school of thought we now refer to as dependency theory.

Neo-Marxism: Michael Hardt and Antonio Negri

Following the end of the Cold War, many Marxists had wondered where they had gone wrong. How could the socialist system implode so quickly and unexpectedly? And how could so many academics who had dedicated decades to research that pertained to the Soviet Union, centrally planned economics, and an interpretation of history as one of exploitation of owners and workers (bourgeoisie and proletariat) not seen it coming? The answer to this question seemed to come in the form of a transformation: It is not that the Cold War had ended in the destruction of the communist ideology and system, but in the way Marxists viewed power. According to what Cynthia Weber has referred to as "a new myth for a new millennium," neo-Marxists developed a new case for opposition and, possibly, revolution by moving the center of exploitation.

In their book *Empire*, leading neo-Marxists Michael Hardt and Antonio Negri associated new developments in trade policies (that gave a significant increase of leverage to wealthy capitalist states) with the rise in what has been referred to as "the new world order." For neo-Marxists, the **new world order** refers to the ways in which large-scale multinational corporations (MNCs), in conjunction with the wealthiest states, have created a new type of imperialism that expands the wealth to the rich (themselves) while continually weakening the economic development of the poor. "By recasting the oppressor as Empire and the oppressed as the multitude, Hardt and Negri restore the basic binary upon which Marxism has long been based."[22] The result is that neo-Marxists have maintained Marxism's commitment to their understanding of history as one that is based on class conflict for a new era of scholars and policymakers and a commitment to active revolution. How? Because neo-Marxists are able to clearly identify the actors involved in the exploitation to both those they label as oppressors and those they label as oppressed, those who maintain the empire of wealthy corporations and those who are now aware of how the wealthy continue to exploit them. It is with this knowledge that neo-Marxists have been able to develop a clearer portrait of who the opposition is and how they might revolt against it.

New world order: *For neo-Marxists this is the way in which the exploitation of the wealthy over the poor will continue. It is best seen in the ways that large corporations have been successful in passing legislation that allows them to lower other poorer countries' tariffs and gain access to their markets, resources, and labor.*

Why So Poor?

Many people tend to use the word *poverty* to describe a condition of extreme financial deprivation. But let's try to humanize this, okay? Many neo-Marxists will look at facts and figures from the developing world and attempt to provide a rationale for their argument. So here are some statistics that might shock you, or at the very least, make you begin to ask the very important question, why?

- In Sub-Saharan Africa, life expectancy has declined from 49 to 46 years of age since 1990. The main reasons for its declining life expectancy are the high infant mortality rate, 100 per 1,000 live births in 2004, and prevalence of HIV among adults is more than 7 percent.

- South Asia has the second lowest gross national income (GNI) per capita ($594) and some of the highest yields of child malnutrition in the world, with **49 percent of children below the standards of weight by age.** In addition, it has the lowest rate of youth literacy—82 percent for males and 65 percent for females—and at 35 percent, the lowest rate of access to sanitation facilities. With only about **12 personal computers per 1,000**, South Asia lags behind other regions in access to personal computers. South Asia is, however, business friendly, requiring only 35 days to start a business in 2005, the lowest among developing regions.

- The Latin American and the Caribbean regions have the highest GNI per capita income of all developing-country regions but the lowest growth of 2.1 percent over the period 1995 to 2004. The region has the highest life expectancy at birth, 72 years, and the lowest under-five mortality rate.

- The Middle East and North Africa have well-developed infrastructures. Over 75 percent of its population has access to improved sanitation facilities and water sources. The region spends heavily on the military; it has the highest of any developing region.

- The developing and transition economies of Eastern Europe and Central Asia grew at 7.2 percent in 2004, doubling a decade low 3.6 percent growth. On a per capita basis, the region has the highest energy use, double that of the Middle East and North Africa and the highest rate of CO_2 per capita emissions of the developing regions.[23]

continued

So what would a neo-Marxist say about such levels of poverty? These levels have been caused by the exploitation of wealthy, multinational corporations working in conjunction with the wealthiest, capitalist states.

> Being an American, you are most likely uncomfortable with the label "Marxist." However, do Marxists and neo-Marxists have a valid point here? If so, on what grounds are they correct? If not, why are they incorrect?

CONSTRUCTIVISM: WE SHAPE OUR OWN EXPERIENCES ABOUT THE WORLD

Constructivism *A school of thought within international relations that examines the impact of values and norms on the behavior of states.*

In the 1980s and 1990s another school of thought emerged in international relations to challenge the dominance of liberalism and realism (neorealism): the constructivist school. Constructivists such as Alexander Wendt and Martha Finnemore believe that realists and neorealists tend to place too much emphasis on the assumptions that anarchy will lead to security and structure in the international system. Instead of assuming (like neorealists) that the international system is materially anarchical (that all states have similar goals toward gaining or protecting wealth) and thus will force states into cooperation, constructivists believe that identity formation based on the states' social practices is a more "realistic" way of analyzing international cooperation/disagreement.

Constructivists tend to believe that the international system is anarchical but do not stress the assumptions about its outcomes. They tend to look at the goals of states, which quite often might not be caused by how they view their power in light of others. In a landmark appraisal of why states adopt certain policy measures, Finnemore argued that states view issues of justice, war and peace, poverty, disease, and other issues from a perspective of social interaction.[24] In other words, individuals in the developing world will view issues of justice or the eradication of poverty differently than other individuals in the developing world and others in the industrialized world. To assume that all states operate according to a "natural" drive toward power, as it is understood by neorealists and liberals, is to deny a basic understanding of human nature: the ability of individuals to construct their own social realities.

Constructivists have, therefore, turned the discussion of international relations inside-out. Instead of assuming (like realists) that states acting in their own national interests determine international stability and create international norms and values, constructivists argue that it is the international community that perpetuates the development of norms *within* states. Thus, constructivists argue that norms emerge from the top (those in positions of authority within the international community) and flow downward, into the domestic realm of the state.

The constructivist Peter Katzenstein wrote a book that detailed this very idea. Katzenstein's, *Cultural Norms and National Security*, examined the political attitudes within Japan before and after the end of World War II and argued that the idea of 'militarism' changed drastically.[25] Katzenstein demonstrated that before the attacks on Hiroshima and Nagasaki in August of 1945, Japan had been considered an aggressive, expansionist military state. However, after its unconditional surrender to the United States and its allies, Japan emerged as a country that not only lacked the legal authority to possess a standing military, but also the political will. For constructivists like Katzenstein, this demonstrates that the international community is not merely a representation of a community of states, but an entity in and of itself able to change the fabric of domestic policies, ideas, identities, and norms. He therefore makes the claim that the best (and often times most overlooked) prediction of how a state will behave is how its own political culture views the norms and values at stake.

SUMMARY

You now understand the ways in which international relations theory has progressed. While those who subscribe to different schools of thought may claim to provide students with the best answers to the problems of war and poverty, you should still be aware that there are no perfect solutions. Realists have consistently argued that power and national security are the primary motivators when explaining international relations but have yet to challenge the popular belief that states have a moral responsibility to protect human rights. On the other hand, idealists have consistently argued that human beings are naturally good and therefore form communities on the basis of morality but have yet to demonstrate why power and security still drive much of the operation of international politics.

This chapter has given you an understanding of the theoretical arguments that have been used in the field of international relations. Inasmuch as there are no standard and accepted "rules" of international politics, this chapter has provided you with the various schools of thought. You may discover that realism makes the most sense to you. Or conversely, you may feel that idealists have a more appropriate way of viewing international law. The value of a chapter like this is to be able to place all of the great debates that surround international relations in a given perspective. Now that you have these tools under your belt, let's look at some historic and current IR situations in Chapters 12 and 13.

KEY TERMS

KEY PEOPLE

WAR, DIPLOMACY, AND THE BEGINNING OF INTERNATIONAL RELATIONS

The members of the Great Powers who met in Vienna in 1815 and created a system of international security that lasted one hundred years.

INTRODUCTION: UNDERSTANDING THE PAST TO MAKE SENSE OF THE PRESENT

This chapter seeks to explain the development of contemporary international relations from a historical perspective. In doing so, we hope to provide you with a fundamental understanding of the ways in which the modern international system has developed over the past 360 years. Although it will not provide you with an exhaustively detailed history like that found in Paul Kennedy's *The Rise and Fall of the Great Powers* or Henry Kissinger's *Diplomacy*, it will offer you a basic framework from which you may better understand the contemporary global arrangement.

It must be remembered that the machinery of international relations—those agents involved in the functioning of foreign policies, such as heads of state, diplomats, civil servants, military personnel, and the like—neither emerged overnight nor in a vacuum. The world of states, or nation-states as they are sometimes called, is a relatively recent phenomenon. For most scholars, modern international relations began in the middle of the seventeenth century as a result of two major developments: the conclusion of the **Thirty Years' War** (1618–1648) and the emergence of the **state** as the primary unit of governance and *sovereignty* as its primary principle of legitimacy.

Following a logical progression this chapter will begin with an examination of the infancy of modern international relations, in other words, those events that occurred in the middle of the seventeenth century that inspired the justification of the state as the most legitimate form of rule. Following this preliminary section, the remainder of the chapter will focus on each century's contributions to the development of international relations. By analyzing the actions of states in relation to one another, we hope to demonstrate that the global stage is just as important as its *actors*. It will end in

© NORTH WIND PICTURE ARCHIVES / ALAMY

Questions to Consider Before Reading this Chapter

1. How did the concept of the balance of power change from the eighteenth century to the nineteenth century?

2. What is realpolitik? Does it accurately portray international relations?

3. Is a balance of power the most effective way of maintaining international security?

4. How did the victorious powers that met at the Congress of Vienna (1815) deal with the defeated power France? How did the victors of World War I that met in Paris (1915) treat Germany? What was the main difference?

5. What is the United Nations and who makes up the membership of the Security Council? Is the Security Council's permanent membership still relevant in today's world?

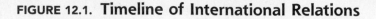

FIGURE 12.1. Timeline of International Relations

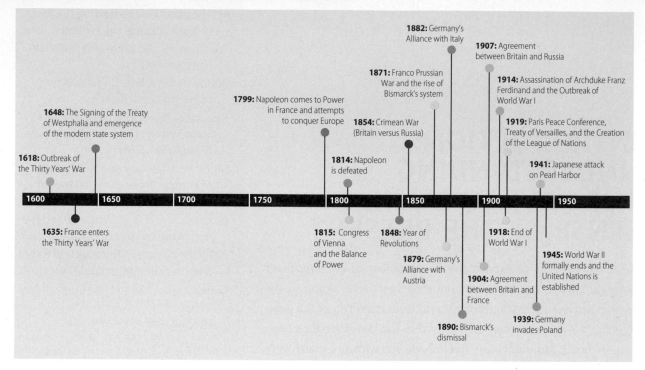

the middle of the twentieth century and the dawn of a new international order led by the emergence of the United States and the Soviet Union.

WHY EUROPE?: AN IMPORTANT QUESTION TO BEGIN

Thirty Years' War: *A war fought in Europe during the period 1618–1648 that was begun by the Catholic states in an attempt to bring the Protestant parts back to the "true" faith. Its conclusion resulted in the modern idea of the state as we know it today and the rise of international relations based on political rather than religious motives.*

Although many political scientists criticize those who view the world through a Western or Eurocentric perspective, the fact is that the structure of modern international relations has been built on the European model of the *state*. Our contemporary perception of legitimate governance is based almost entirely on the interrelated concepts of *sovereignty* (the state as the sole source of authority within its borders) and *territorial integrity* (the state has the right to prevent any aggression within its boundaries); terms that arose in Europe in the middle of the seventeenth century (See Table 12.1). As we will see, the victors of the Thirty Years' War were considered successful because they placed their national interests before other competing loyalties; a notion that was unheard of during most of the medieval period. The following section will present you with an introduction to one of the most important principles of modern international relations, *raison d'état*.

TABLE 12.1. Three Beliefs of the Modern State

Sovereignty	The state is the sole source of authority within its borders.
Territorial integrity	The state has the right to prevent aggression on its borders.
Raison d'état	The national interest. The state places the strength of the state as its primary goal.

RAISON D'ÉTAT: A NEW UNDERSTANDING OF INTERNATIONAL RELATIONS

Most scholars regard the year 1648 as the beginning of the modern period of international relations. The end of the Thirty Years' War (1648) culminated in the perpetuation of a new emphasis on secularism over religion. For centuries, the European continent had been controlled and secured by the twin forces of empire and God. Empires like the Habsburgs and Russian Czars, and the Church in Rome were determined to control large amounts of land and people in order to secure stability. However, by the beginning of the seventeenth century very few regarded either the *empire* or the pope as legitimate forms of rule. The Protestant Reformation questioned papal authority and the dawn of the Enlightenment created a sense of individualism which witnessed a new form of statecraft, the *raison d'état*, and the subsequent emergence of a new understanding of international stability, the balance of power.

Where previous centuries had been defined by the political arrangement of the empire, the seventeenth century was defined by a new arrangement, the state. The state's ascendance as the most viable instrument of governance emerged during the Thirty Years' War as France and its most important statesman, Cardinal Richelieu, employed a new strategy of understanding international relations. This new understanding of international relations based on *raison d'état* became the model of statecraft for the next century.

To best understand *raison d'état,* one must understand the causes and eventual outcomes of the Thirty Years' War. The Thirty Years' War began as a religious conflict fought in Central Europe between the Catholic and Protestant (German-speaking) parts of the Holy Roman Empire. The war ravaged the German territories and eventually involved all of the major European powers. When France entered the conflict in 1635, it did so under a new understanding of international relations. Under its foreign secretary, Cardinal Richelieu, French foreign policy determined its role in the war according to its own national interest rather than any religious one. As Henry Kissinger has pointed out it was this sense of a national interest over that of religious devotion that shattered the previous era and best defined the *raison d'état*. He wrote:

State: *The primary actor in international relations. States (referred to by American students as "countries") have governments, bureaucracies, territory, and people. States are in possession of the ultimate source of authority within its borders and are therefore said to possess sovereignty.*

Sovereignty: *The idea that the government within a state is recognized (domestically and internationally) as the ultimate source of authority to create, implement, and enforce laws.*

Territorial integrity: *The boundaries of any state are to be protected against any acts of aggression and are to be maintained.*

Raison d'état: *Best understood by the modern expression "the national interest" where modern leaders put forth what is best for their own state above all other reasons.*

Secularism: *The belief that religion should be separate from governmental authority and political power.*

Empire: *A political arrangement in which one powerful government is in control of a vast territory and peoples of (possibly) different economic, ethnic, religious groups than the powerful government itself. This configuration dominated the period right before the emergence of the modern state system.*

As a prince of the Church, Richelieu ought to have welcomed Ferdinand's (Emperor of the Holy Roman Empire) drive to restore Catholic orthodoxy. But Richelieu put the French national interest above any religious goals. His vocation as Cardinal did not keep Richelieu from seeing the Habsburg attempt to re-establish the Catholic religion as a geo -political threat to France's security. To him, it was not a religious act but a political maneuver by Austria (Holy Roman Empire was centered in Vienna) to achieve dominance in Central Europe and thereby to reduce France to second-class status.[1]

Richelieu understood that the future lay with France as a political and secular unit; not one bound by religion or the imperial ambitions of empires acting in the name of religion.

In 1648, the Treaty of Westphalia was signed, and the war, often cited as the last of the religious wars in Europe, was over. The Treaty of Westphalia, which was really the result of two peace settlements signed in the cities of Osnabruck and Munster, ushered in a new understanding of governance.[2] The Treaty of Westphalia created a system of rule that ended the dominance of imperial religion, that is, the sway that the Catholic or Protestant churches had over numerous principalities, and called for the breakup of most of the territory known as the Holy Roman Empire. Territories that at one time were considered both part of the Holy Roman Empire and also Catholic, were allowed their political and religious independence. This of course did not mean that the inhabitants of these newly created states were "free" to elect their representatives or voice public opinion, but it did mean that they were now ruled by local authorities who had to grant them protection to practice their faith. If we look at the map of Europe before and after the Thirty Years' War, we can see how the Treaty's agreements changed the landscape.

The end of the war created a general agreement that the French explanation of statecraft was most appropriate. By the late seventeenth century, the notion of *raison d'état* had placed France at the center of European affairs. According to historians Gordon A. Craig, Alexander A. George, and Paul Gordon Lauren, the late seventeenth century witnessed the ascendancy of French culture to incredible heights as its language, culture, and military spread throughout the continent "threatening the independent development of other nations."[4] Although this expansion appeared as a natural result of French power, it also had its shortcomings. The model of effective governance that was in the process of being emulated by other European states challenged France and perpetuated the development of another important step in the evolution of modern international relations, the balance of power.

If there was one thing that this early understanding of European security fostered was the belief that a system of states could work together in order

What Drives Foreign Policy:
Church or State?

The concept of *raison d'état* is usually not that difficult for students living in the twenty-first century to understand because it is based on a logic that students have grown up with. A logic that says that leaders will always act in their own state's interest when it comes to foreign policy and must not be influenced by other things such as personal animosity or religious beliefs. However, this was not always the case.

During the medieval period (fifth to fifteenth centuries) the papacy in Rome (The Roman Catholic Church) held sway over many of the kingdoms and principalities in Europe. This meant the pope had the ability to strongly influence foreign and domestic policy in places under the control of Catholic monarchs. Because Catholics believe that the pope is not only Christ's representative on earth but is also infallible, his political beliefs took on a much more important role than those of other political leaders. In fact Ferdinand II, emperor of the Holy Roman Empire, who took up the cause of restoring Catholicism in Europe during the Thirty Years' War, did so on the basis of his belief that he was doing good for both the pope and God. Ferdinand II is a classic case of the medieval ruler: one who judged foreign policy decisions by his religious convictions rather than what would be practical for his own people.[3] Of course, this led to the eventual collapse of the Holy Roman Empire and the emergence of a number of weakly linked principalities around the larger states of Austria and Prussia. If Ferdinand II had chosen to enter battle according to Richelieu's understanding of the "national interest" then he would have saved thousands of lives and a great deal of territory. Then again, he would never have done so because it would have conflicted with his deep devotion to what he believed was God's will: the restoration at any cost of Catholicism in Europe.

Do you think that religion plays a major role in foreign policy today?

Should foreign policy advisors always behave like Richielieu? Or is there a danger to that type of thinking?

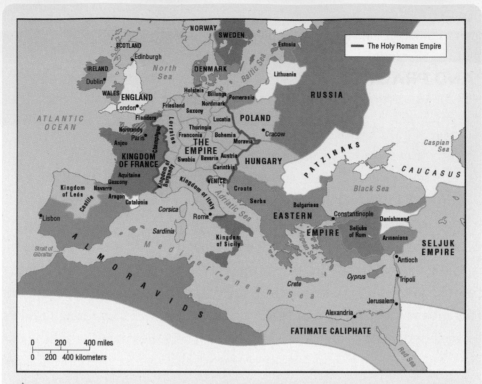

▲ Europe 1100: From the beginning of history until the middle of the 17th century, issues of war and peace were not decided by competing states, but by large empires and small principalities. The world as you know it today simply did not exist.

▲ Europe in 1648: Following the Thirty Years' War, Europe was transformed by a revolution in how international relations was conducted. The ideas of "state" and "sovereignty" became the basis of success in the modern age. Can you see the territorial differences between the two maps? See how wars can change the landscape of a continent?

to prevent one state from gaining too much power. In the late seventeenth century that state was France. Even though France was the dominant state in European affairs, it was not strong enough to dominate all others. Thus we see an early example of the balance of power model. Although it would gain greater visibility and a formal structure following the Congress of Vienna (1815), the seeds of what would become known as the balance of power model were sown much earlier.

BALANCE OF POWER AND THE RISE OF THE STATE SYSTEM

The concept of the balance of power in the late seventeenth and eighteenth centuries came about as a *reaction* to the dominance of its most powerful state: France. However, it was not yet the intentional mechanism it would later become. As Kissinger pointed out:

> If the good of the state was the highest value, the duty of the ruler was the aggrandizement and promotion of his glory. *The stronger would seek to dominate, and the weaker would resist by forming coalitions to augment their individual strengths. If the coalition was powerful enough to check the aggressor, a balance of power emerged; if not, some country would achieve hegemony. The outcome was not foreordained and was therefore tested by frequent wars. At its beginning, the outcome could as easily have been empire—French or German—as equilibrium. That is why it took over a hundred years to establish a European order based explicitly on the balance of power. At first, the balance was an almost incidental fact of life, not a goal of international politics.*[5]

The balance of power model that emerged at the turn of the eighteenth century witnessed an evolution in international relations. States who at one time had joined one another in the pursuit of deterring France from gaining complete dominion over Europe had begun to view foreign affairs in a similarly aggressive manner. Those states with the ability to conquer weaker states did so, finding justification in the belief that it was in their own best interest.

By the middle of the eighteenth century, the game of international warfare and territorial acquisition led to an acceptance of five recognized *great powers* of Europe: France, Great Britain, Russia, Prussia, and Austria. These five powers considered themselves (and consequently were considered) as the bearers of stability on the continent. Although they were not tied to one another in any formal institution or treaty, they realized that their dominance was beneficial to both themselves and more importantly, to the stability of Europe.

According to Craig and George, what developed during the eighteenth century were three principles shared by all of the great powers of Europe. The first of these principles was "a general agreement that it was normal and right that there should be five great powers. The thought of one of them might disappear—that Prussia might actually be destroyed in the Seven Years War, for example—was resisted by all major powers."[6] This unwritten agreement is what many consider the glue that bound Europe together. It was predicated on the belief that if one of the members was destroyed, the ensuing vacuum would engulf all of Europe.

Secondly, "there was general agreement that although the powers might fight each other, the *way* in which they fought should be subject to some regulation."[7] Although there was not an agency to enforce rules of war that had been established in the previous centuries, the great powers of Europe largely adhered to certain norms of military behavior. The destruction caused by the relentless fighting of the Thirty Years' War perpetuated a notion that warfare had limits and that certain military behavior was unacceptable. The writings of Hugo Grotius and in particular, *De jure belli ac pacis* (*On the Law of War and Peace*), published in 1625, analyzed the ways in which warfare was to be conducted. Grotius and others in the *just war* tradition set limits intended to protect civilians, private property, and the means to generate wealth. By the middle of the eighteenth century, these conditions had become part of the military vernacular.

Lastly, Craig and George argue that:

there was a general recognition of the principle of the balance of power, which took two forms: *first, was a general wariness about anything that looked like an attempt at universal domination by a single power . . . and second for the balance of power to work properly, a territorial gain effected in war by one power should be balanced by compensatory gains for other major powers.*[8]

Examples of these factors can be seen throughout most of the eighteenth century with the two most relevant examples being Frederick II's (Prussia) attack on Selesia and the War of the Polish Succession.[9] Both conflicts were designed with limited ambitions in mind. Neither action was considered an act of continental domination because both Prussia and Russia (in the second case) agreed that just as there were five great powers, so too were there weak ones with, of course, the weak ones serving as the beneficiaries of military domination.

What allowed the five great powers of the eighteenth century a degree of success was the balance of power construct. However, as we have already stated,

THEORY AND PRACTICE — Grotius and the Rule of Law

Why do wars have rules? It is an interesting question and one that is often raised during arguments over military behavior. During the first decade of the Thirty Years' War, the scholar Hugo Grotius began to formulate ideas that laws and rules can be developed and agreed upon by combating militaries. In his most famous work, *The Law of War and Peace* (1625), Grotius argued that since war seems to be a natural part of the human experience, it follows that some wars are considered legal and others illegal. Grotius also suggested that just as humanity has defined certain acceptable practices in domestic life, so too must humanity define what is considered acceptable in foreign warfare. Therefore, wartime like peacetime can and must be regulated.

Grotius's masterpiece is divided into three parts. The first part is designed to provide the reader with an understanding of the historical foundations of what is called *just war*; or, the reasons that make war acceptable in certain circumstances. These circumstances are laid out in greater detail in the second part of the book. Grotius concluded that there are three reasons that make war acceptable: self-defense, reparation of injury, and punishment.[10] Essentially, if combatants have been attacked (or are being attacked), have been damaged following an attack, or have been wronged by any means that have hurt the ability of the ruler to rule, it is legally entitled to go to war.

Lastly, and most importantly for this discussion, is Grotius's last section, which deals with behavior on the battlefield. Essentially Grotius makes arguments for what is acceptable conduct during just wars. One of the most striking features of the third part is his constant use of the word, "moderation," which in fact is the word used to title Chapters 11 to 16. While Grotius does allow for a wide array of behavior during times of war, he strongly condemns those acts conducted by members of the military that deliberately harm private citizens and private property. In essence, if military behavior is not behaving in a manner consistent with winning the war and has resorted to humiliation or unreasonable destruction, it is breaking international law and is therefore outlawed.

> **Should there be rules of warfare?**
>
> **If so, who is entitled to decide on these rules of engagement? If not, what will happen to those who refuse to "play by the rules"?**

TABLE 12.2. Balance of Power in Practice

Eighteenth Century: Balance of Power	Reactionary Model	Lack of international agreements and institutions. The five great powers come together only after a state has upset the balance.
Nineteenth Century: Balance of Power	Preemptive Model	Congress of Vienna was formed to prevent the collapse of the great powers system.

the eighteenth-century's understanding of the balance of power was *reactionary* rather than *preventative*. The great powers understood the consequences and the distinct possibility that one state could upset the balance and conquer the continent. Unfortunately, they had not created any international institutions or agreements capable of preventing such an occurrence. So when it finally happened, most of Western Europe was not ready to handle the military and political will of Napoleon Bonaparte, the man who would forever change the landscape of Europe and the European concept of the balance of power. (See Table 12.2, Balance of Power in Practice, to see how the international system changed in the eighteenth and nineteenth centuries.)

NINETEENTH CENTURY AND THE CONCERT OF EUROPE: PREEMPTIVE BALANCE OF POWER

Napoleon's dominance of and reorganization of the continent taught the leaders of Europe's most powerful states a valuable lesson about the balance of power, one that they codified and put into practice. The leaders of the Quadruple Alliance (Britain, Prussia, Russia, and Austria), who had defeated the French army and had driven Napoleon into exile, were determined to create a new type of international arrangement, one that was above all else, capable of preventing continentalwide warfare.

In 1814, the leaders of the Quadruple Alliance signed the Treaty of Chaumont, which brought the Napoleonic Wars to an end. During the final discussions, the leaders determined that they would reconvene the following spring in Vienna, Austria, for an international conference whose sole purpose was the maintenance of security and stability in Europe. The Congress of Vienna (1815), as it came to be known, was the first of its kind, an international conference whose sole purpose was preventative and not solely responsive. This is what it made it so extraordinary for its day.

Up until the Congress of Vienna, conferences were held and treaties were signed with the sole intent of deciding on appropriate reparations and land redistribution. Conferences had traditionally consisted of the *winners* making demands and the *losers*

FIGURE 12.2. The Five Great Powers of Europe

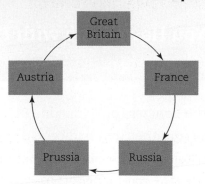

It was believed that as long as the five major powers remained in place and the balance was maintained, peace was assured.

having to agree to them.[11] The Congress of Vienna was something revolutionary because it was not designed to end a war: It was designed to create a future peace. The individuals who met in Austria in the fall of 1814 and the spring of 1815 decided that the balance of power concept needed to be reworked, which meant that it needed to be configured in such a way to ensure that stability was never again disrupted.

So how did they accomplish this? Initially, the Quadruple Alliance was hesitant to include France in the discussions concerning the future of Europe. After all, it was Revolutionary France that led to the disruption of the balance of power and a decade of continental warfare. For many European leaders, the issue of France had to be remedied. Should the state that dominated and consolidated all of the European powers be allowed to participate in the creation of a lasting peace?

After several weeks of negotiations, it was decided that France would at some point in the future, regain its place as one of the five great powers. The Quadruple Alliance realized that France was too powerful to be left out of an international conference whose priority was the establishment of peace. Although it still took several years (1818) for France to be formally included in periodic international conferences, the visionaries that met in Vienna understood that only animosity would emerge within French society and the new French government if French interests were not formally recognized.[12]

Additionally, the powers realized that they had to create a system that proactively maintained stability, so they "stipulated that the great powers would hold periodic conferences of the foreign ministers, 'for the purpose of consulting upon their interests, or for the consideration of measures which shall be considered the most salutary for the purpose and prosperity of Nations and the maintenance of the Peace of Europe.'"[13] This pledge was the first of its kind in international relations. The ministers present at the Congress of Vienna had decided that it was in their collective best interest to actively promote stability by any means necessary. They viewed the system they had created as if it were a grand orchestration of power and politics, a *Concert of Europe*.

Concert of Europe: *The name given to the European balance of power system of the nineteenth century. While many scholars agree that the nineteenth century had several low-level wars (wars fought between some of the great powers), the system that was forged in Vienna proved strong enough to prevent war for almost 100 years.*

What Would You Have Done with France?

ISTOCKPHOTO.COM/ CARACTERDESIGN

If you were attending the Congress of Vienna in 1815 and had been representing one of the countries that had been devastated by France, how would you have treated the new French delegation? Would you have invited them to attend the Congress as an equal participant in the proceedings? Or would you have wanted to punish them to the point where they would no longer be an international threat to the peace and security of Europe? This is a very important set of questions because it allows us to see the great foresight of those diplomats who met in Vienna in 1815. The human impulse would be that of punishment, right? Here is France, the state that has consistently upset the balance of power and has conquered most of the continent. Why would you want to forgive their actions and let them back into the "great powers club"? You would want to cripple them permanently, right? Well, the delegates who met in 1815 gave a resounding no!

Although many of the attendees wanted to make sure that France paid back a number of its wartime costs, which they did, they also realized that a country as large and as powerful as France needed a seat at the table if the great powers were to design a strong international system of security. And that is exactly what happened. France was brought back into the great power system because the Quadruple Alliance realized that it would be dangerous to ignore and possibly isolate them.

This, of course, is the exact opposite of the manner in which Germany was treated after World War I. Instead of realizing that German isolation would make for a much more dangerous international situation in the future, the leaders who met following World War I decided to punish Germany. What was the outcome of such a decision? The rise of Adolf Hitler and the global catastrophe of World War II.

Do you think the balance of power
is an effective form of rule?

Or do you think that a policy of collective
security is more useful?

Which model was pursued after
(a) the Congress of Vienna and (b) World War I?

© ISTOCKPHOTO.COM/SABLAMEK

This proactive mentality provided the nineteenth century with both its greatest strength and weakness. The strength of a proactive balance of power is believed to be greater security. The leadership of Austria and Russia "tried to turn the Quadruple Alliance into an agency that would automatically intervene in the affairs of any country in which there was a revolution or an agitation against the status quo and suppress by force the revolutionary or democratic or liberal movements."[14] Several of the great powers argued that because the spirit of liberalism (i.e., those beliefs that called for greater protection of rights and freedoms)

CourseReader ASSIGNMENT

Log in to **www.cengagebrain.com** and open CourseReader to access the reading:

"The Concert of Europe: A Fresh Look at an International System," in World Politics, Vol. 28. No. 2 (Jan., 1976), pp. 159-174. **by Richard B. Elrod**

In this selection, you will see how the European state system emerged. It will allow you to understand that the nineteenth century witnessed a revolution in international affairs. It will also allow you to understand how the concept of a "balance of power" created a system that was able to maintain European peace and security for almost one hundred years. In a balance of power system, power is distributed among a number of "great" powers who are obligated to maintain the system. As long as the great powers are in agreement, the system is stable. When the powers are in disagreement, the entire system is vulnerable to war.

- *Why did the author feel that it was important to address the Concert of Europe for a modern audience?*
- *What can we learn from studying the nineteenth century?*

THEORY AND PRACTICE — The Balance of Power Updated?

© ISTOCKPHOTO.COM/ DIEGO CERVO

The nineteenth century in Europe is often described as the greatest example for the international relations theory known as the balance of power. Since the leaders of the five great powers in Europe (Britain, France, Prussia, Russia, and Austria) all realized that war was hurtful to the entire system, they decided to create a system that ensured their long-term survival.

A balance of power is reliant on all of its members to maintain the equilibrium. It was understood that if one state became too powerful or too weak, the system would collapse.

In today's world, one could argue that a new "balancing act" is underway, balanced on the strength of nuclear arms and economic development. While the Europeans of the eighteenth and nineteenth centuries understood that stability equaled success, so too do some of our era's largest and most powerful countries. Let's take China and the United States for example. We have arrived at a time where it is best that China

continued

continued

and the United States have become strong allies because it means success for each country's long-term growth and stability.

Right now, the American market consumes many goods created in China. Why? Because China's production costs are much cheaper than U.S. costs. American companies choose to have many of their manufacturing plants in Chinese cities (and elsewhere in Asia) because these locations create a much higher level of profit for them. China, however, is still considered a communist state that enforces wage controls on its workers. This means that workers get paid very low salaries, but the state itself makes great profits from the dealings with American companies. The result is that China has an incredible surplus. Basically if one were to do a basic accounting audit on China, one would see that its credits far exceed its debits. In short, it does not owe countries a lot of money, but a lot of countries owe China.

So why should the United States keep this relationship strong? Because economists will tell you that as China continues to industrialize and more and more Chinese workers move into its cities, they will demand wage increases and a better way of life. Why? Because history shows that this is what happens when countries develop: the citizens want more rights, more freedom, and more safeguards about keeping the money they have earned. Once this happens, China will need to open its borders for more trade in order to attract better businesses to invest there. This is when the United States can step in. While the United States has long given up on its manufacturing sector, it is always looking for new markets to sell its products, and a billion people in China will make a good market.

The same could be said for a number of countries around the world. The European Union, Brazil, India, China, Russia, and the United States are all members of a global market that need each other's support for their individual stability. They make up the largest economies and therefore have the most to lose, not much different than their predecessors in the nineteenth century.

If you were an advisor to President Obama, how would you advise him on China?

Do you think it is in the long-term interest of the United States to maintain a strong alliance with China?

had perpetuated the French Revolution, it was an unacceptable feature of international politics. It was, therefore, continually suppressed for the first three decades after the Congress of Vienna.

It was this joint policy of suppression and military intrusion that gave the Vienna system its greatest weakness. In 1848, Europe was shaken by revolution. So much so, that the year 1848 is now commonly referred to as the Year of Revolutions. Revolutions took place in Sicily and France and then throughout most of Europe. Although they were easily suppressed, it was a wake-up call for the great powers. The design of those that had met in Vienna in 1815 had changed. The Vienna system was still intact and the great powers still maintained a belief in the balance of power, but by the middle of the nineteenth century new states were emerging and a new system was developing.

BISMARCK: THE RISE OF GERMANY, AND THE END OF THE CONCERT OF EUROPE

In 1854, Russia and Britain (supported by France and Piedmont) fought in the Crimean War, the first major war fought in Europe since the Congress of Vienna. Although it was only a limited conflict fought among several of the great powers (Britain aided by France and Piedmont versus Russia), it was significant because it proved that war was neither impossible nor worrisome as long as it was limited in scope, in this case, fought between two or three rivals who possessed limited ambitions.[15] Unfortunately, limited wars made the idea of war become somewhat acceptable. In fact, 15 wars were fought between 1854 and 1870, a sign that limited wars were becoming the norm rather than the aberration.[16]

Of all the wars fought between 1854 and 1870, the last one, the Franco-Prussian War, caused the greatest impact in international politics. The Franco-Prussian War resulted in (1) the creation of a united Germany, (2) the French loss of Alsace-Lorraine (a resource-rich territory) to Germany, (3) a new person in charge of German foreign policy (Otto von Bismarck), and (4) a balance of power system quickly being defined by limited warfare on a continent running out of buffer zones and open territory.[17] Most experts consider these events as some of the most pivotal events of the nineteenth century. With the creation of Germany came the end of the open lands that had separated France from Prussia and Prussia from Austria. This continental buffer zone that had been an integral part of the original design of those at the Congress of Vienna had been swept away.

According to author Paul Kennedy there were two main factors that contributed to Germany's impact on the international balance of power system: location and industrial/commercial/military growth. He writes:

Germany had arisen right in the center of the old European states system; *its very creation had directly impinged upon the interests of Austria-Hungary and France, and its existence had altered the relative position of all of the existing great powers of Europe. The second factor was the sheer speed and extent of Germany's further growth, in industrial, commercial, and military/naval terms.*[18]

THE EUROPEAN EQUILIBRIST

▲ Bismarck needed to keep Germany at the center of European affairs, so he took it upon himself to "juggle" the foreign policies of all the states.

Realpolitik: *The use of practical methods, instead of moral or ideological means, to secure political power. For example, one who engages in realpolitik would assess entry into a war as a calculation of power for one's own country regardless of morality.*

These two features created a great deal of hostility toward the newly unified state. In fact, it was this hostility that caused the German chancellor, Otto von Bismarck, to take action into his own hands.

Bismarck realized that Germany's rise was not welcomed by its neighbors. Yet he also realized that Germany's fate was tied to that of the Concert of Europe. So in order to maintain the balance and to secure German prosperity, Bismarck designed a system of alliances and treaties that placed Germany at the center of European affairs. In doing so, Bismarck changed the concept of the balance of power from one based on the concept of the *raison d'état* to one based on **realpolitik**, a German word that sought to explain international affairs in terms of power and force.

In 1879, Germany signed a secret treaty with Austria-Hungary with the intent of assuring Austrian support in the event of a Russian attack. In doing so, Bismarck created an alliance with Austria-Hungary that protected German interests, gained it one strong ally, and further isolated Russia from European politics. Russia became so concerned by the terms of the treaty, it asked for Germany to reconsider a reformulation of the historic Three Emperors' League (Prussia, Austria, Russia) to make sure that it was not isolated from European affairs.[19] "And that success brought the Italians . . . to Berlin, asking for protection against French attacks on their interests in North Africa—to which Bismarck agreed on condition that the Italians also make a treaty of accommodation with Austria (1882)."[20] As the great powers expanded their colonial reach, Germany had expanded its continental influence to the degree where it was either directly or indirectly allied with every European state, with of course the exception of its most hostile neighbor, France. By the time of Bismarck's dismissal in 1890, France was almost completely isolated by the other powers.

Although Bismarck's policy of alliances via secret treaties was effective in bringing a great amount of order to post–Crimean War Europe and increasing the economic and military dominance of Germany, it had serious consequences. The

How Well Do You Understand Foreign Policy?

As we learned in Chapters 8 and 9, a large part of today's world is considered democratic. Many states hold elections, have representative political parties, and to a degree, a legal system based on the concept of rights. In previous eras, however, this was not the case. Heads of state and diplomats (those who perform foreign policy making) regarded their people as unable to fully understand the nuances of foreign policy. This fact led Metternich (Austria's delegate at the Congress of Vienna in 1815) to assert that foreign policy is not for the "plebs" (or common people) and Bismarck to assert that it is best that people "don't know how laws (like sausages) are made." Their understanding was based on the idea that foreign policy requires quick action of well-informed individuals who know how the system works.

We, however, live in a different era–one that is characterized by public opinion polls and instantaneous media reports. In the United States, public opinion has swayed involvement in wars and attitudes toward returning soldiers. But is the public well informed on foreign affairs? Do you think that your opinion on issues related to national security or diplomacy are as well informed as they need to be? So now what do you think of Metternich and Bismarck?

Before you write them off, think about how well informed you are about foreign policy. Democracies in the twenty-first century will struggle with foreign policy because democracies function in fundamentally different ways than authoritarian states. Democracies (in theory) are based on the will of the people. Those who get elected need the people's votes. Yet, what if the people do not understand all of the issues facing the international community?

Is there any merit to the views of Metternich and Bismarck? Or should they just be regarded as voices from a previous era?

Can wars be conducted according to democratic principles if not all of the combatants are democratic? Better yet, should they?

original design of the Concert of Europe that was constructed by those in Vienna in 1815 was based on preventing continentalwide war through the dual techniques of diplomacy and limited warfare. Bismarck's model was based on realpolitik and secrecy. Realpolitik tends to produce states that join alliances out of fear rather than cooperation because it assumed that states naturally operate according to their *own* interests rather than that of the system.

In the years leading up to the outbreak of World War I, the European system had degenerated into one of militarism and economic tension. As Great Britain, France, and Russia (now openly hostile to Germany because of an economic embargo levied against them) entered into formal alliances (Entente Cordial between France and Great Britain in 1904 and the Anglo-Russian Agreement of 1907), Europe slowly divided into two camps: those friendly to Germany and those unfriendly to Germany. So when the Archduke Franz Ferdinand was assassinated on June 28, 1914, in Sarajevo (still part of the Austrian empire), the alliance system collapsed and Europe became engulfed in World War I. Kennedy has written:

Austria-Hungary's demands upon Serbia, its rejection of the conciliatory Serbian reply, and its attack upon Belgrade led to the Russian mobilization in aid of its Serbian ally. *But that, in turn, led the German General Staff to press for the immediate implementation of the Schlieffen Plan, that is, its preemptive westward strike, via Belgium, against France—which had the further effect of bringing in the British.*[21]

By 1914, the seeds of war had been sown and the rigidity of the post-Bismarckean order had collapsed. When the "war to end all wars" finally ended in 1918, the international system had changed. The world witnessed the simultaneous destruction of the Concert of Europe and the ascent of the United States. Although it would take another world war to witness the emergence of the United States as a *superpower*, American involvement in World War I gave it a seat at the victors' table.

COLLECTIVE SECURITY: THE LEAGUE OF NATIONS AND THE OUTBREAK OF WORLD WAR II

In 1919, the American president Woodrow Wilson entered the Paris Peace Conference with the goal of creating a lasting peace through the realization of the principles of democracy and national self-determination: the belief that independent nations should have the right to govern themselves. What Wilson encountered was a hostile European audience unwilling to take the advice of the American president. Wilson's Fourteen Points representing the notion eventually termed *collective security* was poorly received by Europeans who still regarded the "balance of power" as the most appropriate design for maintaining stable international relations. (See Table 12.3 and what political scientist Karen A. Mingst has determined as the five assumptions of collective security). In a famous quote reflecting this hostility, the French representative Georges Clemenceau commented that while "God gave us the Ten Commandments . . . Mr. Wilson has given us the Fourteen Points." It was as if the European community had decided that certain states had more experience in issues of diplomacy than others and that these "older" states possessed the only voices that mattered. Therefore, the League of Nations which operated under the notion of collective security (that an attack against one member

▲ United States President Woodrow Wilson was the major architect for the creation of the League of Nations.

was to be perceived as an attack against all) was never given an appropriate chance to carry out Wilson's dream. In many ways it was what Lenin described as "still-born from the very first."

It is worth noting though, that Europeans were not the only group concerned with an international institution that mandated equal membership regardless of economic, military, or political might. The American Congress did not like Wilson's vision either. In fact, following the 1919 Congressional elections, the newly Republican-dominated Senate refused the United States' entrance into the League of Nations, claiming that the United States should return to its pre-war ideology of isolationism.

Nevertheless, the individuals who eventually signed the Treaty of Versailles made it clear that Germany would pay dearly for World War I. In fact, the new German government (known as the Weimar Republic) was forced to sign the treaty and claim full responsibility for all losses incurred during the war. This act made it clear that the signatories to the Treaty of Versailles lacked the foresight of their predecessors. We must remember

TABLE 12.3. Karen A. Mingst's Assumptions of Collective Security[22]

1. Wars are caused by aggressive states.
2. Aggressors must be stopped.
3. Aggressors are easily identified.
4. Aggressors are always wrong.
5. Aggressors know the international community will act against them.

that the statesmen who met in Vienna in 1815 faced a similar dilemma. However, unlike their diplomatic heirs, the Vienna statesmen realized that their era's aggressor state, France, was too influential in the international system to be denied an active role in future designs. The leaders who met in Paris 104 years later lacked this particular insight and blamed the new German government for the sins of the previous one.

This mistake has often been cited as one of the major reasons for the revival of German power in the 1930s. However, it is only one part of the flawed response. The other, more critical international error was the poorly designed League of Nations itself. Formally erected in 1919 as part of the Treaty of Versailles, the League of Nations attempted to achieve stability through a policy of collective security. Unfortunately the League's policy of collective security placed an equal share of responsibility and an assumption of power upon all members. For example, each member state possessed an equal vote regardless of its economic or military capabilities. Many felt that this feature created a structure of inadequacy because powerful states could easily be vetoed by weaker ones.

▲ Signers of the Treaty of Versailles

© TRINITY MIRROR / MIRRORPIX / ALAMY

In addition, the League of Nations lacked the support of some of the world's most powerful states. With the absence of both the United States and the Soviet Union (formerly Russia), the League of Nations lacked political credibility. How could an international institution intended to curb warfare do so without the inclusion of its two most powerful states? The answer, of course, is it couldn't. Within two decades of its creation, the political climate of global affairs proved to be too severe for the League. When Nazi Germany invaded Poland on September 1, 1939, and the Japanese attacked the American military base at Pearl Harbor on December 7, 1941, the world witnessed the start of another war of epic proportions and the beginning of a new understanding of international affairs whose outcomes would change the very definition of power itself.

CORRECTING THE LEAGUE AND CONFRONTING A NEW WORLD: THE UNITED NATIONS AND THE END OF WORLD WAR II

In 1945, the world witnessed the emergence of a new understanding of international relations. The international community observed the emergence of two competing superpowers (United States and Soviet Union), two economic ideologies (capitalism and communism), and a multitude of weapons capable of mass destruction. The world that was shaken by World War I was destroyed by World War II. The post–World War I era, defined by its denial of the balance of power and its nonbinding trust in collective security was shattered by World War II. Where World War I ended through exhaustion, World War II ended with mass destruction. The Nazi Holocaust created an environment where the notion of human rights became front and center and the atomic bombings of Hiroshima and Nagasaki reminded the global community that it had entered a new era of unthinkable destruction.

Since its creation on October 24, 1945, the United Nations (UN) has been based on a balancing act. Its configuration is based on a practical assessment of both power politics and representative democracy. Where the League of Nations failed to properly represent the military and economic differences of the world's states, the United Nations was designed to allot power more appropriately. For instance, among the six organs of the United Nations, the UN Security Council sits as a testament to power politics. Composed of five permanent members (the United States, France, Russia, China, and the United Kingdom) and 10 nonpermanent members (whose membership is based on a rotating system of two-year terms, consistent with geographic representation), the Security Council is charged with maintaining international peace and security by the acknowledgment in 1945 that its membership was based on *real* power.

Following World War II the architects of the UN determined that the United States, France, Russia, China, and the United Kingdom were the world's most powerful states. They were therefore given a special status within the overall structure. These permanent five (P5) are the only states with veto power. Although the decisions made by the entire Security Council need to be approved by only 9 out of the 15 members, the permanent members need to provide *unanimous* support for any military action or economic sanction. (See Table 12.4 for the current membership of the United Nations Security Council)

In addition to the Security Council, the United Nations is composed of: the General Assembly (made up of all 192 UN members, designed to provide even the smallest states with a forum for discussion); the Trusteeship Council (made up of the

TABLE 12.4. Current Membership of the UN Security Council

United States *	United Kingdom*	France*	China*	Russia*
Bosnia and Herzegovina (2011)	Gabon (2011)	Lebanon (2011)	Nigeria (2011)	Germany (2012)
Portugal (2012)	India (2012)	South Africa (2012)	Brazil (2012)	Colombia (2012)

Indicates a permanent member of the Security Council.

P5, the Trusteeship Council is to provide guidance to those states who were placed under protection by the UN and are attempting to gain recognition); the Secretariat (headed by the Secretary General, the Secretariat provides much of the administrative and research duties of the United Nations); the Economic and Social Council or ECOSOC (provides research and coordination on a number of issues related to economic development, health, climate change, etc. as well as coordination between **nongovernmental organizations (NGOs)** and specialized agencies like the United Nations Children's Fund and the World Health Organization); and the International Court of Justice (consisting of 15 judges elected by both the General Assembly and Security Council who serve in order to decide disputes between states). Overlooking the East River in Midtown Manhattan on grounds donated by the Rockefeller Family, the UN was designed to promote peace and combat oppression.

Unfortunately, much of the hope and assumed power of the UN was dashed as international relations became dominated by the Cold War system. As the United States and the Soviet Union began to dictate influence around the world, scholars began to question the relevancy of the UN as an agent capable of providing security and preventing war. Because the UN was founded to protect both the sovereignty of states and individual human rights, it sometimes has been unable to prevent warfare and preserve peace. For example, in order for **peacekeepers** to be deployed into a particular region, the permanent members of the Security Council need unanimous support. Although any of the permanent members are allowed to abstain, (decline to vote), agreements to use force have proven difficult. If any of you have seen the movie *Hotel Rwanda* or have read the headlines about the current situation in the Darfur region of the African country of Sudan, you will be able to understand that sometimes the UN is unable to stop mass tragedies. Is this due to its structure? Or is it something else?

These questions have made the relevancy of the UN a constant topic of debate in the international community. Although it must be made clear that the international system has greatly benefitted from the various UN agencies related to the eradication of poverty, education, and women's health and safety in the developing world, it has also proved somewhat ineffective when it comes to stopping large-scale ethnic cleansings and genocides. Perhaps a change in the structure of the institutions of the UN would give it greater strength to promote greater change in the world.

Nongovernmental organizations (NGOs): *Organizations that act independently of states who usually have a particular focus or interest. For example, the organization Doctors Without Borders can be considered an NGO committed to the prevention and treatment of disease in various parts of the world. They are privately funded and provide relief to many people who lack basic health care.*

Peacekeepers: *A group of troops sent as part of a UN mission to maintain a peace agreement in an area that appears troubled.*

FIGURE 12.3 The United Nations System

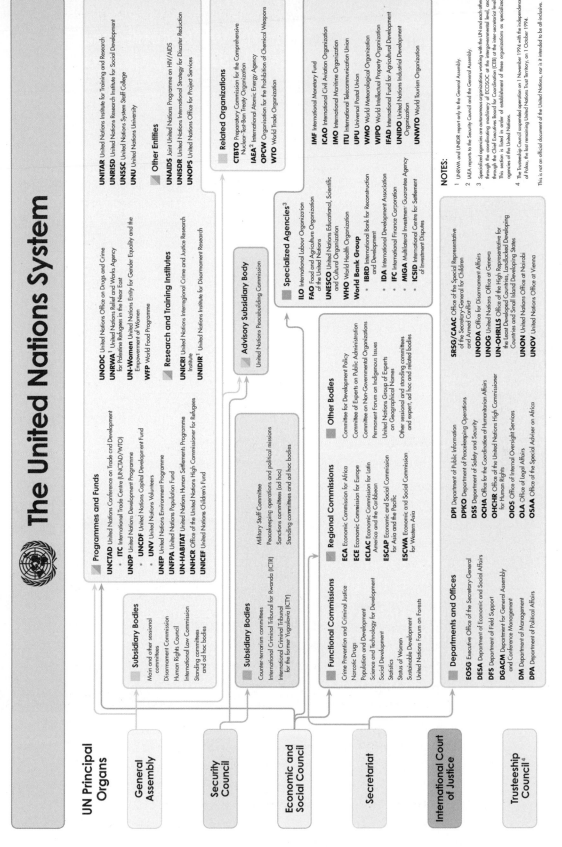

The United Nations System

Should We Reconfigure the UN Security Council?

At the end of World War II, it was decided that there must be a component of the United Nations that is given more authority to provide security on the basis that not all countries are all equal in terms of power. Therefore, it was decided that there must be a Security Council made up of five permanent members, and 10 countries that rotate on a three-year basis based on regional representation. The five permanent members were China, Soviet Union (Russia today), United States, the United Kingdom, and France. Why? Because they had the largest militaries and therefore had the "right" to act as the protectors of international security.

Over the last decade, however, the world has witnessed the emergence of Brazil and India as global leaders. Although their societies are still considered to have high levels of poverty and income inequality when compared to most states in Western Europe and North America, they are quickly developing strong middle classes and strong international financial connections. Should they have a seat at the Security Council? If both Brazil and India are regionally important and globally powerful, then why not give them seats on the Security Council.

> Should the UN Security Council be reconfigured?
>
> Have there been changes in the power relations of the international system?
>
> Currently the United Kingdom and France still reside as permanent members of the Security Council. Are they still two of the most powerful states on earth?
>
> If not, then do they still belong on the Security Council?

SUMMARY

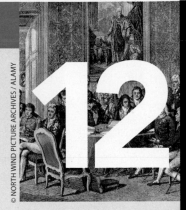

Before reading this chapter you may never have considered the ways in which international relations have evolved over time. In many ways it is not an exaggeration to suggest that we are still living by certain principles that were established almost 400 years ago. Principles such as sovereignty, territorial integrity, *raison d'état,* balance of power, and collective security are still at the heart of many debates related to intervention and security.

Although the world of the twenty-first century (which we will get to in Chapter 13) is in many ways more complex than in previous centuries, it is still linked to many of the institutions and practices of the past. Governments, heads of state, diplomats, militaries, and a host of other public officials continue to dictate foreign policy. Debates over the conduct of state behavior continue to reflect arguments of previous eras, while power as a source of conflict continues to be the dominant goal of those in the international community.

KEY TERMS

Concert of Europe p. 371

Empire p. 363

Nongovernmental organizations (NGOs) p. 382

Peacekeepers p. 382

Raison d'état p. 363

Realpolitik p. 376

Secularism p. 363

Sovereignty p. 363

State p. 363

Territorial Integrity p. 363

Thirty Years' War p. 362

KEY PEOPLE

Otto von Bismarck p. 375

Napoleon Bonaparte p. 370

Ferdinand II p. 365

Hugo Grotius p. 368

Klemens von Metternich p. 377

Cardinal Richelieu p. 363

Woodrow Wilson p. 378

13

THE COLD WAR AND BEYOND: THE RISE OF THE UNITED STATES AND THE EMERGING GLOBAL ORDER

▲ A McDonald's restaurant in Bangalore, India, highlights some of the penetrating forces of the globalized economy.

INTRODUCTION: CONTEMPORARY INTERNATIONAL RELATIONS

This chapter will attempt to explain contemporary international relations, specifically the course of international relations from the beginning of the Cold War to today's post-9/11 world. Therefore this chapter will discuss how international politics shifted from one of bipolarity (a system defined by the presence of two superpowers), to a system marked by a number of competing nonstate and state actors (the present state of world politics). If the Cold War was best defined by nuclear arms, international stability, competing economic ideologies (capitalism and communism), and proxy states (states supported either by the Soviet Union or the United States), the present era is best defined by states and nonstate actors, international instability, and globalization articulated by the presence of unprecedented information communication technology (ICT), neoliberalism, nuclear proliferation, and terrorism.

Because this chapter examines both the Cold War system and that of the contemporary era of international relations, it is important to clarify some of the themes before moving on. First, the discussion of the Cold War examines the major concepts of the era, namely containment and deterrence and the ways in which the system produced what John Lewis Gaddis has referred to as the "Long Peace."[1] It will also look at the ways in which different American foreign policies (Marshall Plan and Truman Doctrine) were employed to maintain American dominance in the world.

Following the brief section that covers the collapse of the Soviet Union, our attention will shift to the current era of international politics by looking at the concept of globalization and the ways that new actors, ideologies, and economic and political forces have challenged the state's ability to govern. It will primarily focus on the ways that multinational corporations (MNCs), transnational terrorist organizations, and nongovernmental organizations (NGOs) have changed the way politics is conducted.

Questions to Consider Before Reading this Chapter

1. What is deterrence? What is containment? How did they define American foreign policy during the Cold War?

2. What best defines the processes known collectively as globalization?

3. How have multinational corporations impeded state sovereignty?

4. What are the differences between domestic, state, international, and transnational terrorism?

5. What are the differences of opinion between Friedman and Zakaria, and Stiglitz? Are the processes of globalization good or bad? Why?

NUCLEAR SECURITY AND COLD WAR POLITICS: CONTAINMENT AND DETERRENCE

The atomic bombings of Hiroshima and Nagasaki forever changed international affairs. Within three days in August of 1945, the United States demonstrated its ability to exert global authority. By 1949, the Soviet Union also possessed this capability. The era which came to be known as the Cold War was defined by this "nuclear tension" and, in fact, created two new understandings about power politics: nuclear deterrence and containment. To best understand these policies, it is best to view them within the time frame of 1945–1991.

Deterrence: *To deter literally means to stop someone from doing something by frightening him or her; dissuasion by deterrence operates by frightening a state out of attacking, not because of launching an attack and carrying it home, but because the expected reaction of the opponent will result in one's own severe punishment.* [27]

Deterrence

Deterrence has always been a strategy of international relations based on the ability of one state to successfully threaten another state from initiating a certain act. As Art and Waltz have suggested,

To deter literally means to stop someone from doing something by frightening him . . . dissuasion by deterrence operates by frightening a state out of attacking, *not because of launching an attack and carrying it home, but because the expected reaction of the opponent will result in one's own severe punishment.* [2]

States are less likely to engage in aggressive behavior if they fear that the reprisal to such behavior would weaken their international position. During the Cold War, however, the gravity of deterrence changed. States were not simply worried about the traditional consequences of their behavior, such as economic sanctions, military invasion, and the like, they were worried about the consequences of nuclear war.

Nuclear deterrence as employed by the superpowers, therefore, created a new understanding of the concept. The best way of understanding nuclear deterrence is to put it within a hypothetical context. As David Krieger explains:

Country A tells country B that if B does X, A will attack it with nuclear weapons. *The theory is that country B will be deterred from doing X by fear of nuclear attack by country A. For deterrence to work, the leaders of country B must also believe that country A has nuclear weapons and will use them. Nuclear deterrence theory holds that even if country A might not have nuclear weapons, so long as the leaders of country B believed that it did they would be deterred.*

The theory goes on to hold that country A can generally rely upon nuclear deterrence with any country except one that also has nuclear weapons or one that is protected by another country with nuclear weapons. *If country B also has nuclear weapons and the leaders of country A know this, then A, according to the theory, will be deterred from a nuclear attack on country B. This situation will result in a standoff. The same is true if country C does not have nuclear weapons, but is under the "umbrella" of country B that does have nuclear weapons. Country A will not retaliate against country C for fear of itself being retaliated against by country B.[3]*

It is within this context that the Cold War is best explained. Both the United States and the Soviet Union stockpiled nuclear weapons in an attempt to stop the other from pursuing aggressive policies outside of each other's spheres of influence.

Containment

From the end of World War II until the end of the 1980s, both *superpowers* carved up much the world into two competing spheres of influence based on each side's economic and political ideologies. The United States, through the **Marshall Plan** and the **North Atlantic Treaty Organization (NATO)** provided protection over its fellow capitalist democracies in Western Europe and Japan while at the same time, the Soviet Union attempted to maintain and spread its communist ideology throughout Eastern Europe through the creation of the **Warsaw Pact**. Realizing that each other had gained unprecedented levels of military and economic strength, the United States and the Soviet Union pursued an antagonistic policy of propping up or destroying pro-American or pro-Soviet regimes around the world.

With the establishment of the Truman Doctrine (1947), the United States pursued a policy that came to be known as **containment**. Based on the arguments of George Kennan, containment policy was designed to stop both the threat of the Soviet Union as an imperial power and communism as an ideology.[4] According to Kennan, "The main element of any United States policy toward the Soviet Union must be that of a long-term, patient but firm and vigilant containment of Russian expansive tendencies."[5] To that end, he called for countering "Soviet pressure against the free institutions of the Western world" through the "adroit and vigilant application of counter-force at a series of constantly shifting geographical and political points, corresponding to the shifts and maneuvers of Soviet policy." Such a policy, Kennan predicted, would "promote tendencies which must eventually find their outlet in either the break-up or the gradual mellowing of Soviet power.[6]

Although the Truman Doctrine was specifically tailored to protect democratic interests in Greece, its overall target knew no boundaries. The Truman Doctrine was designed to allow subsequent American administrations the ability to get involved outside the traditional boundaries of American foreign policy, in other words, beyond the Western Hemisphere.

By the 1950s, communism had become a separate threat, one not necessarily associated with the Soviet Union. In the eyes of American policymakers, the ideology of communism had degenerated into a cancer that was able to infect an entire region. The **domino theory** as it came to be known was based on the threat that if one state was to fall to communism, surrounding states would fall as well.

When China became a communist state in 1949, the United States realized that communism had become volatile in Southeast Asia. Containment policy

Marshall Plan: *The Marshall Plan (named after U.S. Secretary of State George Marshall) provided financial support to Europe following World War II. The United States realized that in order for it to maintain its dominance in areas of trade, it needed strong, reliable European trading partners.*

North Atlantic Treaty Organization (NATO): *The North Atlantic Treaty Organization was established in 1949 and was designed primarily as a military organization among American and European powers. Its original purpose was to prevent Soviet aggression in Western Europe.*

Warsaw Pact: *During the Cold War, the collection of Eastern European states that were controlled by and part of the Soviet Union.*

Containment: *A strategy used in the Cold War designed to stop the spread of Soviet power and communism.*

Domino theory: *The Cold War theory that argued that as soon as one country became communist, the surrounding states would as well.*

THEORY AND PRACTICE

Containment and Deterrence Today?

Are the principles of containment and deterrence still useful today? Or are they tied to a specific time and place, namely the Cold War? For example, is the current U.S. foreign policy designed to contain what it perceives as terrorism? What about its policies toward an emerging Iranian or North Korean nuclear program?

What appeared to make containment and deterrence so successful during the Cold War was the fact that the United States was able to stop the spread of communism by force (Korean and Vietnam wars) and by the *threat* of force, that is, the policy known as mutually assured destruction (MAD). The United States had always ascribed a rational sense of logic to the leadership of the Soviet Union. American foreign policymakers assumed that the Soviet leadership (even as radical as it was portrayed in the press) was unwilling to resort to the employment of nuclear arms because it would mean an end to its own political power. This is generally what we mean by the term *mutually assured destruction*. Country A is unlikely to launch a first strike, because in doing so, it would destroy itself when Country B retaliates.

In today's world, a number of states that either have nuclear arms or the capabilities of acquiring them might behave differently. We have already examined North Korea and its megalomaniacal leader, Kim Jong Il. Will Kim protect his people's interest the way the Soviet's protected theirs? This is one of the great policy questions facing the United States and the rest of the world today.

> **Will the leaders of Iran and North Korea operate as rational actors have in the past?**
>
> **Is it rational to assume that all states operate according to the accepted principles of mutually assured destruction?**

became the major driving force behind the *proxy wars* (wars fought by the superpowers in third party states) in Korea (1950–1953) and Vietnam (1961–1975). Although nuclear deterrence remained as the overarching strategy that caused Gaddis to define the Cold War as the "Long Peace," containment policy was the method employed by the United States to actively stop the spread of communism around the world.[7]

THE LAST DAYS OF COMMUNISM AND THE SOVIET UNION

By the 1980s, the Soviet Union had begun to unravel. Its centrally planned economy, totalitarian social policies, and military problems in Afghanistan (a country it invaded in 1979 to secure access to Middle Eastern oil) had caused its leader, Mikhail Gorbachev, to seek alternatives. Although Gorbachev (and many international observers) initiated the dual policies of **glasnost** and **perestroika** as a way of reviving the socialist system, they proved to be ineffective. Years of political apathy, corruption, national stirrings from those under their control in places like Poland, mixed with an international arms race had caused the Soviet Union to economically and politically implode.

In 1989, when the Berlin Wall fell and Germany had gained reunification, the world began to understand how severely damaged the Soviet Union was. The communist mega-state that was brought to power during the last days of World War I was in a downward spiral. By the end of 1991, the Soviet Union was over and the world was faced with a new international system, one that scholars are still trying to define today.

Glasnost: *Referred to Gorbachev's policy of "openness" in government. It was introduced as a way of shedding light on some of the corruption of the Soviet Union during the 1980s.*

Perestroika: *Another Russian term that means "restructuring." Here it refers to Gorbachev's policy of restructuring the Soviet economy in a way that produced more growth and less government control.*

POST-COLD WAR INSTABILITY: GLOBALIZATION AND THE RISE OF THE NONSTATE ACTOR

On December 25, 1991, the Soviet Union formally dissolved, ending nearly 70 years as a global superpower. Although many of you might not realize the significance of this event, it can easily be considered one of the most important episodes in modern international relations. When trying to imagine the strength of the Soviet Union consider the following: during its time as one of the world's two superpowers, the Soviet Union amassed an empire that stretched from the middle of Europe to the Sea of Japan, possessed nuclear arms, covered 11 time zones, and (by 1991) directly controlled the lives of approximately 293 million people. Its collapse not only shook the political world (by bringing to an end what had become a stable, bipolar Cold

War system), but also changed the way scholars understood some of the most basic terms in international relations.

As we saw in Chapter 12, international relations had been defined by a set of "rules" since the middle of the seventeenth century. With the collapse of the Soviet Union, certain scholars claimed that "the *Westphalian era* seemed to be transitioning into . . . a post-international world," a world whose decision makers are both states and *nonstate actors*.[8] They claimed that the world's most important and legitimate actor, "the state" was in jeopardy of losing its ability to provide a semblance of security in global politics. Although these scholars admitted that the world had been moving away from traditional politics for a number of years, the collapse of the Soviet Union (because of its size, strength, and stabilizing ability during the Cold War) accelerated the process.

By 2001 (and in particular September 11th of that year), scholars had begun to examine international relations according to a new two-tiered approach known as *pluralist-interdependence theory*. **Pluralist-interdependence theorists** argue that the traditional concepts of sovereignty and territorial integrity are no longer capable of explaining the how the world works. Instead, they contend that **nonstate actors** (private corporations, private organizations, or private people), which have traditionally been ignored, have become powerful enough to formulate and carry out policies that have led to a more interconnected world. As a result of this change, they have also developed a term for this new era: globalization.

Globalization, which today has been applied to everything from the penetration of advanced information communication technology to the presence of McDonald's restaurants in Riyadh, Saudi Arabia, was originally coined as a way of trying to explain the causes of new forms of international phenomena. It was designed to bring some sense of order (at least terminologically) to a world that had become increasingly "turbulent."[9] Because globalization has become the buzzword of contemporary international relations, we will use it to examine some of the changes to the international system.

Understanding Globalization

Since the end of the Cold War, scholars have had to find a new way of explaining international politics. For many of them, globalization was that comprehensive term that sought to give scholars a grasp on the changing nature of international affairs. Definitions of globalization abounded over the past decade, but for our purposes it is best to think of it as a turbulent process that has seen new forms of communications, economic policies, and a general weakening of the traditional form of state sovereignty. Richard Haass of the Council on Foreign Relations has provided a great starting point for us. "At its core, globalization entails the increasing volume, velocity and importance of flows within and across borders of people, ideas, greenhouse gases, goods, dollars, drugs, viruses, emails, weapons, and a good deal else."[10] From this well-packed definition, we see that globalization has to do with three basic concepts.

Pluralist-Interdependence theory: *A theory that suggests that the long-standing concepts of sovereignty and territorial integrity are not capable enough of explaining international relations. It therefore argues that nonstate actors like terrorist organizations, nongovernmental organizations, and multinational corporations must be considered vital agents in explaining international affairs.*

Nonstate Actors: *Organizations, businesses, corporations, terrorist groups, and/or private individuals that influence international relations.*

Globalization: *The global process that has witnessed a rise in the free movement and interconnectedness of goods, services, information, and people at the expense of the nation-state.*

WHY POLITICS MATTERS TO YOU!

Globalization of Pop Culture

Have you ever thought about the impact of modern media and how it can affect how the world views American culture? Let's put it in simpler terms: Have you ever thought about how people outside of the United States receive their information about American culture? Not news sources but cultural icons like MTV, MTV2, E! Entertainment Television, Oprah . . . Can you imagine growing up in a restrictive, religious society and only viewing American culture through the lens of MTV? What would you think of American culture if all you saw were cast members of the *Jersey Shore* or a music icon like Lady Gaga? The following personal account might help explain what we mean.

When I was in graduate school, I had the wonderful opportunity of meeting a man visiting the United States from Ukraine. After class one evening, we began discussing American cultural practices and whether or not my girlfriend (now wife) had had a sweet sixteen party. I responded that she had, and it consisted of a little get together of about five of her best friends followed by a sleepover.

He was shocked. He began asking about her family's personal finances and if they had made enough money to survive. At that point, I stopped him, assured him that they were financially secure and asked him why he had thought otherwise. He replied with four simple words: MY SUPER SWEET SIXTEEN. Apparently, there was a show on MTV that chronicled the sweet sixteen celebrations of (extremely) privileged adolescents, called *My Super Sweet Sixteen*.

The show began with the invitation list (one that usually consisted of more than 100 people) and ended with the birthday boy or girl receiving an expensive car or sports utility vehicle. My Ukrainian friend had assumed that most Americans celebrate their sixteenth birthdays in a similar way. When I asked him how many American channels he received, he replied, "One, MTV."

What are the implications of globalization as it relates to the spread of values around the world?

Is there anything wrong with how American values are perceived around the world?

First, it appears that globalization has to do with the "free movement" of items from one place to another; some lawful others unlawful. Second, it appears that globalization has to do with speed. It isn't just that multinational corporations or terrorist groups have an easier time moving their money and people from one place to the next; it is also the fact that because of improvements in information technology and mass transportation they can do so much faster. Lastly, from the above definition, we see that globalization also has to do with the weakening of "state sovereignty" and the emergence of nontraditional sources of authority.

In an age of globalization, many scholars have argued that states, the most traditional authorities in the lexicon of international relations, are losing their ability to regulate the movement of goods, peoples, and services within their borders. As MNCs (e.g., Nike, Walmart, McDonald's, Starbucks,), NGOs (e.g., Greenpeace, Doctors Without Borders, Red Cross/Crescent, Amnesty International), global terrorist groups (e.g., al-Qaeda, Islamic Jihad), and a whole array of other private actors (including you and me) perform their tasks, states are having a difficult time regulating them. Why? In this post-9/11 world, many of these nontraditional actors have more appeal, more money, and fewer restrictions than governments.

For an interesting metaphor on the situation, look at how sociologist George Ritzer explains these processes. Ritzer describes globalization as the process that has seen a change from the "heavy" processes of the state to the "light" processes of the nonstate. His example of al-Qaeda reflects such a metaphor. When one thinks about al-Qaeda and the source of its strength, one always looks to its "light" bureaucracy and its "light" military. This "lightness" makes al-Qaeda very difficult to defeat. As Ritzer writes, "Unlike the armed forces of the United States, al-Qaeda is not a heavy bureaucratic structure, but rather a light "global microstructure. It is Al Qaeda's lightness that gives it many advantages over the extremely cumbersome US military, and the huge bureaucracy of which it is a part, and this helps account . . . for the latter's inability to suppress Al Qaeda or to catch bin Laden."[11] In an era of globalization, where speed is necessary for success, the agents that are "lighter" and can move from state to state with intense agility will be more successful than those that cannot. Currently, the state in many ways still operates the way it has for more than 350 years and is thus a very heavy, cumbersome agent. In the following section we will expand on some of these nonstate actors and exactly how they are limiting state sovereignty.

Neoliberalism and the Power of Multinational Corporations

Multinational Corporations (MNCs):
Companies that have the potential for global reach. In other words, they have the capacity (wealth, technology, personnel) to build, sell, and service products to and from any location in the world.

When the Soviet Union dissolved and with it its centrally planned economic structure, the world witnessed a rise in global markets, that is, places that are "open for business." As the number of markets opened, so too did the strength and wealth of **multinational corporations (MNCs)**. Simply put, MNCs are companies that have the potential for global reach. In other words, they have the capacity (wealth, technology, personnel) to build, sell, and service products to and from any location in the world. Although MNCs such as Nike, Walmart, Starbucks, McDonald's and countless others have been able to act in the international arena for decades, they now have a much greater ability to do so.

For example, if an MNC decides that the country that houses some of its largest factories (say Nike, which has some operations in Indonesia) is allowing its workers to have a minimum wage or the ability to form unions, then it can (and most likely will) quickly move its assets (and managers) out of the country. When you think about this process as it relates to traditional international politics, you will see that in certain parts of the world, these MNCs might actually have more "power" than the states that house them.

WHY POLITICS MATTERS TO **YOU!**

Where Did Your Sneakers Come From?

On March 8, 2002, the following article was printed in the British newspaper *The Independent UK*. Its author, Richard Lloyd Parry focused on the ways in which Nike and Adidas have used their economic power to create favorable financial conditions for themselves, yet unfavorable conditions for their workers in Indonesia. As you make your way through the article, think about your own work experience and some of the things you may take for granted.

Indonesian workers producing sports shoes for the multinational companies Nike and Adidas live in extreme poverty and face prosecution and physical assault for trade union activity, according to a report published yesterday.

Although conditions have improved over the last 18 months, workers are still subjected to verbal abuse, intrusive physical examinations and dangerous conditions.

Timothy Connor, author of the report, *We Are Not Machines*, published in Australia by *Oxfam Community Aid Abroad*, said: "Nike and Adidas have not done enough to address the concerns of human rights groups, consumers and workers themselves."

"Those improvements which have occurred are commendable, and demonstrate that positive change in response to international pressure is possible. Unfortunately they fall well short of ensuring that Nike and Adidas workers are able to live with dignity," he added.

Nike, the world's largest sports shoe company, has 11 Indonesian factories producing up to 55 million pairs of shoes a year. Only one pair in 50 is sold in Indonesia, the majority being exported to the United States.

The company is paying the golfer Tiger Woods $100m (£70m) for a five-year endorsement contract. But full-time workers at its factories are paid as little as $2 (£1.40)

continued

a day. Workers are thus forced to work long hours, and parents with children often have to send them away to be brought up by relatives in other parts of the country, and see them only three or four times a year.

At the Nikomas Gemilang factory in west Java, which produces sports shoes for both Nike and Adidas, half a dozen workers are reported to lose fingers in cutting machinery every year, although there has been a reduction in illnesses caused by poisonous organic solvents used in the process.

In the same factory, female workers are routinely subjected to humiliating physical examinations by company doctors before they are allowed to claim legally mandated but unpaid menstrual leave of two days a month.

Mr. Connor said: "There have been improvements in terms of a reduction in sexual harassment, the availability of sick leave and a reduction in the level of humiliation against workers." One female worker was arrested and imprisoned for a month last year for organizing a strike at the PT Panarub factory, which supplies Adidas. "Fear dominates the lives of these workers," the report concludes. "They are afraid that speaking openly about factory conditions or getting involved in active unions will put their livelihoods in danger."

Chris Helzer, a Nike executive, said the report was not an accurate reflection of working conditions in Indonesia. "Interviewing 35 workers out of 110,000 workers in a country is not at all statistically significant or representative," he said. "On wages, entry-level workers are probably paid five to 10 percent more than the [average minimum wage] amount mandated by the government."

Both Nike and Adidas have said they regularly monitor labor practices in the factories contracted to produce for them and will break off dealings with contractors who do not conform to company standards.

> **Have you ever thought about where your clothing comes from?**
>
> **Do human rights matter to you? Does a company's labor practices play into your choice of clothing?**

© ISTOCKPHOTO.COM/SABLAMEK

Neoliberalism: *The ideology that combines the political principles of classical liberalism (see Chapter 3) with those of neoclassical economics; especially those that argue that the economy must remain unfettered by the government.*

But how did this change in the power structure of states and MNCs occur? Some scholars point to the emergence of the global acceptance of neoliberalism. **Neoliberalism** is the economic ideology that has seemed to have won out in this post–Cold War world. According to David Harvey, neoliberalism is a concept that combines the sentiments of classic liberalism (the idea that one's freedom and liberty are at the center of the human experience) with those of neoclassical economics.[12] The overriding belief is that states, just like individuals, must remain free from government intervention. If taxes are the source of frustration for free individuals in the private, domestic sphere, tariffs are the same source of frustration for businesses in the international sphere. It has been this ideology that has prevailed in the era of globalization. It has also been this ideology that has witnessed the enhanced presence and power of MNCs around the world.

We have already learned that one of the major strengths of governments is their ability to maintain peace and security within their borders. However, we must also realize that economic stability is necessary toward maintaining those goals. If a government, for instance, is unable to provide economic security (jobs, services) to its people, it will most likely collapse. So governments rely on their ability to attract businesses. Why? Because wealthy MNCs provide not only jobs but also tax revenue to pay for programs that better the lives of the citizens.

So when Nike is looking for a location to set up one of its factories, where do you think it will look? What kind of country will it choose? Most likely, it will look for a country with a low tax rate, a cheap labor force, and limited workers' rights. Why? These factors will ensure the highest return on its investment. Nike executives chose to set up a factory in Indonesia because the government promised the best incentives for them. Thus, you could make the argument that Nike has more "power" than the government of Indonesia, at least as it relates to an issue like workers' rights.

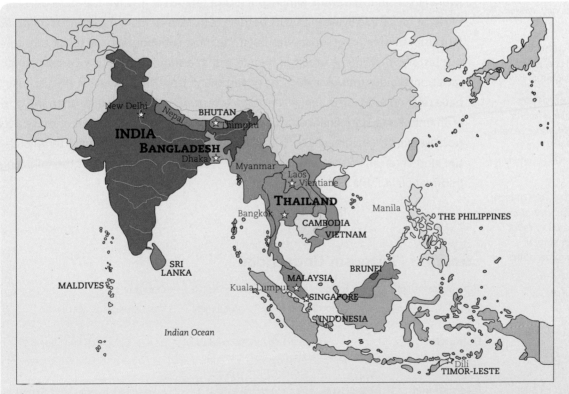

▲ The countries of South Asia and Southeast Asia are prime destinations for many MNCs who see their people as cheap labor. Many of the products purchased in Europe and North America are produced in this region.

But MNCs are not the only private actors giving the state problems. Another type of organization, one with which you are probably much more familiar, is providing the state with many more challenges: global terrorist organizations. The following section will examine some of the problems caused by terrorist organizations.

Transnational Terrorism

In the decades that followed the collapse of the Soviet Union, the world has also witnessed a rise in the number, reach, and strength of terrorist organizations. When at one time terrorist organizations were defined primarily by their opposition to domestic conditions (think the Ku Klux Klan) and their ability to carry out **low-level violence**, today their objections seem to have a global dimension and their abilities appear endless. On September 11, 2001, the world was given a front-row seat to this new type of terrorism that scholars have classified as **transnational terrorism**.

In addition to transnational terrorism (acts of terror carried out by private individuals against foreign targets), IR scholars have identified three other types of terrorism. It is important to show you the differences between them because it helps to emphasize the ways in which globalization has made preventing terrorism so difficult. First is *state terrorism*. Simply put, **state terrorism** is when the state uses acts of terror on people living within its borders (e.g., Nazi Germany). Second is *domestic terrorism*. **Domestic terrorism** has been the most common form of terror throughout history. It is when a group of people within a state target either certain ethnic, racial, or religious groups and/or the government itself. Finally, there is what scholars have referred to as *international terrorism*. **International terrorism** is when the government of one state finances acts of terror against another state. All of these acts possess similar characteristics. But to better understand transnational terrorism—the kind of terrorism that was used on 9/11—we should first consider the following information in Table 13.1.

Low-level violence:
The type of violence traditionally used by terrorist organizations such as hangings, assassinations, intimidation tactics, and bombings of governmental or military installations.

Transnational terrorism:
A type of privately funded, politically motivated violence that involves targets around the world.

State Terrorism: *When a state uses acts of terror on people living within its borders.*

Domestic Terrorism:
A group of people within a state who target either certain ethnic, racial, or religious groups and/or the government itself.

International Terrorism:
When the government of one state finances acts of terror against another state or group within another state.

TABLE 13.1. Terrorism Understood

Type of Terrorism	Description	Example(s)
State	Acts of terror carried out by the government against its own people	Nazi Germany, Soviet Union
Domestic	Acts of terror carried out by private individuals within a country and target ethnic/religious groups and/or the government in power	Ku Klux Klan (KKK), Tamil Tigers
International	Acts of terror carried out by private individuals (but possibly finances by states) across state borders	al-Qaeda, Islamic Jihad, Provisional Irish Republican Army (IRA)

By its very nature, terrorism uses violent means to exact both psychological and physical harm. Think back to the attacks of 9/11. The terrorist attack itself only lasted seconds, but the fear remained much longer. This is what terrorism does. It is designed to disrupt not only the present situation, but also the future. It attempts to psychologically intimidate people through the fear that another attack is imminent.

This definition of terrorism lacks a key component. For an act of violence to be considered an act of terror (and not, for example, a crime) it must be political; in other words, its intent must target those perceived as political enemies. Therefore,

THEORY AND PRACTICE

When Is One a Terrorist and One a Criminal?

What makes one a terrorist instead of an everyday criminal? Have you ever thought about that? Imagine the following scenario and try to see the difference.

Suppose a masked gunman enters a bank. What is it that the bank robber wants? What motivates him? That's easy right? The bank robber's goal is to gain money by robbing the bank and in particular, a bank teller. If in the process someone gets killed (say a teller who refuses to hand over the money), then the bank robber becomes a murderer. He most likely will never be considered a terrorist.

If, however, the gunman who enters the bank is determined to kill the individuals in the bank (customers, tellers, managers, etc.) because he or she believes that the bank, its employees, and its customers are key conspirators of some government or political ideology, the gunman will most likely be considered a terrorist. Why is there such a delineation? From this example we can see that one's *intent* matters greatly when it comes to violence and to determining whether one is a terrorist or an "everyday" criminal. When the public is targeted for *political* reasons, it is an act of terrorism. When the public is targeted for private gain (robbery) and someone gets killed, it is homicide.

Why do you think one's intent matters so much?

Should terrorists be treated differently than criminals? Why?

CourseReader ASSIGNMENT

Log in to **www.cengagebrain.com** and open CourseReader to access the reading:

Samuel P. Huntington, "The Clash of Civilizations," Foreign Affairs, Summer 1993.

In this provocative essay, Samuel P. Huntington argued that ethnic, religious, and geographical differences are responsible for the growth and spread of violence in the world. These differences, Huntington argued, are fundamental and therefore inevitable. In his words, the Islamic world has grown intolerant with "the West" and is committed to its destruction. In many ways, this article created many of the major arguments of the post-9/11 world.

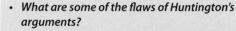

- **What are some of the flaws of Huntington's arguments?**
- **Are some of Huntington's arguments correct? If so, which ones?**

Kishore Mahbubani, "The Dangers of Decadence: What the Rest Can Teach the West," pp. 36-40, in The Clash of Civilizations: The Debate. NY: Council on Foreign Relations, Inc, 1996.

This article, published in 1996, argues that many of the problems that those in the Islamic world have with the "West" have to do with fundamental disagreements over lifestyle choices. The decadent lifestyles of many individuals in Western society hurt the image of the entire region. If the United States is to be successful in its policy of "winning hearts and minds," it must engage in a behavior that other cultures deem acceptable.

- **Are lifestyle choices important to how individuals view the United States?**
- **Should Americans care about how those around the world view their lifestyle choices?**

what ultimately separates a *criminal* from a *terrorist* is his or her intent. The criminal's intent is based on personal gain, while the terrorist's is based on political ideology. Look at the accompanying Theory and Practice box for a common difference between a criminal act and an act of terrorism.

In the United States, the Ku Klux Klan (KKK) has been using acts of terror against its victims, generally minorities in the southern part of the United States, for centuries. It has consistently tried to intimidate ethnic, racial, and religious minorities through violent means such as cross burnings and public hangings. How would you therefore classify the KKK? Since it operates on American soil, and is not supported by the U.S. government (or any other government for that matter), the KKK is considered an example of a domestic terrorist organization. (See Table 13.2 for a list of many of the world's terrorist organizations).

Now, what about al-Qaeda? Al-Qaeda is considered a transnational terrorist organization. Why? Because it conducts its foreign missions without any government direction and is free of government financing. Its former leader, the Saudi billionaire Osama bin Laden who followed an extreme anti-Western, antimodern version of Islam, had carried out acts of terror (or at least claimed responsibility for them) since the late 1980s. Following the end of the **Soviet Afghan War** (in which groups of Afghan rebels aided by the U.S. Central Intelligence Agency successfully defeated the Soviet military), bin Laden founded al-Qaeda or as it is known in Arabic, *The Base*, as way of continuing his violence against those countries he thought were illegitimate, namely those in the West.

The Soviet Afghan War:
A war between the Soviet Union and Afghanistan that lasted from 1979–1989. Waged for easier access to oil, the Soviet-Afghan War saw the presence of American CIA operatives funding and training rebel Afghans.

TABLE 13.2. List of International and Transnational Terrorist Organizations

• Abu Nidal Organization (ANO)	• Lashkar-e Tayyiba (LT) (Army of the Righteous)
• Abu Sayyaf Group	• Lashkar i Jhangvi
• Al-Aqsa Martyrs Brigade	• Liberation Tigers of Tamil Eelam (LTTE)
• Al-Shabaab	• Libyan Islamic Fighting Group (LIFG)
• Ansar al-Islam	• Moroccan Islamic Combatant Group (GICM)
• Armed Islamic Group (GIA)	• Mujahedin-e Khalq Organization (MEK)
• Asbat al-Ansar	• National Liberation Army (ELN)
• Aum Shinrikyo	• Palestine Liberation Front (PLF)
• Basque Fatherland and Liberty (ETA)	• Palestinian Islamic Jihad (PIJ)
• Communist Party of the Philippines/New People's Army (CPP/NPA)	• Popular Front for the Liberation of Palestine (PFLF)
• Continuity Irish Republican Army	• PFLP-General Command (PFLP-GC)
• Gama'a al-Islamiyya (Islamic Group)	• Tanzim Qa'idat al-Jihad fi Bilad al-Rafidayn (QJBR) (al-Qaida in Iraq) (formerly Jama'at al-Tawhid wa'al-Jihad, JTJ, al-Zarqawi Network)
• HAMAS (Islamic Resistance Movement)	• al-Qa'ida
• Harakat ul-Jihad-i-Islami/Bangladesh (HUJI-B)	• al-Qa'ida in the Arabian Peninsula (AQAP)
• Harakat ul-Mujahidin (HUM)	• al-Qaida in the Islamic Maghreb (formerly GSPC)
• Hizballah (Party of God)	• Real IRA
• Islamic Jihad Group	• Revolutionary Armed Forces of Colombia (FARC)
• Islamic Movement of Uzbekistan (IMU)	• Revolutionary Organization 17 November
• Jaish-e-Mohammed (JEM) (Army of Mohammed)	• Revolutionary People's Liberation Party/Front (DHKP/C)
• Jemaah Islamiya organization (JI)	• Revolutionary Struggle
• Kahane Chai (Kach)	• Shining Path (Sendero Luminoso, SL)
• Kata'ib Hizballah	• United Self-Defense Forces of Colombia (AUC)
• Kongra-Gel (KGK, formerly Kurdistan Workers' Party, PKK, KADEK)	• United Self-Defense Forces of Colombia (AUC)

Source: U.S. State Department List of Foreign Terrorist Organizations, 2010.

But hatred does not necessarily translate into action abroad. What has made al-Qaeda so unique is its annual budget. According to the 9/11 Commission report, al-Qaeda requires $30 million per year to carry out its campaign of terror. This means that al-Qaeda has an operating budget that is larger than many of the states in the developing world. It also means that it has more than enough money to acquire and utilize new forms of information technology.

Bin Laden was well versed in the use of cable news and its global reach. According to one CNN report, bin Laden "had a filmmaker with him in Afghanistan when he was fighting the Soviets" while al-Qaeda has had both a media committee and a media spokesman since the 1980s.[13] This has meant that in many ways al-Qaeda has turned a traditional transnational terrorist organization into one that understands the features of globalization.

Now how does this relate to globalization and more importantly to our overall discussion of its impact on state sovereignty? In today's world, terrorists have the ability to use ICT in ways that allow them to not only spread political ideologies, but also money. In much the same way that cyberspace has made life easier for people to buy and sell items (think Amazon.com, or eBay), it too has aided those who perform acts of terror. In this regard, a transnational terrorist organization such as al-Qaeda has successfully used some of the features of globalization to its advantage by attacking traditional forms of governance.

Nuclear Nonproliferation Treaty:
A treaty that came into force in 1970 that was designed to limit the nuclear arsenal of the five members of the UN Security Council and to prevent the proliferation or spread of weapons to states that do not possess them. Currently there are 188 signatories.

WHY POLITICS MATTERS TO YOU!

Nuclear Proliferation and a New Threat of Nuclear War

In 1945, the United States possessed atomic weaponry. In 1949, two states, the United States and the Soviet Union possessed atomic weaponry. By the time the **Nuclear NonProliferation Treaty (NPT)** came into force in 1970, there were five: The United States, the Soviet Union, Great Britain, France, and China (the five permanent members of the United Nations Security Council). Since then, three other states have tested nuclear weapons: India, Pakistan, and North Korea. It is widely believed that Israel also possesses this capability and the country of Iran will possess it before the end of the decade.

So what is the NPT and why has it not ended the threat of nuclear war? Well, the NPT was a treaty (signed in 1968 and brought to force in 1970) that was designed to limit the nuclear arsenals of the major powers (the five permanent members of the Security Council listed above) and to prevent the development of nuclear arms in countries that do not possess them. Unfortunately, not all countries have signed and ratified the treaty, namely Cuba, India, Israel, Pakistan, and North Korea. These countries preferred to pursue nuclear technology and have done so in the name of regional or national security. They argue that nuclear weapons allow them to protect their lands from hostile neighbors.

This had been the main arguments behind Pakistan's pursuit of nuclear weapons. When India, Pakistan's regional aggressor successfully tested its first nuclear weapon in 1974, it created a sense of urgency in Pakistan to develop its own bomb. Thus, Pakistan

continued

continued

through the help of scientist A.Q. Khan developed Pakistan's first nuclear device as a way of balancing Indian aggression.

However, in this era of globalization in which private actors (and private individuals) are gaining greater power over traditional state actors, nuclear proliferation has grown in complexity and danger. Take, for example, the aforementioned A.Q. Khan. In his book *The Inheritance: The World Obama Confronts and the Challenges of American Power*, *New York Times* journalist David Sanger exposes a frightening account of the ways in which A. Q. Khan was able to help countries advance their nuclear programs. After developing the necessary technology to develop nuclear technology in Pakistan, Dr. Khan began a global nuclear operation whose clients included the states of Libya, Iran, and North Korea. Sanger writes:

> The meeting with the Iranians (1986) was the true beginning of what became the Khan network. Iran's shopping list, as pieced together years later by international inspectors, contained all the elements that Khan would later ship to Libya and North Korea: drawings of centrifuges, a few prototypes of the same machines for the Iranians to reverse-engineer, and the layout for a full uranium enrichment plant. They were the building-blocks that Iran would later use to construct its huge enrichment plant in the desert near the city of Natanz, supplied by small centrifuge-manufacturing workshops spread around the country. The process took years; it was not until the summer of 1994 that the Iranians arranged to buy a more sophisticated centrifuge, called the P-2, from Khan and his Malaysian cohort, Buhari Sayed abu Tahir, who ran Khan's operations in Dubai."[14]

This "operation" involved individuals from around the world capable of providing both the knowledge and the equipment to build nuclear arms. A. Q. Khan made it quite clear to all those interested that he could make them a member of the nuclear club.

So, the worry today is both traditional and *non*traditional. If someone like A. Q. Khan was willing to help other states develop nuclear weapons, why wouldn't he sell the information and parts to a well-financed, terrorist organization? This is a major obstacle to nuclear proliferation. During the Cold War, states were the only logical nuclear actors; today this might not be the case.

How can the international community stop this type of proliferation?

How would a realist approach the solution? What about an idealist?

Nongovernmental Organizations: Private Cooperation

Nongovernmental organizations: *Groups that seek to privately help raise awareness and money for specific causes. In many parts of the developing world today, NGOs work in conjunction with governments to care for people dying of disease, victims of natural disasters, environmental causes, and the like.*

Although transnational terrorist organizations and MNCs have dominated much of our media coverage of late, they are not the only actors that have benefited from the forces of globalization. Another category comprises those independent agencies that seek to promote everything from civil society, democracy, economic development, and health care, to human rights, education, technology, and the environment. These nonstate actors, more commonly referred to as **nongovernmental organizations** provide services that bring about the betterment of the human condition. (A look at Table 13.3 will give you a better idea as to the many different types of NGOs.)

Before we begin a brief examination of Doctors Without Borders, an NGO that will highlight some of the basic ways NGOs function, it is important that we explain a few things about NGOs and how they have developed. First, the number of NGOs has dramatically increased over the past 50 years. Following World War II and the collapse of the European empire system, many of the newly created states in the developing world gained their independence were ill-equipped to handle the challenges of governance, for example, providing security and protecting freedoms, and the like. As more and more challenges emerged, so too did the number of NGOs.

Second, as the number of NGOs increased, so did their ability to work with governments and international organizations such as the UN. Although some

TABLE 13.3. Examples and Types of Some NGOs

Children's Issues	Civil Society Outreach Programs	Corruption	Cultural Issues	Democracy	Health	Environment
Child Health Foundation	Advocacy Institute	Standing Committee on Extortion and Bribery	Aid to Artisans Inc.	Ford Foundation	Doctors Without Borders	Greenpeace
Childreach	Centro Latinoamericano de Economia Humana (CLAEH)	Probidad	Institute of Cultural Affairs	International Foundation for Election Systems	International Red Cross and International Red Crescent	African Wildlife Foundation
Coalition to Stop the Use of Child Soldiers	Eastern Caribbean Investment Promotion Service (ECPIPS)	Transparency International	Instituto Mora de Mexico	National Democratic Institute	International Medical Corps	Bahamas National Trust
Children's Defense Fund	Institute of Development Studies		American Association of Museums	U.S. Institute for Peace	Doctors of the World	Envirolink
Christian Children's Fund	International Council on Social Welfare		Piramide	Moviemiento Participacion Ciudadana	Rehydration Project	World Environment Center

**This list is just a small sample of the many NGOs that operate around the world.

governments are less friendly to humanitarian-based NGOs (especially ones that are causing much of the problems the NGOs are trying to solve), most have learned to work well with them. In fact, the World Health Organization (WHO), the major health-related international organization of the United Nations, spends a large portion of its time working with NGOs in the development of health-related policies. This provides the NGOs with the ability to set up clinics on the ground and issue first-hand reports to the United Nations pertaining to potential health crises.

Lastly, through their interactions with international organizations and with states, NGOs have become active participants in the promotion of what we call **global civil society**. Global civil society refers to "the increasing institutionalization of citizen and non-governmental networks in the governance of our complex world."[15] In essence, "the idea of a global civil society is closely related to widespread desires for a more democratic global political architecture."[16] NGOs that seek to promote the development of global civil society help promote ideas like freedoms of speech and the press in places where they are not protected.

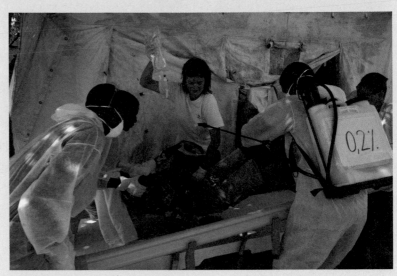

▲ NGOs like Doctors Without Borders seek to help states administer everything from health care, to education, to environmental protection. Here we see a clinic set up by aid workers from Doctors Without Borders providing treatment to individuals who otherwise would have none.

Global civil society:
The ways in which private individuals and NGOs have worked together outside the realm of traditional politics to advance the concepts of human rights and democracy.

Because the concept of a global civil society may seem complex, we have decided to provide you with an example of one of the more prominent NGOs in the world today: Doctors Without Borders (in French, Medecins Sans Frontieres). Although Doctors Without Borders is considered primarily a *health*-based NGO, it still contributes to the development of global civil society because it provides services that strengthen the stability of an impoverished state. It is also a great example of an NGO because it carries with it some basic criteria. See Table 13.3.

NGOs, like Doctors Without Borders, are therefore another set of actors that have proven themselves capable of challenging the traditional sovereignty of the state. Think about it. NGOs like Greenpeace, the Red Cross, the Red Crescent, and/or Doctors Without Borders, perform many of the tasks that states have traditionally performed. Although they do not have the ability to wage war, they do possess many of the state's basic features. NGOs have priorities (environmental, health, human rights), have the ability to conduct research and raise awareness about particular issues, and provide a service to people in a given territory. In many instances, NGOs have even directly challenged states that violate some of their principles.

An NGO in Action: Doctors Without Borders Médecins Sans Frontières

© ISTOCKPHOTO.COM/DIEGO CERVO

Established in 1971 by a number of French health professionals, Doctors Without Borders provides local health care and health education in 60 countries through its staff of 27,000 dedicated individuals.[17] Since it is a privately financed, independent organization its allegiance is to its mission, its board of directors, and those states/international organizations that help to coordinate its agenda. It is not an agent of any particular government. This distinction has allowed it to provide health care to those in need regardless of any political opinions.

According to its website, Doctors Without Borders "provides medical care (emergency help, vaccines, education) to people who are caught in warzones"… or those who have been devastated by disease through the establishment of "clinics and mobile clinics, or (through the) rehabilitation of existing hospitals."[18] In essence, Doctors Without Borders provides services to those who are unable to provide health care for themselves. As it treats patients, it also documents the ways in which societies are failing to provide adequate health care to its most vulnerable. It is this last feature that makes Doctors Without Borders so special: it not only cures the disabled and sick, it sheds light on their stories as well.

Do you think the world will see an increase in NGOs like Doctors Without Borders?

What impact will this have on the nation-state?

© ISTOCKPHOTO.COM/LORENZO COLLORETA

THE VERDICT ON GLOBALIZATION: THE GOOD AND THE BAD

Up to this point, we have discussed some of the ways that globalization has challenged state authority. We have looked at the ways in which MNCs, transnational terrorists, and NGOs have used new sources of technology to their advantages. We have also examined the new nature of nuclear proliferation and the ways in which states are unable to stop it. What we must do at this point, however, is try to determine if the processes of globalization will achieve a more open world that allows more freedom and democracy or a closed world in which human rights are stifled and economic development is ignored. Thus, the chapter will conclude with the appraisals of some noted thinkers and journalists who have written on the topic of *neoliberalism,* namely Thomas L. Friedman and Fareed Zakaria (representing a more positive economic outlook) and Joseph Stiglitz (representing a negative economic outlook of globalization).

Friedman and Zakaria: The World Is Flat and Getting Flatter!

In his book *The World Is Flat, New York Times* best-selling author Thomas L. Friedman paints a rosy picture of globalization and the way that information technology has created a world that is *leveling the playing field* for millions of people in the world and giving hope to the hopeless.[19] Friedman vividly reports that because of **outsourcing** (the process by which certain jobs are being sent to foreign countries), the elimination of Soviet control, advances in information technology, people in China, India, and other parts of the developing world are finding careers as accountants, medical technicians, and other professional jobs and are slowly gaining levels of wealth they once had thought were impossible. For Friedman, the liberalization of the global economy has led to endless possibilities for people once trapped in generational poverty.

Outsourcing: *The practice by which professions from one country (usually wealthy country such as the United States) are sent to other countries where labor laws are less intense, and the pay scale is lower.*

This portrait also seems to describe the rise of China and India (as well as Brazil and Russia) as dominant players in the twenty-first century. If the BRIC (Brazil, Russia, India, and China) countries continue to grow and experience unprecedented levels of wealth and industrial development, the United States may have to understand that its role as the sole superpower is in jeopardy. But if American policymakers attempt to strengthen trade and inspire the BRICs to develop their middle classes and provide more freedoms for their people, the United States will remain a major player. For Friedman it is really that simple: better trade relations and economic growth equals rights and a better life for future generations of Americans. For Fareed Zakaria, it is not only important for the United States, but for the rest of the world as well.

Fareed Zakaria, *Newsweek* editor and international observer, is another optimist when it comes to the processes of globalization. For Zakaria, the world will become more secure as new powers enter the international arena. For Zakaria, the current situation of nonstate actors and political turbulence will be corrected when states begin to realize that the processes of globalization lead to an inevitability: an increase in personal freedom.

In his book *The Post-American World*, Zakaria looks at the ways in which certain states in the developing world (in particular China and India) will become the leaders of the twenty-first century and will have to find better ways of protecting their people's personal freedom. His account of China and its rise is quite telling. For Zakaria, China has a choice. Its leaders can continue to serve as the world's manufacturing base and reach unthinkable levels of wealth all the while restricting Internet usage and limiting personal freedom (and personal wealth), or it can allow its people to experience the kinds of wealth and protection of rights currently seen in the world's democracies. Zakaria, like Friedman, places a lot of faith in the processes of economic development as a motivator for positive change.

THEORY AND PRACTICE ▷ Google versus China

Recently the world witnessed a war between Internet search engine giant Google and the Chinese government. Since 2007 Google has been available to users in China, but only under strict, technological guidelines. In other words, Google was allowed into the Chinese marketplace of ideas, but only according to Chinese censorship laws—kind of like being told you are "free" to play baseball, but the government gets to play umpire and determine the number of balls and strikes. That was until January 12, 2010.

On that date, Google decided to go rogue. It stopped following its agreement with the Chinese authorities and decided to allow Chinese users full access to its services. The way China responds, and the length of time it takes to respond, will be telling indicators of where China wants to be in 10 years. If the Chinese government allows market forces to determine its future, China will dominate the twenty-first century. If it continues to try to maintain its dominance with an iron fist, its future is uncertain.

If you were one of the leading voices in China, how would you handle the new forms of technology?

Would you be threatened by the emerging technologies?

Stiglitz: Globalization and Its Discontents

In his book *Globalization and Its Discontents*, Joseph E. Stiglitz gives the most thorough argument about how globalization has created an international order of corruption and greed for both wealthy corporations and industrialized countries through the politics and policies of the **International Monetary Fund (IMF)**, The **World Bank**, and the **World Trade Organization (WTO)**. These organizations, known collectively as the Bretton Woods institutions (named for the place in New Hampshire where they were created at the end of World War II), are international organizations composed of member states that lend relief money to countries in the developing world. Stiglitz claims that these organizations have taken advantage of the weaknesses of the developing world and gained unthinkable levels of wealth and power as a result.

International Monetary Fund: *An international institution that extends short term aid to states that have been damaged by natural/manmade disasters or war.*

World Bank: *An international institution that provides long term help to states.*

World Trade Organization: *An international organization that seeks to lower barriers to trades in order to make states' economies more competitive.*

Bretton Woods System and Stiglitz's Critique

In the last days of World War II (1944), a number of countries (the United States and its European allies) met in Bretton Woods, New Hampshire, to create three international organizations to help Europe rebuild from the destruction of the war. They then created the IMF designed to provide short-term loans aimed at reconstruction, immediate stability, and to oversee exchange rates; the World Bank designed to provide for long-term stability; and the General Agreement on Tariffs and Trade (GATT), now known as the WTO, which creates policies designed to lessen barriers to trade. As time went on, however, their focus shifted from rebuilding Europe to rebuilding countries in need in the developing world.

Initially, the Bretton Woods System had five key elements. According Boughton (2007) as quoted in Ritzer (2011), they are as follows:

1. Each state that participated needed to create a "'par value' for its currency expressed in terms of gold or in terms of the gold value of the U.S. dollar as of July 1944."[20] As Ritzer points out, this meant that the United States pegged its currency at $35 per ounce of gold, while . . . the figure for Nicaragua was 175 cordobas per ounce. This means that the exchange rate between the two currencies was five cordobas for one dollar.[21]

2. "The official monetary authority in each country would agree to exchange its own currency for those of other

▲ Protesters criticize the policies of the WTO on the grounds that its policies hurt local workers to the benefit of wealthy states and corporations.

countries at the established exchange rates, plus or minus a one-percent margin."[22]

3. The IMF was created and it was mandated that its 40 member states provide some of their gold to its fund.[23]

4. "Member states had agreed to eliminate, at least eventually, 'all restrictions on the use of its currency for international trade.'"[24]

5. "The entire system was based on the US dollar. The US agreed to make the dollar convertible into other currencies or gold at the fixed par value. The dollar in effect became a global currency."[25]

This system, however, has changed significantly since 1944. The U.S. dollar is no longer tied or pegged to gold, the developing world of today has obstacles to growth that were never experienced by the European powers who needed financial help after World War II, and many scholars (including Joseph Stiglitz whom we will examine below) suggest that the policies employed by the IMF, World Bank, and WTO seem to be unrealistic and at times authoritarian toward the states they are trying to help.

One of the strongest contemporary critiques of the Bretton Woods System (and of neoliberal globalization) has been made by renowned economist Joseph Stiglitz. Stiglitz has argued that the policies of the Bretton Woods institutions have in fact made life harder for those in the developing world. Since the IMF and the World Bank operate by providing assistance in the form of loans and assistance packages, they force those countries in the developing world to agree to certain mandates that they must attempt to implement or face the consequences of a subsequent aid package that has less money attached to it. For Stiglitz, some of the demands that the IMF and the World Bank have imposed on those to whom they have provided aid are unreasonable. For example, a very common requirement of the IMF is for the country receiving aid to spend it on economic infrastructure projects only. The result is that government money is no longer spent on clinics, hospitals, or schools. The outcome is that the health of the people worsens and education standards decline; two requirements usually cited as being essential for development.

According to Sebastian Edwards, "Three interrelated policy issues are at the center of Stiglitz's criticism of globalization:

1. In designing reform packages during the 1990s, crucial aspects of the sequencing and pace of reform were ignored. As a result, in many countries, reform was implemented too fast.

2. Advocating (and imposing) capital account liberalization (allowing tons of private money to pour into poor countries without any mechanism for long-term investment).

3. The IMF response to crises (in particular East Asia) was a disaster that made things worse rather than better. In particular imposing fiscal austerity (limitations on spending) while raising interest rates."[26]

For Stiglitz, the pace at which the countries seeking investment were told to reform was too fast and in many ways, left them worse off than they had been before any money was given to them. Countries receiving aid appeared to have been afflicted by a double-edged sword: money going in with high interest rates and an open-door trade policy that hurt domestic development. In other words, as IMF aid went to places in East Asia or the Caribbean, so too did the demands of the WTO to lower trade barriers, which brought foreign competitors into the marketplace, limiting the ability of local industries and farmers to compete and thus, making it almost impossible to pay back the money lent in the first place. For Stiglitz, this became a vicious cycle of aid followed by unreasonable demands.

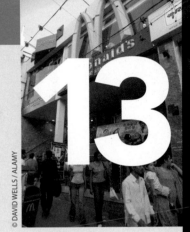

© DAVID WELLS / ALAMY

SUMMARY

So there you have it; the conclusion of our explanation of the development of international relations from the seventeenth to the twenty-first century. In doing so, we hope to have provided you with a good picture of how international politics has moved from one dominated by a handful of European powers to one today dominated by the United States, an array of nonstate actors (MNCs, transnational terrorist groups), and a host of rising developing states.

The world of tomorrow is yet to be written. But now that you are armed with a strong sense of the past, you are better suited for the challenges that remain unknown. Power is still being defined and expanded to suit the needs of a new era. Whether the major powers of the world will resort to violence or try to find diplomatic, peaceful solutions is still unclear. Still, there is always hope when a new generation of students become inspired to make a difference in global affairs. Believe it or not, you have already made such a difference.

KEY TERMS

Containment p. 389

Deterrence p. 388

Domestic terrorism p. 398

Domino theory p. 389

Glasnost p. 391

Global civil society p. 405

Globalization p. 392

International Monetary Fund p. 409

International terrorism p. 398

Low-level violence p. 398

Marshall Plan p. 389

KEY PEOPLE

2008 Bailout of the financial industry Also known as the Emergency Economic Stabilization Act of 2008, this law authorized the U.S. Secretary of the Treasury to spend up to $700 billion to help stabilize the financial industry. The proposal submitted to the House of Representatives was three pages in length.

Abolitionists Members of a political movement that sought to abolish the institution of slavery. The movement in the United States was largely led by William Lloyd Garrison and Frederick Douglas.

Absolutist monarchy A rule by one person who is the creator and enforcer of all legislation. This is in contrast to a "constitutional monarchy," which can be said to describe the governments of Great Britain, the Netherlands, and Spain: all of which have limited monarchical authority and strong representative traditions.

Administrative law Law relating to the authority and procedures of administrative agencies as well as to the rules and regulations issued by those agencies.

Alienation of labor The concept developed by Karl Marx that explained the ways in which modern life removes the worker from the product he/she is creating.

Annapolis Convention An interstate convention called in 1786 to discuss issues of commerce. The meeting was largely seen as a failure because only 5 of the 13 states sent delegations.

Anti-Federalists A political group of the 1780s opposed to the creation of a stronger national government

Anti-Federalists Persons who were generally opposed to both a stronger central government and the ratification of the U.S. Constitution.

Appellate jurisdiction Courts that hear cases on appeal from a lower court. These courts primarily determine whether a legal mistake was made at trial.

Arab Spring Refers to the pro-democratic political movements (2011) spreading throughout the Middle East and Northern Africa.

Aristocracy A government in which power is vested in a minority, consisting of those believed to be best qualified.

Authoritarian states Countries that are characterized by the rule of one person or a few people and tend to prohibit a great many rights and privileges.

Autocracy A type of authoritarian regime where one person is in control of the laws and policies of the state.

Balance of power Historical reference to the ways in which great political powers have attempted to maintain security and to avoid international conflicts. The balance of power concept originated in Europe during the early part of the nineteenth century when five great powers (Great Britain, France, Austria, Russian, and Prussia) dominated international politics and were committed to avoiding war and maintaining each state's position as a dominant power.

Bay of Pigs A bay in South Cuba and the site of an unsuccessful invasion by anti-Castro exiles secretly supported by the U.S. government in 1961.

Behavioralism The school of thought that looks at the "actual" behavior of certain persons or institutions. It is largely data driven and without a strong commitment to values.

Bicameral legislature A legislature that consists of a two-house body, an upper and a lower house. The U.S. Congress and every state legislature except Nebraska's are bicameral.

Bush doctrine The policy formulated by President George W. Bush after the 2001 terrorist attacks on the United States. The doctrine was codified in 2002. The policy marks a break from the decades-old foreign policy of "containment" and asserts that the United States will act unilaterally to "preempt" any threat against the United States.

Carter doctrine A plan announced after the Soviet invasion of Afghanistan in 1979. The Carter doctrine (1980) asserted the United States would use military force to prevent any outside force from gaining control of the Persian Gulf.

Casework When members of Congress use their staff or intervene personally in order to do favors for constituents.

Checks and balances A system of government where each branch of government can limit, amend, and/or nullify the acts of another branch of government.

Civil disobedience The refusal to obey governmental demands or commands especially as a nonviolent and usually collective means of forcing concessions from the government.

Civil law Noncriminal forms of law that guide social relationships between residents. Civil law includes contract law, tort law, or property disputes that typically are settled through financial settlements.

Civil society An indicator of political stability that has been used as a characteristic of democracies. Within a civil society, individuals and organizations promote a diversity of interests and a respect for civil liberties.

Classic realism The school of thought in international relations that sees power as the main goal of each state. In addition, classic realists claim that the state is the main actor in international relations, that it is to be thought of as a unitary actor, and that international politics is inherently chaotic.

Classical liberalism Classical liberalism advocates for a limited government and for greater individual liberties at the political, social, and economic levels of society. John Locke (1632–1704) and Adam Smith (1732–1790) are generally regarded as two leading classical liberals. This movement inspired the American and French Revolutions, and the economic system of capitalism.

Climate change The result of many years of burning high levels of fossil fuels which has caused the earth to heat up.

Cloture A rule in the Senate that requires 60 senators to vote to stop a filibuster.

Cold War The period that began following the end of World War II and was defined by the ideological and political struggle between the United States and the Soviet Union. Both sides made economic and military commitments to states around the world willing to ally themselves to either country. In addition, this era was defined by the prospect of nuclear war, as both sides possessed vast arsenals of nuclear missiles. The era ended with the formal dissolution of the Soviet Union in 1991.

Collective security The idea that an attack on one particular state by another should be understood as an attack against all states.

Colonialism The practice of conquering and incorporating states/territories within the political control of one state; with the "mother country" serving as the core and the colonies as "peripheries." For example, throughout most of the nineteenth and twentieth centuries, Great Britain practiced colonialism because it had controlled a number of states beyond its borders in places as diverse as Ireland, Egypt, and India. Great Britain could be understood as the "core" while its colonies could be understood as the "peripheries"; those groups serving the "mother country" with resources, services, and labor.

Common law Judge-made law that originated in England in the twelfth century, when royal judges traveled around the country settling disputes in each locality according to prevailing custom. The common law continues to develop according to the rule of *stare decisis*, which means "let the decision stand."

Communist state A totalitarian state is one in which power is controlled by the government and whose policies are based on the suppression of religion, nationalism, and private property. In communist states, the economy is said to be centrally planned, that is, prices and salaries are controlled and regulated by the state.

Comparative politics The subfield of political science that examines different types of institutions and issues within different countries. They are usually regionally based. For example, one may do comparative research on the area of the world known as the Middle East.

Concert of Europe The name given to the European balance of power system of the nineteenth century. While many scholars agree that the nineteenth century had several low-level wars (wars fought between some of the great powers), the system that was forged in Vienna proved strong enough to prevent war for almost 100 years.

Concurrent power Powers that are granted to both the national and state government in the U.S. Constitution. The power to tax is an example of a concurrent power.

Confederate form of government A system of government that gives little power to the central government and instead gives power to smaller state governments. The United States adopted a confederate system when it operated under the Article of Confederation system from 1781 to 1787.

Connecticut Compromise The Great Compromise between the large and small states at the Constitutional Convention that called for the U.S. House of Representatives to be apportioned according to the state's population and the U.S. Senate comprised of two senators per state.

Constitutional law Statements interpreting the U.S. Constitution that have been either given approval by lower courts or the Supreme Court, or practiced without being tested in the courts.

Constitutional provisions Constitutional provisions refer to the specific arrangement of the law in any particular country. It refers to exactly what protections individuals have and how the government is able to act.

Constructivism A school of thought within international relations that examines the impact of values and norms on the behavior of states.

Containment A strategy used in the Cold War designed to stop the spread of Soviet power and communism.

Correlation The relationship between two items or variables.

Counterterinsurgency A military strategy that includes military, political, economic, and humanitarian efforts in an attempt to win over the hearts and minds of the domestic population.

Counterterrorism A police or military strategy that employs offensive tactics to preempt or deter future terroristic attacks.

Coup d'etat The violent overthrow of an existing regime.

Criminal law Law that defines crimes against the public order and provides for punishment. Government is responsible for enforcing criminal law, the great body of which is enacted by states and enforced by state officials in state courts. However, the criminal caseload of federal judges is growing.

Cuban missile crisis Crisis between the United States and the Soviet Union as a result of Cuban leader Fidel Castro's decision to allow the Soviet Union to place Soviet nuclear missiles in Cuba in 1961.

Cue-taking Taking a political cue from a respected colleague or party leader when determining how to vote on a particular bill.

Defense of Marriage Act A federal law enacted in 1996 that allows states to not recognize same-sex marriages performed in other states.

Democracy A system of government in which the supreme power is vested in the people and exercised by them directly or indirectly through a system of representation usually involving periodically held free elections.

Demographics Classifications of different groups of people that usually refer to one's race, class, ethnicity, gender, level of wealth, age, place of residence, employment status, level of education, and so on.

Deterrence To deter literally means to stop someone from doing something by frightening him or her; dissuasion by deterrence operates by frightening a state out of attacking, not because of launching an attack and carrying it home, but because the expected reaction of the opponent will result in one's own severe punishment.

Direct democracy A system of democracy whereby citizens directly participate in the decision-making process of government

Disciplined political parties Political parties whose members vote according to the established party platform and rarely vote according to their own consciences.

Doctrine of nullification The doctrine associated with John Calhoun and other states rights advocates in the late 1820s and 1830s asserting that states were within their rights to declare null and void any federal law they believed violated the constitutional rights of states.

Doctrine of original intent The view that judicial decisions should be based on what justices believe to be the original intention of the Founding Fathers when they drafted the U.S. Constitution.

Domestic terrorism

Domino theory The Cold War theory which argued that as soon as one country became communist, the surrounding states would as well.

Earmarks Funds appropriated to a particular bill that do not receive the level of oversight typically associated with the appropriations process.

Eisenhower doctrine The plan announced in 1957 in the aftermath of the Suez Crisis between Egypt, Britain, France, and Israel. Primarily concerned with the Middle East, Eisenhower declared the United States would provide economic aid and/or military support to nations threatened by armed forces of belligerent states.

Eleventh Amendment The judicial power of the United States shall not be construed to extend to any suit in law or equity, commenced or prosecuted against one of the United States by citizens of another State, or by citizens or subjects of any foreign State.

Empire A political arrangement in which one powerful government is in control of a vast territory and peoples of (possibly) different economic, ethnic, religious groups than the powerful government itself. This configuration dominated the period right before the emergence of the modern state system.

Enumerated powers Expressly granted to the government in the U.S. Constitution. The power to declare war, for example, is an enumerated power of Congress that can be found in Article 1, Section 8 of the U.S. Constitution.

Environmentalism A social and political movement that seeks to prevent the further deterioration of our natural resources. Environmentalists primarily believe that all living things, including nonhuman living things, warrant serious consideration when enacting public policy. The movement played a large role in the passage of the Clear Air Act (1970), Clean Water Act (1972), the Endangered Species Act (1973), and a host of other major policies in the United States.

Executive agreements Agreements initiated by the president that involve the United States and a foreign nation that do not require the advice and consent of the Senate.

Executive signing statements Written remarks on congressional legislation made by the president that enable the president to express displeasure with a particular provision of a bill and/or impact the way bills are implemented.

Extradition Clause A clause found in Article IV of the U.S. Constitution that asserts states must surrender criminal offenders to states in which the crime was committed.

Fascist state A totalitarian state in which power is tightly controlled by the government and is derived from extreme nationalist policies. The beliefs of the state are held above those of the individual and each individual is forced into working for the success of the entire state. The concept emerged in Italy in the 1920s under the leadership of Benito Mussolini as an antidemocratic and antisocialist ideology.

Federalist system of government A system of government that divides power between the national and state governments. The system is a number of countries including the United States, Canada, and India.

Federalists Persons supportive of ratifying the U.S. Constitution. Federalists such as Alexander Hamilton and George Washington generally favored a stronger central government. A Federalist Party later emerged under Alexander Hamilton's leadership.

Feminism An organized movement beginning in earnest in the mid-nineteenth century that called for social, political, economic, and familial equality between men and women. Feminism can be broken down into several components, including radical feminism, liberal feminism, and democratic feminism. This movement was successful in securing the passage of the Nineteenth Amendment (1920) to the U.S. Constitution which prohibited states from denying voting rights to women, and continues to push for the ratification of the Equal Rights Amendment.

Feudal system System of economic, political, and social organization that flourished in Europe during the Middle Ages. It was based on the relationship of lord to vassal and the holding of land in feud.

Fifteenth Amendment The amendment that made it illegal to deny voting rights on the basis of race.

Filibuster A formal method used in the Senate in order to stop a bill from coming to a vote. Senators can prevent a vote by making long speeches or by engaging in unlimited debate.

First world countries Countries that receive this distinction are the wealthiest, most industrialized states. The states in this category have the highest levels of wealth and middle classes, highest levels of technology, lowest infant mortality rates (number of children per 1,000 that die before age five), highest life expectancies, and the like.

Fossil fuels Coal, oil, and natural gas.

Fourteenth Amendment The post–Civil War amendment that guaranteed all Americans the rights of due process of law, equal protection of law, and equal privileges and immunities.

Fourth Estate The members of the media. Its roots are found in the days of the French Revolution where society was divided into three groups or estates: the clergy, the nobility, and the masses. The term *fourth estate* was therefore applied to the members of the press who provided commentary on the other official three estates.

Free market system of economics The belief that the market, i.e., the way goods are bought and sold, can and will regulate itself. Adam Smith believed that consumers ultimately control the prices of goods by forcing sellers into competition. Because consumers shop comparatively, businesses that maintain higher prices will be forced out of business. This coincides with the beliefs espoused by classic liberals because the government provides no influence on the price of the goods for sale; it remains limited.

Full Faith and Credit Clause A clause found in Article IV of the U.S. Constitution that requires each state to recognize the civil judgments and public records of other states.

Glasnost Referred to Gorbachev's policy of "openness" in government. It was introduced as a way of shedding light on some of the corruption of the Soviet Union during the 1980s.

Global civil society The ways in which private individuals and NGOs have worked together outside the realm of traditional politics to advance the concepts of human rights and democracy.

Globalization The global process that has witnessed a rise in the free movement and interconnectedness of goods, services, information, and people at the expense of the nation-state.

Greenhouse effect The burning of fossil fuels that results in CO_2 and H_2O being trapped in the atmosphere.

Gridlock A lack of progress on enacting legislation typically caused by partisan and/or institutional infighting.

Hard power Using military and/or economic pressure in a way that allows one state to force another to do something it might not have wanted to do.

House Majority Leader The second-most important person in the House of Representatives. The majority leader assists the speaker in establishing the political agenda in the House.

House Minority Leader The elected leader of the party with minority status in the House of Representatives.

House of Commons The lower house in the British parliament. Members of the House of Commons (known as members of Parliament or MPs) are directly elected by the people and therefore are charged with the duty of passing legislation.

House of Councilors The upper house in the Japanese parliament. It is designed to approve proposed legislation that has already been passed in the lower House of Representatives. However, if it chooses to reject the proposed law, its ruling can be overturned in the House of Representatives by a two-thirds majority vote.

House of Lords The upper house in the British parliament. The House of Lords reflects the history and traditions of British society. Today it serves as a deliberative body that can no longer prevent the passage of legislation, but simply delay it.

House of Representatives The lower house in the Japanese parliament. Its members are voted directly by the people and it is the ultimate source of authority in the legislative process.

Hypothesis An educated guess about a particular experiment.

Imperialism The highest stage of capitalism according to V. I. Lenin. It was the stage at which industrial growth and the banking system become monopolized by a wealthy group of state and industry leaders. For Lenin, it was the stage immediately before the worldwide communist revolution.

Indefinite term Term that is defined by the head of government, not by a constitutional decree. For example, the prime minister of the United Kingdom must call for general elections at some point before a five-year period expires, but its timing is up to his/her discretion.

Institutionalist approach An extralegal approach to judicial decision making that examines how the rules and norms of the court help shape judicial decisions.

International relations The field of political science that studies the way nations interact with one another and the influence of global trends on nation-states.

International terrorism When the government of one state finances acts of terror against another state or group within another state.

Ionians The earliest Greek philosophers who believed in using rationality rather than mythology to understand the universe.

Isolationism The U.S. policy of avoiding alliances with European nations practiced in the nineteenth and early twentieth centuries.

Jacksonian democracy The political philosophy and influence of President Andrew Jackson. The era (1824–1854) was marked with the expansion of democratic rights and started the trend away from political appointments and toward the use of elections to select public officials.

Judicial review The court's power to strike laws that violate the U.S. Constitution. Also the power granted to certain state supreme courts to declare acts and laws passed by legislatures and executives to be invalid if they are in conflict with the state's constitution.

Judiciary Act of 1789 Principally written by Senators Oliver Ellsworth of Connecticut and New Jersey's William Paterson, the Judiciary Act of 1789 established the federal court system that originally included one federal district court per state. Section 13 of the Judiciary Act also granted the Supreme Court the authority to issue a "writ of mandamus" loosely translated to mean "we order," which played a key role in the legal battle associated with the landmark *Marbury v Madison* (1803) case.

Liberalism The school of thought that is centered on the creation of international institutions designed to enhance the natural tendencies of cooperation found in human nature.

Logical reasoning The belief that justices should use logical reasoning on a case-by-case basis as it related to the facts of a particular case.

Logrolling Trading influence or votes among legislators to achieve passage of projects that are of interest to one another.

Lower house A lower house, like the British House of Commons, is designed to best represent the will of the people. Thus, its members are elected directly by the people and their representation is based on population.

Low-level violence The type of violence traditionally used by terrorist organizations such as hangings, assassinations, intimidation tactics, and bombings of governmental or military installations.

Majority-minority district A congressional district that includes a majority of minority voters that increases the probability of electing a minority representative.

Marshall Plan The Marshall Plan (named after U.S. Secretary of State George Marshall) provided financial support to Europe following World War II. The United States realized that in order for it to maintain its dominance in areas of trade, it needed strong, reliable European trading partners.

Marxism Based on the theories associated with Karl Marx (1818–1883), the ideology of Marxism believes almost all conflict in society occurs because of class conflict. Karl Marx pointed to the level of exploitation and social deterioration that occurred during the industrial revolution in the mid-nineteenth century as proof that capitalism primarily fuels human suffering and social alienation. Marx and Friedrich Engels wrote the *Communist Manifesto* in 1848.

McCulloch v. Maryland (1819) The landmark Supreme Court case that expanded the powers of the national government by finding the government had "implied powers" in addition to the expressed powers found in Article 1, Section 8 of the U.S. Constitution.

Military dictatorship An authoritarian government in which political power is controlled and employed by the military. Sometimes it is within the control of the highest ranking official in the military, other times it may be in the hands of a few high-ranking officials.

Missouri Compromise (1820) A political compromise whereby Missouri was admitted into the Union as a slave state and Maine as a free state. The remaining states in the Louisiana territory were divided as slave states in the south and free states in the north.

Modern liberalism Modern liberalism points out potential problems associated with systems of "majority rule" and "equality" by emphasizing the tendency of democracies to degenerate into a tyranny of the majority. Alexis de Tocqueville (1805–1859) and John Stuart Mill (1806–1873) are two leading modern liberal thinkers.

Modernization theorists The most famous is Walt Whitman Rostow. Rostow argued that there is a formula for economic growth and development. Prosperity is based on the ability of certain states to assume an economic formula that will move them from "traditional life" to "mass consumption."

Multiparty parliamentary democracy A democratic state that has more than two active political parties in the legislature.

National Diet The formal name of the Japanese legislature composing the House of Councilors and the House of Representatives.

National interest For realists, states (countries) will always behave in ways that expand their security and protect what they deem as essential to their well-being.

Nation-state system A sovereign state inhabited by people who share political and cultural traditions.

Natural law A body of law or a special principle held to be derived from nature and binding upon human society.

Necessary and Proper Clause Also known as the elastic clause, it is found in the last paragraph of Article 1, Section 8 of the Constitution and expands federal power by granting the federal government all powers that are "necessary" and "proper" to carry out the enumerated powers of Congress.

Neoliberalism The school of thought that says because states are constantly interacting with each other they value cooperation as part of their own self-interest.

New Jersey Plan Proposed by William Paterson at the Constitutional Convention and called for a one-house chamber apportioned according to equal representation of each state.

New world order For neo-Marxists this is the way in which the exploitation of the wealthy over the poor will continue. It is best seen in the ways that large corporations have been successful in passing legislation that allows them to lower other poorer countries' tariffs and gain access to their markets, resources, and labor.

Nixon doctrine Nixon sought to "Vietnamize" the Vietnam War by supplanting American troops with Vietnamese troops. The Nixon doctrine (1969) sought to extricate American forces from the fighting in Vietnam. All U.S. troops were withdrawn four years later in 1973.

Nongovernmental organizations (NGOs) Organizations that act independently of states who usually have a particular focus or interest. For example, the organization Doctors Without Borders can be considered an NGO committed to the prevention and treatment of disease in various parts of the world. They are privately funded and provide relief to many people who lack basic health care.

Nongovernmental organizations Groups that seek to privately help raise awareness and money for specific causes. In many parts of the developing world today, NGOs work in conjunction with governments to care for people dying of disease, victims of natural disasters, environmental causes, and the like.

Normative theory Any theory that examines the way something "should" or "ought" to be rather than focusing on the way something actually "is."

North Atlantic Treaty Organization (NATO) The North Atlantic Treaty Organization was established in 1949 and was designed primarily as a military organization among American and European powers. Its original purpose was to prevent Soviet aggression in Western Europe.

Nuclear Nonproliferation Treaty A treaty that came into force in 1970 that was designed to limit the nuclear arsenal of the five members of the UN Security Council and to prevent the proliferation or spread of weapons to states that do not possess them. Currently there are 188 signatories.

Oligarchy A government in which a small group exercises control over the masses.

Omnibus legislation A large bill that contains several smaller bills.

Original jurisdiction Courts that hear cases for the first time. These courts decide on guilt or innocence or resolve civil disputes on the merits of the facts of the case.

Outsourcing The practice by which professions from one country (usually a wealthy country such as the United States) are sent to other countries where labor laws are less intense, and the pay scale is lower.

Pan-Arab secularism Also known as Arab Nationalism, pan-Arab secularism was a movement designed to create unity among the states of the Middle East and North Africa. It was designed to place secular principles ahead of religious ones. Most experts claim that it was the Arab States' defeat in the Six Day War (1967) with Israel that ended the mass appeal for the movement.

Parliamentary sovereignty A distinction that holds that the legislature is the most powerful source of law making and interpretation.

Parliamentary system A system in which the executive branch is part of the legislature.

Partisan gerrymandering The act of dividing congressional districts to give one political party an unfair advantage in congressional elections.

Patriarchy A concept that is used to define societies that places men in positions of power over women.

Peacekeepers A group of troops sent as part of a UN mission to maintain a peace agreement in an area that appears troubled.

Peloponnesian War The war between Athens and Sparta from 431–404 BCE. Sparta, with the assistance of Persia (now Iran), built a massive fleet that destroyed the Athenian navy at Aegospotami in 405 BCE. The war destroyed Athens.

Perestroika Another Russian term that means "restructuring." Here it refers to Gorbachev's policy of restructuring the Soviet economy in a way that produced more growth and less government control.

Personalized proportional representation system A hybrid approach to selecting party representation that combines elements of the winner-take-all and proportional representation systems.

Platform The ways that political parties articulate their stances on economic, political, and social issues.

Pluralist-Interdependence theory A theory that suggests that the long-standing concepts of sovereignty and territorial integrity are not capable enough of explaining international relations. It therefore argues that nonstate actors like terrorist organizations, nongovernmental organizations, and multinational corporations must be considered vital agents in explaining international affairs.

Pocket veto An indirect presidential veto occurs when a president takes no action on a bill for 10 days and Congress has adjourned.

Political question doctrine The legal view that some political matters should be addressed by the legislative rather than the judicial branch of government.

Political science The academic discipline that seeks to understand the relationship between individuals and political institutions.

Political socialization The process by which one's attitudes and values are shaped.

Positive law A body of law established or recognized by a governmental authority.

Post-behavioralism The school of thought that seeks to combine elements of the traditional approach (especially the idea of values) with those of behavioralism.

Power The ability to persuade others to do what they would not do on their own. Machiavelli asserts that power can be exercised through the use of force, by making threats, and/or by enticing desired behavior by providing gifts.

Presidential system A system in which the executive branch is separate from that of the legislature.

Privileges and Immunities Clause A clause found in Article IV of the U.S. Constitution that assures nonresidents are granted basic privileges and immunities across all states.

Proportional representation systems An electoral system that is designed to send a number of different party representatives to the national legislature.

Proxy state A state that is under some indirect control of another country. It is not a colony per se, but an ally due to economic or military reasons. For example, if a country during times of war gains military or financial assistance, they can be considered to be a proxy state. During the Cold War it was very common for the United States to financially and/or militarily support countries that were opposed to the Soviet Union.

Public opinion polls Surveys that seek to determine how different groups of people perceive political issues.

Quantitative analysis An analysis that uses data to interpret political phenomena. The data may come from survey research or established data sets to better understand the political world.

Quorum A legislative rule that requires a minimum number of legislators to be present in order for a bill to be voted on.

Raison d'état Best understood by the modern expression "the national interest" where modern leaders put forth what is best for their own state above all other reasons.

Rational choice theory The view that judicial decisions are best understood by analyzing the political ideology of justices.

Reagan doctrine Reagan sought to roll back rather than contain Soviet influence. The Reagan doctrine (1985) pledged aid to any nation or group of "freedom fighters," such as the Nicaraguan contras, seeking to defeat the spread of communism.

Realist A school of thought in international relations that emphasizes the furtherance of national interests and military security. Realists primarily believe nations exist within an anarchic international political system, and because of a tendency to distrust international organizations, believe nations must be prepared to militarily defend themselves at all times.

Realpolitik The use of practical methods, instead of moral or ideological means, to secure political power. For example, one who engages in realpolitik would assess entry into a war as a calculation of power for one's own country regardless of morality.

Regime The ruling government in a given country.

Republic A system of government where power lies with the body of citizens who elect representatives to make decisions on their behalf

Republican system of government A system of government in which power is exercised indirectly through representatives that are voted into office by citizens of the state.

RMS *Lusitania* A British cruise liner sunk by a German submarine off the coast of Ireland in 1915, killing almost 1,200 civilians. The outrage caused by the sinking of the *Lusitania* played an important role in the U.S. decision to enter World War I.

Secularism The belief that religion should be separate from governmental authority and political power.

Selective incorporation The process by which many of the Bill of Rights were nationalized into the states.

Senate Majority Leader The elected leader of the majority party in the U.S. Senate. The majority leader is responsible for setting the agenda in the U.S. Senate and plays a role in selecting committee assignments.

Senate Minority Leader The elected leader of the minority party in the U.S. Senate.

Senatorial courtesy The unofficial U.S. Senate custom of rejecting presidential judicial appointees when the nominee from the senator's state is not supported by that state's senior senator of the president's party.

Separate but equal doctrine The legal doctrine established in the *Plessy v. Ferguson* (1896) case that upheld racial segregation laws in the South.

Separation of powers A system of government that is divided between a legislative branch, an executive branch, and a judicial branch of government.

Shays's Rebellion An armed insurrection in Massachusetts led by Revolutionary war hero Daniel Shays. The rebellion targeted attacks on courthouses in an attempt to prevent farm foreclosures.

Skeptics Philosophers who generally agree that nothing can be known with absolute certainty.

Social contract theorists Thinkers beginning in the seventeenth century who sought to explain human nature by looking at the terms by which governments are set up in the first place.

Social contract theory A wide range of theories linked most closely with Thomas Hobbes, John Locke, and Jean-Jacques Rousseau on the most appropriate relationship between the state and the individual. Social contract theorists typically provide an (1) observation on human nature; (2) observation on problems that arise in the absence of government (i.e., precontract state); and (3) a recommendation on a form of government best able to solve these problems.

Social sciences Any number of academic disciplines that seek to understand human behavior. Classically they have been understood to mean anthropology, archaeology, economics, criminology, political science, and psychology.

Soft power Using methods other than military/economic coercion to receive desired outcomes. For example, getting another country to "want" the things we want can create a system of security.

Sovereignty The idea that the government within a state is recognized (domestically and internationally) as the ultimate source of authority to create, implement, and enforce laws.

Speaker of the House The presiding officer of the House of Representatives. The Speaker is the highest-ranking official in the House of Representative. He or she is third in line of succession to the presidency, and is responsible for establishing the political agenda of the body.

Stare decisis A Latin term translated to mean "let the decision stand" that relies heavily on legal precedents established in previous cases.

State The primary actor in international relations. States (referred to by American students as "countries") have governments, bureaucracies, territory, and people. States are in possession of the ultimate source of authority within its borders and are therefore said to possess sovereignty.

State terrorism When a state uses acts of terror on people living within its borders.

Statutory law Law that comes from authoritative and specific law-making sources, primarily legislatures, but also includes treaties and executive orders.

Structural realism The international system that determines the level of power within each state. State power is determined by the prospect of the balance of power within the international system. Sometimes the balance of power within the international system motivates states to pursue aggressive policies; sometimes it stifles them.

Subfields of political science The different content approaches within the overall discipline of political science. It can refer to political theory, American politics, comparative politics, and international relations.

Sunshine laws Laws that require public agencies to open meetings up to the public and to make public information available to the citizens.

Super-Majority vote A congressional vote requiring more than a simple majority vote. The Constitution requires a two-thirds super-majority vote in Congress in five instances: (1) when overriding a presidential veto; (2) when impeaching federal officials; (3) on Senate treaty ratification votes; (4) when removing fellow members for misconduct; and (5) when proposing constitutional amendments.

Supremacy Clause Found in Article VI of the U.S. Constitution, the Supremacy Clause asserts that the Constitution, national laws, and treaties are supreme over state laws when national laws are in compliance the U.S. Constitution.

Territorial integrity The boundaries of any state are to be protected against any acts of aggression and are to be maintained.

The Soviet-Afghan War A war between the Soviet Union and Afghanistan that lasted from 1979–1989. Waged for easier access to oil, the Soviet-Afghan War saw the presence of American CIA operatives funding and training rebel Afghans.

Theory An idea that has been tested that aims to demonstrate a correlation between political phenomena.

Third world countries Sometimes referred to as countries in the developing world. They received this distinction during the Cold War when the world was thought to be divided between a First World (most industrialized states), a Second World (the communist states), and a Third World, the poorest states located everywhere from Africa, to Latin America, Central, South and South East Asia.

Thirteenth Amendment An amendment to the Constitution that abolished the institution of slavery in the United States.

Thirty Years' War A war fought in Europe during the period 1618–1648 that was begun by the Catholic states in an attempt to bring the Protestant parts back to the "true" faith. Its conclusion resulted in the modern idea of the state as we know it today and the rise of international relations based on political rather than religious motives.

Three levels of analysis The three levels of analysis were developed by political scientist Kenneth Waltz as a way to better understand the reasons for conflict. The "three levels" refers to three difference actors involved in warfare: the individual (political leaders, terrorists, etc.), the state (domestic level actors like interest groups, political parties, ethnic or religious groups) and the international community (international tensions that spill over and cause conditions ripe for wars to occur).

Timocracy A government in which the love of honor is the ruling principle.

Totalitarian states States that employ policies and strategies that attempt to completely transform the attitudes and beliefs of the citizens by placing commitment to "the state" as their highest duty.

Traditional conservatism The belief that government should not attempt to change society, but that government should instead merely reflect changes that have already taken place in society. Conservatism believes government should play a role in upholding traditional and religious values, and that social changes should occur incrementally. Edmund Burke is generally regarded as the father of conservatism.

Traditionalism The methodological tradition that seeks to understand if certain government or political institutions are behaving in accordance with how they "ought to behave."

Transnational terrorism The type of privately funded, politically motivated violence that involves targets around the world.

Truman doctrine The foreign policy doctrine formulated by President Harry Truman in 1947 that declared the United States would react against aggression, direct or indirect, that threatened the United States. The doctrine was announced because of instability in Greece and Turkey, but was more widely applied against the Soviet Union.

Twenty-second Amendment A constitutional amendment ratified in 1951 that prohibits a president from serving more than two full terms in office (president may serve up to 10 years if he/she inherits the office as a result of impeachment or death of the previous president).

Tyranny of the majority A chief criticism of democratic systems of government where those in the political majority violate the rights of those in the political minority

Tyrant An absolute ruler unrestrained by law or constitution.

Undisciplined political parties Political parties whose members are free to vote according to their own personal beliefs.

Unicameral legislatures Legislatures that have only one house.

Unitary system of government A system of government where all powers are located in the central government. In this system, regional and local government derive power from the central government. Approximately 150 nations currently have a unitary system of government including Britain, China, France, and Japan.

Upper house An upper house is intended to be removed from the day-to-day activities of the legislature. Thus, it promotes the national interest and provides consultation on serious issues.

USS *Maine* A U.S. battleship that sunk mysteriously in Havana Harbor in Cuba in 1898. The U.S. public blamed the Spanish government for the sinking of the ship. The catchphrase "Remember the *Maine*" played a key role in instigating the Spanish-American War in 1898.

Utilitarianism The belief that the greatest good for the greatest number is the most justifiable course of action.

Utopian society Defined as a "perfect place" and a "place that does not exist."

Variable Features or attributes of social science research. In particular, a variable might look at the relationship between race and voting, age and voting, or religious preference and voting.

Virginia Plan Primarily drafted by James Madison and Edmund Randolph of Virginia. It was proposed at the Constitutional Convention and called for representation in Congress to be apportioned according to the state's population.

Wahabbism A form of Sunni Islam established in the eighteenth century by Muhammed Ibn Abdul-abl-Wahhab. It is considered by most scholars as one of the most conservative interpretations of the Muslim holy book, the Koran.

Warsaw Pact During the Cold War, the collection of Eastern European states that were controlled by and part of the Soviet Union.

Whip Party leaders who work closely with rank-and-file members to ensure individual members vote in accordance with the wishes of party leaders.

Winner-take-all system An electoral system that grants victory to the candidate who receives the majority of votes in his/her district.

NOTES

CHAPTER 1

[1] Thomas M. Magstadt, *Understanding Politics: Ideas, Institutions, and Issues*, 6th ed., Wadsworth Publishing, Belmont, California p. 261.

[2] Emily Hoban Kirby and Kei Kawashima-Ginsberg, "The Youth Vote in 2008," *The Center for Information & Research on Civic Learning and Engagement (CIRCLE)*,at www.civicyouth.org/quick-facts/325.

[3] Ibid

[4] Ibid.

[5] Definitions were gathered from the political dictionary, which can be accessed online at http://www.iamericanspirit.com/politicaldictionary.html. The definition for feminism was gathered from Merriam-Webster dictionary.

[6] See Joan Biskupic, "Ginsburg: Court Needs Another Woman." *USA Today,* October 5, 2009.

[7] Vicki W. Kramer, Alison M. Konrad, and Sumru Erkut, "Critical Mass on Corporate Boards: Why Three or More Women Enhance Governance," a Wellesley Center for Women's Publication, 2006.

[8] Christina L. Boyd, Lee Epstein, and Andrew D. Martin, "Untangling the Causal Effects of Sex on Judging," *American Journal of Political Science*, vol. 54, no. 2 (April 2010).

[9] Dina Refki et al. *"Women in Federal and State Level Judgeships"* A Report for the Center for Women in Government & Civil Society, Rockefeller College of Public Affairs and Policy, University at Albany, State University of New York, Spring 2011 at www.albany.edu/womeningov/judgeships_report_partII.pdf

[10] Dermot Feenan, *"Women at the Bench"* Law Centre (NI) found at http://lawcentre.org/publications/frontline_magazine/454.html

[11] Rania Abouzeid, "Bouazizi: The Man Who Set Himself and Tunisia on Fire." *Time*, January 21, 2011.

[12] "Islam and the Arab Revolutions." *The Economist*, April 2, 2011. p. 11.

[13] See Joseph S. Nye, "Soft Power: The Means to Success in World Politics." Library of Congress, 2004.

[14] Joseph S. Nye, "The Decline of America's Soft Power." *Foreign Affairs,* May/June 2004.

[15] Mike Duvall, "What Makes a Cell Phone Get Smaller? No, It's Not the Price, But You Are Close! Accessed at pdatoday.com. From http://www.pdatoday.com/pdaviews_more/533_0_4_0_M/.

[16] Mike Duvall, "What makes a cell phone get smaller? No, it's not the price, but you are close!" Accessed at pdatoday.com. Accessed at: http://www.pdatoday.com/pdaviews_more/533_0_4_0_M/.

[17] From Sasha Lezhnev and John Prendergast's opinion piece entitled, "Stopping the Flow of Conflict Minerals from Congo to Your Cell Phone," from CNN.com. Accessed at: http://www.cnn.com/2010/OPINION/08/03/congo.conflict.minerals/index.html.

[18]Easton, p. 133.

[19]Ibid, p. 134.

CHAPTER 2

[1]John H. Hallowell and Jene M. Porter, *Political Philosophy: The Search for Humanity and Order* (New York: Prentice Hall, 1997), 1.

[2]Brian R. Nelson, *Western Political Thought: From Socrates to the Age of Ideology* (New York: Prentice Hall, 1996), 6.

[3]Carl J. Richard, *Greeks & Romans Bearing Gifts: How the Ancients Inspired the Founding Fathers* (Lanham, MD: Rowman & Littlefield Publishers, 2008).

[4]Nelson, 6.

[5]For fuller discussion see Dominic J. O'Meara's *Pythagoras Revived: Mathematics and Philosophy in Late Antiquity* (Oxford, U.K.: Clarendon Press Oxford, 1990).

[6]See Michael Frede and Gisela Striker's *Rationality in Greek Thought* (Oxford, UK: Clarendon Press, 1996).

[7]Herbert Ernest Cushman, *A Beginner's History of Philosophy* (Orlando, FL: Houghton Mifflin, 1910), 65–69.

[8]Robert S. Brumbaugh, *The Philosophers of Greece* (Library of Congress, 1964).

[9]A. H. Armstrong, *An Introduction to Ancient Philosophy* (Boston: Beacon Press, 1959).

[10]Hallowell and Porter, 5.

[11]Nelson, 9.

[12]See Plato.stanford.edu/entries/Socrates/

[13]George Klosko, *History of Political Theory: An Introduction* (New York: Harcourt Brace, 1994), 32.

[14]Heather Coffey *Socratic Method* found at http://www.learnnc.org on October 2, 2009.

[15]Nelson, p. 10

[16]See George Novack's *The Origins of Materialism* (Boca Raton, FL: Merit Publishers, 1979), 186–187.

[17]Nelson, p. 14.

[18]G. M. A. Grube, *Plato. Apology. In the Trial and Death of Socrates* (Cambridge, MA: Hackett Publishing, 1975).

[19]Klosko, 41.

[20]Daryl H. Rice, *A Guide to Plato's Republic* (Oxford: Oxford University Press, 1998), 14.

[21]Steven M. Cahn, *Exploring Philosophy: An Introductory Anthology* (Oxford: Oxford University Press, 2000), 373.

[22]See Alain De Botton's introduction in *The Essential Plato* (New York: Quality Paperback Book Club, 1999).

[23]Nelson, 24.

[24]See Francis MacDonald Cornfold, Chapter 1, "Cephalus: Justice as Honesty in Word and Deed" in *The Republic of Plato* (Oxford: Oxford University Press, 1966).

[25]Cornfold, Chapter 3, "Thrasymarchus: Justice as the Interest of the Stronger."

[26]Ibid.

[27]For fuller discussion see Daryl Rice, *A Guide to Plato*, 97–100.

[28]*Plato's Republic,* Book II (434d–435a) found in G.M.A. Grube's translation of Plato's *Republic.*

[29] *Plato's Republic*, Book II (558d–559c, 373d–e, 370a–b, 374a–c, 394e, 423 c–d, 433a, 443b, 453b) found in Grube's translation of Plato's *Republic*.

[30] Net Worth of Members of Congress compiled by the Center for Responsive Politics (www .opensecrets.org/pfds/overview.ph.p?type=w.&year=2008).

[31] *Plato's Republic*, Book II and Book III (376–412b) in G. M. A. Grube's translation of Plato's *Republic*.

[32] Ibid.

[33] Alan Ebenstein, *Introduction to Political Thinkers* (New York: Harcourt College Publisher, 2002), 101.

[34] Ibid., p. 102.

[35] George Klosko, *History of Political Theory: Ancient and Medieval Political Theory* (New York: Harcourt Brace College Publishers, 1994), p. 245.

[36] *Plato's Republic,* Book V (475e–480a, and 596a) in G. M. A. Grube's translation of Plato's *Republic*.

[37] *Plato's Republic*, Book VII (514a–517c) in G. M. A. Grube's translation of Plato's *Republic*.

[38] *Plato's Republic,* Book VIII (547e–548c,555b–557c, 563–564a, 558a) in G. M. A. Grube's translation of Plato's *Republic*.

[39] *Plato's Republic,* Book IX (575a–580c) in G. M. A. Grube's translation of Plato's *Republic*.

[40] *Plato's Republic*, Book III (413b–415b) in G. M. A. Grube's translation of Plato's *Republic*.

[41] C. D. C. Reeve's introduction found in *Aristotle:Politics* (Cambridge, MA: Hackett Publishing, 1998).

[42] *Aristotle's Politics:* Chapter I (1253a–718) in C. D. C. translation of Aristotle's *Politics*.

[43] Joseph Losco and Leonard Williams, *Political Theory: Classic and Contemporary Readings* (Cary, NC: Roxbury Publishing, 2003), 174.

[44] Nelson, 91.

[45] *Aristotle's Politics*: Chapter I (1252a24-1253a38) in T. A. Sinclair's translation of Aristotle's *Politics* (New York Penguin Books, 1992).

[46] See Marjorie Grene's *A Portrait of Aristotle* (Chicago: University of Chicago Press, 1963), 211–226.

[47] *Aristotle's Politics:* Chapter I (1253a9–10) in C. D. C. translation of Aristotle's *Politics*.

[48] Nelson, 54.

[49] See *Aristotle's Rhetoric*, Chapter 1 (http:www.publiciastate.edu/~honeyl/rhetoric/index.html).

[50] Klosko, 126–127.

[51] This definition along with the definitions for civil disobedience, aristocracy, monarch, timocracy, oligarch, tyranny, natural law, and positive law were all found at http://www .merriam-webster.com.

CHAPTER 3

[1] See *Stanford Encyclopedia of Philosophy* at http://plato.stanford.edu/entries/machiavelli/.

[2] Ibid.

[3] Steven M. DeLue *Political Thinking, Political Theory, and Civil Society* (Boston: Allyn and Bacon, 1997), 97.

[4] Niccolo Machiavelli, *The Prince Why Princes Are Praised or Blamed,* in Alan Ebenstein's *Introduction to Political Thinkers* (Library of Congress, 2002), 152.

[5] Brian R. Nelson, *Western Political Thought: From Socrates to the Age of Ideology* (New York: Prentice Hall, 1996), 140.

[6]George Klosko, *History of Political Theory: An Introduction* (New York: Harcourt Brace, 1995), p. 7.

[7]Nelson, 142.

[8]Niccolo Machiavelli, "The Prince: In What Ways Princes Must Keep Faith," in Alan Ebenstein's *Introduction to Political Thinkers* (Library of Congress, 2002), p.155.

[9]Nelson, 144.

[10]Blaine Harden, "North Korea's Hard-Labor Camps: On the Diplomatic Back Burner" in *The Washington Post,* July 20, 2009.

[11]See Genderside Watch, *Case Study: The Anfal Campaign* found at www.genderside.org/case/-anfal_htm.

[12]Frederick the Great, "Should a Prince Keep Faith?" in DeLamar Jensen (ed.), *Problems in European Civilization, Machiavelli: Cynic, Patriot, or Political Scientist?* (Boston: D. C. Heath, 1960), 5. Originally found in the Nelson book on p. 144.

[13]Sheldon Wolin, *Politics and Vision* (Princeton: Princeton University Press, 1960), chapter 7.

[14]Niccolo Machiavelli, *The Prince* (New York: Random House, originally published 1513), chapter 18.

[15]Ibid.

[16]Ibid., "Constant Readiness for War."

[17]Ibid.

[18]Ibid.

[19]Ibid., "Princes Must Avoid Being Despised or Hated.

[20]Ibid., Cruelty and Clemency: Is It Better to Be Loved or Feared."

[21]Machiavelli, *Chapter 8.*

[22]Machiavelli, *Chapter 20.*

[23]Peter Brown, *Strong and Wrong vs. Weak and Right* found at *www.realclearpolitics.com/articles/2007/01/strong and* wrong*vs* weak*and*right, January 15, 2007.

[24]Jack Tapper, *The Brains Behind Bush,* available at http:dir.salon.com/books/feature/2003/011/21/Rove/.

[25]See Brian R. Nelson's explanation in *Western Political Thought,* 150.

[26]Machiavelli, *Chapter 18.*

[27]William H. Honan, "Three Hobbes Essays Renew Debate Over Machiavelli," in *New York Times,* December 20, 1995.

[28]Nelson, 161.

[29]Ibid., 162.

[30]Stephen Hawking, "Galileo and the Birth of Modern Science," *Invention & Technology* (Spring 2009).

[31]Nelson, 163.

[32]See Thomas Hobbes, *Leviathan: The State of Nature* (Chapter VI, "Of the Interior Beginnings of Voluntary Motions, Commonly called the Passions; and the Speeches By Which They Are Expressed"),originally published 1651.

[33]Ibid.

[34]See Thomas Hobbes, *Stanford Encyclopedia of Philosophy* at (*http://plato.stanford.edu/entries/hobbes/*)

[35]Hobbes *Leviathan,* chapter 11.

[36]Ibid.

[37]Ibid.

[38]George Klosko, *History of Political Theory: An Introduction Modern Political Theory* (New York: Harcourt Brace, 1995), 43.

[39]Klosko, 46.

[40]Machiavelli, *The Prince, Chapter 18.*

[41]Klosko, 43.

[42]Hobbes, *Leviathan.*

[43]Ebenstein *Introduction to Political Thinkers* (Fort Worth, TX:Harcourt College Publishers, 2002), 189.

[44]Mitchell Gerber, *Sources: Notable Selections in American Government* (Guilford, CT: Dushkin Publishing, 1996), p. 3.

[45]Reported by Freedom House in *The Economist* on November 16, 2006.

[46]John Locke's "Two Treatises of Government, The State of Nature," found in Ebenstein's *Introduction to Political Thinkers* (Fort Worth, TX, Harcourt College Publishers, 2002) p. 196.

[47]See Seneca Falls Convention (July 19–20) at http://www.npg.si.edu/col/seneca/senfalls1/htm)

[48]Ibid.

[49]James Wiser, *Political Theory: A Thematic Inquiry* (Chicago: Nelson-Hall, 1986), 98.

[50]Klosko, p. 98.

[51]Steven M. DeLue, *Political Thinking, Political Theory, and Civil Society* (Boston: Allyn and Bacon, 1997), 128.

[52]DeLue, 129.

[53]David McLellan, *Karl Marx: Selected Writings* (Oxford, UK: Oxford University Press, 2000), 239.

[54]Nelson, 223.

[55]Ibid., 229.

CHAPTER 4

[1]See www.moticello.org/site/research.and.collection/tje.

[2]Winston Churchill speech in the British House of Commons on November 11, 1947. Found at *Winston S. Churchill: His Complete Speeches, 1897–1963*, edited by Robert Rhodes James, vol 7 (New York: Chelsea House Publishers, 1994), 7566.

[3]Information found at www.ushistory.org/declaration/signers.htm.

[4]Robert L. Lineberry, George C. Edwards, and Martin Wattenberg, *Government In America: People Politics, and Policy* (New York: HarperCollins, 1994), 43.

[5]Jon R. Bond and Kevin B. Smith, *The Promise and Performance of American Democracy* (Belmont, CA: Thomson Wadsworth, 2006), 41.

[6]Barbara A. Bardes, Mack C. Shelley, and Steffen W. Schmidt, *American Government and Politics Today: The Essentials* (Belmont, CA: Wadsworth Thomson, 2000), 39.

[7]Letter from George Washington to Henry Lee Jr. on October 31, 1786. *The Papers of George Washington: Confederation Series*, Library of Congress, vol. 4 pp. 318–320 found at http://lcweb2.loc.gov/ammen/gwhtml/gwhome.html

[8]Letter from Thomas Jefferson to James Madison on January 30, 1787. *The Letters of Thomas Jefferson*, University of Virginia. Available at www.let.rug.nl/usa/p/tj3/writings/brf/jefl53.htm

[9]James MacGregor Burns, J. W. Peltason, Thomas E. Cronin, and David B. Magleby, *Government By the People* (Upper Saddle River, NJ: Prentice Hall, 1997), 8.

[10]Larry Berman and Bruce Allen Murphy, *Approaching Democracy* (*Upper Saddle River, NJ:* Pearson Prentice Hall, 2007), 43.

[11]Bardes, Shelley, and Schmidt, 39.

[12]Charles Beard, *An Economic Interpretation of the Constitution of the United States* (New York: Macmillan, 1913).

[13]See Robert E. Brown, *Charles Beard and the Constitution: A Critical Analysis of "An Economic Interpretation of the Constitution"* (Princeton: Princeton University Press, 1956).

[14]Bardes, Shelley, and Schmidt, 40.

[15]Christopher Collier and James Collier, *Decisions in Philadelphia: The Constitutional Convention of 1787* (New York: Random House, 1986).

[16]Xi Wang, "Building African American Voting Rights in the Nineteenth Century" in *The Voting Rights Act: Securing the Ballot*, ed. Richard M. Valley (Washington DC: CQ Press, 2005).

[17]Paula D. McClain et al., "Rebuilding Black Voting Rights Before the Voting Rights Act" in *The Voting Rights Act: Securing the Ballot,* ed. Richard M. Valley (Washington DC: CQ Press, 2005).

[18]Robert C. Liebermann, "Disenfranchisement and its Impact on the Political System" in *The Voting Rights Act: Securing the Ballot,* ed. Richard M. Valley (Washington DC: CQ Press, 2005).

[19]Michael J. Klarman, "The Supreme Court and Black Disenfranchisement" in *The Voting Rights Act: Securing the Ballot,* ed. Richard M. Valley (Washington DC: CQ Press, 2005).

[20]Colin D. Moore, "Extension of the Voting Rights Act" in *The Voting Rights Act: Securing the Ballot,* ed. Richard M. Valley (Washington DC: CQ Press, 2005).

[21]Ibid.

[22]Alexander Hamilton, James Madison, and John Jay, *The Federalist Papers* (New York: New American Library, 1986).

[23]See Carrie-Ann Biondi's "Aristotle on the Mixed Constitution and its Relevance for American Political Thought," *Social Philosophy and Policy*, vol. 24, p. 176.

[24]*Aristotle's: The Politics,* trans. T. A. Sinclair (London: Penguin Group, 1981), 266–267.

[25]Theodore Lowi, Benjamin G. Ginsberg, and Kenneth A. Shepsle, *American Government: Power and Purpose* (New York: W.W. Norton, 2008), 31.

[26]Hamilton, Madison, and Jay, *The Federalist Papers.*

[27]Walter E. Volkomer, *American Government* (*Upper Saddle River, NJ:* Prentice Hall, 2007), 43.

[28]Burns et al., 44.

[29]Proposition 8, a ballot initiative in California that defined marriage as a relationship between one man and one woman overturned a 2008 California Supreme Court decision that ruled same-sex couples have a right to marry in California. Same-sex marriages performed the passage of Proposition 8 remain valid, but same-sex marriages are no longer performed in California (see National Conference of State Legislatures at http:www.ncls.org).

[30]See the Tenth Amendment to the U.S. Constitution.

[31]See *McCulloch v. Maryland* 4 Wheaton 316 (1819).

[32]See article IV of the U.S. Constitution.

[33]See *Wilson v. Ake*, No. 8:04-cv-1680-T-30TBM, U.S. District Court, Middle District of Florida, January 19, 2005.

[34]E. E. Schattschneider, *Party Government* (New York: Farrier and Rinehart, 1942).

[35]V. O. Key, "A Theory of Critical Elections," *Journal of Politics* 17 (1955): 3–18.

[36]Karen O'Connor and Larry J. Sabato, *American Government: Continuity and Change* (Boston: Allyn and Bacon, 1999).

[37]Lineberry et al., 63.

[38]See *Federalist Paper No. 17*.

[39]Ibid.

[40]See *Federalist Paper No. 10*.

[41]See David R. Mayhew, *Partisan Balance: Why Political Parties Don't Kill the U.S. Constitutional System* (Princeton: Princeton University Press, 2011).

[42]Anthony Champagne, *Congressman Sam Rayburn* (New Brunswick, NJ: Rutgers University Press, 1984).

[43]Bardes et al., 48.

[44]The Twenty-seventh Amendment, which prohibits members of Congress from approving congressional pay increases without first having a intervening election, was ratified more than 200 years later in 1992.

[45]See Albert P. Blaustein, "The U.S. Constitution: America's Most Important Export," in *Issues of Democracy Electronic Journals,* vol. 9, no. 1 (March 2004).

CHAPTER 5

[1]Alexander Hamilton, James Madison, John Jay, *The Federalist Papers* (New York: New American Library, 1986).

[2]The United States Constitution, Article 1, Section 6

[3]See John Locke's *Two Treatise of Government*, found in Peter Laslett's edited *Two Treatise of Government* (New York: Cambridge University Press, 1988).

[4]See Virginia Sloan et al., "Deciding to Use Force Abroad: War Powers in a System of Checks and Balances." The Constitution Project (2005).

[5]See Roger H. Davidson's *"Invitation to Struggle": An Overview of Legislative-Executive Relations*, The Annals of the American Academy of Political and Social Science, vol. 19, no. 1 (1988): 9–21.

[6]Greg Bruno, "U.S. Drone Activities in Pakistan." Council on Foreign Relations, July 19, 2009.

[7]Ibid.

[8]The United States Constitution, Article 1, Section 8.

[9]The United States Constitution, Article 1, Section 2.

[10]The United States Constitution, Article 1, Section 3.

[11]See Federalist Paper #55 in *The Federalist Papers* (New York: New American Library, 1986).

[12]See Federalist Paper #57 in *The Federalist Papers* (New York: New American Library, 1986).

[13]J Pope, *Memoirs of Rt Hon Sir Alexander MacDonald,* vol. 2 (Ottawa, 1894).

[14]See Federalist Paper # 62 in *The Federalist Papers* (New York: New American Library, 1986).

[15]See Federalist Paper # 63 in *The Federalist Papers* (New York: New American Library, 1986).

[16]See C. H. Hoebeke's *The Road to Mass Democracy: Original Intent and the Seventeenth Amendment* (Transaction Publishers, 1995).

[17]See Ralph Rossum's *Federalism, the Supreme Court, and the Seventeenth Amendment* (Lanham, MD: Lexington Books, 2001).

[18]See www.senate.gov/~byrd.

[19]Micheal Barone et al., Politics in America (Washington D.C.: Congressional Quarterly Press, 2002).

[20]Current Biography, "Robert C. Byrd" (Bronx, NY: H. W. Wilson Company, 1978).

[21]Barone et al.

[22]Barone et al.

[23]Daniel Lazare, "The Frozen Republic: How the Constitution Is Paralyzing Democracy" in *Taking Sides: Clashing Views on Controversial Political Issues,* edited by George McKenna and Stanley Feingold (New York: McGraw-Hill/Dushkin, 2001).

[24]Richard S. Beth and Stanley Bach, "Filibusters and Cloture in the Senate," *Report for Congress Congressional Research Service* (March 28, 2003).

[25]Number of cloture votes gathered from the U.S. Senate Web page found at www.senate.gov/page/layout/referecne/cloture_motions/cloturecounts.htm.

[26]Stephen Ansolabehere and Samuel Isaacharoff, "*Baker v. Carr* in Context: 1946–1964" in *Constitutional Law Stories* (M. Dorf, Foundation Press, 2003).

[27]Ann O'M. Bowman and Richard C. Kearney, *State and Local Government*, 3rd ed. (Orlando, FL: Houghton Mifflin Co., 2005).

[28]Lee Epstein and Thomas G. Walker, *Constitutional Law for a Changing America: Institutional Powers and Constraints,* 4th ed. (Washington D.C.: Congressional Quarterly Press, 2004).

[29]Statistical breakdown of current members of Congress comes from Jennifer Manning's *Membership of the 112th Congress: A Profile,* Congressional Research Service (March 1, 2011).

[30]Statistical breakdown of current members of Congress comes from Jennifer Manning's *Membership of the 112th Congress: A Profile,* Congressional Research Service (March 1, 2011). Information on Prorated number of Members of Congress if Congress looked like the American public comes from a 2005 figure used by Larry Berman and Bruce Allen Murphy's in *Approaching Democracy* (Upper Saddle River, NJ: Prentice Hall, 2007), 134.

[31]Mark Rush, "The Voting Rights Act and its Discontents" in Richard Valelly (ed.) *The Voting Rights Act: Securing the Ballot* (Washington DC: Congressional Quarterly Press 2005), 147.

[32]See Karen O'Connor's, *Do Women in Local, State, and National Legislative Bodies Matter? A Definitive Yes Proves Three Decades of Research by Political Scientists."* (http://www.american.edu/oconnor.wandp/)

[33]David R. Mayhew, *The Electoral Connection* (New Haven: Yale University Press, 1974).

[34]Richard F. Fenno Jr., *Congressmen in Committees* (Boston: Little, Brown, 1973).

[35]See World Prison Populations at http://news.bbc.co.uk/2/shared/spl/hi/uk/06/prisons/html/nn2page1.stm.

[36]See "The Sentencing Project: Research and Advocacy for Reform," *Felony Disenfranchisement Laws in the United States.*

[37]Nicholas Thompson, "Locking Up the Vote: Disenfranchisment of former felons was the real crime in Florida." *Washington Monthly,* January/February 2001.

[38]Thomas E. Mann and Norman J. Ornstein, *The Broken Branch* (New York: Oxford University Press, 2006).

[39]John W. Kingdon, *Agendas, Alternatives, and Public Policies* (Boston: Little, Brown, 1984).

[40]Paul Singer, *Members Offered Many Bills But Passed Few*, Roll Call (December 1, 2008).

[41]Singer.

[42]Larry Berman and Bruce Allen Murphy, *Approaching Democracy* (Upper Saddle River, NJ: Pearson/Prentice Hall, 2007).

[43]Sara Collins and Jennifer L. Nicholson, *"Rite of Passage: Young Adults and the Affordable Care Act of 2010,"* The Commonwealth Fund (May 10, 2010).

[44]Collins and Nicholson.

[45]Paul S. Boyer, "Medicare and Medicaid," in *The Oxford Companion to United States History* (New York: Oxford University Press, 2001).

[46]Collins and Nicholson. All information on the impact of the Affordable Care Act on young Americans comes from this study.

[47]Gallup Poll, *Congress's Approval Rating Ties Lowest in Gallup Records.* Available at www.gallup.com (May 14, 2008).

[48]Gallup Poll. *Polling on Congressional Job Approval.* Available at http://www.galluppoll.com (April 6, 2006).

[49]*USA Today* (2006). "USA Today/CNN Gallup Poll." Available at http://www.usatoday.com/news/polls/2006-01-09-poll.htm (January 3, 2006).

[50]*Congressional Ethics: History, Facts, and Controversy* (Washington D.C.: Congressional Quarterly, 1992).

[51]Dean Calbreath and Jerry Kammer, "Contractor Knew How To Grease Wheels." *San Diego Union Tribune* (December 4, 2005).

[52]Charles R. Babcock, "Contractor Linked to Bribery Case Worked Together." *The Washington Post* (November 30, 2005), A-2.

[53]Peter DeLeon, *Thinking About Political Corruption* (Armonk, NY: M.E. Sharpe, 1993).

[54]Bill Muller, "The Keating Five," *The Arizona Republic* (October 3, 1).

[55]Ronald D. Elving, "Senators Cleared By Panel Await Political Judgment," *Congressional Quarterly Weekly Report,* (March 2, 1991).

[56]Dennis F. Thompson, "Mediated Corruption: The Case of the Keating Five," *American Political Science Review* vol. 87, no. 2 (pp. 369–381).

[57]Phil Kuntz, "Cranston Case Ends on Floor with a Murky Plea Bargain," *Congressional Quarterly Weekly Report* (November 23, 1991).

CHAPTER 6

[1]See Open Secrets at www.opensecrets.org/pres/08summary.php?id=no0009638.

[2]Voter turnout numbers gathered from http://elections.gmu/Turnout_2008G.html.

[3]Alexander Hamilton, *The Works of Alexander Hamilton: Comprising His Correspondence and His Political and Official Writings* (New York: Charles S. Francis, 1850), 201.

[4]See Charles C. Thach, Jr., *The Creation of the Presidency, 1775–1789* (Baltimore: Johns Hopkins University Press, 1969).

[5]Letter from James Madison to Virginia delegate Edmund Randolph found at *The Founders Constitution* (Chicago: University of Chicago Press), chap. 6, doc. 9: 367–371.

[6]See Richard Ellis, ed., *Founding the American Presidency* (Lanham, MD: Rowman and Littlefield Publishers, 1999), 9.

[7] James Pfiffner and Roger H. Davidson, *Understanding the Presidency*, (Upper Saddle River, NJ: Longman, 2000), 9.

[8] Michael Nelson, ed., *The Evolving Presidency* (Washington DC: CQ Press, 2004), 1.

[9] Alexander Hamilton, James Madison, and John Jay, *The Federalist Papers* (New York: New American Library, 1986).

[10] See The Center For Information and Research on Civic Learning and Engagement (CIRCLE) at (www.civicyouth.org).

[11] John Hart, "Mr. Hoover's Eligibility for the Presidency," *Virginia Law Review*, vol. 15, no. 5 (March 1929): 476–478.

[12] See the C-Span survey results at http:www.c-span.org/PresidentialSurvey/Overall-Ranking.aspx.

[13] Letter from John Jay to George Washington dated July 25, 1787, found in Alex Heard and Michael Nelson, *Presidential Selection*, (Durham, NC: Duke University Press, 1987), 123.

[14] Senator Patrick Leahy (D-VT) and Senator Claire McCaskill (D-MO) proposed a Senate resolution expressing that Senator John McCain (R-AZ) is a natural-born citizen on April 10, 2008.

[15] Robert E. DiClerico, *The American President* (Upper Saddle River, NJ: Prentice Hall, 1999).

[16] Sidney M. Milkis and Michael Nelson, *The American Presidency* (Washington DC: CQ Press, 2008), 31.

[17] See John Ferling, *Adams vs. Jefferson: The Tumultuous Election of 1800* (New York: Oxford University Press, 2004).

[18] One Electoral College member from Washington DC did not cast a ballot in protest of a controversy in determining the winner in Florida in the 2000 election.

[19] See Jeffrey M. Jones, "Obama's Highest Half-Year Approval Ratings in D.C., Hawaii," Gallup Poll (July 2010), found at www.gallup.com/poll.

[20] Ronald C. Moe, *The President's Cabinet,* in James Pfiffner and Roger H. Davidson, *Understanding the Presidency* (Upper Saddle River, NJ: Longman, 2000), 173.

[21] Moe, 175.

[22] Milkis and Nelson, 41.

[23] L. Gordon Crovitz and Jeremy Rabkin, *The Fettered Presidency: Legal Constraints on the Executive Branch*, (Washington DC: American Enterprise Institute, 1989).

[24] Karen O'Connor, Larry J. Sabato, and Alixandra B. Yanus, *Essentials of American Government: Roots and Reform* (Upper Saddle River, NJ: Longman, 2009), 203.

[25] James Pfiffner, *The President's Broad Power to Pardon and Commute* (July 2007), found at www.heritage.org.

[26] O'Connor, Sabato, and Yanus, 202.

[27] See Mitchel A. Sullenberger's *Congressional Overrides of Presidential Vetoes* for a detailed analysis on presidential vetoes (CRS Report for Congress order code 98–157, April 2004).

[28] George Clinton, *To the Citizens of New York*, found in Pfiffner's and Davidson's, *Understanding the Presidency*, 18.

[29] Arthur Schlesinger Jr., *The Imperial Presidency* (Boston: Houghton Mifflin, 1973).

[30] Richard Neustadt, *Presidential Power: The Politics of Leadership* (New York: John Wiley, 1960).

[31] Samuel Kernell, *Going Public: New Strategies of Presidential Leadership* (Washington DC: CQ Press, 1986).

[32] See Clinton Rossiter's *The American Presidency* (New York: Harcourt Brace, 1960).

[33] DiClerico, 32.

[34]Woodrow Wilson, *Constitutional Government in the United States,* originally published in 1908 (Piscataway, NJ: Transaction Publishers, 2001).

[35]Joseph S. Nye, *Understanding International Conflict* (Boston: Addison Wesley, 1993).

[36]Ibid.

[37]David Abshire, *Foreign Policy Makers: President vs. Congress (The Washington Papers),* (University Press of America, 1979), 36.

[38]Louis Fisher, *Constitutional Conflicts Between Congress and the President* (Lawrence, KS: University of Kansas Press, 2007).

[39]Nye.

[40]Schlesinger.

[41]John Lewis Gaddis, *Strategies of Containment: A Critical Appraisal of Postwar American National Security Policy* (New York: Oxford University Press, 1982).

[42]Ibid.

[43]Abshire, 44.

[44]John Stoessinger, *Why Nations Go To War* (Florence, KY: Wadsworth Publishers, 2000).

[45]Walter Lafeber, *The American Age: United States Foreign Policy at Home and Abroad* (New York: W. W. Norton and Co., 1994), 632.

[46]Ibid.

[47]Gaddis.

[48]Nye.

[49]Lafeber, 646.

[50]Nye.

[51]Spanier and Hook (1995) p. 258.

[52]Presidential address to a joint session of Congress given by President George W. Bush on September 20, 2001.

[53]Ivo H. Daalder and James M. Lindsay, *America Unbound: The Bush Revolution in Foreign Policy* (Washington DC: Brookings Institute, 2003).

[54]Greg Bruno, "U.S. Drone Activities in Pakistan," Council of Foreign Relations, July 19, 2010.

CHAPTER 7

[1]See *Boy Scouts et al. v. Dale* (2000) Supreme Court opinion at http:/caselaw.lp.findlaw.com.

[2]See *Federalist Paper No. 78* in [2]Alexander Hamilton, James Madison, and John Jay, *The Federalist Papers* (New York: New American Library, 1986).

[3]Robert A. Carp and Ronald Stidham, *Judicial Process in America* (Washington DC: CQ Press, 1998).

[4]Ibid., 24.

[5]The United States Constitution, Art. III, Sect. 1.

[6]See James C. Duff's "*Judicial Facts and Figures: Multi-Year Statistical Compilations on the Federal Judiciary's Caseload Through Fiscal Year 2008*" at United States Courts, available at http: www.iscourts.gov/home.aspx.

[7]Ibid.

[8]G. Alan Tarr, *Judicial Process and Judicial Policymaking* (Eagan, MN: West Publishing, 1994), p. 42.

[9]See 2009 Year-End Report on the Federal Judiciary, available at www.supremecourt.gov/publicinfo/year-end/2009report.

[10]Lawrence Baum, *American Courts: Process and Policy* (Boston: Houghton Mifflin, 1998), 310.

[11]Ibid., 264.

[12]See Duff, Table 2.3, September 2009.

[13]See George C. Thomas III, "Double Jeopardy-Mistrials," available at http://law.jrank.org/pages/1019/double-jeopardy.html.

[14]*Encyclopedia of Everyday Law*, "Double Jeopardy."

[15]William J. Brennan, Jr., "*State Supreme Court Judge Versus United States Supreme Court Justice: A Change in Function and Perspective,*" in *University of Florida Law Review,* vol. 19 (1966), 236, found in G. Alan Tarr's *Judicial Process and Judicial Policymaking.*

[16]See National Center for State Courts, *Traffic Violations Caseload,* available at www.ncs.org.

[17]Tarr, 55.

[18]Definitions were taken from Ames MacGregor Burns et al., *Government by the People* (Upper Saddle River, NJ: Prentice Hall, 1997), 335.

[19]Supreme Court Historical Society, *The Court as an Institution,* prepared by the Supreme Court of the United States.

[20]Carp and Stidham, 28.

[21]See Article III of the U.S. Constitution.

[22]Otis H. Stephens, Jr. and John Scheb, *American Constitutional Law* (Florence, KY: Wadsworth, 1999), 272.

[23]George Painter, "The Sensibilities of our Forefathers," available at http:www.gplan/sodomylaws/sensibilities/introduction.htm.

[24]American Civil Liberties Union, "History of Sodomy Laws and the Strategy that Led Up to Today's Decision," available at (http://www.aclu.org/lgby-rights_hiv-aids/history-sodomy-laws.

[25]See Article III of the U.S. Constitution.

[26]Stephens and Scheb, 39.

[27]Ibid., 110.

[28]See *Heart of Atlanta Motel v. United States* (1964) and *Katzenbach v. McClung* (1964) to review how the Interstate Commerce Clause was used to defend the Civil Rights Act of 1964.

[29]Edward S. Corwin, *The Commerce Power Versus State Rights* (Princeton, NJ: Princeton University Press, 1936).

[30]Michael Giuliano, "The Commerce Clause and Civil Rights," available at http://www.lewrockwell.com.

[31]Nancy Lee Jones, *The Americans with Disabilities Act: Statutory Language and Recent Issues,* Congressional Research Service (August 2001).

[32]Ibid.

[33]Lee Epstein and Thomas G. Walker, *Constitutional Law for a Changing America: Institutional Powers and Constraints* (Washington DC: CQ Press,1995), 311.

[34]For more information on the Dred Scott case, see www.watson.org/⬛lisa/blackhistory/scott/casebackground.html.

[35]See *Dred Scott v. Sandford* (1857) decision.

[36]See the Fourteenth Amendment of the U.S. Constitution.

[37]Epstein and Walker, 58.

[38]Ibid., 56.

[39]Ibid., 59.

[40]Ibid., 668.

[41]Ibid., 670.

[42]Stephen Ansolabehere and Samuel Isaacharoff, "*Baker v. Carr* in Context: 1946–1964," in *Constitutional Law Stories* (M. Dorf, Foundation Press, 2003).

[43]Ann O'M. Bowman and Richard C. Kearney, *State and Local Government*, 3rd ed. (Boston: Houghton Mifflin).

[44]Baum, 101.

[45]See Article III of the United States Constitution.

[46]Tarr, 79.

[47]Baum, 106. The successful confirmation of Chief Justice Roberts and Justice Alito included in this number.

[48]Data drawn from the United States Courts, http://www.uscourts.gov/JudgesAndJudgeships/FederalJudgeships.aspx and National Association of Women Judges, http://www.nawj.org/us_state_court_statistics_2010.asp.

[49]Charlie Savage, "Sotomayor Confirmed by Senate, 68–31," *New York Times*, 6 August 2009.

[50]Jone Johnson Lewis, *Sonia Sotomayor Biography*, available at http://womenshistory.about.com/od/publicofficials/p/sotomayor.htm.

[51]Ibid.

[52]Savage.

[53]Tarr, 68.

[54]Information gathered from "*Judicial Selection in the States*," printed by the American Judicature Society.

[55]Carp and Stidham, 265.

[56]Gregory A. Caldeira and John R. Wright, "The Discuss List: Agenda Building in the Supreme Court," *Law and Society Review*, vol. 24, no. 3 (1990); 807–836.

[57]Kenneth A. Manaster, *Illinois Justice: The Scandal of 1969 and the Rise of John Paul Stevens* (Chicago: University of Chicago Press, 2001).

[58]Ibid.

[59]Caldeira and Wright.

[60]Ibid.

[61]John Dean, "What Exactly is Judicial Activism? The Charges Made Against the President's Judicial Nominees," 17 June 2005, available at http:writ.news.findlaw.com/dean/20050617.html.

[62]Tracey E. George and Lee Epstein, "On the Nature of Supreme Court Decision Making," *American Political Science Review*, vol. 82, no. 2 (June 1992).

[63]Epstein and Walker, 14.

[64]Jerome Frank, *Law and the Modern Mind* (New York, 1949).

[65]Adam Liptak, "Justices, 5–4 Reject Corporate Spending Limit," *New York Times*, 21 January 2010.

[66]See Center for Responsive Politics, "Open Secrets" at www.opensecrets.org/news/2010.

[67]See Jeffrey Rosen, "Roberts versus Roberts," *The New Republic*, 2 March 2010.

68Adam Liptak, "Court Under Roberts Is Most Conservative in Decades," *New York Times,* 24 July 2010.

69Larry Berman and Bruce Allen Murphy, *Approaching Democracy* (Upper Saddle River, NJ: Pearson, Prentice Hall, 2007).

70Epstein and Walker, 62.

CHAPTER 8

1Hannah Arendt, *Totalitarianism: Part Three of the Origins of Totalitarianism* (New York: Harcourt Press, 1998).

2Jonathan Alter's, *The Defining Moment: FDR's First Hundred Days and The Triumph of Hope* (New York: Simon and Schuster, 2006).

3Max Wallace's *The American Axis: Henry Ford, Charles Lindbergh, and the Rise of the Third Reich* (New York: St. Martin's Press, 2003), 2–3.

4This quote comes from the *CIA World Fact Book,* at http://www. cia.gov/cia/publications/ factbook/geos/sa.html

5Alexis de Tocqueville, *Democracy in America* (London: Penguin Classics, 2003), 342.

6Ibid, 340.

7From the online *Library of Congress Country Studies* section on the Presidency in Iran, http://lcweb2.loc.gov/cgi-bin/query/r?frd/cstdy:@field(DOCID+ir0128)

8Thomas Paine's *Common Sense* was a pamphlet written in 1776 as an American rallying cry against British colonial rule. It still serves as an interesting discussion on the merits of free government versus that of authoritarianism. A good version of it can be accessed at http://www.earlyamerica.com/earlyamerica/milestones/commonsense/text.html

9Václav Havel, *The Memorandum* (1965) was an attempt at exposing the ills of the Soviet government who had invaded Czechoslovakia in 1963. The plot revolves around the creation and implementation of a new language among office workers unfit to understand it.

10Quoted in Jackson Diehl, "Chavez's Censorship: Where Disrespect Can Land You in Jail," *Washington Post,* March 28, 2005.

11Ibid.

12Ben Bagdikian, *The New Media Monopoly* (Boston: Beacon Publishing, 2004).

13Federal Communication Commission's "About us" page, http://www.fcc.gov/aboutus.html.

14From Common Cause, "The Fallout from the 1996 Telecommunications Act: Unintended Consequences and Lessons Learned," May 9, 2005, http://www.commoncause.org/atf/cf/%7B8A2D1D15-C65A-46D4-8CBB-2073440751B5%7D/FALLOUT_FROM_THE_TELECOMM_ACT_5-9-05.PDF.

15Nikolas van Dam, *The Struggle for Power in Syria: Sectarianism, Regionalism, and Tribalism in Politics.* (London: I. B Taurus, 1996).

16"The Iraqi Baath Party," Aljazeera.net, June 23, 2005, http://english.aljazeera.net/NR/exeres/AFBF5651-45AF-45E7-910E-ECA0AFEA24C1.htm

17McFaul and Stoner-Weiss, "The Myth of the Authoritarian Model," *Foreign Affairs*, January/February 2008, 70–71.

18Tocqueville, 114–115.

[19]Jeremy Bentham's greatest work entitled *An Introduction to the Principles of Morals and Legislation* (1789) examines the concept of utilitarianism defined as giving the greatest number the greatest level of happiness. James Mill's greatest work, *Essay on Government,* continues Bentham's theory of utilitarianism and suggests that democratic governments are the best possible form.

[20]Brian R. Nelson, *Western Political Thought: From Socrates to the Age of Ideology*, 2nd ed. (Upper Saddle River, NJ: Prentice Hall, 1996), 309–310.

[21]Ibid, 311.

[22]The Center for Civil Society, http://www.lse.ac.uk/collections/CCS/what_is_civil_society.htm.

[23]Joey Fishkin, "Democracy: A Citizen's Guide," *Yale Review of Books,* vol. 1, no. 4 (Winter 1998). Available at: http://www.yale.edu/yrb/winter98/review08.htm.

[24]Ibid.

[25]Freedom House, *Freedom of the World Report*, 2000.

[26]Rasmussen Reports, "Partisan Trends: 33.5% of Americans are Republicans, 33.5% Unaffiliated, 33% Democrats", September 1, 2011. Accessed from, http://www.rasmussenreports.com/public_content/politics/mood_of_america/partisan_trends.

[27]Paul Collier, *The Bottom Billion: Why the Poorest Countries Are Failing and What Can Be Done About It*, (New York: Oxford University Press), 39–40.

CHAPTER 9

[1]From *Forum on Federations*. Available at http://www.forumfed.org/en/federalism/by_country/index.php (March 10, 2010).

[2]Bicameral systems that have one house more powerful than the other are known as asymmetric systems. These types of systems have become the norm. There are only a handful of symmetric systems where power is relatively equal among both chambers.

[3]According to Patterson and Mughan, in their edited book *Senates: Bicameralism in the Contemporary World* (1999), only about one-third of all of the states in the possession of a legislature are bicameral. The rest are unicameral, or one-chambered systems.

[4]Robert Rogers and Rhodri Walters, *How Parliament Works,* Fifth edition. Pearson-Longman, 2004, p. 2.

[5]David P. Conradt, *The German Polity,* 8th edition, Pearson-Longman, 2005, p. 190.

[6]In 1999, the House of Lords Act was passed and has changed its configuration. Now the concept of maintaining a sear based on the sole requisite of heredity has been outlawed.

[7]From Hancock, Carman, Castle, Conradt, Peters, et. al. (eds.), *Politics in Europe* (Washington DC: CQ Press, 2011), 38.

[8]Robert Rogers and Rhodri Walters, How Parliament Works, Fifth edition. Pearson-Longman, 2004, p. 288.

[9]Hans H. Baerwald, *Japan's Parliament: An Introduction*, Cambridge University Press, 2010, p. 10.

[10]This quote comes from Tom Todd, a legislative analyst from Minnesota, MN. Available at http://www.house.leg.state.mn.us/hrd/pubs/uni-bicam.pdf. It provides a good rundown of the pros and cons of both types of systems.

[11]From Lewis Rockow's, "Bentham on the Theory of Second Chambers" in *American Political Science Review,* 22, 576-90.

[12]Ibid., p. 583.

[13]In Japan, members of its upper house are elected by the people directly, but the people select the party first and the person second. Thus, the person that eventually wins the seat in the upper house is to a large degree more representative of the party ideology than of the people.

[14]Matthew Paul Zanotelli, *The Failure of the Unicameral Legislature at the State Level in the United States Examined*. A thesis presented to the Honors College at Harvard College, 2002, p. 65. Available at http://www.midwestdemocracy.org/pdf/uni.pdf.

[15]Following the Russian Revolution, the country officially changed its name to the Union of Soviet Socialist Republics, the world's first communist country and began a pattern of invasion and centrally planned and controlled institutions.

[16]To make sure that its ideology and culture expanded properly, Soviet policy created Russian as the official language of its empire. In the eastern part of Ukraine, many of the people continue to see themselves as culturally and linguistically part of Russia.

[17]See Yuri I. Shevchuk's working paper entitled, "Citizenship in Ukraine: Western Perspective," from the Institute on East-Central Europe, March 1996.

[18]Costa Rica was originally a colony of Spain that gained its independence in 1821. It experienced military dictatorships from 1870–1882 and after its civil war in 1948.

[19]From John A. Booth's chapter, "Costa Rica: The Roots of Democratic Stability," in Diamond, Hartlyn, Linz, and Lipset (eds.), *Democracy in Developing Countries: Latin America*, 2nd ed. (Boulder, CO: Lynne Rienner Publishers, 1999): 439.

[20]Ibid., p. 439.

[21]Ibid., p. 443.

[22]Scott Wilson, "Term Limits and Constitutional Tinkering in Latin America." *Washington Post* from June 29, 2009. Accessed online at: voices.washingtonpost.com/44/2009/06/29/term_limits_andconstituional.htm

[23]From Shigeko N. Fukai and Haruhiro Fukui's chapter on Japan from Kesselman, Krieger, and Joseph, et al.'s edited book, *Introduction to Comparative Politics* (Stamford, CT: Wadsworth Publishing, 2008): 231.

[24]Ibid.

[25]David P. Conradt, *The German Polity*, 8th ed. (New York: Longman, 2004): 254.

[26]David P. Conradt's chapter on Germany in M. Donald Hancock, et. Al. *Politics in Europe,* 4th edition, CQ Press, 2007, p. 228.

[27]Ibid.

[28]David Art's *The Politics of the Nazi Past in Germany and Austria,* Cambridge University Press, 2006.

[29]Roskin, Cord, Medeiros, and Jones, *Political Science: An Introduction*, 9th ed. (New York: Longman, 2006): 194.

[30]Donald M. Hancock, et al. *Politics in Europe*, 3d ed. (New York: NY Chatham House Publishers, 2003): 53.

[31]2 U.S.C., Section 2, Elections of Senators and Representatives. Accessed online at: uscode.house.gov/download/pls/02c1.txt

[32]This long caption comes from Steiner and Crepaz, *European Democracies*, 5th ed. (New York: Longman, 2007): 61–62.

CHAPTER 10

[1] From Donald Kagen, Steven Ozment, and Frank M. Turner, *The Western Heritage*, 9th ed., p. 14.

[2] Niccolo Machiavelli, *The Prince,* translated by Peter Bondanella, Oxford University Press, 2005, p. 53.

[3] Ibid, pp. 87–90.

[4] Statistics from U.S. Department of State's Bureau of Near Eastern Affairs, October 2006, http://www.state.gov/r/pa/ei/bgn/3584.htm.

[5] Ibid.

[6] Constitution of the Kingdom of Saudi Arabia, http://www.oefre.unibe.ch/law/icl/sa00000_.html.

[7] Ibid.

[8] Statistics from U.S. Department of State's Bureau of Near Eastern Affairs, October 2006, http://www.state.gov/r/pa/ei/bgn/3584.htm.

[9] Ibid.

[10] From "Saudi Municipal Elections: Gradualism of Reform and Traditional Politics," from the Carnegie Endowment for International Peace, http://www.carnegieendowment.org/publications/index.cfm?fa=view&id=16632

[11] Ghda Karmi's chapter entitled "Women, Islam, and Patriarchalism" in Haideh Moghissi, *Women and Islam: Images and Realities,* Routledge Press, 2005, pp. 168–170.

[12] From Mir Zohair Husain, *Global Islamic Politics*, 2nd ed., 2003, p. 24. The quote from the Koran is from 4:19.

[13] Ibid.

[14] Azmi Bashara's opinion piece entitled, "Reform and the Rentier State," from *Al-Ahram Weekly Online,* June 16–22, 2005. Accessed online at: <http://weekly.ahram.org.eg/2005/747/op2.htm>.

[15] Nina Shea, "This Is a Saudi Textbook. (After the intolerance was removed)," http://www.washingtonpost.com/wp-dyn/content/article/2006/05/19/AR2006051901769_pf.html.

[16] Ibid.

[17] Elie Elhadj, *The Islamic Shield: Arab Resistance to Democratic and Religious Reforms,* Brown Walker Press, 2007, p. 86.

[18] From President George W. Bush's 2002 State of the Union address, http://www.whitehouse.gov/news/releases/2002/01/20020129-11.html.

[19] "Hell on Earth: The West Still Turns a Blind Eye to the World's Most Brutal and Systematic Abuse of Human Rights," *The Economist*, October 22, 2009, http://www.economist.com/node/14699661?story_id=14699661.

[20] Ibid.

[21] From "North Korea's Antique Food Rationing," *Asia Times,* January 15, 2005, http://www.atimes.com/atimes/Korea/GA15Dg01.html.

[22] Both the *CIA World Factbook* and the U.S. Department of State classify Kim JongII's regime as a dictatorship.

[23] From the U.S. Department of State country profile of North Korea found online at http://www.state.gov/r/pa/ei/bgn/2792.htm.

[24]From testimony given at the Senate Committee on Foreign Relations, Subcommittee on East Asia and Pacific Affairs, June 5, 2003. Found online at The Brookings Institution: http://www.brookings.edu/views/testimony/oh20030605.htm.

[25]Ibid.

[26]*CIA World Fact Book on North Korea*, https://www.cia.gov/cia/publications/factbook/print/kn.html.

[27]From the International Churches of Christ website ranking the 20 poorest states in the world, http://www.icochotnews.com/?q=node/1371. (March 29, 2011).

[28]Marcus Noland, "Famine and Reform in North Korea," Working Paper from the Institute for International Economics, 2003, p. 1. Accessed online at http://iie.com/publications/wp/03-5.pdf.

[29]Ibid, pp. 4–5. Noland also quotes Eberstadt, Rubin, and Tretyakova, "The Collapse of Soviet and Russian Trade with North Korea, 1989–1993: Impact and Implications," *The Korean Journal of National Unification* 4, 87–104.

[30]Jim Halley, "With Holes in One, No Matter How You Slice Them Luck Is Vital," *USAToday.com*, http://www.usatoday.com/sports/golf/2006-07-16-hole-in-one_x.htm. (March 29, 2011).

[31]From *The International Institute of Strategic Studies*, Strategic Comments section entitled, "North Korea's Uranium Program Heightens Concern, January 2011, http://www.iiss.org/publications/strategic-comments/past-issues/volume-17-2011/january/north-koreas-uranium-programme-heightens-concern/.

[32]Choe Sang-Hun's article entitled, "N. Korean Leader Dying of Cancer, Report Says," *New York Times,* Asia Pacific section, July 12, 2009. Accessed online at: http://www.nytimes.com/2009/07/13/world/asia/13korea.html

[33]Andrew J. Nathan, "The Tiananmen Papers," *Foreign Affairs*, vol. 80, no. 1 (Jan.—Feb. 2001): 3.

[34]Kristof, "A Reassessment of How Many Died in the Military Crackdown in Beijing," *The New York Times* (June 21, 1989).

[35]"Chinese Dissident Wins Nobel Peace Prize," *The Telegraph* (October 8, 2010).

[36]Mao Zedong as quoted from *The Little Red Book*, found online at: http://www.marxists.org/reference/archive/mao/works/red-book/ch01.htm. (February 24, 2011).

[37]William A. Joseph, Mark Kesselman, and Joel Krieger (eds.), *Introduction to Politics of the Developing World*, (Houghton Mifflin Co., New York: NY, 2007), p. 61.

[38]Ibid, p. 63.

[39]Ibid, p. 63.

[40]Ibid, p. 63.

[41]Catherine Smith, "Egypt's *Facebook* Revolution: Wael Ghonim Thanks the Social Networking Site," http://www.huffingtonpost.com/2011/02/11/egypt-facebook-revolution-wael-ghonim_n_822078.html. (March 31, 2011).

[42]Ibid.

[43]AP report entitled, "China Tightens Rules for Foreign Reporters," *Forbes.com*, February 28, 2011, http://www.forbes.com/feeds/ap/2011/02/28/general-as-china-protest-calls_8331216.html.

[44]Isabella Bennett, "Media Censorship in China," found online at the Council on Foreign Relations homepage at: http://www.cfr.org/china/media-censorship-china/p11515. (March 22, 2011).

[45]Ibid.

46 Joe McDonald, "China on Path to Become Second-Largest Economy," *Huffington Post*, January 21, 2010, http://www.huffingtonpost.com/2010/01/21/china-on-path-to-become-s_n_431189.html.

47 The World Bank's web page entitled "Environment in East Asia and Pacific." The special section on China's Environment. Found online at: http://web.worldbank.org/WBSITE/EXTERNAL/COUNTRIES/EASTASIAPACIFICEXT/EXTEAPREGTOPENVIRONMENT/0,,contentMDK:20266322~menuPK:537827~pagePK:34004173~piPK:34003707~theSitePK:502886,00.html. (March 25, 2011).

48 Quote from James P. Dorian as quoted in Cindy Hurst, "China's Global Quest for Energy," from The Institute for the Analysis of Global Security, p. 3. Accessed online at http://www.iags.org/chinasquest0107.pdf.

49 Cindy Hurst, "China's Oil Rush in Africa," The Institute for the Analysis of Global Security, p. 3. Found online at http://www.iags.org/chinainafrica.pdf. (March 25, 2011).

50 Merriam-Webster dictionary entry of fossil-fuels. Accessed online at http://www.merriam-webster.com/dictionary/fossil percent 20fuel. (March 30, 2011).

51 Joseph Kahn and Jim Yardley, "As China Roars, Pollution Reaches Deadly Extremes," *The New York Times* (August 26, 2007).

52 Ibid.

53 Ibid.

54 BBC, "China Pollution Threatens Growth," February 28, 2011, http://www.bbc.co.uk/news/world-asia-pacific-12595872.

55 Ibid.

56 The World Bank's report from The State Environment and Protection Administration, "Cost of Pollution in China: Economic Estimates of Physical Damages," 2007, pp. xvi–xvii.

57 Ibid, p. xvii.

CHAPTER 11

1 Joseph S. Nye, *Bound to Lead: The Changing Nature of American Power* (New York: Basic Books, 1991).

2 Joseph S. Nye, *The Means to Success in World Politics* (New York: Perseus Books Group, 2004), x.

3 Ibid., 2.

4 Ibid., 2.

5 Harold James, "The Rise of the BRICs and the New Logic of International Politics, *The International Economy* (Summer 2008): 41.

6 Sun Tzu and Ralph Sawyer, *The Art of War* (New York: Basic Books, 1994).

7 From Wellesley College's Classical Studies page, http://www.wellesley.edu/ClassicalStudies/CLCV102/Thucydides—MelianDialogue.html.

8 Department of Defense budget's Web site, http://www.gpoaccess.gov/usbudget/fy09/pdf/budget/defense.pdf.

9 Hans Morgenthau, *Politics Among Nations* (New York: Alfred A. Knopf, 1962).

10 Kenneth Waltz, *Man, the State, and War* (New York: Columbia University Press, 2001).

11 Alan O. Ebenstein, *Great Political Thinkers: From Plato to the Present*, 6th ed. (Florence, KY: Wadsworth Publishing, 1999), 485.

12 Ibid., 485–488.

[13]Robert Axelrod, *The Evolution of Cooperation* (New York: Basic Books, 1984); Robert Keohane, *After Hegemony: Cooperation and Discord in the World Economy* (Princeton: Princeton University Press, 1984).

[14]István Mészáros, "Marx's Theory of Alienation," 1970, Accessed online at: http://www.marxists.org/archive/meszaros/works/alien/

[15]Alan O. Ebenstein, *Great Political Thinkers: From Plato to the Present*, 5th ed. (New York: Harcourt, 1991), 759.

[16]See for example, W.W. Rostow's *The Stages of Economic Growth,* Second Edition, Cambridge University Press, 1971.

[17]Jeffrey D. Sachs, *The End of Poverty* (New York: Penguin Press, 2005), 11.

[18]Richard S. Hillman (ed.), *Understanding Contemporary Latin America*, 2nd ed. (Boulder, CO: Lynne Rienner Press, 2001).

[19]Richard K. Harper and Alfred G. Cuzan, "The Economies of Latin America" in Richard S. Hillman (ed.), *Understanding Contemporary Latin America*, 145.

[20]Ibid.

[21]Ibid.

[22]Cynthia Weber, *International Relations Theory: A Critical Introduction*, 3rd ed. (London: Routledge Press, 2010), 133.

[23]Facts and Figures from World Development Indicators 2006, http://siteresources.worldbank.org/DATASTATISTICS/Resources/reg_wdi.pdf.

[24]Martha Finnemore, *National Interests in International Society* (New York: Cornell University Press, 1996).

[25]Peter Katzenstein, *Cultural Norms and National Security*, Ithaca: Cambridge University Press, 1996.

[26]W.W. Rostow, *The Stages of Economic Growth: A Non-Communist Manifesto* (Cambridge: Cambridge University Press, 1960).

CHAPTER 12

[1]From Henry Kissinger, *Diplomacy* (New York: Simon & Schuster, 1994), p. 59.

[2]Stephen Krasner's chapter entitled, "Globalization and Sovereignty" in David A. Smith, Dorothy J. Solinger, and Stephen C. Topik (eds), *States and Sovereignty in the Global Economy*. (New York: Routledge Press, 1999), p. 44.

[3]Marcilio Toscano Franca Filho's article entitled, "Westphalia: A Paradigm? A Dialogue between Law, Art, and Philosophy, and Science," *German Law Journal*, Vol. 8, No. 10, 962.

[4]Gordon A. Craig and Alexander L. George, *Force and Statecraft*, 3d ed. (New York: Oxford University Press, 1995), 7.

[5]From Henry Kissinger, *Diplomacy* (New York: Simon & Schuster, 1994), p. 67.

[6]Gordon A. Craig and Alexander L. George, *Force and Statecraft*, 2nd ed. (New York: Oxford University Press, 1990), 22.

[7]Ibid, 22.

[8]Ibid, 23.

[9]Craig and George both mention these actions as representative of the first and second examples respectively.

[10]Grotius's book is found online in its entirety at: http://www.lonang.com/exlibris/grotius/

[11]Craig, Gordon A., Alexander L. George, and Paul Gordon Lauren. *Force and Statecraft,* 4th edition, Oxford University Press, 2007, p. 25.

[12]Ibid, 26.

[13]Craig, Gordon A., Alexander L. George, and Paul Gordon Lauren *Force and Statecraft*, 4th edition (Oxford University Press, 2007), 25. The quote they use comes from the actual wording of the Treaty.

[14]Ibid, 28.

[15]Ibid, 29.

[16]Ibid, 33.

[17]Ibid, 33.

[18]Paul Kennedy, *The Rise and Fall of the Great Powers* (New York: Random House, 1987), 209–10.

[19]Craig and George, *Force and Statecraft*, 1990, 38.

[20]Ibid, 38.

[21]Kennedy, *The Rise and Fall of the Great Powers*, 254.

[22]From Karen A. Mingst and Ivan M. Arreguin-Toft, *Essentials of International Relations*, 5th ed. (New York: W.W. Norton and Company, 2011), 273.

CHAPTER 13

[1]John Lewis Gaddis, *We Know Now: Rethinking Cold War History* (New York: Oxford University Press, 1998).

[2]Ibid., 177.

[3]David Krieger, "Nuclear Deterrence, Missile Defenses and Global Instability," April 2001, http://www.wagingpeace.org/articles/2001/04/00_krieger_nuclear-deterrence.htm.

[4]George Kennan, "The Sources of Soviet Conduct," *Foreign Affairs* 25 (July 1947): 566–82.

[5]George Kennan, "The Sources of Soviet Conduct," 1947. Accessed online at: http://www.historyguide.org/europe/kennan.html

[6]From the U.S. Department of State's web page found at http://www.state.gov/r/pa/ho/time/cwr/17601.htm (accessed August 3, 2007).

[7]John Lewis Gaddis, "The Long Peace: Elements of Stability in the Postwar International System," *International Security,* vol. 10, no. 4 (Spring 1986): 92-142.

[8]R. W. Mansbach and Y. H. Ferguson, *World of Polities: Essays in Global Politics* (London: Routledge Press, 2008).

[9]James Rosenau, *Along the Domestic-Foreign Frontier: Exploring Governance in Turbulent World* (New York: Cambridge University Press, 1997).

[10]Richard Haas, "Sovereignty and Globalization," http://www.cfr.org/publication/9903/sovereignty_and_globalisation.html (February 17, 2006).

[11]George Ritzer, *Globalization: The Essentials* (Hoboken, NJ: Wiley-Blackwell Publishers, 2011), 9.

[12]David Harvey, *A Brief History of Neoliberalism* (London: Oxford University Press, 2005).

[13]Henry Schuster, "Al Qaeda's Media Strategy," CNN.com, January 30, 2006.

[14]David E. Sanger, *The Inheritance* (New York: Crown, 2009), 34–35.

[15]Richard Langhorne, *The Essentials of Global Politics* (London: Hodder Arnold Press, 2006), 112.

[16]Ibid., 112.

[17]Doctorswithoutborders.org.

[18]Ibid.

[19]Thomas L. Friedman, *The World Is Flat: A Brief History of the Twentieth Century* (New York: Farrer, Strauss, and Giroux, 2005).

[20]As quoted in Ritzer's book, *Globalization,* 58. This quote originally was made by James Boughton in his chapter entitled, "Bretton-Woods System," in Jan Aart Scholte and Roland Robertson's edited book, *Encyclopedia of Globalization* (New York: MTM Publishing, 2007).

[21]Ritzer, *Globalization*, 58.

[22]Boughton's chapter entitled, "Bretton Woods System" from Scholte and Robertson's edited book, *Encyclopedia of Globalization*, as found in Ritzer's *Globalization*, 58.

[23]Ritzer, *Globalization*, 58.

[24]Ibid., and Boughton, 107.

[25]Ritzer, *Globalization,* 59.

[26]Sebastian Edwards, book review entitled "Review of Joseph E. Stiglitz's *Globalization and Its Discontents* (Cambridge: National Bureau of Economic Research, September 9, 2002), 253.

[27]From Robert J. Art and Kenneth J. Waltz, *The Use of Force: International Politics and Foreign Policy*, as quoted in Paul G. Lauren, Gordon A. Craig, and Alexander L. George, *Force and Statecraft*, 4th ed.(New York: Oxford University Press, 2006), 177.

INDEX